To Dunni
A book full of \
a very wise wo

love
Clive xx
8/4/2009

GW01392959

Yoruba Proverbs

Yoruba Proverbs

OYEKAN OWOMOYELA

University of Nebraska Press, Lincoln and London

The publication of this volume
was made possible by a generous
gift from Nancy Sack Stevens.

© 2005 by the Board of Regents
of the University of Nebraska
All rights reserved
Manufactured in the United
States of America
∞
Set in Minion by Tseng.
Designed by Dika Eckersley.
Printed by Thomson-Shore, Inc.
Library of Congress Cataloging-
in-Publication Data
Owomoyela, Oyekan.
Yoruba proverbs / Oyekan
Owomoyela.
p. cm.
Parallel English and Yoruba.
Includes bibliographical
references.
ISBN 0-8032-3576-3 (cloth: alk.
paper) — ISBN 0-8032-0495-7
(electronic: alk. paper)
1. Proverbs, Yoruba. 2. Proverbs,
Yoruba — Translations into
English. I. Title.
PN6519.Y6097 2005
398′.996333 — dc22
2004065911

To William and Berta Bascom, in memoriam,
and to the Yoruba sages

Contents

Part Four

HUMAN NATURE

Part Five

RIGHTS AND RESPONSIBILITIES

Part Six

TRUISMS

Acknowledgments

It has been forty years since I embarked on the work whose fruition is this volume, and I have incurred substantial debts of gratitude to several people along the way, which I can only partially acknowledge here. I had collected only slightly more than two hundred proverbs when Bernth Lindfors, a fellow graduate student at UCLA, suggested that we collaborate on publishing some of them. The successful outcome of our joint effort was a major influence on my decision to persist with the project and aim for as comprehensive a treasury as I could assemble.

At various times I turned for help to knowledgeable scholars in the field, who were unstinting with their advice and comments; for these I thank Isidore Okpewho, Rowland Abiodun, and Toyin Falola, the last of whom became so taken with the project that he periodically sent me some gems of which I had been unaware. In an earlier publication I acknowledged the large contribution I received from the collection of William and Berta Bascom. I reiterate my gratitude here, both for their service to Yoruba studies and especially for the encouragement I received from Berta, and for her generous help and hospitality when I visited her in Berkeley in connection with my work on this project. I wish she had lived to see the publication she promoted so enthusiastically. I also acknowledge Alan Dundes's incisive input, even if I frustrated him with some of my methodological choices.

I cannot adequately express my gratitude for the help and encouragement I have consistently received from my friend and colleague in the English Department at the University of Nebraska–Lincoln, Linda Ray Pratt; the instances and forms they took are numerous and various and best left unspecified. John Turner of our Classics Department is another friend and colleague who applied his computer expertise to creating a Yoruba font for me at a time when none was commercially available. The task was time-consuming, but he embraced it without complaint, and I thank him.

I am also grateful for the funding I received from the Research Council of the university to purchase computer hardware, and from the College of Arts and Sciences in the form of faculty development fellowships. The financial help and the released time that went with the fellowship were a great help. The University of Nebraska Press has acknowledged the generous assistance of Nancy Stevens in making this publication possible; I wish to join the press in the acknowledgment, and to add the name of Susan Norby of the University of Nebraska Foundation, who interested Ms. Stevens in the project. Finally, and by no means least, I thank my wife and chief motivator, Joan, for her constant support and for keeping me focused on the finish line.

I am certain that in spite of the help, advice, and comments from the people I have listed and others, some errors will be found in the following pages, whether in translation, in explication, or in typing. They are entirely my responsibility, and I hope that they do not detract significantly from the value of the collection.

Yoruba Proverbs

Introduction

I t is customary to translate the Yoruba *òwe* into English as "proverb," a choice that is justified by the close correspondence of the verbal formulations the words designate in their respective cultures. Not surprisingly, therefore, scholars familiar with the English genre expect to find its features (or properties) and variations replicated in the Yoruba; in other words, they expect that a study of *òwe* will disclose a form in all essential particulars like the proverb. Accordingly, they expect discussion of Yoruba *òwe* to account for such subgenres of the English proverb as aphorisms, apothegms, Wellerisms, and so forth. Examples of such forms do occur in the huge corpus of Yoruba *òwe* — if not exactly as in the English, at least close enough to pass. But ferreting out Yoruba correspondences to the English subgenres, although a useful comparative exercise, has little relevance to understanding the Yoruba concept and usage of *òwe*, which do not exactly coincide with those of the English proverb.

ENGLISH PROVERBS, TRUE AND FALSE

Representative of the Western conception of the proverb is the view that it is an ancient and popularly accepted encapsulation of wisdom. Citing the Greek origin of the word and its literal meaning, "wayside saying," Edward Hulme comments that the word is roughly equivalent to "adage," and his use of the biblical passage "Israel shall be a proverb and a byword among all people" as an example suggests that a proverb may also be a *material* model (4). In addition, he invokes both Aristotle's definition as quoted by Synesius — "A proverb is a remnant of the ancient philosophy preserved amid many destructions on account of its brevity and fitness for use — and also Agricola's description of the form as "short sentences into which, as in rules, the ancients have compressed life" (5–6).

Jan Brunvand introduces a significant criterion for determining what is a proverb and what is not when he writes that "the true proverb is always a complete sentence," thus distinguishing it from other (or false) proverbs, and further that the true proverb "never varies more than slightly in form, and usually expresses some general truth or wisdom" (52). Moreover, "the majority of true proverbs are metaphorical descriptions of an act or event applied as a general truth," whereas false proverbs, in addition to not being complete sentences, are not fixed and "seldom express any general wisdom" (53). The latter include proverbial phrases; proverbial comparisons such as "greedy as a pig" and "clear as mud"; Wellerisms; miscellaneous proverbial insults, retorts, and wisecracks such as "Is the Pope Catholic?"; and euphemisms such as "It's snowing down south" for "Your slip is showing" (54).[1]

The customary inclusion of assorted metaphorical verbal formulations in collections and discussions of the proverb elicited the following complaint from Roger Abrahams: "The study of proverbs has been severely complicated by the grouping of conventional conversational devices that share almost nothing but their brevity and their traditional currency. Almost certainly this complication is due to the fact that proverb dictionaries were written not for the purpose of defining this genre but for storing any device useful in developing oratory techniques. Thus these compendia contained not only true proverbs but hyperbolizing devices, such as traditional exaggerations, that were useful in ornamenting extemporized formal speech" (123). The rhetorical devices that are mistaken for proverbs, according to Abrahams, are "formulaic intensifiers [which] exist for no other reason than to decorate speech. These are devices of hyperbole; they take an ongoing argument and lend it wit and color" (123–24).

The existence of several words in the English language that often substitute for "proverb" would seem to suggest that each one signifies a subtle or significant variation. In fact, though, that does not appear to be the case. Although Hulme, as we have seen, says that "adage" is "fairly equivalent" to "proverb," he makes hardly any distinction when he uses the term "apothegm," the word which, as he notes, Lord Bacon favored for his 1625 collection *Apothegms New and Old*. An example of the apothegms in that collection comes from Psalm 27:14, "He that blesseth his friend with a loud voice, rising in the morning, it shall be counted a curse to him," whose import is, in effect, "Excessive and ostentatious praise amounts to denunciation" (Hulme 44). Dictionary definitions of the various designations support Hulme's practice in this regard.[2]

The Wellerism, however, is a bona fide subgenre of the proverb with a distinguishing structural peculiarity: it comprises a direct quotation that is attributed to a person, plus a facetious tag specifying the context (or occasion) of the quotation. Abrahams describes it variously as a cliché, a "dialogue-proverb," and a joking device (122), and Brunvand as a "quotation proverb" (53). According to Archer Taylor, the form is more ancient than the Charles Dickens character for which it is named, and its more recent examples tend to incorporate puns. Taylor cites among others: "'It won't be long now' (or 'That's the end of my tail'), said the monkey when he backed into the lawn mower" ("Wisdom" 8). Another often cited example is "'I see,' said the blind man, as he picked up his hammer and saw."

One consensus requirement for a proverb seems to be that it must be short and to the point, in other words, that it be pithy, succinct, terse, or brief. Thus Hulme (6–7) quotes Chambers to the effect that "proverbs are pithy, practical, popular sayings"; Annandale, that it is "a short and pithy sentence"; and the dictionary compiler Worcester, that it is "a common or pithy expression which embodies some moral precept."

THE YORUBA ÒWE

Yoruba language and speech practices do feature forms that are practically, if not exactly, identical with the English proverb, but not all of them will qualify as *òwe* for the Yoruba speaker. On the other hand, some verbal forms that come under the general rubric of *òwe* in Yoruba do not have equivalents in the English proverb corpus. Perhaps the best approach to understanding the Yoruba concept of *òwe*, therefore, is to begin with an etymology of the word.

Òwe seems to be formed from the contraction of *ò-wé e*, literally "something that wraps it." The root is the verb *wé* (wrap [something] around [something else]). The initial *ò* is the vowel prefix that in Yoruba lexicology converts a verb to a noun, the particular vowel depending on the particular verb; it functions like the English suffixes "-ist," "-er," and "-or." The phrase *wé e* (wrap it) becomes *we* in the contraction characteristic of everyday speech. I am suggesting that the word is *òwe* rather than *òwé,* a combination of *ò* (an agent that . . .) and *wé* (wraps), because the object pronoun "it," in this case the midtoned "*e*" is appended to the combination. (Yoruba is a tone — or tonal — language with high, mid, and low tones. These are indicated on the vowels and the nasals *n* and *m* by acute and grave marks for the high and low tones respectively, the midtone carrying no mark.)

To say in Yoruba that one thing may be compared with or to another, one says "*fi* (noun 1) *wé* (noun 2)," literally "use (n1) to wrap (n2)," or, more idiomatically, "wrap (n1) around (n2)." The formulation reveals an important Yoruba view of what happens when one likens something to someting else: one brings the two items into as close proximity as possible in order to make their qualities observable side by side or in (virtually) the same space; one intertwines them, in other words. Corroboration for this suggestion comes from the term for another verbal genre that has close affinities with *òwe*: namely, *àlọ́,* the riddle. The root of *àlọ́* is *lọ́,* which also means "wrap [something] around [something else]," and in this case the initial nominalizing vowel is *à.* What the riddle does, of course, is to describe some essential feature of an object or situation (the answer to the riddle) in terms of a different thing or situation that shares that feature (the clue). For example, for a person's two eyes a Yoruba riddle offers as its clue a set of twins that inhabit the same house without ever seeing each other. (Folktales are also sometimes termed *àlọ́* because they are parables for occurrences other than those they literally narrate.)

Reduced to its essence, therefore, *òwe* is a speech form that likens, or compares, one thing or situation to another, highlighting the essential similarities that the two share. In Yoruba usage it is always at least one *complete* sentence. Although the language is rich in phrases, descriptions, and idioms that resemble some of the false English proverbs cited above, the Yoruba do not recognize these as *òwe*. For example, the epithet *Ṣámúgà, eléyín ọkọ́* (*Ṣámúgà,* with hoes for teeth), often used with the elaboration *kòróun fálejò ó wayín sáwo* (lacking the wherewithal to entertain a visitor, he scoops teeth into a dish), which refers to a person with protruding teeth, is called not *òwe* but *eébú,* insult. The same is true of this chant (in Ifon dialect):

Máà gbédòn yún óko,
àíké orí è ó tóó lagi
[Don't carry an axe to the farm,
the axe on his head will do for splitting wood.]

Other figurative idioms that parallel the English pseudoproverb but would not qualify as *òwe* (true *or* false) in Yoruba include such sayings as *kóyán láì dúró gbọbẹ̀* ([to] take some pounded yam but not tarry to receive some stew) and *bá esẹ̀ sòrò* ([to] engage in conversation with one's legs), both of which mean "to make a hasty exit from a threatening scene"; and *fi àáké kórí* ([to] hang an axe on one's head), meaning "to assume a rigid and unyielding position in a discussion." The Yoruba speaker would also distinguish between *òwe* and both *àfiwé* (comparison, such as *Ó ga tópẹ*: he, she, or it is as tall as a palm tree) and *àpèjúwe* (description). I have, however, included formulations that, even though they seem at first glance to lack the requisite qualities of one, actually make proverbial statements. An example is entry 5235, which makes a statement about maidens.

Among Yoruba *òwe* there are formulations that, like Wellerisms, combine direct quotations and contexts, albeit not always in exactly the same manner as in the English versions. Two examples: *"Ọlórun má pèé o gbọ́kan,"* *àdúrà olè* ("'God, don't let on that you heard a thing,' the thief's prayer"); and the colonial-era *"Háó fò duù?" lòyìnbó fi ńjẹ̀bà lÓrígo* ("'How for do?' is the white man's resigning rationalization for eating *ẹ̀bà* at Orígo"). *Ẹ̀bà*, a starchy food made from cassava grains, is a plebeian staple among the Yoruba, much less favored than such elites among foods as *iyán* (pounded yam) and *ìrẹsì* (rice). And Orígo is a station on the Yoruba stretch of the Lagos-Kano railway line; being an inconsequential stop, it did not rate a government guesthouse like the ones dispersed strategically around the colonies, provided with some basic necessities for the comfort of touring colonial officials, and maintained by cook-stewards competent to offer close imitations of European culinary fare. The expression *Háò fò duù?* is a Yoruba rendering of "How for do?" itself a pidgin version of "What to do?" or "What is one to do?" or "What option does one have?"

Here are five other possible candidates for the designation of "Welleristic" *òwe*:

- *"Mo mỌ̀bàrà, mo mỌ̀fún,"* *tí kò jé kí eyelé kọ́ àparò nÍfá.* "I know Ọ̀bàrà, I know Ọ̀fún," which discouraged the pigeon from teaching Ifá to the partridge. (Because the partridge claims, falsely, to know it all, he blocked his own opportunity to learn Ifá from the pigeon.)

- *"Sún mọ́hùn-ún, a ó sọrò ilé-e wa,"* *tí kò jé kí àlejò di onílé.* "Make room, we are about to perform our lineage ritual," which keeps the sojourner from becoming a permanent resident. (As long as citizens exclude immigrants from full participation in civic activities, the latter will not become fully integrated into the population.)

- *"Òní ló ńmọ,"* *ìjà òle.* "It will all end today," the lazy person's fighting motto. (The lazy person enters into a fight with the consoling knowledge that it will end sometime.)

- *Òní "Mò ńlọ," òla "Mò ńlọ,"* *tí kò jé kí àlejò gbin awùsá.* Today, "I am leaving"; tomorrow, "I am leaving," which keeps the sojourner from planting *awùsá*.

(*Awùsá,* usually translated as "wallnut" (wall-nut), is the fruit of a tree that takes years to mature and bear fruit.)

- "*Kò dùn mí, kò dùn mí,*" *àgbàlagbà m̀bú ọpa lẹ̀ẹ̀mẹfà nítorí iyán alẹ́ àná.* "It does not bother me, it does not bother me," yet a grown man curses by invoking *ọpa* on account of last night's pounded yam. (The person concerned was obviously excluded from the meal the previous night, and his injured behavior belies his protestation of nonchalance.)

In proverbs of this sort the phrase *tí kò* (meaning "that prevents" or "that keeps . . . from") is sometimes replaced with *kò* (prevents) alone.

The use of the English term "Wellerism," although it certainly serves a useful purpose in comparative discussions, may give pause to African and Africanist scholars leery of possible charges that they are subscribing to the representation of African forms in Western terms. Alan Dundes's essay on the subject is of particular interest in this regard. His primary intention is to demonstrate, with Yoruba examples, the widespread (perhaps worldwide) incidence of this type of proverb. With the aid of the Yoruba informant Ayodele Ogundipe, he lists ten examples that qualify as Wellerisms by virtue of their containing direct quotations. Most of them do incorporate direct quotations in the original Yoruba, and some are close enough in form to English Wellerisms to pose no difficulties. For example, in his number 7— "*Ṣé kí nfidí hẹ?*" *làfòmọ́ fi ńdi onílé* (my transcription), which he translates, "'Shall I sit awhile?' says the parasite before becoming a perma- nent dweller" (116) — the translation is adequate, although it would be better ren- dered "'May I *perch* awhile?' is the ruse that eventually makes the parasite the homeowner." In other instances, however, the proverbs are forced into the cate- gory, inasmuch as the direct quotations the author and informant attribute to them are absent in the original Yoruba. For example, for the Yoruba original *Adìẹ ńjọkà, ó ńmu omi, ó ńgbẹ òkúta pé-pè-pé mì, síbè-síbè ó ní òun ò léhín* (again, my transcription), they provide the following translation: "'I have no teeth,' com- plains the chicken which eats corn, drinks water, and swallows pebbles" (114), whereas the correct translation is, "The chicken eats corn, it drinks water, it swal- lows small pebbles, and yet it claims that it has no teeth." Obviously, the Yoruba original has undergone some radical manipulation in order to make a Wellerism out of it.

In addition to what we might describe as "true" *òwe,* the Yoruba have a popu- lar verbal form whose title includes the word *òwe* as a modifier: the allusive songs known as *orin òwe,* literally "proverb songs," which make indirect and usually disparaging references to unstated targets. They are normally expressions of an- tagonism, as the meta-proverb *Ìjà ló dé lorín dòwe* ("It is the commencement of a quarrel that turns a song into a proverb") makes clear. Although such songs most often characterize domestic quarrels, especially among women, they also feature prominently in popular entertainment songs — for example, in the lyrics of *jùjú* music. Professional rivalry among *àgídìgbo* musicians in the 1960s gave rise to the following lyrics:

Kélégbé megbé
Kélégbé megbé
A jùmò gbálùmáyà pò
Kélégbé megbé
[Let cohorts know their equal
Let cohorts know their equal
We may all, alike, wrap our bosoms around drums
Yet, let cohorts know their equal]

The target of the song, though not named, would have realized that he was intended, as would those privy to the quarrel. The following was an interlude in a high-life dance number a few years later:

Òfófó ilé yìí á yera
Òfófó ilé yìí á yera
Ká má gbodò sòrò
Ká má gbodò jenu wúyé
Òfófó ilé yìí á yera
[The tale bearer in this household must make way
The tale bearer in this household must make way
One dares not talk
One dares not whisper
The tale bearer in this household must make way]

Also akin to Hulme's usage of the term "proverb" to designate a material model is the Yoruba usage of *òwe* as in the saying *Ikú tó pa ojúgbà eni-í pòwe móni* ("The death that kills one's age mate speaks to one proverbially"). The *òwe* in this case is not a verbal statement but a visible phenomenon or an event from which an observer can draw a lesson.

Another difference: the constant in the definitions of the English proverb that it is pithy, concise, succinct, brief, terse, and so on, is not *always* true of the Yoruba *òwe*, which is sometimes quite long-winded. For example, there is nothing pithy about the following: *Gbogbo eranko ìgbé pé, wón ní àwon ó fi ìkokò se asípa; nígbà tó gbó inú è-é dùn; sùgbón nígbà tó se, ó bú sékún; wón ní kí ló dé? Ó ní bóyá wón lè tún ro òràn náà wò kí wón ní kì íse béè mó* ("All the animals in the forest assembled and decided to make Hyena their secretary; he was happy to hear the news, but a short while later he burst into tears; asked what the matter was, he replied that perhaps they might revisit the matter and reverse themselves"). The import, depending on the user's intention, could be either that even in times of good fortune one should be mindful of the possibility of reversal, or that one should not so focus on the negative as to be incapable of enjoyment.

THE AESTHETICS OF *ÒWE*

Isidore Okpewho, one of the most influential scholars of African traditional verbal artistry, has decried the tendency on the part of non-African scholars to minimize the aesthetic properties of these texts, a tendency he blames in part on their limited or sometimes nonexistent command of the pertinent languages. His *African Oral Literature* is an elaborate illustration of the sophisticated artistry in African traditional texts, including brief forms such as the proverb.

Discussion of the proverb in Western folklore scholarship has characteristically acknowledged the aesthetic aspects of the form. Roger Abrahams describes proverbs as "among the shortest forms of traditional expression that call attention to themselves as formal artistic entities." He goes on to illustrate their use of "all of the devices we commonly associate with poetry in English: meter, binary construction and balanced phrasing, rhyme, assonance and alliteration, conciseness, metaphor, and occasional inverted word order and unusual construction" (119). Brunvand also observes that "proverbs exhibit most of the stylistic devices of poetry. They have *meter . . . rhyme . . . slant rhyme . . . alliteration . . . assonance . . . personification . . . paradox . . . parallelism . . .* and several other poetic characteristics" (56; original emphasis). To these he adds figures of speech, which occur in proverbs as well as in "proverbial comparisons." Also worth mentioning is Alan Dundes's essay "On the Structure of the Proverb."

With regard to the Yoruba *òwe*, Ayo Bamgbose, the dean of Yoruba scholars, and Olatunde Olatunji have written seminal essays on its artistic qualities and especially on its structure; both point out that it shares central aesthetic features with Yoruba poetry in general. Since my earlier collection *A Kì í* includes a brief discussion on the subject, what follows only advances my argument in that work, elaborating upon and clarifying some of its assertions and qualifications.

Bamgbose highlights the use of lexical contrast and lexical matching in Yoruba proverbs (and poetry), which he explains as "the bringing together of two or more lexical items in such a way as to exhibit a semantic contrast or correspondence" and offers examples (*Grammar* 83, 84, 85). The contrasted items, which occur in identical locations in parallel sentences, are sometimes antonyms and sometimes synonyms (or items that belong in the same semantic range), and sometimes they are unrelated. For example, in the formulation

Ó *mú* ọkùnrin
Ó *sì mú* obìnrin
[He captured *men*
He also captured *women*]

ọkùnrin (men) and *obìnrin* (women) are antonyms. In the following,

Èhìnkùlé lòtá *wà*
Ilé laṣeni *ńgbé*
[The *enemy* lives in the back yard
The abode of the *person who inflicts injury* is the home]

òtá (enemy) and *aṣeni* (inflictor of injury) are synonyms (*laṣeni* is contracted from *ni aṣeni*), or at least exist within the same semantic range.

At times the proverb takes advantage of the existence of different words in the language that designate the same thing more or less exactly, resulting in the sort of wordplay in

Àjànàkú *kì í ya aràrá*
Ẹni erin-*ín bí erin ní ńjọ*
[The elephant does not turn out dwarfish
The child sired by an elephant takes after an elephant]

The lexical item *Àjànàkú* (elephant) in the first part matches *erin* (elephant) in the second, with the difference that the first word carries the suggestion of mightiness. But in

Ohun tówá lọ sí Ṣókótó
Wà nínú àpò-o ṣòkòtò

Ṣókótó (a city in northern Nigeria) and ṣòkòtò (trousers) are unrelated.

Olatunji, for his part, lists as the main features of Yoruba proverbs: a prescriptive function (meaning the outlining of rules of conduct); a characteristic sentence form (which might be simple, complex, sequential, or parallel); a high incidence of lexical repetition and contrast; and terseness (175). In addition, he cites "tonal counterpoint": that is, contrast in the tones of lexical items that occur in identical locations in parallel sentences. In the example already cited above,

Èhìnkùlé lòtá wà
Ilé laṣeni ńgbé

the high tone of the final syllable in the second line contrasts with the low tone of the corresponding syllable in the first sentence. Another good example is,

Ohun tí a ní kí ọgbọ́ gbọ́ ni ọgbọ́ ńgbọ́
Ohun tí a ní kí ọgbà gbà ni ọgbà ńgbà
[Whatever we tell ọgbọ́ to hear is what ọgbọ́ hears
Whatever we tell ọgbà to accept is what ọgbà accepts]

The high tones on the pair *ọgbọ́* and *gbọ́* in the first line give way to low tones on *ọgbà* and *gbà* in the second.

One characteristic of proverbs that comprise three lines is that the first two follow a parallel construction, whereas the concluding line deviates. Characteristically, the first two lines repeat a concept as a lead-in to the real message of the proverb, which the third line delivers with a flourish, as it were. Here are examples:

• *Ẹní da eérú leérú ńtò*
   Eléte lète ńyé
   Ohun a bá ṣe ní ńyéni

[The person who throws ashes is the one ashes follow
The person who proposes is the one to whom the proposal is understood
What one does is what one understands]

- *Ìhín ilé*
  Òhún ilé
  Òjò kì í rò kó pa ọmọ adìẹ
  [Here a home
  There a home
  The rain does not fall and drench a chicken]

- *À ńkólé ikin*
  À ńyòdèdè imò
  Hòrò nilé àgbékéhìn
  [Although we build a house of thatch
  Although we construct a porch of palm leaves
  The grave is the final home]

In each of the three examples the burden of the saying, its main thesis, is couched in the last line: "What one does is what one understands"; "The rain does not fall and drench a chicken"; and "The grave is the final home."

A Syllogistic Quirk

Another feature that is not peculiar to proverbs but characterizes Yoruba rhetoric represents a logical non sequitur which Yoruba usage, however, accommodates. Consider this proverb:

Pípé là ńpé gbón
A kì í pé gò
[Assembling is what we do in order to be wise
We do not assemble to become foolish]

Roughly comparable in its import to the English saying "Two heads are better than one," it asserts that a certain problem is not amenable to individual tackling but demands the pooling of communal wisdom: we must put our heads together if we wish to come up with a wise solution and not a foolish one. The proverb thus recommends assembling, *pípé,* as opposed to its opposite, which would be *àdáṣe,* as in *Àdáṣe ní ńhunni; àjọṣe kì í hunni* ("Going it alone is what gets one in trouble; collaborating with others does not get one in trouble").

We might conceptualize the argument as follows: the desired end is wisdom (arriving at a wise decision), and the means recommended is assembling (*pípé*), not unilateral action (*àdáṣe*). One would expect the argument to be as follows: *Assembling* is what people do in order to be wise, not *going it alone.* Let the goal (*gbón* or *gbígbón*) be *x,* the means (*pípé*) be *y,* and the alternative not recommended (*àdáṣe*) be *z*; thus, in order to achieve the end *x*, the means must be *y*, not *z*. We may then represent the argument as follows:

$$y \dashrightarrow x$$
$$z \longrightarrow\!\!/\!/\!\longrightarrow x.$$

But the proverb does not follow that reasoning. It says, *assembling* is what people do in order to be wise; people do not assemble *to be foolish* (*gò*), or *w*. Schematically, therefore,

$$y \dashrightarrow x$$
$$y \dashrightarrow\!\!/\!/\!\longrightarrow w$$

The last phrase it offers as the undesirable eventuality is not a contrast to the action being recommended, *assembling*. It would fit better, logically, in the formulation:

> *Gbígbọ́n là ńpé gbọ́n*
> *A kì í pé gọ́*
> [*Wisdom* is what we achieve by assembling
> We do not assemble to achieve *folly*]

Humor (or Wit)

A further inescapable quality characterizing Yoruba *òwe* is the humor many of them display. It derives, as in other texts and other cultures, from a variety of devices: different forms of ironies (situational, verbal, and others), hyperbole, understatement, deliberate shock (especially in vocabulary), and so forth. Often it is a result of tongue-in-cheek cleverness, as in

> *A gbọ́ tajá*
> *A gbọ́ tẹran*
> *Èwo ni tàgùntàn lórí àga?*

The literal translation is

> We hear that of the dog
> We hear that of the goat
> What about that of the sheep on a chair?

Alternatively,

> One could understand if it was a dog
> One could understand if it was a goat
> But what about a sheep on a chair?

Idiomatically it says, "One can tolerate the eventuality in the case of a dog, and one can tolerate it in the case of a goat, but who ever heard of a sheep on a chair?" The fact, though, is that not even a goat or a dog is conceivable, or acceptable, on a chair. The proverb refers to, and plays on, the expression *tajá teran*—literally "dogs and goats inclusive"—the Yoruba equivalent of the English "every Tom, Dick, and Harry." One would usually employ the phrase to indicate that all comers had (for example) taken advantage of a situation to intrude into one's affairs, even (and especially) those whom one would exclude as being no better than dogs or goats. One reluctantly suffers them, therefore, as unwelcome necessities imposed by misfortune. The enormity of the outrage implied in the situation the proverb describes, likened to a sheep's usurpation of a chair, is easily conceivable. The proverb's statement that one can tolerate a dog, or even a goat, on the chair is not to be taken seriously but seen as tongue-in-cheek.

Comparable to the foregoing in facetiousness, in incorporating an ironic twist that somewhat undercuts what the proverb professes to assert, is

Kàkà kí gbajúmò je òpòló
Eni tí yó pa kònkò fún un yó jàáde
[Rather than that a popular person would have to eat a toad
Someone who will kill a frog for him or her will emerge]

The idea is, of course, that worthy and well-respected persons will never be reduced to suffering indignities, because people will rush to their aid. The indignity the proverb chooses for illustration is the eating of a toad, a disgusting if not abominable prospect. The relief it suggests, though (the eating of a frog instead), is in Yoruba thinking just about equally disgusting. The point of the proverb is made, but tongue-in-cheek.

This next example differs somewhat in structure but also incorporates the tongue-in-cheek element:

Àgbààgbà ìlú kì í péjo kí wón je ìfun òkété
Àfi iyán àná
[The patriarchs of a town will not assemble and eat the intestines of a bush rat
Only stale, day-old pounded yams]

If the prospect of venerable patriarchs eating the intestines of a bush rat is belittling at best, their eating stale pounded yams is not much better.

The type of humor in the foregoing examples is familiar to students and speakers of Yoruba in such ironic praises as

Ó lóhun tóyìnbó ò ní
A-biná-ko-n-du-létí-aso
[He or she has what even the white man lacks
Blessed with plump lice in the seams of his or her clothing!]

In Yoruba culture a great deal of importance attaches to whatever utterance issues out of the mouth. Speech being the highest form of utterance, the Yoruba approach it with deliberate care, taking great pains to avoid careless, casual, or thoughtless statements whose damage might outlast lifetimes. The proverb

> Ẹyin lòrò
> Bó bá balè, fífó ní ńfó
> [Speech is an egg
> When it drops on the floor what it does is shatter]

bears witness to this concern. In addition, the Yoruba speaker strives to ensure that the idea he or she wishes to communicate reaches its target ungarbled and in as unmistakable a form as possible. If an explanation for such care is necessary, one need only remember the importance of relationality in close-living communalism, especially when speech also happens to be the most available and therefore most common transactional medium. In such a context, to paraphrase another proverb, the judicious—not simply correct—application of speech causes the kola nut to emerge from the pocket, whereas careless use brings out the sword from its scabbard.

Resort to proverbs is the most important and most effective strategy the Yoruba have devised to optimize the efficaciousness of speech. The culture's richness in them, of which this collection provides evidence, bears out the Yoruba insistence that bereft of proverbs, speech flounders and falls short of its mark, whereas aided by them, communication is fleet and unerring. Accordingly, the Yoruba assert,

> Òwe lẹsin òrò
> Bí òrò-ó bá sọnù, òwe la fi ńwá a
> [The proverb is the horse of speech
> When speech is lost, the proverb is the means we use to hunt for it]

Proverbs, often incisive in their propositions and terse in their formulation, are deduced from close observation of life, life forms and their characteristics and habits, the environment and natural phenomena, and sober reflection on all these. Because proverbs are held to express unexceptionable truths, albeit with some qualification, their use in a discussion or argument is tantamount to an appeal to established authority. This is one reason for their virtual indispensability in formal and informal verbal interactions in Yoruba society. They accordingly pervade all other major forms of verbal texts, whose effectiveness their presence enhances.

Just as the formulation of proverbs involves considerable creativity, so does their application—a fact that is sometimes discounted in exercises that attempt to assign definitive applications to specific sayings. Creativity in their use transcends simply knowing a great number of proverbs and the "correct" situation(s) in which to apply them. Such competencies certainly count for much, but competence is a far cry from effectiveness, which comes, in part at least, from the ability to deploy proverbs in ways that are not only appropriate but also demonstrate some ingenuity on the part of the user in seeing applicability where others might not. An original application causes a momentary disorientation on the part of the hearer, followed by an intimation of some affinity between the subject (or situation) under discussion and the content (or proposition) in the proverb, and finally a recognition of the brilliance of the analogy involved.

Discussion of the rhetorical raison d'être of proverb use speaks incidentally to their utility or function. Writing about proverbs in the Nigerian context, John Messenger lists what I describe as their "active" roles — "as a means of amusement, in educating the young, to sanction institutionalized behavior, as a method of gaining favor in court, in performing religious rituals and association ceremonies, and to give point and add color to ordinary conversation" (64). The Yoruba scholar Olowo Ojoade, focusing on what I term their "passive" functions, describes them as "an open sesame for the workings of the native mind, manners and customs, traditional wisdom, religion, ideas and ideals, feelings, modes of thought, principles of conduct, and philosophy" (20). Another scholar, William Bascom, summarizes all the foregoing into four functions — passive and active and all positive — that proverbs perform for society: they mirror its culture; they afford its members a means of psychological and emotional release through venting otherwise prohibited expressions; they aid in education and socialization; and they maintain conformity to accepted patterns while validating institutions, attitudes, and beliefs ("Four Functions" 279–98).

The eminent Yoruba art scholar Rowland Abiodun offers an example of a proverb that connects in obvious and not so obvious ways with the values of its culture:

> Kójú ó má rìíbi
> Esè loògùn-un rè
> [For the eyes to see no evil
> The legs are the medicine]

("Medicine" here means something like "talisman.") The import is that the legs bear the responsibility of transporting the eyes (and their owner, of course) away from locations that might harbor evil. The saying echoes others such as Kò séni tó mo ibi tí orí ńbá esè-é rè ("There is no person who knows where the head will accompany the legs").

The proverb, Abiodun points out, is a discursive explanation of a phenomenon in Yoruba (and African generally) figurative sculpture: the preference for full figures over busts. Whereas in some traditions it is permissible for the artist to represent a subject with a bust, the Yoruba figure must include the torso (the chest), the hands, the legs, and the feet, for all these parts are indispensable to the integrity, and the fortunes, of the person represented. Moreover, whereas in Western iconography the human form is represented according to the Aristotelian idea of beauty, in which the proportions are as close to real-life ones as possible, in African portraiture the representation of the human body answers to a different aesthetic principle, one that can be described as "metaphorical": it assigns relative size to parts of the body on the basis of their metaphysical importance. Accordingly, the head, in reality usually about a seventh of the body in size, takes up as much as a third of the total height of the sculptural image. The same theory explains the disproportionately large breasts of female images.

Finally, the relative brevity of proverbs in comparison with other traditional verbal texts — tales, epics, panegyrics — gives them a functional advantage over the more complex ones. Their characteristic conciseness permits easy recall and versatile application — at any time and on any occasion. Since their use in effect represents an invitation to pause and enter a laboratory where the matter in hand can be scrutinized under the lens of the wisdom of the ages, it offers individuals an opportunity to engage in what Victor Turner says the whole group does on liminal occasions, proverbs playing the role of the "performative genres" or "social dramas" that characterize those occasions (99–106).

GENDER AND PROVERBS

Certain proverbs raise questions concerning a most important issue: gender. The presence in the Yoruba òwe corpus of derogatory (at least on the surface) statements about women deserves some comment.

Students of Yoruba culture are familiar with the reverence with which the Yoruba regard womanhood. It results from the importance they attach to the practically absolute dependence of human existence on the woman: she is the only pathway through which people come into existence, and whatever a man's contribution to the process, it cannot compare in importance or in the awesome psychic implications of the truth that every human being begins incarnation as an anatomical part of a woman, concealed in the protection of her body, drawing sustenance from her, and relying completely on her for some nine months. Not even the test-tube innovations of science have succeeded in doing away with the woman's contribution. The newborn's dependence on her continues long after birth, for unlike the offspring of lower animals, those of humans require years of nurturing before they can survive on their own. Writing about the earliest stages in the history of hominids, Gerder Lerner observes, "Only the mother's arms and care sheltered the infant from cold; only her breast milk could provide the nourishment needed for survival. Her indifference or neglect meant certain death" (40). The mysteries and perils of pregnancy, fetal development, and parturition also play a crucial role in determining the Yoruba apprehension of womanhood — with awe, humility, and profound appreciation. As one would expect, therefore, Yoruba folklore — proverbs no less than tales and other forms — testifies to this reverence and awe for *womanhood* and — to a lesser extent, admittedly — for women.

Nevertheless, the casual observer might point to Yoruba social practices and to such elements of folklore as irreverent and facile references to women and female genitalia as proof that the Yoruba woman is no more than a despised object, tolerated only insofar as she can give pleasure and satisfaction to men. But that conclusion is at variance with the reality and inconsistent with the reverential regard described above; such radically conflicting attitudes can hardly coexist in an organization that lays claim to any significant degree of coherence. The intelligent conclusion must be that the *apparent* contradictions are susceptible to explanations that would reveal hidden consistencies and that any analysis that discounts either perception—reverence for women or *seeming* disregard for women—is bound to result in misrepresentation and misunderstanding.

I suggest that those manifestations of *apparent* male disparagement of or irreverence toward women may be evidence of the almost oppressive impulse (even necessity) to accord near veneration to womanhood: they are arguably stratagems to relieve some of the tension born of the imperative of veneration. People often rebel by finding occasions to engage in just those behaviors that are socially proscribed, the grossness of the rebellion proportionally reflecting the intensity of the pressure in the prescribed direction. Among instances from the Western experience, comedy, we learn, probably came into being as a response to the excessive urge to seriousness and somberness in tragedy, and—closer to our times—the irreverent revels and elaborate ceremonial mockeries of sacred rituals that inmates of monasteries and nunneries in medieval Europe indulged in were supposedly responses to the constraints of excessive asceticism. Similarly, in the Yoruba scene, the annual Òkè 'Bàdàn procession in Ibadan—its ribald sexual vocalizations and demonstrations graphically illustrated with props in the form of modeled genitalia—provides the people with a liminal space for otherwise forbidden performances and an interlude to recharge their ability to face again their regulated lives.

TRUTH, AESTHETICS, AND ETHICS

Thus far my discussion of proverbs in general and Yoruba *òwe* in particular has deferred consideration of certain controversial issues that exist among proverb scholars. I have considered the aesthetics to some extent as well as the utilitarian value of the proverb. The question now is, how crucial is either of those in the life of the proverb? At issue are contentions like Lawrence Boadi's that ascribing a primarily didactic or utilitarian function to proverbs is "too pragmatic and limiting and excludes much about certain aspects of the proverb as an art form. It ignores the importance that some societies attach to linguistic and literary features associated with the proverb, especially the sharp wit, the sarcasm, the humor, the rhetoric, and, indeed, all the aesthetic and poetic values of language use." Using proverbs from the Akan (an ethnic group in Ghana) as his examples, Boadi asserts that their primary function is "aesthetic or poetic and not didactic" (183). He presses his challenge to the utilitarian argument by noting that whereas a speaker can in most cases realize the intention of "putting across a point, exhorting, admonishing, or concealing a fact" without the use of proverbs, he nevertheless resorts to them "because he wishes to embellish his language with a poetic dimension, or demonstrate to his opponent his superior sophistication, education, eloquence, or sensitivity in the use of language"; in Boadi's experience, "brilliant speakers [who] use proverbs . . . are motivated in the main by a desire to heighten their message poetically" (184).

Having made his case with regard to the *user* of proverbs and the secondariness of utility, Boadi goes on to make a similar case with regard to the audience and also the moral dimension and truth claim of proverbs: "the varied emotional and intellectual reactions" to proverbs depend more on their aesthetic value, "the quality of the imagery and of the wit," than on their "moral content or truth value." He accordingly proposes a hierarchy ranging from "highly valued proverbs used in serious discussions and debates, generally by adults" to "little-valued ones used by non-adults or by adults with children, especially during classroom instruction. . . . The more concrete and unusual the imagery, the higher the proverb rates" (185).

It is quite untrue, though, that imagery and wit always trump utility, moral content, or truth value. Scholars nowadays have, to be sure, discredited the once current idea that African art is exclusively (or almost exclusively) utilitarian, but I believe that even so, Boadi's judgment is quite revolutionary. Without getting into a rehash of the arguments for utility, I would simply cite Boadi's own evidence in rebuttal. He contends (or grants) that the purpose of the speaker who resorts to proverbs is "putting across a point, exhorting, admonishing, or concealing a fact." That being the case, it would stand to reason that whatever strategy the speaker adopts is chosen *in order to ensure* that ultimate end. It is safe to assume that the speaker would not resort to any embellishment that would undermine the message and abort its intended outcome. Further, Boadi maintains with reference to his lower-rated proverbs that "any serious adult public speaker who *hoped to drive a point home to his audience* and used these proverbs to illustrate his argument would be judged an incompetent speaker" (186; emphasis added). One assumes that he would be judged even more incompetent if he used no proverbs at all. Boadi thus incidentally, and inadvertently, testifies to the *utility* of the proverb and its *efficacy* as a device "to drive a point home." He goes on, helpfully, to observe that the Akan value rhetoric more than do most societies: "The importance attached to brilliance and imaginativeness in public speech," he says, "leads those who aspire to enter traditional public life and hope to exert influence, especially in the courts and in politics, to cultivate the use of striking images" (186). Finally, he claims that "the proverb is an important aspect in the training of courtiers, who are required to show brilliance, wit, and sophistication in debates" (189). In short, the attraction of proverbs to those who aspire to public life is in their effectiveness in enhancing the aspirants' prospects for success, and the purpose of training courtiers, of course, is to turn out not artists but *effective and persuasive* speakers.

With regard to moral content and truth value (and Boadi's proposed hierarchy), I believe we can readily grant that native speakers do not evaluate all proverbs equally, and that those displaying greater wit and more arresting imagery are adjudged more pleasing than the more prosaic ones. But a proverb that has no truth value, however inventive or striking its imagery, is of no value. Although the intrusion of the classroom into the discussion, of course, unfortunately drags it into the modern age, might not one legitimately ask what the traditional locale would be, and what the occasion, for the use of low-rated proverbs? Proverbs, let us remember, achieve part of their educational purpose, that part involving the socialization and instruction of the youth, precisely and *necessarily* in their use *in the presence of the young.* And whereas in such pursuits as drumming, for example, the instructors or mentors make accommodations for young neophytes, giving them roles and instruments commensurate with their limited, less developed physical competence, proverb users make no such allowances for a presumed mental or rational underdevelopment in youthful listeners. There is, in other words, no such thing as *òwe ọmọdé* (children's proverbs) — not to my knowledge, anyway. If a statement, any statement, deliberately employs esoteric language comprehensible only to people privy to some mystery or some specialized knowledge, then it would exclude uninitiated adults and children alike. Boadi's point would be valid, though, if he referred to raunchy, off-color formulations, for responsible adults would normally abstain from their use in the presence of children. But he means *imagery* as such.

Furthermore, Boadi's bold declaration that "native speakers are sensitive to the poetic value of proverbs whether or not these contain a moral truth" (185) constitutes a serious problem. What, one wonders, does he mean by "moral truth"? Saying that people are sensitive to (in other words, applaud) proverbs whether or not they are based on a *universally accepted* truth, or whether or not they uphold an *approved* or *consensual* view of morality, is one thing; saying that people approve of them even when they are devoid of *any* sort of truth or morality is quite another.

Kwame Gyekye's view of the relative importance of aesthetics and truth value in Akan proverbs is significantly different from Boadi's. For Gyekye, the goal of the proverb is to establish what is real and true. The wise person (*onyansafo*), he asserts, "reflects, imagines, intuits, and then condenses these reflections, imaginings and intuitions in proverbs." From human experience he synthesizes what is "ultimately real and true," which is then "distilled in proverbs." With regard to "moral truth" (or morality), Gyekye observes that the aim of Akan philosophers is to gain a "comprehensive understanding of the world and human life and conduct." They not only describe reality but also recommend "how human beings ought to live and what their values ought to be — hence the existence of many proverbs relative to morality. The wise person of the Akan community," he declares, "is essentially a speculative philosopher" (64).

So useful do Akan sages find proverbs, according to Gyekye, that when during his research he asked people to give the meanings of such concepts as fate or destiny (*nkrabea*), they usually resorted to proverbs. He concludes, therefore, that "in the view of the Akan wise person, analysis of propositions cannot dispense with experience" (65). I might corroborate this valorization of experience with a Yoruba proverb. In Duro Ladipọ's opera *Ọba Kò So* a messenger arrives at Ọba Ṣàngó's palace from the Ẹdẹ outpost to report on conditions there. Asked if he is certain of what he is reporting, he responds rhetorically, *Ng ó ha yó kí mmá mọ̀?* ("Would I be satiated and not know?"). To experience something is to know it, or to really know something is to experience it.

In *A Kì í,* my earlier collection, I argued against excessive claims about proverbs' infallibility, specifically the sort some scholars derived from John Messenger's claim that in some Nigerian courts, cases were decided on the basis of a skillful application of proverbs. I pointed out that in the same essay Messenger noted that the judges went to great lengths, including employing mediums, to ascertain the merit of each litigant's case. Few Africans, I argued, believe proverbs to be incontrovertible; "most people realize that a number of the sayings make assertions that are evidently tenuous" (6). That is a far cry, though, from denying the relevance of truth.

The difficulty of making any valid general statement about the truth value of proverbs as a whole results from certain obvious facts, one being what one writer described a century ago as their "stopped-clock" aspect (*Spectator* 694): a stopped clock is right, or "truthful," twice every twenty-four hours but wrong, or "false," the rest of the time. Let me cite two Yoruba examples. The first says,

> Ilé olóore kì í jó tán
> Tìkà kì í jó kù
> [The house of a good person never burns completely
> That of a wicked person never burns partially]

The other asserts,

> Àṣeṣílẹ̀ làbọ̀wábá
> Ẹní bá ṣu sílẹ̀ á bọ̀ wá béṣinṣin
> [What one sets aside (or leaves behind) is what one returns to find
> Whoever leaves excrement behind will return to find flies]

The "truth" in the first proverb is that good people will never lack succor when they are in need, whereas evil people will never find people to come to their aid. The second teaches that one reaps what one sows. If the "truth" in these proverbs is consistent with the prevailing ethos of the society, then surely they purvey a "moral" truth. Even though empirical knowledge tells us that the houses of good people sometimes do collapse completely, whereas those of wicked people may not collapse at all, or, again, that one might sometimes leave excrement behind and return to find a sapling rather than flies, that fact is immaterial. A "moral truth" does not have to be absolutely and *invariably* valid to be relevant. As Barry Hallen has astutely observed, "Proverbs do not introduce themselves to us as universal truths, as generalizations that always apply. Their pith, their point, their punch is situational or context-dependent to an essential degree" (141). To insist on invariable, empirical verifiability as the measure of proverbs' truthfulness would therefore be to deny nearly all of them any claim to truth. According to that standard, "Haste makes waste" would be untrue, as would "Every cloud has a silver lining."

Archer Taylor quotes Lord John Russell's definition of the proverb as "one man's wit and all men's wisdom" (Taylor "Wisdom"). Notwithstanding the consensus implied in the attribution of the wisdom to "all men" (these days, one would rather say "all people"), one needs no more than a casual knowledge of a culture's proverbs to discover that they are not always consistent with one another, that for every one that asserts a "truth" there will be others that contradict it. The proverb

Àsòrò àìlàdí ló pa Elempe àkókó
Tó ní igbá wúwo ju àwo
[Speaking without elaborating is what killed Elempe the First
Who said calabash is heavier than china]

is clarified with the information that Elempe the First got himself killed by assert-ing that calabash was heavier than china, when the penalty for being proved wrong was execution.[3] In the verification process, it turned out that calabash was lighter than china, mass for mass. The poor man failed to specify that he was speaking of heavily loaded calabash and empty china. The proverb advises people to spell things out and not stint on explanation. On the other hand, the proverb

Òrò púpò, iró ló ḿmú wá
[A lot of words only entail lies]

makes an opposite or conflicting assertion. Similarly, the advice in *Àgbájo owó la fi ńso àyà* ("It is with fingers bunched together that one strikes one's breast"), meaning that there is strength in numbers, contradicts the injunction implied in *Olómú dá omú ìyá è gbé* ("Each breast-feeding child must lift its mother's breast by itself"). I return to this point later.

In my earlier collection I noted instances in which, in response to some prov-erbs' contestable assertions, subsequent wits have coined rebuttals. I cited among other examples the original proverb *Orí kì í burú lówòó* ("A head is never bad in a group"—meaning that a single person in a crowd cannot be selectively beset with ill fortune), to which a wit has retorted, *Orí a máa burú lówòó; bí a bá sòkò lójà enìkan ni yó bàá* ("A head may be bad in a group; if one throws a stone in a market it will hit one person") (*A Kì í* 6–7). One scholar has recently given such rebuttals the grandiose name "postproverbials" (Raji-Oyelade).

Whereas we might decide to dispose of a stopped clock because of the tiny per-centage of the time during which it speaks true, we cannot so dispense with prov-erbs that are similarly true in a comparable percentage of circumstances. The rea-son is that the truth they affirm when they *are* true is fundamental, and, to repeat Okpewho's words, based on "intimate observation of human experience and of the surrounding nature." Many make philosophical, epistemological, and moral as-sertions that are consistent with the dominant ethos of the community. Olatunji's assignment of a prescriptive function to the Yoruba proverb (175) is understand-able only to the extent that proverbs are believed to accord with the morality of the group. In other cases, of course, proverbs are true because they present known contrasting, even oppositional, strains to the dominant ethos.

The Good, the Bad, and the Expedient

An important fact to bear in mind is that African societies are not as simple and their mentality and world view not as jejune as some people might suppose. For that reason, one who looks for simple, uncomplicated concepts of truth and morality among them will go astray. With regard to "good" and "bad" in Yoruba thought, one might go so far as to contend that a significant Nietzschean strain exists in it, something consistent with what that controversial speaker remarked about Herbert Spencer, "who considers the concept *good* qualitatively the same as the concepts *useful* or *practical;* so that in the judgments *good* and *bad,* humanity is said to have summed up and sanctioned precisely its unforgotten and unforgettable experiences of the *useful practical* and the *harmful impractical*" (Nietzsche 161).

To the extent that the "useful practical" — in other words, the expedient — places self-interest above all else, including charity, equity, and even honesty, proverbs that sanction it could be adjudged in one view "immoral," or at best "amoral," and one will find several such proverbs in the Yoruba corpus. An acquaintance once provided me with an eloquent demonstration of the cynicism that supposedly explains some instances of a sense of community. He cited the proverb

> *Bí o bá ńgbọ́ "Gbe! Gbè! Gbe!"*
> *Tí o ò bá wọn gbé e*
> *Èhìnkùlé ẹ ni wọ́n ḿbọ̀ wá gbé e dà sí*
> [If you hear "Haul it! Haul it! Haul it!"
> And you don't join them in hauling it
> It is to your backyard they will come to dump it]

One can understand the proposition that if, for example, the community was engaged in a beautification project that involved removing eyesores from public view and dumping them in less public places, the workers might choose as their dump site a readily available property whose owner was not involved in the cleanup or not around to protect it. In that case, participation in such a public, communal project might indicate not public spiritedness so much as self-interest. But the occasion of my acquaintance's employment of the proverb was even more cynical. He used it as the Yoruba equivalent of the English "If you can't beat them, join them" to urge the expediency of participating in the raid on public funds by well-positioned officials during the infamous Abacha regime of the 1990s.

Another applicable proverb,

> *O ṛ́ẹsè-ẹ wèrè o ò bù ú ṣoògùn*
> *Níbo lo ti máa rí tọlọgbọ́n?*
> [You come upon the footprint of an imbecile and you do not take some of
>   the soil for your juju
> Where will you find the footstep of a sane person?],

refers to the belief that magical charms made with soil taken from a person's footprint are powerfully effective against the person, and the care people take, therefore, not to leave their footprints carelessly about where their enemies might have access to them. The proverb's admonition is to take advantage of the vulnerable, because you will probably never find a mentally competent person to so misuse.

Consider also

Ẹni tí ò gbọ́n lààwẹ̀ ńgbò
[Only the foolish suffer the hunger pangs of fasting]

and

Ọgbo-ọgbọ́n làgbàlagbà-á fi ńsá fún ẹranlá
[It is with dissembling that a venerable man (gender specificity intended)
    flees from a wild beast]

Normally, a person fasting should suffer the pangs of hunger which constitute the sacrifice that is the whole point of fasting. And a venerable man does not flee from danger but confronts it manfully. But the two proverbs pooh-pooh such sentiments. In both, the injunction is to do the expedient thing for one's comfort and safety, even if it is something normally forbidden or "not done." The better part of valor is discretion, they say.

The users of such proverbs could be speaking tongue-in-cheek, not seriously recommending or justifying the propositions in their sayings, just as they could be in dead earnest. Evidently, proverb use lends itself to cynicism, and one cannot always be sure when a proverb is cynical and inconsistent with approved morality (and the user's true belief and intention) and when it is a reliable expression of a society's mores (and the user's true inclination).

Relativity of "Truth" and Ethics

Such uncertainty indicates, if nothing else, the need for some guide to understanding the proverbs and *how* they mean. Some of the confusion about them would disappear if, for instance, we were mindful that they are sensitive to what one could describe as the relativity of "truth" and ethics. The resolute relativism of Yoruba proverbs is the import of

Kòkòrò tó jẹfọ́ jàre ẹfọ́
Ìwọ̀n lewéko ńdára-á mọ
[The insect that eats the vegetable is vindicated (in any case brought) by the
    leaf
Leaves should be moderate in their attractiveness]

A modern Western court should quite properly be scandalized if a rape defendant (male or female) were to cite it as a defense! A similar sentiment is evident in a less objectionable form in

Bí a bá ńkìlọ̀ fólè
Ká kìlọ̀ fónísu ẹ̀bá ọ̀nà
[As we reprimand the thief
Let us also reprimand the owner of the yams beside the path]

Incidentally, this last may record a shift in morality in the Yoruba world, for there was a time when a dealer could leave his commodities unattended, simply indicating the asking price alongside the goods: leaving so many pebbles, for example, to indicate so many cowries. Those wishing to purchase any of the items offered for sale would help themselves and leave the correct amount. The returning owner would find the rest of the merchandise and the price of the purchased goods waiting undisturbed. Any merchant who displays such trust today could be judged extremely foolish, if not insane.

That said, however, I must acknowledge the existence and usage of proverbs that are downright inconsistent with generally accepted behavior and are immediately recognized as such. No Yoruba person who hears

> Òyìnbó ò fólè
> Ó fẹ́ ìyára
> [The white man does not like stealing
> He admires nimbleness]

mistakes its moral contrariety, at least in the context of Yoruba values, even though its truth with regard to the perceived morality of the white man (in Africa) is not in question. What it says, in plain language, is that stealing is not an admirable thing, but if you are good enough at it to get away with it (or if you can find a clever lawyer to argue your case), go for it! Like the earlier proverbs about doing what is expedient, if its use is not in jest, it is probably cynical.

Raymond Firth's discussion of Maori proverbs illustrates their problematic tendency toward inconsistency, both with one another and with accepted usage, and consequently their capability to confound whoever places implicit confidence in them as evidence of the culture's mores. Whereas the people place a high value on hospitality, he notes, their proverbs (whakatauki) are very often antihospitable, urging people "not to be too lavish in their gifts, to consume their food themselves before visitors arrive and they are deprived of the greater share of it, and not to grant undue hospitality without the prospect of some equivalent in return" (249).

The question legitimately arises, then, how does one tell when to take a proverb seriously and when with a grain of salt? In this regard there is no substitute for a close knowledge of the society concerned and its values. Knowing when a proverb first came into use (and to what end) would also be helpful but is impossible or, at least, unrealistic and in any case inconsistent with the spirit of proverbs and of traditional oral texts (creative and otherwise) generally.

Firth's representation of the Maori as inveterately hospitable enables him (and us) to conclude that proverbs enjoining the opposite of hospitality are facetious, and our knowledge of Yoruba society similarly enables us to determine that antisocial Yoruba proverbs are facetious. That is, of course, because we are able to see the proverbs synchronically. Viewed diachronically, an intentionally facetious proverb might come to express group ethos after the society has undergone significant social and ethical changes. Thus, whereas the Yoruba proverb enjoining one to take advantage of vulnerable people might have been facetious on its creation, one can credibly argue that it accords with the prevailing morality in much of Yorubaland today. The same goes for the advice to "join them if you can't beat them."

Authoritarianism (Unanimism)

One weighty objection to reliance on proverbs comes from the Ghanaian philosopher Kwasi Wiredu, for whom they represent a check on youthful aspiration and development. According to him, they are a means through which African traditional cultures enforce unquestioning obedience to elders and curtail curiosity and independence of thought in the young. African proverbs, which he describes as "concentrations of practical wisdom," are marvelous in clinching arguments and reinforcing morals, he says, but "it is rare to come across ones which extol the virtues of originality and independence of thought" (4). An American colleague of mine made a point not dissimilar to Wiredu's on looking through my collection of proverbs. He noted with considerable interest the large number of entries in the first category, especially in that section dealing with self-knowledge, on knowing one's place and not exceeding it—in other words, not overreaching. He remarked that the preoccupation in Western societies is exactly opposite to the one my collection indicates: in the West people are *encouraged* to overachieve, to dream the impossible dream.

Wiredu's opinion is curious, especially his assertion about the paucity of proverbs that encourage the youth to be original and enterprising. It is easy to see, though, why some do regard certain proverbs as discouraging ambition. Among the Yoruba, for example, the well-bred person is always careful to avoid the embarrassment and disgrace that come from being cut down to size after any arrogant act of self-overvaluation. Since part of avoiding disgrace is avoidance of overreaching, of biting off more than one can chew, the wealth of proverbs that caution, in effect, "Know your place and do not exceed it" is understandable. Examples include

Awòlúmátèé, ìwòn ara è ló mò
[The person who enters a town and avoids disgrace achieves the feat because
    he or she knows his or her place]

and

Bí a ti mọ là ńkú
Olongo kì í kú tìyàn-tìyàn
[One dies [or crashes] according to one's weight
The robin does not die with a resounding noise]

Still, the perception that proverbs encouraging people to strive for excellence, to overachieve, to climb every mountain and be limited only by their imagination are a Western monopoly is false, as the proverbs in my section on industry show. The Yoruba also encourage adventure, achievement, and the pursuit of excellence while decrying and even ridiculing indolence and shiftlessness. The following proverbs suffice as proof:

> *O ò ṣági lógbẹ́*
> *O ò ta ògòrò lófà*
> *O dédìí ọpẹ o gbẹ́nu sókè ò ńretí*
> *Ọ̀fẹ́ ní ńro?*
> [You did not cut a wound into the tree
> You did not shoot an arrow into the palm tree
> You arrive at the base of the palm tree and you lift up your mouth
>   expectantly
> Does it drip sap for free?]

The proverb refers to the necessary actions one must perform before expecting to get wine from the palm tree—drilling a hole at the top and collecting the sap in a container. The message is that one must struggle in order to triumph, make an effort in order to gain a prize. A second example,

> *Iwájú iwájú lòpá ẹ̀bìtì ńré sí*
> [Forward, forward is the direction in which the staff of the [tripped] snare
>   springs]

is usually employed in a prayer that a person's fortunes may always advance, but it also expresses the belief that one must always aspire to move forward, to be better tomorrow than one is today.

With particular reference to the young, another proverb says,

> *Ọmọ tí yó jẹ́ẹ́ àṣàmú*
> *Kékeré ló ti ńṣẹnu ṣámú-ṣámú*
> [A child that will turn out to be peerless
> It is from childhood that he or she distinguishes himself or herself]

Another adds,

> *Ọmọ tó káwọ́ sókè ló fẹ́ ká gbé òun*
> [It is the child that lifts up its arms that asks to be picked up]

The child who just sits *may* be picked up, but the one who raises its arms aids its cause considerably. The idea is that when opportunities present themselves, one must still make an effort to take advantage of them, and a child is employed in the imagery because the logic that applies to the adult applies to children also. In that regard, remember that even in Western societies people are cautioned against biting off more than they can chew (Brunvand 56) and advised to cut their coats according to their sizes.

As for the preponderance of entries in my first category, the explanation resides in the premium the Yoruba place on how other people regard them. They jealously guard their image and public perception, taking care to keep whatever might detract from their good reputation well hidden, left behind in the confines of the family compound, before they venture abroad. Here are two pertinent proverbs in this regard:

Ilé ẹni la ti ńjẹ òkété onídodo
[It is within the confines of one's home that one eats a cane rat with a tumor]

Bánidélé là ḿmọ ìṣe ẹni
Èèyàn gbé òkèèrè níyì
[Going home with a person is how one knows his or her ways
People enjoy good repute when they live at a distance]

The first proverb acknowledges the sentiment that one's home is one's castle and that one may do as one likes, even behave dishonorably, in its privacy. The second refers to the expectation that though one's guard is usually down at home, those who venture outside will be on their best—perhaps uncharacteristically good—behavior. The proverbs advise, in effect, "Be what you *wish* to be at home but what you *should* be abroad."

Nativism

One last word on actual or implied disparagement of proverbs. In his *Proverbs, Textuality, and Nativism in African Literature,* the Yoruba scholar Adélékè Adéèkó discusses African creative writers' use of traditional elements in their works, and African critics' use of traditional criteria in evaluating these works—usages that he characterizes as "nativist engagements" (ix). In spite of the quite interesting observations and commentary in the book, his lumping together of traditional resources under the unmistakably pejorative designation "nativism" suggests, perhaps unintentionally, a dismissive attitude toward traditional (or non-Western) resources and approaches. The appearance of the book (in 1998) coincided with the increasing desire among African scholars, in response to an intellectual current in the West, to distance themselves from such concepts as race, nationalism, and other means of suggesting, if not asserting, differences among humankind. The discountenancing and disparaging of such distinguishing categories have proved especially attractive to those Africans (philosophers for example) who believe that attempts to resuscitate and revitalize traditional resources—those that European colonizing and civilizing efforts of the past several centuries have repressed or done away with—amount to some sort of recidivism. Describing African cultural resources and their use as "nativism" is therefore unfortunate. This is not to deny the impulses driving "the process of transnationalization," as Achille Mbembe sets them out in a recent essay, but it is to challenge the assumption that transnationalism (or transnationality) is self-evidently preferable to an African specificity or difference.

Among suggestions made to me about what information to supply for the entries in this collection are several that I have decided against including.

Sources

On several occasions I have had to explain my refusal to heed a demand that I supply the sources of the proverbs in my collection. Such a request would make good sense with regard to certain performative texts, especially elaborate ones such as epics, *ìjálá* (hunters' chanted poetry), and *iwì egúngún* (masqueraders' chants), which always bear the unique and unmistakable stamp of the performer. But hardly ever does a user's individual signature inflect proverb usage, in either Yoruba or English (as an example) proverbs in general. Do we know the source of "Two heads are better than one" or "Haste makes waste"?[4] Where we do know the sources for English proverbs—Shakespearean ones, for example, such as "The better part of valor is discretion"—it is because we are in that case dealing with a *literary* tradition.

The debate on the importance of authorship in literary scholarship and analysis is not irrelevant in this context. Western literary theory has gone back and forth in its effort to locate the meaning or significance of a text, posing such questions as: Does it reside in the mind of the author of the text?

Is it a stable phenomenon with a stable relationship with its medium?

Is it something (whatever that might be) that the reader makes of it?

Does it matter in this regard who the author is, and should we care?

Is the unattributed text not, like anonymous legal documents, more venerable than one whose creator we know? (see Eagleton 67–90)

The quality of being unattributed is, moreover, consistent with the Yoruba de-emphasizing of the individual, especially with regard to the formulation and enunciation of things done and not done.[5] The authority belongs to the people, the supraindividual entity, whose dictates, unlike those of an individual we may or may not respect, we are not inclined to challenge.

Asking a Yoruba person to cite his source for a proverb that he has heard perhaps a thousand times in his life, the first time as a child, is in any case quite unrealistic. That is not to say, however, that he could never possibly identify when and where he first heard a certain proverb or number of proverbs. I do recall the first occasion when I heard certain proverbs used, and the identity of the persons who used them. For example, I first heard *Gbọ-gbọ-gbọ lọwọ́ ńyọ ju orí* (4232) from Bọla Ige in Ibadan in 1983, when he was governor of Ọ̀yọ́ State; *Ìka tó tọ́ símú là ńnà símú* (3399) from Victor Olunlọyọ in Ibadan in 1983, when he was campaigning in the Ọ̀yọ́ State gubernatorial race; *Eni tó bá ńje lábé-ẹ Jẹ́gẹ́dẹ́ ló ńpè é nÍgi Àràbà* (2079) from Ayọ Ayọrinde, a friend in Lincoln, Nebraska, in the late 1970s; and *Dì ẹ̀ndì lòpin-in sinimá* (4914) from Toyin Falọla some time in the late 1990s and somewhere in the United States. In no case, though, was any of these "sources" the originator of the proverb in question. Identifying someone who uses a proverb as its source would be, in my thinking, preposterous and somewhat arrogant. What right, I mean, do I have to glorify *my* "source" (as defined above) as *the* source of a proverb, simply because I first heard it from him or her, when someone else could earlier have heard another person use the same proverb? My assigning it to "X" would privilege me in a way that neither "X" nor I deserve.

Proverbs are communal property, and the Yoruba experience differs from that which, according to Kwesi Yankah, obtains among the Akan, to whom the office of "professional proverb custodian" is apparently unique. "After a speaker has composed or effectively used a proverb, particularly in a conflict interaction," Yankah tells us, "she may register it with the custodian and narrate the circumstances that triggered the proverb. . . . The custodian then moves from ward to ward narrating the proverb and the circumstances of its original use to the public" (79).

Historical Markers

Embedded in some proverbs are bits of dating information that reveal approximately when they came into being. These are usually references to identifiable historical events, sometimes to historical personalities, and sometimes to items whose advent is associated with historical developments, such as the introduction of foreign religions (Christianity and Islam) or the arrival of Europeans. Proverbs that incorporate historical markers permit an approximate determination of the time when they came into use. An event referred to in a proverb obviously predates it, and one that is about a historical figure probably originated during the lifetime or soon after the demise of that person. In

> *Olọ́run ò pín dọ́gba*
> *Sajiméjò-ọ́ ju Kòròfo*
> [God has not apportioned things equally
> The Sergeant Major outranks the Corporal]

the mention of British military ranks bears witness to the prior establishment of British presence and institutions. One could further narrow the temporal space in which the proverb probably came into being by suggesting that it postdated the establishment of the British West Africa Frontier Force and the recruitment of local soldiers into its ranks.

The proverb

> *Ìmàlé sọ̀rọ̀ òjó kù*
> *Ó ní Olọ́rún sán-ìn sí i*
> [The Muslim spoke and thunder rumbled
> He said God has signed off on the matter]

provides two different markers. First, there is the mention of *Ìmàlè,* a practitioner of Islam, and then there is the evidence of authentication he offers, God's endorsement *by signature,* for the habit of signing a document as an indication of agreement or acknowledgment is associated with the European incursion into the Yoruba world.

Other proverbs with historical markers, specifically references to the presence of Europeans, include

Adìẹ kòwé
Òyìnbó kà á tì
[The chicken wrote something
The white man cannot read it]

With its reference to literacy and the knowledge of writing, this one was a popular derogatory comment on bad calligraphy during colonial days, particularly in the primary schools, where penmanship was an important part of the curriculum. Similar in its referents is

Òyìnbó tó ṣe lẹ́ẹ̀dì ló ṣèrésà
[The same white man who made the lead pencil also made the eraser]

Apart from referring to the new phenomenon of writing and its associated paraphernalia, it incidentally also acknowledges the culture's endorsement of unsentimental pragmatism.

"Dì ẹ́ǹdì" lòpin-in sinimá
["The End" is the end of the cinema show]

acknowledges a new form of entertainment and propaganda and therefore dates to some time after the Colonial Film Unit introduced cinema featuring propaganda shows during the colonial period.

The following proverb refers to both a historical figure and a historical event:

Akíni ńjẹ́ akíni
Afinihàn ńjẹ́ afinihàn
Èwo ni "Ọ kú, ará Ìbàdàn" lójúde Ṣódẹkẹ́?
[A greeter is a greeter
A betrayer is a betrayer
What is the motive for "Hello, Ibadan native," in front of Ṣodẹkẹ's home?]

It certainly originated in the late nineteenth century during the Yoruba wars and in the lifetime of one General Ṣodẹkẹ, who led the Ẹ̀gbá in their conflict with Ibadan (see Ajayi and Smith). During that conflict, a person from Ibadan caught in Abẹokuta, and especially in front of General Ṣodẹkẹ's residence, would be assumed to be up to no good.

The extent and precision of timing that these proverbs allow is limited, though, and insufficient caution on that score can lead to errors such as Dupẹ Oduyọye's too precise determination of a proverb's dating on the basis of its internal referent. Of the proverb

Aláàrù tó jẹ búrẹ́dì
Awọ orí ẹ̀ ló ńjẹ
[The head porter who eats bread
Is eating the scalp off his head]

he says that it "dates about 1850 — first contact of the Yoruba with wheat bread and the English word bread. . . . It was fashionable but more expensive than the local staples." His dating suggests that the proverb's appearance followed immediately upon the introduction of wheat bread into the Yoruba world. He does say "*about* 1850," but how elastic is "about" in this instance? In fact, all we can say, in the absence of any more specific evidence, is that it originated sometime *after* the introduction of the food. If we were able to ascertain the proverb's first appearance in a collection, then of course we would be entitled to assert that it originated sometime between the introduction of wheat bread and the date of that publication. There is no doubt, though, that the proverb has been around for a long time.

Contextualization

My argument for not contextualizing each proverb — that is, placing it in an actual usage situation, as some well-meaning readers have suggested — is similar to the one against identifying sources. Whereas one would certainly contextualize other forms of traditional verbal performance if one intended to make their cultural, transactional significance evident, my caveat with regard to proverbs is that they are incidental to *all* other forms of oral performance and discourse, and there are usually no occasions dedicated to their use. A collector can arrange to hear an informant tell short stories, or may happen on storytelling sessions; one can ask an informant to recite some *oríkì* (praises), *rárà* (brides' nuptial chants), or *ìjálá;* one might be present where a performance is taking place; and one may ask a *babaláwo* to recite *Ifá* divination verses or perhaps have the opportunity to see divination in action. In all such cases (with the possible exception of command performances) a description of the context would be useful, and the identity of the "sources" or informants would be of interest: *context,* because we would wish to understand the who, the why, the how, and the wherefore of the performance; *identity,* because each performer brings personal idiosyncrasies to the act, sometimes modifying the text or otherwise putting an individual stamp on the total event.

In his discussion of the significant role the audience plays in shaping performances, Okpewho cites instances in which the performer altered his text, either in deference to the sensitivities of particular audiences or to avoid trouble with the law (57–63). The proverbs that could possibly cause offense in certain quarters are insignificantly few, and can be so tagged, but not every proverb merits such attention. Although suggesting possible contexts for each proverb might be interesting, any suggestion would simply be one of several possibilities. (I did suggest occasions on which each of the proverbs in *A Kì í* might be used, but in that book I was dealing with a fraction of the material in this collection, and the benefit of doing the same in this volume would not be commensurate with the increase in heft it would entail.)

Original Dialects

I have also balked at the call for the use of "original dialects" — Ekìtì, Ẹ̀gbá, Ìjẹ̀sà, Ìjẹ̀bú, Oǹdó, Ọ̀yọ́, and so forth — in my transcription of the proverbs. The desire to "fix" pan-Yoruba proverbs in such a manner is, again, inappropriate and alien to the spirit of proverbs. It is true that were we able to fix these sayings in the ways that some scholars would like — determining who originated them, when, where, and why, the original dialect for each one, and the like — we could make some interesting deductions that we currently cannot make. I am not certain, though, that our inability to perform such exercises is any real loss. Having presented reasons why I believe efforts at such fixing are not only unnecessary but, more important, misguided, I here stress the epistemic consideration: what is in keeping with the Yoruba way and, indeed, the African way. The African way does not countenance the chiseling of texts in stone, as it were, with the exception of sacred (ritual) materials, and even these are fixed not according to authorial attribution, dating, and so forth but by core content. In general, traditional oral materials (including elaborate ones such as the *Kambili,* the *Mwindo,* and the *Ozidi*) live in their not being canned, in their being able to respond to each occasion and each audience according to the dialectal, idiosyncratic, or any other particularity of the performer (Okpewho 105–15). Their true and ideal mode of existence is not in their recorded, published, and therefore preserved, form but in their *potentiality,* which is actualized anew at each performance or, in the case of proverbs, at each utterance. It is in this form that texts lend themselves to the salutary quality of revisability, enabling a people to reinvent itself and its history according to its ever-evolving sense of itself.

ORGANIZING THE COLLECTION

The thousands of proverbs presented in this volume — here numbered consecutively within categories for ease of reference and cross-reference — made necessary a number of decisions about their format, their transcription and translation (and import), and their categorization and sequence.

Presentation

In this introduction I have rendered the proverbs most often in verse form rather than in running prose in order to acknowledge their poetic qualities. As my examples illustrate, one can present them in single lines, in couplets, in triads, or in quatrains, depending on each individual case. I have not chosen that option in the body of the collection, however, for considerations both of space and of most common usage — in common "prosaic" communication.

Nor have I adopted the suggestion that I present each and every proverb with "interlinear" translation. According to that call, the proverb

Ẹni tí ó bá ńje lábẹ́-ẹ Jẹ́gẹ́dẹ́
Ní ńpè é nÍgi Àràbà

would be rendered as follows:

Ẹni	*tí*	*ó*	*bá*	*ńje*	*ní abẹ́-ẹ*	*Jẹ́gẹ́dẹ́*
Person	that	he/she	happens to	customarily eat	at underneath (of)	Jẹgẹdẹ

Ní	*ńpè*	*é*	*ní Igi*	*Àràbà*
It is [that]	customarily addresses	him	as Tree	Silk-cotton

Each such rendering would then necessarily be followed by an idiomatically correct translation — a most extravagant use of space. But my main objection has more to do with ideology than with paper conservation. If the desire were to provide illustrations of the peculiarities of Yoruba syntax with particular reference to proverb construction, one or two illustrations like the one above would suffice. If, on the other hand, the intention were to enable linguists who do not speak the language to do linguistic analyses of it with the aid of such presentation, then one must insist that such assistance would not be in the service of good linguistic practice. I believe that as with English, French, German, Japanese, or Russian, whoever would claim expertise in the culture's literary texts, and the competence to carry out linguistic analyses of them, should have a sound knowledge of the language. A scholar lacking the requisite language tool should collaborate with another who *is* adequately equipped. Adherence to such a requirement would reduce the incidence of such texts as Ryszard Pachocinski's *Proverbs of Africa,* which suffers from the author's lack of knowledge of the languages concerned and therefore constitutes a disservice both to the cultures and to any nonspeaker of the language(s) who might take the book as a reliable resource.

The Yoruba language is quite supple in its structure, permitting, for example, what one might describe as a modified shorthand in the conveyance of meaning. I refer to the possibility of eliding certain (auxiliary) syntactic elements from a sentence structure, elements that nonetheless continue to be understood and whose omission does not affect the semantic integrity of the statement. One set of proverbs that proves quite interesting and challenging in this regard has as their subjects noun clauses that are made up of the pronoun *Ẹni* (Person), followed by an adjective clause comprising a relative pronoun, an appositive pronoun referring back to the initial pronoun, a subjunctive, and, lastly, the defining (or delimiting) quality. The following example clarifies what I mean:

Ẹni tí ó bá ńje lábẹ́-ẹ Jẹ́gẹ́dẹ́
Ní ńpè é nÍgi Àràbà

It translates, literally, as

> Person that he or she happens to customarily eat under Jẹgẹdẹ
> Is the person who calls him a silk-cotton tree,

and the entire first line constitutes the subject. Yoruba construction permits the omission of some or all of the elements between Ẹni and ńjẹ (customarily eat) without detracting from the completeness of the message. We could thus have Ẹní bá ńjẹ lábẹ-ẹ Jẹgẹdẹ . . . or Ẹni tó bá ńjẹ lábẹ-ẹ Jẹgẹdẹ . . . or even Ẹní ńjẹ lábẹ-ẹ Jẹgẹdẹ . . . The form in which I have entered such a proverb (which depends on the form in which it occurs most frequently in speech) affects its placement in my alphabetization scheme (explained below).

Orthography

I have departed from some current practices not to be contrary but in order to live up to the expectation that tone marks will reliably guide the reader to the correct pronunciation of the written text. Therefore, I have chosen to include the tone that indicates a genitival relationship between two nouns, for example bàbá-a Wálé (Wálé's father or, more appropriately, father-of Wálé), where the midtone a stands in place of the elided but understood midtone ti (of). The final vowel of the substantive word (in this case bàbá, father) is always reduplicated and always assigned the midtone of the elided word, regardless of its original tone and regardless of the initial tone of the cognate (in this case Wálé). Thus

> okọ́-ọ wa   [our hoe]
> okọ-ọ wa   [our husband]
> okò-ọ wa   [our vehicle]

In other instances where the tone of an elided word is retained to indicate its graphical absence but understood presence (usually in the reduplication of the preceding vowel), I have continued the practice of using a hyphen between the original vowel and its reduplication. The tone of the reduplicated vowel is always high, regardless of the tone of the original vowel, because the reduplication indicates the elision of a high-toned pronoun ó (he, she, or it). Thus

> okọ́-ọ́ lọ   [the hoe (it) went]
> okọ-ọ́ lọ   [the husband (he) went]
> okò-ọ́ lọ   [the vehicle (it) went]

The pronoun ó is elided, but its tone is assimilated into the following verb. Note, though, that in the case of okọ́-ọ́ lọ, because the original vowel already carries a high tone, it is usually not reduplicated in speech but simply rendered as okọ́ lọ. In rapid speech "the husband went" would also be rendered as okọ́ lọ, making a possible ambiguity ("the husband went" *or* "the hoe went"), which is however resolved by the context and common sense.

The use of a hyphen in cases of reduplicated vowels has the added advantage of reducing the possibility of confusion in cases of nasalized vowels. Because in writing such a vowel, an *n* is attached to it, its reduplication could result in confusion for the reader if the hyphen were left out. For example, in the case of *agbọ̀n-ọ́n kún* (the basket [it] was full), simply writing *agbọ̀nọ́n kún* would leave a reader wondering what the word *agbọ̀nọ́n* was or meant. Where the reduplicated vowel stands for a direct object, though, I have not connected the vowels with a hyphen: for example, *A kì í dájọ́ Orò ká yè ẹ́* (One does not set the date for an *Orò* rite and then ignore it). I have also used a hyphen to separate the two syllables in a diphthong if it is nasalized, as in *ọ̀fọ́n-ọ̀n* (house rat). In speech, especially rapid speech, when the verb has a high tone, its final sound and the mid-tone extension representing the direct object come together to form a diphthong, a glide from high to midtone. Most often, indeed, the high part becomes completely elided, leaving only the midtone. Thus, *Bí o bá ńgbọ́ Gbé e! Gbè! Gbé e!* eventually becomes *Bí o bá ńgbọ́ Gbe! Gbè! Gbe!*

Furthermore, I have preferred to indicate the pronunciation in cases where the future auxiliary *yó* (will, shall) occurs — in other words, to indicate the associated low tone by incorporating it in the main verb, which assimilates and retains the tone: thus, *yó jàáde* (will emerge) rather than *yóò jáde*. The same is true of the negative *má* as in *má jòó* (not dance), which others would render as *máà jó* or (in Ayo Bamgbose's orthography) *má jó*. I have maintained that practice in all cases where a high-toned proposition (such as *sí*, meaning "to" or "into" or "toward") is followed by a low-toned object (like *ìlú*, meaning "town"), in which case I have written *sílùú* rather than *síìlú* or *sí .lú*.[6]

I have also departed from the more or less standard practice of spelling the Yoruba word for "person" or "human being" as *ènìà* (alternatively *ènìyàn*). My preference is *èèyàn*, which I believe to be more accurate from the standpoint of both etymology and semantics. The word incorporates the belief that each human being on the verge of incarnation kneels before the Creator and chooses what path he or she will pursue in life. The path, or fate, is *à-kúnlè-yàn* ("what one chooses on one's knees," or "what one kneels to choose"). Thus, the choosing agent is *èè-yàn* ("one who chooses"). The Yoruba speaker knows that in pronouncing the word the nasalization begins at the point of sounding the *y*, almost as though one were saying *èè-nyàn*. The original orthographers, not thinking of etymology, based their orthography on sound. (Note that in *ènìà* the final vowel would be nasalized because of the effect of the preceding *n* sound, unless the speaker made a deliberate (and I would say unnatural) effort otherwise. The same mistaken process led to the spellings *aiyé* instead of *ayé* (world) and *ẹiyẹ* instead of *ẹyẹ* (bird), both of which I have corrected.

Furthermore, my rendering of the nasalized vowels differs from what some writers of Yoruba would prefer in such words as the place name *Ìbàdàn* and such nouns as *iyán* (pounded yam), *ọ̀nà* (path), *itàn* (story), and *ọkàn* (heart). Some writers would prefer *Ìbàdòn, iyón, ònò, itòn,* and *okòn.* As there is no uniformity in pronunciation across Yorubaland, the choice poses no difficulty.

Finally, in those cases where a proverb employs a characteristic statement to stand for a character, I have hyphenated the entire statement (e.g., 3025) or, alternatively, placed it within quotation marks (e.g., 433) or sometimes both (23).

Classification Scheme

In his introduction to *The Yoruba: History, Culture, and Language,* the Yoruba historian and scholar J. Adebọwale Atanda testifies that the basic motivating force for the Yoruba is the desire to have a good life. It is why they worship *òrìṣà* (divinities) and why, if one *òrìṣà* fails to deliver, the people turn away from that divinity. "Hence the saying," he says, "*Òrìṣà, bí o ò le gbè mí, ṣe mí bí o ti bá mi* (*Òrìṣà,* if you cannot improve my lot, do not worsen it)." He continues, "But it must be added that a seeming rebellion against an *òrìṣà* did not mean abandoning religion. It meant turning to another *òrìṣà,* another agent, to seek the good" (24; diacritics added). Roland Hallgren, writing about the Yoruba a few years earlier, had given his study of their traditional religious culture the title *The Good Things in Life,* explaining that for the Yoruba "the desire for 'the good things in life' is sanctioned not only by traditional religion but also by the entire culture" (13). Indeed, one of the comments one hears the Yoruba make about any person who has lived a good life is *Ayé yẹ é* ("Life suited him or her well"), and one of their wishes for a person to whom they are well disposed is *Ayé á yẹ é* ("Life will suit you well"). The underlying, somewhat Calvinistic world view holds that if the gods favor a person, the evidence will be manifest in *this* life in the guise of the person's access to such good things as wealth — especially wealth in children, relatives, people (friends), and the like — as well as health, a good reputation, and so forth. Proverbs, being designed in one way or another to aid people in negotiating the sometimes tricky path through life, would then presumably be concerned also in one way or another with the conditions for the enjoyment of a good life.

Furthermore, the reduction of the concept "wealth" to an abundance of people around one, as in *Ẹni tí ò lówó a léèyàn . . .* ("Whoever lacks money should have people . . ."), or the equation of wealth (in clothing) with abundance of children, as in *Ọmọ laṣọ* ("Children are garments"), lends credence to the claim that the maintenance of good relations is of crucial importance in Yoruba social life. That includes relations with one's immediate family, with other members of the community, with total strangers, with the poor and the destitute, with fauna, with flora, with nature itself, with the supernatural, and not least with the self.

By relations with the self (or oneself) I mean those that constitute "self-care," encompassing such things as self-knowledge, comportment, and habits — qualities, that is, that reflect on the self but do not necessarily involve or affect others. An example is the import of the proverb *Eégún tó jó tí kò tàpá, àbùkù ara ẹ* ("The masquerader that dances and does not kick up his legs, the disgrace is his [alone]"). Quite different are habits that affect (or reflect on) oneself in the first instance but *also* cause offense to others, as in the sense of the proverb *Àìfinipeni, àìfèèyàn-*

pèèyàn, lará oko-ó fi ńsán ìbàńtẹ́ wọ̀lú ("A lack of proper regard for others, a lack of proper regard for people, is what emboldens the country bumpkin to venture into town clad only in a loincloth").

It was in accordance with the foregoing considerations that I arrived at my classification categories by posing the question "What are the conditions for having a good life?" I came up with three answers:

One must be a good person, or be considered a good person.
One must be fortunate.
One must have good relationships.

Having determined those factors, I was faced with the reality that certain conditions in life fall outside the realm of possible human control and are unaffected by human qualities, judgment, actions, or relationships. The human condition itself is an example. I make a distinction here between things existential and the accident of fortune; proverbs concerned with the latter occupy a category of their own. Furthermore, there are such proverbs that deal with human rights and responsibilities which would not fit in the other groupings and therefore have a separate one to themselves. My concluding category comprises a large number of sayings that express truisms about Life, the World, Human Experience, and so forth.

My final groupings are therefore as follows:

Category 1 is devoted to the qualities that make a good person: caution, honesty, moderation, patience, perspicaciousness, prudence, reasonableness, reliability, resilience, sagacity/wisdom, savoir faire (worldly wisdom), self-control, self-knowledge, self-respect, and thoughtfulness.

Category 2 encompasses those things that conduce to the good life, material and otherwise: happiness, health, wealth, longevity, and good name (good repute).

Category 3 is made up of relational observations and prescriptions, those things that conduce to good relations, and things to do, to mind, and so forth: behavioral do's and don'ts regarding the divine and the Supernatural, the community in general, the family, friends, other people and elders, strangers, the less fortunate, and nature (flora and fauna).

Category 4 embraces statements (and observations) on human nature, existential, congenital, and the like: dependence on fate (for example), the finitude of human life, the opacity of the future.

Category 5 comprises observations on rights and responsibilities: the right to life, to be oneself, to human dignity, to patrimony, and to property; included also are statements on the responsibilities that go with rights as well as the belief in just deserts.

Category 6 is the catchall home for the rest, or miscellaneous: general comments and truisms about life, the world, human behavior, and the like.

These six categories constitute the collection. Each of Parts 1 through 5 comprises several sections or chapters (Part 6 has only one), within each of which the proverbs appear in alphabetical order. (I use the word-by-word alphabetization system and treat a hyphenated element as a single word. Note, however, that the Yoruba alphabet differs from the English in omitting C, Q, V, X, and Z but adding Gb (one letter), Ẹ, Ọ, and Ṣ. The full sequence including upper and lower case is as follows: A a, B b, D d, E e, Ẹ ẹ, F f, G g, Gb gb, H h, I i, J j, K k, L l, M m, N n, O o, Ọ ọ, P p, R r, S s, Ṣ ṣ, T t, U u, W w, Y y.)

The problem of classification is not an easy one to resolve, as other proverb scholars have pointed out. I have always argued that it is something of a presumption to classify proverbs according to usage—that is, according to the situations in which they may be applied or the values they address—because proverbs are multivalent and are available for diverse usages, depending upon the acumen and creativity of the user. Classification on the basis of usage involves making a judgment that a particular proverb is available for one particular application out of several possibilities. Yet since the aim of classification is to establish discrete categories, with as little overlap as possible, assigning a proverb to multiple usages would undermine that aim.

Having pointed out the absurdity of classifying only alphabetically, Hulme shows that even classification by subject, though it has advantages, is not without difficulties, for "we very soon find that we come to something that declines to be thus pigeon-holed," while "others . . . might with almost equal appropriateness find a home under three or four headings" (51). Indeed, it is possible, even likely, given that some proverbs can be (and are) employed in different situations, for one to place a proverb one way one day and another way the next day. Thus, because I completed the classification not at one sitting but over a period of several months, there is bound to be some inconsistency in my assignment. An entry that could have been classified under "relationships" at one sitting could quite conceivably have wound up under "reasonableness" at another. I offer as an instance the proverb *"Múwá! Múwá!" lapá eyẹlé ńké* ("'Bring! Bring!' is the cry of the pigeon's wings"). It is part of a man's complaint about the incessant demands of his girlfriend—a rather inconsiderate girlfriend, or a rather greedy girlfriend, or a rather unreciprocative girlfriend. At the first pass (during the process of translating and explaining), the implied lack of consideration was what struck me; later (at the classification stage), it was the lack of reciprocation—the woman's constant taking without ever *giving*. As I have just indicated above, I could also have classified it under "greed."

I readily concede that my scheme is open to legitimate objections. To some extent the headings are quite arbitrary. I could have devised a very different scheme with different rubrics, and I suspect that other scholars could come up with alternatives that might be better than mine. It would be quite easy, and free of controversy, for example, to group proverbs according to the real-life objects they employ as the bases for their declarations or observations, the experiential sources of their metaphorical constructions: does a proverb base its meaning on analogy to human relations, or on natural phenomena, or on observed animal behavior, or . . . ? I would not be unduly perturbed, therefore, if someone else chose to take up that task; indeed, I would embrace the prospect. One of my major intentions in compiling this treasury has always been to make it available for a variety of uses, not least as data for legitimate scholarly investigations and manipulations. Suggestions by other scholars with regard to explication, usage, and classification different from mine would be consistent with that intention.

Duplications

Readers will find that I have sometimes tagged proverbs as variants of other proverbs often listed in quite different sections. The seeming discrepancy is actually no discrepancy at all, because, as I have sought to stress, any given proverb can be invested by its user with values and meanings that differ from occasion to occasion. That flexibility also explains why other users might offer explications different from the ones I have provided for some of these proverbs.

The same applicability to different occasions and instances may also somewhat excuse my inadvertent repetitions. Although I have made an effort to avoid duplications — as distinct from variants — of proverbs, I am certain that I have not been successful in eliminating them all. One problem has been the difficulty of remembering so many sayings and recognizing an entry toward the end of the collection as a duplicate of something near the beginning. This problem will disappear, though, with the envisaged digitization of the entire corpus as a searchable electronic document. The Electronic Text Center of the University of Nebraska–Lincoln has completed a pilot project that involved the digitization of about two thousand of the proverbs, thus demonstrating the feasibility of converting the entire collection to an electronic format publishable on the Internet (see http://libr .unl.edu:2000/yoruba). If the required funding materializes, interested scholars and users will be able to access the entire collection on the World Wide Web.

NOTES

1. Brunvand is, of course, following Archer Taylor, whose examples he borrowed and who includes others such as "Once in a blue moon," "As blue as the sky," and "You can never tell" (5–6) within his rather liberal conception of the proverb. Wolfgang Mieder, whose monumental *Encyclopedia of World Proverbs* lists 18,520 entries, seems to support the view that a proverb is a sentence, inasmuch as practically all his examples are complete sentences, with rare exceptions such as "Much ado about nothing" (his 67), "Many kinsfolk and a few friends" (8,654), and "Slow and sure" (14,643).

2. *American Heritage College Dictionary* defines *proverb* as "a short pithy saying that expresses a basic truth or practical precept"; *apothegm* as "a terse, witty, instructive saying; a maxim"; *maxim* as "a succinct formulation of a fundamental principle, general truth, or rule of conduct"; and *aphorism* as "a terse statement of a truth or opinion; an adage," and

"a brief statement of a principle." Evidently, elaborations on the differences among what these various words—adage, aphorism, apothegm, maxim, proverb—designate may be no more than intellectual hairsplitting.

3. The reference is presumably to Elempe, a fifteenth-century king of the Nupe people. Yoruba historians identify him as the maternal grandfather of Ṣàngó, to whose court he attempted to retire after his disgrace and flight from Ọ̀yọ́ (Hodgkin 31, 110).

4. Wolfgang Mieder identifies "Two heads are better than one" as an English proverb (1986:221), whereas G. L. Apperson credits it to Homer in the *Iliad,* 10.224 (655).

5. This observation is not at variance with Rowland Abiodun's argument that the Yoruba sometimes acknowledge and celebrate the authorship of works of art. He deals with sculptors mainly, a form of art that is quite visible and whose practice is often a lineage profession, but he also acknowledges the fact of anonymity, with reasons, even in this case.

6. For a discussion of assimilated tones in Yoruba, see Bamgbose, "Assimilated," 1–13.

ONE

The Good Person

On humility, self-control, self-knowledge, self-respect, and self-restraint

1. *A di gàárì sílẹ̀ ewúrẹ́ ńyojú; ẹrù ìran rẹ̀ ni?*
We prepare the saddle, and the goat presents
itself; is it a burden for the lineage of goats?
(Goats that know their place do not offer
their backs to be saddled. This is a variant
of 4.)

2. *A fi ọ́ joba ò ńṣàwúre; o fẹ́ẹ́ jẹ Olọ́run ni?*
You have been crowned a king, and yet
you make good-luck charms; would you
be crowned God? (Being crowned a king is
about the best fortune a mortal could hope
for.)

3. *A fijó gba Awà; a fijà gba Awà; bí a ò bá jó,
bí a ò bá jà, bí a bá ti gba Awà, kò tán bí?*
By dancing we take possession of Awà [a
woman's name]; through fighting we take
possession of Awà; if we neither dance nor
fight but take possession of Awà anyway, is
the result not the same? (Why make a huge
production of a matter that is easily taken
care of?)

4. *A gbé gàárì ọmọ ewúrẹ́ ńrojú; kì í ṣe ẹrù
àgùntàn.*
We lift a saddle and the goat scowls; it is no
burden for a sheep. (The goat has no cause
to scowl, because no one will condescend to
ride it anyway. This is a variant of 1.)

5. *A kì í bá ọba pàlà kí ọkọ́ ọba má ṣàn-ánni
lẹ́sẹ̀.*
One does not share a farm boundary with
a king without getting one's feet gashed by
the king's hoe. (One should be cautious in
dealing with people in authority. Compare
1354.)

6. *A kì í bẹ̀rù ikú bẹ̀rù àrùn ká ní kí ọmọ ó kú
sinni.*
One does not so fear death and disease that
one asks that one's child die before one.
(One should not be more concerned with
saving oneself than with saving one's dependents.)

7. *A kì í bínú àátàn ká dalẹ̀ sígbẹ̀ẹ́.*
One does not get angry with the rubbish
dump and discard one's rubbish into the
bush. (One should not act in unreasonable
and harmful ways because of anger.)

8. *A kì í bínú orí ká fi fìlà dé ìbàdí.*
One does not get angry with one's head and
therefore use one's cap to cover one's buttocks. (Do not cut off your nose to spite
your face.)

9. *A kì í bọ òrìṣà lójú òfón-ọ̀n; bó bá dalẹ́ a
máa tú pẹpẹ.*
One does not sacrifice to a god in the presence of a house rat; otherwise, when night
falls it invades the rafter shelves. (Do not do
things that might constitute temptation to
others.)

10. *A kì í dàgbà má làáyà; ibi ayé bá báni là ńjẹ ẹ́.*
One does not become an adult and yet lack courage; one lives life as it finds one. (One should do what is fitting for one's station in life.)

11. *A kì í dá ọwọ́ lé ohun tí a ò lè gbé.*
One does not lay hands on a load one cannot lift. (One should not overreach.)

12. *A kì í dájọ́ orò ká yẹ ẹ́.*
One does not set the day for an *orò* rite and then ignore it. (One must not let important matters slide.)

13. *A kì í dákẹ́ ká ṣìwí; a kì í wò sùn-ùn ká dáràn.*
One does not keep quiet and yet misspeak; one does not silently contemplate the world and yet get into trouble. (A careful and cautious person seldom gets into trouble.)

14. *A kì í dé Màrókọ́ sin eléjọ́.*
One does not arrive at Màrókọ́ ahead of the litigant.[1] (One should not take charge of other people's business.)

15. *A kì í fi gbèsè sọ́rùn sọ̀sọ́.*
One does not carry debt around one's neck and live like a dandy. (One should discharge one's obligations before indulging in extravagance.)

16. *A kì í fi ìka ro etí, ká fi ro imú, ká wá tún fi ta ehín.*
One does not use one's finger to clean one's ear passages, use it to pick one's nose, and then use it to pick one's teeth. (One should always behave with decorum.)

17. *A kì í fi orí wé oríi Mokúṣiré; bí Mokú kú láàárọ̀ a jí lálẹ́.*

One does not liken one's fortune to Mokúṣiré's; if Mokú dies in the morning, he resurrects at night.[2] (Never emulate people who know tricks you don't.)

18. *A kì í fi pàtàkì bẹ́ èlùbọ́; ẹní bá níṣu ló ńbẹ́ ẹ.*
One does not come by yam flour because of one's importance; only people who have yams can make yam flour. (One cannot eat importance.)

19. *A kì í fini joyè àwòdì ká má lè gbádìẹ.*
One cannot be given the title "eagle" and yet be incapable of snatching chickens. (One should be able to live up to expectations.)

20. *A kì í gbé sàráà kọjá-a mọ́ṣáláṣí.*
One does not carry alms beyond the mosque. (Excess brings disgrace.)

21. *A kì í gbọ́ "Lù ú" lẹ́nu àgbà.*
One never hears "Beat him or her up" in the mouth of an elder. (Elders resolve disputes; they do not goad disputants on.)

22. *A kì í gbọ́n ju ẹni tí a máa dífá fún.*
One cannot be wiser than the person for whom one will consult the Ifá oracle.[3] (It is better to listen to the supplicant rather than put words in his or her mouth. Compare the two following entries.)

23. *A kì í gbọ́n tó Báyìi-ni-ngó-ṣe-ǹkan-àn-mi.*
One cannot be as wise as "Thus-will-I-do-my-thing." (Never impose your preferences

---

2. The name Mokúṣiré means "I play at dying."

3. Ifá, the Yoruba divination system, is based on an extensive library (the Ifá corpus) of case histories, precedents, and remedies. It comprises sixteen major chapters (*Odù*), each divided into sixteen subchapters (*omo Odù*, the children of *Odù*).

---

1. Màrókọ́ is a place-name and the site of a court.

on other people in their own affairs. Compare the following two entries.)

24. *A kì í gbón tó "Èmi-lóni-í."*
One cannot be as wise as "I-am-the-owner." (One should not presume to know as much about a thing as the owner of it. Compare the foregoing and following entries.)

25. *A kì í gbón tó ẹni tí ńtannijẹ.*
One is never as wise as the person deceiving one. (The deceiver always has the advantage of the dupe. Compare the preceding two entries.)

26. *A kì í jayé ọba ká ṣu sára.*
One does not so luxuriate in one's majesty that one shits on oneself. (Lack of moderation and decorum will bring disgrace to even the most elevated person.)

27. *A kì í jẹ oyè ẹnu ọ̀nà kalẹ́.*
One does not bear the title of gatekeeper even until nighttime. (As one advances in age, so should one's responsibilities advance in gravity and importance.)

28. *A kì í kó èlé ṣèṣọ́.*
One does not live fashionably on borrowed money. (Live within your means.)

29. *A kì í kórira òfọ́n-ọ̀n ká finá bọ ahéré.*
One does not so hate the bush rat that one sets one's farm hut alight. (One should not destroy oneself simply to get at one's enemy.)

30. *A kì í kọ́ àgbàlagbà pé bó bá rún kó rún.*
One does not teach an elder that what has been crushed should remain crushed. (An elder should know when a matter should end.)

31. *A kì í kọ ẹlẹ́sin ká tún lọ fẹ́ ẹlẹ́sẹ̀.*
One does not divorce a horse rider and

go marry a pedestrian. (One should ever progress, never regress.)

32. *A kì í lé èkúté ilé ẹni ká fọwọ́ ṣẹ́.*
One does not shoo the mouse in one's house and break one's hand. (One should be safe from hazards in one's own home.)

33. *A kì í mọ́ egbò fúnra ẹni ká sunkún.*
One does not treat one's own sore and yet cry from the pain. (One should know one's own pain threshold.)

34. *A kì í mọ ìyá Òjó ju Òjó lọ.*
One does not presume to know Òjó's mother better than Òjó himself does. (Never claim to know a thing better than the people closest to it. Compare the next entry.)

35. *A kì í mọ ọ̀nà ọgbà ju ọlógbà lọ; ẹní múni wá là ńtẹlé.*
Do not presume to know the way to or around a garden better than the owner of the garden; always follow the person who brought you. (Never presume to have a better knowledge of a matter than has the person most intimately involved. Compare the preceding entry.)

36. *A kì í mọ̀-ọ́ rò bí ẹléjọ́.*
One never knows how to present it like the owner of the case. (No one can know better than the person himself or herself where it hurts most and what relief is needed.)

37. *A kì í mú oko lọ́nà ká sèmẹ́lẹ́; tajá teran ní ńbúni.*
One does not farm a plot by the road and neglect its care; every dog and goat would ridicule one. (Never expose yourself to insult by behaving badly in public view.)

38. *A kì í ní agbára kékeré ṣe èkejì.*
One does not offer to second a combatant in spite of one's negligible strength. (Never

attempt more than you have the power to accomplish.)

39. *A kì í ní òkánjúwà ká mò; ará ilé eni ní ńso fúnni.*
One does not know that one has covetousness; it is one's kin who so inform one. (Often, only those close to one can recognize and point out one's flaws.)

40. *A kì í pe ìyàwó kó kan alárenà.*
One does not summon the wife and so involve the go-between. (People should mind their own business.)

41. *A kì í peni láko eran ká sorí bòró.*
One does not enjoy the designation "He Goat" and yet sport a smooth [hornless] head. (A person should live up to his or her billing.)

42. *A kì í pèlú òbo jáko.*
One does not join a monkey in roaming the bush. (Do not join others in their madness.)

43. *A kì í síwájú eléèédé.*
One does not conclude for the person who says, "Èédé . . ." (Never presume to know what someone else intends to say.)[4]

44. *A kì í yàgò fún elésin àná.*
One does not get out of the way for a person who rode a horse yesterday. (Past glory avails little in the present.)

45. *A kì í yàgò fún "Mo gun esin rí o!"*
One does not get out of the way for "I used to ride a horse!" (People should not expect to live on past glory. The preceding entry is a variant.)

46. *A lésu sílè páńdòrò-ó já lù ú; èlé mbénì?*
We group yams in lots, and the fruit of the sausage tree drops among them; does it count as complement to a lot, or as gratuity? (The fruit might look something like a yam, but it does not belong with yams.)

47. *À mbáni mú adìe à ńforúnkún bó; bówó bá ba òkókó, a ò ní fún aládìe?*
One helps to catch a chicken and scrapes one's knees; having laid hands on the chick, will one not hand it over to the owner? (One should not be overzealous in helping others, especially when no benefit will accrue to one from the effort.)

48. *À mbèrù alájá, ajá sebí òun là mbèrù.*
One shows deference to the dog's owner, and the dog thinks the deference is to it.[5] (A person who has a powerful patron mistakenly believes that the respect he enjoys from others is due to his or her own qualities, whereas it is reflected from the patron.)

49. *À ńgé e lówó, ó mbo òrùka.*
His hand is being severed, yet he is slipping on a ring. (The person has been judged undeserving of a hand; it is an affront, therefore, for him or her to adorn the fingers—an indication of heedlessness.)

50. *A ní ká wá eni tó léhìn ká fomo fún, abuké ní òun rèé; ti gànnàkù èhìn-in rè là ńwí?*
One seeks a person with a prominent back as suitor for one's daughter, and the humpback presents himself; who spoke of protruding back? (Since the expression that translates as "prominent back" is an idiom meaning a proud pedigree. the humpback makes a rather embarrassing mistake. Compare 55.)

---

4. In Yoruba numeration *èédé* . . . indicates a certain amount (or figure) "less than . . .": *èédógún*, for instance, is fifteen (five less than twenty); *èédégbèrin* is seven hundred (one hundred less than eight hundred).

5. In Yoruba usage one would not apply personal pronouns to animals, even though Yoruba pronouns are not differentiated by gender.

51. *A ní Tanlúkú ò mò-ó jó, Tànlùkù wá gbè é lésè.*
People say that Tanlúkú is a poor dancer, and Tanlùkù comes to his aid. (A person who is as helpless as the person in trouble should not offer to rescue him/her.)[6]

52. *À ńjà ìbàntè è léhìn, ó ńjà tará iwájú.*
His loincloth is being stripped from behind, yet he is stripping those of the people ahead of him. (Attacks on him do not stop him from belaboring his enemies.)[7]

53. *À ńsòrò olè, aboyún ńdáhùn; odiidi èèyàn ló gbé pamó.*
We speak of stealing, and a pregnant woman intervenes; she herself is concealing a whole person. (Her condition makes her guilty of concealment.)

54. *À ńsunkún Awúgbó, Awúgbó ò sunkún ara-a è.*
We lament Awúgbó's plight; Awúgbó does not lament his own plight. (The person the proverb is aimed at is too daft to realize his or her sorry plight.)

55. *À ńwá eni tí a ó fomo fún, olòsì ńyojú.*
We seek a person to give a child to [in marriage], and a worthless person presents himself. (People should know their place and not overrate themselves. This is a variant of 50.)

56. *À ńwónà àti fi asiwèrè sílè, ó ní bí a bá dé òkè odò ká dúró de òun.*
People are scheming to shake an imbecile from their company, and he asks that they wait for him on reaching the bank of the river. (If people are seeking ways of getting rid of a person, that person should not lay down his conditions for remaining with them.)

57. *A ò lóbìnrin à ńdá oóyò sí; bí a bá dá oóyò sí ewúré ni yó je é.*
Without having a wife, a person spares oóyò[8] to grow; if it flourishes, it is destined to be food for goats. (The vegetable is used in stews, and stews are for wives to cook.)

58. *A ò mo ohun tí Dárò-ó ní kó tó wí pé olè-é kó òun.*
One does not know what Dárò owned before he claimed to have been robbed. (The poor person conveniently blames his poverty on thieves. This is a variant of 410.)

59. *A ò mo ohun tí eléwé-e gbégbé ńtà kó tó so pé ojà ò tà.*
One does not know what the seller of *gbégbé* leaves was selling before she started complaining about the slow market. (The seller of goods nobody wants blames her fortune on the slow market.[9] This is a variant of 411.)

60. *A pè ó lómo erín-màgbon ò ńyò; ìwo pàápàá ló mì í?*
You are described as the child of the elephant that swallows coconuts, and you rejoice; are you the one who swallows coconuts? (The description honors the father, not the person being addressed.)

61. *A rí èyí rí ni tonílé; a ò rí èyí rí ni tàlejò; bónílé bá ní ká je é tán, àlejò a ní ká je é kù.*

---

6. As the names suggest, the one is a virtual clone of the other; the aid the one offers will not make the other any better as a dancer.

7. The proverb recalls the *oríkì* (praise poem) of Ògèdèmgbè, the nineteenth-century Ìjèsà warrior, which says, *À ńlé e bò léhìn, ó ńlé ará iwájú lo* ("He is being pursued from behind, and yet he is in pursuit of people in front").

8. *Corchorus olitorius,* or Jew's Mallow (Tiliaceae); see Abraham 533.

9. *Gbégbé* leaves are used for making charms that enable the user to transport himself instantly over long distances.

"Its like has been seen before" is what the host says; "No one has ever seen its like before" is what the guest says; if the host says that we should empty the plate, the guest should argue for leaving a little. (A host might minimize his hospitality, but the guest should praise it; if the host is lavish, the guest should not be greedy.)

62. *A rígi lóko ká tó fi ọmọ̀ gbé ìlù.*
We saw other trees in the bush before we settled on ọmọ̀ for making drums.[10] (One should never presume to be the only possible answer to every challenge.)[11]

63. *A sìnkú tán, alugbá ò lọ; ó fẹ́ẹ́ ṣúpó ni?*
The funeral is over, but the calabash beater does not take his leave; does he want to inherit a wife?[12] (This proverb has the same import as 653.)

64. *Aaka ò gbé ọ̀dàn; igbó ní ńgbé.*
The hedgehog does not live in the grassland, only in the forest. (Certain things are proper; certain things are not.)

65. *Àáyá yó níjọ́ kan, ó ní ká ká òun léhín ọ̀kánkán.*
The colobus monkey ate its fill one day and asked that its front teeth be knocked out. (Excessive happiness made the animal careless.)

66. *Aáyán ati eèràà ṣígun, wọ́ ní àwọ́n ńlọ mú adìẹ; àlọ la rí, a ò rábọ̀.*
Cockroach and ant make ready for war and say they are off to capture chicken; we see their departure but not their return. (Never forget your limitations. Compare 4714.)

67. *Aáyán fẹ́ẹ́ gẹsin; adìẹ ni ò gbà fún un.*
The cockroach would ride a horse; it is the chicken that does not allow. (A cockroach that stirs in the presence of a chicken is as good as dead. Compare 68 and 133.)

68. *Aáyán fẹ́ẹ́ jó; adìẹ ni ò jẹ́.*
The cockroach would dance; it is the chicken that does not allow. (This is a variant of the previous entry. Compare also 133.)

69. *Aáyán kì í yán ẹsẹ̀ erin; èèyàn kì í yán ẹsẹ̀ ìrọ̀.*
A cockroach does not trip an elephant; a human being does not trip a chimpanzee. (One should not take on adversaries one cannot match.)

70. *Àbá ni ikán ńdá; ikán ò lè mu òkúta.*
The termite is only striving; it can never eat a rock. (Though termites may make their tunnels on a rock, the rock will be safe.)

71. *A-báni-gbé kì í yáná; a-bọ̀rìṣà kì í sun òtútù; eyin gégé kì í gbé àwùjọ; ilé kannáà ni wọ́n kọ́ fún àwọn mẹ́tẹ̀èta.*
A guest does not warm himself by the fire; a priest or priestess does not sleep in the cold; a delicate egg does not live in a crowd; the same house was built for all three. (Know yourself and your place.)[13]

72. *A-bánijẹun-bí-aláìmọra, ó bu òkèlè bí ẹgbọ́n ìyá ẹ̀.*
He-who-eats-with-one-without-self-restraint

---

10. *Cordia millenii* (Boraginaceae) is used for making *bẹ̀mbẹ́* drums, large drums with a deep sound.

11. Other trees may feel superior to ọmọ̀ in other regards, but they cannot beat it as drum material.

12. A calabash is the dried, cut-off bottom part of a gourd, often used as a bowl and sometimes as a percussion instrument. The calabash beater is someone employed to clear evil spirits ahead of the funeral procession by means of a charm-laden calabash.

---

13. All three propositions are similar in indicating conditions that are inappropriate: that a visitor take over the seat by the fireplace, that the priest or priestess be without shelter, or that delicate eggs be crushed together.

breaks off morsels like his mother's senior. (When eating in company, one should be restrained. A man eating with the child of his younger sister need show no such restraint.)

73. *A-bèèrè kì í sìnà.*
He who asks the way does not lose his way. (One should admit one's weaknesses. Compare 760.)

74. *À-bí-ì-kọ́; à-kọ́-ì-gbà; òde ló ti ńkọ́gbọ́n wálé.*
A-child-that-was-never-taught-how-to-behave, a-child-that-was-taught-but-refused-to-heed-instruction: it is from outside the home that he will learn wisdom. (Look well to your child's upbringing.)

75. *A-binú-fùfù ní ńwá oúnjẹ fún a-binú-wẹ́rẹ́-wẹ́rẹ́.*
A volatile-tempered person secures food for a mild-tempered person. (Whatever good fortune might have been meant for the volatile person will wind up in the lot of the mild-mannered person.)

76. *Aboyún kì í jó bèmbé: a-bodò-ikùn-kèrèbètè.*
A pregnant woman does not dance to *bèmbé* music: pendulous-stomached woman. (One should match one's actions to one's circumstances.)[14]

77. *Àbọ̀ ejò kì í gbé isà.*
Half a snake does not live in a burrow. (One should act according to one's circumstances.)

78. *Abùlàngà kì í ṣasán: bíyàá ò lọ́rọ̀, baba a lówó lówó.*
The arrogant person is not arrogant for

nothing; if his mother is not wealthy, his father must be rich. (There is, or should be, some basis for one's strutting.)

79. *Abùléra òfọ́n-òn: ó ní ojó tí ológbò-ó ti bí òun ò ìtí-ì dá a ní báríkà.*
Mouse-that-does-not-know-its-place: it says that since the day the cat delivered [a baby], it has not gone to offer congratulations. (Never forget your vulnerabilities and limitations.)

80. *Àbúrò kì í pa ẹ̀gbọ́n nítàn.*
The younger person does not give the older person history lectures. (One should not exceed one's station.)

81. *Àbúrò rẹ ńdáṣọ fún ọ, o ní o ò lo elékuru; ta ní ńlo alákàrà?*
Your junior brother [or sister] buys clothing for you, and you say you will not wear anything with bean-grits patterns; who has the right to opt for clothing with a bean-fritter pattern? (One should act in accordance to one's station in life.[15] Compare 318.)

82. *A-dá-má-lè-ṣe àdàbà tí ńdún bèmbè.*
Start-something-it-cannot-finish dove makes bombastic noises. (Bombast often masks fickleness.)

83. *Adẹ́tẹ̀ẹ́ ní òun ò lè fún wàrà, sùgbọ́n òún lè yí i dànù.*
The leper says he may not be able to squeeze out milk, but he can spill it. (Even feckless people can cause some damage.)

84. *Adẹ́tẹ̀-ẹ́ rí wèrè, ó kán lùgbé.*
The leper sees a mad person and dashes into the bush. (A person who should be ostracized ostracizes others.)

---

14. *Bèmbé* is a type of music named after the bass drum that it employs; the dancing to this music is close to stomping.

15. Presumably * èkuru* is a less desirable meal than *àkàrà*, but the beggar cannot (or should not) presume to exercise a choice.

85. *Adétè-é sòrò méjì, ó fikan puró; ó ní nígbàtí òun lu ọmọ òun lábàrá, òun já a léèékánná pàtì.*
The leper said two things, one of them being a lie; he said after he had struck his child with his palm, he also pinched him severely with his nails. (One fools only oneself when one claims to have done the impossible.)

86. *Adìẹ funfun ò mọ ara ẹ̀ lágbà.*
The white chicken does not recognize itself as an elder. (One should act one's age always.)[16]

87. *Adìẹ ò bí yọyọ kú yọ̀.*
A chicken does not give birth to a multitude of chicks and die of the exertion. (Children should not be the death of their parents.)[17]

88. *Adìẹ tó ṣu tí kò tò, ara-a rẹ̀ ló kù sí.*
The chicken that shits and does not piss retains the rest in its body. (Self-deprivation hurts the person concerned, not anyone else.)

89. *Adígbónránkú ńfikú ṣeré.*
Death-feigning-beetle flirts with death. (If one persists in flirting with disaster, disaster is likely to befall one.)[18]

90. *A-dìtan-mọ́ èsúó; ó ní èkùlù ló bí ìyá òun.*
The red-flanked duiker, desperate to claim relationship, says that its mother was born of a crested duiker. (Never make preposterous claims of kinship.)

91. *Adití ò gbọ́, "Yàgò!"*
The deaf do not hear, "Make way!" (Cautionary words are lost on reckless people.)

92. *À-fà-tiiri ni tìyàwó; bí a bá fà á tí kò tiiri, ó ní ohun tó ńṣe é.*
Resisting-while-being-pulled is the proper behavior for a bride; if she is pulled and does not resist, something is the matter with her. (However eager the bride, she must appear coy and shy; one should behave with decorum appropriate to one's position.)

93. *Àfi ohun tí a kì í tà lójà lẹrú kì í jẹ.*
The only thing a slave cannot eat is something not available in the market. (A slave has no choice.)

94. *Afínjú ní ńjẹ iwọ; ọmọ̀ràn ní ńjẹ obì; màrí-màjẹ ní ńjẹ awùsá.*
It is a finicky person who eats *iwọ*; it is a sagacious person who eats kola nut; it is someone not squeamish about what he eats that eats *awùsá*.[19] (People are what they eat; each to his or her own taste.)

95. *Afínjú wọ ọjà ó rìn gbẹndẹkẹ; òbún wọ ọjà ó rìn sùẹ̀sùẹ̀; òbùn ní ó ru ẹrù afínjú relé.*
The fashionable person enters the market and walks in a leisurely manner; the filthy person enters the market and walks in a sluggish manner; it is the filthy person that will carry the fashionable person's load to the house for him or her. (Good breeding confers great advantages.)

96. *Afínjúu Ààre; ó fi àkísà dí orùbà; ó ńwá eniire-é bá sú epo.*

---

16. White hair is associated with age, and the chicken's white feathers compare with white hair. The chicken, of course, is unaware of the implications of age among humans.

17. The proverb was obviously suggested by the usual description of a chicken as *ọlọ́mọ-yọyọ*, mother of a flock of chicks.

18. The beetle in question plays dead whenever it is touched.

19. *Iwọ* is a substance from the brimstone tree, *òrúwọ*, whose sap is used in weaning children from breast-feeding because of its bitterness (see Abraham 489). *Awùsá* is the fruit of the vine *Tetracarpidium conophorum*; the English name by which people refer to it is wallnut.

Fashionable woman of Ààre, she cocks her oil jar with a rag, and she expects good people to buy oil from her. (Never compromise on cleanliness and good character.)

97. *Afínjú-u póṇpólà, ogé kun osùn láìwè.*
Unusual-fashionable-person, the preener anoints herself with camwood without taking a bath. (Cleanliness should be more than a matter of appearance.)

98. *Àfòpiná tó fẹ́ẹ́ paná-a súyà; ẹrán pò sí i.*
The moth tries to put out the barbecue fire; the meat becomes more plentiful. (A person who foolishly attempts dangerous tasks courts destruction. This is a variant of the following entry.)

99. *Àfòpiná tó ní òun ó pa fìtílà, ara è ni yó pa.*
The moth that attempts to kill [put out] the oil lamp will kill itself. (It is unwise to take on an adversary one knows can destroy one.)

100. *Afójú tó dijú, tó ní òún sùn, ìgbàtí kò sùn ta ló rí?*
The blind person who shuts his eyes and says he is asleep, when he was not asleep, whom did he see? (The deceiver deceives himself or herself.)

101. *A-fònú-fóra ní ńfi òsì jó bàtá.*
It is a person who is both incapable of thought and shameless that dances to *bàtá* music while in poverty.[20] (Know your place and live according to your circumstances.)

102. *Àgó tó gbó ṣáṣá, èbìtí pa á; áṁbòṣì olóóṣè a-bara-kùòkùò.*
The nimble, sprightly rat fell victim to the trap; how much more the sluggish, sickly

mouse. (If the green wood is consumed, the dry wood has no prayer.)

103. *Àgùnbánirò ní ńfojúdini.*
It is the person taller than another who shows no respect for the other. (Even in a company, each person should know his or her relative station.)

104. *Àgbà ajá kì í bàwòjé.*
A grown dog does not deface its skin. (Decorum goes with age.)

105. *Àgbà ìmàle kì í káṣo kórùn.*
A Muslim elder does not throw a sheet over his shoulder for clothing. (One should behave as is proper for one's position.)

106. *Àgbà kán ṣe bẹ̀ẹ̀ lÓgùn; Yemaja ló gbé e lọ.*
An elderly person tried it [something] in the river Ògùn; the river goddess carried him away. (Thoughtless emulation of others could be disastrous.)

107. *Àgbà kì í faàrò họ ìdí kó má kan funfun.*
A grown person does not scratch his buttocks in the early morning without showing some whiteness. (Improper behavior brings disgrace.)[21]

108. *Àgbà kì í ṣerée kí-ló-bá-yìí-wá?*
An elderly person does not engage in the kind of play that provokes the comment, "What brought all this about?" (Elders should show decorum. See 126.)

109. *Àgbà kì í ṣorò bí èwe.*
An elderly person does not perform rituals like a youth. (The elder's performance should be commensurate with his station and status.)

---

20. *Bàtá* is a kind of music reserved for affluent people.

21. The dry skin will be chafed.

110. *Àgbà kì í wà lójà kórí ọmọ titun wó.*
An elder who is not present at a market permits a child's head to rest askew. (Elders must not permit untoward happenings in their presence.)[22]

111. *Àgbá òfìfo ní ńpariwo; àpò tó kún fówó kì í dún.*
It is an empty barrel that is noisy; a sack full of money makes no sound. (Persons of little worth make the most noise.)

112. *Àgbà tí kò lésè nílè a lógbọ́n nínú.*
An elder who has no substance should have cunning. (One should know one's limitations and how to compensate for them.)[23]

113. *Àgbà tí kò mọ ìwọ̀n ara-a rè lodò ńgbé ló.*
It is an elder who does not know his limitations that is washed away by a river. (Elders who cannot swim will be cautious near rivers.)

114. *Àgbà tí kò nítìjú, ojú kan ni ìbá ní; ojú kan náà a wà lógangan iwájú-u rè.*
An elder without self-respect might as well have only one eye, that one eye being in the center of his forehead. (Shamelessness does not become an elder.)

115. *Àgbà tí yó tẹ̀ẹ́, bó fárí tán, a ní ó ku járá ẹnu.*
An elder courting disgrace, after his head has been shaved, says, "Now, how about shaving the beard [as a gratuity]?" (One should know how far one may go before one suffers disgrace.)

116. *Àgbà tó bú ọmọdé fi èèbú-u rè toro.*
An elder who insults a youth makes a present of his own insult. (Only those who show respect for others may expect respect in return. Compare the preceding and following entries.)

117. *Àgbà tó fi ara-a rè féwe lèwe ńbú.*
It is an elder who delivers himself unto youths that the youth will insult. (If one wants to be respected, one should respect oneself. Compare the preceding two entries.)

118. *Àgbà tó mọ ìtìjú kì í folè ṣeré.*
An elder who is wary of disgrace will not play at stealing. (Anything that smacks of stealing will disgrace an elder.)

119. *Àgbà tó torí ogójì wọ ìyẹ̀wù: igbawó ò tó ohun à-mú-ṣèye.*
The elder who escapes into his inner chamber because of 40 cowries: 200 cowries are not enough for casual spending.[24] (One must act as one's station demands. Compare 2891.)

120. *Àgbààgbà ìlú ò lè péjọ kí wọn ó jẹ ìfun òkété, àfi iyán àná.*
The elders of the town will not assemble and eat the intestines of a bush rat, only stale pounded yams. (People should behave in ways that befit their station.)[25]

121. *À-gbàbọ̀-ọ ṣòkòtò, bí kò fúnni lésè a ṣoni; rẹ́múrẹ́mú ni ohun ẹni ńbani mu.*

---

22. Babies are carried on their mothers' backs, and when they fall asleep their heads may loll crookedly. Since the mothers cannot see behind them, responsible people are required to call their attention to a baby's crooked posture.

23. The phrase *ní ẹsẹ̀ nílè*, literally "to have feet on the ground," means to have substance or influence.

24. Cowries (or cowrie shells) are small, nutlike, white seashells that were used as currency in parts of West Africa before the arrival of Europeans. They continue to adorn traditional ritual regalia.

25. Pounded yam is made by using a mortar and pestle to pound cooked and peeled yams into a paste, which is eaten with a stew. The prescription of *stale* pounded yams is a humorous twist, since that is not the sort of food that self-respecting people would choose to eat, although it is certainly better than rat intestines.

Borrowed trousers: if they are not too tight around the legs, they will be too loose; one's own things fit one exactly. (Borrowed articles are never like one's own.)

122. *Àgbà-ìyà tí ńmùko ọnìní: ó ní nítorí omi gbígbóná orí-i rè ni.*
Worthless elderly person who is eating corn gruel worth one-tenth of a penny: he says he only wants the hot water on top of it. (One should act according to the demands of one's status.)

123. *Àgbàlagbà akàn tó kó sí garawa; yègèdè, ojú tì í.*
The elderly crab that enters into a bucket is thoroughly disgraced. (One should avoid potentially disgraceful actions.)

124. *Àgbàlagbà kì í ṣe lágbalàgba.*
An elder should not behave in an unbecoming manner. (One should behave according to one's status.)

125. *Àgbàlagbà kì í wẹwọ́ tán kó ní òun ó jẹ si.*
An elder does not wash his hand and then decide to eat more. (An elder should know his mind.)[26]

126. *Àgbàlagbà kì í yọ ayọ̀-ọ kí-ló-báyìí-wá?*
An elder does not rejoice in a manner that would provoke, "What brought all this about?" (Moderation and decorum in everything. This is identical in intent with 108.)

127. *Àgbàlagbà tí ò kí Ààrẹ ńfi okùn sin ara-a rè.*
An elder who does not greet the Ààrẹ tries a [hanging] rope for size.[27] (One must avoid actions that will place one at grave risk.)

128. *Àgbàlagbà tó ńgun ọpẹ, bó bá já lulẹ̀ ó dòrun.*
An elder who climbs palm trees: if he crashes from the tree, he will find himself in heaven. (An elder should know better than to climb palm trees; one should not court danger. Compare 223; see also 1500.)

129. *Àgbàlagbà tó wẹwù àṣejù, ẹtẹ́ ni yó fi rí.*
An elder who wears the garment of immoderation will find disgrace because of it. (Immoderation brings disgrace.)

130. *Àgbàrá ba ọnà jẹ́, ó rò pé òún tún ọnà ṣe.*
The rain flood ruins the path believing that it is repairing it. (Ignorance or incompetence in tackling a task often leads to unintended results.)

131. *Agbára wo ló wà lọ́wọ́ igbá tó fẹ́ẹ fi gbọn omi òkun?*
What strength does the calabash have at its disposal that makes it attempt to scoop up all the water in the ocean? (People should not overreach.)

132. *Àgbéré àwòdì ní ńní òun ó jẹ ìgbín.*
It is an overreaching kite that proposes to eat snails. (Know your limits. See 1997.)[28]

133. *Àgbéré laáyán gbé tó ní òun ó jòó láàárín adìẹ.*
The cockroach overreaches itself when it says it will dance in the company of chickens. (The chickens will eagerly peck it to death. Compare 67 and 68.)

134. *Àgbéré lẹyẹ ńgbé; kò lè mu omi inú àgbọn.*
The bird only attempts the impossible; it

---

26. Traditionally, the Yoruba eat with their fingers, and washing one's hand after eating is a sign that one is done.
27. *Ààrẹ* is a high chieftaincy title.

---

28. The kite is notorious for swooping down to grab chicks with its talons, but the snail's hard shell makes it invulnerable to the bird.

cannot drink the milk in a coconut. (One should know one's limits.)

135. *Àgbéré-e sìgìdì tó ní ká gbé òun sójò: bí apá ti ńya nitan ńya; kidiri orí ò lè dá dúró.*
The overreaching mud idol that asked to be put in the rain: as the arms fell off, so did the thighs; the rounded head could not support itself. (One should know one's limitations.)

136. *Ahọ́n ni ìpínnlẹ̀ ẹnu.*
The tongue is the border of the mouth. (There is a limit to everything.)

137. *Àì-jonilójú lọ́sàn-án ní ḿmúni jarunpá luni lóru.*
Lack of regard for a person during the day makes one kick the person during the night as one tosses restlessly in sleep. (Familiarity breeds contempt.)[29]

138. *Àì-kúkú-joyè, ó sàn ju, "Ẹnuù mi ò ká ìlú" lo.*
Not-assuming-the-position-of-ruler-at-all is far better than, "My word is not heeded by the people." (A person who does not assume a responsibility is better off than a person who takes it on and fails to fulfill it.)

139. *Àì-lápá làdá ò mú; bí a bá lápá, ọmọ owú tó-ó gégi.*
It is a deficiency of biceps that blunts the machete; if one has strong biceps, one can cut trees with a cudgel. (One should not blame one's deficiencies on one's tools.)

140. *Àì-lè-jà ni à ńso pé, "Ojúde baba-à mi ò dé ìhín."*
It is inability to fight that prompts one to say, "My father's front yard does not extend

this far." (A coward will find any excuse to avoid a just fight.)

141. *Àì-mọ̀-kan, àì-mọ̀-kàn ní ḿmú èkúté-ilé pe ológbò níjà.*
It is severe ignorance that prompts a mouse to challenge a cat to a fight. (Never taunt an adversary you cannot handle.)

142. *Àìsí èèyàn lóko là ḿbá ajá sọ̀rọ̀.*
It is the absence of people on the farm that brings one to converse with a dog. (But for unfortunate circumstances, one would not deign to associate with certain people.)

143. *Àìsí-ńlé ẹkùn, ajá ńgbó.*
The leopard being away from home, the dog barks. (When the master is away, the minion will strut. See the following entry, and also 146.)

144. *Àìsí-ńlé ológbò, ilé dilé èkúté.*
The cat being away from home, the house becomes a domain for mice. (People will take advantage of any relaxation of supervision. See the previous entry.)

145. *Àìso àbà ló m: éye wá jẹ̀gbá; ẹye kì í jẹ̀gbá.*
The failure of the *àbà* tree to fruit brought the bird to eating garden egg; ordinarily, birds would not eat bitter tomato. (But for unavoidable misfortune, one would not have been reduced to the demeaning circumstance in which one finds oneself.)

146. *Ajá kì í gbó níbojì ẹkùn.*
A dog does not bark in the leopard's lair. (One must defer to one's superiors. See also 143.)

147. *Ajá kì í lọ ságinjù lọ sọdẹ ẹkùn.*
A dog does not go into the wild to hunt a leopard. (One should not attempt feats one is unqualified to accomplish.)

---

29. It is sometimes necessary for a person to share a sleeping mat with a superior, but one in awe of the superior would not forget oneself even in sleep.

148. *Ajá kì í rorò kó ṣọ́ ojúlé méjì.*
A dog is never so fierce that it can guard two doorways. (One cannot serve two masters simultaneously.)

149. *Ajá mọ ìgbẹ́; ẹlẹ́dẹ̀-ẹ́ mọ àfọ̀; tòlótòló mọ ẹni tí yó yìnbọn ìdí sí.*
A dog knows excrement; a pig knows a mud pit; a turkey knows to whom to direct its fart. (People should know who are their peers and who are not.)

150. *Ajá ò gbọdọ̀ dé mọ́sálásí ìkókò ṣàlùwàlá.*
A dog dares not go to a wolf's mosque to make ablutions. (One should not exceed one's station.)[30]

151. *Ajá rí epo kò lá; ìyá-a rẹ̀ẹ́ ṣu ihá bí?*
The dog sees palm oil but does not lick it; did its mother excrete palm-nut pericarp? (One should not be unreasonably squeamish.)

152. *Ajá tó ńlépa ẹkùn, ìyọnu ló ńwá.*
A dog that chases a leopard is seeking trouble. (One should not overreach oneself.)

153. *Ajá tún padà sí èébì-i rẹ̀.*
The dog returns to its vomit. (To accept what one has once rejected is to lose face.)

154. *Àjàjà ṣoge àparò, abàyà kelú.*
The uncharacteristically spruced-up partridge swells its chest. (The nouveau riche always goes to extremes in consumption.)[31]

155. *Àjànàkú ò tu lójú alájá; o-nígba-ajá ò gbọdọ̀ tópa erin.*
The elephant does not break and run at the sight of dogs; a person with two hundred dogs dares not stalk an elephant. (Even two hundred dogs are no match for an elephant.)

156. *Àjàpá ní kò sí oun tó dà bí oun tí a mọ̀ ọ́ṣe; ó ní bí òún bá ju ẹyìn sẹ́nu, òun a tu èkùrọ́ sílẹ̀.*
Tortoise says there is nothing quite like expertise in one's calling; it says if it puts a palm fruit into its mouth, it spits out a palm nut. (Nothing succeeds like expertise.)

157. *Àjàpá ní òun tí ìbá só ló sùn yí, bẹ́ẹ̀ni ẹni bá sùn kì í só.*
Tortoise argues that it that might have farted but was sound asleep, and, surely, those that sleep do not fart! (Some defenses are so transparent as to be frivolous.)

158. *Àjàpá ńlọ sájò, wọ́n ní ìgbà wo ni yó dèé, ó ní ó dìgbàtí òun bá té.*
Tortoise set out on a journey and, asked when it would return, replied that it would be after it had earned disgrace. (Certain people will not change course until they are disgraced.)

159. *Àjátì àwọn ní ńkọ́ òrofó lógbọn.*
It is a loosely hung net that teaches the fruit pigeon a lesson. (Careless, imprudent persons have their nemesis waiting for them.)

160. *À-jẹ-ì-kúrò ní ńpa ẹmọ́n; à-jẹ-ì-kúrò ní ńpa àfẹ̀; à-jẹ-ì-kúrò ní ńpa máláàjú.*
Feeding-without-leaving kills the Tullberg's rat; feeding-without-departing kills the spotted grass mouse; feeding-without-departing kills the *máláàjú* rat. (Lack of moderation leads to death.)

161. *À-jẹ-pọ̀ ni tàdán.*
Eating-until-vomiting is the trait of the bat.

---

30. The proverb has added force because dogs are considered unclean by Muslims and are not allowed near mosques. See 561.

31. For some reason the Yoruba consider the partridge an unfortunate and lowly bird.

(This observation on a being with no self-restraint could also be a wish that a person not benefit from something he or she has appropriated.)

162. À-jẹ-tán, à-jẹ-ì-mọra, ká fi ọwọ́ mẹ́wẹ̀ẹ̀wá jẹun ò yẹ ọmọ èèyàn.
Eating-absolutely-everything, eating-with-abandon, eating with all ten fingers is unworthy of human beings. (People should not be slaves to food.)

163. À-jókòó-àì-dìde, à-sọ̀rọ̀-àì-gbèsì, ká sinni títí ká má padà sílé: àì-sunwọ̀n ní ńgbẹ̀hìn-in rẹ̀.
Sitting-without-getting-up, speaking-without-waiting-for-responses, walking people on their way and not turning back: unpleasantness is what they breed. (Excess and self-forgetfulness in anything bring unpleasant results.)

164. Àkàtàm̀pò ò tó ìjà-á jà; ta ní tó mú igi wá kò ó lójú?
The bow cannot fight, but who dares confront it with a stick? (A stick is no match for a bow.)

165. Àkíìjẹ́ mú òrìṣà níyì.
Refusal-to-acknowledge-salutations enhances the god's dignity. (Distancing oneself from ordinary people lends one prestige.)

166. Àkísà-á mọ iwọ̀n ara-a rẹ̀, ó gbé párá jẹ́.
The rag knows its place; it remains quietly on the rafters. (A person of low standing should not call attention to himself or herself.)

167. Àkókó inú igbó ní àwọn lè gbé odó; ọpọ̀lọ́ lódòó ní àwọn lè ló ìlẹ̀kẹ̀; awúrebé ní àwọn lè hun aṣọ.
Woodpeckers in the forest say they can carve mortars; frogs in the stream say they can string beads; and awúrebe say they can weave cloth. (Misplaced self-confidence leads the creatures into empty boasts.)[32]

168. Akórira ò ní ǹkan; ọ̀dùn ò sunwọ̀ fún ṣòkòtò.
An overly squeamish person owns nothing; raffia cloth is no good for trousers. (Excessive squeamishness renders one helpless and destitute.)

169. Akú, nkò ní omitooro-o rẹ̀ ẹ́ lá; àìkú, nkò níí pè é rán níṣẹ́.
Dead, I will not eat its broth; alive, I will not send it on an errand. (One need pay no mind to a person who can in no way affect one's fortune. Compare 2188.)

170. Àkùkọ adìẹ fi dídájí ṣàgbà; ó fi ṣíṣu-sílẹ̀ ṣèwe.
The rooster shows its maturity by its early rising; it shows its lack of maturity by defecating on the floor. (Nobody is free of some blemish.)

171. Aláàńtètè: ó jí ní kùtùkùtù ó ní òun ó dàá yànpọ̀n-yànpọ̀n sílẹ̀.
The cricket arises in the morning and vows to perform wonders. (The puny person's boasts are always empty.)

172. Aládàá ló làṣẹ àro.
It is the owner of the machete who exercises authority over mutual laborers. (One yields authority to one's host, or the owner of the property.)[33]

---

32. The woodpecker's habit has some slight resemblance to the carving of a mortar (for a mortar and pestle); the eggs of frogs have some slight resemblance to strung beads; and the action of awúrebe (an archaic word for some animal) resembles weaving, but in each case the product is not quite what humans have in mind.

33. The owner of the machete in this case is the person on whose farm mutual-help workers are engaged.

173. *Aláìnítìjú lọ kú sílé àna-a rẹ̀.*
A shameless person goes to die in his in-laws' house. (One should never demean oneself with unbecoming actions.)

174. *Alákòró kì í sá fógun.*
A wearer of a battle helmet does not flee from war. (A warrior does not run from battle.)

175. *Aláǹgbá kì í lérí àti pa ejò.*
A lizard does not boast that it will kill a snake. (People should not propose what they cannot accomplish.)

176. *Aláṣejù ajá ní ńlépa ẹkùn.*
It is an overreaching dog that chases leopards. (One should not challenge people one cannot match.)

177. *Aláṣejù, baba ojo.*
The immoderate person, greatest of cowards. (Immoderation is a cloak for cowardice.)

178. *Aláṣejù ní ńgbébọ kojá ìdí èṣù; a-gbé-sàráà-kojá-a-mọ́ṣáláṣí.*
It is an immoderate person who carries his offering past Èṣù's shrine; one-who-carries-his-alms-past-the-mosque.[34] (It is a grievous fault not to observe discreet limits.)

179. *Aláṣejù, pèrè ní ńtẹ́; àṣéjù, baba àṣeté.*
The immoderate person easily finds disgrace; immoderation is the father of disgrace. (Immoderation brings disgrace. See also 206.)

In the traditional mutual-help arrangement, the owner of the farm being worked on is the person in authority.

34. Èṣù, gatekeeper before shrines and messenger to the Creator and to Ifá (god of divination), is much feared because of his capacity for mischief. Erroneously, Christians equated him with their Devil and folklorists with the Trickster.

180. *Aláṣejù tí ńpoko ní baba.*
Overzealous wife calls her husband "father." (The wife who calls her husband "father" carries respect beyond reasonable limits; one should not be overzealous observing proprieties.)

181. *Aláṣọ àlà kì í jókòó sísọ̀ elépo.*
A person dressed in white does not sit at the stall of a palm-oil seller. (One should not expose oneself to abuse or danger.)

182. *Aláṣọ-kan kì í ná ànárẹ.*
A person who has only one set of clothing does not bargain until he is wet. (A person with meager resources should husband them judiciously. See also the following entry.)

183. *Aláṣọ-kan kì í ṣeré òjò.*
A person who has only one set of clothing does not play in the rain. (See the preceding entry.)

184. *Alátiṣe ní ḿmọ àtiṣe ara-a rẹ̀.*
The person who must settle his or her affair knows best how to plan to go about doing so. (One should not second-guess others or try to make their decisions for them.)

185. *Àlejò kì í lọ kó mú onílé dání.*
The visitor does not take his or her leave and take the host along. (Each person must confront his or her destiny alone.)

186. *Àlejò kì í pìtàn ìlú fónílé.*
The visitor does not recount the history of the town for the host. (Never presume to know more than the custodian of knowledge.)

187. *Àlémú ò yẹ àgbà; àgbà kì í ṣe ohun àlémú.*
To be pursued does not become an elder; an elder does not cause himself to be pursued. (Elders should always behave in ways that would cause them no disgrace.)

188. *A-lu-dùndún kì í dárin.*
The *dùndún* player does not lead a song. (A subordinate does not set policy.)[35]

189. *Àmòtékùn-ún fara jọ ẹkùn, kò lè ṣe bí ẹkùn.*
The *àmòtékùn* looks like a leopard, but it cannot do what a leopard can do.[36] (Looking a part does not indicate an ability to play the part.)

190. *Amùrín ò sunwọ̀n, ó yí sáró.*
The lizard is not good-looking to start with, and it slips into indigo dye. (A person who has enough flaws should not seek ways to add to them.)

191. *Ànán-mánàán ẹtú jìnfin; oní-mónìí ẹtú jìnfin; ẹran mìíràn ò sí nígbó léhìn ẹtu?*
Yesterday the antelope was caught in a pit trap; today the antelope is caught in a pit trap; is there no other animal in the forest besides the antelope? (If the same person repeatedly finds himself or herself in difficulties others are able to avoid, one should look to the person's character for the explanation.)

192. *Apá ẹkúté-ilé ò ká awùsá; kìkìi yíyíkiri ló mọ.*
The mouse cannot get a grip on the *awùsá* nut; all it can do is roll it around. (Some people are beyond any schemes by their enemies.)

193. *Àpárá ńlá, ìjà ní ńdà.*
Excessive ribbing unfailingly leads to a fight. (Jokes should have limits.)

194. *Àpárá ńlá ni iná ńdá; iná ò lè rí omi gbése.*
The fire is being most overbearing; there is nothing fire can do to water. (This entry has the same application as the following one.)

195. *Àpárá ńlá nikán ńdá; ikán ò lè mu òkúta.*
The termite is being most overbearing; a termite cannot eat a rock. (Certain people do not know their place; certain people are beyond the reach of their adversaries. Compare the preceding entry.)

196. *Àpọ́nlé ni "Fọ́maànù"; ẹnìkan ò lè ṣe èèyàn mẹ́rin.*
Calling a person a foreman is only a mark of respect; nobody can be four men. (People whose positions earn them respect should not forget themselves, or people would forget their positions. See the following entry.)[37]

197. *Àpọ́nlé ni "Ìyá-a Káà"; ìyá kan ò sí ní káà tí kò lórúkọ.*
Calling a person "Mother of the Compound" is only a mark of respect; there is no mother in the compound who does not have a name. (People in a position of respect should not forget that respect can be withdrawn. See the preceding entry.)

198. *Ará okó ní òún gbọ́ fínrín fínrín; ta ló sọ fun bí kò ṣe ará ile?*
The bush dweller says he heard a rumor; who told him, if it was not a town dweller? (People should not presume to instruct those who know better than they.)

199. *Ara-àìbalè, olórí àrùn.*
Restlessness, father of all diseases. (No disease is greater than hyperactivity.)

---

35. *Dùndún* is a minor drum in the traditional "talking drum" ensemble.

36. *Àmòtékùn* is a variety of leopard that the Yoruba consider inferior to the "real" leopard.

37. The proverb plays on "foreman," which it deliberately mistakes for "four men."

200. Àrífín ilé ò jẹ́ ká jẹ òròmọ adìẹ.
Fear of losing face within one's home dissuades one from eating day-old chicks. (A
person who would retain esteem among his
or her peers must not act beneath himself or
herself.)

201. À-rí-ì-gbọdọ̀-wí: baálé ilé ṣu sápẹ.
Something-seen-but-unmentionable: the
man of the house shits in the saucepan.
(When an illustrious person does the unmentionable, no one dares speak. See the
following entry also.)

202. Àrí-ì-gbọdọ̀-wí, baálé ilé yọkun lémú.
Something-seen-but-unmentionable: the
man of the house walks around with mucus
dripping from his nose. (When a venerable
person acts like a fool, few dare tell him so.
See the preceding entry.)

203. Arólẹ̀kẹ̀ ò rọ bàtà; gbẹ́dó-gbẹ́dó ò rọ
ojúgun.
The bead maker cannot fashion a shoe; the
mortar carver cannot manufacture a shinbone. (People should stick to what they are
qualified to do.)

204. Àṣá kì í rà kádìẹ gbé kòkòrò dání.
When a kite hovers, a chicken does not
hang on to an insect. (When a great danger threatens, one does not wait for small
favors.)

205. A-ṣe-bòròkìnní-má-kìíyè-sábíyá, gbogbo
abíyá dóṣe.
He-who-lives-in-style-but-pays-no-
attention-to-his-armpits: both armpits are
taken over with foamy filth. (Attention to
detail is integral to good character or breeding.)

206. Àṣejù baba àṣeté; ẹtẹ́ ní ńgbẹ̀hìn àṣejù;
àgbàlagbà tó wẹ̀wù àṣejù ẹtẹ́ ni yó fi rí.

Lack of moderation is the father of disgrace;
disgrace comes of immoderation; a grown
person who clothes himself in immoderation will find disgrace. (Immoderation leads
to disgrace. This is a more elaborate form of
179.)

207. À-sé-kú làgbàlagbà ńṣẹ òràn.
Denying-until-death is the way an old person denies a matter. (One must never admit
to doing something unworthy of one's position.)

208. Àṣẹ̀sẹ̀yọ màrìwò, ó ní òun ó kan ọrun;
àwọn aṣáájúu rẹ̀-ẹ́ ṣe bẹ́ẹ̀ rí?
The newly emerged palm frond says it will
touch the sky; did those that came before it
do so? (Ambition should be tempered with
realism. See the following entry.)

209. Àṣẹ̀sẹ̀yọ ògọmọ̀ ó ní òun ó kan ọrun;
àwọn aṣáájú ẹ̀-ẹ́ ṣe bẹ́ẹ̀ rí?
(This is a variant of the previous entry, using
a different name, ògọmọ̀, for "palm frond.")

210. Aṣiwèrè èèyàn ní ńsọ pé irú òun ò sí; irúu
rẹ̀-ẹ́ pọ̀ ó ju ẹgbàágbèje lọ.
Only an imbecile says there is no one else
like himself; the likes of him are many more
than several thousands. (There is no one the
likes of whom the world has never seen.)

211. Aṣọ à-fọ̀-fún ò jẹ́ ká mọ olówó.
Clothes washed clean make identifying the
rich person impossible. (A poor person who
looks to his or her appearance appears rich.)

212. Aṣọ tó kuni kù ní ńjẹ́ gọgọwú.
Whatever clothing one is left with is one's
best. (One makes the most of what one has.)

213. A-ṣúra-mú ò tẹ́ bọ̀rọ̀.
A person who is mindful of his or her image
is not easily disgraced. (People take one as

one presents oneself. Compare the following entry.)

214. À-tẹ́-è-ká ni iyì ọlọ́lá; sálúbàtà ni iyì ọlọ̀tọ̀; bá a bá gbéra lágbèéjù ọba ni wọ́n ńfini íse.
Spreading-the-mat-without-rolling-it-back-up is the mark of the wealthy; sandals are the mark of the illustrious; if one sings one's praise too loudly, one is liable to be made a king. (People take one as one presents oneself.)

215. À-wín-ná-wó ò yẹni; à-gbà-bọ̀-ọ ṣòkòtò ò ye ọmọ èèyàn; bí kò fúnni lésè a dòrògí; ohun ẹni ní ńyẹni.
Borrowing-money-to-spend does not speak well of one; borrowed trousers do not become a person: if they are not tight around the legs, they are difficult to remove; it is one's own things that fit. (One should not live beyond one's means.)

216. Àwòrò tí a ò bá lù kì í luni.
A priest you do not hit does not hit you. (A person who wants to be respected must respect others.)

217. A-wọlú-má-tèé, ìwọ̀n ara-a rè ló mọ̀.
One-who-enters-a-town-and-maintains-his-or-her-reputation does so because he or she knows his or her place. (Self-knowledge guarantees one's reputation.)

218. Àwúrèbeé ní òún lè yẹnà; ta ní jé tọ ònà àwúrèbe?
Àwúrebe says it can make a path; who would wish to follow a path it makes? (One should not offer one's services where one's abilities are inadequate.)[38]

219. Ayọ̀ àyọ̀jù làkèré fi ńṣẹ́ nítan.
It is excessive rejoicing that breaks the frog's thigh. (Immoderate happiness breeds unhappiness.)

220. Àyọ̀-yó ni bàtá à-jó-fẹ-ehín.
Dancing to bàtá music and exposing one's teeth is excessive happiness. (Happiness should know moderation.)

B

221. Babaaláwo kì í bèrè ẹbọ àná.
The diviner does not ask for yesterday's sacrifice. (One should not demean oneself by demanding piddling favors.)[39]

222. Bẹbẹlúbẹ ò ì tíì débẹ̀, ibẹ̀ ló ńbọ̀.
The busybody is not there yet, but he is on his way. (There is no keeping a nosy person out of others' affairs.)

223. Bí a bá dàgbà à yé ogun-ún jà.
When one becomes old, one stops warring. (An elder should leave off things that are a mark of youth. Compare 128 and 1500.)

224. Bí a bá fi inú wénú, iwọ là ńjẹ.
If we compare notes with others, we wind up eating bile. (Comparing fortunes with others is likely to leave a bitter taste in one's mouth.)

225. Bí a bá ńbá ọmọdé jẹun lóko, gànmù-ganmu imú ẹni ní ńwò.
If one eats with a youth on the farm, he stares at the protrusion of one's nose. (Too much familiarity with youth breeds contempt.)

---

38. The reference is apparently to an insect that makes paths in the sand.

39. Diviners hold back for their own use some of the items they prescribe for sacrifice.

226. *Bí a bá ńgúnyán, kòmẹsẹ̀ á yọ.*
If one prepares pounded yams, the uninvited should depart. (The well-bred visitor should make an exit when the hosts turn to intimate affairs.)

227. *Bí a bá ti lè ṣe là ńwí; a kì í yan àna ẹni lódì.*
One admits to one's limits; one does not cease speaking to one's relatives-in-law. (One should not let an inability to fulfill a formal obligation prevent one from fulfilling essential obligations.)

228. *Bí a bá ti mọ là ńdé; a-láì-lẹ́sin kì í dé wọ̀nwọ̀n.*
One arrives according to one's worth; a horseless person does not arrive with the noise of hoofs and stirrups. (One should act according to one's worth. See also the following entry.)

229. *Bí a bá ti mọ là ńkú; olongo kì í kú tìyàntìyàn.*
One dies according to one's weight; the robin does not die and make a resounding noise [on hitting the ground]. (One acts according to one's worth. See also the previous entry.)

230. *Bí a bá tọ̀ sílẹ́, onípò a mọ ipò.*
If someone wets the bed, each person should know where he or she slept. (In the event of a crime, the guilty should not attempt to shift the blame to others.)

231. *Bí a bá wí pé ó dọwọ́-ọ babaláwo, babaláwo a ló dọwọ́ Ifá; bí a bá ní ó dọwọ́ àgbà ìṣègùn, àgbà ìṣègùn a ló dọwọ́ Òsanyìn; bí a bá ní ó dọwọ́ ààfáà tó gbójú, a ní ó dọwọ́ Ọlọ́run ọ̀gá ògo.*
If one says that a matter now lies in the hands of the Ifá priest, the Ifá priest says it lies in the hands of Ifá; if one says that it lies in the hands of the venerable medicine man, the venerable medicine man says it rests in the hands of the god of herbs; if one says it rests in the hands of the formidable Muslim priest, he says it is in the hands of God the most glorious. (All achievements are creditable to the powers that make them possible, not to the agents.)

232. *Bí a kò bá dásọ lé aṣọ, a kì í pe ọ̀kan lákìísà.*
If one has not acquired one garment after another, one does not call the first one a rag. (One may not disdain an old tool until one is able to replace it.)

233. *Bí a kò bá lè dá Tápà, Tápà kì í dáni.*
If one cannot throw a Nupe man in a wrestling match, he should not throw one. (If one fails, one should at least avoid disgrace.)

234. *Bí a kò bá lọ sóko iró, a kì í pa á mọ́ni.*
If one does not go to the farm of lies, lies are not told against one. (If one does not lay oneself open to lies, one is not lied about.)

235. *Bí a kò bá ṣèké, a kì í fi ẹtẹ́ kú.*
If one has not been false, one does not die in disgrace. (One's honesty is one's vindication.)

236. *Bí a kò bá tí ì jókòó, a kì í nasẹ̀.*
If one has not yet sat down, one does not stretch one's legs out. (Until one has thoroughly secured one's position, relaxation is premature.)

237. *Bí a kò bá tí ì lè kọ́lé àgó là ńpa.*
If one is yet unable to build a house, one makes a tent. (One should neither overreach oneself nor refrain from striving.)

238. *Bí a kò bá tó baba ọmọọ ṣe, a kì í pe alákàrà.*

If one lacks the wherewithal to act like a father to a child, one does not summon the seller of bean fritters. (If one has no means of offering hospitality, one should not invite visitors.)

239. *Bí a kò bá tó ìyà-á kò tí à ǹkọ̀ ọ́, àjẹkún ìyà là ńje.*
If one lacks the means to reject suffering and attempts to reject it, one's suffering simply multiplies. (Whoever cannot defend himself or herself must learn forbearance.)

240. *Bí a ó ti tó kì í jẹ́ ká hùwà búburú; bí a ó ti mọ kì í jẹ́ ká hùwà rere.*
The heights one will reach keep one from evil deeds; the ordained limit to one's greatness keeps one from doing good deeds. (A person's achievements are enhanced or limited by the person's character.)

241. *Bí àgbà kò bá ṣe ohun ẹ̀rù, ọmọdé kì í sá.*
If an elder does not do something fearful, the youth do not flee. (Youth responds to age according to how age acts.)

242. *Bí ajá rójú ẹkùn, a pa rọ́rọ́.*
When the dog sees the eyes of the leopard, it keeps very still. (In the presence of one's betters, one keeps one's place.)

243. *Bí àjànàkú ò bá rí ohun gbémì, kì í ṣe inú gbẹndu sódẹ.*
Unless an elephant had swallowed something, it would not turn its bloated stomach to the hunter. (Unless a person has some resource to rely on, he or she does not tempt fate.)

244. *Bí ayá bá mojú ọkọ, alárìnnà a yẹsẹ̀.*
When the wife has got to know the husband, the marriage broker makes way. (Once one's task is done, one removes oneself.)

245. *Bí ayé bá ńyẹni, ìwà ìbàjẹ́ là ńhù.*
If life is being good to one, one is likely to act disgracefully. (Prosperity breeds temptations to misbehave.)

246. *Bí baálẹ̀-ẹ́ bá ńtàkìtì, òrógi là ńbá emẹsẹ̀.*
If the chief is turning somersaults, the messenger should be found standing erect. (The great may indulge themselves, but the lowly must keep their heads.)

247. *Bí eegbọ́n bá so mọ́ ajá lẹ́nu, akátá là ńní kó já a?*
If a tick fastens onto a dog's mouth, does one ask a jackal to dislodge it? (A person of great substance is not asked to minister to a person of no substance. See also the next entry.)

248. *Bí eegbọ́n bá so ayínrín nímú, adìẹ kọ́ ni yó ja.*
If a tick clings to a fox's nose, it is not a chicken that will remove it. (The prey is not sent to minister to a predator. See also the preceding entry. Compare 283.)

249. *Bí èèyàn bá ní kò sí irú òun, àwọn ọlọgbọ́n a máa wòye.*
If a person says there is no one like him or her, wise people maintain a contemplative silence. (A person who thinks he or she is peerless fools no one but himself or herself.)

250. *Bí ẹkùn ò bá fẹ, ẹsẹ là ńpè é.*
If a leopard does not act mighty, one refers to it as a cat. (A person who acts beneath his station loses some respect.)

251. *Bí ẹlébọ ò bá pe ẹni, àṣefín ò yẹni.*
If the person offering a sacrifice does not invite one, intruding is not proper. (It is bad form to intrude into other people's affairs.)

252. *Bí ìlàrí bá féé té, a ní kí ọba ó ṣe?*
When a courtier seeks disgrace, he asks,
"What can the king do?" (If one does not
show respect for one's patron, one courts
disgrace.)

253. *Bí iná bá dun ọbè, a dá ọ̀rọ̀ sọ.*
If the fire gets at the stew, the stew will burst
into speech. (If the excitement is strong
enough, coyness disappears.)

254. *Bí kò sí àkópọ̀, kí lewúrẹ́ wá dé ìsọ adìẹ?*
Were it not for the fact that they were trans-
ported together, what would a goat want
in the chicken's stall? (Necessity brings
together people who would otherwise have
nothing to do one with another).

255. *Bí kò sí tòbùn èèyàn, ta ni ìbá jí lówùúrọ̀
tí kò bójú ṣáṣá?*
But for a person of filthy habits, who would
wake in the morning and not wash his or
her face clean? (Antisocial people betray
themselves by their habits.)

256. *Bí mo bá torí oko kú ng ó rò fáhéré; bí
mo bá torí ògèdè kú ng ó rò fódò; bí mo bá
torí alábàjà òkìkí kú, ng ó rò fórí-ì mi.*
If I die on account of a farm, I will lay my
case before the hut; if I die on account of
bananas, I will lay my case before the river;
if I die on account of the famous woman
with facial scarification, I will lay my case
before my head. (Were I to die for a woman,
the forces ordering my fortune would know
why.)[40]

257. *Bí ó di ọdún mẹ́ta tí ẹkùn-ún ti ńṣe òjòjò,
olugbe la ó ha rán lọ bẹ ẹ̀ wò?*
If it has been three years since the leopard
took ill, is it a monkey that one sends to

ask its condition? (Even though one may
be down on one's luck, there are yet certain
propositions one would consider insulting.)

258. *Bí òfé ti ńfò la ti ṁmọ̀ ó láko eye.*
It is by its flight that the parrot proves itself
a formidable bird. (One shows one's quality
through one's accomplishments.)

259. *Bí ojú bá rí, ẹnu a dáké.*
When the eyes see, the mouth remains quiet.
(The mouth does not reveal everything the
eyes see.)

260. *Bí ojú kò bá rí, ẹnu kì í sọ nǹkan.*
If the eye does not see, the mouth says nothing. (The mouth can tell only what the eye
sees.)

261. *Bí ojú kò bá ti olè, a ti ará ilé è.*
If the thief feels no shame, members of his
household should. (A person's disgrace must
concern his relatives.)

262. *Bí ojú onílé bá mọ tíntín, tí ojú àlejòó tó
gbòǹgbò, onílé ní ńṣe oko àlejò.*
Even though the host's eyes are tiny, and
the guest's eyes are huge, it is the host who
holds sway over the guest. (The host is lord
over the guest.)

263. *Bí òkú fẹ, bí kò fẹ, ká bi ọmọ olókùú
lèèrè.*
Whether the funeral is grand or is not, one
should ask the heir of the dead. (Only those
most intimately concerned know the close
truths of an affair and should be asked about
them.)

264. *Bí olóde ò kú, òdee rè kì í hu gbégi.*
If the owner of a yard does not die, his yard
is not overgrown with wild grass. (If one
does not die, one is able to look after one's
affairs.)

---

40. This is apparently the plaint of a man besotted
by his attraction to a woman.

265. *Bí olóúnjẹẹ bá rojú à fi àìjẹ tẹ́ ẹ.*
If the owner of the food is reluctant to share,
one disgraces him by refusing to eat. (The
best way to treat a miser is to refuse anything
from him.)

266. *Bí ọdún bá dún, bọnnọnbọ́nnọ́n a pàwọ̀
dà.*
When the year is done, the *bọnnọnbọ́nnọ́n*
tree changes its color. (When the seasons
change, one changes one's habits.)

267. *Bí ọjàá bá tú tán, a ku olórí-i pàtẹpàtẹ, a
ku àgbàÀgbà sà-ǹkò sà-ǹkò lójà; bífá bá pèdí
tán, ìwò-ǹwọ̀ a dìde.*
When the market disperses, only the head of
the market women remains; only the venerable elders remain; when Ifá has had his say,
the genius that consults him arises. (When
a matter is done, those involved should
disperse.)

268. *Bí ọjọ́ ewúrẹ́ bá pé, a ní kò sí ohun tí
alápatàá lè fi òun ṣe.*
When a goat's day [to die] arrives, it says
there is nothing a butcher can do to it. (A
person who does not recognize and heed
danger courts death.)

269. *Bí ọlẹ́ ò lè jà, a lè kú tùẹ̀.*
If a lazy man cannot fight, he should be able
to die disgracefully. (A person who cannot
defend his rights should yield to death.)

270. *Bí Ọlọ́run ò ṣe ẹni ní baba, à fi ìyànjú ṣe
bí àgbà.*
If God does not make one a father, one
strives to act like an elder. (Even if one has
no influence, one strives to act responsibly.)

271. *Bí ọmọdé bá fẹ́ẹ́ ṣìṣe àgbà, ọjọ́ orí-i rẹ̀ ò
nií jẹ́.*
If a youth attempts to act like an elder, his
age will stop him. (A youth does not have
what it takes to be an elder.)

272. *Bí ọmọdé bá gun òkè àgbà, ó ńláti gbọ́n.*
If a child ascends the height of maturity, he
or she must become wise. (Wisdom goes
with age.)

273. *Bí ọmọdé bá ńṣe ọmọdé, àgbà a máa ṣe
àgbà.*
When a child is being a child, an elder must
remain an elder. (One should not permit
other people's misbehavior to deflect one
from the proper course.)

274. *Bí ọmọdé ńléri bébé, tí kò ní baba, ti
baba là ńṣe.*
If a child brags a great deal but has no father,
one acts the part of a father. (One should
not deal too harshly with a child who has no
one to direct him or her.)

275. *Bí Ọya ńkọ lórun, bí Ṣàngó ńjó láyé,
kò nií burú fún baba kó ní ó dọwọ́ ọmọ òun
lọ́run.*
Even if the goddess Ọya sings in heaven
and the god Ṣango sings on earth, matters
cannot be so bad for the father that he will
say it is all up to his dead child in heaven.
(Even in suffering, one should never disgrace
oneself.)[41]

D

276. *Dídákẹ́ lerín dákẹ́; àjànàkú ló legàn.*
The elephant has only chosen to remain
silent; to the elephant belongs the forest.
(The mighty need not proclaim their importance. Compare 4136.)

---

41. The proverb refers to the Yoruba belief that the
dead have the power to protect their living survivors.
Normally, though, the living look to the spirits of dead
elders for such protection, never to the spirits of their
dead children.

277. *Dìgbòlugi-dìgbòlùuyàn ò jẹ́ ká mọ ajá tòótọ́.*
The mad dog, and the person who behaves like a mad dog, both make it impossible for one to know the real dog. (He who acts like a dog makes himself the equal of a dog.)

E

278. *Eegun àjànàkú: ó há ìkokò lẹ́nu.*
An elephant's bone: it sticks in the wolf's mouth. (A person has overreached himself or herself and is paying the price of folly.)

279. *Eégún ju eégún; òrìṣá ju òrìṣà; Pààká lé onísàngó wọ̀gbẹ́.*
Some masqueraders are greater than others; some gods are greater than others; the masquerader *Pààká* chases the Ṣango worshiper into the bush. (Every company has its hierarchy; each person should know his or her place.)

280. *Eégún ò na obìnrin lágọ̀; obìnrín tú kíjìpá ìdí-i rẹ̀, ó fi na eégún.*
The masquerader did not hit a woman with his shroud, but the woman unwraps her home-woven wrapper and hits the masquerader with it. (A person is fortunate to have been overlooked by trouble, but he or she goes to deliberately provoke it.)[42]

281. *Eégún pẹ́ lóde, ó fẹtẹ̀ òkè dáhùn; wọ́n ní, "Baba kú àbọ̀," ó ní, "Hì ì ì."*
The masquerader stayed too long on parade and was reduced to speaking with his upper lip. They said, "Welcome, father," and he responded, "He-e-e-e." (A person who has disgraced himself speaks softly.)

282. *Eégún wọlé, ó ní òun ò rí Ejonto; Ejontó ní, "Àkísà ni, àbí kíní wọlé?"*
The masquerader enters a house and claims he did not see Ejonto; Ejonto asked, "Is that a rag that entered the house, or what?" (A person who disregards one earns one's disregard.)

283. *Eegbón so mọ́ àyìnrín lẹ́nu, a ní kí adìẹ wá yán an jẹ; adìẹ mọ̀ pé òun náà oúnjẹ àyìnrín.*
A tick fastens on a fox's mouth and a chicken is asked to peck it off; the chicken, though, knows that it itself is food for a fox. (One wastes one's time inviting others to endanger themselves. Compare 248.)

284. *Èèyàn bí ọ̀bọ lòbọ ńya láṣọ.*
Only people like monkeys have their clothing torn by monkeys. (Those who consort with undesirables are likely to have their reputation soiled.)

285. * Èèyàn ò ríbi sùn, ajá ńhanrun.*
Humans have no place to sleep, and a dog is snoring. (A lowly person lays claim to what his or her betters lack.)

286. * Èèyàn tí ò nítìjú ojú kan ni ìbá ní, a gbórín a tó tẹsin.*
A shameless person deserves to have only one eye, that one as large as a horse's. (Human endowments are wasted on graceless people.)[43]

287. *Ejò kì í ti ojú Ààrẹ gun ogbà lọ.*
A snake does not escape over the fence while

---

42. Women are forbidden to approach masqueraders, on pain of being whipped, and are supposed to run into hiding whenever masqueraders are about.

43. The proverb plays on *ìtìjú*, literally "the pushing at the eyes," which is the Yoruba word for shame. A person who is insensitive to "the pushing at the eyes" certainly can do without a second eye, and the one he or she does have can be as large as possible, since it will be insensitive to pushing, and the disfigurement would mark the person as grotesque while having no effect on him or her.

a warrior watches.[44] (One does not permit disaster on one's watch; one must live up to the expectations of one's position.)

288. *Èmí dáko okòó, ìwọ dáko okòó, ò ńpèmí ní mùkọ-mùkọ.*
I bought 20 cowries' worth of corn pap, and you bought 20 cowries' worth of corn pap, and you call me a corn-pap addict. (One should not criticize others for flaws that are also one's lot. Compare 555.)

289. *Èmi ìwòfà, ìwọ ìwòfà, o ní babá ní ká gbowó wá; o dá tìrẹ sílẹ̀ ná?*
I am a pawn, you are a pawn, and you tell me the creditor sent you to collect his money; have you repaid yours? (Whoever will correct others should first take care of his or her own failings.)

290. *Epo ni mo rù; oníyangí má ba tèmi jẹ́.*
It is palm oil that I am carrying; sandman, do not ruin my fortune. (I am cautiously going about my own business; let no one bring trouble my way.)

291. *Erin kì í fọn kọ́mọ-ọ rẹ̀ ó fọn.*
An elephant's trumpeting is never answered by its young's trumpeting. (Lowly people should not emulate illustrious ones.)

292. *Èrò ònà ni yó ròhìn ọkà tó gbó.*
It is people who use the path that will spread the word about mature corn. (A noteworthy accomplishment need not advertise itself.)

293. *Èsúrú ṣe fújà ó tẹ́ lọ́wọ́ oníyán; aláǹgbá ṣe fújà ó tẹ́ lọ́wọ́ ògiri; Ọlámọnrín àjàpá ṣe fújà ó tẹ́ lọ́wọ́-ọ mi.*
Èsúrú yam forgets itself and loses favor with the maker of pounded yams;[45] the lizard forgets itself and falls into disfavor with the wall; tortoiselike He-who-will-remain-nameless forgets himself and loses all regard with me. (A person who does not know his or her place soon suffers disgrace.)

294. *Etí lobìnrín fi ńgbọ́ ohùn orò.*
It is only with the ears that a woman hears the voice of Orò. (One must not intrude into affairs that do not concern one; undesirable people should be kept in the dark about important or delicate matters.)[46]

295. *Èwo ló tó ẹ̀kọ-ọ́ gbà nínú ewé ìrúgbàá?*
Which among the leaves of the locust-bean tree is adequate to receive corn loaf? (Certain feats are beyond certain people; people should not presume to do things beyond their capabilities.)[47]

296. *Èwo ni ti Síkírá nílùú Ìwó.*
What business does Sikirat have in the town of Ìwó? (One should not intrude into matters that do not concern one.)[48]

297. *Ewújù tí yóò tú ọpẹ: gbogbo ehín è ni yóò kán tán.*

---

the starch content is so low that it is not suitable for pounding.

46. Orò is a secret divinity connected with the secret supreme political and juridical council known as Ògbóni or Òṣùgbó. His cult is forbidden to women; at the sound of the bull-roarer announcing his public outings, women must go into hiding. A man who is not a member of the cult also runs the risk of being killed if he intrudes into its rites even accidentally. (When lower-cased, the word orò is used as a generic term for rites or rituals.)

47. Corn loaves are cooked wrapped in large leaves, much larger than the leaves of the locust-bean tree, which are inadequate for the purpose. The proverb plays on gbà (to receive) and the end of ìrúgbàá (gbà á), which means "receive it," or "accommodate it."

48. Sikirat is a Muslim name for a woman; the town of Ìwó is, presumably (as far as this proverb is concerned), a stranger to Islam.

---

44. In this case *Ààrẹ* is the short form of the highest Ọ̀yọ̀ military title, *Ààrẹ Ọ̀nà Kakaǹfò.*

45. *Dioscurea dumetorum* (see Abraham 324);

The cane rat that attempts to uproot a palm tree will lose all its teeth in the attempt. (One should not attempt a task for which one is not qualified.)

298. *Ewúrẹ́ kì í bíni ká lọ sísọ̀ àgùntàn lọ jẹ̀.*
If sired by a goat, one does not go foraging in the realm of sheep. (One should keep to one's proper company.)

299. *Ewúrẹ́ ò wí pé òun ò ṣọmọ àgùntàn; àgùntàn ló wí pé òun ò ṣọmọ ewúrẹ́.*
The goat did not say it was not sired by the sheep; it was the sheep that said it was not sired by the goat. (The goat would like to associate with the sheep, but the sheep would not associate with the goat; "superior" people reject association with "inferior" people, not the other way around.)

Ẹ

300. *"Ẹ fà á wọlé" ló yẹ ẹlẹ́sin.*
"Lead it into the stable" is what becomes a horseman. (To be able to afford a horse but not a groom is something of a disgrace.)

301. *Ẹ jẹ́ ká mí, ẹ jẹ́ ká simi; èèyàn ní ńfidí èèyàn jókòó; èèyàn ìbá ṣe bí Ọlọ́run kò níí jẹ́ ká mí.*
Let us breathe, leave us in peace; the fashion is for people to sit on their behinds; were humans in the position of God, they would not permit people to breathe. (People are wont to be too full of their authority; it is a good thing they have less power over others than God does.)

302. *"Ẹ kú-ulé" ò yẹ ará ilé; "Ẹ kú atìbà" ò yẹni tí ńtàjò bọ̀; ẹni tí ò kí ẹni, "Kú atìbà"-á pàdánù "Ẹ kú-ulé."*
"Greetings to you, housebound ones" is improper for the housebound to utter; "welcome home" is not proper for the person

arriving from a trip; whoever fails to give "welcome" to the person returning does himself or herself out of "greetings, housebound." (Whoever does not extend courtesies cannot expect to receive courtesies. Compare 4520.)

303. *Ẹ̀bìtì ẹnu ò tàsé.*
The mouth trap never misses. (The mouth easily accomplishes even impossible feats.)

304. *Egbẹ́ ẹni là ńgúnyán ewùrà dè.*
It is for one's peers that one makes pounded yam with *ewùrà* yams. (One may take liberties only with one's peers.)

305. *Ègbèrì ò mọ̀ pé arẹwà kì í gbé èkú; gbogbo ehín kin-kìn-kin lábẹ́ aṣọ.*
The novice does not know that a good-looking person does not wear a masquerade; all his perfectly white teeth are concealed beneath the cloth. (It is a foolish person who conceals his or her endowments.)

306. *Ègbọ́n ṣíwájú ó so aṣọ kó; àbúrò-ó kẹ́hìn ó wèwù; bí a ò mọ̀lẹ, ọ̀lẹ ò mọ ara-a rẹ̀?*
The elder walks in front, a loincloth draped over his shoulder; the younger walks behind, wearing a garment; if people cannot tell which one is shiftless, does he not know himself? (The shiftless person cannot hide his shiftlessness either from himself or from others.)

307. *Ẹlẹ́dẹ̀ ńpàfọ̀ ó rò pé òún ńṣoge.*
The pig wallows in mud but thinks it is being a dandy. (People who lack good judgment are never aware of their own misbehavior.)

308. *Ẹlẹ́dẹ̀ ò mèye.*
A pig does not know what is becoming. (Some people do not know fitting behavior.)

309. *Eléèèdé ńlọ èèdé, o ní "Èèdégbèta ni àbí èèdégbèfà?"; èwo lo gbé níbè?*

A person says he has lost an unspecified amount of money, and you ask if the amount is 500 cowries or 1,100 cowries; which amount did you steal? (A person who is too inquisitive about other people's affairs raises suspicions about his or her motives.)

310. *Elééfà kì í lọ ẹẹfà-a rè ká sọ pé o di ìjẹfà tí a ti jẹun.*

When a person proclaims the loss of six articles, one does not respond by saying one has not eaten in six days. (If one can offer no help to a person in trouble, one should not complicate the person's plight.)

311. *Ẹni à bá fi sóko kó dàparò, ó ní òun ẹni ilé.*

The person one would leave on the farm hoping he would become a partridge boasts that he is the indispensable presence of the household. (An unwanted person believes himself to be indispensable.[49] See the following three entries also.)

312. *Ẹni à bá tà ká fowó-o rè ra àdá: ó ní ìyà àdá ńjẹ òun.*

A person who should be sold for money to purchase a machete bemoans his lack of a machete. (A person who is only most grudgingly tolerated in a company complains about his lack of privileges. This is a variant of the preceding and the following two entries.)

313. *Ẹni à bá tà ká fowó-o rè ra àtùpà: ó ní òun à-jí-tanná-wò-lóru.*

A person who should be sold for money to purchase a lamp boasts that he is one-people-light-lamps-to-admire-at-night. (A person most unwanted in a company regards himself or herself as the soul of the party. This is a variant of the preceding two and the following entries.)

314. *Ẹni à bá tà ká fowó-o rè ra èbù: ó ní èlé òún kó ọòdúnrún.*

A person one would sell for money to purchase quartered yams for planting claims that he has enough earnings to buy three hundred yam pieces. (A person considered worthless and expendable makes claims to equal rights. This is a variant of the preceding three entries.)

315. *Ẹni à ńgbé gègè ni yó ba ara-a rè jé.*

It is the person who is revered that will disgrace himself or herself. (People who are placed on pedestals have ample opportunities to topple themselves.)

316. *Ẹní bá dẹ ojú-u rè sílè á rímú-u rè.*

Whoever gazes downward will see his or her nose. (Whoever comports himself or herself indecorously will be disgraced.)

317. *Ẹní dádé ti kúrò lómọdé.*

The person who wears a crown has outgrown childhood. (A high office carries high responsibilities with it.)

318. *Ẹni tí a bá ńdáṣọ fún kì í ka èèwò.*

The person who is clothed by others does not list what he will not wear. (Those who depend on the charity of others must be satisfied with whatever they can get. Compare 81.)

319. *Ẹni tí a fé yàtò sí ẹni tó ní kò sí irú òun.*

A person one loves is different from a person who says there is no one like himself or herself. (One's worth is more a matter of what other people think than what one thinks of oneself.)

---

49. The Yoruba word for the partridge, *àparò*, can be rendered etymologically as *à-pa-rò* (something one kills and boasts about killing), because the bird is desirable for stew meat.

320. *Ẹni tí a gbé gun ẹlẹ́dẹ̀, ìwọ̀n ni kó yọ̀ mọ; ẹni tó gẹsin, ilẹ̀ ló ḿbọ̀.*
The person whom people have seated on a pig should moderate his or her strutting; even a horse rider will eventually come down to earth. (One should not let good fortune go to one's head; circumstances do change.)

321. *Ẹni tí a lè gbé kì í dawọ́.*
A person who can be lifted does not hang limp. (There is no point in resisting the irresistible.)

322. *Ẹni tí à ḿwò láwò-sunkún ḿwo ara-a rẹ̀ láwò-rẹ́rìnín.*
A person whose appearance moves one to tears is moved to laughter by his own appearance. (The miserable person has no notion of his own miserableness.)[50]

323. *Ẹni tí a ò fẹ́, àlọ́ ò kàn án.*
A person whose company is not desired gets no turn at riddling. (A person not wanted in a group should not press his or her rights. Compare the following entry.)

324. *Ẹni tí a ò fẹ́ nílùú kì í jó lójú agbo.*
A person not welcome in the town does not take a turn in the dancing circle. (A person not wanted in a group should keep a low profile. Compare the preceding entry.)

325. *Ẹni tí ìbá hùwà ipá ò hùwà ipá; ẹni tí ìbá hùwà ẹ̀lẹ̀ ò hu ẹ̀lẹ̀; òkùn tó nígba ọwọ́, tó nígba ẹsẹ̀ ńhùwà pẹ̀lẹ́.*
The person one would expect to be reckless is not reckless; the person one would expect to be cautious is not cautious; the millipede with two hundred arms and two hundred legs behaves very gently. (Even though one

has a great deal of weight, one should still tread lightly.)

326. *Ẹni tí kò lè gbé eèrà, tí ńkùsà sí erin, títẹ́ ní ńtẹ́.*
A person who lacks the strength to lift an ant but rushes forward to lift an elephant ends in disgrace. (One should know one's capabilities and limit oneself to what one can accomplish.)

327. *Ẹni tí kò rí ayé rí ní ńsọ pé kò sẹ́ni tó gbọ́n bí òun.*
It is a person with limited experience of life who thinks there is none as wise as he. (No wise person claims he or she is the best there is.)

328. *Ẹni tí kò tó gèlètè kì í mí fín-ìn.*
A person who is not huge in stature does not breathe heavily. (One should match one's strutting to one's accomplishment.)

329. *Ẹni tó tan ara-a rẹ̀ lòrìṣà òkè ńtàn: àpọ̀n tí ò láya nílé, tó ní kí òrìṣà ó bùn un lọ́mọ.*
It is the person who deceives himself that the gods above deceive: a bachelor who has no wife at home but implores the gods to grant him children. (It is self-deceit to expect the gods to do everything for one who has not lifted a finger on his or her own behalf.)

330. *Ẹni tó tijú tì í fún ara-a rẹ̀.*
The person who is self-aware protects his or her own reputation thereby. (Good character benefits the owner more than others.)

331. *Ẹnìkan kì í jẹ "Àwá dé."*
Nobody is entitled to say, "Here we come." (However mighty, a person is still only one person.)

332. *Ẹran kí la ò jẹ rí? Ọ̀pọ̀lọ́ báni lábàtà ó ba búrúbúrú.*
What sort of meat is it the likes of which

---

50. This proverb is usually a comment directed at a particular person rather than a general proposition or observation.

one has never tasted? A toad comes upon one at the swamp and cowers in fright. (A person for whom one has no use wastes his or her time if he or she goes to great lengths to hide from one.)

333. Èrùkọ́ ńṣe bí ọkọ́.
The haft of the hoe is behaving like a hoe. (A certain person is putting on airs to which he or she is not entitled.)

334. Èṣọ́ kì í gba ọfà lẹ́hìn; iwájú gangan ní ńfi-í gba ogbẹ́.
A palace guard does not receive arrows in his back; he suffers wounds only in front. (One must act in a manner that befits one's station.)

335. Èwọ̀n tó tó ọpẹ ò tó-ó dá erin dúró; ìtàkùn tó ní kí erin má ròkè ọ̀dàn, tòun terin ní ńlọ.
A chain as thick as a palm tree cannot stop an elephant; the vine that proposes to stop the elephant from going to the grassland will go with the elephant. (Whoever attempts to stop an irresistible force will be swept along by it.)

336. Èyá ló bí mi, ẹkùn ló wò mí dàgbà, oló-gìnní gbà mí tọ́; bí kò séran lóbẹ̀ nkò jẹ.
I was born of a monkey, I was raised by a leopard, I was adopted by a cat; if there is no meat in the stew I will not eat it. (I will not act in a way inconsistent with my upbringing.)

337. Ẹyẹ akòko-ó ní òun le gbẹ́ odó; ta ní jẹ́ fi odó akòko gúnyán jẹ?
The woodpecker boasts that it can carve a mortar; whoever used a mortar carved by the woodpecker to make pounded yam? (The puny person's best efforts cannot amount to much.)

338. Ẹyẹ ò lè rí omi inú àgbọn bù mu.
A bird cannot get at the liquid inside a coco-nut to drink. (One should not attempt the impossible.)

339. Ẹyẹ tó fi ara wé igún, ẹ̀hìn àdìrò ní ńsùn.
Whatever bird emulates the vulture will find itself behind the cooking hearth. (People who have everything to lose should not emulate those who have nothing to lose.)

F

340. Fáàárí ọ̀bọ ò ju inú ìgbẹ́ lọ.
The monkey's showing off is limited to the confines of the forest. (One may be esteemed in one's own locality and be quite unknown in another.)

341. Fálànà gbọ́ tìrẹ, tara ẹni là ńgbọ́.
Falana, look to your own affairs; one's attention should be focused first on one's own affairs. (People should keep their noses out of other people's business.)[51]

G

342. Gànràn-gànràn ò yẹ ẹni a bí ire.
Unrestrained and thoughtless behavior does not befit a well-born person. (One should behave in a manner that reflects well on one's family.)

Gb

343. "Gbà jẹ" ò yẹ àgbà.
"Take this and eat it" does not become an elder. (It better becomes an elder to give than to go begging.)

---

51. Falana is a proper name that has come to be associated with uninvited intrusion into other people's affairs.

344. *"Gbà mí, gbà mí!" ò yẹ àgbà; àgbà kì í ṣe ohun àlémú.*
"Save me, save me!" does not become an elder; an elder should not do something that will make him the object of pursuit. (One should behave in a manner that befits one's station. Compare the entry that follows.)

345. *"Gbà mí, gbà mí!" ò yẹ eégún; "ẹran ńlémi bọ̀" ò yẹ ọdẹ.*
"Save me, save me!" does not befit a masquerader; "An animal is chasing me!" does not befit a hunter. (One should act in ways that become one's station.[52] Compare the preceding entry.)

346. *"Gba wèrè," "Ng ò gba wèrè" lọjà-á fi ńhó.*
"Accept imputation of imbecility"; "I will accept no imputation of imbecility" is the explanation for market noise. (One may have no means of avoiding insult from others, but it is always in one's power to reject insults.)[53]

347. *Gbogbo èèyàn ní ńsunkún-un Bá-njọ; ṣùgbọ́n Bá-njọ ò sunkún ara è.*
Everybody laments Banjo's fate, but Banjo does not lament his own fate. (Some people remain blissfully unaware of their own misfortune, even though the misfortune is obvious to others.)

348. *Gbogbo ẹgbẹ́ ńjẹ Má-yè-lóyè, ò ńjẹ Sáré-pẹgbẹ́.*

Everybody is taking the title *Máyèlóyè* (May-you-never-lose-the-title), but the title you receive is *Sáré-pẹgbẹ́* (Run-and-assemble-the-associations' members: in other words, Courier or Messenger). (The addressee is backsliding among his or her peers but believes he or she is doing rather well.)

349. *Gbogbo ọ̀rọ̀ ní ńṣojú èké.*
The busybody is privy to all matters. (There is nothing the busybody will admit he or she does not know about.)

350. *Gbọ̀n-ọ́n-gbọ̀n-ọ́n kan ò sí, àfi ẹni tó bá ńti ara è.*
There is no cause for staggering about, except for the person pushing himself or herself. (Some people make more trouble for themselves than others can ever make for them.)

I

351. *Ìbàjẹ́ ọjọ́ kan ò tán bọ̀rọ̀.*
The disgrace one incurs in one day does not disappear that soon. (Reputations are easy to destroy but most difficult to repair.)

352. *Ibi tí a bá pè lórí, a kì í fi tẹlẹ̀.*
Whatever one names as the head, one does not tread the floor with it. (Never misuse or abuse your prized possessions or attributes.)

353. *Ibi tí a fi ara sí lara ńgbé.*
Wherever one situates the body, there it inhabits. (One should confine oneself and one's activities to the appropriate spheres. See the following entry.)

354. *Ibi tí a fi iyọ̀ sí ló ńṣomi sí.*
Salt dampens only the place where it is placed. (One should confine one's activities to the proper arena. See the preceding entry.)

---

52. *Eégún*, masqueraders supposed to be the incarnations of dead ancestors, are themselves objects of terror. Fright does not become them.

53. The expression *Gba wèrè*, translated as "Accept imbecility," means "acquiesce in being treated like an imbecile." The back-and-forth haggling during market transactions is here seen as each bargainer proposing terms to the interlocutor, who would be an imbecile to accept them.

355. *Ibi tí a pè lórí ní ńhurun.*
The part one names the head is the one that grows hair. (One should act in accordance to one's station.)

356. *Ibi tí a ti mú ọlẹ ò kúnná; ibi tí a ti mú alágbáraá tó oko-ó ro.*
The place where a lazy person was apprehended bears no marks; the place where a powerful man was apprehended is broad enough to plant a farm. (A worthy person, even if eventually vanquished, will leave signs of powerful resistance behind.)

357. *Ibi tí a ti ńpìtàn ká tó jogún, ká mọ̀ pé ogún ibẹ̀ ò kanni.*
Where one must recite genealogies in order to establish one's claim to inheritance, one should know that one really has no claim to patrimony there. (One need not go to great lengths to establish one's claim if it is legitimate.)

358. *Ibi tí ayé bá eni ni a ti ńjẹ ẹ̀.*
Where life catches up with one, there one lives it. (One lives according to the conditions one finds oneself in.)

359. *Ìbọ́n dídá olówó ló ní kíwòfà rín rín rín kó sọ àdá nù.*
It is the master's engaging in silly antics that affords the pawn the opportunity to laugh so hard that he tosses his cutlass away. (If the person in charge behaves irresponsibly, then those over whom that person has charge have an excuse for irresponsible behavior also.)

360. *Idà ahun la fi ńpa ahun.*
It is with its own sword that one kills the tortoise. (Each person carries his or her own bane.[54] Compare 5019.)

361. *Idà ńwó ilé ara ẹ̀ ó ní òún ńba àkò jẹ́.*
The sword is destroying its own home, and it says it is ruining the scabbard. (Said of a person whose actions will eventually recoil on him or her, even though the person thinks that he or she is hurting others. Compare 1167.)

362. *Ìdí méjèèjìí tó olúwa-a rẹ̀-ẹ́ jókòó.*
The two buttocks are sufficient for their owner to sit on. (One should be satisfied with one's own resources.)

363. *Igúnnugún bà lé òrùlé; ojú tó ilé ó tó oko.*
The vulture perches on the roof; its eyes see the homestead as well as the farm. (Said of a busybody whose eyes get into everything.)

364. *Ìgbà tí sìgìdìí bá fẹ́ẹ́ ṣe eré ẹ̀tẹ́ a ní kí wọ́n gbé òun sójò.*
When the clay statue hankers for disgrace, it asks to be placed in the rain. (A person who so forgets himself or herself as to overreach will wind up in disgrace.)[55]

365. *Ìgbà wo ni Mákùú ò níí kú? Mákùú ò mọ awo ó ńbú opa; Mákùú ò mọ iwẹ̀ ó ńbọ́ sódò.*
When will (or how can) Maku avoid the danger of dying? Maku does not know the mysteries of the cult yet he joins in its vows; Maku does not know how to swim, and yet he jumps into the river. (A person who will not cooperate in safeguarding himself or herself frustrates the efforts of others.)[56]

366. *Ihò wo lèkúté ńgbé tó ní iṣẹ́ ilé ńdíwọ́?*
What sort of hole does the rat live in that

of the shell behind the neck until it comes apart. That part of the shell is known as the tortoise's sword.

55. *Sìgìdì* is a clay image one makes of one's enemy and endows by means of incantations with the power to harm the enemy in his or her dreams. Although thus endowed with supernatural powers, if it is placed in the rain it will crumble.

56. The name Mákùú (*má kùú*) means "Do not die."

54. Customarily, the tortoise is killed by pulling out the head and rubbing the neck against the sharp edge

makes him say that household work pre-occupied it? (One should not oversell oneself.)

367. *Ìjàkùmọ̀ kì í rin ọ̀sán; ẹni a bí ire kì í rin òru.*
The wild cat never roams in daylight; a well-bred person does not wander around in the nighttime. (People who care about their reputation should stay away from questionable actions.)

368. *Ìjàlọ ò lè gbé òkúta.*
The brown ant cannot lift a boulder. (One should not attempt a task that is beyond one's capability.)

369. *Ìjokòó ẹni ní ḿmúni da ewé ẹ̀kọ nù.*
How one sits causes one to carry the leaves used to wrap corn meal to the dump. (People treat one the way one presents oneself.)[57]

370. *Ìjọba ńpè ọ́ o ní ò ḿmu gàárí lọ́wọ́; ta ní ni ọ́, ta ní ni omi tí o fi ḿmu gàárí?*
The government summons you, and you say you are busy eating cassava grains soaked in water; who owns you, and who owns the water with which you are eating the cassava? (When the law summons, one has no option but to heed the summons.)

371. *Ilé kì í jó kí baálé ilé tàkakà.*
A house does not burn while the landlord lounges with indifference. (One must not ignore matters of grave concern to oneself. Compare the following entry.)

372. *Ilé kì í jó kí oorun kun ojú.*
A house does not burn and fill the eyes with sleep. (One must not ignore grave matters. Compare the previous entry.)

---

57. It is the manner of one's sitting in a company that causes one to be selected as the right person to clear the garbage.

373. *Ilé-ni-mo-wà kì í jẹ̀bi ẹjọ́.*
"I-was-in-my-home" is never the guilty party in a dispute. (One does not get into trouble by minding one's own business.)

374. *Ìlù kan ò tó Ègùn jó; bí a bá lù fún un a máa lu àyà.*
One drum is not enough for an Ègùn person to dance to; if one drums for him, he too will play a rhythm on his chest. (Said of a person who is never satisfied with whatever others do for him/her but must always make some adjustment.)

375. *Iná ńjó ògiri ò sá, ó wá ńgbá gẹẹrẹ gẹẹrẹ sómi.*
Fire burns and the wall does not run from it; now it moves threateningly toward water. (A person who is powerless against others should not make threatening moves.)

376. *Inú burúkú làgbà ńní, àgbà kì í ní ojú burúkú.*
An unpleasant inside is what a venerable elder should have; a venerable elder should not have an unpleasant mien. (One should not permit the way one really feels to push one into unseemly behavior.)

377. *Ipa ọgbẹ́ ní ńsàn; ipa ohùn kì í sàn.*
The wound left by a cutlass may heal, but the wound left by speech does not heal. (Injury inflicted through speech is impossible to heal.)

378. *Ìpàkọ́ onípàkọ́ là ńrí; enìẹ́lẹ́ni ní ńrí tẹni.*
One sees only other peoples' occiputs; only others can see one's own. (One usually pays closer attention to other people's faults than to one's own, of which others are quite aware. Compare 3888.)

379. *Ìpénpéjú ò ní enini; àgbàlagbà irùngbọ̀n ò ṣe òlòó.*
The eyelashes do not make dew; a venerable

old beard does not behave like an ingenue. (Some habits are fitting for one's station; others are not.)

380. *Ìréjẹ ò sí nínúu fọ́tò; bí o bá ṣe jókòó ni o ó bàá ara-à rẹ.*
There is no cheating in photography; it is just as you sit that you will find your image. (One's public perception depends ultimately on one's self-presentation.)

381. *Irú aṣọ ò tán nínu àṣà.*
The likeness of a particular type of cloth is not lacking among those in fashion. (No one has a monopoly on certain qualities. Compare the following entry.)

382. *Irú erin ò tán ní Àlọ́.*
The likeness of an elephant is not scarce in Àlọ́.[58] (Nobody is one of a kind. Compare the preceding entry.)

383. *Ìrùkẹ̀rẹ̀ kì í yan Ifá lódì; oge, dúró o kí mi.*
The horse-tail whisk does not shun Ifá; high-fashion maiden, pause awhile and give me a greeting. (One should not neglect to say hello to other people.)[59]

384. *Ìsáǹsá ò yọ ẹ̀gún; ìsáǹsá kì í káwo ọbẹ̀.*
The fugitive does not stop to pull a thorn [from his or her feet]; the fugitive does not stop to clear dinner dishes. (A person who has committed a crime does not wait around to be caught.)

385. *Ìṣẹ́ ò ti ibìkan mú ẹni; ìyà ò tibìkan jẹ èèyàn; bí o bá rìnrìn òsì, bí o bá ojú ìṣẹ́ wọlú, igbá-kígbá ni wọn ó fi bu omi fún ẹ mu.*
Destitution does not attach to one at a particular place; suffering does not attack a person at a particular place; if one walks like a wretch into a town, if one looks like a loser when when one enters a town, it is with a miserable calabash that the people will offer one water to drink. (People treat one the way one presents oneself.)

386. *Ìtàkùn tó tó ọpẹ kò tó pé kérin má lọ; ìtàkùn tó pé kérin má lọ Àlọ́, tòun terin ní ńlọ.*
A vine as thick as a palm-tree trunk will not stop an elephant; whatever vine attempts to stop an elephant from going to Alo will go with the elephant instead. (A powerless person will not stop a mighty person from doing what he wants; one who attempts it invites suffering for himself.)

387. *Ìwà ní ńjo oníwà lójú.*
Character is always remarkable (or good) in the opinion of its owner. (One naturally approves of one's own character.)

388. *Ìwọ̀fà ní ńmú ìwọ̀fà jó.*
A pawned person always dances with a pawned person. (People should know who share their station and confine their dealings to them.)

389. *Ìwọ̀n eku nìwọ̀ ìtẹ́; olongo kì í gbé tìmù-tìmù.*
The measure of the rat is the measure of the nest; a robin does not live on a cushion. (One should cut one's garment according to one's size.)

390. *Ìwòsí ní ńba ilé àgbà jẹ́.*
Trading insults brings ruin to an elder's home. (An elder who fails to maintain harmony among the members of his household will see it destroyed.)

391. *Ìyàwó tó na ọmọ ọbàkan, ọ̀rọ̀ ló féé gbọ́.*
The wife who whips a relative of her hus-

---

58. Àlọ́, mythical city of elephants, is also a jungle.

59. Ìrùkẹ̀rẹ̀, horse-tail whisk, is one of the tools for consulting Ifá, the Yoruba oracle.

band is asking for stern rebuke. (One should not engage in inappropriate actions.)[60]

J

392. *Jéjé leégún àgbà ńjó.*
Sedately is the way an elderly masquerader dances. (Grown-up people should behave in a decorous manner.)

393. *Jòkùmò-ó ṣe bí ẹlú, aró la bè lówè.*
The *jòkùmò* plant looks like the indigo plant; it is the indigo dye, though, we have use for. (One should know and employ the appropriate materials for one's tasks.)

K

394. *Ká ríni lóde ò dàbí-i ká báni délé.*
To see a person in the streets is not the same as going home with the person. (To really know a person, one must see the person where he or she lives.)

395. *Ká ríni sòrò fúnni ò dàbí-i ká sòrò fúnni ká gbà.*
Having people to advise one is nothing like knowing how to take advice. (Nobody can help anyone who will not help himself or herself.)

396. *Ká wí fún ẹni ká gbó; ká sòrò fúnni ká gbà; ká bèrè ọnà lówó èrò tó kù léhìn káyé baà lè yẹni.*
If one is spoken to, one should listen; if one is advised, one should heed the advice; one should seek direction from straggling wayfarers in order that one's life might be pleasant. (It is wise to heed advice, and it is

wise to seek direction from those who have greater experience. Compare the preceding and the following entries.)

397. *Ká wí fúnni ká gbó; ká sòrò fúnni ká gbà; à-wí-ìgbó, à-gbó-ìgbà ní ńfi igbá àdánù bu omi mu.*
If one is spoken to, one should listen; if one is advised, one should accept the advice; refusal to listen to speech and refusal to accept advice leads to using the calabash of deprivation as a drinking cup. (Refusal to heed advice leads to deprivation. Compare the following two entries.)

398. *Ká wí ká gbà ló yẹ ọmọ èèyàn.*
To heed advice is what best becomes a human being. (One should heed advice. Compare the preceding two entries.)

399. *Ká wí ogún, ká wí ọgbòn, "Ng ò fẹ́, ng ò gbà" lasiwèré fi ńpèkun òràn.*
Whether one speaks twenty times or speaks thirty times, "I do not like it, and I will not accept it" is how the imbecile ends the discussion. (The incorrigible person will never listen to reason.)

400. *Kàkà ká dòbálè fún Gàmbàrí, ká rójú ká kú.*
Rather than prostrate oneself in homage or obeisance to a Hausa person, one should rather die. (An expression of Yoruba superciliousness toward the Hausa.)

401. *Kàkà kí àgbò ké, àgbò a kú.*
Rather than cry out, the ram will die. (A grown man must know how to hide his pain.)

402. *Kàkà kí bàbá ran ọmọ ní àdá bọ oko, oníkáluku a gbé tìẹ.*
Rather than the father carrying the son's cutlass home from the farm, each will carry his own. (People may withhold their respect

---

60. A wife is expected to accord respect to the relatives of her husband, even very young ones, especially those born into the family before she married into it.

from one, but one should not abet their insolence.[61] Compare 404.)

403. *Kàkà kí iga akàn ó padà sẹhìn, a kán.*
Rather than bend backward, the crab's claws will break. (Death is to be preferred to retreat.)

404. *Kàkà kí kìnìún ṣe akápò ẹkùn, ọlọ́dẹ a mú ọdẹ è ṣe.*
Rather than the lion serving as carrier for the leopard, each will hunt separately. (One would rather leave a company than remain in it and be subordinate to those one considers inferior. Compare 402.)

405. *Kékeré lòpọ̀lọ́ fi ga ju ilẹ̀ lọ.*
The toad is only slightly taller than the earth. (Said of people who behave as though they are superior to others though have little reason to believe so.)

406. *Kí ẹrú mọ ara è lẹ́rú; kí ìwọ̀fà mọ ara è níwọ̀fà; kí ọmọlúwàbí mọ ara è lẹ́rú Ọlọ́run ọba.*
Let the slave know himself or herself as a slave; let the pawn know himself or herself as a pawn; let the well-born person know himself or herself as the child of God.[62] (Everybody should know himself or herself and his or her station in the scheme of things.)

407. *Kì í dọwọ́-ọ baba kó ló di ọwọ́ ọmọ.*
Responsibility does not devolve on the father only for him to say it is his son's duty. (An elder must do his or her duty and not shove it on the youth.)

408. *Kí ni ànfàníí kẹtẹkẹtẹ̀ lára kẹtẹkẹtẹ́ à-gùn-fẹsẹ̀-wọ́lẹ̀?*
What is the point of bragging about an ass which, when one rides on it, one's feet drag on the ground? (It is pointless to make too much of a virtually worthless thing.)

409. *Kí ni apárí ńwá ní ìṣọ̀ onígbàjámọ̀?*
What does a bald man want in the stall of the barber? (One should stay out of places where one has no business. Compare 412.)

410. *Kí ni Dáàró ní kó tó sọ pé olè-é kó òun?*
What did Dáàró own before he claimed he was robbed? (Said of a person who could do nothing in the best of circumstances but blames his or her lack of success on certain eventualities. This is a variant of 58.)

411. *Kí ni eléwé-e-gbégbé ńta tí ó ńsọ pé ọjà ò tà?*
What is it that the seller of *gbégbé* leaves has to sell that she complains that the market is slow? (Said of people who have fundamental problems but complain only of the symptoms.[63] This is a variant of 59.)

412. *Kí ni ìbá mú igún dé ọ̀dọ̀-ọ onídìrí?*
What would take the vulture to the stall of the hairdresser? (One should stay away from places where one has no business. Compare 409.)

413. *Kí ni ó yá àpọ́n lórí tó fisu síná tó ńsúfèé pé "bí a ti ńṣe ni inú ńbí wọn"?*
What has the bachelor to feel so superior about that while he is roasting yams, he is whistling the song, "What one does fills them with jealousy"? (Said of people who are arrogant even though they have no basis for pride.)

414. *Kí ni onígbá ńṣe tí aláwo ò lè ṣe?*
What is the calabash owner doing that the

---

61. The proper thing is for the son to carry the cutlass for the father.

62. *Iwọ̀fà* (pawn) is a person whose temporary services one acquires in return for a loan of money.

63. *Gbégbé* leaves are of little use to anyone. They are reputed to have magical powers, though.

china plate owner cannot do? (Whatever one can accomplish, those better placed or better endowed can accomplish also.)

415. *Kí ni orí ńṣe tí èjìká ò lè ṣe? Èjìká ru ẹrù ó gba ọ̀ọ́dúnrún; orí ta tiè ní ogúnlúgba.*
What can the head do that the shoulder cannot do? The shoulder carried a load and earned 300 cowries; the head sold its own for 220 cowries. (One should not be foolish enough to think that the person who has more power and standing than oneself cannot accomplish what one has accomplished.)

416. *Kí ni wọ́n ti ńṣe Àmọ́dù nÍlọrin? Ewúrẹ́ ńjẹ́ bẹ̀ẹ̀.*
What use do the people of Ilorin have for Ahmadu? Even goats are so named. (Said to express the overabundance of some commodity being discussed.)[64]

417. *Kíjìpá laṣọ òlè; òfì laṣọ àgbà; àgbà tí ò ní tòfì a rójú ra kíjìpá.*
Durable hand-woven cloth is the material for shiftless people; loom-woven cloth is the material for the elders; whichever elder cannot afford loom-woven cloth should strive for durable hand-woven cloth. (If one cannot have the perfect thing, one should strive to have at least something.)

418. *Kò rà, kò lówó lọ́wọ́, ó ńwú tutu níwájú onítumpulu.*
He does not buy, he has no money, yet he sits sulkily before the seller of bean fritters. (Said of people reluctant to accept the fact that they cannot have what they wish.)

419. *Kò sí ẹni tó dùn mọ́ àfi orí ẹni.*
There is no one pleased [by one's success] except one's own head. (Few people genuinely wish that one should succeed.)

420. *Kò sí mi lájọ àjọ ò kún: ara ẹ̀ ló tàn jẹ.*
Without-me-in-an-assembly-the-assembly-is-not-complete deceives only himself or herself. (Whoever thinks he or she is indispensable is self-deceived.)

421. *Kò sí ohun tí Ṣàngó lè ṣe kó jà lẹ̀ẹ̀rùn.*
There is nothing Sango can do to enable himself to rage in a drought. (One cannot transcend one's nature.)[65]

422. *Kò-sí-nílé kì í jagun ẹnu tì.*
He-was-not-at-home never fails to prove his valor with his mouth. (Said of a person who vows that had he been around when something happened, he would have performed wonders.)

423. *Kó-tán-kó-tán lajá ńlá omi.*
Swiftly-consumed-swiftly-consumed is the way a dog laps up water. (Said of people who attack good things with excessive greed.)

L

424. *Labalábá fi ara ẹ̀ wéye, kò lè ṣe iṣe eye.*
The butterfly likens itself to a bird, but it cannot do what a bird can do. (Attempts to emulate those better endowed and qualified than oneself always prove futile. Compare the following entry.)

425. *Lábúlábú fara wé aró, kò lè ṣe bí aró; pòpòndó fara wé àgbàdo.*
Ash mixed with water likens itself to indigo dye, but it cannot do what the dye can do;

---

64. At the time Nigeria became independent in 1960, one of the most powerful politicians was Ahmadu Bello. The people of Ilorin did not care much for him, apparently, and one person there named his goat after him.

---

65. Being the god of thunder, Sango can rage only during the rainy season.

the large red bean likens itself to corn.[66]
(One should know better than to attempt
to overreach one's capabilities. Compare the
preceding entry.)

426. *Lágbájá ìbá wà a di ìjímèrè; ẹni tó bá
níwájú di oloyo?*
Were So-and-So alive, he would transform
himself into a brown monkey; did the person who preceded him ever transform himself into any kind of monkey? (One should
not make excessive claims when there is no
basis for them.)[67]

427. *Láká-ǹláká ò ṣéé fi làjà; ọmọ eégún ò ṣéé
gbé ṣeré.*
A limp is no great asset for a person wishing to stop a fight; a masquerader's child is
no easy playmate. (One should know one's
limits and also what one would be ill advised
to attempt.)

428. *Lásán kọ́ là ńdé ẹtù; ó ní ẹni tórí ẹ̀ ńbá
ẹtù mu.*
One does not wear an *ẹtù* cap as a matter
of course; only certain people have heads
suited for such a cap.[68] (Not every person is
made for greatness.)

429. *Lékèélékèé ò yé eyin dúdú; funfun ni wọ́n
ńyé eyin wọn.*
Cattle egrets never lay black eggs; only white
eggs do they lay. (Ony certain types of behavior are suitable for people in certain
positions.)

---

66. In the traditional indigo dyeing process a mix-
ture of ash and water is used for fixing the dye. *Pòpòǹdó*
is *Canavalia* (Papilonaceae); see Abraham 556.

67. The proverb in all probability refers to the *alárìnjó* contests of itinerant performing masqueraders,
during which they claim to transform themselves into
animals and reptiles. *Oloyo* is another name for the
brown monkey.

68. *Ẹtù* is a rich cloth cap that only the prosperous
wear.

430. *Má tẹ̀ẹ́ lọ́wọ́ oníle, má tẹ̀ẹ́ lọ́wọ́ àlejò;
lọ́wọ́ ara ẹni la ti ńtẹ́.*
Save face with members of your household,
and save face with complete strangers, such
a person loses face with himself or herself.
(A person too careful about his or her reputation will end up losing regard for himself
or herself. Some situations call for doing
away with decorum.)

431. *Màlúù ò lè lérí níwájú ẹsin.*
A cow may not boast in the presence of a
horse. (One should acknowledge and defer
to those better able than oneself.)

432. *Mànàmáná ò ṣéé sun iṣu.*
Lightning is no good for roasting yams.
(Many instances of boasting lack the sub-
stance to back them.)

433. *"Ǹbá wà lÓyọ̀ọ́ mà ti so ẹsin"; àgùntàn-
an rẹ̀ á níye nílẹ̀yí.*
"Were I at Ọ̀yọ́ I would own a horse by
now"; he should have numerous sheep to
his name in this town. (What a person has
accomplished in his or her present circumstances is a good indication of what the person has the potential to do in more favorable
circumstances.)

434. *Mélòó lÈjìgbò tí òkan ẹ̀ ńjẹ́ Ayé-gbogbo?*
How large a community is Ejigbo that one
of its settlements is named Ayegbogbo [the
whole world]? (One should be modest in
one's claims.)

435. *Mo dàgbà mo dàgó, aré ọmọdé ò tán
lójúù mi.*
I have become old and wise, but childish
play has not ceased to appeal to me. (There
is something of the youth that lingers even
in age. Compare the following entry.)

436. *Mo dàgbà tán èwe wù mí.*
Having grown old, I miss youthfulness. (One does not appreciate one's youth until one has lost it. Compare the preceding entry.)

437. *"Mo dára, mo dára," àìdára ní ńpèkun è.*
"I am beautiful, I am beautiful" has ugliness as its conclusion. (Whoever is infatuated with his or her attractiveness will end up being despised by all.)

438. *"Mo gbón tán, mo mòràn tán" kì í jé kí agbón lóró bí oyin.*
"I am all-wise, I am all-knowing" kept the wasp from having as much venom as the bee. (Whoever will not listen to instruction will learn nothing.[69] Compare the next four entries.)

439. *"Mo mÒbàrà mo mÒfún" ti kì í jé kí àwòko kó òpèèrè nÍfá.*
"I am versed in Òbàrà and versed in Òfún," the boast that discourages àwòko from teaching òpèèrè Ifá verses. (Disdain for advice or instruction leaves a person in ignorance. Compare the preceding and following three entries.)

440. *"Mo mò-ó gùn" lesin ńdà.*
"I am an expert horseman" is usually the one thrown by a horse. (Assuming that one knows it all causes one grief. Compare the preceding two and the following two entries.)

441. *"Mo mò-ó gún, mo mò-ó tè" niyán ewùrà-á fi ńlémo.*
"I know how to pound and I know how to marsh" is what causes pounded yam made with wateryam to be lumpy. (Knowing it all can be disastrous. Compare the preceding three and the following entry.)

442. *"Mo mò-ó tán" lOrò-ó fi ńgbé okùnrin.*
"I know it all" is the reason for Orò's carrying a man away. (Knowing it all leads to disaster.[70] Compare the four preceding entries.)

443. *"Mo mòwòn ara-à mi" kì í sèrèké èébú.*
"I am jealous of my dignity" does not hurl insults at others. (A person who wishes to maintain his or her dignity must not by his or her actions invite insults.)

444. *"Mo yó" ńjé "mo yó," "mo kò" ńjé "mo kò"; jeun ńsó, àgbà òkánjúwà ni.*
"I am full" means "I am full"; "I decline" means "I decline"; eating with abandon, that is the father of all greediness. (One should not accept every invitation to the table.)

N

445. *"Ng óò gba owó-ò mi lára sòkòtò yìí"; ìdí làgbàlagbà ńsí sílè.*
"I will get my money's worth out of these trousers"; the grown man only winds up exposing his bare buttocks to the world. (One should not insist on squeezing every last ounce of use out of a perishable article.)

446. *Níbo lo forúko sí tí ò ńjé Làmbòròkí?*
Where did you discard all other names and pick for yourself the [unpleasant] name Làmbòròkí? (Where did you leave good manners and pick up unbecoming and unacceptable behavior?)[71]

447. *Nígbàtí à ńto okà a ò to ti emó si.*
When we were stacking the corn, we did

---

69. The idea is that the bee listened attentively to instructions on how to pack venom in its sting, but the wasp thought it knew it all.

70. Even know-it-alls need to remember that a man who is not a member of Orò's cult runs the risk of being killed if he intrudes into its rites even accidentally.

71. This proverb is used to chastise people and to order them to snap out of their bad habits.

not stack some for the brown rat. (People should keep their hands off other people's property unless they have been asked to help themselves.)

448. *Nígbàtí o mọ̀-ọ́ gùn, ẹsin ẹ-ẹ́ ṣe ṣẹ́ orókún?*
Since you claim to be a seasoned rider, why has your horse gone lame? (An expert does not produce flawed goods.)

449. *Nígbàwo làpò ẹkùn-ún di ìkálá fọ́mọdé?*
Since when did a tiger-hide sack become a thing a child uses to harvest okro? (People should not presume to lay claim to things or functions that are far beyond their station.)

450. *Nlánlá lọmọ abuké ńdá: ó ní "Ìyá, ìyá, òun ó pọ̀n."*
The humpback's child has presented a formidable dilemma: he cries, "Mother, mother, carry me on your back!" (A dependent who demands of one what one cannot provide is intent on showing one up.)

O

451. *Ó bọ́ lọ́wọ́ iyọ̀ ó dòbu.*
Salt loses its good quality and becomes like saltpeter. (A person who has been written off loses all regard.[72] See the next entry.)

452. *Ó bọ́ lọ́wọ́ oṣù ó dàràn-mọ́jú.*
The moon loses its esteem and shines all night long. (A person who overstays his or her welcome ceases to be valued. See the previous entry.)

453. *O dájú dánu, o ò mọ ẹ̀sán mẹ́sàn-án.*
Your eyes flinch not and your mouth is un-stoppable, but you do not know nine times nine. (Too much mouth often indicates too little substance.)

454. *Ó di àwùjọ sòkòtò kí ládugbó tó mọ ara rẹ̀ Lábèṣè.*
Not until the gathering of trousers will Ládugbo know itself as a miscreant. (Some people will not learn the truth about themselves until they are openly disgraced.)

455. *Ó di ọjọ́ alẹ́ kábuké tó mọ̀ pé iké kì í ṣọmọ.*
Not until the end of days will the humpback realize that a hump is not a child. (People seldom learn wisdom until it is too late.)

456. *O kò mọ ẹwà lóńjẹ à-jẹ-sùn.*
You do not know what black-eyed peas are like for dinner. (Addressed to a person who is not mindful of the repercussions of his or her behavior.)[73]

457. *Ò ńjàgbònrín ẹsín lọ́bẹ̀, o ní o ti tó tán.*
You are reduced to eating last year's antelope in your stew, and yet you claim to have attained the height of good fortune. (A hard-up person who claims to be prosperous deceives himself or herself.)

458. *O ru ládugbó ò ńrera; kí ni ká sọ fẹ́ni tó ru Òrìsà-a Yemoja?*
Because you are carrying a huge pot, you strut; what would one say to the person carrying the divinity Yemoja? (Never assume to be more important than you are, especially when there are really more important people around.)

459. *Ó tọ́ kí eégún lẹ́ni lóko àgbàdo, èwo ni ti Pákòkò láàrin ìlú?*
It might be seemly for a masquerader to

---

72. When the Yoruba have written someone off as irremediably worthless, they say, *Ó bọ́ lọ́wọ́ ẹ̀* ("It has all slipped from his or her hands").

73. Black-eyed peas eaten for dinner cause heart-burn and great thirst.

chase one off a corn farm, but it is not seemly for Pákòkò to chase one in the middle of town.[74] (A person who is in no position to exercise authority over another should not presume to do so.)

460. *Ó ye ẹni gbogbo kó dínwó aró, kò ye atòólé.*
It is fitting for everybody to bargain to reduce the cost of dyeing clothes, but not the bed wetter. (The person in desperate need of a thing cannot afford to be finicky.)

461. *Ó ye ẹni gbogbo kó sọ pé iṣu ò jiná, kò ye alubàtá.*
Everybody has a right to say the yams are not well cooked, but not the *bàtá* drummer. (People should not be too quick to complain about conditions they helped to engineer.[75] Compare 459.)

462. *Ó ye ẹni gbogbo kó sọ pé "Ọlọrun a-ṣèkan-má-kù," kò ye akúkó.*
Everyone can justifiably say, "God, who has left nothing undone," but not a eunuch. (People should not act as though they are unaware of their flaws.)

463. *Odò kékeré lalákàn-án ti lè fọ epo; bó bá di àgàdàm̀gbá tán, odò a gbé alákàn lọ.*
It is only in a small stream that the crab can make its oil; when it becomes huge and swift, the river sweeps the crab away. (When times are easy, there is little one cannot attempt.)

464. *Òfin ni yó sọ ara ẹ̀; ìyàwó tí ǹna ọmọ ìyálé.*

The law will assert itself, [as in the case of] a junior wife flogging the child of the senior wife. (Whoever transgresses should expect more or less automatic repercussions.)

465. *Ogun tí olójúméjìí rí sá ni olójúkan-án ní òun ńlọ jà.*
The war that the two-eyed person saw and fled is the same the one-eyed person vows he will join. (A comment on overreaching people who attempt feats that have defeated their betters.)

466. *Ohun méjì ló ye Èṣọ́: Èṣọ́ jà, ó lé ogun; Èṣò jà ó kú sógun.*
Only two things are proper for a warrior: the warrior goes to war and drives the enemy off; the warrior goes to war and dies in battle. (One should not act in a way that is not proper or becoming.)

467. *Ohun tí à ńtà là ńje; kì í ṣe ọrọ̀ oní-kẹrosíìnì.*
What one sells is what one eats; that does not apply to the kerosene seller. (One should be mindful of the peculiarities of one's situation.)

468. *Ohun tí eèrá bá lè gbé ní ńpè ní ìgànnìkó.*
Whatever the ant is able to carry is what it says is its full measure. (One should match one's desires to what one can afford.)

469. *Ohun tí ìrè-ẹ́ ṣe tó fi kán lápá, aláàǹtèté ní kí wọ́n jẹ́ kí òun ó ṣe è.*
That which the cricket attempted and broke a thigh, the *aláàǹtèté* asks to be permitted to attempt. (Some fools never learn from others' mistakes.)[76]

470. *Ohun tí kò tó okòó kì í jẹ àgbà níyà.*
A thing that is not worth the least amount of money should not prove a hardship for

---

74. Pákòkò is a very minor *eégún* (masquerader), as distinct from the major ones that strike terror into people.

75. The idea is that there was insufficient wood to cook the yams because so much wood had been used to make the *bàtá* drum.

---

76. *Aláàǹtètè* is a type of cricket.

an elder. (One should not be defeated by insignificant problems.)

471. *Ohun tí wèré fi ńse ara è, ó pò ju ohun tó fi ńse omo elòmíràn lo.*
What the imbecile does to himself is far worse than what he does to others. (Said when a person intending to injure others in fact does himself or herself greater injury.)

472. *Ohun tó seé faga là ńfaga sí; èwo ni, "Ìwòyí àná mo ti na ànaà mi fága-fàga"?*
One boasts only about things proper to boast about; whoever heard of the boast, "By this time yesterday I had given my parent-in-law the beating of his life"? (One should not cheerfully and boastfully embrace disgrace.)

473. *Ohun tó yeni ló yeni; okùn òrùn ò ye adìe.*
Whatever is becoming for a person is what is becoming; a noose is not becoming for a chicken.[77] (One should always confine one's actions to those that are proper and becoming.)

474. *Ojú àlejò la ti ńje gbèsè; èhìn-in è là ńsan án.*
It is in a visitor's presence that one gets into debt; it is in her absence that one repays the debt. (One does not estimate how much hospitality is costing until one's visitor has departed. Compare 3454.)

475. *Ojú baba ara: a-wón-bí-ojú; a-sòró-dà-bí-àgbà.*
The eye, father of the body: nothing is as valuable as the eye; nothing is as difficult to achieve as the status of elder. (What is most precious is most difficult to achieve.)

---

77. A tag to the proverb goes *Bó bá ye é, teni tí ńfà á ńkó?* ("Even if it is, what about the person pulling it?").

476. *Ojú iná kó lewùrà ńhurun.*
It is not in the presence of the flame that water yam grows hair. (One dares not strut when one's bane is around. Compare 1743.)

477. *Ojú kì í pón baálé ilé kó fowó gbálè ilé è.*
A head of a household is never so hard up that he sweeps his compound with his bare hands. (However desperate one might be, there are certain things one must not stoop to do.)

478. *Ojú kì í pón babaláwo kó bèrè ebo àná.*
An Ifá diviner-priest is never so hard up that he asks for yesterday's sacrifice. (One should not permit hardship to lead one to demeaning behavior.)

479. *Ojú kì í pón edun kó deni ilè; ìsé kì í sé igún kó di ojúgbà adìe.*
The colobus monkey is never so reduced in circumstances that it becomes a land-hugging creature; the vulture is never so badly off that it becomes the equal of a chicken. (No matter what one's misfortune, one should maintain one's dignity.)

480. *Ojú kì í pón òkú òrun kó ní kí ará ayé gba òun.*
A dead person cannot be so desperate as to appeal to a living person for deliverance. (However bad one's circumstances might be, one should use good sense in determining where to turn for help.)

481. *Ojú kì í pónni ká fàbúrò eni saya.*
One should not become so desperate that one takes one's younger sister as wife. (Desperation should not preempt propriety.)

482. *Ojú kì í pónni ká fàkísà bora.*
One should never be so benighted that one covers oneself in rags. (Despite adverse circumstances, one should strive to maintain one's dignity.)

483. *Ojú kì í pọ́nni ká pọ́n léhìn.*
One's circumstances do not so deteriorate
that one becomes red in teeth. (Adverse
circumstances should not keep one from
attending to essential matters.)

484. *Ojú ò rọ́lá rí: ó bímọ ẹ̀ ó sọ ọ́ ní Ọláni-
yọnu.*
A person only newly acquainted with
wealth: he has a son and names him Ọlani-
yọnu.[78] (The nouveaux riches will always call
attention to themselves with their ostentatious consumption.)

485. *Ojú ò ti oníṣègùn, ó ní àna òun ńkú lọ.*
The medicine man lacks all shame, he announces that his parent-in-law is dying. (If
one cannot do what is expected, one should
at least not broadcast one's shame.)

486. *Ojú ti agbọ́n; agbọ́n láfà kò léro.*
Shame upon the wasp; the wasp has a nest
but no honey. (There is a limit to how much
one can emulate others.)[79]

487. *Òkété pèlú ọmọ ẹ̀-ẹ́ di ogboogba sínú ihò;
nígbà tí ìyá ńfehín pàkùrọ́, ọmọ náà ńfehín
pa pèlú.*
The giant bush rat and its child become
equals in their hole; the mother cracks palm
nuts with her teeth, and the child does the
same thing. (Too much familiarity makes
comrades of people who are quite distant
from each other in standing.)

488. *Òkùnkùn ò mẹni ọ̀wọ̀; ó dífá fún "Ìwọ́ tá
nìyẹn"?*
Darkness does not know who deserves deference; it consulted the oracle Ifá for "Who
might you be?" (People who wander about

in darkness cannot expect to be treated with
deference. This is a variant of 511.)

489. *Olóbìnrin kan kì í pagbo ìja.*
A person who has only one wife does not
form a circle for a fight. (A person who does
not have enough helping hands should not
embark on ventures that are too ambitious.)

490. *Olójúkan kì í tàkìtì òró.*
A one-eyed person does not attempt standing somersaults. (One should limit one's
ambition to one's capability.)

491. *Olómele kì í sọ pé igi yó dàá lóde lóla.*
The *omele* drummer does not vow that there
will be an earth-shaking performance on
the morrow. (If one has no say, one should
avoid making projections or promises.)[80]

492. *Olówó jẹun jẹ́jẹ́; òtòṣì jẹun tìpà-tìjàn;
òtòṣì tí ḿbá olọ́rọ̀ rìn, akọ ojú ló ńyá.*
The rich man eats slowly and at leisure;
the poor person eats fast and with anxiety;
the poor man who keeps company with a
wealthy man is exceeding his station. (One
should keep to comrades whose station is
similar to one's own.)

493. *Olówó ní ḿbá olọ́rọ̀-ọ́ rìn; egbẹ́ ní ḿbá
egbẹ́ ṣeré.*
It is a rich person that keeps company with a
wealthy person; only people of equal standing play together. (One should associate with
one's equals.)

494. *Olówó ní ńjẹ iyán ẹgbàá.*
It is a rich person that eats pounded yams
worth 2,000 cowries. (One's level of consumption reflects the depth of one's pocket.)

495. *Olóyè kékeré kì í ṣe fáàárí níwájú ọba.*
A minor chief should not act garrulously in

---

78. The name means "Wealth entails such headaches!"

79. Using *afà* and *èro* for hive (nest) and honey is
nonstandard Yoruba.

80. The *omele,* the smallest drum in the *dùndún*
ensemble, is usually played by an apprentice drummer.

the presence of a king. (One should know one's station and act accordingly.)

496. *Òní, etú jìnfin, òla, etú jìnfin; etu nìkan leran tó wà nígbó?*
Today, the antelope falls into the ditch; tomorrow, the antelope falls into the ditch; is the antelope the only animal in the forest? (If a person is the only one misfortune always visits, there is probably something the person is doing to invite it. See 1777.)

497. *Oníbàjé ò mora; oníbàjé ńlo sóko olè ó mú obìnrin lo; okó kó akọsu, ìyàwó kó ewùrà.*
The shameless person does not know what is fitting; the shameless person is off to raid a farm, and he takes his wife along; the husband steals staple yams, and the wife steals water yams. (A man who involves his family in his questionable ventures has sunk to the lowest depths.)

498. *Oníbàtá kì í wọ mósálásí kó ní "Lèmámù ńkó?"*
The *bàtá* drummer does not enter a mosque and ask, "Where is the *imam*?" (One should know just where one is welcome and how to behave there.)[81]

499. *Onífunra àlejò tí ńtètè ṣe onílé pèlé.*
The excessively attentive visitor extends hospitality greetings to the host. (One should not assume other people's functions.)

500. *Onígègé fílèkè dópò; onílèkè ìbá gbowó, kò rórùn fílèkè so.*
The person with a goiter offers a ridiculously low price for beads; were the beads seller to accept her offer, she would have no neck to string the beads around. (One can always find a ruse to get one out of embarrassing situations.)

501. *Onílé ńje èso gbìngbindò; àlejò-ó ní kí wón ṣe òun lówó kan èwà.*
The host is eating the fruits of the *gbìngbindò* tree; the visitor asks to be treated to some black-eyed peas. (When one's benefactor is experiencing hardship, one should be realistic in one's requests of him.)

502. *OníSàngó tó jó tí kò gbọn yèrì: àbùkù-u Sàngó kó; àbùkù ara è ni.*
The Sango worshiper who dances and does not shake his skirt: he does not disgrace Sango but himself.[82] (A person who does not live up to his potential disgraces only himself. See the following entry.)

503. *OníSàngó tó jó tí kò tàpá, àbùkù ara è.*
The Sango worshiper who dances and does not kick his legs disgraces himself. (A person who skimps on what is expected of him disgraces himself. See the preceding entry and its note.)

504. *On-iṣèépé-igí bímọ ó sọ ọ́ ní Ayò-ó-kúnlé; ayò wo ló wà lára ìṣépé igi?*
The seller of twigs for firewood has a child and names him Ayòókúnle [Joy-fills-this-home]; what sort of joy is to be found in firewood twigs? (One should not make too much of nothing.)

505. *Ònpè ní ńfa olá; òjípè kì í fa olá.*
It is the person who does the summoning that assumes airs; the person subject to summons does not assume airs. (One should know one's place, especially in the company of more illustrious people.)

506. *Oòrùn, kó tìe wò ká má bàá Olójó wí.*
Sun, go set so one does not blame the owner of the day.[83] (Subordinates should not be-

---

81. The *bàtá* drum and ensemble are associated with traditional deities and their worship and are therefore out of bounds in a mosque.

82. Sàngo worshipers wear skirts, and good Sàngo dancing requires skirt shaking.

83. Olójó ("Owner of the day") is another designation for God.

have in a manner that would bring their
superior to disrepute.)

507. *Orí àgbà-á níyì, ó sàn ju orí àgbà-á fó lọ.*
The-elderly-person's-head-deserves-respect
is better than The-elderly-person's-head-
is-damaged. (An elder who enjoys respect
is better off than one who is insulted by
others.[84] Compare 519.)

508. *Orí awọ là ṁbágbà.*
It is on the hide that one finds the elder.[85]
(One should always live up to what others
expect.)

509. *Orí-i kí ní ńyá àpọ́n tó ńsúfèé? Nítorí pé
yó gùn-ún-yán fúnra è yó nìkan jẹ́?*
What is the cause of the bachelor's elation
that makes him whistle? That he will make
pounded yams for himself and eat it by himself? (A bachelor with no one to share his
life and his meals has nothing to be cheerful
about.)

510. *Orogún ìyá ẹ-ẹ́ dáṣọ fún ọ o ní kò balẹ̀;
mélòó nìyá ẹ-ẹ́ dá fún ọ tó fi kú?*
Your mother's co-wife made a garment for
you, and you complain that it is not long
enough; how many did your mother make
for you before she died? (People dependent
on charity should be grateful rather than
difficult to please.)[86]

511. *"Òru ò molówó" nIfá tí à ńdá fún "Ìwọ ta
nìyẹn?"*
"The dark of night knows not who is a
wealthy person" is the oracle one delivers to
"Who might that be?" (Nighttime wanderers

should be prepared for indignities. This is a
variant of 488.)

512. *Òtòlò-ó jẹ, òtòlò-ó mu, òtòlò-ó fẹsẹ̀ wé ẹsẹ̀
erin.*
The water buck ate, the water buck drank,
the water buck compared its limbs to an
elephant's. (Satiation leads to excess.)

513. *Oúnjẹ ọmọ kékeré a máa wọ àgbà nínú;
òrùka ọmọ kékeré ni kì í wọ ágbá lọ́wọ́.*
A youth's food can enter the stomach of an
elder; it is only a youth's ring that cannot
slip onto an elder's finger. (An elder may
take advantage of the youth in certain respects, but in some others an elder must
respect his status.)

514. *Owó èyẹ ò sú ẹni-í san; tòràn ni ò
súnwòn.*
People have no difficulty paying the money
for glorious events; it is the money for
trouble that is unpleasant to pay. (The
troubles one goes into for honorable purposes are really a pleasure; not so the trouble
to extricate oneself from problems.)

Ọ

515. *Ọbẹ̀ kì í gbé inú àgbà mì.*
A stew does not slosh around once inside an
elder. (An elder should know how to keep
confidences.)

516. *Òbún ríkú ọkọ tìrànmọ́; ó ní ọjọ́ tí ọkọ
òún ti kú òun ò fi omi kan ara.*
The filthy person takes advantage of her
husband's death for blame; she says since
her husband died, she has not violated her
person with water. (Shiftless people will
latch on to any excuse to shirk duties.)

517. *Ògà-ǹ-gà lọmọ-ọ mi ńjẹ́, ẹ má pe ọmọ-ọ
mi ní Ògò-ǹ-gò mọ́! Èwo lorúkọ rere níbẹ̀?*
My child's name is Ògàǹgà; don't you call

---

84. *Orí ẹẹ́ fó!* ("Your head is split") is an insult.
85. Elders often sit on cowhides when they relax or
adjudicate disputes.
86. The proverb assumes that wives would not ordinarily extend generosity toward the children of their
co-wives.

my child Ọ̀gòǹgò any more! Which of the two is a good name? (A choice between two bad things is no choice at all.)

518. Ògègé ò léwà; lásán ló fara wésu.
The poisonous cassava has no attraction; it resembles a yam only in vain. (No imitation can be as good as the real thing.)

519. Ọjọ́ àgbà-á kú sàn ju ọjọ́ àgbà-á té.
The day an elder dies is far better than the day an elder is disgraced. (Death is preferable to disgrace. Compare 507.)

520. Ọjọ́ kan là ṁbàjé, ọjọ́ gbogbo lara ńtini.
Only one day brings disgrace to a person; the shame is felt every day. (The thoughtless act of a moment mars one's reputation for a long time. See the following entry.)

521. Ọjọ́ kan ṣoṣo là ńté; ojoojúmọ́ lojú ńtini.
It takes only one day to disgrace oneself; the shame is a daily affair. (Fleeting indiscretions have lasting effects. See the preceding entry.)

522. Ọjọ́ tí alákàn-án ti ńṣepo, kò kún orùbà.
In all the days the crab has been making oil, it has not filled a pot. (Said of people who have labored long but have nothing to show for all their effort.)

523. "Ọjọ́ tí mo ti ṁbọ̀ ng ò rírú è rí": olúwa è-é mọ iwòn ara è ni.
"In all the days I have walked this earth, I have never seen the like": that person knows his place. (If one knows one's place, one will be spared humiliation.)

524. Òkánjúwà àgbà ní ńṣo ara è dèwe.
It is an avaricious elder that turns himself into a child. (An elder who cannot control his appetite asks to be treated like a child.)

525. Òkánjúwà alágbàà ní ńgarùn wo eégún.
It is an insatiable chief of the masqueraders'

cult that stands on tiptoe to watch a performing masquerader. (It is unseemly to be too greedy, especially when everything is at one's disposal anyway.)

526. Ọkùnrin kì í ké, ako igi kì í ṣoje.
A man does not cry; hardwood does not ooze sap. (Fortitude is the mark of a man.)

527. Ọlọgbọ́n kan ò ta kókó omi sáṣọ; òmòràn kan ò mọ oye erùpè ilè.
No wise man ever ties water in a knot in his cloth; no knowledgeable person can tell the number of grains of sand on the earth. (There are certain feats that are beyond even the most accomplished of men.)

528. Ọlọgbọ́n ò tẹ ara è nífá; òmòràn ò fi ara è joyè; abẹ tó mú ò lè gbé èkù ara è.
The wise person does not consult the Ifá oracle for himself; the knowledgeable person does not install himself as chief; the sharp knife does not carve its own handle. (The strongest and wisest of men still would need the service of other people at some time.)

529. Ọmọ àì-jọbè-rí tí ńja epo sáyà.
A child new to eating stews: he shows himself by dripping palm oil on his chest. (Upstarts will betray themselves by their misuse of their new-found fortune.)

530. Ọmọ onílè á tè é jéjé.
The owner of the earth treads gently on it. (Responsible people do not always do as they can, but behave as is proper.)

531. Ọmọ ọba Ọ̀nà Ìṣokùn ńfi ehín gé ejò, ọmọ ọba kan-án ní òun kì í jẹ é; ìlú wo lọmọ ọba náà-á ti wá?
The prince of Ọna Ìṣokùn [a ward in Ilésà] is sharing out snake meat with his teeth, and another prince says he does not eat such a thing; where did that prince come from? (If your betters are reduced to an expedient,

you would be foolish to say it is beneath you.)

532. Ọmọdé dáwọ́tilẹ̀, ó ní òún tó ọbọ; bó tó ọbọ, ó tó gègè àyà-a rẹ̀?
A child rests his hand on the earth and claims it is as big as a monkey [chimpanzee]; even if the child is as big as a monkey, is its chest as big as the monkey's? (Equality is more than mere physical resemblance.)

533. Ọmọdé ní ẹẹ́ta lówó, ó ní kí Èṣù wá ká ṣeré owó; ẹẹ́ta-á ha tó Èṣùú sú epo lá?
A child has 3 cowries in hand and challenges Èṣù to a game played for money; will 3 solitary cowries suffice for Èṣù to purchase palm oil to lick?[87] (People who come into some money for the first time are wont to overestimate their sudden worth.)

534. Ọmùtí gbàgbé iṣẹ́; alákọrí gbàgbé ọla.
The drunkard ignores his misery; the ill-fated person forgets tomorrow. (Irresponsible people often indulge themselves instead of taking care of their pressing problems.)

535. Ọnà ọ̀fun ò gba egungun eja.
The throat cannot accommodate fish bones. (Everybody and everything have some limitation.)

536. Òràn ò dun ọmọ ẹṣin; a mú ìyá ẹ̀ so, ó ńjẹ oko kiri.
Problems make hardly any impression on the foal of a horse; its mother is tied down, but it grazes nonchalantly about. (Said of people who show no concern for the afflictions of those close to them.)

537. Ọ̀rọ̀ bọtí-bọtí ò yẹ àgbàlagbà.
Speech like drunken babble does not befit a venerable person. (Responsible adults should be very careful about what they say.)

538. Ọ̀rọ̀ ò dùn lẹ́nu ìyá olè.
Speech is not pleasant in the mouth of the mother of a thief. (There is little a miscreant can say that will impress people.)

539. Ọ̀rọ̀ wo ló wà lẹ́nu alaṣọ pípọ́n?
What sort of speech can there be in the mouth of the person whose clothes are brown from dirt? (People with blemishes should keep a low profile.)

540. Ọsán pọ́n o ò ṣán ẹ̀kọ; oòrún kan àtàrí o ò jẹ àmàlà; àlejò-ó wá bà ọ ní ìyẹ̀tàrí oòrùn o ò rí ǹkan fún un; o ní "Njẹ́ ng ò níí tẹ́ lọ́wọ́ ẹ̀ báyìí"? O ò tíì tẹ́ lọ́wọ́ ara ẹ, ká tó sẹ̀sẹ̀ wá wípé o ò tẹ̀ẹ́ lọ́wọ́ ẹlòmíràn tàbí o ò níí tẹ́?
The sun rises and you do not eat corn meal; the sun moves directly overhead and you do not eat yam-flour meal; a visitor arrives for you when the sun is just past the overhead position and you have nothing to entertain him with; and you ask, "Am I not in danger of being disgraced in his eyes"? Aren't you already disgraced in your own eyes? Never mind whether you may be disgraced in others' eyes or not. (What one thinks of oneself is every bit as important as what others think of one.)

541. Ọsìn ò lè mú àwòdì òkè; Bámidélé lòsín lè mú.
The fish eagle cannot catch the kite flying on high; it can only catch Bamidele.[88] (Said of people who will confront only weaklings rather than people who match them in strength.)

---

87. Èṣù is the unpredictable god in the Yoruba pantheon; his favorite food is palm oil.

88. Bámidélé is a male name. The proverb is probably based on the play between ọ̀sín, the name for the vulturine fish eagle, and Ọsìn, a male name that is sometimes used as a designation for a king. Bámidélé (which means "Come home with me") indicates that the possible prey is one that is readily at hand.

542. Ọṣọ́ olọ́ṣọ́ọ́ ò yẹni; ṣòkòtò àgbàbò ò yẹ ọmọ èèyàn.
One never looks good in other people's finery; borrowed trousers do not fit the borrower. (One should not be a habitual borrower.)

543. Ọwọ́ àìdilẹ̀ ní ńyọ koríko lójú àna ẹ̀.
Idle hands are the ones obliged to remove grass specks from their in-law's eyes. (People who are unemployed can expect to be asked to perform all sorts of belittling tasks.)

544. Ọ̀wọ́n là ńra ògo, ọ̀pọ̀ là ńra ọ̀bùn, iyekíye là ńra ìmẹ́lẹ́.
Honor is always bought dear, filthiness cheap, and idleness at an indifferent price. (Nothing is more difficult to come by than honor.)

545. Ọ̀yájú-u baálé ní ńpàdé ìbòsí lọ́nà.
It is a reckless homeowner who is met with alarms when he ventures outside. (A patriarch who misbehaves earns disgrace.)

P

546. Pamí-nkú obìnrín ṣorí bẹmbẹ sọ́kọ.
A masochistic woman hardens her head against her husband. (Obstinacy only invites harsh punishment.)

547. Pátápátá alágbẹ̀dẹ ò ju ilé àrọ lọ.
The most one can expect of the blacksmith is confined to the smithy. (There is a limit to a person's bragging.)

548. Pẹ̀lẹ́ larẹwà ńrìn; jẹ́jẹ́ lọmọ olọ́jà ńyan.[89]
Carefully is the manner in which a beautiful person walks; gently is the manner in which a prince steps. (Gently and carefully are the best ways to take life.)

549. Pẹ̀lẹ́-pẹ̀lẹ́ nijó àgbà; ara gbogbo ló di àkísà tán.
An elderly person's manner of dancing must be very gentle, because the whole body has become worn to a rag. (Elderly people should not overexert themselves.)

550. Pẹ̀tẹ̀pẹ́tẹ̀ Ìjẹ̀sà, ó ta sẹ́ni lára kò wọ́n.
The mud of the Ìjẹ̀sà: it splashes on one and will not be washed off.[90] (Disgrace is not easily washed away. Compare 1877.)

S

551. San là ńrìn; ajé ní ńmúni pá kòrò.
Straight and upright is the way one would walk; it is money that forces one to sneak about. (When one is in debt, one's freedom of movement is compromised.)

552. Sesere ńdá gọ́ọ́bú; oníkamẹ́sàn-án ńgbé síbí.
The insignificant thing is attempting an earth-shaking feat; the person with only nine fingers is lifting a spoon. (Said of a person overreaching.)

553. Sún mọ ọ̀hún, sún mọ́ ìhín! Bí a bá kan ògiri ilé-e baba ẹni, ṣe là ńdúró gboin-gboin.
Move away, move over here! When one moves until one is against the walls of one's father's house, one stands steadfast. (There

---

89. Olọ́jà, literally "owner of the market," is another designation for the Yoruba ọba (king), because the market is customarily just outside the palace.

90. Most probably this is a riddle doing double duty as a proverb. The answer to the riddle Pẹ̀tẹ̀pẹ́tẹ̀ ọnà Ìjàyè, atasíníláramáwọ́ọ́n ("The mud along Ìjàyè way that splashes on one and cannot be removed") is facial scarification: the permanent scars of marks cut into the face during childhood. Each clan had its own distinguishing pattern of scarification; members could easily identify one another thereby when they chanced to meet in strange lands.

must be a limit to how much one will back down before enemies.)

Ṣ

554. *Ṣàgbà-ṣàgbà ò níí ṣé àgbà títí láí.*
The elderly person who acts his proper part will always be respected as an elder. (If responsible people wish to be retain other people's respect, they must always act like elders.)

555. *Ṣágo ńbúgò, ó ló ṣenu gbáṣóró.*
The demijohn insults the bottle, saying the latter has a long snout. (It is silly to pick a blemish one shares as the basis for insulting others; the pot should not call the kettle black.)

556. *Ṣàkì ńṣe bí òrá, egungun ńṣe bí ẹran.*
The tripe presents itself as fat; the bone presents itself as meat. (One should not pretend to be what one is not.)

557. *Ṣáláporẹ́ ò mọ egbẹ́ ẹ̀ nínú omi.*
Ṣáláporẹ́ [a tiny fish] does not know its peer inside water. (One should know who one's peers are and not overstep one's bounds.)

558. *Ṣe bóo ti mọ, ẹlẹ́wà-a Ṣàpọ́n.*
Moderate your preening and strutting, beautiful woman of [the town of] Ṣàpọ́n. (Do not overreach, and do not be too full of yourself.)

T

559. *"Ta ní ḿbẹ níbẹ̀?" làgbẹ́ fi ńsán ìbàntẹ́ wọlú.*
"Who is there whose opinion matters?" is the attitude that makes the farmer come into town dressed only in a loincloth. (People

who make a spectacle of themselves show no regard for others. Compare 3313.)

560. *Ta ní mọ Òkolo lÓyọ̀ọ́?*
Who knows Òkolo in [the city of] Ọ̀yọ́?[91] (Said of people who are of no account but act as though they matter.)

561. *Ta ní ńjájá ní mọ́sálásí?*
What would a dog be doing in a mosque? (Said to tell off people who are not wanted in a company. See the entry that follows and also 4105.)

562. *Ta ní ńjẹun tájá ńjùrù?*
At whose dinner table is the dog wagging its tail?[92] (Said to tell off people who make their presence felt when they should rather make themselves scarce. Compare the preceding entry.)

563. *Tẹ̀tẹ̀ kì í té.*
Spinach is never disgraced.[93] (May one never know disgrace.)

564. *Tòlótòló mọ eni tó ńyìnbọn ìdí sí.*
The turkey knows toward whom it farts. (People must be careful in choosing the people they presume to approach with familiarity. Compare 3399.)

W

565. *Wèrè èèyàn ní ńwípé irú òun ò sí; irú ẹẹ́ pọ̀ ó ju ẹgbàágbèje lọ.*
Only an imbecile asserts that there is none like him or her; his or her like numbers

---

91. Òkolo is not a Yoruba personal name but one used by the ethnic group Ijọ.

92. The Yoruba do not consider dogs to be preferred company.

93. The play is on the syllable *tè*, which occurs in *tẹ̀tẹ̀* (spinach) and *té* (to be disgraced).

more than millions. (No one is incomparable.)

566. *Wọ́n ńpe gbẹ́nàgbẹ́nà ẹyẹ àkókó ńyọjú.*
The call goes out for a carpenter, and the woodpecker presents itself. (One should not think too much of one's capabilities.)

Y

567. *"Yan àkàrà fún mi wá ká jìjọ jẹ ẹ́": àìtó èèyàn-án rán níṣẹ́ ní ńjẹ́ bẹ́ẹ̀.*
"Go buy bean fritters for me so we can eat them together": that spells uncertainty about one's right to send the person addressed on an errand. (People in authority should not be tentative in asserting their authority.)

568. *Yíyẹ́ là ńyẹ́ Òkóró sí tí à ńpè é nígi obì; obì tí ì bá so lórí è ní ńya abidún.*
It is only a mark of respect when one calls Òkóró a kola-nut tree; any kola nut that might grow on his head would turn out to be slimy. (People who enjoy the respect of others should not make the mistake of overestimating their importance.)

On perspicaciousness (good judgment, perceptiveness), reasonableness, sagacity, savoir faire, wisdom, and worldly wisdom

A

569. *A bímo kò gbón, a ní kó má ṣàà kú; kí ní
ńpa omo bí àìgbón?*
A child lacks wisdom, and some say that
what is important is that the child does not
die; what kills more surely than lack of wisdom? (A foolish child is not much better
than a dead child.)

570. *A débo fún igúnnugún, ó ní òun kò rú;
a débo fún àkàlà, ó ní òun kò rú; a débo fún
eyelé, eyelé gbébo, ó rúbo.*
A sacrifice was prescribed for the vulture,
but it refused to sacrifice; a sacrifice was
prescribed for the ground hornbill, but it
declined to sacrifice; a sacrifice was prescribed for the pigeon, and it gathered the
prescribed materials and made the sacrifice. (The vulture and the ground hornbill
were unfortunate in comparison with the
pigeon, because they did not carry out the
prescribed sacrifice.)[1]

571. *A fowó mú ajá o lo, a sèsè ńfi ìka méjì
pè é.*
We grab a dog with the hands and it escapes;
thereafter we beckon it with two fingers. (If
both hands cannot detain a dog, two fingers
from a distance will not bring it back.)

572. *A fún o lóbè o tami si; o gbón ju olóbè lo.*
You are given some stew and you add water;
you must be wiser than the cook. (Adding
water is a means of stretching stew. A person who thus stretches the stew he or she
is given would seem to know better than
the person who served it how much would
suffice for the meal.)

573. *A kì í bó sínú omi tán ká máa sá fún
òtútù.*
One does not enter into the water and then
run from the cold. (Precautions are useful
only before the event.)

574. *A kì í dá aró nÍsokùn; àlà là ńlò.*
One does not engage in a dyeing trade
in Ìsokùn; people there wear only white.
(Wherever one might be, one should respect
the manners and habits of the place.)

575. *A kì í dá erù ikùn pa orí.*
One does not weigh the head down with a
load that belongs to the belly. (Responsibilities should rest where they belong.)

576. *A kì í du orí olórí kí àwòdì gbé teni lo.*
One does not fight to save another person's
head only to have a kite carry one's own
away. (One should not save others at the
cost of one's own safety.)

---

1. The Yoruba name for pigeon, *eyelé*, means "house
bird." The domestication of the pigeon gives it a higher
status than that enjoyed by other birds.

577. *A kì í duni lóyè ká fọnà ilé-e Baálẹ̀ hanni.*
One does not compete with another for a chieftaincy title and also show the competitor the way to the king's house. (A person should be treated either as an adversary or as an ally, not as both.)

578. *A kì í fá orí lẹ́hìn olórí.*
One does not shave a head in the absence of the owner. (One does not settle a matter in the absence of the person most concerned.)

579. *A kì í fi àgbà sílẹ̀ sin àgbà.*
One does not leave one elder sitting to walk another elder part of his way. (One should not slight one person in order to humor another.)

580. *A kì í fi àì-mọ̀-wẹ̀ mòòkùn.*
One does not dive under water without knowing how to swim. (Never engage in a project for which you lack the requisite skills.)

581. *A kì í fi ara ẹni ṣe oògùn àlọ̀kúnná.*
One does not use oneself as an ingredient in a medicine requiring that the ingredients be pulverized. (Self-preservation is a compulsory project for all.)

582. *A kì í fi aṣọ ṣèdìdí yọwó.*
One does not leave cloth in a bundle while bargaining over it. (It is wise to know what one is negotiating to buy.)

583. *A kì í fi ejò sórí òrùlé sùn.*
One does not go to bed while a snake is on the roof. (Never let down your guard while danger still lurks. Compare 589.)

584. *A kì í fi ẹ̀jẹ̀ ìbálé pa tírà; alákoto ò bí abo ọmọ.*
One does not smear blood [from a woman's deflowering] on a Muslim charm; a devirgined woman does not give birth to a "female" child.[2] (One must not do the forbidden if one does not expect trouble.)

585. *A kì í fi ẹran ikún gbọn ti àgbọ̀nrín nù.*
One does not brush off antelope meat with squirrel meat. (Never prefer something of little value to something of great value.)

586. *A kì í fi ẹ̀tẹ̀ sílẹ̀ pa làpálàpá.*
One does not ignore leprosy to treat a rash. (More serious problems deserve more immediate attention.)

587. *A kì í fi idà pa ìgbín.*
One does not use a sword to kill a snail. (Remedies should be commensurate with the problem.)

588. *A kì í fi ìgbín sọkọ̀ sórìsà.*
One does not throw a snail at a god. (Service to the worthy should be performed with decorum, not with insult.)

589. *A kì í fi iná sórí òrùlé sùn.*
One does not go to bed while there is a fire on one's roof. (Better take care of problems before relaxing. Compare 583.)

590. *A kì í fi ìtìjú kárùn.*
One does not because of shyness expose oneself to a disease. (Never be too shy to speak out on your own behalf.)

591. *A kì í fi ìyá ẹní dákú ṣeré.*
One does not as a joke say one's mother has collapsed. (Never trifle with serious matters.)

592. *A kì í fi ogun dán ẹ̀ṣọ́ wò.*
One does not tease a warrior by saying there

---

2. Muslims are squeamish about blood from the deflowering of a woman. *Alákoto* here refers to a promiscuous woman, whose child one cannot expect to be well behaved. A "female" child means a well-behaved one (of either sex); a "male" child is not.

is a war [or an invasion]. (Do not play with a loaded and primed gun.)

593. *A kì í fi ohun ṣọ́wọ́ búra.*
One does not hide something in one's hand and yet swear [that one knows nothing about it]. (It is foolish to tempt fate; the dishonest person exposes himself or herself to the possibility of discovery.)

594. *A kì í fi ohun-olóhun tọrẹ bí kò ṣe tẹni.*
One does not make a gift of property that is not one's own. (Never be too free with other people's property.)

595. *A kì í fi oko sin fún ìwọ̀fà.*
One does not hide the farm from the pawned worker. (It does not make sense to prevent a servant one has hired from doing what one hired him to do.)

596. *A kì í fi olórí ogun ṣe ìfagun.*
One does not position the commander of the army at the rear of the column. (The best foot is the one to put forward.)

597. *A kì í fi oníjà sílẹ̀ ká gbájúmọ́ alápẹpẹ.*
One does not leave the person one has a quarrel with and face his lackey. (Focus rather on your main problem, not a side-show.)

598. *A kì í fi owó du oyè-e alágbára.*
One does not rely on money to contest a chieftaincy reserved for the strong. (Money won't buy everything.)

599. *A kì í fi olá jẹ iyọ̀.*
One does not consume salt according to one's greatness. (Too much of a good thing can be dangerous.)

600. *A kì í fi ọ̀nà ikùn han ọ̀fun.*
One does not show the throat the way to the stomach. (Do not presume to know better than the expert. See the following entry.)

601. *A kì í fi ọ̀nà odò han ikún.*
One does not show the squirrel the way to the river. (Telling someone what he or she already knows is silly. See the preceding entry.)

602. *A kì í fi ọ̀rọ̀ sílẹ̀ gbọ́ ọ̀rọ̀.*
One does not ignore one matter to attend to another matter. (Every obligation deserves attention.)

603. *A kì í gbá ẹni tó yọbẹ mú.*
One does not grab hold of a person who has pulled a knife. (Prudence and caution are imperative in dealing with dangerous people.)

604. *A kì í gbé àwòrán gàgàrà ká má fi ọwọ́ ẹ ti nǹkan.*
One does not carve a tall statue without resting its hand on something. (Everybody needs some support.)

605. *A kì í gbé ẹran erin lérí ká máa fẹsẹ̀ wa ihò ìrè.*
One does not carry elephant meat on one's head and dig cricket holes with one's big toe. (If one is blessed with plenty, one should not keep chasing after trifles.)

606. *A kì í gbé odò jiyàn-an ọṣẹ́ hó tàbí kò hó.*
One does not sit by a river and argue whether the soap will foam or will not foam. (Where the claim can be put to the test, verbal argument is foolish. Compare 4861.)

607. *A kì í gbé ọ̀pọ̀lọ́ sọnù ká tún bèrè-e jàǹto.*
One does not throw a toad away and inquire after its young. (Commiseration after injury is hypocritical.)

608. *A kì í gbójú-u fífò lé adìẹ àgàgà; a kì í gbójú-u yíyan lé alágẹmọ.*
One should not expect flight from the flightless chicken; one should not expect striding

from a chameleon. (To expect the impossible is to delude oneself.)

609. *A kì í gbọ́ ejọ́ ẹnìkan dájọ́.*
One does not deliver a verdict after hearing only one side. (Justice requires impartiality and a full hearing.)

610. *A kì í jẹ "Mo férè-ẹ́" lóbẹ̀.*
One does not eat "I almost" in a stew.[3] (What one missed narrowly, one cannot enjoy at all.)

611. *A kì í ka igún mọ́ ẹran jíjẹ.*
One does not list vultures among edible meats. (Certain things one does not stoop to do.)

612. *A kì í ka ilé òrìṣà kún ìlú.*
One does not count a god's grove as part of the town. (Do not list questionable items as part of your wealth.)

613. *A kì í ka oyún inú kún ọmọ ilẹ̀.*
One does not count a fetus among living children. (Never count your chickens before they are hatched.)

614. *A kì í ka ọmọ fún òbí.*
One does not enumerate children for the parents. (Do not presume to know better than those most intimately involved.)

615. *A kì í kọ ọmọ-ọ́ bí ká sọ ọ́ ní Èwolódé?*
One does not so resent having a child that one names it What-is-this-that-has-happened? (Childbirth is always a happy event.)

616. *A kì í léku méjì ká má pòfo.*
One does not chase two rats and avoid coming up with nothing. (Never try to go in two directions at once. See also 935.)

617. *A kì í lọ́mọ lẹ́hìn kọ oúnjẹ.*
One does not have children at one's rear and yet refuse food. (No amount of anger or distress should keep one from looking after one's dependents.)

618. *A kì í mọ ọkọ ọmọ ká tún mọ àlè-e rè.*
One does not acknowledge the husband for one's child and also acknowledge her illicit lover. (Never betray trust or connive at betraying it.)

619. *A kì í mú ìbọn tetere.*
One does not hold a gun carelessly. (Always be careful in handling dangerous matters.)

620. *A kì í mú oko mú ejọ́ kí ọkan má yẹ̀.*
One does not opt to work on the farm and also opt to go argue one's case and avoid neglecting one or the other. (One cannot do two mind-absorbing tasks at once. Compare 623 and 645.)

621. *A kì í mú ọmọ ọ̀ndópọ̀ dè.*
One does not chain the child of a person who offers too low a price for one's wares. (It is not a crime to make an offer that might be unacceptable.)

622. *A kì í mú ọmọ òṣì lọ sí Ìlọ́rọ̀.*
One does not take a child destined for poverty to Ìlọ́rọ̀.[4] (A person cannot transcend his or her destiny.)

623. *A kì í múlé móko kọ́kan má yẹ.*
One does not devote oneself to the home and devote oneself to the farm and not wind up neglecting one of them. (One cannot go

---

3. The quoted element is short for "I almost hit the prey I was aiming at."

4. Ìlọ́rọ̀ is an Ìjèṣà township whose name translates as "Town of Riches."

in two opposite directions at once. Compare 620 and 645.)

624. *A kì í ní ẹgbàá nílé wá ẹgbàá ròde.*
One does not have 1,000 cowries (or six pence) at home and go chasing abroad for 1,000 cowries. (Only the promise of a greater fortune should tempt one to neglect what one already has.)

625. *A kì í pa asínwín ilé, nítorí ọjọ́ tí tòde yó bàá wá sílé.*
One does not kill the imbecile within one's home, because of the day when the one from outside might visit. (One should cultivate one's own madness; one might need it to combat others' madness.)

626. *A kì í pa igún, a kì í jẹ igún, a kì í fi igún bọrí.*
One does not kill the vulture; one does not eat the vulture; one does not offer the vulture as a sacrifice to one's head. (Certain behaviors are beyond the pale.)

627. *A kì í pé kí òṣìkà ṣe é ká wò ó.*
One does not dare a wicked person to do his worst. (Never tempt evil people to do their evil.)

628. *A kì í peni lólè ká máa gbé ọmọ ẹran jó.*
One does not suffer the reputation of being a thief and yet go seeking to dance with kids [baby goats]. (It is foolish to behave in ways that will confirm people's evil opinion of one.)

629. *A kì í rán ọ̀lẹ wo ojú ọjọ́ àárọ̀.*
One does not send a shirker to go see what the morning looks like outside. (Never rely on the advice of people who have a vested interest in the matter being considered.)

630. *A kì í re nísun lọ dà síbú.*
One does not collect water from a spring to

dump in the deep. (Do not rob the poor to further enrich the wealthy.)

631. *A kì í rí adìẹ nílẹ̀ ká da àgbàdo fún ajá.*
One does not see chickens about and throw one's corn to the dog. (Always direct help where it will be appreciated and where it will do some good.)

632. *A kì í rí àjẹkù orò.*
No one ever sees the leavings of the god Orò. (What must be consumed must be completely consumed.)

633. *A kì í rí bàtá nílẹ̀ ká fẹnu sín in jẹ.*
One does not see a *bàtá* drum on the ground and use one's mouth to mimic its sound. (Too much talk about a problem is useless when a practical solution has presented itself. One should not make a person's case for him or her when that person is present.)

634. *A kì í rí ewé nílẹ̀ ká fọwọ́ fámi.*
One does not see leaves lying about and scoop up feces with one's bare hand. (Take advantage of whatever aids are available to you.)

635. *A kì í rí ẹni ranni lẹ́rù ká yọké.*
One does not find helpers willing to help with one's load and yet sprout a hump on one's back [from carrying too heavy a load]. (Always avail yourself of offered help.)

636. *A kì í rí ojú ẹkùn ká tọ́ ẹkùn.*
One does not see the look on a leopard's face and then taunt the leopard. (It is foolish to invite disaster needlessly on one's own head.)

637. *A kì í sá fún àjíà ká dìgbò lu eégún.*
One does not run from the herald of the masquerader and collide with the masquerader himself. (Never court a greater disaster in an attempt to avert a minor one.)

638. *A kì í sin àlè kojá odò; ohun tí ńṣe oṣé ò tó ǹkan.*
One does not walk one's secret lover across a river; the causes of huge disasters are usually insignificant in themselves. (If one is engaged in a dangerous venture, one should not also cast discretion to the wind.)

639. *A kì í sọ pé abẹ Òyó mú; nígbà náà ni yó sọ pé bẹ́ẹ̀ ni òun ò tíì pọn.*
One does not tell an Òyó person that his knife is sharp, for only then will he say he has not even honed it yet. (Offer no braggart any opportunity to resume his bragging. Compare 3480.)

640. *A kì í sọrọ ìkọkọ lójú olófòófó.*
One does not discuss secret matters in the presence of a tattler. (Be careful with your secrets.)

641. *A kì í sùn jẹ́rìí ìdí.*
One cannot be asleep and also be able to vouch for one's anus. (Assert only those things you know for certain.)[5]

642. *A kì í ṣe fáàárí ẹ̀ṣẹ́ dídì sómọ adétè.*
One does not flaunt one's ability to make a fist in the face of a leper's child. (Never make fun of people because of their affliction. See also the following entry.)

643. *A kì í ṣe fáàárí itọ́ dídà sómọ a-kú-wárápá.*
One does not drool in jest in the presence of the child of an epileptic. (Never make fun of afflicted people by mimicking their affliction. Compare the preceding entry.)

644. *A kì í ṣoore tán ká lóṣòó tì í.*
One does not do a favor and then camp by

it. (Having done some good, do not hang around to compel gratitude.)

645. *A kì í ṣòwò méjì kéran má jẹ òkan.*
One does not engage in two trades without having one consumed by goats. (One cannot effectively manage two enterprises at once. Compare 620 and 623.)

646. *A kì í ti ojú ogun wéfọ́n.*
One does not wait until the heat of the battle to start looking for palm-leaf midrib.[6] (Always make your preparations well ahead of the event.)

647. *A kì í ti ojú on-íka-mẹ́sàn-án kà á.*
One does not count the fingers of a person who has only nine in his or her presence. (One must be discreet in speaking about other people's flaws and deformities.)

648. *A kì í tijú bá baálé ilé jẹ akátá; bó bá mú, ìwọ náà a mú tìẹ.*
One should not be too embarrassed to eat a jackal with one's host; as he helps himself, one also helps oneself. (Never be too bashful to adopt the ways of the people among whom you find yourself.)[7]

649. *A kì í wá alásọ-àlà nísọ̀ elépo.*
One should not look for a white-clad person in the stall of palm-oil sellers. (One should know the likely places to look for whatever one seeks.)

650. *A kì í wà nínú ìṣẹ́ ká perin tọrẹ.*
One does not wallow in poverty and yet kill an elephant for public distribution. (Always live according to your circumstances.)

651. *A kì í wíjọ́ọ wíwò ká jàre.*
One does not complain about being looked

---

5. A sleeping person cannot be sure whether he farted or not.

6. Palm-leaf midrib is the material out of which arrows are made.

7. A jackal is apparently no enticing food.

at and be vindicated. (One should not complain that other people are doing what one
is also doing.)

652. *A kì í yin ọmọdé lójú ara ẹ̀; ìfàsẹ́hìn ní
ńkángun ẹ̀.*
One does not praise a child in his presence;
only backsliding results. (Children should
not be praised too highly; they should
always be made aware that they can be even
better.)

653. *A kúnlẹ̀ a pàgbò, alubàtá ní "ojú ò
férakù"; o fẹ́ bá wọn ṣúpó ni?*
We kneel and sacrifice a ram, and the *bàtá*
drummer shows reluctance to take his leave;
does he wish to inherit a wife?[8] (One should
always know when to take one's leave. See
1287. This is similar in import to 63.)

654. *A lé tẹ̀mbẹ̀lẹ̀kun jìnnà bí ẹnipé kó bọ́ jù
sígbó.*
One chases conspiracy away, as though
one would have it disappear into the bush.
(No one should want anything to do with
conspiracy.)

655. *À ńfọ̀tún tẹ́ní, à ńfọ̀sì tú sòkòtò, obìnrín
ní a kò bá òun gbọ́ tọmọ.*
One spreads a mat with the right hand while
removing one's pants with the left hand; yet
the woman complains that one is not helping her quest for a child.[9] (Some people are

incapable of recognizing and acknowledging
favors.)

656. *À ńgba òròmọ adìẹ lọ́wọ́ ikú, ó ní wọn ò
jẹ́ kí òun jẹ láàtàn.*
One struggles to save the chick from certain
death, and it complains that one is prevent-
ing it from foraging at the dump. (Chicks
foraging at the dump are easy prey for kites.)

657. *À ńgbèjà Ọ̀jàá, Ọ̀jà ní ta ní ńjà lẹ́hìnkùlé
òun?*
We fight in defense of Ọ̀jà, and Ọ̀jà asks who
is fighting in his back yard.[10] (Some people
do not acknowledge or appreciate favors.)

658. *A ní ìrókò ni yó pa ọmọdé, ó bojú-wẹ̀hìn;
òòjọ́ ní ńjà?*
One curses a child that *ìrókò* will kill him,
and he glances to his rear; does the curse
take effect immediately?[11] (The child obviously does not know that the fact that he
does not die immediately in no way invali-
dates the curse. Compare 1847.)

659. *A ní kí olókùnrùn ṣe tó, ó ní òun ò lè ṣe
tó, tò, tó.*
The invalid is asked to say, "*Tó*," and he
complains that he cannot keep saying, "*Tó,
tò, tó.*" (He has expended more effort in his
refusal than he would have in complying.)[12]

660. *A ní kọ́mọ má kùú, o ní kò jọ bàbá kò jọ
ìyá.*
We strive to keep a child from dying, and
you say he resembles neither the father nor

---

8. The kneeling and sacrificing described here are
the final activities in funeral obsequies. Thereafter, the
immediate survivors of the deceased turn to practical matters, such as distributing the dead man's wives
among themselves for support; hired drummers are
certainly not welcome in such matters. The greeting *ojú
ò férakù,* meaning literally "the eyes do not [have not]
miss[ed] one another," is spoken on leave-taking, but it
suggests that the person departing is really still present
in spirit.

   9. The woman in question obviously has severe

difficulty in reading intentions and is unappreciative to
boot.

   10. Note the play on the syllable *jà,* which as a word
means "fight" and forms the main part of the name Ọ̀jà,
which can be taken to means "a person who fights."

   11. The *ìrókò* tree is believed to house frightful
spirits.

   12. The sound *tó* suggests something that requires
minimal effort, especially in diction.

the mother. (The person addressed has his or her priorities reversed.)

661. "À ńjùwón" ò ṣéé wí léjọ́; ìjà ìlara ò tán bọ̀rọ̀.
"We are driven by envy of them" is a bad case to make; a quarrel spawned by jealousy is not easy to settle. (Quarrels whose causes cannot be openly admitted will not readily end.)

662. À ńkì í, à ńsà á, ó ní òun ò mọ ẹni tó kú; a ní, "Alákàá egbàá, a-bisu-wọ̀rọ̀-wọ̀rọ̀-lóko, a-bàgbàdo-tàkì-tàkì-légàn"; ó ní, "Ọlọ́dẹ ló kú, tàbí ìnájà?"
We recite someone's praise names, we intone his attributes, and a person says he does not know who died; we say, "He of the two hundred granaries, he whose yams are plentiful on the farm, he whose corn is abundant in the fields," and the person asks, "Is the dead person a hunter or a trader?" (A person for whom everything must be spelled out, a person who cannot make deductions from the most obvious hints, is daft indeed. See the following entry.)

663. À ńkì í, à ńsà á, ó ní òun ò mọ ẹni tó kú; ó ńgbọ́, "Ikú mẹ́rù, Ọ̀pàgá, a-bisu-ú-ta-bí-òdòdó, a-lábà-ọkà, a-roko-féyẹ-jẹ"; ó ní, "Àgbẹ̀ ló kú, tàbí ọ̀nájà?"
We recite someone's praise names, we intone his attributes, and a person says he does not know who died; he hears, "Death takes a renowned man, a titled man, whose yams spread like petals, who possesses barns of corn, whose fields are a bounty for birds," and he asks, "Is the dead man a farmer or a trader?" (This is a variant of the preceding entry.)

664. À ńsọrọ̀ elégédé, obìnrín ḿbèrè ohun tí à ńsọ, a ní ọ̀rọ̀ ọkùnrin ni; bí a bá kó elégédé jọ, ta ni yó sè é?
We are discussing pumpkins; a woman asks

what we are discussing, and we respond that it is men's talk; after we have gathered the pumpkins, who will cook them? (The woman, certainly. There is no point in excluding her from a matter that will eventually involve her anyway.)

665. À ńsọrọ̀ obìnrin, a ní ká sọ́ bàrà ká lọ gbin bàrà sódò; ta ní máa báni pa á?
We speak of women, and someone suggests that we hedge our words and go plant watermelon by the stream; who will help in harvesting it? (This is a variant of the preceding entry.)[13]

666. A rí i lójú, a mọ̀ ọ́ lẹ́nu; òsòwò ọṣẹ kì í pọ́n-wọ́-lá.
One can tell by looking, and one can tell by taste; a soap seller does not lick her fingers. (Soap is recognizable as soap, and anyone who has ever tasted it knows that one does not lick fingers caked with soap. Each trade has its don'ts. See 794.)

667. A ta bàbà, a fowó-o bàbà ra baba.
We sell guinea corn, and with the copper coins we redeem the old man.[14] (With what one has one seeks one's goals. See the following entry.)

668. A ta bàbà a fowó-o bàbà ra bàbà.
We sell guinea corn, and with the guinea-corn money we buy guinea corn. (This variant of the previous entry suggests that for all one's efforts and exertions, one has not significantly altered one's circumstances.)

---

13. The proverb features a play on the word bàrà, which is both the word for watermelon and an adjective describing an evasive course.

14. The saying is more a play on the syllables ba-ba (as to both the different tones they can bear and their different meanings) than a real proverb. Bàbà means guinea corn, and owó-o-bàbà (literally "guinea-corn money") means copper coin, because guinea corn is copper-colored.

669. Ààrẹ ńpè ọ́ ò ńdÍfá; bÍfá bá fọọre tí Ààrẹ fọbi ńkọ́?
The *Ààrẹ* summons you and you consult the oracle; what if the oracle says all will be well, and the *Ààrẹ* decrees otherwise? (There is no point in attempting to restrict the action of an absolute authority.)[15]

670. Àáyá bọ́ sílẹ̀, ó bọ́ sílé.
The colobus monkey jumps to the ground; it runs for home. (When danger lurks, the wisest course is to run for safety.)

671. Àáyá gbọ́n, Ògúngbẹ̀-ẹ́ sì gbọ́n; bí Ògúngbẹ̀-ẹ́ ti ḿbẹ̀rẹ̀ ni àáyá ńtiro.
The colobus monkey is wily, but so is Ogungbẹ; as Ogungbẹ crouches, so the monkey tiptoes. (The prey that knows its stalker's tricks is safe.)

672. Àbá alágẹmọ lòrìṣà ńgbà.
The gods heed what chameleon proposes.[16] (One should heed the advice of trusted friends and advisers.)

673. Àbá kì í di òtítọ́; ojo ni kì í jẹ́ ká dá a.
Plans do not automatically bear fruit; only the fainthearted do not make plans. (Although plans may never bear fruit, people should still make them. Compare the following entry.)

674. Àbá ní ńdi òtítọ́; ojo ni kì í jẹ́ ká da.
Attempts result in achievement; it is faintheartedness that keeps one from making an effort. (Without striving, one accomplishes nothing. Compare the preceding entry.)

675. Àbàtì àlàpà: a bà á tì, a bá a rẹ́.
Unfinished, abandoned wall: unable to master it, one befriends it. (One reconciles oneself to matters one cannot control.)

676. A-bayé-jẹ́ kò ṣéé fìdí òràn hàn.
A treacherous person is not someone to tell profound matters to. (One should keep one's secrets from treacherous people.)

677. Abẹ́rẹ́ ò ṣéé gúnyán.
A needle cannot be used to make pounded yams. (Some tools are inadequate for some tasks.)

678. Abẹ́rẹ́ tó wọnú òkun ò ṣéé wá.
A needle that drops into the ocean defies finding. (Some tasks are hopelessly impossible to accomplish.)

679. Abiyamọ, kàgbo wàrà; ojọ́ ńlọ.
Nursing mother, make the herbal decoction in good time; the day is waning. (Attend to duties on time.)

680. Abiyamọ kì í rìn kó ṣánwọ́ ahá.
A nursing mother does not venture away from home without a cup. (She must be prepared to feed the baby.)[17]

681. Abiyamọ́ purọ́ mọ́mọ-ọ rẹ̀ jẹun.
The nursing mother lies against her child to secure food. (One uses every ruse available in the interest of one's well-being.)

682. Abiyamọ́ ṣọwọ́ kòtò lu ọmọ-ọ rẹ̀.
A nursing mother cups her palm to strike her child. (Discretion is the better part of discipline.)

---

15. The proverb came into being in the days of Kurunmí the *Ààrẹ* (military ruler) of Ìjaye in the 1820s. He was so powerful and so feared that people believed even oracles could not deflect him from any course he chose to follow.

16. In Yoruba tradition the chameleon is a trusted servant of the gods. In the myth of creation it was the chameleon that was sent down to the newly formed earth to determine whether it was firm enough yet for habitation.

17. *Ahá,* a cup cut out of a small calabash, is used in force-feeding babies.

683. *Àbòṣé kì í ṣe iṣẹ́ òòjọ́; iṣẹ́-ẹ baba ẹni ní ńgbani lójọ́ gan-an.*
Spare-time work is no profession; it is an assignment from one's father that takes all of one's day. (One does not waste one's time on trifles or hobbies.)

684. *Àbùkún layé gbà.*
The world accepts only adding on. (Supplement rather than deplete.)

685. *Adánilóró fagbára kọ́ni.*
He who disappoints teaches one to be more resourceful. (Once disappointed or injured, one learns to be self-reliant.)

686. *Adétè ò gbọdọ̀ dúró de eléépín.*
A leper must not wait for a bearer of abrasive leaves [*eépín*].[18] (Know your weaknesses.)

687. *Adétè-ẹ́ ní òún ṣẹ́ òràn kan de àwọn ará ilé òun; ó ní bí òún bá lọ sídàálè, wọn ò jẹ́ fi kàn-ìn-kàn-ìn òun wè.*
The leper says that he trusts his relatives on a certain matter; he says when he goes on a journey, they would not dare use his sponge to wash themselves. (People have a knack for skirting dangerous or distasteful situations.)

688. *Adìẹ ìrànà ní ńṣíwájú òkú.*
It is the votive herald-chicken that precedes a dead person.[19] (Matters must be attended to in their proper sequence.)

689. *Adìẹ ò lè ti ìwòyí sunkún ehín.*
A chicken cannot at this late date bemoan its lack of teeth. (Everything at its proper time.)

690. *Adìẹ ò lórúnkún ejó.*
A chicken has no knees for cases.[20] (One should steer clear of actionable behavior.)

691. *Adìẹ rí aláásàà, ó pa ìyẹ́ mọ́.*
The chicken sees the snuff seller and enfolds its wings. (When one sees potential danger approaching, one should take precautions.)[21]

692. *Adìẹ-odò ò ṣéé bọ ìpọ̀nrí.*
Waterfowl is no good as a sacrifice to Ìpọ̀nrí.[22] (One should use only tools proper to the task at hand.)

693. *Àdó gba ara è télẹ̀, ká tó fi oògùn sí?*
Could the small gourd save itself, before we put charms into it? (Do not seek protection from a helpless person.)[23]

694. *A-faṣé-gbèjò ńtan ara-a rẹ̀ jẹ.*
He-who-would-collect-rainwater-in-a-sieve deceives himself. (The shiftless person hurts himself more than others.)

695. *A-fàtẹ́lẹwọ́-fanná kì í dúró.*
He-who-carries-live-coals-in-his-palm does not tarry. (A person who has a pressing problem has no time for socializing.)[24]

696. *Àféèrí kan ò ju ká rí igbó ńlá bọ́ sí lọ; ẹbọ kan ò ju ọ̀pọ̀ èèyàn lọ; "Òrìsá gbé mi lé àtète" kan ò ju orí ẹsin lọ.*

---

18. *Ficus asperifolia* (see Abraham 161).

19. As part of Yoruba funerary rites, a chicken is sacrificed to clear evil forces off the way of the deceased's spirit.

20. It is customary for litigants in Yoruba courts to state their cases on their knees. The proverb builds on the fact that chickens have no knees and, therefore, cannot kneel to state cases.

21. Snuff sellers use chicken feathers to sweep the snuff from the grindstone.

22. Ìpọ̀nrí is a god for which the appropriate sacrifice is a chicken.

23. Àdó is a tiny gourd in which people keep charms, often serving as talismans.

24. Before the advent of matches, people who wished to start a fire took live coals from an established fire to start their own.

There is no disappearing trick better than the availability of a dense forest to disappear into; there is no sacrifice more efficacious than having many people on one's side; there is no "The gods have elevated me" that is higher than the back of a horse. (Practical and realistic moves are more reliable than mysterious expectations.)

697. *Aféfé ńda ológìì láàmú; oníyèfun ṛora.*
The wind is making life difficult for the seller of liquid cornstarch; corn-flour seller, you had better watch out! (When even those better situated are defeated, one must be prepared for tough times.)

698. *A-fi-tiè-sílè-gbó-teni-eléni: ògànjó ni wón ńsìnkú-u rè.*
He-who-neglects-his-own-affairs-to-care-for-others'-affairs: it is in the middle of the night that his burial is carried out. (Do not sacrifice your self-interest to take care of others.)

699. *Àfòmó ńse ara-a rè, ó ní òún ńse igi.*
The creeper is destroying itself, but it thinks it is destroying its host. (The host's death will also be the parasite's death.)

700. *Àgádágodo ò finú han ara-a wọn.*
Padlocks do not share their secrets with one another. (Some secrets one should not divulge to others.)

701. *Àgùntàn ò jí ní kùtùkùyù se enu bọbọ.*
A sheep does not wake in the morning and droop its mouth. (One should not dawdle in the morning.)

702. *Àgbà òsìkà ńgbin ìyà sílè de ọmọ-ọ rè.*
A wicked elder sows suffering for his children. (One's character often affects the fortunes of one's children. Compare 1306 and 3307.)

703. *Àgbà ṣoore má wo bè.*
Elder, do a favor and remove your eyes from it. (Do not advertise your acts of kindness or pointedly await acknowledgment of them.)

704. *À-gbà-bó ò di teni.*
A foster child does not become one's own child. (There is nothing like having one's own. Compare 2800.)

705. *Àgbàdo kì í ṣe èèyàn; ta ní ńrí ọmọ léhìn eèsún?*
The maize plant is not a human being; who ever saw children on the back of elephant grass? (One should not overestimate the value of things.)[25]

706. *Àgbàká labiyamọ ńgbàjá mọ́ ọmọ-ọ rè.*
It is completely and securely that a mother [bearing her child on her back] supports the child with a strip of cloth.[26] (One must be thorough in discharging one's responsibility.)

707. *Àgbàlagbàá ṣenú kerendẹn; èyí tó máa ṣe ńbẹ níkùn-un rè.*
An elder shows a smooth belly to the world, but what he will do is known to him. (Be a person of thought and action, not of words.)[27]

---

25. When the maize plant develops fruits, the Yoruba say, "*Ó yọ ọmọ,*" literally, "It has sprouted a child." The expression does not, however, mean that the people believe the plant is human. Elephant grass is almost identical to maize in size and looks, even though it bears no fruit.

26. After strapping her child to her back, a mother prevents the child from sliding down by passing a strip of cloth, *òjá,* under the child's buttocks and around to the mother's front, there tying it snugly.

27. The proverb derives from the fact that *inú* (or *ikùn*) means both "mind" and "stomach." The expression *mọ inú* means "to know (someone's) mind," but to see a person's stomach is not to know the person's mind.

708. *Àgbèję ò korò nílé ńlá.*
Pumpkin is never bitter in a big household.
(When one is in need, one cannot be too
choosy.)[28]

709. *A-gbé-òòdè bí òfé, a-mọ-ara-í-ré bí oódẹ;*
a débọ fún òfé, òfé ò rú, agánrán gbébọ, ó
rúbọ; àsèhìnwá àsèhìnbò òfé di ará Òyó,
agánrán di ará oko; wón rò pé òfé ò gbón.
Òfé, dweller-in-the-corridor, forward as
oódẹ; a sacrifice was prescribed for *òfé,* but
he did not offer it; *agánrán* went ahead and
offered the sacrifice; in the end *òfé* became
a citizen of Ọyọ, while *agánrán* became a
dweller in the bush; and people thought *òfé*
was foolish.[29] (Never second-guess people
who are better informed than you are.)

710. *Àgbìgbò, rọra fò, ọdẹ ti dé sóko; àgbìgbò*
tí ò bá rọra fò á bọ́ sápò ọdẹ.
Big-headed bird *àgbìgbò,* fly warily, for the
hunter has arrived in the forest; any *àgbìgbò*
that does not fly warily will wind up in the
hunter's bag. (Conditions are hazardous; it
behooves everyone to take care.)

711. *Àgbò dúdú kọjá odò ó di funfun.*
The black ram crosses the river and becomes
white.[30] (Propitious events can drastically
change a person's fortunes for the better.)

712. *Àgbokan là ńrọ́ Ifá adití.*
It is with full voice volume that one recites
divination verses for the deaf. (One cannot
be too subtle with the daft.)

---

28. The size of the household, and the need to feed
the many mouths, makes even the pumpkin with its
slightly bitter taste acceptable food.

29. *Òfé, oódẹ (odíde, odídẹré),* and *agánrán* are all
types of parrots. Because *agánrán* is considered favored
by the gods, it is usually sacrificed to them, while *òfé,*
which is not so favored, is spared that fate.

30. This is also a riddle, to which the answer is soap.
The traditional soap is blackish in color.

713. *Àgbọn kì í ṣe oúnjẹ ẹyẹ.*
Coconut is no food for birds. (Some things
and some people are immune to some types
of danger; one should not attempt the impossible.)

714. *Ahún dùn; kò tóó jẹ fúnni.*
Tortoise meat is delicious, but there is not
enough of it to make a meal. (One should
husband one's resources wisely.)

715. *Ahún ńre àjò, ó gbé ilé-e rẹ̀ dání.*
Tortoise embarks on a journey and takes
his house along.[31] (One's dearest possessions
deserve the closest attention.)

716. *Ahún wọnú orù, ó ku àtiyọ.*
Tortoise has entered into a narrow-necked
pot; now, getting out is a problem. (One
should consider the possible consequences
of one's actions before acting.)

717. *Àìgbọn ni yó pa Iṣikan; a ní ìyáa rè-ẹ́ kú,*
ó ní nígbàtí òún gbọ́, ṣe ni òún ńdárò; bíyàá
ẹní bá kú àárò là ńdá?
Foolishness will be the death of Iṣikan; he
is told that his mother has died, and he says
that when he heard the news, he sorely la-
mented the tragedy; if one's mother dies, is
it lamentation that is called for? (The well-
bred person is always mindful of his or her
obligations.)

718. *Àì-gbọn-léwe ni à-dàgbà-di-wèrè.*
Lack-of-wisdom-in-youth is imbecility in
adulthood. (The man turns out just as the
child was; the grown person acquires his
traits in childhood.)

719. *Àì-mò-ó-gbé-kalè leégún fi ńgba ọtí.*
It is ineptitude-in-setting-it-down that

---

31. The observation suggests that the animal is so
concerned about its possessions that it must carry its
house along on every journey.

makes the wine a spoil for the *eégún* [i.e., that causes the wine to be spilled]. (Ineptitude makes an impossible job of the easiest tasks.)[32]

720. *Àì-mọwọ́-ọ́-wè ni àì-bágbà-jẹ; ọmọ tó mọwọ́-ọ́ wè á bágbà jẹ.*
Not-knowing-how-to-wash-one's-hands is not-eating-with-elders; a person who knows how to wash his hands will eat with elders. (To qualify to live in society, one must learn the social graces.)[33]

721. *Àìpé, "Tìrẹ nìyí" ní ḿbí ayé nínú.*
Neglecting to say, "Here is yours" is what incites the earth's anger. (Failure to take account of people's possible influence on one's affairs incites their anger. As long as one assumes humility, people will let one be.)[34]

722. *Àì-roko, àì-rodò tí ńṣápé fún eégún jó.*
Not-going-to-the-farm, not-going-to-the-river claps for masqueraders to dance. (It is an idler who makes music for masqueraders to dance.)

723. *Àì-sòrò ní ḿmú ẹnu rùn.*
It is abstention from speaking that makes the mouth smell. (One should always say one's piece in a discussion.)

724. *Ajá èṣín ò mọdẹ.*
A dog born a year ago does not know how to hunt. (One learns from experience and maturity.)

725. *Ajá là bá kí; ẹse ò pẹran fúnni jẹ.*
One should rather commend the dog; the cat does not kill meat for one to eat. (Assign commensurate values to your assets.)

726. *Ajá ti eré-e rèẹ̀ bá dánilójú là ńdẹ sí ehoro.*
It is a dog in whose speed one has faith that one sics at a hare. (One entrusts important tasks only to those one can trust. This is a variant of 729 and 2433.)

727. *Ajá tí ò létí ò ṣé-é dègbẹ.*
A dog without ears is no good for stalking prey. (A person who cannot be instructed is useless.)

728. *Ajá tó gbé iyọ̀, kí ni yó fi ṣe?*
A dog that swipes salt, what will it do with it? (Do not expend your effort on senseless ventures.)

729. *Ajá tó lè sáré là ńdẹ sí egbin.*
It is a swift dog that one sends after a Kobe antelope. (This is a variant of 726 and 2433.)

730. *Ajàkàṣù ò mọ̀ bí ìyàn-án mú.*
The person who eats large helpings does not care that there is a famine. (Greed knows no thrift.)

731. *Àjànàkú kúrò léran à ńgọ dè.*
The elephant is not among the ranks of animals one lies in ambush for. (The wise person puts some distance between himself and a formidable adversary.)

732. *Àjànàkú ò ṣéé rù.*
The elephant is impossible to carry. (Some tasks are impossible to accomplish.)

---

32. The Yoruba expression *"Eégún gbà á,"* meaning literally *"Eégún* [the incarnated spirit of the ancestors] has appropriated it," is a way of saying, "It is lost to people."

33. Washing one's hands before meals is both a health requirement and a mark of social grace. It is a minimum requirement for the privilege of joining the elders at meals.

34. This belief is reflected in the practice of paying homage to *ayé* (meaning literally "the world" but in fact the people of the world) before embarking on any venture; the gesture, people believe, will safeguard their venture from ill will.

733. *Àjàpá ní kò sí oun tó dà bí oun tí a mò*
ọ̀ṣe; ó ní bí òun bá ńrìn lóko èpà, ọ̀kọ̀ọ̀kan a
máa bọ́ sóun lẹ́nu.
Tortoise says there is nothing quite like what
one knows how to do; it says when it walks
through a peanut farm, peanuts keep popping one by one into its mouth. (When one
does what one is a true expert at doing, it
seems like performing magic.)[35]

734. *Àjàpá ní ojọ́ tí òun ti jágbọ́n-ọn òo lọ̀rùn*
ò ti wọ òun mọ́.
Tortoise says that since the day it learned
the trick of saying yes, its neck has ceased to
shrink. (One who says yes to every request
avoids a great many arguments.[36] See 923
and 983.)

735. *Àjàpá ńyan lóko; aláìlóye-é ní ó jọ*
pẹ́pẹ́yẹ.
The tortoise struts on the farm; the senseless
person says it resembles a duck. (It is indeed
a fool who cannot discern the obvious.)

736. *Àjẹ́gbà ni ti kọ̀nkọ̀.*
Croaking-in-relays is the mark of frogs. (It is
in the nature of sheep to follow and to lack
initiative.)

737. *Àjẹ̀kù là ńmayo.*
Remnant-leaving is the indicator of satiation. (How one lives will show how well off
one is.)

738. *Àjẹ̀kù làgbẹ̀ ńtà.*
It is the leavings from his table that the
farmer sells. (One takes care of one's own
needs before one disposes of the excess. See
4137.)

739. *Àjẹsílẹ̀-ẹ gbèsè tí ò jẹ́ kí ẹgbèfà tóó ná.*
Long-standing debt, that makes 1,200 cowries insufficient to spend. (Existing debts eat
new fortunes away.)

740. *A-jí-má-bọ̀ọ́jú: tí ńfi ojú àná wòran.*
A-person-who-rises-in-the-morning-
without-washing-his-face: one who sees
things with yesterday's eyes. (A person who
does not keep his eyes peeled for developments is ever behind time.)

741. *Àjímú kì í tí.*
The task one takes on upon waking in the
morning does not flounder. (The task to
which one gives the highest priority does
not suffer.)

742. *Àjò kì í dùn kódídẹ má rèWó.*
The journey is never so pleasant that the
parrot does not return to Ìwó.[37] (The sojourner should never allow the pleasantness
of his or her sojourn to obliterate thoughts
of returning home. See the following entry.)

743. *Àjò kì í dùn kónílé má relé.*
The journey is never so pleasant that the
traveler does not return home. (The traveler
should never forget his or her home. See the
previous entry.)

---

35. The point in this, as in the next proverb, is that
there is really no trick to what Tortoise does, only the
expected; what is important is that the animal knows
how to do it.

36. The explanation is that Tortoise was one in the
company of more powerful animals who, whenever
they had heavy loads to carry, sent for Tortoise, but that
animal always refused to oblige, whereupon they gave
it powerful blows on the head. At times, in order to
avoid such blows, Tortoise would carry the loads at the
expense of its weak neck. Finally it learned to say "Yes"
to every request but to escape when the animals were
not looking. The moral is that one may agree to every
request, but one does not have to follow through.

37. Parrots are associated with Ìwó, a town to
which they faithfully return after their seasonal migra-
tions—a relationship that recalls that of the swallows to
Capistrano.

744. *Àjòjí lójú, ṣùgbọ́n kò fi ríran.*
A stranger has eyes, but they do not see. (A stranger's eyes are blind to the intricacies of his or her new surroundings.)

745. *À-jókòó-àì-fẹ̀hìntì bí ẹní nàró ni.*
Sitting-without-leaning-the-back-against-something is like standing. (Never do things by half measures.)

746. *A-ká-ìgbá-tà-á náwó ikú.*
He-who-plucks-the-African-locust-bean-tree-seeds-to-sell spends death's money. (Whoever engages in a dangerous venture more than earns his or her pay.)

747. *Àkámọ́ ẹkùn-ún níyọnu.*
A cornered leopard poses problems. (One should be wary in deciding what prey to stalk.)

748. *Àkísà aṣo la fi ńṣe òṣùká.*
A rag is what one uses as a carrying pad. (One's most valuable possessions are not for careless use.)

749. *Àkó balẹ̀, ó fi gbogbo ara kígbe.*
Àko hit the ground and cried out with its whole body.[38] (A person who needs help should not be coy in asking.)

750. *Akòpẹ Ìjàyè ò gbọ́ tiẹ̀, ó ní ogún kó Agbo-roode.*
The palm-wine tapper of Ijaye, instead of looking to his own affairs, says Agboroode has been destroyed by invaders. (The wise person learns from others' misfortunes instead of gawking at them.)

751. *Aláàárù kì í ru ẹṣin.*
The porter cannot carry a horse. (Certain tasks are impossible to accomplish.)

---

38. *Àko*, the dry leaf stem of a palmlike tree, makes a resonant clatter when it falls to the ground.

752. *Aláàjàá gbé e sókè, o ní, "Kó ṣe!"; o mọ̀ bí ibi lówí tàbí ire?*
The wielder of the incantation rattle lifts it, and you respond, "May it be so!"; do you know whether he has invoked good or evil? (One should be certain about what is happening before one intervenes or becomes involved.)

753. *Alágbàfọ̀ kì í bá odò ṣòtá.*
A washerman does not harbor a grudge with the river. (One does not turn one's back on one's means of livelihood.)

754. *Alákataṁpòó ṣe bí ọ̀bọ ò gbọ́n; ọ̀bọ́ gbọ́n; tinú ọ̀bọ lòbọ́ ńṣe.*
The person with the crossbow thinks that the monkey is not clever; the monkey is clever, but it is following its own strategy. (It matters nothing to be derided as long as you know what you are doing and why.)

755. *Alákì*ìsà ní ńtójú abẹ́rẹ́ tòun tòwú.*
It is the owner of rags who makes sure that needle and thread are available. (Each person looks after his her own interests.)

756. *Aláńtakùn, bí yóò bá ọ jà, a ta ká ọ lára.*
When the spider wants to engage an enemy, it spins its web around it. (The attentive person can detect signs of hostility before it occurs. Also, one makes good preparations before embarking on a venture.)

757. *Aláńtakùnún takùn sí ìṣasùn, ṣíbí gbọludé.*
The spider has spun its web in the saucepan; the spoon takes a holiday. (In the absence of the proper tools, one cannot fault the laborer for being idle.)

758. *Aláṣedànù tí ńfajá ṣọdẹ eja.*
A wastrel uses a dog to stalk fish. (It is folly to employ an impossible tool for a given task.)

759. *Àlejò bí òkété là ńfi èkùró lò.*
It is a visitor like a giant rat to whom one offers palm nuts. (One should approach other people as their stations dictate.)

760. *Àlejò tó bèèrè ọ̀nà kò níí sọnù.*
A stranger who asks the way will not get lost. (One should be willing to admit one's ignorance and seek direction. Compare 73.)

761. *Àlùkò ò ní ohùn méjì; "Ó dilé" lagbe ńké.*
The woodcock has but one statement: "Ó dilé" ["Time to head for home"] is the cry of the touraco. (One should know when the time is ripe to start home.)

762. *Àlùsì ẹsè tí ńfa koríko wòlú.*
Disaster-causing legs [that] drag weeds into town. (A person who will bring disaster on others behaves like the wayward foot that drags weeds into town.)

763. *Amọ̀nà èsí kì í ṣe amọ̀nà ọdúnníí.*
The person who knew the way last year does not necessarily know the way this year. (The person whose knowledge does not grow with the times soon becomes ignorant.)

764. *Amọ̀rànbini Ọ̀yọ́, bí o bá gbé kete léri, wọn a ní oko lò ńlọ tàbí odò.*
People-who-know-the-answer-yet-ask-the-question, natives of Ọ̀yọ́, if they see you carrying a water pot, ask whether you are on your way to the farm or the stream. (If the answer is plain to see, one does not ask the question.)

765. *Amùṣùà àgbẹ̀ tí ńgbin kókò.*
A wastrel farmer [that] plants coco yams.[39] (It is a wastrel farmer that plants an inferior crop.)

766. *Àpà èèyàn ò mọ̀ pé ohun tó pọ̀-ọ́ lè tán.*
A wastrel does not know that what is plentiful can be used up. (A wastrel knows no thrift.)

767. *Àpà-á fi owó méwèèwá bọ ẹnu; àpà, a-bìjeun-wọ̀mù-wọ̀mù.*
The wastrel puts all ten fingers into his mouth; wastrel, a-person-who-eats-with-abandon. (A wastrel is immoderate in his eating.)

768. *Apajájẹẹ́ ní èrù adìẹ ńba òun.*
The-person-who-kills-and-eats-dogs claims to be afraid of chickens. (A hardened criminal pretends to have scruples about mere peccadilloes.)

769. *Àpàkòmọ̀rà, tí ńgẹsin lóri àpáta.*
A-shiftless-person-who-knows-not-what-things-cost rides a horse on rocks. (A person who has no part in paying for a thing is seldom careful in using it.)

770. *A-pé-é-jẹ kì í jẹ ìbàjé.*
A person who waits patiently for a long time before eating will not eat unwholesome food. (Those who are patient will have the best of things.)

771. *Àpèmọ́ra là ńpe Tèmídire.*
It is in furtherance of one's own fortune that one calls the name Temidire. (Each person must advance his or her own interests.)[40]

772. *Àpọ́n dògí ó ṣàrò.*
When a bachelor becomes old, he makes his own cooking fire. (One should make provisions for the future in one's youth.)

---

39. Coco yams, *Colocasia esculentum* (Araceae), also known as taro, are a variety of yams that the Yoruba eat only for want of something better. Farmers would rather plant a more favored variety.

40. The name Temidire means "My affairs have prospered." Although the name indicates that the bearer is the fortunate one, the person who calls the name says "My . . . ," thereby invoking his or her own good fortune.

773. *Ara è lara è: ṣòkòtò ọlọ́pàá.*
A little bit of it is a little bit of it: the police-man's short pants. (Leave nothing to waste, for one can always find some use for the smallest remnant.)[41]

774. *Ara kì í rọni ká ṣégi ta.*
If one has the wherewithal to live a life of ease, one does not gather firewood for sale. (One who has found success does not persist in grubbing.)

775. *Ara kì í tu ẹni káká, kí ara ó rọni koko, ká má leè jíkàkà dífá.*
One cannot be so much at ease, or so much in pain, that one cannot wake early to con-sult the oracle.[42] (Whatever one's condition, one does what one must do.)

776. *Ará òrun ò ṣẹtí aṣọ.*
Natives of heaven do not sew their hems.[43] (The uninitiated do not know the customs of a place.)

777. *A-rìn-fàà-lójú-akégàn, a-yan-kàṣà-lójú-abúni, abúni ò lówó nílé ju ẹnu-u rẹ̀ lọ.*
One-who-saunters-in-front-of-detractors, one-who-struts-before-abusers: those who abuse one have no money at home, only their mouths. (One's best course is to ignore detractors and insulters; all they have is their mouths.)

778. *Arìngbèrè ni yó mùú oyè délé; asárétete ò róyè jẹ.*
The person who walks casually is the one who will bear a title home; the person who runs fast has no title to show for his efforts. (The spoils do not necessarily go to those who exert themselves most. Compare 1357.)

779. *À-ró-kanlè laṣọ ayaba; à-wà-kanlè ni ti yàrà.*
Wrapping-from-waist-to-the-floor is the style of the queen's wrapper; digging-down-to-the-deepest-bottom is the requirement of the dry moat. (Whatever one has to do, one must be thorough and not satisfied with half measures.)

780. *Arúgbó ọ̀ndágbèsè: ó ní mélòó ni òun óò dúró san níbẹ̀?*
The old person who incurs debt: he says how much of it will he be around to pay? (A person whose days are numbered can afford to take on long-term obligations freely.)

781. *A-sáré-lówó ńbẹ lọ́nà ogun; A-pọ̀sẹ̀sẹ̀ ńbẹ lọ́nà èrò; Bó-pé-títí-ng-ó-là ńbẹ lábà, ó ńjẹ èsun iṣu.*
He-who-hurries-after-riches is on his way to battle; He-who-has-in-abundance is off on his travels; Sooner-or-later-I-will-be-rich is back in his hut, eating roasted yams. (Wealth comes to those who exert them-selves, not to those who wait for it to find them.)

782. *À-sìnkú-àì-jogún, òsì ní ńtani.*
Burying-the-dead-without-sharing-in-the-inheritance leads one to poverty. (One should have something to show for one's efforts.)

783. *Asínwín ní òun ó ti iná bọlé; wọ́n ní kó má ti iná bọlé; ó ní òun ó sáà ti iná bọlé; wọ́n ní bó bá tiná bọlé àwọn ó sọ ó si; ó ní ìyẹn kẹ̀ ìkan.*
The imbecile said he would torch the house; he was asked not to torch the house; he said he certainly would torch the house; he was

---

41. Colonial policemen's notoriously short uniform pants gave rise to the suggestion or speculation that they were made out of remnants.

42. This is a reference to the incumbency on the priests of daily consultation with Ifá.

43. *Ará òrun* is the designation for masqueraders who are supposed to be the incarnated spirits of dead ancestors. Their costume is cloth shrouds, usually of variegated strips that they do not bother to hem.

told that if he torched the house, he would be thrown in it; he said, "That casts the matter in a different light." (Even an imbecile becomes sane when his life is at stake.)

784. A-ṣo-aré-dìjà ní ńjẹ̀bi ẹjọ́.
One-who-turns-play-into-a-fight is always guilty. (One should take a jest in the spirit of jest.)

785. A-sọ̀kò-sádìẹ-igba, òkò ní ńsọ tí ilẹ̀-ẹ́ fi ńsú.
One-who-throws-stones-at-two-hundred-chickens will be engaged in stone throwing until nightfall. (Tackling a job with inadequate tools makes the job interminable.)

786. Àṣàyá kì í jẹ́ kí ọmọ ọ̀yà ó gbọ́n.
Roughhousing keeps the young of the cane rat from learning wisdom. (A person who takes life as a jest does not learn to be wary.)

787. A-ṣe-kó-súni, ẹrú-u Ségbá; ó fọ́ akèrègbè tán ó lọ sóde Ọ̀yọ́ lọ gba oníṣẹ́ wá; bẹ̀ẹni egbàà lowọ́ oníṣẹ́.
He-who-frustrates-one, Ségbà's slave; he broke a gourd and went to Ọ̀yọ́ town to hire a calabash stitcher; and a stitcher's fee is six pence.[44] (There is nothing one can do in the face of ingrained folly.)

788. À-ṣe-sílẹ̀ làbọ̀wábá; ẹni tó ṣu sílẹ̀ á bọ̀ wá bá esinsin.
What-is-put-aside is what-is-there-to-find; he who puts excrement aside will return to find flies. (One reaps what one sows.)

789. À-sẹ̀sẹ̀-tọ́-ọtí-wò okùn-un bàntẹ́ já; bí a bá mu àmuyó ńkọ́?
One taste of wine and the belt snaps; what would happen in the event of drunken-

ness? (One should match the response to the stimulus.)

790. Aṣiwèrè èèyàn lòjò ìgboro ńpa.
It is an imbecile who is soaked in the rain in the middle of a town. (Only an imbecile ignores a refuge when one is available.)

791. Aṣiwèrè èèyàn ní ńgbèjà ìlú-u rẹ̀.
Only an imbecile gets into a fight in defense of his town. (A town's cause is no business of any one individual.)

792. A-ṣoore-jókòó-tì-í, bí aláìṣe ni.
A-person-who-does-a-favor-and-squats-by-it is like a-person-who-has-done-no-favor. (One should not dwell on what favor one has done.)

793. Aṣòroójà bí ìjà ọjà; onítìjú ò níí sá; ẹni tí ńnà án ò níí dáwọ́ dúró.
Difficult-to-fight is the fight of the marketplace; the self-conscious person will not run, and the person beating him up will not stop. (Too much concern with appearances exposes one to occasional inconveniences.)

794. A-sòwò-ọṣẹ kì í pa owó ńla.
A trader in soap does not make big money. (One's success cannot exceed one's enterprise. See 666.)

795. Aṣọ funfun òun àbàwọ́n kì í ré.
White cloth and stains are not friends. (A person of good breeding does not associate with an ill-bred person.)

796. Aṣọ ìrókò ò ṣéé fi bora.
Cloth fashioned from the bark of the ìrókò tree cannot be wrapped around one's body. (Always use the proper material for the job at hand.)

---

44. The name Ségbá (sé igbá) here means "Calabash stitcher" or, literally, "Stitch Calabash."

797. Aṣọ tá a bá rí lára igún, ti igún ni.
Whatever cloth one finds on the vulture be-

longs to it. (The vulture may lack feathers, but it does not borrow from other birds. Compare 4355.)

798. *A-ṣọ́-èhìnkùlé ba ara-a rẹ̀ nínú jẹ́; ohun tó wuni là ńṣe nílé ẹni.*
He-who-spies-on-others-from-behind-their-walls upsets himself; one does as one pleases in one's home. (What one does in the privacy of one's home is nobody else's business.)

799. *Àtàrí ìbá ṣe ìkòkò ká gbé e fún òtá yẹ̀wò; a ní ó ti fọ́ yányán.*
If one's head was a pot and one gave it to an enemy to inspect, he would say it was irretrievably broken. (An enemy is not one to trust with one's destiny.)

800. *Atégùn ò ṣéé gbé.*
The wind is impossible to carry. (Certain propositions are unrealizable.)

801. *Àtẹ́lẹwọ́ ò ṣéé fi rúná.*
The palm of the hand is not good for stoking fires. (One should not attempt difficult tasks without the proper resources.)

802. *Atipo ò mọ erèè; ó ní, "Bàbá, mo réwé funfun lóko."*
Atipo does not recognize beans; he says, "Father, I saw white leaves on the farm." (Ignorance is a curse.)

803. *Àtònímòní ò tó àtànọ́mànọ́.*
All-day-long is no match for since-yesterday. (The person who has endured since yesterday takes precedence over the person who has endured all day.)

804. *A-tọrọ-ohun-gbogbo-lọ́wọ́-Ọlọ́run kì í kánjú.*
The-seeker-of-all-things-from-God does not yield to impatience. (The supplicant must be patient for an answer.)

805. *A-wí-fúnni-kó-tó-dáni, àgbà òmùjà ni.*
He-who-alerts-one-before-he-throws-one is a past master of wrestling. (One would be wise to avoid adversaries confident enough to show their hands beforehand.)

806. *À-wí-ìgbọ́, àfọ̀-ọ̀-gbọ́ tí ńfi àjèjé ọwọ́ mumi.*
He-who-will-not-listen-to-talk, he-who-will-not-listen-to-counsel drinks water with the bare hand. (The obstinate child drinks with the bare hand, even though it is unsatisfying.)

807. *Àwítẹ́lẹ̀ ní ńjẹ́ ọmọ gbẹ́nà; ọmọ kì í gbẹ́nà lásán.*
Previous-instruction enables a child to understand coded speech; a child does not naturally understand codes. (A clever child reflects the instruction he or she has received.)

808. *Awo aláwo la kì í dá lẹ́ẹ̀mejì.*
It is another person's divination that one does not repeat. (One might not put oneself out for others, but will do so for oneself.)

809. *Àwòdì òkè tí ńwo ìkaraun kòrò, kí ni yó fìgbín ṣe?*
The hawk in the sky eyes the snail shell slyly; what will it do with a snail? (One should not waste time on a task one cannot master.)

810. *Awọ erin ò ṣéé ṣe gángan.*
The elephant's hide cannot be used to fashion a *gángan* drum. (Employ the proper material for the task at hand.)

811. *Awọ ẹlédẹ̀ ò ṣéé ṣe gbẹ̀du.*
The hide of a pig is no use for making the *gbẹ̀du* drum. (Certain materials are of no use in some applications.)

812. *Awọ ẹnu ò ṣéé ṣe ìlù.*
The skin of the mouth cannot be used to

fashion a drum.[45] (Employ the proper materials for the task at hand.)

813. *Àyàn ò gbẹdùn.*
The *àyàn* tree does not accept an axe.[46]
(Certain approaches must be rejected as improper.)

814. *Àyangbẹ ejá dùn; ṣùgbọ́n kí la ó jẹ kéjá tó yan?*
Dry smoked fish is delicious, but what is one to eat before the fish is smoked? (Although one must look to the future, one must also take care of the present.)

815. *Ayé ńlọ, à ńtọ̀ ọ́.*
The world goes forth, and we follow. (One lives according to what life confronts one with.)

816. *Ayé ò ṣé-é bá léri; wọ́n lè ṣeni léṣe.*
The world is not a thing to exchange threats with; it can inflict disaster. (Be wary in dealing with the world.)[47]

817. *Ayé ò ṣé-é finú hàn; bí o lógbọ́n, fi síkùn ara-à rẹ.*
The world does not deserve to be trusted; if you have a store of wisdom, keep it in you. (People of the world are not reliable; whatever wisdom one wishes to pass on should be reserved for one's own use.)

B

818. *Baálé àìlọ́wọ̀ ni àlejò àìlọ́wọ̀.*[48]
An unsolicitous host makes for a visitor

with no deference. (The visitor responds according to his reception.)

819. *Baálẹ̀ àgbẹ̀-ẹ́ ní òun ò ní nǹkan-án tà lọ́run, kí owó okà òún ṣáà ti pé.*
The chief of farmers says he has nothing to go to heaven to sell; all he cares about is fair payment for his corn. (If one does not ask for too much, one will not have to die to get it.)

820. *Baba-ìsìnkú ò fọmọ-ọ rẹ̀ sọfà; alábàáṣe ńfọmọ-ọ rẹ̀ kówó.*
The executor does not pawn his child; his helper pawns his own. (The obligated person holds back, whereas the helper risks his all.)

821. *"Báyìí là ńṣe" níbìkan, èèwọ̀ ibòmín-ìn.*
"This is what we do" in one place is taboo in another. (Different people, different ways.)

822. *Bí a bá bá aṣiwèrè gbé, a ó gba odì ọlogbọ́n; bí a bá bá ewé iyá sọtè, a ó ṣe eléko.*
If one lives with a maniac, one incurs the enmity of the wise; if one shuns *iyá* leaves, one offends the corn-gruel seller. (Keeping bad company alienates good people; to shun a person is to shun that person's friends.)

823. *Bí a bá bá ẹrán wí, ká bá ẹ̀rán wí.*
As one castigates *ẹrán*, one should also castigate *ẹ̀rán*.[49] (If both sides in a dispute deserve blame, one should apportion it accordingly. Compare 826.)

824. *Bí a bá fi owó ọ̀tún na ọmọ, à fi owó òsì fà á mọ́ra.*
If one whips a child with the right hand, one embraces it with the left. (A child deserving punishment yet deserves love.)

45. The reference here is obviously to the cheeks.
46. The *àyàn* tree is used for house posts and for carving drums; it is the *àyán* tree that is used for axe and hoe handles.
47. "The world" here stands, of course, for people at large.
48. The word *baálé* also means both landlord and husband.
49. The entities *ẹrán* and *ẹ̀rán* are imaginary beings which, as indicated by their names, are practically interchangeable.

825. *Bí a bá jèwọ́ tán èrín là ńrín; bí a bá yó tán orun ní ńkunni.*
After a joke one gives way to laughter; after satiation one gives way to sleep. (The action should match the occasion. Compare 833.)

826. *Bí a bá kìlọ̀ fólè, ká kìlọ̀ fóníṣu ẹ̀bá ọ̀nà.*
As one warns the thief, one should also warn the owner of the wayside yams. (The offender and the tempter both deserve blame. Compare 823.)

827. *Bí a bá ní mọ̀, ọ̀mọ̀ràn a mọ̀ ọ́.*
If one says "Know," the knowledgeable will know it. (The perceptive person can detect meaning in the slightest of signs.)

828. *Bí a bá ńsunkún, à máa ríran.*
While one weeps, one can still see. (However accommodating one is, one should never take leave of one's good judgment.)

829. *Bí a bá ránni níṣẹ́ ẹrú, à fi jẹ́ tọmọ.*
If one is sent on an errand like a slave, one carries it out like a freeborn. (The well-bred person removes the flaws in a message sent through him, or a task given him to perform.)

830. *Bí a bá ránti ojó kan ìbálé, ká ránti ojó kan ìkúnlè abiyamọ, ká ránti kan abẹ́ tí ńtani lára.*
If one remembers the day of [the loss of] virginity, one should also remember the day of a woman's delivery, and one should remember the vagina that smarts. (As one takes one's pleasures, one should be mindful of the pains that make them possible.)

831. *Bí a bá rí èké, à ṣebí èèyàn rere ni; à sọ̀rọ̀ ságbọ̀n a jò.*
When one sees a devious person, one mistakes him for a good person; one talks into a basket and it leaks. (It is easy to mistake a bad person for a good one and to place trust in that person.)

832. *Bí a bá rí òwúrọ̀, alẹ́ ńkọ́?*
Although one has seen the morning, what about nighttime? (Nobody should be judged until he or she has reached the end of his or her days.)

833. *Bí a bá sọ̀rọ̀ tán, ẹrín là ńrín; bí a bá yó tán orun ní ńkunni.*
When one is done discussing a matter, one laughs; when one is satiated, sleep claims one. (When a matter has been taken care of, one turns one's attention in the appropriate direction. Compare 825.)

834. *Bí a bá ṣe ohun ńlá, à fi èpè gba ara ẹni là.*
If one has committed a great offense, one frees oneself by swearing [innocence]. (One's greatest duty is self-preservation.)

835. *Bí a bá ta ará ilé ẹni lópọ̀, a kì í rí i rà lówọ̀n-ọ́n mọ́.*
If one sells a member of one's household cheap, one will not be able to buy him back at a great value. (Once one has besmirched the name of a person one is close to, one cannot later wipe it clean.)

836. *Bí a kò bá gbé ọ̀pọ̀lọ́ sọ sínú omi gbí-gbóná, ká tún gbé e sọ sí tútù, kì í mọ èyí tó sàn.*
If one does not throw a toad into hot water and then throw it into cold water, it does not know which is better. (It takes a change in circumstances to make one appreciate good fortune.)

837. *Bí a kò bá gbọ́n ju àparò oko ẹni lọ, a kì í pa á.*
If one is not more clever than the partridge on one's farm, one cannot kill it. (To succeed, one must be more clever than one's adversary.)

838. *Bí a kò bá rádànán, à fòòbè ṣebo.*
If one cannot find a [full-sized] bat, one

sacrifices a [smaller] house bat. (One makes do with what one can find. See also the next entry.)

839. *Bí a kò bá rígún a ò gbọdọ̀ ṣebọ; bí a ò bá rí àkàlà a ò gbọdọ̀ ṣorò.*
If we cannot find a vulture, we may not offer a sacrifice; if we cannot find a ground hornbill, we may not carry out a ritual. (Nothing can be accomplished in the absence of the requisite materials. Compare the previous entry.)

840. *Bí a kò bá torí iṣu jẹ epo, à torí epo jẹṣu.*
If one does not eat oil because of yams, one will eat yams because of oil. (If one does not perform a duty because one likes it, one performs it because it is the right thing to do.)

841. *Bí a kò bímọ rí, a kò ha rómọ léhìn adìẹ?*
If one has never had a child, has one not seen chicks flocking after chickens? (Children are no novelty to anyone.)

842. *Bí a kò ránni sójà, ọjà kì í ránni sílé.*
If one does not send a message to the market, the market does not send a message to one at home. (Without making an effort, one cannot expect rewards.)

843. *Bí a kò ṣe ọdẹ rí, a kò lè mọ ẹsè-ẹ kò-lọ-ibèun.*
If one has never hunted, one would not know the tracks of "it-did-not-go-that-way." (One is an ignoramus in a trade that is not one's own.)

844. *Bí alẹ́ bá lẹ́, à fi ọmọ ayọ̀ fún ayọ̀.*
When night comes, one gives the *ayọ̀* seeds to *ayọ̀*.[50] (When the time comes, one puts an end to whatever one is doing.)

845. *Bí alẹ́ bá lẹ́, bọnnọ-bọ́nnọ́ a rẹ̀wẹ̀sì.*
When night falls, *bọnnọ-bọ́nnọ́* goes limp.[51] (There must be an end to every struggle and every exertion.)

846. *Bí alẹ́ kò lẹ́, òòbẹ̀ kì í fò.*
If night does not fall, the house bat does not fly. (All actions must await their auspicious moments.)

847. *Bí apá ò ká àràbà, apá lè ká egbò ìdí-i rè.*
If the arms cannot encompass the silk-cotton tree, they may encompass its root. (If one is no match for the father, one may be more than a match for the child.)

848. *Bí àrùn búburú bá wọlú, oògùn búburú la fi ńwò ó.*
If a terrible epidemic descends on a town, it is confronted with a terrible medicine. (One matches the medicine to the disease.)

849. *Bí eégún ó bàá wọlè, orò ní ńṣe.*
A masquerader who wishes to disappear into the ground cries "*Orò!*" (A person intending to do something extraordinary should give prior warning.)

850. *Bí ẹlẹ́rẹ̀kẹ́ régérégé bá ro ẹjọ́-ọ tirè̩ tán, kó ránti pé ẹlẹ́rẹ̀kẹ́ mẹ́ki á rí rò.*
After the person with smooth cheeks has stated his or her case, he or she should remember that the person with blemished cheeks will have something to say. (The person who looks good owing to the efforts of his or her subordinates should remember that they also deserve some credit.)

851. *Bí eré bí eré, àlàbọrùn-ún dèwù.*
Like play, like play, the makeshift cape be-

---

50. *Ayọ̀* is a game played with the smooth, hard of the *Heloptelea grandis* (Ulmaceae) tree (see Abra-

51. *Bọnnọ-bọ́nnọ́* is another name for the tree *ayùnrẹ́*, whose leaves droop when night falls. The term could also apply to a person noted for restlessness.

ham 84), using a board with twelve scooped holes. It is popular in many parts of the continent.

came a dress. (Imperceptibly, a stop-gap arrangement has become the status quo.)

852. *Bí igí bá wó lu igi, tòkè là ńkọ́ gbé.*
If trees fall atop one another, one removes the topmost one first. (One should attend to affairs according to their urgency.)

853. *Bí ikún bá jẹ, bí ikún bá mu, ikún a wo oòrùn alẹ́.*
When the squirrel has eaten, when the squirrel has drunk, the squirrel looks at the setting sun. (Whatever one does, one should mind the passing of time.)

854. *Bí ilẹ̀-ẹ́ bá laná, òpòlọ́ á fò gun igi.*
If the earth catches fire, the toad will hop on a tree. (If your position becomes untenable, seek refuge elsewhere.)

855. *Bí ilú bá dá sí méjì, tọba òrún là ńṣe.*
If the town is split in two, one does the will of the heavenly king. (If there is a division in one's group, one takes the side God would favor.)

856. *Bí iṣẹ́ kò pẹ́ ẹni, a kì í pẹ́ iṣẹ́.*
If a task does not delay one, one does not drag it out. (Tasks that are easy should be finished promptly.)

857. *Bí kò bá tíì rẹ ìjà, a kì í là á.*
If a fight is not yet spent, one does not intervene to end it. (One cannot end a fight that is not yet over.)

858. *Bí kókó bá dáni, a kì í jẹ orí ìmàdò; bí a bá jẹ orí ìmàdò, a kì í lọ sí àwùjọ pọ́npó; bí a bá lọ sí àwùjọ pọ́npó, ìwòn ara ẹni là ńmọ̀.*
If one is tripped by a protruding object, one should not eat a warthog's head; if one eats a warthog's head, one should not go to a gathering of cudgels; if one goes to a gathering of cudgels, one should know one's place and act accordingly. (If unforeseen

circumstances force one to engage in risky behavior, one should be that much more careful.)

859. *Bí nǹkán bá tán nílẹ̀, ọmọ ẹbọ a bọ́ síjó, àwọn tó wà níbẹ̀ a múra àti lọ.*
At the conclusion of a ceremony the acolyte commences to dance, and the onlookers prepare to make their exit. (One should not hang around after one's business is done.)

860. *"Bí o bá já ng ó so ọ́"; kókó yó wà láàárín-in rẹ̀.*
"If you break I will retie you"; there will be a knot in it. (Something repaired is seldom the same as something unspoilt.)

861. *Bí o kò gbọ́ Ègùn, o kò gbọ́ wòyọ̀-wòyọ̀?*
If you do not understand Ègùn, do you not recognize signs that someone is speaking? (One may not understand what a person says, but one will be able to tell that the person is speaking.)

862. *Bí o máa ṣe aya Olúgbọ́n ṣe aya Olúgbọ́n; bí o máa ṣe aya Arẹsà ṣe aya Arẹsà, kí o yéé pákòkò légbẹ̀ẹ́ ògiri; ẹni tí yó ṣe aya Olúfẹ̀ a kógbá wálé.*
If you will be a wife to the *Olúgbọ́n,* be a wife to him; if you will be a wife to the *Arẹsà,* be a wife to him and stop sneaking around hugging walls; a person who would be the wife of the *Olúfẹ̀* must gather her affairs into the house.[52] (Once one has chosen a course, one should commit oneself completely to it.)

863. *Bí obìnrin ò bá gbé ilé tó méjì, kì í mọ èyí tó sàn.*
If a woman has not lived in at least two homes, she never knows which is better.

---

52. The persons named are titled people, whose wives would therefore be expected to be above reproach.

(Unless one has tasted some adversity, one does not appreciate good fortune.)

864. *Bí ojú bá mọ́, olówò a gbówò; ọ̀rànwú a gbé kẹ́kẹ́; ajagun a gbé apata; àgbè a jí tòun tòrúkọ́; ọmọ ọdẹ a jí tapó tọrán; ajíwẹsẹ a bá odò omi lọ.*
When day breaks, the trader takes up his trade; the cotton spinner picks up the spindle; the warrior grabs his shield; the farmer gets up with his hoe; the son of the hunter arises with his quiver and his bows; he-who-wakes-and-washes-with-soap makes his way to the river. (When morning comes, everybody should embark on something useful.)

865. *Bí ojú bá rí ọ̀rò, a wò ó fín.*
When the eyes come upon a matter, they must look hard and well. (Imperfect understanding causes difficulties.)

866. *Bí ojú ọmọdé ò tó ìtàn, a bá àwígbọ́.*
If a youth's eyes do not witness a story, they should be good for hearsay. (If one does not witness something, one learns from those who did.)

867. *Bí olósùn-ún bá lọ osùn, ara-a rẹ̀ ní ńfi dánwò.*
When the camwood-powder seller grinds the powder, she tests it on her own body. (One tries a remedy on oneself before offering it to others.)

868. *Bí òrìṣá bá mú ẹléhìn, kí abuké máa múra sílẹ̀.*
If the gods take a person with a protruding back, the humpback should make ready. (If a person like you suffers a certain fate, you too are at risk.)

869. *Bí òwe bí òwe là ńlùlù ògìdìgbó; ọlọgbọ́n ní ńjó o; ọ̀mọ̀ràn ní ńsìí mọ̀ ọ́.*
Like proverbs, like proverbs one plays the

ògìdìgbó music; only the wise can dance to it, and only the knowledgeable know it.[53]
(Only the wise can follow subtle discourses.)

870. *Bí òwe bí òwe nIfá ńsọ̀rọ̀.*
Like proverbs, like proverbs are the pronouncements of [the oracle god] Ifá. (The most profound speech is indirect and subtle.)

871. *Bí ọ̀bùn ò mọ èrè, a mọ ojú owó.*
If the filthy person does not know profit, he should know his capital. (If a person cannot improve a matter, he should at least not worsen it.)

872. *Bí ọkùnrín réjò, tóbìrín pa á, à ní kéjò má ṣáà lọ.*
If a man sees a snake, and a woman kills it, what matters is that the snake does not escape. (One should not be a stickler about roles.)

873. *Bí ọlọgbọ́n bá ńfi wèrè se iṣu, ọ̀mọ̀ràn a máa fi gègé yàn án.*
If a wise person is cooking yams in an insane way, a knowing person picks them up with stakes. (If a person tries to mislead you, find your own direction.)

874. *Bí Ọlọ́run-ún bá ti fọtá ẹni hanni, kò lè pani mọ́.*
Once God has revealed your enemy, that enemy can no longer kill you. (Knowledge neutralizes dangers.)

875. *Bí ọmọ́ bá jágbọ́n-ọn kíké, ìyá-a rẹ̀ a jágbọ́n-ọn rírè é.*
If a child learns the trick of crying, the mother learns the trick of consoling him or her. (One must be ready to adapt to cope with any situation. See the next entry also.)

---

53. Ògìdìgbó is the royal ceremonial music of Ọ̀yọ́.

876. *Bí ọmọ bá jágbọ́n-ọn kíkú, ìyá ẹ̀ a jágbọ́n-ọn sísin.*
If a child learns the trick of dying, his mother should learn the trick of burying. (One should learn to meet wiles with wiles. See also the preceding entry.)

877. *Bí ọmọ bá yó, a fikùn han baba.*
When a child is full, he shows his stomach to his father. (When one accomplishes one's goals, one feels like celebrating. Also, one should show appreciation to one's benefactor.)

878. *Bí ọmọdé bá dúpẹ́ ore àná, a rí tòní gbà.*
If a child expresses gratitude for yesterday's favor, he will receive today's. (The grateful person encourages others to do him more favors. Compare 3467.)

879. *Bí ọmọdé bá ḿbẹ́ igi, àgbàlagbà a máa wo ibi tí yó wòó sí.*
If a youth is felling a tree, an elder will be considering where it will fall. (Unlike the youth, the elder is mindful of consequences.)

880. *Bí ọmọdé bá mọ ayò, ẹyọ la ó fi pa á.*
If a child is an adept *ayò* player, one defeats him with single seeds. (A precocious child may be almost but not quite as accomplished as an adult.)

881. *Bí ọmọdé bá ṣubú a wo iwájú; bí àgbá bá ṣubú a wo ẹ̀hìn.*
When a youth falls, he looks ahead; when an elder falls, he looks behind. (The youth is mindful of what his superiors think of him; the elder is mindful of what the young think of him. Compare 3365.)

882. *Bí ọmọdé kọ iyán àná, ìtàn la ó pa fún un.*
If a child refuses yesterday's pounded yams, it is stories one treats the child to. (A person who boycotts a meal or some entitlement simply deprives himself or herself of some benefits.)

883. *Bí ọmọdé ò bá rí oko baba ẹlòmíràn, a ní kò sí oko baba ẹni tó tó ti baba òun.*
If a youth has never seen another person's father's farm, he says nobody's father's farm is as large as his father's. (Until one has seen other people's great accomplishments, one is overly impressed by one's own.)

884. *Bí òrán bá pẹ́ nílẹ̀, gbígbọ́n ní ńgbọ́n.*
If a problem remains long enough, it becomes clever. (If one keeps at it long enough, one will find the solution for any problem.)

885. *Bí ọwọ́ ò bá ṣeé ṣán, à ká a léri.*
If the arms cannot be swung, one carries them on one's head. (If one cannot do as one would, one does what one can.)

886. *Bí sòbìyà yó bàá degbò, olúgambe là á wí fún.*
If guinea worm is becoming an ulcer, one should inform *olúgambe*.[54] (When a problem arises, one must consult those who can solve it.)

887. *Bí túlàsí bá di méjì, ọ̀kan là ḿmú.*
When emergencies number two, one concentrates on one. (Concentrate on one problem at a time.)

888. *"Bùn mi níṣu kan" kì í ṣáájú "Ẹ kú oko òo."*
"Give me one yam" does not precede "Greetings to you on the farm." (One does not ask a favor of or transact any business with any person without first exchanging pleasantries. Compare 1249.)

---

54. A medicine for treating guinea worm.

889. *Dà-á-sílè-ká-tun-pín, ogún ijóun, a ò pín in re.*
The recent throw-it-all-on-the-floor-that-we-may-redistribute-it inheritance was not well distributed the first time around. (Whatever needs to be done again must not have been done well the first time.)

890. *Dídì ní m̀mú abẹ mú.*
It is wrapping that makes a knife sharp. (Only by taking great care of them does one keep one's possessions in good shape.)

891. *Díẹ̀-díẹ̀ nimú ẹlédèé fi ńwọgbà.*
It is bit by bit that the nose of the pig enters the fence. (A small problem, if not attended to, becomes unmanageable.)

892. *Dífá-dífá ò fìfá sẹré.*
The diviner does not take Ifá lightly. (One should not be careless about one's livelihood.)

893. *Dùgbẹ̀-dùgbẹ̀ kì í fi eyin-in rẹ̀ sílẹ̀.*
The egg-bearing spider never leaves its eggs behind. (One does not turn one's back on one's treasure.)

894. *Dúró o kíkà; bí o ò dúró kíkà, ìkà a ba tìrẹ jẹ́.*
Stop and say hello to the wicked; if you do not say hello to the wicked, the wicked will find problems for you. (One's best defense against wicked people is ingratiation.)

895. *Ebi ńpa mí ọlóṣẹ ńkiri; ìgbà tí ng ò wẹnú ng ó ṣe wẹ̀de?*
I am hungry, and the soap seller hawks her wares; when I have not washed my inside, how can I wash my outside? (One must order one's priorities sensibly.)

896. *Ebi ò pàJèṣà ó lóun ò jẹkọ Ọ̀yọ́; ebí pa ọmọ Obòkun ó jẹ ori.*
The Ijeṣa person is not hungry, and he rejects corn loaf prepared by an Ọ̀yọ́ person; when hunger gripped the son of Obokun [an apellation for Ijeṣa people], he ate *ori* [the Ọ̀yọ́ name for corn loaf]. (It is when one is not desperate that one is choosy.)

897. *Ebi ò pàmọ̀le ó ní òun ò je àáyá; ebí pa Súlè ó jọbọ.*
The Muslim is not hungry, and he vows he will not eat a red colobus monkey; hunger gripped Suleiman, and he ate a monkey. (A desperate person is seldom finicky.)

898. *Eégún Ẹ̀gbá, Ẹ̀gbá ní ńfọ̀.*
The Ẹ̀gbá masquerader must needs speak Ẹ̀gbá.[55] (One should speak to others in a manner that is fitting and that will facilitate one's business with them.)

899. *Eégún tí yó gbeni là ńdáṣọ fún; òrìṣà tí yó gbeni là ńsìn; bi igí bá gbè mí mà kó obì mà bọ igi.*
It is the masquerader that succors one that one makes shrouds for; it is the god that succors one that one worships; if a tree succors me, I will take kola nuts and worship the tree. (One should confine one's efforts to profitable ventures and one's service to appreciative people.)

900. *Eégún tí yó ṣe bíi Lébé, Lébé ni yó dà; èyí tí yó tàkìtì bí Olúfolé, òfurugbàdà ni yó ta á.*
The masquerader that will perform like Lébé must become like Lébé;[56] the one that will somersault like Olúfolé [meaning "Great-One-Jumps-a-House"] must perform his feat in the open spaces. (One must prepare oneself and gather one's resources before one attempts momentous tasks.)

---

55. Ẹ̀gbá is another designation for the people of Abẹ́òkúta and their language.

56. An *alárìnjó* (itinerant dancer) type.

901. *Ejò-ó rí ihò tó há ó kó wọ̀ ọ́; ìyá-a rẹ̀-ẹ́ lọ́wọ́ àti fà á yọ?*
A snake sees a tight hole and crawls into it; has its mother hands to pull it out? (One had better be certain to be able to extricate oneself before venturing into tight spots.)

902. *Elékuru kì í kiri lóko.*
The seller of steamed ground beans does not hawk her wares on a farm. (One wastes time attempting to sell things to those who produce them.)

903. *Èló là ńra adìẹ òkókó, tí à ńgba ọmọ-ọ rẹ̀ sìn?*
How much does a hen cost that one would contract to raise chicks for the owner?[57] (Certain obligations are not worth the trouble.)

904. *Èmi-ò-níí-fẹ́-obìnrin-tẹ́nìkan-ńfẹ́, olúwarẹ̀ ò níí fẹ́ obìnrin ni.*
I-will-court-no-woman-being-courted-by-another-man will court no woman at all. (A person who wants exclusive rights to a woman — or anything — will look for a long time and in vain.)

905. *Èmi-ò-níí-ṣu-imí-le-imí, olúwarẹ̀ ó rìn jìnnà ààtàn.*
I-will-not-defecate-on-existing-excrement will walk a good distance into the bush. (People who are too finicky will pay in effort and delay for their habits.)

906. *Èpè la fi ńwo èpè sàn.*
Curses are the antidote for curses. (One matches the remedy to the affliction.)

907. *Epo ló ṣeé jẹṣu; àkàsọ̀ ló ṣeé gun àká; obìnrín dùn-ún bá sùn ju ọkùnrin lọ.*
It is palm oil that goes best with yams; it is a ladder that is best for climbing granaries; a woman is more pleasant to make love to than a man.[58] (Certain things are fit for certain purposes; not just anything will do anytime.)

908. *Epo lojú ọbẹ̀.*
Palm oil is the countenance of stew.[59] (One should be particularly attentive to that one ingredient or thing whose absence mars the entire project.)

909. *Eré là ńfọmọ ayò ṣe.*
All one does with *ayò* seeds is play. (One should take time for pleasure when one may.)

910. *Èrò kì í mọ ibùsọ̀ kọ́rùn ó wọ́ ọ.*
A wayfarer does not know the location of the rest stop and yet has his neck crushed from the weight of a heavy load.[60] (One should measure one's exertions to suit one's capacity.)

911. *Ète lẹ̀gbọ́n; ìmọ̀ràn làbúrò; bí-a-ó-ti-ṣe lẹ̀kẹta wọn.*
Intention is the eldest; contemplation is the next; and plan of action is the third. (First there is the goal, then a contemplation of it, and finally a plan for attaining it.)

912. *Ètò lòfin kìn-ín-ní lóde ọ̀run.*
Order is the first law in heaven. (Whatever one does, one must be orderly.)

913. *Ewúrẹ́ ò ṣe-e fiṣu ṣó.*
A goat is not a wise choice as the guard over yams. (Do not entrust your affairs to your enemy.)

---

57. People sometimes agreed to raise domestic animals for other people in the hope of sharing in the offspring.

58. The proverb obviously speaks from a man's point of view.

59. The Yoruba believe that the more palm oil goes in, the better the stew.

60. The neck may be crushed because loads are often carried on the head.

914. Èyí tó yẹ ará iwájú, èrò ẹ̀hìn fiyè sílẹ̀.
[To] what turned out favorably for those
going ahead, you coming behind, pay close
attention. (Learn from the examples of
others.)

Ẹ

915. Ẹ̀bẹ̀ là m̀bẹ ọ̀ṣìkà pé kó tún ìlú-u rẹ̀ ṣe.
One can only remonstrate with a wicked
person to urge him or her to improve his or
her town. (Gentle pleas are the only likely
means of getting contrary people to do what
is right.)

916. Ẹbọ díẹ̀, òògùn díẹ̀, ní ǹgba aláìkú là.
A little sacrifice, a little medicine, is what
keeps the one who does not die alive. (One
should not place all one's faith in a single
solution to a problem.)

917. Ẹbọ ẹnìkan là ǹfi ẹnìkan rú.
It is a sacrifice on behalf of only one person
that demands only one person as offering.
(Extraordinary problems demand extraordinary solutions.)

918. Ẹ̀ẹ̀kan lejò ǹyánni.
One gets bitten by a snake only once. (The
same disaster does not befall one more
than once; after the first time one learns to
avoid it.)

919. Ẹ̀fẹ̀-ẹ́ dèfẹ̀ iyán; a paláwẹ́ ẹ̀kọ baálé ilé ní
ẹ̀ ńpèun bí?
The teasing involves pounded yam; the corn
loaf is unwrapped, and the father of the
household asks, "Did someone call me?" (A
person who wants something badly will not
let a little teasing put him or her off taking
it. See the next entry.)

920. Ẹ̀fẹ̀-ẹ́ dèfẹ̀ iyán; ò báà gbémi lulẹ̀ ng ó
bàá ọ jẹun.

The teasing involves pounded yam; even if
you throw me on the ground, I will eat with
you. (No amount of teasing will stop me
from doing what I have in mind. Compare
the preceding entry.)

921. Ẹgbẹ́ ẹni kì í wọ́n láyé ká wá a lọ sọ́run.
One does not, upon failing to find suitable company in this world, go looking in
heaven. (If one cannot find what one wants,
one should learn to do without it.)

922. Ẹjọ́ a-fẹ́ni-lóbìnrin là ńwí; a kì í wíjọ́
a-fẹ́ni-lọ́mọ.
One may complain about a person who
courts one's wife but not about a person
who courts one's daughter. (One should not
pursue causes without good grounds.)

923. Ẹlédèé ní ojó tí òun ti jágbọ́n-ọn hùn, ojó
náà ni ọ̀rọ̀ ò ti nìun lára mọ́.
The pig says since the day it learned to reply
to every statement with a grunt it has not
got into any trouble. (A person who says
nothing seldom gets in trouble. This is a
variant of 734 and 983.)

924. Ẹléjọ́ ṣa èyí tó wù ú wí.
The person with complaints pursues the
most pressing ones. (One should concentrate on one's most pressing problems.)

925. Ẹlẹ́nu-ú tóó rí sá.
An overly loquacious person is someone to
flee from. (Be wary of loquacious people.)

926. Ẹni à ńwò kì í wòran.
The person people have gathered to watch
should not himself or herself be a spectator.
(One should not ignore one's problems to
dwell on those of others.)

927. Ẹni a óò gbé òkú-u rẹ̀ sin, a kì í sọ pé ó
ńrùn pani.
One does not complain that a corpse one

will have to bury stinks. (One should not run down a person or thing that will eventually devolve to one's care.)

928. Ẹni a pé kó wáá wo kọ̀bì: ó ní kí nìyí kọ́bi-kọ̀bi?
The person invited to take a look at the throne-room extension exclaims, "What a maze of apartments!"[61] (One should not waste one's breath expressing the obvious.)

929. Ẹni a wí fún ko gbọ́; ẹni a fọ̀ fún kó gbà; èyí tí ò gbọ́ yó fìlẹ̀ bora.
Whomever people speak to should listen; whomever people instruct should accept instruction; the one who does not listen will be covered by the earth. (Refusal to heed advice can be deadly.)

930. Ẹni àìgbọ́n pa ló pọ̀; ẹni ogbọ́n pa ò tó ǹkan.
People killed by folly are innumerable; people killed by wisdom are few. (Few things kill more surely than folly.)

931. Ẹní bá ríkun nímú ọlọ́jà ní ńfọn ọ́n.
Whoever sees mucus in the nose of the king is the one who cleans it. (Tactless or indiscreet people usually rue their bad judgment. Compare 962.)

932. Ẹní bá tó ẹni-í gbà là ńké pè.
One appeals only to those capable of helping. (Do not seek the aid of feckless people.)

933. Ẹní du ara-a rẹ̀ lóyè Apènà: kó tó jẹ ẹran ọ̀fẹ́, ó dọrun.
Whoever deprives himself of the title of Apènà will wait until he dies before tasting

free meat.[62] (If one does not grab opportunities when they present themselves, one is in for a difficult life.)

934. Ẹní gbọ́n juni lọ ní ńtẹni nífá.
It is someone wiser than oneself who consults the oracle. (Take advice only from those qualified to offer it.)

935. Ẹní léku méjì á pòfo.
Whoever chases after two rats will catch neither. (One who pursues two or more objectives at once is likely to achieve neither. Compare 616.)

936. Ẹní máa ké ìbòsí á pa baba-a rẹ̀ jẹ.
Whoever wishes to raise an alarm will have to murder his father. (Whoever acts without cause will have to justify his action by manufacturing a cause.)

937. Ẹní rúbọ òrìṣà-á gbọ́dọ̀ rú ti èèyàn kí ebọ-ọ́ tó gbà.
Whoever offers a sacrifice to a deity must also offer a sacrifice to humans in order for the sacrifice to be efficacious. (One can please the gods and yet run afoul of humans.)

938. Ẹni tí a bá fi orí-i rẹ̀ fọ́ àgbọn ò níí jẹ níbẹ̀.
The person on whose head a coconut is broken will not share in eating it. (Whoever takes foolhardy risks in pursuit of an end seldom lives to enjoy it.)

939. Ẹni tí a bá ńbá nájà là ńwò, a kì í wo ariwo ọjà.
One pays attention to the person with whom one is bargaining, not to the commotion of

---

61. The kọ̀bì is an extension of the palace used for audiences, or for other purposes of state, or as a veranda; its approaches are necessarily mazelike, a fact to be taken for granted.

62. Apènà is the title of the second-ranking member of the powerful Ògbóni cult. The holder leads the procession in funerary rites and is free to enter and eat in any house.

the marketplace. (One should keep mind on one's business and leave extraneous matters aside.)

940. Ẹni tí a wífún kó gbọ́; ẹni tí kò gbọ́, tara-a rẹ̀ ni yó dà.
Let the person one advises pay heed; the heedless person places himself at risk. (Those who refuse instruction lay the foundation for their own ruin.)

941. Ẹni tí ẹ̀gún gún lẹ́sẹ̀ ní ńṣe lákàńláká tẹ̀lé alábẹ́rẹ́.
It is the person with a thorn in his foot who limps to the person with a needle. (The person in need of help should make some effort in his own behalf and not expect the helper to make all the necessary effort.)

942. Ẹni tí kò gbọ́n làǎwẹ̀ ńgbò.
Only the unwise hunger while fasting. (The resourceful person can find a way around any difficulty.)

943. Ẹni tí kò mọ iṣẹ́-ẹ́ jẹ́ ní ńpàǎrà lẹ̀ẹ̀mejì.
It is a person who does not know how to carry out instructions that is forced to repeat his or her efforts. (One saves time and effort by doing things right the first time.)

944. Ẹni tí kò mọ ọba ní ńfọba ṣeré.
Only a person who does not know the king trifles with the king. (The wise person recognizes potential danger and avoids it.)

945. Ẹni tí ó lè jà ni yóò kúnlẹ̀ kalẹ́.
It is the incorrigible fighter who has to remain on his or her knees until nightfall. (The person who cannot stay out of a fight will spend his or her time incessantly stating cases.)

946. Ẹni tí yó bọ Ògún, yó ra ọjà-a tirẹ̀ lọ́tọ̀.
The person who will worship Ògun will keep his or her market purchases separate

from those of others. (If one's priorities are incompatible with those of others, one parts company with them.)

947. Ẹni tí yó fò yó bẹ̀rẹ̀.
The person who will leap must first crouch. (One must make adequate preparations for any project.)

948. Ẹni tí yó mu ẹ̀ko fòrò, yó bàá ọmọ ẹléko ṣeré.
Whoever wishes to eat steaming corn pap will play with the child of the seller. (One must ingratiate oneself with the person from whom one expects a favor. This is a variant of the next entry.)

949. Ẹni tí yó mu ẹ̀ko ọ̀fẹ́ yó bàá ọmọ ẹléko ṣeré.
The person who wishes to eat free corn pap will play with the seller's child. (Nothing comes free. Compare the preceding entry.)

950. Ẹni tí yó sòwò àlè, ẹní-i rẹ̀ ní ńká; ẹni tí yó sòwò-o Ṣàngó, ààjà-a rẹ̀ ní ńrà.
Whoever chooses concubinage as a practice must provide herself with a sleeping mat; whoever chooses Ṣàngò's trade [one to do with metal] must purchase his magical rattle. (One prepares according to what is proper for one's chosen trade.)

951. Ẹni tí yó yàáni lówó, tí kò níí sinni, ohùn ẹnu-u rẹ̀ la ti ńmọ̀.
The person who will lend money and will not keep pestering one for repayment, one can tell from the tone of his or her voice. (The way people talk is a good indication of their character.)

952. Ẹni tó bá da omi síwájú á tẹ ilẹ̀ tútù.
Whoever throws water ahead will step on cool earth. (The future will look kindly on those who look well to the future. Compare 1360.)

953. Ẹni tó bá fi ojú àná wòkú, ẹbọra a bọ́ ọ
lásọ.
Whoever looks at the dead with yesterday's
eyes will be stripped naked by the spirits.
(One behaves toward people according to
the heights they have attained, not according
to the way they used to be.)[63]

954. Ẹni tó bá máa jẹ ọ̀pọ̀ló a jẹ èyí tó léyìn.
If one must eat a toad, one should eat one
with eggs. (If one must suffer, one might as
well do so with panache.)

955. Ẹni tó bá máa lu ọ̀ṣùgbó a lu ńlá; kékeré
egbèfà, ńlá egbèfà.
Whoever will smite a secret-cult priest had
better smite an important one: for a lowly
one, 1,200 cowries in fines; for an important
one, 1,200 cowries. (If the penalty for a small
offense is the same as that for a grievous one,
one might as well throw all caution to the
wind.)

956. Ẹni tó bá máa mú ọ̀bọ a ṣe bí ọ̀bọ.
Whoever wishes to catch a monkey must act
like a monkey. (To succeed against an adversary, or with a person one desires, one must
suit one's approach to the other's ways.)

957. Ẹni tó bá mọ ìdí ọ̀ràn tẹ́lẹ̀ ní ńbu àbùjá
èké.
It is a person who has prior knowledge of
the facts of a matter that can foil a devious person's attempts to skirt them. (Prior
knowledge is the surest weapon against lies.)

958. Ẹni tó bá ní igbà-á lò, bí igbà-á bá já, kó
dúró so ó.
If one must use a tree-climbing rope and it
breaks, one must pause to repair it. (One

must make time to attend to necessary
chores.)

959. Ẹni tó bá pẹ́ lórí imí, ẹṣinṣin kẹ́ṣinṣin yó
ò bá a níbè̀.
Whoever prolongs his or her defecating will
be visited by a host of flies. (Nothing good
comes of dawdling over what one must do.)

960. Ẹni tó bá rántí Efuji, kó má fi ore ṣe ẹṣin.
Whoever remembers Efuji should show no
kindness to any horse.[64] (Remember those
who have caused you injury and remember
to show them no favor.)

961. Ẹni tó bá rántí ojọ́ ní ńṣe ọmọ òkú pẹ̀lé;
ta ní jẹ́ ṣe ọmọ eégún lóore?
Those who gratefully remember past favors
extend compassion to the survivors of the
deceased; who would rather show compassion to the child of a masquerader? (When
a good person dies, the survivors inherit the
good will of those who remember him or
her well.)

962. Ẹni tó bá sọ pé ẹsẹ̀ eégún ńhàn ní ńwá
abẹ́rẹ́ lọ.
Whoever announces that the legs of the masquerader are showing is the one who goes
in search of a needle. (Some sights the eyes
must not acknowledge seeing.[65] Compare
931.)

963. Ẹni tó bá yá ìwọ̀fà egbàá, tòun tirẹ̀ ní ńlọ
ata kúnná.
Whoever hires a pawn for only sixpence will
join the pawn in grinding pepper. (Whatever comes too cheaply is sure to work
unsatisfactorily. Compare 4523.)

---

63. The dead are believed to acquire powers beyond
those possessed by the living; one would earn a dead
person's displeasure, therefore, by continuing to regard
him or her as though still among the living.

---

64. Efuji is a legendary Ègbá woman who died from
being thrown by a horse.

65. It is taboo for any part of a masquerader's body
to show. If one notices any part showing, it would be
wise to keep the fact to oneself.

964. Ẹni tó dùbúlẹ̀-ẹ́ ṣe oògùn ìjàkadì tán.
The person who remains prone has perfected the charm for wrestling. (The wise person forestalls problems.)

965. Ẹni tó fi irun dúdú ṣeré, yó fi funfun sin enieléni.
Whoever plays around with his or her black hair will serve others with his or her white hair. (If one wastes one's youth, one spends one's old age struggling for a living.)

966. Ẹni tó fi owó-o rẹ̀ ra ẹsin, kò níí jẹ́ kó ṣe àrìnjẹ́.
Whoever paid his or her own money for a horse will not let it be sacrificed for a good luck charm. (One guards one's treasures jealously.)

967. Ẹni tó gbajúmọ̀ tí kò mọ èèyàn-án kí, òun òbúrẹ́wà egbéra.
The dandy who does not know how to extend greetings to people is no different from a boor. (Good looks without the social graces amount to nothing.)

968. Ẹni tó máa tẹ́ òkú ọ̀pọ̀ló, yó nìí ilé ògbóni tirè lótò.
Whoever wishes to lay a dead toad in state will have to build his own cult shrine separately. (Whoever wishes to do the absurd should not expect the cooperation or approval of others.)

969. Ẹni tó máa yáni lẹ́wù, ti ọrùn-un rẹ̀ là ńwò.
If a person offers to lend one a dress, consider what he or she has on. (One should be discriminating about those from whom to accept favors.)

970. Ẹni tó mi kùkùtẹ́, ara-a rẹ̀ ní ńmì.
The person who shakes a tree stump shakes himself. (Whoever takes on an invincible adversary fashions his or her own defeat.)

971. Ẹni tó mọ ẹtu ní ńkì í ní "òbèjé, ẹlẹ́sẹ̀ owò."
It is someone who knows the duiker intimately who can recite its praise, "spindle-legged duiker." (Only those deeply involved in a profession are versed in its jargon.)[66]

972. Ẹni tó ńṣápẹ́ fún wèrè jó, òun àti wèrè òkan-ùn.
The person who claps for a mad person to dance to is no different from the mad person. (Whoever joins the imbecile's games is himself or herself an imbecile.)

973. Ẹni tó pa kẹ́tẹ́kẹ́tẹ́ yó ru káyá ẹrù.
The person who kills the donkey will carry a heavy burden. (Whoever is careless with his or her resources will pay dearly in the future.)

974. Ẹni tó ránṣẹ́ sí orò-ó bẹ̀wẹ̀ fún àìsùn.
Whoever sends for Orò is contracting for sleeplessness.[67] (Whoever deliberately provokes trouble should be prepared for a difficult time.)

975. Ẹni tó re Ìbàdán tí kò dé ilé Olúyọ̀lé, oko igi ló lọ.
Whoever goes to Ibadan and does not visit Oluyọle's house has merely gone wood gathering.[68] (Whoever misses the principal sight of any place might as well not have visited the place at all.)

976. Ẹni tó rúbọ tí kò gba èèwọ̀, bí ẹni tó fi owó ẹbọ ṣòfò ni.

---

66. It is one of the expectations of the hunting profession that hunters know the conventional praises of the animals they encounter in their trade. The quoted phrase comes from the hunters' praise for the duiker. See Babalọla 88–91; Abraham 199.

67. Orò, the secret cult forbidden to women, is much feared by all.

68. Olúyọ̀lé was an illustrious king of Ibadan in the 1830s.

The person who makes a sacrifice but does not follow the prescribed taboos is just like someone who throws away the money for the sacrifice. (A person who knows the remedy but does not apply it is as badly off as the person who does not know the remedy at all.)

977. Eni tó sọ ẹlẹ́dẹ̀ lékùró, oúnjẹ ló fún un.
The person who throws palm nuts at a pig gives food to it. (One does not douse a fire by throwing oil on it.)

978. Eni tó torí òtútù fi ọmọrí odó yáná ò gbọdọ̀ retí a-ti-jẹyán.
Whoever because of cold weather uses the pestle as kindling to warm himself or herself must not expect to eat pounded yams. (One should not jeopardize one's long-term interests by indulging in immediate gratifications.)

979. Enu àìmẹ́nu, ètè àìmétè, ní m̀mú òràn bá ẹ̀rẹ̀kẹ́.
A mouth that will not stay shut, lips that will not stay closed are what bring trouble to the cheeks. (The words that the mouth and lips allow to escape usually bring the slap to the cheek; a person who cannot keep his or her mouth shut often lands in trouble.)

980. Enu ehoro ò gba ìjánu.
A rabbit's mouth does not accept a leash. (Do not adopt an inappropriate remedy for a problem.)

981. Ẹ̀rẹ̀kẹ́ ni ilé ẹ̀rín.
The cheeks are the home of laughter. (Suit the means to the project.)

982. Ẹ̀rù bíbà ní m̀múni pe àjẹ́ ní ará ire.
It is fear that makes one call witches the good people. (It is wise to curry the favor of fearful or malicious people.)

983. Ẹ̀rù-u hòo kì í wọni lórùn.
"I agree" is not a load that causes one's neck to shrink. (Saying one agrees, even when one does not, spares one a great deal of headache. Compare 734.)

984. Ẹ̀sín alátọ̀sí ò sí lọ́wọ́ òkóbó.
The ridiculing of the person with gonorrhea does not belong with the eunuch. (Do not ridicule a person whose condition is no worse than yours.)

985. Ẹyẹ igbó kì í mọ fífò ọ̀dàn.
The bird of the forest does not know how to fly in the grassland. (In a strange environment, one becomes a dunce.)

986. Ẹyẹ ńwá àtifò, wọ́ ńsọ òkò sí i.
A bird is preparing for flight, and people throw stones at it. (One needs little encouragement to do what one is determined to do anyway; being forced to do what one wishes to do anyway is no punishment.)

F

987. Fi ìjà fún Ọlọ́run jà; fọwọ́ lérán.
Leave the fighting to God; sit back and watch. (Leave those who have injured one to God's judgment and punishment.)

988. Fimí-pamọ́-kí-npa-ọ́ làrùn ńjẹ́.
Hide-me-and-I-will-kill-you is the name a disease answers to. (A concealed disease is a deadly thing.)

Gb

989. "Gba ọmọ fún mi kí nrèdí"; bí ìdí ò bá ṣe-é re ká gbọ́mọ fọ́lọ́mọ.
"Hold my child for me so I may wiggle my buttocks"; if one cannot wiggle one's buttocks, one should return the child to its

mother.[69] (One should not place oneself
in difficulty in order to help others out of
difficulty.)

990. *Gbogbo ẹranko ìgbẹ́ pé, wọn ní àwọn ó
fi ìkokò ṣe aṣípa; nígbà tó gbọ́ inú ẹ̀-ẹ́ dùn;
ṣùgbọ́n nígbà tó ṣe ó bú ṣẹ́kún; wọ́n ní kí ló
dé? Ó ní bóyá wọ́n lè tún ọ̀ràn náà rò kí wọ́n
ní kì í ṣe bẹ́ẹ̀ mọ́.*
All the animals of the forest assembled and
decided to make Hyena their secretary;
Hyena was happy, but a short while later it
burst into tears. Asked what the matter was,
it said perhaps they might reconsider and
reverse themselves. (Some people can be relied upon to find the sad aspect of the most
fortunate event. This is a variant of a proverb with Tortoise as the named character.)

I

991. *Ìbéèrè kì í jẹ́ kí ẹni ó sìnà; ẹni tí kò lè
béèrè ní ńpọ́n ara ẹ̀ lójú.*
Asking [directions] keeps one from losing
one's way; the person who refuses to ask is
responsible for his or her own difficulties.
(One should not be too obstinate or too
proud to seek help when one needs it.)

992. *Ibi tí a bá ńgbé la ti ńgbàwìn; à-rà-àì-
san ni ò sunwọ̀n.*
One's home is a legitimate place to buy
things on credit; what is bad is avoiding payment. (There is nothing wrong in seeking
favors from those close to one; what is bad is
not returning favors.)

993. *Ibi tí a gbé epo sí a kì í ṣo òkò síbẹ̀.*
One does not throw rocks at the place where
one has one's palm oil stored. (One should

always protect one's base or where one's best
interests lie.)

994. *Ibi tí à ńgbé là ńṣe; bí a bá dé ìlú adẹ́tẹ̀ à
di ìkúùkù.*
One should live according to the customs
and fashions of the place one finds oneself
in; if one lands in the city of lepers, one
should make a fist [i.e., conceal one's fin-
gers]. (While in Rome, do as the Romans
do.)

995. *Ibi tí a ti gùn, ibẹ̀ la ti ńrọ̀.*
Where one began one's climb, there one
effects one's descent. (One must not shift
the problems originating in one context to
another, unrelated context.)

996. *Ibi tí a ti ńjẹun bí ikun bí ikun, a kì í
sọ̀rọ̀ bíi kèlèbẹ̀ bíi kèlèbẹ̀ níbẹ̀.*
Where one is eating food like mucus, one
should not speak of matters like phlegm.
(One must be careful not to bring up matters
that are too sensitive for present company.)

997. *Ibi tí o máa sùn lo tẹ́ ọmọ sí.*
It is precisely where you will eventually
have to sleep that you have laid down your
child to sleep. (Said of a person deceiving
himself or herself in the futile hope that
a transparent ruse will work to his or her
advantage.)

998. *Ibi tí òjò-ó ti ńpa igún bọ̀-ọ́ jìnnà; ta ní
rán igún níṣẹ́?*
The vulture has endured the drenching rain
from a great distance, but who sent the vulture on an errand? (If one's choices land one
in difficulty, one should not blame others.)

999. *Ibi tí òjò-ó bá ọjọ́ ní ńpa á sí.*
Wherever the rain catches up with the day,
there it drenches it. (One should do what
one has to do as the opportunities present
themselves.)

---

69. When Yoruba women dance, they like to wiggle
their buttocks, a feat that is difficult when they have
children strapped to their backs, as is the custom.

1000. *Ibi tí oníyònmòntìí ṣubú sí, ibẹ̀ ló ti tà á tán.*
Wherever the *yònmòntì* [food made from beniseed] seller falls, there she has sold all her wares.[70] (It makes no sense to dwell on unrecoverable disasters.)

1001. *Ibi tí oyín gbé ńhó, tí àdó ńhó, ìfun ò dákẹ́ lásán.*
As the bees hum and the small calabash containing charms hums, the intestine does not keep silent.[71] (No matter what other people's preoccupations are, one should not ignore one's own problems.)

1002. *Ìdí òwò ni òwòó gbé tà.*
It is at its home base that a company or trade prospers. (One would be wise to protect one's base.)

1003. *Igún ṣoore ó pá lórí, àkàlà-á ṣoore ó yọ gẹ̀gẹ̀; nítorí ojọ́ mìíràn kẹni ó má ṣe oore bẹ́ẹ́ mọ́.*
The vulture did others a favor and became bald in return; the hornbill did others a favor and developed a goiter in return.[72] (In the future, one should not do those kinds of favors.)

1004. *Igúnnugún ò torí abẹ párí.*
The vulture did not go bald for fear of the razor. (One's actions are not determined by one's fear of any person.)

1005. *Ìgbà ara là ńbúra.*
One swears when it is time to swear. (Everything in its proper time.)

1006. *Igbá là ńpa, a kì í pa awo.*
It is a calabash that one cuts decorative patterns on; one does not cut patterns on china plates. (What is appropriate treatment for one thing may be inappropriate for another.)

1007. *Ìgbà òjò ńlo, ìgbà ẹ̀rùn ńlo, a ní ká dí isà eku kó le; ìgbà wo la óò tó wá peku nàá?*
The rainy season passes, the dry season passes, and the suggestion is that the rat's burrow be sealed up tight; when will the time be ripe to kill the rat? (One must do what needs to be done while there is still time rather than resort to transparent temporizing ruses.)

1008. *Ìgbà tí a bá dóko làárọ̀ ẹni.*
The time of one's arrival on the farm is one's dawn. (People must not be slaves of time but use time to their own advantage. Compare the following entry.)

1009. *Ìgbà tí a bá rẹ́ni lòwúrọ̀ ẹni.*
Whenever one first sees a person, that is that person's morning. (One does what one has to do when it is convenient to do it. Compare the preceding entry.)

1010. *Igbá tó gbédè là ńpè lóṣùwọ̀n.*
It is a calabash that understands one's language that one describes as a measure.[73]

---

70. *Yònmòntì* cannot be scooped up after it has spilled on the ground. The seller taking some to the market hopes to sell it all, but if she falls along the way and spills it, she is left with nothing to sell, just as though she has sold it all.

71. The stomach will rumble to announce its hunger, even as the bees busily attack and the medicine man busily consults his charms.

72. According to a folktale, Vulture agreed to take sacrifices to heaven on behalf of the other creatures when there was a great drought. The sacrifices were accepted, and torrential rain began to fall while Vulture was still on its way back. When it arrived back on earth, no one would offer it shelter from the rain, which beat it so severely that it became bald.

---

73. Traders in such things as grains or flour use calabashes as measures, and they resort to dexterous tricks to control just how much the measure will hold from transaction to transaction: that is, a good measure responds to the owner's wishes.

(One places one's confidence only in those of the same mind.)

1011. *Ìgbín ìbá má mò-ó jẹ ìbá ti kú síjù.*
Had the snail been careless in its foraging, it would have died in the bush. (However disadvantaged one might be, one could still thrive if one took life easy. Compare the following entry.)

1012. *Ìgbín ìbá má mò-ó jẹ kò tó okòó.*
Had the snail been careless in its foraging, it would not [have grown large enough to] be worth 20 cowries. (With caution, one can offset the effects of any handicap. Compare the previous entry.)

1013. *Ìgbín kì í pilẹ̀ aró, àfè ìmòjò kì í pilẹ̀ àràn.*
The snail never embarks on a dyeing trade, and the spotted grass mouse never digs for àràn. (One should stick to habits that are proper for oneself.)[74]

1014. *Igbó lẹranko ńgbé.*
The forest is the home for animals to live in. (Everything in its proper place.)

1015. *Ìgbònwó ti kékeré yọké.*
The elbow develops a hump right from its youth. (Said of a precocious person.)[75]

1016. *Ìjà ní ńpa onítìjú; ogun ní ḿpa alágbára.*
A street fight is the death of a bashful person; warring is the death of a strong man. (One should not court danger or disaster simply to avoid losing face.)

1017. *Ìjó ní ḿbóṣọ, ìjà ní ḿbọ́ ẹwù.*
It is dance that strips one of one's cloth; it is a fight that takes off one's shirt. (Different situations call for different responses.)

1018. *Ikúdú pa ẹsin à ńyọ̀; ó ḿbọ̀ wá pa ọmọ èèyàn.*
An abandoned well kills a horse and we rejoice; it will in time kill a human being. (We should take other people's misfortunes as a reminder that we are not immune to such misfortunes.)

1019. *Ilé ajá là ńwá ìwo lọ?*
Is a dog's house the place to go in search of horns? (One should not bark up the wrong tree.)

1020. *Ilé olóńjẹ là ńdèbìtì àyà sí.*
It is in the home of a person who has food that one sets one's chest like a trap. (People usually position themselves where they imagine there is something to gain.)

1021. *Ilẹ̀ nìjòkò ńjókòó de ìdí.*
It is on the ground that the stool sits to await the buttocks. (One should maintain one's place and not, for example, go out of the house to receive a visitor.)

1022. *Ìlẹ̀kẹ̀ àmúyọ, a kì í sin kádìí tán.*
One does not string decorative beads all around one's waist. (One should not deploy all one's resources at once.)[76]

1023. *Ìloro là ńwọ̀ ká tó wọlé.*
One enters the porch first before one enters the house. (Everything in its proper order.)

1024. *Ìlọ-ọ́ yá; oníbodè Atàdí, wọ́n kó o nílé, wọ́n gbà á lóbìnrin, ọpẹ̀lẹ̀ tó ní òun ó fi wádìí òràn, ajá gbé e, ọmọ ẹ tó lé ajá láti gba ọpẹ̀lẹ̀,*

---

74. *Àràn* is an insect that the field rat eats, but not the spotted grass mouse.

75. The point of the elbow compares to the humpback's affliction, which is here construed as properly an affliction of old age. The elbow, however, always has the point, even when it is quite young.

76. *Ìlẹ̀kẹ̀ àmúyọ* are highlighting beads interspersed with others, not made into whole strings by themselves.

ó yí sí kàṅga; oníbodè Atàdí wá dáhùn ó ní, "Ìlọ-ọ́ yá."

It is time to get out of here; the gatekeeper of Atadi, his home was burglarized; his wife was taken from him; the divining string he was going to use to investigate matters was snatched by a dog; his son who ran after the dog to retrieve the divining string fell into a well. The gatekeeper of Atadi then spoke up and said, "It is time to get out of here." (When a place becomes too hot for a person, he or she should know it is time to get out.)

1025. *Iná èsìsì kì í jóni léèmejì.*
The fire of the stinging tragia plant does not burn a person twice. (One should learn a lesson from the first bad experience.)

1026. *Iná kúkú ni yó ba ọbè ará oko jé.*
Too much fire will ruin the stew of a bushman. (An ignorant person's ignorance will ruin whatever venture he or she embarks on.)

1027. *Iná tó ńléri omi á kù sọnù.*
The fire that challenges water will die off. (It is foolhardy to take on a power one is no match for.)

1028. *Ìpàṣán tí a fi na ìyálé ṁbẹ láàjà fún ìyàwó.*
The whip used on the senior wife is resting on the rafters waiting for the new wife. (Do not assume that the misfortune that befell those who went before will pass you over.)

1029. *Ìròrẹ ò le-è jà ó múlé ti agbọ́n.*
Ìròrẹ cannot fight, so it makes its home close to the wasp's.[77] (If one is weak, one should befriend the strong.)

---

77. *Ìròrẹ* denotes fledglings, but in this case it is apparently some kind of flying insect.

1030. *Isó inú èkú, à-rá-móra.*
The fart within a masquerader's shroud [is] something to be endured. (The insult one cannot escape from, one has to endure.)

1031. *Ìṣeńṣe ewúrẹ́, kágùntàn fiyè sí i.*
The fate that has befallen the goat, the sheep should bear in mind. (One should learn from the fates of others.)

1032. *Iṣu ta iṣu ò ta, òkòòkan là ńwúṣu lébè.*
Whether the yams are large or not, it is one by one that they are extracted from the heap. (There is no task so small or insignificant that it does not deserve care and attention.)

1033. *Ìtórò tó so lóko tí kò fẹhìntì, aféfẹ́ oko ní ńtú u.*
The lemon plant that grows in the bush and does not support itself against something will be uprooted by the forest breeze. (A weak person who has no support will fall victim to puny forces.)

1034. *Ìwò-o ọlọgbọ́n ò jọ ti aṣiwèrè.*
The way a wise person looks at things is different from the way an imbecile does. (A wise person considers matters in a more rational way than an imbecile does.)

1035. *Ìyàwó mi ò sunwọ̀; nítorí ọmọ ni mo ṣe fẹ́ ẹ; ẹni mélòó la ó wìí fún tán?*
"My wife is not good looking, but I married her for the sake of children"; to how many people will one give that explanation? (One should not embark on the endless and futile task of justifying one's decisions to others.)

1036. *Ìyàwó sọ ọ̀rọ̀ kan tán: ó ní ìyálé òun a-bẹnu-funfun-bí-ẹgbodò.*
The junior wife has said what will be her last; she said the senior wife's mouth is as white as the new yam. (Said of people who have done the unthinkable. Compare the following entry.)

1037. Ìyàwó ṣe òràn kan tán; ọkọ è-ẹ́ ṣe òràn-an nkò-jẹ-mọ́.
The wife has done the unpardonable; her husband has adopted an I-will-not-eat-any-longer attitude. (Said of people who have caused unpardonable offense. Compare the preceding entry.)

J

1038. "Já ilé ẹ kí mbá ẹ kọ́ o"; ìtẹ́ èèkàn kan ní ńfúnni.
"Unroof your house and I will help you re-roof it" usually gives one only one bundle of thatching grass. (One relies on other people's promise of help only at one's own risk.)

1039. Jùrù-fẹ̀fẹ̀ jùrù-fẹ̀fẹ̀, ewúrẹ́ wọ ilé àpọn jùrù-fẹ̀fẹ̀; kí làpọ́n rí jẹ tí yó kù sílẹ̀ féwúrẹ́?
Busily wagging its tail, busily wagging its tail, a goat enters a bachelor's house busily wagging its tail; what does a bachelor have to eat whose leftover the goat can have? (One wastes time expecting largesse from a destitute person.)

K

1040. Kàkà kí ọmọdé pàgbà láyò, àgbà a fi ọgbọ́n àgbà gbé e.
Instead of permitting defeat by a child in a game, an elder should resort to elderly wiles. (An elder should save face and protect his standing by all means available.)

1041. Kékeré egbò ní ńgba ewé iyá; àgbà egbò ní ńgba ègbèsì; tilé-wà-tọ̀nà-wá egbò ní ńgba ìgàn aṣọ.
A small sore calls for the balsam tree leaf; a big sore takes an ègbèsì leaf; a huge ulcer calls for a whole bolt of cloth. (Remedies must fit the complaint.)

1042. Kéré-kéré leku ńjawọ; díẹ̀-díẹ̀ leèrà ńbọ́ ìyẹ́.
Bit by bit the rat consumes the leather; gently, gently the ant sloughs its skin. (Use caution in all enterprises.)

1043. Kì í jẹ́ kí etí ẹni di kì í jẹ́ kí inú ẹni dùn.
Whatever keeps one from being deaf to certain things keeps one from being happy. (Learn to turn a deaf ear to certain things for the sake of your peace of mind.)

1044. Kì í ṣe gbogbo ẹni tí ńṣe "Ẹni Ọlọ́run bùn ó bùn mi" là ńfún ní nǹkan.
It is not to every person who says "Whoever has received some bounty from God should give to me" that one gives alms. (One should be judicious as to those to whom one shows kindness.)

1045. Kí ni à ńwọ̀ nínú-u ṣòkòtò mẹ́ta ọ́ọ́dún-rún?
What is there to wear in a pair of trousers bought at three for 300 cowries, or three a penny? (Much ado about a worthless thing.)

1046. Kí ni fìlà yó ṣe lórí ògógó? Ata ni yó ṣi.
What would a cap be doing atop the ògógó mushroom? Pepper will remove it. (Super-fluous adornments make no sense when one goes to battle or engages in strenuous work.)

1047. Kí ni ìyá aláṣọ ńtà tó yọ ẹgba lọ́wọ́? Ewúrẹ́ ńjẹ wúlìnì?
What does the cloth-selling woman have to sell that she carries a whip in her hand? Do goats eat woolen fabrics? (One should not engage in meaningless or unnecessary activities.)

1048. Kíkọ́ ni mímọ̀, òwe àjàpá.[78]
Learning is knowing: Àjàpà's proverb.[78] (To know, one must learn.)

---

78. The anecdote connected with this proverb states that once Àjàpá (Tortoise and Trickster) made a basket so speedily that people asked in astonishment how it was done and Àjàpá responded with the proverb.

1049. *Kò sí aláásàà tí ńta ìgbokú; gbogbo wọn ní ńta oyin.*
There is no snuff seller who will advertise her ware as awful; they all say they are selling honey. (Everybody presents himself or herself in the best light. Compare the following entry.)

1050. *Kò sí alámàlà tí ńsọ pé tòun ò yi; alá-dàlú nìkan ló sòótọ́.*
There is no yam-flower meal seller who will advertise her ware as fluffy; the *àdàlú* seller alone speaks the truth.[79] (One puts the best face on one's own affairs. Compare the preceding entry.)

1051. *Kò sí ẹni tí kò mọ ogbọ́n-ọn ká fẹran sẹ́nu ká wá a tì.*
There is nobody who does not know the trick of putting meat in the mouth and making it disappear. (Nobody is a complete fool.)

1052. *Kókó ló kọ́kọ́ dé orí, tàbí orí ló kọ́kọ́ dé kókó?*
Was it the lump that first got to the head, or the head that first got to the lump? (A chastisement for someone attempting to reverse the order of precedence.)

1053. *Kóńkólóyo: èyí tó ní tèmi.*
A rather small thing: this is enough for me. (However small it is [usually a child], one is glad to have it.)

1054. *Kóró-kóró là ńdá Ifá adití.*
Very loud is the way one consults Ifá for a deaf person. (One should match one's actions to the circumstances. Or, one should err on the side of repetitiousness in cautioning an obstinate person.)

1055. *"Kùbẹ̀rẹ̀, ká roko ìpére." Ó ní èyí tí òún lọ òun òì bọ̀.*
"Kubere, let us go to the bush where small snails are picked." He said the last such trip he went on, he has not returned from. (When one has not recovered from the consequences of a venture, one is not ready to embark on another.)

L

1056. *Lójú òpè, bí-i kọ́logbọ́n dàbí òle.*
As far as the dunce is concerned, the wise person should be shiftless. (The worthless person always wishes others were equally worthless.)

M

1057. *"Máa jẹ́ ǹsọ́" lòyá fi ńju ẹmọ́ lọ.*
"Go on feeding" is what makes the cane rat fatter than the Tullberg's rat.[80] (Excessive consideration for others can be disadvantageous.)

1058. *"Màá kó ẹrú, màá kó ẹrù" là ńbá lọ sógun; ọ̀nà lẹnìkẹta ńbáni.*
"I will capture slaves and I will capture loot" are what one has in mind on departure for a war; the third comes upon one only along the way.[81] (Too often one is so preoccupied with the good aspects of a proposition that the bad aspects sneak up on one.)

1059. *Màjèsín dóbò àkọ́kọ́, ó sáré yọ okó síta, ó ní Olúwa-á ṣeun.*
The tender youth has sex for the first time ever, pulls out his penis prematurely, and

---

79. *Àdàlú* is a meal made with black-eyed peas. A number of condiments go into it: hence the name, which means something like "a concoction of various ingredients."

80. The Tullberg's rat is supposed to have told the cane rat to eat first of their common food. The latter fed rather well, leaving little for the former to eat.

81. The third thing that surprises the soldier along the way is death.

says "God be praised!" (A novice knows not how to relish good things.)

1060. *Mójú-kúrò nílé ayé gbà; gbogbo òrò kó ló séé bínú sí.*
Judicious forbearance is the wise approach to the world; not every matter deserves anger. (The best way to live is to ignore petty annoyances.)

N

1061. *Ní ìlú tí a ò ti fé eyelé, adìe yóò sòwón níbè.*
In a town that does not welcome pigeons, chickens will be very scarce. (Onerous things will not be countenanced where easy obligations are not.[82] See the following variant.)

1062. *Ní ìlú tí a ò ti fé eyelé, tí a ò fé adìe, irú eye wo ní yóò jí wòn lójú orun?*
In a town that does not tolerate pigeons and does not tolerate chickens, what sort of bird will awaken them from sleep? (A person who will not be pleased by anything will simply have to do without everything. See also 1061.)

1063. *Ní inú Ifá ni Fá-túmò-ó wà.*
It is within Ifá that one finds Fátúmò.[83] (Every problem bears the seeds to its own solution.)

1064. *"Níbo ló gbé wà?" nìyájú ekùn.*
"Where is it?" is a great insult to the leopard. (One should be smart enough to hide one's ignorance about things one should know.)[84]

1065. *Nígbàtí owó ò tí ì gbón lojú nsepin.*
It is when the hands have not learned wisdom that the eyes ooze matter. (A wise person will know how to manage and conceal his shortcomings.)

1066. *Nítorí adití lòjó fi nsú; nítorí afójú ló se nkù.*
It is for the benefit of deaf people that rain clouds gather; it is for the benefit of the blind that thunder rumbles. (The wise person should be able to read portents and take precautions.)

1067. *Nítorí èèyàn la se nní owó òtún; òsì là bá lò.*
It is on account of people that one has a right hand; one could do with only a left hand otherwise. (One must learn the grace that is appropriate for decent company.)[85]

1068. *Nítorí-i ká lè ríbi gbé e la se nse oyàn sódó.*
It is in order to have a means of lifting it that one carves breasts [handles] on the mortar. (One should anticipate problems and prepare solutions for them.)

O

1069. *Ó di kan-nu-rin kan-nu-rin, agogo Ògúntólú.*
All one hears is noise without pattern, like that of Ògúntólú's bell. (The statements being made are senseless.)[86]

---

82. The logic is that chickens are far easier to care for than pigeons.

83. Fátúmò is a proper name that means "Ifá [the Oracle] interprets."

84. The leopard is so self-important that it will take offense if anybody should ask where it was, or which it was, among other animals.

85. People eat with with the right hand and use only the left hand for dirty jobs. The left hand has consequently come to be associated with filthiness, disrespect, and so forth. One would not, for example, offer something with the left hand to a person one respects.

86. The reference to Ògúntólú, a proper name, is obscure.

1070. *O fẹ́ẹ́ joyè o ní o-ò ní-í jà.*
You aspire to taking a chieftaincy title, and you say you will not get into a fight. (It is self-deceit to wish for something without being prepared for the struggle that getting it demands.)

1071. *O fi awọ ẹkùn ṣẹbo àìkú; ẹkùn ìbá má kùú ìwọ ìbá rawọ è ṣoògùn?*
You use a leopard's skin as an ingredient for medicine to hold off death; had the leopard not died, would you have had access to its hide for the medicine? (One should not chase impossible dreams.)

1072. *O jó nÍfọ́n Ifọ́n tú; o jó lÉjìgbò Èjìgbó fàya bí aṣọ; o wá dé Ìlá Ọ̀ràngún ò ǹkàndí; gbogbo ìlú òrìṣà ni wọ́n ní kí o máa bàjẹ́ kiri?*
You danced at Ífọ́n town and Ífọ́n became desolate; you danced at Èjìgbò and Èjìgbò was split asunder like a rag; now you came to Ìlá Ọ̀ràngún and you commenced to wiggle your buttocks; were you given a mission to ruin all towns associated with gods?[87] (A person who has the reputation for causing disasters should not be given freedom of action anywhere.)

1073. *O kò bá ìsín máwo, o ò bá ìrókò mulè; abẹ́rẹ́ ẹ-ẹ́ bọ́ sómi o ní o ó yọ ọ́.*
You made no secret pact with minnows, and you entered into no covenant with the ìrókò tree, yet when your needle dropped into the stream, you proposed to retrieve it. (Unless one has superhuman powers, one should not attempt the impossible. The following two entries are variants.)

1074. *O kò bá òkun máwo, o ò bá ọ̀sà mulè; abẹ́rẹ́ ẹ-ẹ́ bọ́ sódò o ní o ó yọ ọ́.*
You made no secret pact with the lagoon, and you entered into no covenant with the ocean, yet when your needle dropped into the stream, you proposed to retrieve it. (Unless one has extraordinary means, one should not attempt the impossible. This and the following entry are variants of the foregoing one.)

1075. *O kò bá Ọya máwo, o ò bá Ògún mulè; abẹ́rẹ́ ẹ-ẹ́ bọ́ sódò o ní o ó yọ ọ́.*
You made no secret pact with Ọya, and you made no covenant with Ògún,[88] yet your neddle dropped into the river and you proposed to find it. (One should not embark on missions for which one has not made adequate preparations. Compare the preceding two entries.)

1076. *O kò lu òmìrán lóru, ò ńlù ú lósàn-án.*
You did not hit the giant at night, but you hit him in daylight. (One should court trouble only if and when one has some cover.)

1077. *O kò wọ bàtà nínú ẹgún ò ńsáré; o lágbára màlúù?*
You wear no shoes on the thorny path and yet you are running; do you have a cow's [hoof] power? (Unless one is well fortified, one should not court danger.)

1078. *O kò-ì mú ẹrú, o ní Àdó ni ò ó tà á fún.*
You have not captured a slave, but you are already saying you will sell him or her only to an Àdó [Benin City] person. (One should not use a commodity before one has it.)

1079. *O ló-o fẹ́ẹ́ jọba o ní o-ò nìí ṣÒgbóni, o-ò níí pé lóyè.*
You propose to become a king, but you refuse to join the Ògbóni society; you will not last long on the throne. (Whoever

---

87. All the towns mentioned are associated with important gods and cults.

88. Ọya is the goddess of rivers and seas, and Ògún is the god of metals.

wishes to prosper must observe the conditions for prosperity.)[89]

1080. *Ò ḿbẹ oníṣègùn, o ò bẹ asínwín; bí oníṣègùn-ún ṣe tí asínwín ò gbà ńkọ́?*
You are pleading with the medicine man but not with the demented person; what if the medicine man produces the medicine and the demented person refuses it? (When two steps are required to accomplish a purpose, one should not take one and slight the other.)

1081. *"Ó ḿbọ̀, ó ḿbọ̀!" la fi ńdẹ́rù ba ọmọdé; bó bá dé tán èrù a tán.*
"It's coming! It's coming!" is what one says to frighten a child; after it has arrived it loses all its terror. (Looming problems often cause consternation out of all proportion to their real damaging force. Compare 3268.)

1082. *O ní kí ará ọ̀run ṣe oore fún ọ, bẹ́ẹ̀ni o rí ẹni tí eégún ńlé, tó fá lóbẹ̀ lá.*
You pray to the being from heaven to grant you a boon, yet you can see the person who is being chased by the masquerader and whose stew the masquerader has consumed. (One should not expect to receive better treatment from a person who is known to be vicious to others.)[90]

1083. *Ó ńti ilé bọ̀ kò ra ẹgbẹ; ó dé oko tán ó ní ẹgbẹ ni oníkú èkọ.*
Leaving home, he did not purchase dried meat; after arriving on the farm, he says dried meat is the indispensable thing to eat corn loaf with. (One should make provisions against one's future needs.)

1084. *O rí etí adẹ́tẹ̀ o fi san okòó; kò nípọn tó ni, tàbí kò rè dèdè tọ́?*
You see a leper's ears and you value them at 20 cowries; do they lack sufficient thickness or are they not red enough? (Said of someone who applies the wrong value to things.)

1085. *O rí ẹsè-ẹ wèrè o ò bù ú ṣoògùn; níbo lo ti máa rí tologbọ́n?*
You see the footprint of an imbecile and you do not take soil from it to make a charm; where will you find the footprint of a wise person?[91] (One should take advantage of the weak and vulnerable, because one will not be able to take advantage of the strong.)

1086. *O rojọ́ láàárọ̀ o ò jàre, ó dalẹ́ o ní kọ́ba dúró gbọ́ tẹnu ẹ; ohun tó o wí láàárọ̀ náà kọ́ lo máa wí lálẹ́?*
You state your case in the morning and are not vindicated, yet at nightfall you plead with the king to delay a bit and listen to what you have to say; isn't what you have to say in the evening the same thing you said in the morning? (Repeated stating will not make a bad case a good one.)

1087. *O sá fún ikú, o bọ́ sí àkọ̀ idà.*
You run from death and seek refuge in a scabbard. (Said of a person who has got into a worse predicament than the one he or she was fleeing from.)

1088. *"Ó ṣe mí rí"; ògbó adìẹ rí àwòdì sá.*
"I have experienced it before"; a grown chicken flees at the sight of a kite. (One learns to run from danger once one has recognized it as such.)

---

89. Aspirants to chieftaincy titles often engage in bitter competition.

90. The detail about the *egúngún* eating the poor person's stew suggests that the person praying to him as a being from heaven should have realized that the stew-eating figure was no heavenly being.

---

91. Soil taken from a person's footprints is supposed to be a particularly good ingredient for making potent and usually evil charms against that person.

1089. *Ó ti ojú orun wá ó ńfọ ẹnà; ó ní "ẹ jẹ́ ká máa ji ní mẹ́mu-mẹ́mu."*
He woke up from sleep and spoke in scrambled language; he said, "Let us wake it in moos." (An ignorant person will always make stupid suggestions. See 1848.)

1090. *O wà láyé, mo wà láàye, ò ḿbi mí bí ọ̀rún ṣe rí.*
You are on earth [alive] and I am on earth, and yet you ask me what heaven is like. (Said of a person seeking information from someone in no better position to know than the seeker.)

1091. *Ó yẹ kí eégún mọ ẹni tó mú àgbò so.*
It is proper that the masquerader know who tethered the ram. (One should acknowledge those who have done one some favor.)[92]

1092. *Obìnrin ò gbé ibi tó máa rọ̀ ọ́ lọ́rùn.*
A woman never remains where her wellbeing rests. (Women seldom know until it is too late which home would best suit them.)

1093. *Òbò ò ṣéé ṣe àlejò.*
The vagina is not a thing for showing hospitality. (Good things are not good for all purposes.)

1094. *Odídẹrẹ́ dawo, ìkó ìdí è-ẹ́ dògbẹ̀rì.*
The parrot becomes fully initiated into the secrets; his tail feather becomes a noninitiate. (The person being propped up achieves great glory, but his backer loses his standing.)[93]

1095. *Odó iyán ò jẹ́ gún ẹlú; odó ẹlú ò jẹ́ gúnyán; àtẹ tá-a fi ńpàtẹ ìlẹ̀kẹ̀, a ò jẹ́ fi pàtẹ ọ̀rúnlá.*

The mortar used for pounding yams will not do for pounding indigo leaves; the mortar for pounding indigo leaves will not do for yams; the tray on which beads are displayed for sale will not do for displaying dried okro. (Each object has its proper uses.)

1096. *Òdú kì í ṣe àìmọ̀ olóko.*
The *òdú* vegetable is not something the farmer does not know. (An indication that a matter under discussion is not such a secret after all.)

1097. *Ogún kì í pọ̀ ká pín fún aládùúgbò.*
The inheritance is never so abundant that one shares it with neighbors. (However abundantly one is blessed, one should manage one's resources wisely.)

1098. *Ogún mbókòó? Òwe aṣiwèrè.*
Twenty or a score? An imbecile's puzzle. (Trust an imbecile to pose stupid questions.)

1099. *Ohùn àgbà: bí kò ta ìgún, a ta èbù.*
An elder's voice: if it does not yield yams ready for pounding [for food], it will yield yam seedlings ready for planting. (There is some value in whatever comes out of an elder's mouth.)

1100. *Ohun tí a bá pàdé ò jọ ohun tí a rí tẹ́lẹ̀.*
That which one comes upon is nothing to compare with what one has always had. (No new friend or find can be as valuable as the one you have had for some time.)

1101. *Ohun tí a ni la fi ńkẹ́ ọmọ ẹni.*
It is what one has that one uses to spoil one's child. (One should not go beyond one's means simply to make a good impression on others.)

1102. *Ohun tí a ò rí rí lèèwọ̀ ojú.*
It is something one has never seen before that is taboo for the eyes. (Whatever one has

---

92. The tethered ram would be an offering to the masquerader.

93. The parrot's colorful tail feather (*ìkó*) is the bird's main attraction, the chief reason why it is valued.

encountered before cannot be too much to accommodate.)

1103. *Ohun tí a ṣe nílé àna eni, "Ojú ńtì mí" kúrò níbè.*
What one does in the home of one's parents-in-law leaves no room for "I am bashful." (One must not be reticent in doing whatever one must do.)[94]

1104. *Ohun tí kò jé káṣo pé méjì ni ò jé kó dú.*
The same thing that keeps one from having more than one item of clothing also keeps that one from getting blackened by dirt. (Misfortune teaches fortitude; scarcity teaches thrift. Compare 1106.)

1105. *Ohun tí kò jé kí oko pò ni ò jé kó mó.*
Whatever limits the size of a farm is the same thing that makes it overgrown with weeds. (A basic defect will manifest itself in sundry ways. The sentiment here is the opposite of that of the preceding proverb.)

1106. *Ohun tó fóni lójú ló ńjúwe ònà fúnni.*
Whatever deprives one of sight is the same thing that shows one the way. (Misfortune teaches those it afflicts how to cope with it. Compare 1104.)

1107. *Ohun tó jo oun la fi ńwé ohun; èpo èpà ló jo ité èlíri.*
It is what resembles a thing that one compares it with; peanut shells are most like the nest of the rodent *èlíri*. (One should observe propriety in dealing with respectable people.)

1108. *Ohun tó ní òun óò béni lórí, bó bá síni ní filà, ká dúpé.*

If a thing that vows to decapitate one only knocks off one's hat, one should be thankful. (If misfortune turns out to be far milder than expected, one should give thanks. Compare the following entry.)

1109. *Ohun tó ní òun óò ṣeni lérú, tó wá ṣeni níwòfà, ká gbà á.*
If whatever promised to make one a slave only makes one a pawn, one should accept one's fate. (One should gratefully accept a fate that turns out more merciful than it might have been. Compare the preceding entry.)

1110. *Ohun-a-lè-ṣe, tó forí ṣo àpò òwú; wón ní ṣe bó rí yangí nílè, ó ní "Ohun a bá lè ṣe là ńlérí sí."*
Ohunalèṣe dashes his head against a sack of cotton wool; people asked if he did not see the rock nearby; he replied, "One should vow to do only what one can safely accomplish." (Attempt only feats that will cause no headache.)[95]

1111. *Òjò òì dá a ní kò tó tàná.*
It has not yet stopped raining, and some observe that todays's rainfall is not as much as yesterday's. (One should not arrive at conclusions until one has all the facts.)

1112. *Òjòwú ò já gèlè; kooro ló lè já.*
The jealous woman does not snatch her headgear off; all she can do is threaten a fight. (Some people are all mouth and no action.)[96]

---

94. The necessity to impress parents-in-law often mandates behavior one would not contemplate elsewhere and in other circumstances.

95. The name Ohunalèṣe (*Ohun-a-lè-ṣe*) means "That which one can accomplish."

96. When a woman makes ready for a fight, she removes her headgear and ties it around her waist. A woman who merely crowds her adversary (*já kooro sí i*) is not ready to fight.

1113. *Òjòwú ò léran láyà.*
The jealous woman lacks flesh on her chest.
(Excessive jealousy eats up the jealous.)

1114. *Ojú àwo làwó fi ńgba ọbẹ̀.*
It is on its face that a plate accepts soup.
(One should not delegate matters crucial to
oneself to others.)

1115. *Ojú kan làdá ńní.*
A cutlass has only one edge. (One should
concentrate on one matter at a time.)

1116. *Ojú kì í pọ́nni ká fi pọ́nlẹ̀.*
One should not because of one's suffering try honing one's eyes on the ground.[97]
(Difficulties should not lead one to foolish
behavior.)

1117. *Ojú kì í pọ́nni ká mu ìsápá; òùngbẹ kì í
gbẹni ká mu ẹ̀jẹ̀.*
One is never so desperate that one drinks
red sorrel juice; one is never so thirsty that
one drinks blood. (Desperation must never
push one beyond the bounds of acceptable
behavior.)

1118. *Ojú kì í ti àgbà lóru; jagun a lọ́sọ̀ọ̀
gọ́ńgọ́.*
An elderly person does not become embarrassed under cover of darkness; the stalwart
squats nonchalantly.[98] (One can do whatever
one pleases when no eyes are watching.)

1119. *Ojú kì í ti eégún kó má mọ̀nà ìgbàlẹ̀.*
A masquerader is never so shamed that
he cannot find his way to the secret grove.

---

97. The phrase *ojú pípọ́n*, from which the proverbs
in this series are formulated, means "red eyes," supposedly the sign of suffering. *Pọ́n* can mean both "to be
red" and "to hone." Hence the wordplay in this proverb.

98. A reference to squatting in a roadside bush at
night to defecate.

(One cannot become so shamed abroad that
one cannot return to the embrace of one's
home.)

1120. *Ojú la fi m̀mọ àìsí epo; ẹnu la fi m̀mọ
àìsíyọ̀; ọbẹ̀ tí ò bá lépo nínú òkèèrè la ti m̀mọ̀
ọ́.*
It is with the eyes that one tells the absence
of palm oil; it is with the mouth that one determines the absence of salt; if a stew lacks
oil, it is the eyes that will tell. (In some matters the evidence of the eyes is enough to
reveal all one needs to know.)

1121. *Ojú tó rò nirorẹ́ ńsọ.*
Pimples attack only faces that are delicate.
(Other people always take advantage of
gentle people.)

1122. *"Òkè ìhín ò jẹ́ ká rí tòún" ò ṣéé pa lówe
nílé àna eni.*
"The nearer hill kept me from seeing the
farther one" is not a proverb to use in one's
parents-in-law's home. (There are some
obligations one cannot sidestep with flippant
excuses.)

1123. *Okó ilé kì í jọ obìnrin lójú, àfi bó bá dó
tìta.*
The penis at home never impresses the
woman, unless she fucks one outside the
home. (One hardly ever appreciates what
one has until one has flirted with, and has
been disappointed by, alternatives.)

1124. *Oko kì í jẹ́ ti baba àti tọmọ kó má nìí
àlà.*
Farms do not, by virtue of belonging to a
father and his son, lack boundaries. (Even
close relatives may benefit from good
fences.)

1125. *Oko mímọ́ ṣe-é ro; ọ̀nà mímọ́ dùn-ún
tọ̀; gbogbo ìyàwó dùn-ún gbàbálé; aṣọ ìgbà-á
ṣe-é yọ.*

A clean farm is a pleasure to weed; a clean-swept path is a pleasure to tread; all new wives are a pleasure to deflower; the new fashionable cloth of the season is a pleasure to wear. (Everybody loves performing the most pleasant of chores.)

1126. *Okotorobo-ó tùyẹ́ sílẹ̀ ọmọ titún ńgbe jó; ó ní ó rọ òun lórùn lòún tu ú?*
Okotorobo, a bird, casts away a feather, and a young chick picks it up to dance with; the one who shed the feathers asks, would I have discarded it if it was not a nuisance? (One should be careful before taking over things that others have rejected.)

1127. *Okotorobo-ó yé eyin sílẹ̀, àdàbà ńgarùn wo eyin ẹléyin.*
Okotorobo the bird lays an egg, and the turtledove stretches its neck to inspect the egg that does not belong to it. (One should mind one's own business.)

1128. *Òkú ẹran kì í ti ajá lójú.*
A dog is never too squeamish to eat a carcass. (If one's means are limited, one cannot be too choosy.)

1129. *Olè tó gbé fèrè ọba ò róhun gbé.*
The thief who stole the king's bugle could find nothing to steal. (There can be no rational explanation for acts of utter senselessness.)

1130. *Olé tó jí kàkàkí: níbo ni yó ti fọn ọ́n?*
A thief who stole a bugle: where will he blow it? (One should not waste one's efforts chasing something one can never use.[99] Compare 1766.)

1131. *Olóhun kì í rí ohun ẹ̀ kó pè é lórò.*
The owner will not see what he owns and

call it a fearful abomination. (One cannot be afraid of what one owns.)

1132. *Olóhun-ún dolè; "Gbà bù jẹ́" dolóhun.*
The owner becomes a thief; "Take this and eat" becomes the owner. (The tables are turned: the rightful owner is displaced by a usurper.)

1133. *Olóògùn ní ńṣe bí a-láigbọ́-mòràn; bí ogun ó bàá wọlú ọlogbọ́n là ńfọrò lọ.*
The medicine man behaves like a person impervious to wise counsel; if war threatens a town, the person to consult for counsel is the sage. (Trust in wisdom rather than in magical charms.)

1134. *Olórìṣà tó da kiriyó: ọjọ́ tó gbọ́ dùrù orí ijó lẹsẹ̀-ẹ́ kán sí.*
The idol worshiper who became a Christian: the day he first heard the organ play, he lost his legs dancing. (Old habits die hard.)[100]

1135. *Olòsì ọmọ ní ńfọwọ́ òsì júwe ilé-e baba-a ẹ̀.*
It is a worthless child that points the way to his father's house with his left-hand fingers. (One should show proper regard for one's own patrimony.)

1136. *Olóúnje-ẹ́ tó-ó bá kú.*
Someone who has food is worth dying with. (Food is a good enough reason to cast one's lot with another person.)

1137. *Olówe lalásẹ̀ òrò.*
A person who knows proverbs has the last word in a dispute. (There is no authority like proverbial authority.)

---

99. A *kàkàkí* bugle was used exclusively to announce the presence of a king.

100. Traditional worship is done to drumming and dancing, whereas the music in church is not for dancing.

1138. *Olówó á wá; aláwìn á wá; ìlú tí à ǹgbé la gbé ńgbàwìn; à-rà-àì-san ni ò súnwòn.*
Those who have money will come, and those who will buy on credit will come; it is in one's town that one buys on credit; failure to pay up eventually is what is bad. (There is nothing bad about buying on credit as long as one eventually pays.)

1139. *Olówó pèlù o ò jó; ojó wo lo máa rówó pe tìe?*
A rich person engages a dance band and you do not dance; when will you have the money to hire your own band? (One should take advantage of every opportunity to supply one's deficiencies.)

1140. *Òmùgò èèyàn ni ḿbóbìnrin mulè; ojó tóbìnrín bá mawo lawó bàjé.*
Only a foolish person enters into a secret pact with a woman; the day a woman knows a cult mystery is the day it is exploded. (Never trust a woman.)

1141. *Òmùgò ní ńgbé ígunnu; ologbón ní ńgbowó.*
It is the fool that wears the Nupe masquerade;[101] it is the wise person that collects the monetary gifts. (The wise person chooses the most profitable option available.)

1142. *Onígègé filèkè dópò; adámú fi sàárà san egbèta.*
The goitered person sets a low price on beads; the person with a blocked nose repays 6,000 cowries with alms. (One usually sets little value on what one cannot use.)

1143. *Onígi ní ńfigi è dópò.*
It is the firewood seller who sets a low price for his wares. (People take their cue from the owner of a thing in placing a value on it. Compare the following entry.)

1144. *Onígbá ní ńpe igbá è ní àìkàrágbá káyé tó fi kólè.*
It is the owner of the calabash who first called it a broken piece of gourd before the world used it for scooping dirt. (If one does not value what one has, other people will value it even less. Compare the preceding entry.)

1145. *Onígbèsè tí ńpa àpatà eyelé.*
The habitual debtor butchers a pigeon for sale. (The debtor is desperate, because there is not much meat to a pigeon, and few people eat pigeons anyway.)

1146. *Oníṣègùn tó so pé díè ò tó òun, òfo ni yó fowó mú.*
The medicine man who is dissatisfied with a modest payment will wind up with nothing. (One should not demand too much from people who are in dire straights.)

1147. *Ooré pé, aṣiwèrè-é gbàgbé.*
The favor is long past; the imbecile forgets. (Only an imbecile forgets a favor even long after it was done.)

1148. *Oòrùn kì í je iṣu àgbà kó má mobè.*
An elder does not lose his yams to the sun without knowing where the event happened. (A grown-up person should know where he went wrong and make amends accordingly.)

1149. *Oòrùn kì í là kínú bí olóko.*
The sun does not shine and cause displeasure in the farmer. (Everybody welcomes an auspicious event. See also 1164.)

1150. *Orí òkéré popo láwo; bí a wí fómo eni a gbóràn.*
The squirrel's head sits in a plate like a lump; if one counsels one's child, it should listen. (Refusal to listen to counsel leads to disaster.)

---

101. On Nupe people, see note 15 to 1371.

1151. *Orí tí yó jẹ igún kì í gbọ́; bí wọ́n fun ládìẹ kò níí gbà.*
The head that is destined to eat a vulture cannot be saved; if a chicken is offered to it, it will refuse. (The person destined to suffer will manage to succumb to the suffering despite efforts by others to save him or her.)

1152. *Orí tó kọ ẹrù, owó ní ńnáni.*
A head that refuses [to carry] loads will cost its owner some money. (It costs money to have others do what one refuses to do for oneself.)

1153. *Orin tí ò ṣoro-ó dá kì í ṣòro-ó gbè; bí ó bá ní "héééé," à ní "hááádá."*
A song that is not difficult to lead is not difficult to follow; if the leader sings "haaaay," one responds "haaaah." (One expends on a task only the amount of effort commensurate with it.)

1154. *Orín yí, ìlù-ú yí padà.*
The song changes, and the drumming changes to suit. (One should match one's behavior to one's circumstances.)

1155. *Òrìṣà tó ní tÒgún kì í ṣe ọ̀nà ò ní rí ńnkan jẹ lásìkò tó fẹ́.*
The god that says matters pertaining to Ògún are irrelevant will not find anything to eat when he or she wishes. (Humor those in a position to punish you.)

1156. *Òṣùpá lé a ní kò gún; ẹni tọ́wọ́ ẹ̀-ẹ́ bá to kó tún un ṣe.*
The moon appears, and people say it is not straight; whoever can reach it, let him go and right it. (It is pointless to complain about things one can do nothing about.)

1157. *Òtòṣì ò gbọ́ tìṣẹ́ ẹ̀ ó ní ogún kó àparò; ọdẹ rorò.*
The destitute person does not look to repair his fortune; he says the partridge has been captured in a war, for the hunter is merciless. (Rather than deal with their own problems, people sometimes gloat over the troubles of others.)[102]

1158. *Owó kì í lóye kómọ kú sẹ́rú.*
If the amount of money is known, a child cannot die in slavery.[103] (One does not endure adverse conditions when one is capable of the effort to escape them. The following proverb is something of a variant.)

1159. *Owó kì í yéye kómọ ó kú.*
If money is available in abundance, a child does not die. (One should spare no expenses to take care of one's children or one's affairs. See the previous entry.)

1160. *Owó la fi ńfiná owó; bí egbèrún bá so lókè, igbió la fi ńká a.*
Money is what one uses to kindle the fire for money; if 1,000 cowries grow from the branches above, one uses 200 cowries to pluck them. (Without some expenditure there can be no profit.)

1161. *Owó la fi ńlògbà; ọgbọ́n la fi ńgbélé ayé.*
It is with money that we secure pleasures; it is with wisdom that one secures a good life. (Riches are desirable, but wisdom is more valuable.)

1162. *Owó ní ńpa ọjà òmòràn.*
It is money that brings a knowing person's trading to a conclusion. (A wise trader knows how to use his money to make his offer successful.)

---

102. The expression *ogun-ún kó,* "to be carried off or captured in a war," means to be in serious trouble.
103. The reference is to the practice of pawning oneself or a relative for a loan. If the amount is not infinity, the redemption of the pawn cannot be an insurmountable problem.

1163. *Owó tómọdé bá kókọ́ ní, àkàrà ní ńfi-í rà.*
The first money a youth comes into he spends on bean fritters. (Young people seldom know how to manage wealth.)

1164. *Òwú kì í là kínú bí olóko.*
The cotton seed does not open and thus anger the farmer. (The success of a venture does not make one angry. See 1149.)

1165. *Owú pani ju kùmmọ̀.*
Jealousy kills more surely than a cudgel. (Jealousy is a dangerous thing.)

1166. *Òyìnbó Òkè Eléérú, ó ṣubú sóde Alóba; kùmmọ ni yó gbe dìde.*
The white man from Òkè Elérú; he collapses in front of Alóba's compound; cudgels will help him up. (A person who becomes disabled where he is at his enemy's mercy can expect rough handling.)[104]

Ọ

1167. *Òbẹ ńwólé ara ẹ̀ ó ní òún ńba àkọ̀ jé.*
The knife is destroying its own home; it says it is ruining the sheath. (Said of people whose actions will hurt them more than they will hurt other people. Compare 361.)

1168. *Ọbẹ̀ tí baálé kì í jẹ, ìyálé ilé kì í sè é.*
The sort of stew the man of the house will not eat, the woman of the house should not cook. (One should not do what one knows one's comrades hate.)

1169. *Òdè ọmọ ńfi ìdò ṣeré.*
An idiot child plays with *ìdò* flowers. (A simpleton does not know the value of anything.)

---

104. The suggestion is that the white man had earned the enmity of a certain person named Alóba.

1170. *Ọ̀dẹ̀dẹ̀ ò gba òró, àfi abẹ́ ọdán.*
The porch does not accommodate standing people; only the shade of the *ọdán* [banyan tree] does. (An invitation to repair to another place outside other people's earshot to discuss confidential matters.)

1171. *Ọ̀fàfà fohùn ṣakin.*
The tree bear wins renown with its voice. (The loud person attracts attention.)

1172. *Ọgbọ́n a-dákọ-kéré ò tó ti a-yọwó-má-rà.*
The cunning of the person who skimps on the measure of her corn meal is not as great as that of the would-be purchaser who refuses to buy. (One does not have to patronize a dishonest trader.)

1173. *Ọgbọ́n dùn-ún gbọ́n; ìmọ́ dùn-ún mọ̀.*
Wisdom is a good thing to have; knowledge is a good thing to have. (Always seek wisdom and knowledge.)

1174. *Ọgbọ́n ju agbára.*
Wisdom is greater than strength. (Always prefer wisdom to strength.)

1175. *Ọgbọ́n kì í tán.*
Wisdom is never used up. (There will always be a place and some use for wisdom.)

1176. *Ọgbọ́n la fi ńgbé ayé.*
One needs wisdom to live in this world. (Wisdom is indispensable.)

1177. *Ọgbọ́n lajá fi ńpa ìkokò bọ Ifá.*
It is cunning that the dog employs in order to sacrifice a wolf to Ifá. (A cunning person can get the better of people far more powerful than he.)

1178. *Ọgbọ́n ní ńṣégun; ìmọ̀ràn ní ńṣẹ́ ètẹ̀.*
Cunning wins battles; knowledge defeats plots. (Cunning and knowledge will help one prevail.)

1179. Ọgbọ́n ọlọgbọ́n la fi ńsọgbọ́n; ìmọ̀ràn ẹnìkan ò tọ́ bọ̀rọ̀.
One learns wisdom from other people's wisdom; one person's knowledge does not amount to anything. (Wisdom and knowledge are best shared.)

1180. Ọgbọ́n ọlọgbọ́n ò jẹ́ ká pe àgbà ní wèrè.
Other people's wisdom saves the elder from being called a lunatic. (The person who can learn from others will avoid a lot of embarrassment.)

1181. Ọgbọ́n tí ahún gbọ́n, èhìn ni yó máa tọ ti ìgbín.
The cunning of the tortoise will always rank behind that of the snail. (Some people cannot hope to be more cunning than certain others.)

1182. Ọgbọ́n tí ọ̀pọ̀ló fi pa ẹfọ̀n ló fi ńjẹ ẹ́.
The same cunning with which the toad killed the buffalo will show it how to eat the prey. (If a person has proved himself capable of doing the impossible, one should not doubt that he can accomplish another impossibility.)

1183. Ogbọọgbọ́n làgbàlagbà-á fi ńsá fún ẹranlá.
It is with cunning that a grown man runs away from a bull. (A grown person should know how to avoid disaster without losing face.)

1184. Ọjọ́ eré là ńjiyàn ohun.
It is on a playful occasion that one argues about matters. (Arguments conducted in jest conceal some serious import.)

1185. Ọjọ́ tí ìlù-ú bá ńlu onílù, iṣẹ́ mìíràn-án yá.
The day the drum begins to beat the drummer is the day he should seek another employment. (One should know when to abandon an unprofitable proposition.)

1186. Ọjọ́ tí olówó ńṣẹbọ ni à-wà-jẹ-wà-mu ìwòfà.
The day the person who did the hiring makes a sacrifice is the day the hired hand eats and drinks. (The poor will eat when the rich provide a feast.)

1187. Ọ̀kéré ńsunkún agbádá; èyí tí àjàò-ó dá lẹ́sìí kí ló fi ṣe? Ṣebí igi ló fi ńgùn.
The squirrel weeps for want of a stately garment; the garment the àjàò bird made last year, what did it do with it? Was it not tree climbing it used the garment for? (It is silly to hanker for something one cannot use anyway.)

1188. Ọkọ́ ọlọ́kọ́ la fi ńgbón èkìtì.
It is other people's hoe that one uses to clear a mound of rubbish. (One is usually more respectful of one's own property than that of others.)

1189. Ọ̀kọ̀ọ̀kan là ńyọ ẹsẹ̀ lábàtà.
One at a time is how one extricates one's feet from a mire. (The best way to approach a problem is systematically. Compare 1870. The following entry is a variant.)

1190. Ọ̀kọ̀ọ̀kan là ńyọ ẹsẹ̀ lékù.
One at a time is how one removes one's legs from a masquerade costume. (The best way to approach a problem is systematically. Compare the preceding entry.)

1191. Ọkùnrin jẹ́jẹ́ a-bìwà-kunkun.
An easygoing man's gentle mien hides a strong disposition. (The quiet type is often a tough customer.)

1192. Ọlọ ò lọ ló dé Ìbarà? Ìbarà a máa ṣe ilé ọlọ?

If the grindstone did not move, how did it get to Ìbarà? Is Ìbarà the home of grindstones? (People do not travel from home without some reason.)[105]

1193. *Olọ́gbọ́n dorí eja mú; òmùgọ́ dìrù-u rẹ̀ mú.*
The wise person grabs a fish by the head; the fool grabs it by the tail fin. (The wise person knows better than a fool the best way to handle a situation.)

1194. *Olọ́gbọ́n jẹni bí ẹmùrẹ́n; aṣiwèrè jẹni bí ìgbòngbòn.*
The wise person bites one like a mosquito; the mad person bites one like a gadfly. (Cautiousness will get one to the goal far more successfully than brashness.)

1195. *Ologbọ́n ló lè mọ àdììtú èdè.*
Only a wise person can decipher the meaning of speech. (The deep meanings and nuances of an utterance are for only the wise to understand.)

1196. *Olọ́gbọ́n ńdẹ ihò, òmòràn-án dúró tì í; olọ́gbọ́n ní "Háà, ó jáde!" Òmòrán ní "Háà, mo kì í!" Olọ́gbọ́n ní "Kí lo kì?" Òmòrán ní "Kí nìwọ náà-á ló jáde?"*
The cunning man is watching a hole, and the knowledgeable person is standing by him; the cunning man exclaims, "Ha, it has sprung out!" The knowledgeable person responds, "Ha, I have grabbed it!" The cunning person asks, "What did you grab?" The knowledgeable person asks in turn, "What did you say sprang out?" (Two matched wits are in contest.)

1197. *Olọ́gbọ́n ni yó jogún ògo; aṣiwèrè ni yó ru ìtìjú wálé.*

The wise child will inherit glory; the idiot child will bring shame home with him. (A wise child is to be preferred to an idiot.)

1198. *Olọ́gbọ́n ọmọ ní ḿmú inú-u bàbá è dùn; aṣiwèrè ọmọ ní ḿba inú ìyá è jẹ́.*
A wise child gladdens the heart of his father; an imbecile child saddens the heart of his mother. (Every parent would prefer a wise child to an idiot.)

1199. *Olọ́jà kì í wípé kójà ó tú.*
The owner of the market never wishes the market to be disrupted. (People always want the best outcome for their ventures.)

1200. *Olọ́tí kì í mọ ọmọ è lólè.*
The wine seller never realizes that his child is a thief. (One is always blind to the flaws of those one loves.)[106]

1201. *Olọ́tòọ́ ní tòun ọ̀tọ̀; ìyá è-ẹ́ kú nílé, o gbé e lọ sin sóko.*
Olọ́tò says his ways are different; his mother dies at home, and he takes her to the farm for burial. (The unconventional person will always do things differently.)[107]

1202. *Ọmọ atiro tó ra bàtà fún bàbá è, ọ̀rọ̀ ló fẹ́ẹ́ gbọ́.*
The child of a cripple who bought shoes for his father is asking for a stern lecture. (One must not be thoughtless in one's actions.)

1203. *Ọmọ ẹní dàra, bí-i ká fi ṣaya kó.*
One's child may be beautiful, but one cannot make her one's wife. (Not all attractive propositions can be pursued.)

---

105. The play is on the syllable *lọ* (which means "to go") in the word *ọlọ*, grindstone.

106. The wine seller leaves his child in charge and does not realize that he has been cutting the wine with water.

107. *Olọ́tò* means "One who is different."

1204. Ọmọ eni eléni ò jọ ọmọ eni; ọmọ eni ì-bá jiyán, ọmọ eni eléni a jèkọ.
Other people's children are not like one's own; when one's child eats pounded yams, other people's children will eat corn-meal loaf. (One always favors one's own children over those of others.)[108]

1205. Ọmọ eni kì í gbọnsè ká fi eèsún nù ú nídìi.
One does not, after one's child defecates, wipe the child's anus with the abrasive elephant grass. (We do not deliberately injure those who look to us for protection.)

1206. Ọmọ iná là ńrán síná.
It is the child of fire that one sends on an errand to fire. (It is best to match the remedy to the problem.)

1207. Ọmọ tí ò ní baba kì í jìjà èbi.
A fatherless child should not engage in an unjust fight. (Never provoke trouble unless you have strong backers. Compare 3136.)

1208. Ọmọdé kékeré ò mọ ogun, ó ní kógun ó wá, ó ní bógún bá dé òun a kó síyàrá ìyá òun.
A small child does not know what war is like; hence he says that war should break out, for when it does he will go hide in his mother's room. (Ignorance often leads people to bite off much more than they can chew.)

1209. Ọmọdé kì í mọ àkókò tí kúrò-kúròó fi ńkúrò.
A small child never knows when kúròkúrò takes its leave.[109] (Youth is a stranger to etiquette or protocol.)

1210. Ọmọde kì í mọ ìtàn, kó mọ à-gbọ́-wí, kó mọ ojó tí a ṣe èdá òun.
A child does not know so much history and know so much hearsay that it knows the day of its creation. (However knowledgeable a youth might be, some deep knowledge would be beyond him.)

1211. Ọmọdé kì í mọ ori-í jẹ kó má ràá a lénu.
A child is never so careful about eating corn meal that it does not smear the meal on its mouth. (A youth may be clever but will inevitably make some mistakes.)

1212. Ọmọdé kì í ní iná níle kí tòde má jòó o.
A child does not have fire at home and therefore escape being burned by the fire abroad. (Being secure and well respected in one's home does not save one from vicissitudes outside the home.)

1213. Ọmọdé mọ sáárá, sùgbọn kò mọ àlòyí.
A child knows snuff but does not know how to grind and turn the tobacco. (A child is good at consuming but not at procuring.)

1214. Ọmọdé ní wọn ńjẹ igún, bàbá è-é ní wọn kì í jẹ ẹ́; ó ní ẹnìkán jẹ ẹ́ rí lójú òun; bàbá è-é ní ta ni? Ó ní eni náà ò sí.
A child says that people do eat vultures, and its father says people do not; the child says someone did eat a vulture in its presence; its father asks, who? The child says the person is dead.[110] (The youth who attempts to challenge the wisdom of the elders will find himself tripped up by his own mouth.)

---

mean "one who departs." The idea here is that the child does not know the right time to leave a place.

110. The phrase kò sí in Yoruba means "there is none" or "there is not . . ."; when attached predicatively to a person, it is a euphemism meaning that the person is dead. In this case the statement that the person died does double duty in that it also *literally* supports the father's assertion.

---

108. The assumption, of course, is that this mother has charge of both her own children and thos of others.

109. Kúrò means "leave" or "depart." Kúrò-kúrò, in accordance with Yoruba word formation, would thus

1215. *Ọmọdé ò mèfọ́, ó ńpè é légbòġi.*
A child does not recognize a vegetable and calls it medicine. (An uninformed person will inevitably make a fool of himself or herself. Compare the following two entries.)

1216. *Ọmọdé ò mọ oògùn, ó ńpè é léfọ́ọ́, kò mọ̀ pé ikú tó pa baba òun ni.*
A child does not know medicine, and he therefore calls it vegetables; he does not recognize it as what killed his father. (People may call disasters on their own heads out of ignorance. Compare the previous and following entries.)

1217. *Ọmọdé ò moògùn ó ńpè é légùn-ún.*
A child does not know medicine and says it is a thorn.[111] (The ignorant person knows not the value of anything. Compare the previous two entries.)

1218. *Ọmọdé yìí, máa wò mí lójú, eni (tí) a bá lọ sóde là ńwò lójú.*
Child, keep your eyes on me; one keeps one's eyes on the person who takes one visiting. (Always pay attention to what your guide and instructor does and tells you to do.)

1219. *"Ọmọ-ọ̀ mi ò yó" la mọ̀; "ọmọ-ọ̀ mí yó, sùgbọ́n kò rí sáárá fẹ́," a ò mọ ìyẹn.*
"My child did not have enough to eat" we understand; "My child had enough to eat but had no snuff to snort" we do not understand. (People should care for their children, not spoil them with overindulgence.)

1220. *Ọ̀mọ̀ràn ní ḿmọ oyún ìgbín.*
Only a sage knows the pregnancy of a snail.

(Deep wisdom is the gift of only a select few.)

1221. *Ọ̀pá gbóńgbó ní nṣíwájú agbọ́ọni.*
It is a small walking stick that goes before the person who walks a path overhung with foliage that is wet with morning dew. (One uses the tools or weapons at one's disposal to tackle challenges.)

1222. *Ọpẹ́ ló yẹ ẹrú.*
Gratitude is what befits the slave. (People should be grateful for whatever charity they receive.)

1223. *Ọ̀pẹ̀lẹ̀ èèyàn, bí a ò bá gbé e lulẹ̀, kò níí lè fohùn ire.*
A person who is like the divining string: unless you throw him down, he will not talk sense.[112] (Some people respond only to force.)

1224. *Ọ̀pọ̀lọ́ ní kéjò máa kálọ; ìjà òún di ojú ọ̀nà.*
The toad tells the snake to follow it, for it does not fight except by the roadside. (Weaklings always make sure that saviors are around before they get into a fight.)

1225. *Ọ̀pọ̀lọ́ ní òun lè sín ìlẹ̀kẹ̀; ta ní jẹ́ fi ìlẹ̀kẹ̀ ọ̀pọ̀lọ́ sídìí ọmọ-ọ ẹ̀?*
The toad boasts that it knows how to string beads; who, though, would put a toad's beads around his child's waist? (Not just anything will do for discriminating people.)

1226. *Ọ̀pọ̀lọ́ ńyan káńdú-kàndù-káńdú lójú eléguúsí; eléguúsí ò gbọdọ̀ yí i láta.*
The toad struts nonchalantly before the person cooking ègúsí stew; the person cooking

---

111. *Oògùn* may refer to medicine or to charms. Much of Yoruba medicine is herbal; one can imagine a child who sees only thorns where a person knowledgeable about herbs would see a potent source of medicine.

112. *Ọ̀pẹ̀lẹ̀* is the string the Ifá priest (*babaláwo*) divines with by casting it on the ground and reading the pattern of the nuts strung on it.

the ẹ̀gúsí stew will never add it to the ingredients. (A person outside one's jurisdiction may well taunt one.)

1227. Ọ̀pọ̀lọ́ ò mọ̀nà odò, ó dà á sí àwàdà.
The toad does not know the way to the stream and turns matters into a jest. (When one is stumped, one covers one's embarrassment with laughter.)

1228. Ọ̀pọ̀lọpọ̀ òjò ní ńlé eégún wọlé kẹri-kẹri.
It is a deluge that chases the eégún masquerader indoors indefinitely. (When problems become overwhelming, one has no choice but to succumb to them.)

1229. Ọ̀ràn kan la fi ńṣòfin ọ̀kan.
One problem serves as the basis for a law that will apply to another case. (Experience establishes a precedent for future occurrences.)

1230. Ọ̀ràn ọlóràn la fi ńkógbón.
From other people's problems one learns wisdom. (One should learn from other people's vicissitudes.)

1231. Ọ̀ràn tí ò sunwọ̀n, konko ńṣojú.
A matter that is unpalatable hardens the eyes. (When one is in the wrong, one hides behind braggadocio.)

1232. Ọ̀rọ̀ kì í gbórín ká fi ọ̀bẹ bù ú, ẹnu la fi ńwí i.
A problem is not so formidable that one attacks it with a knife; one tackles it with the mouth. (The weightiest problem is resolvable through discussion and negotiation.)

1233. Ọ̀rọ̀ la fi ńjẹ omitooro ọ̀rọ̀.
Words are the things with which to savor the delicious broth of words. (It is with words that one resolves all problems.)

1234. Ọ̀rọ̀ rere ní ńyọ obì lápò; ọ̀rọ̀ búburú ní ńyọ ọfà lápó.
Good talk brings the kola nut out of the pouch; provocative talk draws the arrow out of the quiver. (Judicious language defuses problems, whereas thoughtless talk aggravates them.)

1235. Ọ̀rọ̀ tí ọlọgbọ́n bá sọ, ẹnu aṣiwèrè la ti ńgbọ́ ọ.
Whatever a wise man says will be heard repeated by the nitwit. (Rumormongers always distort the news they hear from reliable sources.)

1236. Ọ̀rọ̀ tó dojú rú di ti ọlọ́rọ̀, ayé á dèhìn.
A problem that is too complicated to resolve becomes the sole responsibility of the person concerned, whom the world leaves to his or her devices. (People will help one only so far; in the end each person must confront his or her problems alone.)

1237. Ọ̀rọ̀-ọ́ ni òun ò nílé; ibi tí wọ́n bá rí ni wọ́n ti ńsọ òun.
Discourse says it has no home; people engage in it wherever they please. (Any place is a good place for an exchange of views.)

1238. Ọsán gbé ojú ọrun le kókó; bó bá wọ odò, a di ò-rò-pòjò-pòjò.
The bowstring is taut while it remains on the bow; dipped into the river, it becomes very soft indeed. (One thrives on one's home ground where conditions are ideal; in hostile territory one becomes helpless.)

1239. Ọ̀sán ọrun ò pón; ẹni tó bá yá kó máa bá tiẹ̀ lọ.
It is not yet noon in heaven;[113] whoever is anxious to get there may go ahead by him-

___
113. Noon is considered the time after which one may properly pay a visit.

self or herself. (One is not eager to join others in deadly adventures.)

1240. *Ọwọ́ asiwèrè ni a gbé ńbá apá yíya.*
It is in the hands of an imbecile that one finds a severed arm. (Simpleminded people do not know how to cover their tracks or get rid of the evidence.)

1241. *Ọ̀wọ̀-ọ kókó la fi ńwọ igi; ọ̀wọ̀ òrìṣà la fi ńwọ àfín.*
The regard one has for the knob is that with which one clothes the tree; the regard one has for the gods is the same that one invests the albino with.[114] (One extends one's regard for certain people to those associated with them.)

R

1242. *Rà á ire, gà á ire; ìpéńpéjú ni àlà-a fìlà.*
Press it well on the head, puff it out; the eyebrow is the limit for the cap. (One may be free to use one's possession as one pleases, but there are still some conventions to observe.)

1243. *Ràdà-ràdà-á mọ ibi tí ó ńrè.*
The meandering person knows where he is headed. (A person who seems without a purpose may be engaged in something known to himself or herself.)

1244. *Rírí tí a rí igún la fi ńta igún lófà.*
It is because one sees the vulture that one shoots arrows at it. (One who does not make oneself available will not present a target for people's hostility.)

---

114. The knob is the toughest part of any tree. The albino, like other so-called afflicted people, is considered by the Yoruba to be a special ward of the gods.

S

1245. *"Sìn mí ká relé àna," ó wẹ̀wù ẹtù.*
"Go with me to my in-laws' home," and he wore a garment made from rich handwoven material. (Said of a person who attempts to steal other people's glory whom he or she is supposed to be helping.)

1246. *Sọ̀rọ̀ kí ọlọ́rọ̀ gbọ́, àbùkù ní ńfi kanni.*
Spreading rumors into the ears of the subject of the rumor brings disgrace to the speaker. (One should refrain from rumormongering.)

Ṣ

1247. *Ṣàngó kì í jà kó mú ilé aró.*
Sango does not fight and destroy the enclosure for dyeing. (Some people are beyond the reach of some nemesis.)

1248. *Ṣàngó ní òun ní ńkó ọkùnrin suuru bá jà; Èṣù ní bí-i tòun? Ṣàngó ní kí tÈṣù kúrò.*
Sango says he gathers people around him to fight together; Èṣù asks if Sango includes people like him, and Sango says Èṣù is the exception. (No one wants to engage in any venture with an unpredictable troublemaker.)

1249. *"Ṣe mí nísu" ní ńṣíwájú "ẹ kúuṣẹ́" bí?*
Does "Give me some yam" go before "Hello there, you working man"? (It is bad form to ask people for favors before you greet them. This is a variant of 888.)

1250. *Ṣèkèrè ò ṣéé fọpá na.*
The beaded musical gourd is not something to play with a stick. (Always apply the proper tool to the job.)

1251. *Ṣẹ́kẹ́-ṣẹkẹ̀-ẹ́ dára, ṣùgbọ́n alágbẹ̀dẹ ò rọ ọ́ fún ọmọ ẹ̀.*

Handcuffs are pretty, but the blacksmith does not fashion them for his own child. (When trouble is being distributed, one always wishes to exempt one's own people.)

1252. *Sútà ò nílé; ìkóríta lÈṣù ńgbé.*
Perfidy has no home; the home of Èṣù is the crossroads. (No one makes room in his or her home for an abomination.)

T

1253. *Ta lèèyàn nínú ẹrú Ààrẹ? A ní Ìdaganna la wá wá, ẹ ní Ìdakolo?*
Which of the Ààrẹ's slaves is a person of any account? We said we came looking for Ìdaganna, and you ask, "Ìdakolo?" (Said to indicate that one's auditor is making nonsense out of the sense one is making. Also, there is nothing to choose between two worthless things.)

1254. *Ta ní jẹ́ jẹ ọṣẹ kó fọgìrì fọṣọ?*
Who would eat soap and wash clothes with fermented beans? (Who would seek unease when ease is available?)

1255. *Ta ní mòdí òjò, bí kò ṣe Ṣàngó?*
Who can know the secret of the rain if not Ṣango? (Only those privy to mysteries can explain mysterious events.)

1256. *Tábà tí ò dùn, ẹnu ò tà á.*
Snuff that is not pleasant, the mouth cannot sell. (No amount of talk will make something unpleasant become pleasant.)

1257. *"Tèmi ò sòrò," tí kì í jẹ kọ́mọ alágbẹ̀dẹ ní idà.*
"Mine is not urgent" prevents the son of the blacksmith from owning a sword. (The person who always yields to others will never get anywhere.)

1258. *Tẹni ní ńjọni lójú; eèrà-á bímọ-ọ rẹ̀ ó sọ ọ́ ní òyírìgbí.*
One's own thing is what one finds impressive; the ant has a child and names it The-one-who-rolls-mightily-around. (One always tends to overestimate the worth of one's own possession.)

1259. *Tẹni ntẹni; bí àpọ́n bá sun iṣu a bù fọ́mọ-ọ rẹ̀.*
One's own is one's own; when a man without a wife roasts yams, he cuts a piece for his child. (One makes do with what one has.)

1260. *Tètẹ́ ní ńṣíwájú eré sísa.*
A child's learning to walk comes before running. (One should observe some order in what one does.)

1261. *Tìẹ́ sàn, tèmí sàn, lolókùnrùn méjì-í fi ńdìmú.*
"Your condition is better; my condition is better" is what gets two invalids into a fight. (Fools will fight over the most stupid things.)

1262. *Tinú òlẹ lòlẹ ńjẹ; aṣiwèrè èèyàn ni ò mọ èrú tí yó gbà.*
The lazy person eats the products of his native wisdom; only a fool does not know what devious way will be fruitful. (If one lacks industry, one had better be resourceful.)

W

1263. *Wàrà-wàrà là ńyọ oró iná.*
When one is on fire, one's reaction is extremely agile. (Do not delay in exacting vengeance for a wrong. Compare 1266.)

1264. *Wèrè-é dùn-ún wò, kò ṣé-é bí lómọ.*
An imbecile makes an entertaining spectacle

but not as one's own child. (One might be tolerant of simplicity or irresponsibility in other people but not in one's own relatives.)

1265. *Wèrè-é yàtò sí wéré; wéré kì í ṣe wèrè; ìjá yàtò sí eré.*
Madness differs from the singing of Islamic songs; the singing of Islamic songs is not madness; fighting is different from playing. (One should not confuse jesting with quarreling.)

1266. *Wéré-wéré lọmọdé ńbọ oko èèsì.*
A child's journey home from a nettle bush is fast indeed. (Painful problems enforce quick attention. Compare 1263.)

1267. *Wò mí lójú, wò mí lẹ̀ẹ̀kẹ́; ẹni a bá lọ sóde là ńwò lójú.*
Keep your eyes on my face, and keep your eyes on my cheeks; one keeps one's eyes on the person with whom one goes visiting. (People should not cultivate wandering eyes.)

1268. *"Wo ọmọ-ò mi dè mí": ó ńlo kíjìpá mẹ́ta gbó; mélòó ni ọlọ́mọ-ọ́ máa lò gbó?*
"Look after the child for me": she wears three durable hand-loomed wrappers to tatters; how many would the mother of the child herself wear out? (The caretaker should not use up all his own resources for the benefit of his or her employer.)

1269. *Wolé-wolé kì í wolé agbọ́n láì tẹ́.*
The sanitary inspector does not inspect a wasp's home without coming to grief. (One should be cautious in performing one's duties.)

1270. *Wọ́n ní, "Afọ́jú, o ò tanná alẹ́." Ó ní àtòsán àtòru, èwo lòún rí níbẹ?*
People said, "Blind man, you did not light a lamp." He asked, night or day, which one would his eyes register? (One should not waste efforts in procuring things one cannot use.)

1271. *Wọ́n ní, "Afọ́jú, ọmo-ò re-é pẹran." Ó ní kò dá òun lójú, àfi bí òún bá tọ́ ọ wò.*
They said to the blind man, "Blind man, your son has killed game." He responds that he cannot believe them until he has tasted the meat. (Always insist on positive proof.)

On caginess, caution, moderation, patience, and prudence

A

1272. *A bu omi lámù a rí eégún; kí ni ẹni tó lọ sódò lọ ọ̀nmi yó rìí?*
We scoop water from the water pot and see a masquerader; what will the person who goes to draw water at the river find?[1] (If a person exposed to minimal risk cries disaster, what would the person exposed to much greater risk do?)

1273. *A fún ọ nísu lÓyọ̀ọ́ ò ńdúpẹ́; o rígi sè é ná?*
You are given yams at Ọ̀yọ̀ and you rejoice; have you secured wood to cook them? (Never assume that a propitious beginning assures a successful conclusion.)[2]

1274. *A ki ẹsẹ̀ kan bọ odò omí fà á; bí a bá wá ti mejèèjì bọ̀ ọ́ ńkọ́?*
One dips one leg into the stream and the water tugs at it; what if one had dipped both legs in it? (Repercussions should not be disproportionate to the act.)

1275. *A kì í bá ẹlẹ́nu jìjà òru.*
One does not fight at night with a braggart. (Never get into a competition with a braggart unless a witness is present.)

1276. *A kì í bú ọba onígẹ̀gẹ̀ lójú àwọn ẹ̀ẹ̀yàn-án rẹ̀.*
One does not insult a king with a goiter in the presence of his people. (Never expose yourself to repercussions with careless speech or indiscreet behavior.)

1277. *A kì í du orí olórí kí àwòdì gbé tẹni lọ.*
One does not fight to save another person's head only to have a kite carry one's own away. (One should not save others at the cost of one's own safety.)

1278. *A kì í fi ìkánjú lá ọbẹ̀ gbígbóná.*
One does not eat scalding stew in a hurry. (Patience is best in delicate or difficult matters.)

1279. *A kì í gbélé gba ọfà láìlọ ogun.*
One does not sit at home, not going to war, and yet be shot with an arrow. (One should be safe in one's own home.)

1280. *A kì í kánjú tu olú-ọrán; igba ẹ̀ ò tó-ó sẹbẹ̀.*
One does not gather olú-ọrán mushrooms in haste; two hundred of them are not enough to make a stew. (Certain tasks demand patience if they are to come out right.)

---

1. During the *eégún* season people who follow pathways (like those leading to rivers) are likely to run into masqueraders on the way from *ìgbàlè*, their secret groves.

2. The rejoicing is premature because the Ọ̀yọ́ people supposedly tantalize strangers with deceptive generosity.

1281. *A kì í rídìí òkun; a kì í rídìí ọsà; ọmọ-oní-gele-gele kì í jẹ́ kí wọ́n rídìí òun.*
One never sees the bottom of the ocean; no one ever sees the bottom of the lagoon; a well-bred woman will never expose her buttocks to anyone. (People should not expose their innermost secrets to all and sundry.)[3]

1282. *A kì í rójú ẹni púrọ́ mọ́ni.*
One does not look into the eyes of a person and still tell a lie against that person. (It is always easier to do evil to people who are absent.)

1283. *A kì í sọ̀rọ̀ orí bíbẹ́ lójú ọmọdé; lọ́rùnlọ́-rùn ni yó máa wo olúwa-a rẹ̀.*
One does not speak of a beheading in the presence of a child; otherwise, his gaze will be fixated on the neck of the person concerned. (Never discuss a secret in the hearing of a person whose behavior will give the secret away.)

1284. *À ńgba òròmọ adìẹ lọ́wọ́ ikú, ó ní wọn ò jẹ́ kí òun jẹ láàtàn.*
One struggles to save the chick from certain death, and it complains that it is prevented from foraging at the dump. (Chicks foraging at the dump are easy prey for kites.)

1285. *A nísẹ́ isẹ́ ẹ, o ní ò ńlọ sóko; bó o bá lọ sóko ò ḿbọ̀ wá bá a nílé.*
You are told that a job is your responsibility, and you say you are on your way to the farm; you may be on your way to the farm, but the job will be there on your return. (One may devise stratagems to defer carrying out one's duties, but they are unlikely to make others carry them out.)

1286. *À ńsa kẹ́kẹ́, aájò ẹwà ni; à ḿbàbàjà, aájò ẹwà ni.*
Marking one's face with *kẹ́kẹ́* is a quest for beauty; marking one's face with *àbàjà* is a quest for beauty.[4] (The pains one takes to adorn oneself are for a good end.)

1287. *A sìnkú tán, alugbá ò lọ; ó fẹ́ẹ́ sụpọ́ ni?*
The funeral is over, but the calabash beater does not take his leave; does he want to inherit a wife?[5] (This proverb has the same import as 653.)

1288. *Aaka ò gbé òdàn; igbó ní ńgbé.*
The hedgehog does not live in the grassland, only in the forest. (Certain things are proper; certain things are not.)

1289. *Àáké tí ńgégi-í kọsẹ̀, gbẹ́nàgbénà-á bu ẹtù sórí.*
The axe that cuts wood stumbles, and the carver anoints his head with medicinal powder. (The evildoer's conscience will not let him or her rest.)[6]

1290. *Àáyá kan-án bẹ̀ ọ́ wò; igba wọ́n ti rí ọ.*
If a single colubus monkey sees you, be sure that two hundred of them have seen you. (A secret disclosed to one person is as good as published for all.)

1291. *Abẹ ní ḿbẹ orí; oníṣẹ́ àtẹ́lẹsè ní ḿbẹ ọnà; bèbè ìdí ní ḿbẹ kíjìpá; bí a dáwọ́-ọ bíbẹni, a tán nínú ẹni.*
The razor begs the scalp; the wayfarer's soles beg the path; waist beads beg the home-

---

3. The expression *rí ìdí*, literally "see the bottom [of]," also means "discover the guarded secrets [of]."

4. *Kẹ́kẹ́* and *àbàjà* are both patterns of facial scarification.
5. The calabash beater is employed to clear evil spirits ahead of the funeral procession by means of the calabash.
6. Both the axe and the carpenter are offenders against wood; the carpenter takes the axe's stumbling as a bad omen.

woven cloth; when the begging is done, one lets matters drop. (One is placated by a person close to one; afterward, one allows oneself to be appeased.)

1292. *Abẹ́rẹ́ bọ́ sómi táló; Ọ̀dọ̀fín ní òun-ún gbọ́ "jàbú!"*
The needle makes an almost inaudible sound when it drops into the water; Ọ̀dọ̀fin said he heard a loud splash.[7] (Excessive exaggeration amounts to lying.)

1293. *Abiyamọ, kàgbo wàrà; ojọ́ ńlọ.*
Nursing mother, make the herbal decoction in good time; the day is waning. (Attend to duties in time.)

1294. *Àbùlẹ̀ ní ḿmú aṣọ tọ́; ẹni tí kò tójú àbùlẹ̀ yó ṣe ara-a rẹ̀ lófò aṣọ.*
Patching extends the life of clothes; whoever does not save materials for patching deprives himself or herself of clothing. (Everything has its use; conserve your resources.)

1295. *Àdàbà ńpògèdè, ó rò pé ẹyẹlé ò gbọ́; ẹyẹlé gbọ́, títiiri ló tiiri.*
The dove recites incantations, thinking that the pigeon cannot hear; the pigeon hears, only pretending to sleep. (Never mistake a peron's easygoing demeanor for cowardice or folly.)

1296. *Adìẹ ńjẹkà, ó ḿmumi, ó ńgbé òkúta pé-pẹ̀-pẹ́ mì, ó ní òun ò léhín; ìdérègbè tó léhín ńgbé irin mì bí?*
The chicken eats corn, drinks water, even swallows small pebbles, and yet complains that it lacks teeth; does the goat that has teeth swallow steel? (One should be content with one's lot.)

1297. *Àdó gba ara ẹ̀ tẹ́lẹ̀, ká tó fi oògùn si?*
Could the small gourd save itself, before we put charms into it?[8] (Do not seek protection from a helpless person.)

1298. *Àdóìṣí loògùn ọrọ̀.*
Choosing-a-base-and-maintaining-it is the medicine for wealth. (One should not be a rolling stone.)

1299. *Àféfé tó wọlé tó kó aṣọ iyàrá, ìkìlọ̀ ni fún ẹni tó wọ tiẹ̀ sọrùn.*
The wind that enters the house and carries off the clothes in the bedroom is a warning to those who wear theirs around their necks. (When disaster befalls the most formidable people, those less formidable should take warning.)

1300. *Àfojúdi ìlẹ̀kẹ̀ ní ńjé "Erú-kò-ní."*
It is an impertinent bead that is named "The-slave-does-not-own-its like."[9] (One must be mindful of how one's actions might affect others.)

1301. *Àgékù ejò, tí ńsoro bí agbọ́n.*
Partially severed snake stings like a wasp. (A wounded adversary is a vicious one.)

1302. *Àgúnbàjẹ́ ni tolódó.*
Pounding-until-it-is-ruined is the habit of the owner of the mortar. (One should exercise restraint in using what one has in abundance.)

1303. *Àgùntàn bòlòjò ò gbàgbé eléèrí bọrọ̀.*
The big, fat sheep does not soon forget the provider of corn bran. (One remembers one's benefactor.)

---

7. *Ọ̀dọ̀fin*, a chieftaincy title, serves here as a proper name.

8. *Àdó* is a tiny gourd in which people keep charms, often serving as talismans.

9. The insinuation is that whoever does not have its like is no better than a slave.

1304. Àgùntàn ńwò sùn-ùn; ogbón inú pé egbèje.
The sheep stares blankly, but its cunning stratagems number 1,400. (Looks are deceptive.)

1305. Àgùntàn ò jí ní kùtùkùtù se enu bobo.
A sheep does not wake in the morning and droop its mouth. (One should not dawdle in the morning.)

1306. Àgbà òsìkà ńgbin iyà sílè de omo-o rè.
A wicked elder sows suffering for his children. (One's character often affects the fortunes of one's children. Compare 702 and 3307.)

1307. Àgbè ò dáso lósù, àfodún.
A farmer does not make new clothes monthly, only annually. (The reward for one's labor is often a long time coming.)

1308. Àgbè tó bá pé nílé ò níí ko oko òsán.
A farmer who tarries in the house will not object to hoeing the farm in the afternoon. (He who dallies makes his tasks that much more difficult.)

1309. À-gbèrù-àì-wèhìn lòpálábá fi gbàgbé iyá è sílè.
Picking-up-one's-load-without-checking-one's-rear caused the piece of broken bottle to forget its mother on the ground. (The broken bottle suffered its fate, perhaps, because it was not careful about what it "carried." The hasty traveler leaves his goods behind.)

1310. Agbójúlógún fi ara-a rè fósì ta.
He-who-places-his-hopes-on-inheritance delivers himself to destitution. (One should secure one's own living.)

1311. Àgbóká etí olóràn á di.[10]
The ear that will insist on hearing everything will go deaf. (There is some benefit to ignoring certain things.)

1312. Àgbókànlé ò pani lébi.
A thing in which one reposes one's trust does not make one hunger. (One's reserve guarantees one's supplies.)

1313. Àìfesòké ìbòsí ni kò séé gbè.
An alarm raised without moderation finds no helpers. (If the person who raises an alarm puts people off by his or her methods, they will not come to his or her aid.)

1314. Àìgbóràn, baba àfojúdi.
Disobedience, father of disregard. (To disobey people is to show a lack of regard for them.)[11]

1315. Àìlèfohùn ní ńsáájú orí burúkú.
Inability to speak out precedes misfortunes. (A person who will not speak on his or her own behalf suffers the consequences.)

1316. Àìròròso ìyàwó tó wí pé èkúté-ilé yó je ide; bèèni Mójide nìyálé-e rè ńje.
The junior wife could find nothing to say, and said that the mice in the house will eat brass; the senior wife of the household happens to be named Mójide [Omo-ó-je-ide, meaning "Child eats brass"]. (Veiled insults directed at an adversary are as potent as any other sort of provocation.)

1317. Àìsàn là ńwò, a kì í wo ikú.
One treats an illness; one does not treat

---

10. In plainer Yoruba the statement would be Àgbóká letí olóràn-án fi ńdi.

11. The formulation baba àfojúdi means both "father of disregard" and "father-type disregard": in other words, an extraordinary degree of disregard.

death. (If one neglects an illness until death intervenes, the treatment comes too late. Compare 1356.)

1318. *Àìtètèmólè, olèé mólóko.*
Because of the delay in apprehending the thief, the thief apprehends the owner of the farm. (One must be alert in dealing with slippery people; otherwise, they turn the tables.)

1319. *Ajá ilé ò moḍeé ṣe.*
A domesticated dog does not know how to hunt. (Pampering kills initiative.)

1320. *Ajá kì í dán-nu "Kò séwu" lókò ẹkùn.*
A dog does not boast "No danger" in a leopard's bush. (Never sneer at obvious danger.)

1321. *Ajá tí yó sọnù kì í gbọ́ fèrè ọdẹ.*
A dog destined to be lost does not hear the hunter's whistle. (No matter what help one may render, one cannot save an ill-fated person.)

1322. *Ajá tó rí mọ́tò tó dúró fi ara-a rẹ̀ bọ Ògún.*
A dog that sees a motor vehicle and stands in its way makes itself a sacrifice to Ògún. (A person who needlessly endangers himself or herself deserves his or her fate.)

1323. *Àjànàkú tí a gbé ọ̀fin sílẹ̀ dè, erin-ín mojú; erin ò bá ibẹ̀ lọ.*
One digs a pit in the path of the elephant, but the elephant can read signs; the elephant does not go that way. (The alert person will thwart an enemy's machinations.)

1324. *Àjẹ́ ńké, òkùnrùn ò paradà; ó lówó ẹbọ nílé.*
A witch proclaims her presence and an invalid does not make way; he must have money for sacrifices at home. (One need

not fear a scourge for which one has the remedy.)

1325. *Ajẹnifẹ́ni, èkúté ilé.*
One-that-bites-and-blows-on-the-wound: the house mouse.[12] (Be wary of adversaries who pose as friends.)

1326. *Àkàlàmàgbò-ó ṣoore ó yọ gègè lọ́rùn.*
The ground hornbill did a favor and developed a goiter. (Good deeds sometimes come back to haunt the doer. Compare 1783 and 1787.)

1327. *Akánjú jayé, ọrun wọn ò pé.*
People who live impatiently: their going to heaven is not far off. (Reckless living leads to early death.)

1328. *Àkèekèé ò ṣé-é dì níbò.*
A scorpion is not a thing to close one's palms on. (Some matters call for extreme caution.)

1329. *Àkèekèé rìn tapótapó.*
The scorpion travels accompanied by venom. (The stalwart is never unprepared to answer a call.)

1330. *Àkèekèé ta Kindo lẹpọ̀n, ará ilée Labata ńrojú; kí ló kàn án níbẹ̀?*
A scorpion stung Kindo in the testicle, and a person from Labata's household frowns in dismay; what business is it of his? (One should not take on matters that are not one's business.)

1331. *Àkọ̀ tó bá bá ọbẹ dìtè á gbọgbẹ́ láti inú.*
A sheath that engages in a dispute with a knife will suffer an internal wound. (Never court the anger of a person in a position to inflict injury on you.)

---

12. The bite hurts, but the animal also soothes so as to be able to continue hurting its victim.

1332. *Akóbáni lèkúté-ilé; ejò kì í jàgbàdo.*
The mouse is a bringer of disaster to the innocent; snakes do not eat corn. (Bad company brings bad fortune.)

1333. *Àlá tí ajá bá lá, inú ajá ní ńgbé.*
Whatever dream the dog dreams remains inside the dog. (Keep your own counsel.)

1334. *Aláàárù kì í so pé kí ajé se òun pa; eléŕù ńkó?*
The hired carrier does not ask to die from his efforts; what would the owner of the merchandise ask? (One should not assume other people's responsibilities and risks.)

1335. *Alágbàró ò yege; aláso á gbà á bó dòla.*
She who borrows a wrapper skirt to wear is not home free; the owner of the cloth will take it back tomorrow. (There is nothing like having one's own.)

1336. *Alángbá tó fojú di erè, ikùn ejò ni yó bàá ara-a è.*
A lizard that views a python with disregard will find itself in the belly of the snake. (Whoever disdains obvious danger will suffer dire consequences.)

1337. *Alápàáńdèdè ńjayé lébé-lébé.*
The sparrow enjoys life carefully. (The best way to live is carefully.)

1338. *Alára ò lè wí pé kò dun òun, ká ní ó kú àìsùn, ó kú àìwo.*
The owner of the body does not say that he is in no pain, while we insist on commiserating with him for his sleeplessness and his restlessness. (One does not commiserate with a person who does not admit his or her misfortune).

1339. *Alárìnjó tí yó jòó, kó ti ìwòyí mú esè kó le kó kó kó.*
The person who will engage in itinerant

dancing should look to his legs in good time. (Before embarking on a trade, one should hone one's tools.)

1340. *Aláwàdà ló lè soko òsónú; eni tí kò lénu mímú tete ò lè soko alápepe.*
Only a good-humored person can make a good husband for an ill-humored woman; a person whose mouth is not sharp cannot make a good husband for a hyperactive woman. (Incompatible natures cannot make a good marriage.)

1341. *Àlejò tó wò nílé-e Póngilá, Póngilá ní, "Ìwo ta ni?" Àlejò-ó ní òun Bugije; Póngilá ni, "Tòò, ló dájú igi-i tìre lótò."*
The visitor arrived at the home of Póngilá [Lickwood], and Póngilá asked him, "Who are you?" The visitor replied, "I am Bugije" (Bitewood). Póngilá said, "Well, you had better go find yourself some wood elsewhere." (Do not encourage people to take advantage of you or abuse your generosity.)

1342. *Àlo ti alábaun; àbò ti àna-a rè.*
To Tortoise belongs the outward trip; to his father-in-law belongs the return. (The person in the right in a dispute, if he or she is too vindictive, quickly becomes the one in the wrong. Compare 1482.)[13]

1343. *Àlùkerese ò mò pé olóko-ó ládàá.*
The weed did not know that the farmer had a machete. (The evildoer does not consider the response of the person wronged.)

1344. *Àmòjù là ńmo ekùn-un Sàáré.*
Sàáré always goes too far in his description

---

13. The proverb is based on a folktale in which Tortoise stole yams from the farm of his father-in-law. The latter caught Tortoise and tied him up by the path, where people going to their farms saw him and justified the father-in-law. When on their return in the evening they saw Tortoise still tied up, however, people began to scold the father-in-law for the excessive punishment, especially considering his relationship to Tortoise.

of a leopard. (An immoderate display of
knowledge soon backfires.)[14]

1345. *Àpáàdì ló tó ko iná lójú.*
Only a potsherd has what it takes to confront a live coal. (Only a person capable of
facing a situation should take it on. Compare 1984.)

1346. *Apatapara-á pa ara-a rè lájùbà; ẹni tí
yó ko là ńwòye.*
Apatapara kills himself in the wilderness;
who will carry him is now the question.
(One should not outstrip one's help.)

1347. *Àpò tí a kò fi ọwọ́ ẹni dá sòro-ó kiwọ́ bọ̀.*
A pocket one did not make with one's own
hand is a difficult one to dip one's hand into.
(One should keep one's hands in one's own
pockets.)

1348. *Ará Ìbàdàn kì í ságun; à ó rìn séhìn ni
wọ́n ńwí.*
Ibadan people do not run from war; what
they say is, "We will fall back a little." (There
are ways of avoiding battle without seeming
to do so.)

1349. *À-rí-ì-gbọdò-wí, à-rí-ì-gbọdò-fọ ni ikú
awo.*
Something-seen-but-unmentionable,
something-seen-but-unspeakable is the
death of a guardian of the mysteries. (The
eyes sometimes see things that are too
sacred for the mouth to mention.)

1350. *Àrísá iná, àkòtagìrì ejò; àgbà tó réjò tí
kò sá, ara ikú ló ńyá a.*
Fire, something-one-sees-and-flees; snake,
something-one-sees-and-jumps; an elder
who sees a snake and does not flee flirts
with death. (Fire and snakes are not things
to take lightly, and elders should not be
embarrassed to flee from danger.)

1351. *Àròkàn ní ḿmú à-sun-ùn-dá wá; ẹlékún
sunkún è ó lọ.*
Going-from-one-sad-thought-to-another
results in endless weeping; the person weeping does his weeping and departs. (If one
keeps thinking sad thoughts, one will ever
remain miserable; if one must be sad, one
must observe some limits.)

1352. *Arọ ò nasè kan dí ọ̀nà.*
A cripple does not block the road with his
legs. (A person with a handicap should not
challenge those who are not handicapped.)

1353. *Arọ tí kò lésè nílè-ẹ́ lógbón nínú.*
A cripple who has no legs to stand on has
wisdom inside him. (Whatever one's handi-
caps, one will have some asset.)

1354. *Aróbasá ò sojo.*
He-who-flees-on-seeing-the-king is no coward. (One's safest course is to steer clear of
those in authority. Compare 5.)

1355. *Arúgbó soge rí; àkísà-á lògbà rí.*
The old person was once a dandy; the rag
was once in fashion. (Those who are favored
should remember that times and circumstances do change.)

1356. *Àrùn là ńwo; a kì í wokú.*
One treats a disease; one does not treat
death. (We should attend to problems before
they become unmanageable. Compare 1317.)

---

14. The story behind the proverb is of a boy who
ran home panting because he had seen a leopard in the
forest. Grateful that the animal did not kill his son, the
father killed a cock as a sacrifice. The boy went on to
describe how huge the animal was, and the father, even
more thankful, killed a he-goat for sacrifice. Then the
son spoke of how the animal went from okro plant to
okro plant to eat the fruits. The father knew, of course,
that only antelopes eat okro, and he scolded the son for
not killing the game and bringing it home.

1357. *Asárétete ní ńkojá ilé; arìngbèrè ni yó rìi oyè je.*
The fast runner will run past his home; the leisurely stroller is the one who will win the title. (A fast start does not guarantee success. Compare 778.)

1358. *Àṣá ḿbá eyelé ṣeré, eyelé ńyò; eyelé ńfikú ṣeré.*
The kite plays with the pigeon, and the pigeon rejoices; the pigeon is courting death. (An enemy who pretends friendship is even more dangerous.)

1359. *Àsàyá kì í jé kí omo òyà ó gbón.*
Roughhousing keeps the young of the cane rat from learning wisdom. (A person who takes life as a jest does not learn to be wary.)

1360. *Àsesílè làbòwábá; eni tó da omi síwájú á telè tútù.*
What one puts aside is what one returns to find; whoever dumps water ahead of him or her will step on wet earth. (One reaps what one sows. This is a variant of 952.)

1361. *Àsèsèwón ológbò ní ńjìyà; bó bá pé títí a tó eku-ú pa.*
Only the newly weaned cat suffers; eventually it will learn to kill mice. (A child may be helpless today but not in the future.)

1362. *Asòroówò bí èwù àsejù.*
Difficult-to-wear is like the garment of immoderation. (Wearing the cloak of immoderation exposes one to difficulties.)

1363. *Ata-á kéré; ìjá jù ú.*
Pepper is small; its fight is much bigger. (One should not judge people by their size.)

1364. *Ataare-é réni tún ìdí-i rè ṣe ó ńfi òbùró sèsín; òbùró ìbá réni tún ìdí-i rè ṣe a sunwòn jú ataare lo.*
Alligator pepper has someone to tend it, and it mocks the *òbùró* tree; had the *òbùró* tree someone to tend it, it would look better than alligator pepper. (A person enjoying a run of good fortune should not deride the less fortunate; if they had been similarly favored, there is no telling what they might have accomplished.)

1365. *Atàkò fó eyin àparò: ohun ojú ńwá lojú ńrí.*
Person-who-stones-and-breaks-partridge's-eggs: the eyes find what the eyes seek. (The culprit is asking for trouble, and he will not be disappointed.)

1366. *Atèhìnrógbón agétí ajá; a gé e létí tán ó fabe pamó.*
A-creature-that-learns-wisdom-in-reverse-order, dog-with-severed-ears: after its ears have been severed, it hides the razor. (Prevention makes sense only before the disaster.)

1367. *Àtélewó eni kì í tanni.*
One's palm does not deceive one. (One's trust is best placed in one's own resources.)

1368. *Atoro-ohungbogbo-lówó-Olórun kì í kánjú.*
The-seeker-of-all-things-from-God does not yield to impatience. (The supplicant must be patient for an answer.)

1369. *Àwòfín ní ḿmú òré bàjé; fírí là ńwo eni tí ńwoni.*
Persistent staring ruins a friendship; look only glancingly at those looking at you. (A battle of looks does not help a friendship.)

1370. *Ayáraròhìn, aya ode, ó ní oko òun-ún pa èkínní, ó pa èkefà.*
The impatient reporter, wife of the hunter, says that her husband killed the first and killed the sixth. (The impatient reporter is likely to outstrip her report.)

1371. *Àyé gba ògùnmọ̀ ó ránṣẹ́ sí òdú; àyé gba Tápà ó kólé ìgunnu.*
The cultivated vegetable is contented, so it sends for its wild variety; the Nupe [Fulani][15] person is so comfortable that he builds a tall house. (When one enjoys a life of ease, one is tempted to overreach.)

1372. *Ayé ò ṣéé fipá jẹ.*
Life is nothing to enjoy heedlessly. (Life demands caution.)

B

1373. *"Bá mi mádìẹ" kì í fi orúnkún bó.*
"Help me catch a chicken" does not scrape his knees. (Overzealousness in helping others is a fault.)

1374. *Baálé ilé kú, wọ́n fi olókùnrùn rólé; ẹkún ńgorí ẹkún.*
The man of the house died and they put an invalid in his place; weeping climbs upon weeping. (People known to be unsuitable should not be entrusted with important affairs.)

1375. *"Baálé pè mí nkò wá," òhànhàn ní ńpa wọ́n.*
"The patriarch of the compound called me but I did not respond" dies of anxiety. (A person who defies his or her main succor heads for ruin.)

1376. *Bánú sọ, má bàà èèyàn sọ; èèyàn ò sí; ayé ti dèké.*
Counsel with your inside, not with people; [good] people are no longer to be found; the world has turned false. (There is no one to trust but oneself.)

1377. *Bí a bá bu ìrè jẹ, ká bu ìrè sápò.*
If one takes a bite of a cricket, one should put a little in one's pocket. (Even if one has only a little, one should still save something for the morrow.)

1378. *Bí a bá bú ọba, à ṣẹ́; bí a bá bú ọ̀ṣọ̀run, à ṣẹ́.*
If one insults the king, one denies doing so; if one insults the chief minister, one denies doing so. (One may disdain authority, but should not expose oneself to punishment for doing so. Compare the following entry and 4475.)

1379. *Bí a bá bu ọba tí a ṣẹ́, ọba a fini sílẹ̀.*
If one insults a king and denies doing so, the king leaves one in peace. (One should not be held accountable for an insult one recants. Compare the preceding entry and 4475.)

1380. *Bí a bá dáké, tara ẹni a báni dáké.*
If one keeps silent, what is in one's body keeps silent as well. (If one does not disclose one's problems, one can expect no help.)

1381. *Bí a bá fa àgbò féégún, à fi okùn-un rẹ̀ sílẹ̀.*
If one drags a sheep to present to a masquerader, one lets go of its leash. (When one has made a gift of something, one should forget about it.)

1382. *Bí a bá fẹ́ràn òrẹ́ ẹni láfẹ̀ẹ́jù, bó bá forígbún, ìjà níńdà.*
If one loves one's friend beyond reason, when that friend bumps his or her head, a fight results. (Friendship that knows no limits is a burden.)

1383. *Bí a bá fi dídùn họ ifàn, a ó họra dé eegun.*
If one scratches an itch as long as the sensation is pleasant, one will scratch down to the

15. An ethnic group in the Sahelian areas of West Africa, also known as the Fulbe.

bone. (Even pleasures should be pursued in moderation.)

1384. *Bí a bá fi ojú igi gbígbẹ wo tútù, tútù-ú lè wó pani.*
If one approaches a dried-up tree as one would a green one, it is likely to crash and crush one to death. (One should be alive to the peculiarities of whatever situations one finds oneself in.)

1385. *Bí a bá fi ọdún mẹ́ta pilẹ̀sẹ̀-ẹ wèrè, ọjọ́ wo la ó bunijẹ?*
If one takes three years to prepare for madness, when will one start biting people? (Preparations for an action should not be endless. See also the following entry.)

1386. *Bí a bá fi ọdún mẹ́ta ṣánpá, ọdún mélòó la ó fi fò?*
If one spends three years flapping one's arms, how many years will one take to fly? (Preparations for an action should not be interminable. See also the previous entry.)

1387. *Bí a bá fi ọwọ́ kan fọmọ fọ́kọ, ọwọ́ mẹ́wẹ̀ẹ̀wá kì í ṣeé gbà á mọ́.*
If one gives a girl away in marriage with one hand, ten hands will not suffice to take her back. (Mistakes made casually are seldom easy to correct.)

1388. *Bí a bá lé ẹni, tí a kò bá ẹni, ìwọ̀n là ḿbá ẹni-í sọ̀tá mọ.*
If one chases a person and does not catch up, one should moderate one's hatred of the person. (Envy should not turn into hatred.)

1389. *Bí a bá ní ká bẹ́ igi, a ó bẹ́ẹ́ èèyàn.*
If one attempts to cut a tree, one will cut people. (If one behaved toward certain people as they deserve, one would offend innocent people.)

1390. *Bí a bá ní ká jẹ èkuru kó tán, a kì í gbọn ọwọ́-ọ rẹ̀ sáwo.*
If one wishes to clean one's plate of dry bean grits, one does not keep scraping the remnants from one's fingers onto the plate. (If one wishes a quarrel to end, one does not keep recalling its cause.)

1391. *Bí a bá ńjà, bí í kákú là ńwí?*
Even though we are quarreling, should we wish each other dead? (Quarrels should stop short of death wishes.)

1392. *Bí a bá ńretí òfò, ká fi ohun tọrẹ.*
If one expects a loss, one should make a gift of what one has. (Rather give things away than lose them.)

1393. *Bí a bá perí ajá, ká perí ìkòkò tí a ó fi sè é.*
If one talks of the dog, one should also talk of the pot one will use to cook it. (If one proposes a momentous action, one should also consider the consequences.)

1394. *Bí a bá róbìnrin à lérí ogun; bí a bá róbìnrin à sọ̀rọ̀ ìjà; bí a dé ojú ogun à ba búbú.*
When one sees women, one boasts of war; when one sees women, one talks of battle; when one gets to battle, one lies low. (Before women, one protects one's image; in battle, one protects one's life.)

1395. *Bí a bá sọ pé ẹyẹ ni yó jẹ ojú ẹni, bí a rí tí-ń-tín, a ó máa sá lọ.*
If one has been told that a bird will eat one's eyes, when one sees the tiniest of birds, one takes to one's heels. (Given prior warning of a peril, take extraordinary precautions.)

1396. *Bí a bá sọ̀kò sí ààrín ọjà, ará ilé ẹni ní ḿbà.*
If one throws a stone into the marketplace,

it hits someone from one's household. (Random acts of wickedness are likely to affect those close to one.)

1397. *Bí a bá sòrò fún olófòófó, ajádìí agbòn la sọ ọ́ sí.*
Whatever one says to a talebearer one says to a basket that has lost its bottom. (Words whispered to a talebearer are in effect broadcast.)

1398. *Bí a bá sí ìdí ẹni sókè, ọmọ aráyé á rọ omi gbígbóná sí i.*
If one exposes one's anus to view, people will fill it with hot water. (If one exposes one's vulnerability to people, one will be done in.)

1399. *Bí a bá wí a dàbí òwe; bí a ò bá wí a dàbí ìjà.*
If one speaks, it sounds like speaking in proverbs; if one does not speak, it seems like picking a fight. (In certain delicate situations no option is safe.)

1400. *Bí a kò bá láyà-a rìndòrìndò, a kì í jẹ aáyán.*
If one's stomach is not immune to nausea, one does not eat roaches. (One should avoid things one cannot stomach.)

1401. *Bí a kò bá lè kú, ìpẹ̀ là ńgbà.*
If one is unable [or unwilling] to die, one accepts consolation. (Unless you want to die of grieving, allow yourself to be consoled.)

1402. *Bí a kò bá lè mú ọkọ, a kì í na obìnrin-in rẹ̀.*
If one is no match for the husband, one does not hit the wife. (Never provoke a fight you cannot fight.)

1403. *Bí a kò bá lówó aládìn-ín, à jẹun lójúmọmọ, à gbálẹ̀ sùn wàrà.*
If one has no money for lamp oil, one eats in the daytime and sweeps the house and

goes to sleep in good time. (One's plans and actions should fit one's resources.)

1404. *Bí a kò bá ní èsè èfà, a kì í kó iṣu ọjẹ.*
If one does not have 1,200 cowries in savings, one does not purchase yams worth 1,400 cowries. (One's aspirations should match one's means.)

1405. *Bí a kò bá rí wọlé-wọde a ò gbọdọ̀ wọlé ọba.*
If one cannot find the official gatekeeper, one dares not enter the king's palace.[16] (Always ask leave before venturing into another person's domain.)

1406. *Bí a kò bá rígún, à fàkàlà sẹbọ.*
If one cannot find a vulture, one sacrifices a hornbill. (One makes do with what one has.)

1407. *Bí a kò bá ṣe fún ilẹ̀, a kì í fi ọwọ́ sọ ọ́.*
If one has done nothing for Earth, one does not swear by it. (One cannot expect sustenance where one has not cultivated.)

1408. *Bí a kò rówó ra ẹrú, à sọ adìẹ ẹni lórúkọ.*
If one has no money to buy a slave, one gives one's chicken a name. (One should somehow make do with what one has and be content.)

1409. *Bí a ó ti ṣe é ní ńfi ara-a rẹ̀ hàn.*
How it will be accomplished will reveal itself. (The way to accomplish a task will always reveal itself.)

1410. *Bí aáṣẹ bá ti ńfò, bẹ́ẹ̀ la ti ńsọkọ̀ sí i.*
It is according to the flight pattern of the standard-winged nightjar[17] that one throws

---

16. *Wọlé-wọde*, literally "enter-come out," is another designation for the *ẹmẹsẹ* or *ẹmẹ̀wà*, the king's chief messenger.

17. A bird characterized by erratic flight.

stones at it. (One responds according to the situation one is confronted with.)

1411. *Bí adìẹ bá gbélẹ̀ a ya òpìpì.*
If a chicken always keeps to the ground, it becomes flightless. (Whatever endowment one has, one loses it if one neglects it.)

1412. *Bí àjànàkú ò bá gbẹ́kẹ̀lé fùrò, kì í mi òdù àgbọn.*
If an elephant is not sure of its anus, it does not swallow whole coconuts. (Unless one can cope with the consequences, one does not engage in an action. Compare 1427.)

1413. *Bí àjẹ́ bá mupo, ojú-u rẹ̀ a rò.*
Once a witch has drunk oil, she calms down. (After one has achieved one's goal, one should relax.)

1414. *Bí alágbára-á bá jẹ ọ́ níyà, fẹrín sí i.*
If a powerful person mistreats you, burst into laughter. (Never protest against victimization by one against whom you can do nothing.)

1415. *Bí alágẹmọ-ọ́ bá fẹ́ẹ́ kọjá, ìjàm̀pere ò ní-í jà.*
When the chameleon wishes to go by, the black ants refrain from stinging. (The cautious person is immune to the dangers that beset others.)

1416. *Bí alẹ́ bá lẹ́, adẹtẹ̀ a rìn, a yan.*
When night falls, the leper walks and struts. (Night is a welcome cloak for blemishes. This is a variant of 1429.)

1417. *Bí àṣá bá m̀bínú, sùùrù ló yẹ ọlọ́jà.*[18]
If the kite is displaying anger, the best re-sponse for the trader is patience. (One must learn forbearance in the face of provocation.)

1418. *Bí awó ti ńlù lawó ti ńjó.*
As the initiate of mysteries drums, so the initiate of mysteries dances. (One's actions are best suited to the circumstances.)

1419. *Bí bàtá bá ró àrójù, yíya ní ńya.*
If the *bàtá* drum sounds too loud, it tears. (Excess leads to disaster. See also 1430.)

1420. *Bí ekòló bá kọ ebè, ara-a rẹ̀ ni yó gbìn sí i.*
If a worm makes a heap, it is itself that it will plant in it. (The consequences of a person's actions will fall on that person's own head.)

1421. *Bí èsù ikú bá ńṣe ìgbín nìgbín ńyẹ́yin.*
It is when the snail wants to invite death that it lays eggs.[19] (A person who knows an action will be disastrous but carries it out anyway deserves what he gets.)

1422. *Bí ẹja bá sùn, ẹja á fi ẹja jẹ.*
If fish sleep, fish will devour fish. (If one does not wish to be taken advantage of, one must be ever watchful.)

1423. *Bí ẹlẹ́hìnkùlé ò sùn, à pé lẹ́hìnkùlé-e rẹ̀ títí; bó pẹ́ títí orun a gbé onílé lọ.*
If the owner of the back yard does not sleep, one stays in the back yard for a long time; sooner or later the owner of the house will fall asleep. (Patience accomplishes all ends.)

1424. *Bí ẹlẹ́jọ́ bá mọ ẹjọ́-ọ rẹ̀ lébi, kì í pẹ́ níkùnúnlẹ̀.*
The person involved in a case who acknowledges guilt does not last long on his or her knees. (Penitence invites leniency.)

---

18. *Ọlọ́jà*, literally "the owner of the merchandise" or "the owner of the market," is also used as a designation for a king, inasmuch as he owns the main market, which is usually sited outside the palace.

---

19. Snails supposedly die after laying eggs.

1425. *Bí ẹnìkán bá fojú di Orò, Orò a gbé e.*
If anyone defies the Orò mystery, it does
away with him or her. (Whoever disdains
potential dangers eventually pays for the
disdain.)

1426. *Bí ẹnìkán ṣe ohun tí ẹnìkan ò ṣe rí,
ojú-u rẹ̀ á rí ohun tí ẹnìkan ò rí rí.*
If a person does what no one has ever done
before, his eyes will see what no one has ever
seen before. (Those who do unusual things
should expect unusual consequences.)

1427. *Bí ìdí ìkokò kò bá dá a lójú, kì í gbé
egungun mì.*
If the wolf does not have faith in its anus, it
does not swallow bones. (One should not
attempt a thing whose repercussions one
cannot withstand. Compare 1412.)

1428. *Bí ìfà bí ìfà lọmọdé fi ńdáràn wọlé.*
As though he were stumbling on treasures,
thus a youth brings trouble into the household. (A youth seldom realizes what actions
will involve his household in trouble.)

1429. *Bí ilé bá dá, adẹ́tẹ̀ a rìn, a yan.*
When the house is deserted, the leper will
walk and strut. (When one is unobserved,
one does as one pleases. This is a variant of
1416.)

1430. *Bí ìlùú bá dún àdúnjù, yó faya.*
If a drum makes too much noise, it breaks.
(Disaster follows excess. See also 1419.)

1431. *Bí iná bá jóni, tó jó ọmọ ẹni, tara ẹni là
ńkọ́ gbòn.*
If one is on fire and one's child is on fire, one
douses one's own fire first. (Without first
attending to one's own needs, one cannot
attend to those of others.)

1432. *Bí iṣu ẹní bá funfun, à fọwọ́ bò ó jẹ.*
If one's yam is white, one eats it furtively. (It
would be unwise to flaunt good fortune.)

1433. *Bí kò bá sí oníṣẹ́ iṣẹ́ ò leè lọ; bí kò bá sí
olọ́wẹ̀ a kì í ṣọ̀wẹ̀; àkèhìnsí olọ́wẹ̀ là ńṣípá.*
If the owner of the job is absent, the job does
not progress; if the person who engaged
the help is absent, no help is given; when
the back of the person who engaged help is
turned, one lifts one's hands from the job.
(The employee is most industrious under
the supervision of the employer.)

1434. *Bí o máa ra ilá ra ilá, bí o máa gba ènì
gba ènì; ọmọdé kì í wá sójà Agbó-mẹ́kùn kó
wá mú eku.*
If you wish to buy okro, buy okro; if you
wish to receive a gratuity, do so; a child
does not come to a tiger hunt and catch rats.
(One's deeds should be appropriate to the
location.)

1435. *Bí obìnrín bá wọgbó Orò, a ò lè rí àbọ̀-ọ
è mọ́.*
If a woman enters the ritual grove of the Orò
cult, no one will ever see her return. (Any
person who engages in forbidden action
courts destruction.)

1436. *Bí ògbó eni ò bá dánilójú, a kì í fi gbárí
wò.*
If one does not trust one's cudgel, one does
not try it on one's own head. (One should
not swear by something about which one is
not certain. Compare 2020.)

1437. *Bí ojú alákẹdun ò dá igi, kì í gùn ún.*
If the monkey is not certain about a tree, it
does not climb it. (One should not embark
on projects one cannot accomplish.)

1438. *Bí ojú onísó ò bá sunwọ̀n, a kì í lọ̀ ọ́.*
If the face of the person who farted is baleful, one does not make a big fuss about the
fart. (Do not incite a person who is spoiling
for a fight.)

1439. *Bí ológbò-ó bá pa eku, a fi ìrù-u rẹ̀ delé.*
When a cat kills a mouse, it uses the tail as a

sentry. (One should save something of one's fortune for the future.)

1440. *Bí ológbò-ó bá sè ńpa ẹmọ́, à mọ̀ pé ó máa lọ.*
When a cat begins to kill guinea pigs, one knows it is ready to go.[20] (A person who embarks on improper behavior invites ostracism.)

1441. *Bí olówe-é bá mọ òwe-e rè, tí kò já a, èrù ìjà ḿbà á ni.*
If the butt of a proverb recognizes but does not acknowledge it, he is afraid of a fight. (A person who has reason to take offense but does not is avoiding a fight.)[21]

1442. *Bí òní ti rí, òla ò rí béè; ni babaláwo-ó fi ńdífá lọ́rọọrún.*
As today is, tomorrow will not be; hence the diviner consults the oracle every five days. (Since no one knows the future, one must constantly reassess one's decisions.)

1443. *Bí onísú bá fi iṣu-u rè se èbé, ọgbọ́n a tán nínú a-tu-èèpo-jẹ.*
If the owner of the yams cuts them for porridge, the person who gleans what sticks to the peelings is at a loss for what to do. (If the perennial victim learns to protect himself, the victimizer is stumped.)[22]

1444. *Bí ooré bá pọ̀ lápòjù, ibi ní ńdà.*
If goodness is excessive, it becomes evil. (There can be too much of even a good thing.)

1445. *Bí òwe ò bá jọ òwe, a kì í pa á.*
If a proverb does not apply to a situation, one does not use it. (One's comparisons should be apt.)

1446. *Bí ọmọ ẹni bá dára, ká sọ pé ó dára; bí-i ká fi ṣaya ẹni kọ́.*
If one's daughter is beautiful, one may acknowledge that she is beautiful but may not marry her. (However much one is attracted to a forbidden thing, one must avoid it.)

1447. *Bí ọmọdé bá dárí sọ apá, apá á pá; bó bá dárí sọ ìrókò, ìrókò a kò ó lọ́nà.*
If a child strikes his head against the mahogany-bean tree, the tree will kill him; if he strikes his head against the ìrókò tree, the tree will accost him on his way.[23] (Whoever incites a terrible force to fight will rue his folly.)

1448. *Bí ọmọdé ò rí àjẹkù-u kìnìún nínú igbó, a ní kí ẹran bí ẹkùn ó pa òun.*
If a child has not seen the leavings of a lion in the forest, he prays that he might be killed by an animal like the leopard. (One is likely to disdain forces the extent of whose powers one is ignorant of.)

1449. *Bí ọnà-á dé orí àpáta, níṣe ní ńpin.*
When a trail comes to a rock, it ends. (When an insurmountable obstacle intervenes, efforts must stop.)

1450. *Bí òràn-án bá ṣú òkùnkùn, à bẹ̀ ẹ́ wò lábẹ́.*
If a matter is dark, one peeps at it under cover. (If the facts of a matter are a close secret, one should quietly investigate it.)

1451. *Bí òràn ò tán, ibì kan là ńgbé; arékété lohun ńṣe.*
If a problem is not finished, one stays in place; it is the overeager person who comes

---

20. Guinea pigs are kept as pets.
21. *Olówe* (owner of the proverb) in this instance means the person to whom the proverb is applied.
22. Yams cut for porridge leave no remnants sticking to the peels.

---

23. Both of these trees are reputed to be homes for fearful spirits.

to grief. (One should await the outcome of a confused situation before taking further action.)

1452. *Bí ọtí bá kún inú, ọtí á pọmọ; bí oòrùn-ún bá pọ̀ lápọ̀jù a sọ ọmọ di wèrè; bí a bá lóba lánìíjù a sínni níwín; tètè ègún pọ̀ lódò o di olú eri.*
If wine fills the stomach, it intoxicates a child; if there is too much sun, it makes a child go insane; if one has too much authority, one goes mad; spinach that grew in too great abundance by the stream became ordinary weed. (Excess in anything is evil.)

1453. *Bí ọwọ́ ò bá tẹ èkù idà, a kì í bèrè ikú tó pa baba ẹni.*
If one has not laid one's hand on the hilt of the sword, one does not ask what killed one's father. (Until one is able, one should not attempt to right an injustice.)

1454. *Bíbi là ḿbi odò wò ká tó wọ̀ ọ́.*
One asks a river before one enters it. (One must study well any situation before becoming involved in it.)

1455. *Bọ̀rọ̀kìnní àṣejù, oko olówó ni ḿmúni lọ.*
Excessive devotion to fashion leads one to pawn oneself. (Excessive trendiness depletes a person's resources.)

1456. *Bọ̀rọ̀kìnnín lòtá ilú; afínjú lọba ńpa.*
The dandy is the enemy of the town; it is the finicky person that the king kills. (The people of a town may envy a dandy, but it is the reckless person who comes to grief.)[24]

D

1457. *Dàda ò leè jà, ṣùgbọ́n ó lábùúrò tó gbójú.*
Dada cannot fight, but he has a brave younger brother. (One who may not be able to do much has relatives to take up his cause.)

1458. *Dágun-dágun Kaletu tí ńdá ìbejì lápá.*
Troublemaker of Kaletu breaks the arms of a twin. (A person who provokes someone with powerful champions is a troublemaker.)

1459. *Dá-mìíràn-kún-mìíràn tí ńpa àpatà eyẹlé.*
One-who-commits-crimes-atop-crimes: he butchers pigeons for sale. (Refers to a hardened criminal who piles crimes on crimes.)[25]

1460. *Dàńdógó kojá èwù àbínúdá; bí a bá ko ẹni tó juni lọ, a yàgò fún un.*
Dàńdógó is not something to make in a huff;[26] one makes way for a person who is too much for one. (One should know one's limits. Compare 2026.)

1461. *Dá-ǹkan-dá-ǹkan, tí kì í dáṣọ, tí kì í dẹwù.*
Originator-of-problems: he does not make a cloth and does not make a dress. (What a troublemaker brings is trouble, never anything useful.)

E

1462. *Èèyan má-jẹ́ẹ́-kí-èèyàn-kú ḿbẹ níbòmíràn; bó-le-kú-ó-kú ḿbẹ nílé-e wa.*
The save-the-person-from-death type

24. The idea is that the dandy knows his place, even if he incites envy, whereas the finicky person who is afraid of death refuses to show respect for the king in the usual way—by prostrating himself—and therefore loses his head.

25. Killing a pigeon is bad enough; cutting it up for sale worsens the crime.
26. Dàńdógó is an expensive and elaborate traditional garment.

of people abounds elsewhere; the let-
the-person-die-if-he-or-she-wishes type
abounds in our house. (It is not our way
to stop people bent on destroying themselves. Also, we do have evil people in our
home.)

1463. Èèyàn-án ní oun ó bà ọ́ jẹ́ o ní kò tó bẹ́ẹ̀;
bí ó bá ní o ò nùdí, ẹni mélòó lo máa fẹ furọ̀
hàn?
A person vows to disgrace you, and you
respond that there is no way he can succeed; if he spreads the word that you did not
clean yourself after defecating, to how many
people will you display your anus? (No one
is immune to malicious defamation.)

1464. Èké tan-ni síjà ẹkùn, ó fi ọrán sísẹ́ sápó
ẹni.
The devious person goads one to confront
a leopard and fills one's quiver with broken
arrows. (It is dangerous to follow a devious
person's counsel.)

1465. Eku ò gbọdọ̀ ná ojà tí ológìnni dá.
A mouse dares not visit a market established
by a cat. (One should not deliberately court
disaster.)

1466. Eku tí yó pa ológìnni ò níí dúró láyé.
The mouse that attempts to kill a cat will
not live long on this earth. (It is foolhardy to
take on powers that can destroy you.)

1467. "Èmi ló lòní, èmi ló lọla" lọmọdé fi
ńdígbèsè.
"Today belongs to me; tomorrow belongs to
me" is the attitude that pushes a youth into
debt. (Lack of foresight leads to disaster).

1468. Èmi ò wá ikún inú agbè fi jiyán; ṣùgbọ́n
bíkún bá yí sínú agbè mi mo lè fi jiyán.
I will not go looking for a squirrel in my
gourd to eat with pounded yam; but if a
squirrel falls into my gourd, I will eat it with

pounded yam. (I will not steal, but neither
will I refuse a lucky find.)

1469. Èpè-é pọ̀ ju ohun tó nù; abẹ́rẹ́ sọnù wọ́n
lọ gbé Ṣàngó.
The cursing is far in excess of what is lost: a
needle goes missing, and the owners invoke
Ṣango. (One's reaction to a situation should
be commensurate to it. This is a variant of
the following entry.)

1470. Èpè-é pọ̀ ju ohun tó nù lọ; abẹ́rẹ́ sọnù a
gbé ṣẹ́ẹ́rẹ́ síta.
The curse is out of all proportion to the
lost article: a needle is lost and [the owner]
brings out a magic wand. (One should not
overreact to events. Compare the preceding
entry.)

1471. Eré-e kí lajá ńbá ẹkùn ṣe?
What sort of sport is it that the dog engages
in with the leopard? (One should know
better than to court disaster.)

1472. Èrò kì í jéwọ́-ọ "Mo tà tán."
The trader never confesses, "I sold all my
wares." (People are ever loath to disclose the
extent of their good fortune.)

1473. Eṣinṣin ò mọkú; jíjẹ ni tirẹ̀.
The fly does not heed death; all it cares to
do is eat. (The fly will persist in attacking
an open sore, heedless of death; nothing will
keep an addict from the thing he or she is
addicted to.)

1474. Èṣù ò ṣejò; ẹni tó tẹ ejò mọ́lẹ̀ lẹbá ńbá.
There is no disaster stalking the snake; it is
whoever steps on a snake that is in trouble.
(It is not the snake inadvertently stepped on
that is in peril; it is the person who inadvertently steps on the snake.)

1475. Etí mẹ́ta ò yẹ orí; èèyàn mẹ́ta ò dúró ní
méjì-méjì.

Three ears are unbecoming for the head; three people cannot stand in twos. (Good things are not good in all situations; one can have too much of a good thing.)

1476. *Ewú logbó; irùngbòn làgbà; máamú làfojúdi.*
Gray hair shows age; a beard shows maturity; a mustache shows impudence. (One's appearance in a group sometimes indicates one's attitude toward the group.)[27]

1477. *Ewúrẹ́ jẹ ó relé; àgùntán jẹ ó relé; à-jẹ-ì-wálé ló ba ẹlẹ́dẹ̀ jẹ́.*
The goat forages and returns home; the sheep forages and returns home; the pig's flaw is its habit of not returning home after foraging. (There is nothing wrong with traveling, as long as one knows when to go home.)

1478. *Ewúrẹ́ kì í wọlé tọ ìkokò.*
A goat does not venture into the lair of a wolf. (Never knowingly put yourself in harm's way.)

1479. *Èyí ayé ńṣe ng kà sàì ṣe; bádìẹ-ẹ́ máa wọ ọ̀ọ̀dẹ̀ a bẹ̀rẹ̀.*
Whatever the rest of the world does, I will not forswear; when a chicken wants to enter the porch, it stoops. (One should not violate established custom.)

1480. *Èyí ò tófò, èyí ò tófò: fìlà ìmàle-ẹ́ kù pẹ́tẹ́kí.*
"This is no great loss; this is no great loss": the Muslim's cap dwindles to almost noth-ing.[28] (If one keeps dispensing one's property only a little at a time, soon little will be left.)

Ẹ

1481. *Ẹ pa Ayéjẹnkú, ẹ pa Ìyálóde Aníwúrà; ìgbà tí ẹ pa Ìyápò ẹ gbàgbé ogun.*
You killed Ayéjẹnkú and killed Ìyálóde Aní-wúrà; but when you killed Ìyápò, you forgot about wars.[29] (Past misbehaviors might have gone unpunished, but the latest will have dire repercussions.)

1482. *Èbi alábaun kì í gbèé dèbi àna-a rè.*
Tortoise's guilt is not long in becoming its parent-in-law's. (Incommensurate retaliation soon transfers public sympathy from the aggrieved person to the culprit. See 1342.)

1483. *Èbìtì ò peèrà tó ṣe pèlépèlé; ẹnu eni ní ńpani.*
A trap does not kill an ant that is cautious; it is one's mouth that turns out to be one's death. (The cautious will live long on the earth; the incautious engineers his or her own death.)

1484. *Èbìtì tí ò kún ẹmó lójú, òun ní ńyí i lépòn séhìn.*
It is a trap that the giant rat disdains that wrenches its testicles backward. (Dangers

---

27. *Máamú* (*máa mú*), here used for mustache, means "keep drinking," since when a mustached person takes a drink, some liquid clings to the mustache — for later drinking. The proverb presumably refers to the practice of drinking from a communal cup or bowl; in that situation a person who wears a mustache invites others to drink from a vessel in which he has washed his mustache.

28. The reference is to the skull cap associated with Muslims. The idea is that once it was much larger, but then the owner raised no objection to successive requests for just a little piece of it. His response each time is that he can afford to give up just a little bit.

29. The references are to real events and real people in Ibadan history in the 1870s. The three named persons are notables: Ìyálóde [Ẹfúnsetán] Aníwúrà, the leader of the women in the community; Ayéjẹnkú, a person of worth; Ìyápò, apparently a great warrior whose demise placed the community at risk.

that one belittles are likely to cause great havoc.)

1485. Èèkan ṣoṣo lọmọ ńsín tí à ńní "à-sín-gbó, à-sín-tọ́."
It is when a child sneezes only once that one wishes for the child "Sneeze and grow old, sneeze and live long." (Casual responses are appropriate only for minor difficulties; if the difficulties grow serious, more appropriate measures must be adopted.)

1486. Ègbá mòdí Ọbà; ẹni tó gbénisánlè-ẹ́ lè pani.
The Ègbá know the secrets of Ọbà town; whoever throws a person has the ability to kill the person. (Whoever holds a person's secret has some power over that person, just as the wrestler who can throw his opponents can probably also kill him.)

1487. Egbẹ́ eja leja ńwẹ̀ tò; egbẹ́ eye leye ńwọ́ lé.
Fish swim in a school of their own kind; birds fly in a flock of their own kind. (One should seek and keep the company of people of one's own station.)

1488. Èhìn àjànàkú là ńyọ ogbó; ta ní jẹ́ yọ agada lójú erin?
It is after the demise of the elephant that one brandishes a cudgel; who dares draw a scimitar in the face of an elephant? (One can be brave after the danger has been removed. This is a variant of 1764.)

1489. Èhìn ní ńdun ol-ókùú-àdá sí.
It is the back of the man with a blunt cutlass that suffers. (A person who does not make adequate preparations for a task or test will rue his or her negligence. Compare 1598.)

1490. Èkọ tí kò bá léwé làgbà ńgbà.
It is corn loaf with no leaf wrapping that the elder takes. (One who is careless with one's property is likely to lose it.)[30]

1491. Ẹkùn kì í yan kí ajá yan.
A leopard that struts is not answered by strutting from a dog. (One should recognize danger and avoid it.)

1492. Ẹlédè tó kú légbodò ló ní ká fòun jẹyán.
It is a pig that dies at the time of the harvesting of new yams that asks to be eaten with pounded yam. (If one puts oneself in harm's way, one deserves what one gets.)

1493. Ẹléjọ́ kú sílé, aláròyé kú síta gbangba.
The person involved in an affair dies at home; the spokesperson dies out in the open. (The busybody's fate is worse than that of the person involved in the affair.)

1494. Ẹlékún sunkún ó bá tirẹ̀ lọ; aláròpa ìbá sunkún kò dáké.
The person with a cause to cry cries and departs; a person whose mind never leaves a problem will never stop crying. (One should not keep harping on one's injuries.)

1495. Ẹlérù ní ńgbé ẹrù ká tó ba ké ọfẹ.
The owner of the load must first lift it before one lends one's encouragement. (Only those who make an effort on their own behalf deserve help from others.)

1496. Èlúlùú, ìwọ ló fòjò pa ara-à rẹ.
Lark-heeled Cuckoo, it was you that got yourself drenched in the rain. (Whatever your difficulty is, you brought it on yourself.)

1497. Ẹni àjò ò pé kó múra ilé.
The person for whom a journey has not

---

30. Àgbà (elder) should not be taken literally here; the proverb plays on the syllable gbà (take from), the sense being that what-takes (construed here as a-gbà) takes only what is unprotected.

been profitable should prepare to return home. (One should know when it is time to go home.)

1498. Ẹní bá fẹ́ abuké ni yó ru ọmọ-ọ rẹ̀ dàgbà.
Whoever marries a humpbacked woman will carry her child on his back until the child is weaned. (One who knowingly gets himself or herself into a difficulty will bear the consequences.)

1499. Ẹní bá fẹ́ arúgbó gbẹ̀hìn ni yó sìnkú-u rẹ̀.
The last spouse of an old person will bury him or her. (One should weigh the obligations an enterprise will entail before embarking on it.)

1500. Ẹní bá mọ ayé-é jẹ kì í gun àgbọn.
Whoever knows what makes for a good life never climbs coconut palms. (Whoever cares about his or her welfare does not live dangerously. Compare 128 and 223.)

1501. Ẹní bá mọ ayé-é jẹ kì í jà.
Whoever knows how to enjoy life does not enter into a fight. (The best way to enjoy life is to avoid conflict.)

1502. Ẹní bá mọ iṣin-ín jẹ a mọ ikú ojú-u rẹ̀-é yọ.
Whoever knows how to eat Akee apple must know how to remove its deadly raphe. (One should be sure of one's capabilities before attempting dangerous feats.)[31]

1503. Ẹní bá na Ọ̀yẹ̀kú á ríjà Ogbè.
Whoever whips Ọ̀yẹ̀kú will have Ogbè to

answer to.[32] (If one assaults a protected person, one should be prepared to answer to his or her protector.)

1504. Ẹní bá pé kí àkàlà má jòkú, ojú-u rẹ̀ lẹyẹ ńkọ́kọ́ yo jẹ.
Whoever says the ground hornbill should not eat carrion will be the first to lose his or her eyes to the bird. (Whoever tries to prevent the inevitable will be trampled in the process of its occurring. Compare 2192.)

1505. Ẹní bá rọra pa eèrà á rí ifun inú-u rẹ̀.
Whoever takes great care in killing an ant will see its innards. (One must handle delicate matters carefully.)

1506. Ẹní bá sọ púpọ̀ á ṣìsọ.
Whoever talks a lot will misspeak. (It is best to be a person of few words.)

1507. Ẹní bẹni-í tẹ́ni.
Whoever pleads with one makes one lose face. (A beseecher places the beseeched at risk of losing face.)[33]

1508. Ẹní dáríjini sètẹ́ ejọ́.
The one who forgives defuses the dispute. (Once the aggrieved person is pacified, there is no further point in pursuing the case.)

1509. Ẹní dúró de erín dúró dekú; ẹní dúró defọn-ón dúró dèjà; ẹní dúró de eégún alágangan, ọ̀run ló fẹ́-ẹ lọ.
Whoever waits in a charging elephant's path waits for death; whoever waits in a

---

31. Iṣin, Akee apple, is a fruit whose fleshy part is eaten raw or cooked. Its raphe, or seam, is deadly and must be carefully removed before the flesh is consumed (see Abraham 323).

32. Ogbè is the chief of the chapters that make up the Ifá divination corpus; Ọ̀yẹ̀kú is one of the junior chapters. These chapters are regarded as spirits.

33. The idea is that whatever one's justification might be and however great the beseecher's unworthiness, one who refuses his or her plea is likely to appear heartless.

buffalo's path waits for an attack; whoever tarries before a fleet-footed masquerader hankers for a trip to heaven. (Whoever sees trouble approaching and does not flee courts disaster.)

1510. *Ẹní fi ìpọ́njú kọ ẹyìn á kọ àbọn; ẹní fi ìpọ́njú rojọ́ á jẹbi ọba; ẹní fi ìpọ́njú lọ gbẹ́ ìhò á gbẹ́ ìhò awọ́nrínwọ́n.*
Whoever gathers palm fruits in desperation will gather unripe ones; whoever states his or her case in desperation will be adjudged at fault by the king; whoever digs a hole in desperation will dig out an iguana lizard.[34] (Nothing turns out well if done in desperation. Easy does it.)

1511. *Ẹní gúnyán kalẹ̀ yóò júbà ọbẹ̀.*
A person who has made pounded yams must pay homage to the stew. (The prudent person cultivates the source of what he or she needs.)

1512. *Ẹní gbé adìẹ òtòṣì-í gbé ti aláròyé.*
Whoever steals a poor person's chicken steals from an incessant complainer. (One should choose one's adversaries with prudence.)

1513. *Ẹní kánjú jayé á kánjú lọ sọ́run.*
Whoever is in a hurry to enjoy life will go to heaven in a hurry. (Patience is what life calls for.)

1514. *Ẹni méjì kì í bínú egbinrin.*
Two people do not hold a grudge and refuse reconciliation. (If there is to be any hope of ending a quarrel, at least one of the parties must be willing to make up.)

1515. *Ẹni òyìnbó féràn ní ńtì mọ́lé.*
It is the person the white man likes that the white man incarcerates. (Whoever becomes too friendly with a white man deserves what the white man does to him. A favorite, being more likely to take liberties with his or her benefactor, is more likely to get in trouble than the unfavored.)

1516. *Ẹní ṣe òràn Ìjẹ̀bú: etí ẹ̀ á gbọ́ ìbon.*
Whoever provokes an Ìjẹ̀bú person, his or her ears will hear gunshot. (If one incites a bellicose person, one asks for trouble.)[35]

1517. *Ẹni tí a bá ńbá ṣiṣẹ́ kì í sọ̀lẹ; bórí bá túnni ṣe a kì í tẹ́ bọ̀rọ̀.*
The person being lent a hand does not malinger; one whom Providence favors is not easily disgraced. (One should make the most of unexpected good fortune and not squander the opportunity it presents. Compare 2064.)

1518. *Ẹni tí a bá ńmú ìyàwó bọ̀ wá fún kì í garùn.*
The person to whom a bride is being brought does not strain his neck [to see her from a distance]. (One should not be unduly impatient for what is coming toward one anyway.)

1519. *Ẹni tí a bá ti rí kì í tún ba mọ́lẹ̀ mọ́.*
A person who has been seen has no further need of hiding. (Once the damage is done, prevention comes too late.)

1520. *Ẹni tí a fẹ́-ẹ́ sunjẹ kì í fẹpo para lọ jókòó sídìí iná.*
A person being eyed for barbecuing does not baste himself with oil and sit by the

---

34. The digging of holes in this case would normally be for the purpose of finding something edible: a crab, for instance. An iguana is not only unsuitable as food but is also considered dangerous.

---

35. The Ìjẹ̀bú are an ethnic group reputed to possess powerful and fearful charms with which they are believed to attack their enemies.

fire. (One should not facilitate one's own undoing.)

1521. Ẹni tí a lù lógbòó mẹ́fà, tí a ní kó fiyèdénú: ìgbà tí kò fiyèdénú ńkó?
A person is hit with a cudgel six times and then urged to learn forbearance; what other option does he or she have? (A victim with no access to any remedy needs no advice to let matters drop.)

1522. Ẹni tí a ò lè mú, a kì í gọ dè é.
One does not lie in ambush for an adversary one is no match for. (Pick fights only with those over whom you can prevail. Compare 4201.)

1523. Ẹni tí a ò lè mú, Ọlọ́run là ńfi lé lọ́wọ́.
An adversary over whom one cannot prevail one leaves to God's judgment. (If your adversary is too much for you, let God attend to him or her.)

1524. Ẹni tí ńsáré kiri nínú-u pápá ńwá ọ̀nà àti jìn sí kòtò.
The person who runs about in the bush courts the danger of falling into a ditch. (Reckless action can lead to disaster.)

1525. Ẹni tí ó bá mu ọtí ogójì á sọ̀rọ̀ okòó.
Whoever drinks 40 cowries' worth of wine will talk 20 cowries' worth of talk. (A little wine opens the way for even less information.)

1526. Ẹni tí ó bá obìnrin kó lọ sílé-e rẹ̀ yó sùn nínú èrù.
A man who goes with a woman to her house will sleep in fear. (Illicit acts carried on indiscreetly are attended by great anxiety.)

1527. Ẹni tí ó ba ogún-un baba rẹ̀ jẹ́, ó ja òkú ọ̀run lólè, yó sì di ẹni ìfibú.
Whoever ruins his or her father's bequest robs the dead and becomes a person of reproach. (We must keep faith with our ancestral heritage.)

1528. Ẹni tí ó bá wọ odò ni àyà ńkò, àyà ò fo odò.
It is the person who enters a river who is terrified, not the river. (It is the person who takes on an invincible adversary, not the adversary, who has a problem.)

1529. Ẹni tí ò fẹ́ẹ́ wọ àkísà kì í bá ajá ṣe eré-e géle.
A person who does not wish to wear rags should not engage in rough play with a dog. (People should avoid situations that might earn them disgrace.)

1530. Ẹni tí ó jìn sí kòtò-ó kọ́ ará ìyókù lógbọ́n.
The person who falls into a ditch teaches others a lesson. (One learns from the experiences of those who have gone before.)

1531. Ẹni tí ó mú u lórí ní ó kú, ìwọ tí o mú u lẹ́sẹ̀-ẹ́ ní ó ńjòwèrè.
The person holding it by the head says it is dead; you who are holding it by the feet say it is going through death throes. (Novices should not presume to be more knowledgeable than the experts.)

1532. Ẹni tí ó tọ odò tí kò dèhìn yò bàá Olúwẹri pàdé.
Whoever follows the river without turning back will come face to face with Oluweri.[36] (Whoever persists in courting danger will eventually find it.)

1533. Ẹni tí ò tóni-í nà ò gbọdọ̀ ṣe kọ́-ń-dú síni.
A person who is not strong enough to beat you up should not adopt a threatening pose

---

36. Said to be a river goddess.

toward you. (People should not challenge forces they cannot withstand.)

1534. Ẹni tí ó yá egbàafà tí kò san án, ó bẹ́gi dí ọ̀nà egbèje.
The person who borrows 1,200 cowries and does not pay them back blocks the path of 1,400 cowries. (A person who defaults in little things does himself or herself out of the opportunity for larger benefits.)

1535. Ẹni tí Orò-ó máa mú ṁba wọn ṣe àìsùn Orò.
The person who will be the sacrificial victim of Orò is joining in the revelry on the eve of the sacrifice. (The intended victim innocently helps in making preparations for his or her own demise; if there is the slightest possibility of peril, one should not act carelessly.)

1536. Ẹníkan kì í fi ọ̀bẹ tó nù jẹṣu.
No one eats yams with a lost knife. (People are loath to admit they are at fault in any matter.)[37]

1537. Ẹnu eye ní ṁpẹye; ẹnu òrofó ní ṁpòrofó; òrofó bímọ méfà, ó ní ilé òun-ún kún sọ́sọ́sọ́.
The bird's mouth is its death; the green fruit pigeon's mouth is its death; the pigeon hatches six chicks and boasts that its house is bursting at the seams. (To boast about good fortune is to invite predators. See 1539 and 1540.)

1538. Ẹnu iná ní ṁpa iná; ẹnu èrò ní ṁpa èrò.
The mouth of the louse is its death; the mouth of the nit is its death. (Reckless persons bring disaster on their heads by their own actions.)[38]

1539. Ẹnu ni àparò-ó fi ṁpe ọ̀rá; a ní "Kìkì ọ̀rá, kìkì ọ̀rá!"
With its own mouth the partridge invites its own ruin; it cries, "Nothing but fat, nothing but fat!"[39] (Conspicuous display of one's good fortune invites predators. Compare 1537 and 1540.)

1540. Ẹnu òfòrò ní ṁpa òfòrò; òfòrò-ó bímọ méjì, ó kó wọn wá sébàà ọ̀nà, ó ní "Ọmọ-ọ̀ mí yè koro-koro."
The squirrel's mouth summons its death; the squirrel has two children, takes them to the edge of the path, and says, "My children are hale and well indeed." (Excessive boasting about one's good fortune invites predators. Compare 1537 and 1539.)

1541. Ẹnu tí ìgbín fi bú òrìṣà ní ṁfi-í lọlẹ̀ lọ bá a.
The same mouth with which the snail insults the god is the one on which it crawls to the god.[40] (The person who insults a powerful person will in time eat his or her words before the person insulted.)

1542. Ẹnu-ù mi kọ́ ni wọ́n ti máa gbọ́ pé ìyá oba-á lájẹ̀ẹ́.
It is not from my mouth that people will learn that the king's mother is a witch. (I will not place myself in jeopardy by speaking dangerous truths; one should not acknowledge or comment on everything one sees.)

1543. Ẹrè òkèọ̀dàn ni yó kìlọ̀ fún a-l-áròó-gbálẹ̀ aṣọ.

---

37. Once a knife is lost, no one will admit that he or she used it last.

38. If lice and nits did not bite, no one would know of their presence and crush them.

39. The proverb is based on the call of the partridge, which is here suggested to be what attracts the attention of the hunter. Ọ̀rá is "fat," but it can also mean "being eliminated."

40. Snails are used as sacrifices to some gods. The suggestion is that snails crawl mouth down because a snail once insulted a god.

The mud on the plains will teach a lesson to the person whose loincloth has a train sweeping the ground. (The thoughtless person will learn wisdom when his or her thoughtlessness comes home to roost.)

1544. Èrù kọ́ ní m̀ba ọpẹ tó ní ká dá òun sí, nítorí ẹmu ọ̀la ni.
It is not out of fear that the palm tree pleads to be allowed to stand; it is on account of tomorrow's palm wine.[41] (What we have the good sense to preserve today will yield benefits for us in the future.)

1545. Ẹṣin iwájú ni ti ẹ̀hìn ǹwò sáré.
The leading horse is the one by which the followers set their pace. (One takes example from those that have gone before.)

1546. Èsọ̀ èsọ̀ la fi ńlá ọbẹ̀ tó gbóná.
Slowly, slowly is the way to eat soup that is scalding hot. (The more dangerous the task, the greater the care required.)

1547. Ètẹ́ ní ńgbẹ̀hìn aláṣejù.
Disgrace is the reward of excess. (Lack of moderation results in disgrace.)

1548. Ẹyẹ kí lo máa pa tí ò ńfi àkùkọ ṣe oògùn àtẹ̀?
What sort of bird do you hope to kill that you use a cock as the birdlime charm?[42] (It is unreasonable to expend something of great value in pursuit of something of lesser value.)

1549. Ẹyin adìẹ ò gbọdọ̀ forí sọ àpáta.
A chicken egg should not strike its head against a rock. (It is unwise to take on forces one cannot withstand.)

1550. Ẹyin lọ̀rọ̀; bó bá balẹ̀ fífọ́ ni ńfọ́.
Words are eggs; when they drop on the floor, they shatter into pieces. (Words are delicate things; once spoken, they cannot be retrieved.)

F

1551. Fáàárí àṣejù, oko olówó ní m̀mú ọmọ lọ.
Intemperate dandyism lands a youth on a creditor's farm as a pawn. (Squandered resources bring destitution.)

1552. Fẹ̀hìntì kí o rí iṣẹ́ èké; farapamọ́ kí o gbọ́ bí aṣeni-í ti ńsọ.
Sit back and and you will see how a devious person operates; conceal yourself and you will hear how those who seek others' destruction speak. (One must be cagey in order to learn the truth about unreliable people.)

1553. Fi ẹ̀jẹ̀ sínú, tu itọ́ funfun jáde.
Keep your red blood inside and spit out clear saliva. (Never show your hand to your enemy or let your words or action reveal your intentions.)[43]

1554. Fi ohun wé ohun, fi ọ̀ràn wé ọ̀ràn; fi ọ̀ràn jì ká yìn ọ́.
Liken one thing to another, liken one matter to another; forgive and forget and earn people's praise. (Rather than permit an

---

41. Palm tees are tapped for wine by hacking off some of the leaves to expose the pulp at their base and then punching a hole in the pulp. Palm wine is the milky juice that oozes out of the incision and ferments as it collects in a gourd or bottle tied to the tree.

42. "Birdlime" is a sticky trap for birds to which a charmed or magical item may be added to make it more effective.

43. This proverb is sometimes used as a criticism of deceitful people who appear to be friends but are full of ill will: Ọmọ aráyé fẹjẹ sínú tutọ́ funfun jáde ("Human beings keep their blood inside and spit out clear saliva").

offense to recall earlier ones, one should forgive and forget. This is a variant of 3298.)

1555. *Fi òràn sínú pète èrín; fi ebi sínú sunkún ayo.*
Keep your troubles inside and laugh heartily; keep your hunger hidden and pretend to weep from satiation. (One should keep one's woes to oneself and show a happy face to the world.)

1556. *Fò síhìn-ín fò sóhùn-ún làkèré fi ńsé nítan.*
Jump this way, jump that way is how a frog breaks its thigh. (Restlessness lands people in trouble.)

G

1557. *Ganganran ò séé kì mólè; a-gúnni-lówó-bíi-sosoro.*
A sharp object is not something to grab for; [it is] a-thing-that-pierces-one's-hand-like-a-sharp-instrument. (Dangerous things must be handled very carefully.)

1558. *Gìdì-gìdì ò mólà; ká sisé bí erú ò da nǹkan.*
Scurrying around does not ensure prosperity; working like a slave results in nothing. (One does not necessarily prosper by working oneself to death.)

1559. *Gùdùgudu ò túra sílè léékan.*
Poisonous yam has never lost its skin.[44] (A certain person has never been known to be off his or her guard.)

1560. *Gùdùgudu-ú kan légbò kán-ín-kán-ín.*
Poisonous yam's roots are sour indeed. (The

---

44. One would not bother to peel a poisonous variety of yam.

subject is something one must stay away from, for encounter with it is unpleasant.)

Gb

1561. *"Gbà sókè" ni "Gbà sókò"; ohun tá a bá so síwájú là ḿbá.*
"Put this above [ashore]" equals "Put this in the boat"; it is what one throws ahead that one finds in one's path. (One reaps the rewards of the good one sows.)

1562. *Gbéjò-gbéjò ò gbé okà.*
No snake dancer dances with a cobra. (There are some perils even the bravest of people should not court. Compare the following entry.)

1563. *Gbéran-gbéran ò gbé ekùn.*
No animal pilferer ever pilfers a leopard. (There are some risks even the most brazen risk taker would be wise to avoid. Compare the preceding entry.)

1564. *Gbígbòòrò là ńse ònà igi.*
The path along which a log will be rolled must be made wide enough. (One should make provisions adequate for the task ahead.)

1565. *Gbogbo ajá ní ńje imí: èyí tó bá je tiè bénu laráyé ńpè ní dìgbòlugi.*
All dogs eat excrement, but only those that smear their mouths with it are described as rabid. (No one is without blemish, but one must keep one's flaws within reasonable bounds. Compare 1567.)

1566. *Gbogbo ìjà nìjà; bóo gbémi lulè mà mó e lójú láko láko.*
Every way of fighting is a legitimate way of fighting. If you are strong enough to throw me, I will fight back by looking at you with absolute disdain. (One must know

one's limitations, especially when up against insurmountable odds.)

1567. *Gbogbo obìnrin ló ńgbéṣẹ́, èyí tó bá ṣe tiẹ̀ láṣejù laráyé ńpè láṣẹ́wó.*
All women are unfaithful; only those who know no moderation are put down as whores. (Nobody is without blemishes; the important thing is to keep them from getting out of hand. Compare 1565.)

1568. *Gbólóhùn kan Agán tó awo-ó ṣe.*
Just one utterance by the masquerader Agán is sufficient to effect many wonders.[45] (The truly competent person need not strain overmuch to accomplish much.)

1569. *Gbólóhùn kan la bi elépo; elépo ńṣe ìrànrán.*
One asks only one question of the palm-oil seller, but she rambles endlessly on. (A person plagued by a bad conscience makes endless excuses when asked simple questions.)

1570. *Gbólóhùn kan-án ba ọ̀rọ̀ jẹ́; gbólóhùn kan-án tún ọ̀rọ̀ ṣe.*
One solitary statement muddies an entire affair; one solitary statement clears all the confusion. (A single sentence can cause irreparable damage; a single sentence can also repair the greatest relational damage.)

I

1571. *Ìbẹ̀rẹ̀ òsì bí ọmọ ọlọ́rọ̀ là ńrí.*
At the beginning of one's penury one seems like the child of most prosperous parents. (A course of action that will lead to disaster often has a pleasant beginning.)

45. Agán (or Agón) is one of the more formidable Yoruba masqueraders; he was traditionally employed to execute witches.

1572. *Ibi ìṣáná la ti ńkíyè sóògùn.*
From the time one makes one's boasts, one should begin to mind one's charms [or juju]. (One should always match one's vows with adequate preparation to effectuate them.)

1573. *Ibi rere làkàsọ̀-ọ́ ńgbé solẹ̀.*
The ladder always rests on a propitious spot. (A prayer that one may always land at a fortunate place.)

1574. *Ibi tí a gbọ́n mọ là ńsòwò-o màlúù mọ.*
One should limit the depth of one's involvement in cattle trading to the extent of one's astuteness. (Be careful not to put at risk more than you can afford, or to get in over your head.)

1575. *Ibi tí à ńlọ là ńwò, a kì í wo ibi tí a ti ṣubú.*
One should keep one's eyes on where one is going, not where one stumbled. (The best course of action is not to dwell on setbacks but to face the future resolutely.)

1576. *Ibi tí a ti ńwo olókùnrùn la ti ńwo ara ẹni.*
Just as one cares for the sick, one should also care for oneself. (One should be as solicitous of one's own welfare as of others'.)

1577. *Ibi tí akátá ba sí, adìẹ ò gbọdọ̀ débẹ̀.*
Wherever the jackal lurks, the chicken must give the place a wide berth. (Keep as clear of known dangers as possible.)

1578. *Ibi tí inú ḿbí aṣẹ tó, inú ò gbọdọ̀ bí ìkòkò débẹ̀; bínú bá bí ìkòkò débẹ̀, ẹlẹ́kọ ò ní-í rí dá.*
The cooking pot must never harbor a grudge to the same extent that the sieve does; if the pot does so, the corn-meal trader will have nothing to sell. (The more power

one has, the more one should exercise restraint.)[46]

1579. *Ibi tí ó mọ là ńpè lómọ.*
Where it stops, there one designates "child." (When one reaches the end of a matter, or the end of a road, one should acknowledge the end.)[47]

1580. *Ìbínú baba òsì.*
Anger [is the] father of hopelessness. (Anger achieves no good but may backfire on whoever expresses it. Compare 1582.)

1581. *Ìbínú lọbá fi ńyọ idà; ìtìjú ló fi ḿbẹ́ ẹ.*
It is in anger that the king draws his sword; it is shame that makes him go through with the beheading. (Once one begins an injudicious action on impulse, one may have to carry it through to avoid embarrassment.)

1582. *Ìbínú ò da nǹkan; sùúrù baba ìwà; àgbà tó ní sùúrù ohun gbogbo ló ní.*
Anger accomplishes nothing; forbearance is the father of character traits; an elder who has forbearance has everything. (Forbearance will avail one everything, whereas anger will always prove futile. Compare 1580.)

1583. *Ìbínú ò mọ̀ pé olúwa òun ò lẹ́sẹ̀ ńlẹ̀.*
Anger does not know that its owner has no legs to stand on. (Anger does not know prudence.)

1584. *Ìbìṣéhín àgbò kì í ṣojo.*
A ram's stepping backward is not indica-

tive of cowardice. (One should not mistake for indecisiveness a person's deliberateness before acting.)

1585. *Ìbọn-ón ní apátí kò lápátí, taní jẹ́ jẹ́ ká kojú ìbọn kọ òun?*
Whether a gun has a trigger or not, who would calmly permit it to be pointed at him or her? (One should not take foolish chances.)

1586. *Ì-dún-kídùn-ún òyo ni wọ́n fi ńsọ òyo nígi; ì-fọ̀-kúfọ̀ ògbìgbì ni wọ́n fi ńta ògbìgbì lókò; ì-je-kúje àdán ní ńfi-í tẹnu pọ̀ fẹnu ṣu.*
It is the incessant chattering of the Pataguenon monkey that causes people to belabor it with sticks; it is the annoying sounds of the *ògbìgbì* bird that causes people to throw stones at it; it is indiscriminate feeding that causes the bat to ingest food and excrete with the same mouth. (A person's mouth may be his or her death.)

1587. *Ìfẹ́ àféjù lewúrẹ́ fi ḿbá ọko-ọ rẹ̀ hu irùngbọn.*
It is excessive love that induces the goat to grow a beard in sympathy with her mate. (In all things, moderation is advisable.)

1588. *Ìfi ohun wé ohun, ìfi òràn wé òràn, kò jẹ́ kí òràn ó tán.*
Citing comparable things and recalling similar occurences [in the past] make ending a quarrel impossible. (Refusal to forget the past prevents reconciliation.)

1589. *Ìfunra loògùn àgbà.*
Wariness is the elders' most efficacious juju. (The person who is always wary will avoid much grief.)

1590. *Igi ganganran má gùn-ún mi lójú, òkèèrè la ti ńwò ó wá.*
"Protruding twig, do not poke me in the eye"; one must keep one's eyes on the twig

---

46. In a sense, both the pot that cooks the corn meal and the strainer used to separate the starch from the *eèrí* (bran) are containers, but the pot holds all the material put into it; the strainer permits some to escape. That action is here represented as a manifestation of anger. If the pot were to behave like the strainer, there would be no food left.

47. This is a play on the words *mọ* (which indicates "limit" or "extent") and *ọmọ* (which means "child").

from a distance. (Don't wait until problems arise before preparing to deal with them.)

1591. *Igi tó bá bá Ṣàngó lérí, gbígbẹ ní ńgbẹ.*
Whatever tree engages in a contest of threats with Ṣango will suffer the fate of drying up. (Never take on an adversary too tough for you to handle.)

1592. *Igúnnugún gbọ́n sínú.*
The vulture conceals a lot of wisdom in itself. (Even a person who appears foolish may be quite astute.)

1593. *Ìgbà ara ḿbẹ lára là ḿbù ú tà.*
It is when there is a surfeit of flesh on the body that one cuts some of it for sale. (One makes a gift only of one's surplus.)

1594. *Igbá dojúdé ò jọ ti òṣónú, tinú igbá nigbá ńṣe.*
That a calabash faces downward is no antisocial sign; the calabash is only acting according to its nature. (One should not read evil intent into others' innocent actions.)

1595. *Ìgbà tí a bá ní kí Ègùn má jà ní ńyọ̀bẹ.*
It is only when one pleads with the Ègùn person [from Porto Novo or Àjàṣẹ́ in present-day Benin Republic] that he draws his knife. (Said of people who redouble their efforts belatedly, just when they are supposed to break off.)[48]

1596. *Ìgbà tí a bá perí àparò ní ńjáko.*
Just as the talk turns to the partridge, it shows up to raid the farm. (Said of a person who plays into his or her adversary's hand just when the adversary most wants to injure him or her.)

---

48. The Ègùn serve the Yoruba as favorite butts of jokes.

1597. *Igbá tó fó ní ńgba kasẹ létí; ìkòkò tó fó ní ńgba okùn lọ́rùn.*
It is the broken calabash that has iron staples driven into its edges; it is the cracked pot that has its neck tied with a rope. (It is the person who makes trouble who is visited with repercussions.)

1598. *Ìgbẹ̀hìn ní ńyé olókùúàdá.*
It is only at the end that the person with a blunt cutlass realizes his error. (Sometimes wisdom comes too late to salvage lost opportunities. This is a variant of 1489.)

1599. *Ìgbín ńràjò ó fìlé è ṣẹrù.*
The snail sets out on a journey and makes a load of its house. (Said of people who are overly possessive of their goods or turf.)

1600. *Ìgbín tó ńjẹ ní màfọn, tí ò kúrò ní màfọn, ewé àfọn ni wọn ó fi dì í dele.*
A snail that forages at the base of the African breadfruit tree and never leaves the base of the African breadfruit tree will be taken home wrapped in the leaf of the African breadfruit tree. (One should know when to quit, or else one will wind up in trouble.)

1601. *Ìhàlẹ̀-ẹ́ ba ọṣọ́ èèyàn jé.*
Empty boasts ruin a person's reputation. (One's mouth should not be more powerful than one's arms.)

1602. *Ìjẹńjẹ àná dùn méhoro; ehoró rebi ìjẹ àná kò dẹ̀hìn bọ̀.*
Yesterday's food find so delighted the hare that it went to the spot of yesterday's feeding and never returned. (Persistence in risky ventures leads to disaster.)

1603. *Ìjímèrè tó lóun ò ní-í sá fájá, ojú ajá ni òì tí-ì to.*
The brown monkey vows it will not run

from a dog, only because the dog has not caught a glimpse of it. (The coward may boast as much as he or she wishes, until the real test materializes.)

1604. *Ijó àjójù ní ńmú kí okó eégún yo jáde.*
Unrestrained dancing is what causes the masquerader's penis to become exposed. (One should exercise restraint in performing even pleasurable activities.)

1605. *Ìkánjú òun pèlé, ogboogba.*
Haste and patience end up the same. (Great haste offers no advantage over patience.)

1606. *Ìkekere ńfòrò ikú sèrín.*
Ikekere [a type of fish] is treating a deadly thing as something to laugh about. (One should not take serious or deadly matters lightly.)

1607. *Ìkóeruku èèwò Ifè; ajá kì í gbó níbòji ekùn.*
Carrying dust is taboo in Ifè; no dog dares bark in the shadow of the leopard. (One should not engage in forbidden or dangerous acts.)

1608. *Ìkòkò ńsesu enìkan ò gbó; isú dénú odó ariwó ta.*
Yams cook in a pot and nobody knows, but when the yams get into the mortar, alarms sound. (Matters disclosed only to prudent people can be contained, but once they leak to irresponsible persons, they become broadcast.)

1609. *Ìkókó omo tó towó bo eérú ni yó mò bó gbóná.*
The newborn child who thrusts its hand into ashes will find out for itself if they are hot. (Experience best teaches that one should avoid dangerous ventures.)

1610. *Ikú ńde Dèdè, Dèdè ńde ikú.*
Death stalks Dede, and Dede stalks death.[49]
(Said of a person whom people are after but who does everything to become even more vulnerable.)

1611. *Ikún ńjògèdè ikún ńrèdí; ikún ò mò pé ohun tó dùn ní ńpani.*
The squirrel is eating a banana, and the squirrel is wagging its tail; the squirrel does not know that it is what is sweet that kills. (Overindulgence in good things can result in serious problems.)

1612. *Ìlara àlàjù ní ńmúni gbàjé, ní ńmúni sésó.*
Excessive envy of others causes one to take on witching and makes one become a wizard. (Too much envy leads to antisocial behavior.)

1613. *Ilé nÌjèsà-á ti ńmúná lo sóko.*
It is from the home that the Ìjèsà person takes fire to the farm. (The wise person assembles all the materials needed before embarking on a venture.)

1614. *Iná kì í wo odò kó rójú sayé.*
Fire does not enter into a stream and yet retain the opportunity to live. (Whoever ventures into dangerous situations deserves the repercussions.)

1615. *Iná ò sé-é bò máso.*
Fire is not something one conceals under one's clothing. (One should not hide one's pressing problems but seek help.)

1616. *Ìnàkí kì í ránsé ìjà sékùn.*
The baboon does not send an ultimatum to

---

49. *De* is "stalk," and the proverb plays on that word by redoubling it as the name of the subject.

the leopard. (People should not challenge forces they are no match for.)

1617. *Inú ẹni lorúkọ tí a ó sọ ọmọ ẹni ńgbé.*
It is inside oneself that the name one will name one's child resides. (One should not broadcast one's secrets to the whole world.)

1618. *Inúure àníjù, ìfunra atèébú ní ḿmù wá báni.*
Too much good will toward others engenders suspicion and attracts insults. (One can be too good to others.)

1619. *Ìpàkọ́ là ńdà sẹ́hìn ká tó da yangan sénu.*
One throws back the head first before throwing corn into the mouth. (One should not put the cart before the horse.)

1620. *Ìpàkọ́ ò gbọ́ sùtì, ìpẹ̀hìndà ò mọ yẹ̀gẹ̀ yíyẹ̀.*
The occiput does not recognize contempt; a turned back does not see a disdainful gesture. (The best response to insults is to disregard them.)

1621. *Isà tí ò lójú Alalantorí ńdẹ ẹ́, ámbọ̀ntorí àgbá ikún.*
Alalantori watches a hole without a visible opening, how much more a squirrel's burrow. (A person who watches his or her pennies is not likely to be careless with dollars.)

1622. *Isán ni à ḿmọ olè; ìtàdógún là ḿmọ dọ́kọ-dọ́kọ.*
The thief is exposed on the ninth day; the woman who sleeps around is exposed on the seventeenth day.[50] (Bad habits can be

kept secret only so long; they are eventually exposed.)

1623. *Ìṣẹ́ kì í pani; ayọ̀ ní ńpani.*
Misfortune does not kill; it is indulgent happiness that kills. (Indulgence kills more surely than want.)

1624. *Iṣẹ́ tí a kò ránni, òun ìyà ló jọ ńrìn.*
A task one was not asked to do usually travels in the company of punishment. (One usually rues doing things one has no business doing.)

1625. *Itọ́ tí a tu sílẹ̀ kì í tún padà re ẹnu ẹni mọ́.*
The saliva one has spat out does not return to one's mouth. (Once one has said something, one cannot take it back.)

1626. *Ìtọ́jú ló yẹ abẹ́rẹ́.*
Safekeeping is what is appropriate for a needle. (One should pay special attention to matters that are very delicate.)

1627. *Ìtọsẹ̀ ló nìlú.*
Close investigation keeps the affairs of the town in order. (Investigating matters well before acting helps maintain harmony in a group.)

1628. *Ìwà òní, ẹjọ́ ọla.*
Today's behavior [causes] tomorrow's problem. (The foolish behavior of the present sows the seeds of difficulties for the future.)

1629. *Ìyá là bá bú; bí a bú baba ìjà ní ńdà.*
One would be wiser to insult [another person's] mother; if one insults the father, a fight would certainly ensue. (One should measure one's insults in order to avoid a fight; a father is valued well over a mother.)

1630. *Iyán àmọ́dún bá ọbẹ̀.*
Next year's pounded yam will still find some

---

50. People who had been caught stealing were exposed to the public every nine days, and women who had been caught in illicit relationships were exposed every seventeenth day.

stew. (Whenever one's good fortune comes will be time enough to enjoy it.)

1631. *Iyán mú, ìrẹ́ yó; ìyàn-án rò, ìrẹ́ rù.*
A famine rages and the grasshopper grows fat; the famine subsides and the grasshopper grows lean. (One should husband one's resources wisely and save for lean times in times of plenty.)

1632. *Ìyàwó la bá sùn; ọkọ ló lóyún.*
The wife was the one made love to, but it is the husband who got pregnant. (The person directly involved in a matter does not make as much fuss as the person only tangentially involved.)

1633. *Ìyàwó ò fohùn ó fójú.*
The bride does not speak, and she is also blind. (Persons newly arrived in a place or a company should shut their mouths and open their eyes so that they learn the customs before speaking.)

1634. *Ìyẹ̀wù kan sọsọ ò lè gba olókùnrùn méjì.*
One single room will not do for two invalids. (Make adequate provisions for whatever one contemplates doing.)

J

1635. *Já ewé ọ̀pọ̀tọ́ kí o ríjà eèrùn; jáwé bọ ẹnu kóo ríjà odi.*
Pluck a fig leaf and be attacked by soldier ants; put a leaf in your mouth and be attacked by the deaf.[51] (Whoever takes unnecessary risks will very likely face dangerous consequences.)

1636. *Jayé-jayé fi ẹ̀lẹ̀ jayé; báyé bá já kò ní àmúso.*
You reveler, do things in moderation; if the string of life is cut, there is no retying it. (One should observe moderation in all things.)

1637. *Jẹ ẹ́ kí o yó oògùn ni kò sunwọ̀n.*
Eat-your-fill-of-it medicine is no good. (Anything without measure is dangerous.)

1638. *Jẹ́ kí ọmọ ó ti ọwọ́ ìyá ẹ̀ kú wá.*
Let a child die at his or her own mother's hands. (One should not become involved in the affairs of a person intent on his or her own ruin.)

K

1639. *Kàkà kí ó sàn lára ìyá àjẹ́, ó fi gbogbo ọmọ bí obìnrin; eye ńgorí eye.*
Instead of mother witch's affairs improving, all the children she bears turn out to be female; birds climb upon birds.[52] (Despite all efforts, the fortunes of a person may continue to be bad.)

1640. *Kàkà kí ọmọ ó bẹ̀bẹ̀ ọ̀ràn, òmíràn ni kò ní-í ṣe mọ́.*
Instead of apologizing for past misbehavior, a child should rather guard against a repetition. (One should look to the future and not dwell on past mistakes.)

1641. *Kànìké tìtorí oókan kùngbé.*
Kànìké set fire to the forest on account of a single cowry shell. (It makes no sense to lose control of oneself over trifling matters.)[53]

---

51. Fig leaves are usually infested with soldier ants, and the deaf are supposed to be insulted by anyone who places a leaf in his or her mouth.

52. Witches are believed to change into birds for trips to their nocturnal covens or when they go on any errand.

53. One cowry shell was the very smallest amount in traditional Yoruba currency.

1642. *Kékeré ejò, má foore ṣe é.*
However small the snake, show it no mercy.
(Better to be safe than sorry.)

1643. *Kékeré la ti ńpa ẹkàn ìrókò; bó bá dàgbà ọwọ́ kì í ká a mọ́.*
One kills the roots of the ìrókò tree while it is still a sapling; when it matures it is out of control. (One should take care of problems before they become unmanageable.)

1644. *Kékeré nìmàlé ti ńkọ́ ọmọ ẹ̀ lóṣòó.*
The Muslim teaches his children how to squat from their youth.[54] (One should do things in a timely manner.)

1645. *Kèrègbè tí kò lọ́rùn ni yóò júwe bí àgbẹ̀ ó ti so òun kọ́.*
The neckless gourd will itself indicate to the farmer how to tie it up. (A difficult person prompts others as to the best way to handle him or her.)

1646. *Kèrègbè tó fọ́ a padà léhìn odò.*
The broken gourd ceases plying the river. (One should know when to stop pursuing an adversary.)

1647. *Kí a baà lè mọ̀ pé àjàpá ṣe ògbóni, wọ́n ní "Káàbò"; ó ní "Awo àbí ọ̀gbèrì?"*
Just so that people might know that Àjàpá [the tortoise] has joined the secret society, he was greeted, "Welcome"; he responded, "Initiate or a novice?"[55] (Said of those who unnecessarily flaunt their accomplishments. Compare the next entry.)

1648. *Kí a baà lè mọ̀ pé Wòrú pa awó, wọ́n ní "Káàbò"; ó ní "Kẹnkẹn làpò."*

Just so that people might know that Woru killed a partridge, he was greeted, "Welcome"; he responded, "My hunting-bag is full!" (Said of people gratuitously proclaiming their accomplishments when no one is interested. Compare the preceding entry.)

1649. *Kí á fọn fèrè, ká jámú sí-i, òkan yóò gbélè.*
Between blowing a flute and wriggling the nose, one [action] will have to go. (No one can hope to perform two conflicting activities at the same time.)

1650. *Kí á jìnnà séjò tí a ò bé lórí; ikú tí yó panni a jìnnà síni.*
One should stand far back from a snake that has not been beheaded; the death that would kill deserves a wide berth. (One should recognize dangerous situations and keep away from them.)

1651. *Kí á lé akátá jìnnà ká tó bá adìẹ wí.*
One should first chase the jackal away before reprimanding the chicken. (Get rid of the immediate danger before reprimanding those who caused it.)

1652. *Kí a máa re tábà ká máa wòkè, kọ́jọ́ tó kanrí ká wo oye ìka tí yó kù.*
Let us keep on cutting tobacco leaves to pieces while looking up, and let us see at day's end how many fingers will be left. (One should pay close attention when one is engaged in dangerous work.)

1653. *Kí á ṣiṣẹ́ ká lówó lọ́wọ́ ò dàbí-i ká mọ̀-ọ ná.*
To work and make a great deal of money is nothing like knowing how to spend it. (Riches are nothing if one does not know how to use the wealth.)

1654. *Kí á ta sílẹ̀ ká ta sẹ́nu, ká má jẹẹ́ kí tilẹ̀ pọ̀ ju ti inú igbá lọ.*

---

54. The reference is to the squatting posture Muslims adopt during their ablutions.
55. The point is that one does not have to be an initiate to offer ordinary greetings to a person, and initiates are not barred from responding to greetings from noninitiates.

Let us place some on the ground and put some in the mouth, but let what is placed on the ground be more than what is left in the calabash.⁵⁶ (One should do one's duty by others but not at the expense of providing for one's future.)

1655. *Kí á tan iná pa agbọ́nrán, ká fọpá gbọoro pejò, ká dìtùfù ká fi gbọ̀wè lọ́wọ́-ọ Sàngó; ní ìṣojú-u Mádiyàn lagará ṣe ńdáni.*
Let us light a lamp to kill the wasp; let us use a long stick to kill the snake; let us light a torch to secure the help of Ṣango; when one is face-to-face with Mádiyàn [enter-into-no-dispute], one runs out of patience. (One should adopt the appropriate solution for every problem instead of engaging in long disputes.)

1656. *Kí á tó mọ̀ pé kíjìpá kì í ṣe awọ, ó di ọdún mẹ́ta.*
Before one realizes that tough hand-woven cloth is not leather, three years will have passed. (It may take time, but one will eventually realize that no one is invulnerable to misfortune.)

1657. *Kì í bọ́ lọ́wọ́ èèyàn kó bọ́ sílẹ̀; ọwọ́ ẹlòmíràn ní ḿbọ́ sí.*
It never slips out of a person's hand and falls to the ground; it always drops into someone else's hand. (Other people always stand ready to appropriate whatever one carelessly lets slip through one's fingers.)⁵⁷

1658. *Kì í ṣe ojú-u kòlòkòlò ladìẹ ti ńjẹ.*
It is not in the presence of the fox that the chicken forages nonchalantly. (One would

be foolish to let down one's guard when one knows that danger is nearby.)

1659. *Kì í tán nígbá osùn kó má ba àlà jẹ́.*
The calabash of camwood is never so empty that it cannot soil white cloth. (Some people or conditions are so unredeemable that no matter what one does, they persist in being evil. Compare 2183 and 4617.)

1660. *Kì í tètè yé oníbúrédì; ó dìgbà tó bá di mẹ́ta kọ́bọ̀.*
The bread seller never learns in time, not until his ware has become three a penny. (People rarely learn to mend their ways until they have suffered some reverses.)

1661. *Kì í tètè yéni: òwe ńlá ni.*
One never learns in good time: that is a profound proverb. (People tend always to learn wisdom too late.)

1662. *Kí ni ó yá apárí lórí tó ńmòòkùn lódò?*
What got into the bald person that made him or her swim underwater? (One should not unnecessarily endanger oneself.)⁵⁸

1663. *Kí ni ológìní ńwá tó fi jóna mọ́le? Ṣòkòtò ló fẹ́ẹ́ mú ni, tàbí ẹrù ní ńdì?*
What was the cat doing that caused it to be burnt in a house fire? Was it looking for its trousers or gathering its property? (One should not put oneself in the path of avoidable dangers.)

1664. *Kí oníkálùkù rọra ṣe é; ìfẹjú òbò ò lè fa aṣo ya.*
Let everybody take matters easy; the vagina cannot tear a cloth by gaping at it. (Overexcitement accomplishes little; it is far better to take life easy.)

---

56. It is customary when one eats to place a little of the food on the ground for the ancestors.

57. The expression *Ó bọ́ lọ́wọ́*, "It has slipped out of the hands of," expresses the sentiment that the person is no longer worth bothering about.

58. The proverb is based on the proposition that a bald person underwater could be mistaken for some aquatic animal.

1665. *Kìtì ò mọ́là; ká sịsẹ́ bí ẹrú ò da nǹkan.*
Sudden pouncing does not capture greatness; working like a slave does not ensure
anything. (One does not guarantee greatness
for oneself by slaving.)

1666. *Kò sí ajá tí kì í gbó; àgbójù ajá là ńpè ní
dìgbòlugi.*
There is no dog that does not bark; excessive barking by a dog is what makes people
say it is rabid. (No person is without a flaw;
unbounded flaws are what give people a bad
reputation. Compare 1565.)

1667. *Kò sí ìgbà tí a dá aṣọ tí a ó rílẹ̀ fi wọ́.*
There is no time one makes a dress that
one lacks opportunities to wear it casually.
(There will always be time to enjoy what one
has worked for; one should not be unduly
impatient.)

1668. *Kò sí ohun tí ńle tí kì í rọ̀.*
There is nothing that gets hard that does
not eventually become soft. (Every problem eventually becomes solved somehow.
Compare 1670.)

1669. *Kò sí ohun tí sùúrù-ú sè tí kò jinná.*
There is nothing that patience cooks that is
not well cooked. (Forbearance overcomes all
things.)

1670. *Kò sí ohun tó lọ sókè tí kò ní padà wá
sílẹ̀.*
There is nothing that goes up that will not
eventually come down. (One should not be
too impatient in anticipating the inevitable.
Compare 1668.)

1671. *Kò sí ohun tó yára pa ẹni bí ọ̀rọ̀ àsọjù.*
There is nothing that kills faster than talking too much. (One should govern one's
mouth.)

1672. *Kọko-kọko ò jẹ́ ká mọ ẹni tí ọ̀ràn ńdun.*
The woman who divorces husbands at the

least provocation does not allow one to
know when a matter really hurts. (Habitual
overreaction defuses real alarms.)

1673. *Kọ́kọ́rọ́ àṣejù, ìlẹ̀kùn ètẹ̀ la fi ńṣí.*
The key of excess is usually good only to
open the door of disgrace. (Excess brings
disgrace.)

1674. *Kòkòrò tó jẹfọ́ jàre ẹfọ́; ìwọn lewéko
ńdára mọ.*
The insect that eats the vegetable wins the
case against the vegetable; leaves should observe moderation in their attractiveness. (A
person enticed to a crime is not as guilty as
the person who did the enticing.)

1675. *Kùkùté kan kì í fọ́ni lépo lẹ́ẹ̀mejì.*
No one stump can break one's oil pot twice.
(The same disaster should not befall a person twice; one usually learns from experience.)

1676. *Kùn yún, kùn wá bí ikọ̀ eèrà .* Hurry
forth and hurry back like a messenger ant.
(Said of people who are too restless to stay
still.)

L

1677. *Làákàyè baba ìwà; bí o ní sùúrù, ohun
gbogbo lo ní.*
Common sense [is] the father of good character; whoever has patience has everything.
(Common sense and patience are the chief
qualities one must have. Compare 1582.)

1678. *Làálàá tó ròkè, ilẹ̀ ní ḿbọ̀.*
A worrisome problem that soars to the
heavens must eventually come down. (No
difficulty is without its end.)

1679. *Labalábá kì í bá wọn nájà ẹlégùn-ún;
aṣọ-ọ è á fàya.*

The butterfly does not join others at a market of thorns; otherwise, its cloth will be shredded.[59] (One should know one's limitations and act accordingly. Compare the following entry.)

1680. *Labalábá tó dìgbò lègún, aṣo è á fàya.*
The butterfly that collides with a thorn will have its cloth shredded. (One should be wise enough to know one's nemesis and avoid it. Compare the preceding entry.)

1681. *Lù mí pé, lù mí pé làpón fi ńlu ọmọ è pa.*
It is by gentle but persistent beating that the bachelor beats his child to death. (People not used to caring for delicate articles soon destroy them by mishandling.)

M

1682. *Màà jẹ iṣu; màà jẹ èrú; ibi ayo ló mọ.*
I will eat a whole yam; I will also eat a slice of yam; satiation ends it all. (The greediest appetite will not survive satiation.)

1683. *Má bà á loògùn ètè.*
Avoiding contact is the only medicine for leprosy. (The best way out of trouble is not to get into it in the first place.)[60]

1684. *Má bàá mi ṣeré tí kèrègbé fi gba okùn lórùn.*
Do not ask me to play the sort of game the gourd played and got a rope around its neck. (Do not ask me to endanger myself needlessly.)

1685. *Má fi iyán ewùrà gbọ́n mi lóbè lọ sóko egàn.*
Do not eat up my stew with pounded yam made from water yams before your trip to the forest farm. (Do not use up my meager resources on your way to a place of plenty.)[61]

1686. *"Má fi okoò mi dá ònà," ọjọ́ kan là ńkọ ọ́.*
"Do not cut a path through my farm" is a protest one must make some day. (Whoever does not take a stand to protest the violation of his or her rights will continue to have them violated.)

1687. *"Má fi tìrẹ kọ́ mi lórùn" là ńdá fún apènà àti òwú.*
"Do not hang your trouble around my neck" is the oracle delivered to the shuttle and the weft thread. (Do not involve me in your problems as the weft thread got the shuttle entangled.)

1688. *Má fikánjú jayé, awo ilé Alárá; má fi wàà-wàà joyè, awo Òkè Ìjerò; ayé kan ńbẹ léhìn, ó dùn bí ẹní ńlá oyin.*
Do not go impatiently about enjoying life: the oracle delivered to the [royal] Alárá household; do not rush into chieftaincy: the oracle for the people of Òkè Ìjerò; there comes another life in the future that is as delicious as licking honey. (Whoever goes about life with patience will reap untold enjoyment from it.)

1689. *Má ṣe jáfara; àfara fírí ló pa Bíálà; ara yíyá ló pa Abídogun.*
Never be sluggish; sluggishness killed Bíálà, but then overeagerness killed Abídogun. (One should avoid extremes in all things.)

1690. *Mábàjẹ́ ò jé fi aṣo è fún ọlẹ bora.*
Mábàjẹ́ will never think of giving his cover-

---

59. The cloth here refers to the butterfly's wings.
60. The proverb is obviously from the days when there was no cure for leprosy.

61. Water yam (*Dioscurea alata*) is a poor make-do for preparing pounded yams. The objection is that the person addressed is eating up stew that is valuable or scarce even though made with second-rate pounded yams.

ing cloth to a shiftless person to use. (Whoever values his or her property will not entrust it to worthless people.)[62]

1691. *"Méè-wáyé-ejó" fomo è fóko méfà.*
Méèwáyéejó ["I did not come to live a life of litigation"] gave his daughter to six suitors all at once. (If one wishes to avoid trouble, one should avoid actions certain to result in trouble.)

1692. *Méjì-i gbèdu ò sé-é so kó.*
Two *gbèdu* drums are too much to hang on one's shoulders. (Some propositions are simply too much for anyone to tackle.)

N

1693. *"Ng óò wó o kágbó" èhìn-in rè ni yó fi lànà.*
"I will drag you through the bush" will have to clear a path with his own back. (Whoever is determined to make trouble for others must be prepared to take some trouble himself. Compare 3140 and 4819.)

1694. *Nítorí ará ilé la se ńdá sòkòtò ará oko dára.*
It is with the town dweller in mind that one makes the bush person's trousers well. (One's products are one's advertisement, regardless of whether the recipient knows their quality. Compare 1699.)

1695. *Nítorí-i ká lè simi la se ńse àì-simi.*
It is to be able to rest that one forgoes rest. (One labors in the present to provide for one's future. Compare the following entry and also 1698.)

1696. *Nítorí-i ká má jìyà la se ńyá Májìyà lófà.*

It is in order not to suffer that one pawns Májìyà. (One should not suffer the misfortune one has done everything to avoid.[63] Compare the preceding entry and also 1698.)

1697. *Nítorí ojó tí ó bá máa dáràn la se ńsomo lórúko.*
It is in anticipation of the day a child will get into trouble that one gives it a name. (Each individual has a name and is therefore an independent agent responsible for his or her own actions.)

1698. *Nítorí òla la se ńsòní lóore.*
It is with tomorrow in mind that we do favors for today. (What one sows determines what one reaps. Compare 1695 and 1696.)

1699. *Nítorí ologbón la se ńdá èwù asiwèrè kanlè.*
It is with the wise person in mind that one makes the idiot's garment full length. (One who cares about his or her reputation will perform obligations well even when the recipient has no power over him or her. Compare 1694.)

1700. *Nnkan méta la kì í pè ní kékeré: a kì í pe iná ní kékeré; a kì í pe ìjà ní kékeré; a kì í pe àìsàn ní kékeré.*
Three things one must never treat as of little consequence: one must never treat fire as of little consequence; one must never treat a quarrel as of little consequence; and one must never treat an illness as of little consequence. (Attend to every potential problem early before it gets out of hand.)

---

62. The name Mábàjé means "Spoil not."

63. The name Májìyà means "Suffer not." The suggestion is that the speaker has either taken Májìyà as a pawn to work for him or has sent Májìyà away as a pawn to perform the obligations the speaker had taken on.

O

1701. *O bá ẹ̀fọ̀n lábàtà o yọ̀bẹ sí i; o mọ ibi ẹ̀fọ̀n-ọ́n ti wá?*
You come upon the carcass of a buffalo in the marshes and you pull out your butchering knife; do you know where the bush cow came from? (People should not lay claim to things whose procurement they know nothing about.)

1702. *Ó dé orí akáhín àkàràá deegun.*
In the mouth of a toothless person, bean fritters become like bones. (To the shiftless person even the easiest task is onerous.)

1703. *Ó dé ọwọ́ aláròóbọ̀ ó di nínà.*
When goods get into the hands of the retailer, they become objects to haggle about. (A shopkeeper is a difficult person to obtain a good bargain from. Compare 4702.)

1704. *O kò rí àkàṣù ò ńpata séfọ́ọ́.*
You have not found corn loaf and yet you are readying the vegetable stew. (Said of a person too eagerly anticipating a favor that might not materialize.)

1705. *O lọ sÍjẹ̀bú ẹ̀ẹ̀kan, o ru igbá àṣẹ bọ̀ wálé.*
You made only one trip to Ìjẹ̀bú and you returned with a calabash of charms. (Said of a person on whom the impact of an experience is all out of proportion.)[64]

1706. *Ò ńbá obìnrin ẹ jà ò ńkanrí mọ́nú; o máa nà á lóògùn ni?*
You quarrel with your wife and you put on a baleful look; do you propose to use an evil charm on her? (One should moderate one's response to annoyances.)

1707. *"Ó ńbọ̀, ó ńbọ̀!" ẹ̀wọ̀n là ńso sílẹ̀ dè é.*
"Watch out, watch out, for here it comes!"

---

64. The saying is obviously a reference to the reputation of the Ìjẹ̀bú for powerful charms.

For such a thing one would best prepare a snare. (If the thought of something fills one with apprehension, one should plot to defeat it.)

1708. *Ó ní ibi tí tanpẹ́pẹ́ ńgbèjà ẹ̀yìn mọ.*
There is a limit to the protection that black stinging ants can offer palm fruits. (There is a limit to the help one can expect from others.)

1709. *Ó ní ohun tí àgbá jẹ tẹ́lẹ̀ ikùn kó tó sọ pé èyí yó òun.*
The elder ate something to line his stomach before he said that what [little] was before him would suffice to sate his hunger. (The prudent person prepares himself or herself for all eventualities. Compare the following.)

1710. *Ó ní ohun tí àgbá jẹ tẹ́lẹ̀ ikùn kó tó sọ pé ìyà-á yó òun.*
The elder ate something to line his stomach before he said his suffering was enough food for him. (Even when one is prostrated by grief, one does not ignore one's need to survive. Compare the preceding entry.)

1711. *Ó ní ohun tí ìbòsí ràn nínú ìjà.*
Raising an alarm or calling for help goes only so far to aid someone in a fight. (No matter what help a person in trouble receives, he or she will still be in for some grief.)

1712. *Ó pẹ́ títí aboyún, oṣù mẹ́sàn-án.*
The longest respite for the pregnant woman is nine months. (Sooner rather than later, the day will arrive when one must fulfill one's obligation or pay one's debt.)

1713. *O rí àgbébọ̀ adìẹ lójà ò ńta geere sí i; ìba ṣe rere olúwa rẹ̀ ò jẹ́ tà á.*
You see an adult chicken at the market and you eagerly go for it; if it was of any value, would the owner sell it? (People should

think carefully before they assume obligations.)

1714. *O só pa mí mo pónnu lá, o bojúwèhìn
mo dòbálè, o tiwó bògbé; o féé dè mí ni?*
You foul the air in my face and I lick my
lips; you glance back and I prostrate myself
before you and yet you stretch your hand
into the bush; would you tie me up? (Said
by a long-suffering person who has quietly
taken a great deal of abuse, when the abuser
persists in his or her ill treatment.)

1715. *O síwó nílé o kò san, o dóko o ńsí ìkòkò
ògèdè wò, o bímo o so ó ní Adéśínà; bí śíśí ò
bá sìn léhìn rẹ, o kì í sìn léhìn-in śíśí?*
You borrow money at home and you refuse
to repay it; you arrive on the farm and open
the pot containing plantains for inspection; and when you have a baby you name
it Adéśínà; if *śí-śí* does not leave you alone,
why don't you leave it alone? (Obsession
with anything is bad.)[65]

1716. *O wà lórùn òpẹ ò ńbá Olórun sèlérí.*
You are perched at the lofty neck of the palm
tree and you are bandying words with God.
(Said of a person who taunts more powerful adversaries even when he or she is in a
vulnerable position.)

1717. *Obìnrin bẹẹrẹ: òsì bẹẹrẹ.*
Innumerable wives, innumerable problems. (Whoever adds wives to wives adds
problems to problems.)

1718. *Obìnrin tó gégi nígbó Orò, ó gé àgémo.*
A woman who cuts wood in the grove of
Orò has cut her last. (Whoever tempts a
fate that is known to strike unfailingly has
tempted her last.)

1719. *Òbò-ó ní ìtìjú ló mú òun sápamó sábẹ
inú, sùgbón bí okó bá dé, òun á sìnà fún un.*
The vagina says it is coyness that caused it
to hide below the belly, but if a penis shows
up, it will open the way for it. (Modesty does
not indicate a lack of ability or willingness
to act decisively.)

1720. *Odídẹrẹ ní wọn ò lè tí ojú òun yan òun
mó ẹbọ; bí wón bá ńdÍfá, òun a sá wọlé.*
The parrot says no one will prescribe it as a
sacrifice in its presence; when it sees people
consulting the oracle, it will go hide in its
closet. (The smart person should always
distance himself or herself from disaster.)

1721. *Odídẹrẹ ńwolé hóró-hóró bí ẹnipé yó
kòó sílé; àgbìgbò nòwòràn ńwohò igi bí ẹnipé
kò tìbẹ jáde.*
The parrot eyes the cramped house as
though it would enter; the big-headed bird
ágbìgbò eyes the hole in the tree as though
it did not emerge from there. (Some people
fail to appreciate their assets, while others
envy them what they have.)

1722. *Òfèèrèfé ò sé-é fẹhín tì.*
A chasm is nothing to lean on. (One should
not trust in emptiness.)

1723. *Ogun àgbótélè kì í pa aro.*
A long-foreseen war does not kill a cripple.
(One must take advantage of foreknowledge
to protect oneself. Compare 2237.)

1724. *Ohun à ńjẹ là ńtà; bí epo òyìnbó kó.*
What one eats is what one sells; but not
like kerosene. (One must be selective about
which of one's just desserts one will accept.)[66]

---

65. The proverb plays on the word *śí*, which can
mean "borrow" or "open." The name Adéśínà means
"The crown (or king) opens the way."

66. The proverb would make better sense if the two
balancing phrases were reversed: what one sells is what
one eats.

1725. *Ohun gbogbo, ìwọn ló dùn mọ.*
All things are good or pleasing only to a point. (One should observe moderation in all things.)

1726. *Ohun gbogbo kì í pẹ́ jọ olóhun lójú.*
It is never long before a thing becomes invaluable to the owner. (A person always attaches excessive value to his or her possessions. Trust a person to exaggerate their value, especially when they are damaged or coveted by others.)

1727. *Ohun gbogbo kì í tó olè.*
Nothing ever satisfies a thief. (Greed and covetousness are the marks of a thief.)

1728. *Ohun gbogbo là ńdiyelé; ṣùgbọ́n kò séni tó moye ara-a rẹ̀; ẹ̀jẹ̀ ò fojú rere jáde.*
Everything has its price, but no one knows his or her own worth; bloodshed never has a good cause. (People should not devalue their own lives by exposing themselves to unnecessary danger.)

1729. *Ohun tí a bá máa jẹ a kì í fi runmú.*
One does not sniff at what one will eventually eat anyway. (Don't sneer at what you will eventually embrace.)

1730. *Ohun tí à bá ṣe pẹ̀sẹ̀, ká má fi ṣe ìkánjú; bó pẹ́ títí ohun gbogbo a tó ọwọ́ ẹni.*
That which one should do slowly and carefully one should not do in a hurry; sooner or later everything comes within one's reach. (One should not shirk present responsibilities in the pursuit of a distant goal.)

1731. *Ohun tí a bá tẹjúmọ́ kì í jóná.*
Whatever one trains one's eyes upon will not get charred. (Matters to which one devotes one's undivided attention will not go awry.)

1732. *Ohun tí a fi ẹ̀sọ̀ mú kì í bàjẹ́; ohun tí a fagbára mú ní ńnini lára.*

Whatever one handles gently will not be ruined; it is what one attempts with force that causes grief. (A gentle approach will accomplish much, whereas a forceful approach is likely to complicate matters.)

1733. *Ohun tí a fún ẹlẹ́mọ̀ṣọ́ ní ńṣọ́.*
It is what one gives to a caretaker to look after that he looks after. (One would best focus only on the task assigned.)

1734. *Ohun tí a ò pé yó dẹrù ní ńdiṣẹ́.*
It is always something one does not expect to be a load that eventually becomes a huge task. (Matters that one considers of little significance have a way of becoming insoluble problems.)

1735. *Ohun tí a rí la fi ńbọ párá ẹni; bí igi tíná ńbẹ lẹ́nu è kọ́.*
One uses whatever one can find to fill gaps in one's roof; that does not apply to a faggot spewing flames. (Every seemingly sensible generalization has exceptions.)

1736. *Ohun tí ajá rí tó fi ńgbó ò tó èyí tí àgùntán fi ńṣèran wò.*
That which a dog sees and barks at is nothing compared to what the sheep contemplates in silence. (Some people make mountains out of other people's molehills.)

1737. *Ohun tó bá wu olókùnrùn ní ńpa á.*
Whatever the invalid craves is what spells his or her death. (Whatever one is addicted to is likely to prove one's undoing.)

1738. *Ohun tó bá wu ọmọ-ọ́ jẹ kì í run ọmọ nínú.*
Whatever a child craves will not give him or her a stomachache. (One is always willing to endure sacrifices in order to have whatever one craves.)

1739. *Òjijì là ńrómọ lọ́wọ́ alákẹdun.*
It is all of a sudden that one sees a baby in

the arms of the colobus monkey. (One need not announce ahead of time what feat one will perform.)

1740. *Òjò kan kì í báni lábà ká jìjàdù òrò-ó so; bí ègbón bá so tán, àbúrò á so.*
When people are trapped in a hut by a downpour, there is no sense in fighting to get a word into the discussion; after the older person has spoken, the younger person will speak. (When there is a surfeit of a commodity, there is no sense in scrambling to get some of it.)

1741. *Òjò ńrò, Orò ńké; atókùn àlùgbè tí ò láso méjì a se ògèdèmgbé sùn.*
The rain is falling, and the call of the secret cult is sounding loudly outside; the shuttle that lacks a change of clothing will sleep naked. (If one has not made provisions for rainy days, when they come one must suffer the attendant hardship.)

1742. *Ojú abe ò sé-é pónlá.*
The edge of a razor is not a thing to lick. (Never engage in dangerous behavior.)

1743. *Ojú àwòdì kó ladìe ńre àpáta.*
It is not in the watchful presence of a kite that a chicken strolls to a rock. (One does not engage in culpable activity in the presence of those charged with upholding discipline. Compare 476.)

1744. *Ojú ìmàle ò kúrò lótí, ó bímo è ó so ó ní Ìmórù-máhá-wá.*
The Muslim cannot take his mind off liquor; he has a child and named him Ìmórù máhá wá.[67] (One's addiction will always mani-

fest itself, however much one might hide it. In a variant, the father names the child Lèmámù.)[68]

1745. *Ojú kan làdá ńní.*
A machete can have only one edge. (One should be true to one calling or relationship and not philander.)

1746. *Ojú kan náà lèwe ńbágbà.*
It is at the same place that the youth will come up on the elder. (Sooner or later the youth becomes an elder; patience is all.)

1747. *"Ojú là ńgbó re ònà Ìbàdàn"; ó fi ogún òké gbàdí.*
"It takes a great deal of fortitude to set out for Ibadan"; he ties his money around his waist.[69] (One should take the necessary precautions when one embarks on a dangerous venture.)

1748. *Ojú ní ńkán okolóbìnrin; àlè méjì á jà dandan.*
The husband of the wife is only being unduly hasty; in time two concubines will inevitably quarrel. (One should not be overly anxious for results that are inevitable anyway.)

1749. *"Ojú ò férakù" tó ta ajá è lókòó; ó ní bó bá jé bèè ni wón ńtà á won a máa tún ara-a won rí.*
"We-might-see-each-other-again" sold his dog for 20 cowries; he said if that is how things are sold, they might well see each other again. (If someone sells you an item at

---

67. Ìmórù is the Yoruba rendering of the Arabic name Umar; the Yoruba version in full would be *Ì mú orù*, meaning "the taking up of a wine cup"; the *máhá wá* [*mú ahá wá*] attached at the end means "bring a wine cup."

68. Lèmámù is the Yoruba rendering of Imam; here it suggests the name *Lè-máa-mu*, which means "Maintain the ability to drink."

69. The road to Ibadan is in this case taken to be full of peril from ambushers. The person involved must be brave indeed when the amount of money he ties around his waist is considerable.

a ridiculously low price, you may expect to see that person again soon.)

1750. *Ojú ológbò lèkúté ò gbọdọ̀ yan.*
In the presence of the cat the mouse must not saunter. (One cannot afford to be careless in the presence of powerful enemies.)

1751. *Ojú tí kì í wo iná, tí kì í wo òòrùn; ojú tí ḿbáni dalẹ́ kọ́.*
Eyes that cannot stand lamplight and that cannot stand sunlight are not eyes that will last until the twilight of one's life. (From early indications, one can tell what friendships or possessions will prove lasting. Compare the next entry.)

1752. *Ojú tí yóò báni dalẹ́ kì í tàárọ̀ ṣepin.*
The eyes that will last one until nighttime will not start oozing matter at the dawn. (Relationships that will last will not become onerous right at the start. Compare the preceding entry.)

1753. *Ojúkòkòrò baba òkánjúà.*
Covetousness [is] the father of envy. (The envious and the covetous are similar.)

1754. *Ojúlé ló bá wá; ẹ̀bùrú ló gbà lọ; ó dífá fún àlejò tí ńfẹ́ obìnrin onílé.*
He entered through the front door, but it was through a hidden shortcut that he sneaked away; the Ifá oracle was consulted for the visitor who had an affair with his host's wife.[70] (Whoever abuses hospitality will depart in disgrace.)

1755. *Òkèlè gbò-ǹ-gbò-ó fẹ ọmọ lójú toto.*
A huge morsel forces the child's eyes wide open. (A person who bites off more than he can chew will suffer in the process of trying.)

1756. *Òkèlè kan ní ńpa àgbà.*
Only one morsel kills an elder. (The smallest thing, if not accorded the proper attention, can be the death of even the most powerful person.)

1757. *Òketè baba ogun: bí a ṣígun, olúkúlùkù ní ńdi òketè-e è lọ́wọ́.*
Large bundle, father of all wars: when preparing for war, each person prepares his bundle to take along. (For all tasks, adequate preparations are mandatory.)

1758. *Òkété tó bọ́ ìrù-ú mọ̀ pé ìpéjú ọjà ọrún òun ló sún.*
The giant bush rat that has its tail stripped by a trap knows that it is its visit to the fifth-day market that was postponed. (One should take a near-disaster as a warning.)

1759. *Òkìpa ajá la fi ḿbọ Ògún.*
It is a mature and sizable dog that one sacrifices to Ògún. (One should use material proper for the occasion.)

1760. *Òkò àbínújù kì í pẹye.*
A stone thrown in anger does not kill a bird. (Whatever one does in anger is likely to go awry.)

1761. *Oko ni gbégbé ńgbé.*
The farm is where *gbégbé* belongs.[71] (Everything in its proper place.)

1762. *Òkò tí eyẹ bá rí kì í pẹye.*
A missile that a bird sees will not kill the bird. (If one sees danger approaching, one will take precautions.)

---

70. The formulation is typical of several in which a leading statement describing a situation is followed by the statement *Ó dífá fún* ("He consulted the Ifá oracle for") and then by a description of the behavior that leads to the condition described at the opening.

71. See note 9 to 59 about the magic of *gbégbé* leaves.

1763. *Òkóbó ò lè fi alátòsí sèsín.*
The eunuch cannot make fun of the person with gonorrhea. (A person who has a blemish should not make fun of other people's blemishes.)

1764. *Òkú àjànàkú là ńyọ ogbó sí; ta ní jé yọ agada séerin?*
It is a dead elephant one approaches with a cutlass; who would dare draw a machete to attack an elephant [that is alive]? (One dares taunt a powerful adversary only when he has been neutralized. This is a variant of 1488.)

1765. *Okùn àgbò kì í gbèé dorí ìwo.*
It is never long before a ram's tethering rope slips to its horns. (Seemingly minor difficulties soon become unmanageable problems.)

1766. *Olè kì í gbé gbèdu.*
No thief steals a *gbèdu* drum.[72] (One should not attempt a risky business one has no hope of pulling off. Compare 1130.)

1767. *Olójútì logun ńpa.*
It is those who worry about their image who die in war. (Discretion and a thick skin are sometimes much better than valor.)

1768. *Olóògbé ò jéwó; atannijẹ bí orun.*
The dozing person does not confess; nothing deceives like sleep. (One can always feign sleep to avoid engaging in discussions.)

1769. *Olóòlà kì í kọ àfín.*
The facial scarifier does not scarify an albino's face. (There are some tasks that are beyond the scope of experts.)

1770. *Olórìṣá gbé àája sókè, wón ní ire ni; bí ire ni, bí ibi ni, wọn ò mò.*
The cult priest raises his divining wand and the worshipers proclaim the omen good; whether it is good or bad they do not know. (It is foolhardy to presume to know what is in other people's minds.)

1771. *Omi là ńkọ́-ọ́ tè ká tó tẹ iyanrìn.*
Water is the first thing one's foot encounters before it encounters the sand. (One should attend to the most urgent matters first.)

1772. *Òní, adìẹ̀ mí sìwò; ọ̀la, adìẹ̀ mí sìwò; ọjọ́ kan la óò fé àìwọlé adìẹ kù.*
Today, my chicken has gone to roost in the wrong place; tomorrow, my chicken has gone to roost in the wrong place; someday soon the errant chicken will disappear permanently. (Little errors, if not checked, will result in a major blunder. See the following two entries.)

1773. *Òní, babá dákú; ọ̀la, babá dáku; ọjọ́ kan ni ikú yóò dá baba.*
One day, the patriarch collapsed; the next day the patriarch collapsed; one day death will throw the patriarch.[73] (Frequent close calls with death will eventually lead to real death. Compare the foregoing and following entries.)

1774. *Òní, ẹsín dá baba; ọ̀la, ẹsín dá baba; bí baba ò bá yé ẹsin-ín gùn, ọjọ́ kan lẹsin óò dá baba pa.*
One day, the horse threw the patriarch; the next day the horse threw the patriarch; if the patriarch does not stop riding the horse, one day the horse will throw him to his death. (One should take warning from little disasters. See the foregoing two entries.)

1775. *Onígbàjámò ńfárí fún ọ, ò ńfọwó kàn án wò; èwo ló máa kù fún ọ níbè.*

---

72. This kind of drum is too hefty to carry away, and where would the thief play it anyway?

73. *Dákú,* meaning "collapse" or "faint," can also be a contraction of *dá ikú,* meaning "throw death in a wrestling match."

The hair scraper is scraping your head, and you are feeling your scalp with your hand; what do you expect will be left for you there? (Once the end is clear, one should stop being anxious about developments.)

1776. *Onílé ńrelé wọ́n ní oǹdè ńsá; oǹdè ò sá, ilé ẹ̀ ló lọ.*
The homeowner heads for home and they say the guard is on the run; the guard is not on the run but merely heading home. (A strategic retreat to regroup is not the same as giving up the fight.)

1777. *Ònímónìì, ẹtú jìnfín; òlamọ́la, ẹtú jìnfín; ẹran mìíràn ò sí nígbó ni?*
Today, the antelope falls into a ditch; tomorrow, the antelope falls into the ditch; is there no other animal in the forest? (If the same person gets into trouble every time, the person needs to look to himself or herself. See 496.)

1778. *Onínúfùfù ní ńwá oúnjẹ fún onínúwẹ́rẹ́-wẹ́rẹ́.*
Always it is the hot-tempered person that finds food for the even-tempered person. (The even-tempered person will always have the advantage of the hot-tempered person.)

1779. *Oníṣu ní ḿmọ ibi iṣú gbé ta sí.*
The owner of the yams is the one who knows where the mature yams are. (One should not presume to know more about an affair than the person most intimately involved.)

1780. *Onísùúrù ní ńṣe ọkọ ọmọ Aláhúsá.*
Only the patient person will win the daughter of the Hausa man. (Patience overcomes all obstacles.)

1781. *Oókan ni wọ́n ńta ẹṣin lọ́run; ẹni tí yó lọ ò wọ́n; sùgbón ẹni tí yó bọ̀ ló kù.*
Horses sell for only one cowrie in heaven; there is no shortage of people who will go

there, but who ever returns from there? (Setting out on dangerous ventures is the easiest thing in the world, but their repercussions prove to be unspeakable.)

1782. *Oókan-án sọni dahun; eéjì-í sọni dàpà.*
One cowrie makes one a miser; two cowries make one a spendthrift. (One who has little seems a miser; one who has plenty becomes careless with money.)

1783. *Ooré di erè lÁwẹ́; àwọn igúnnugún soore wọ́n pá lórí.*
A favor has turned to mud in Awẹ́ town; the vulture did a favor and went bald.[74] (One should be careful about doing favors, lest they come back to haunt one. Compare 1787.)

1784. *Òòrẹ̀ ní ńṣégi tí a ó fi wì í.*
The porcupine itself will procure the wood with which it will be roasted.[75] (The incautious person will provide the instrument for his own undoing.)

1785. *Oore òfé gùn jùwàásù.*
The benediction is longer than the sermon. (Said of people who are long-winded.)

1786. *Oore tí Agbe ṣe lÓfà, ó dagbe.*
The favor Agbe did in Òfà town reduced him to begging. (One should learn from Agbe's example and be prudent in doing favors.)

1787. *Oore tí igúnnugún ṣe tó fi pá lórí, tí àkàlá ṣe tó fi yọ gègè, a kì í ṣe irú ẹ̀.*
The sort of favor the vulture did by going

---

74. Awẹ́ is a town near Ọ̀yọ́; the proverb refers to an incident in which someone did a favor and reaped disaster, as did the vulture; see note 72 to 1003 for the story.

75. The porcupine's quills are here likened to kindling.

bald, the sort of favor the ground hornbill did by developing a goiter, one does not do it. (One should not do favors that will result in one's own ruin. Compare 1326 and 1783.)

1788. *Ooré pọ̀, a fìkà san án.*
The favor was excessive; it was repaid with wickedness. (Too great a favor provokes enmity.)

1789. *Orí ejò ò ṣé-é họ imú.*
The head of a snake is nothing to scratch one's nose with. (Never expose yourself to unnecessary danger.)

1790. *Orin ní ńṣíwájú ọ̀tè.*
Singing goes before plotting. (People about to engage in a plot will first spar to sound one another out.)

1791. *Orin tí a kọ lánàá, tí a ò sùn, tí a ò wo, a kì í tún jí kọ ọ́ láàárọ̀.*
The song that we sang yesterday, without sleep, without respite, we do not resume singing in the morning. (Yesterday's problems should be gone with yesterday.)

1792. *Òrìṣà kékeré ò ṣé-é há ní pápá.*
A small god is not a thing to hang from the rafters. (Some things may seem insignificant yet must not be taken lightly.)

1793. *Òròmọ-adìẹ ò màwòdì; ìyá è ló màṣá.*
The young chick does not know the eagle; it is its mother that knows the kite. (The young are neither as experienced nor as careful as the old.)

1794. *Oṣé ní ńṣíwájú ẹkún; àbámọ̀ ní ńgbẹ̀hìn òràn; gbogbo àgbà ìlú pé, wọn ò rí oògùn àbámọ̀ ṣe.*
Hissing goes before crying, and had-one-but-known comes at the conclusion of an unfortunate matter; all the elders in the town assembled, but they could find no anti-dote for had-we-but-known. (One can only regret an error once it has been committed; there is no undoing it.)

1795. *Oúnjẹ tí a ó jẹ pé, a kì í bu òkèlè-e rẹ̀ tóbi.*
Food that one expects to last one does not eat in huge handfuls. (Wise husbandry is the medicine for lasting prosperity.)

1796. *Owó ò bá olè gbé.*
Money does not live with a thief. (A thief and money are incompatible neighbors; never trust a thief with money.)

1797. *Òwúyé; a-ṣòro-ó-ṣọ bí ọ̀rọ̀.*
A hush-hush matter [is] difficult to utter as speech. (The matter under reference is so delicate it almost does not bear speech.)

1798. *Oyún inú: a kì í kà á kún ọmọ-ọ tìlẹ̀.*
One does not count a pregnancy as a child already delivered. (One should not treat anything hoped for as though it were already in hand.)

Ọ

1799. *Òbánijà ní ḿmọ ìjagun ẹni.*
Only those we struggle with know our strategies. (Only through close association does one know other people.)

1800. *Òbàrà gba kùmmọ̀; ó dífá fún a-láwìì-ì-gbọ́.*
Òbàrà received a cudgel blow; it consulted the Ifá oracle for a disobedient child.[76] (The obstinate person is asking for cudgel blows.)

1801. *Òbàyéjé, tí ńru gángan wòlú.*
Purveyor of general disaster, who carries

---

76. Òbàrà is one of the subchapters of the Ifá corpus (see note 3 to 22).

a *gángan* drum into town. (Apostrophe addressed to troublemakers.)[77]

1802. *"Ọbẹ̀ lọmú àgbà" ló pa onígbaǹso Ògòdò.*
"Stew is the breast milk of adults" is what killed the calabash repairer of Ògòdò town. (Addiction kills.)

1803. *Ọbẹ sìlò-ó ḿbáni ṣeré a ní kò mú, bí eré bí eré ó ńpani lọ́wọ́.*
The *sìlò* knife is playing with one, and one says it is not sharp, just as in play it slashes one's hand. (Be careful not to underestimate people who do not advertise themselves; otherwise, they will have you prostrate before you know what is happening.)

1804. *Ọbẹ̀ tóo sè tílé fi jóná wàá sọ ọ́.*
The sort of stew you cooked and set the house on fire, you will explain. (You must explain the unheard-of behavior that resulted in such a disaster.)

1805. *Ọbẹlẹ̀wò bẹlẹ̀wò; bí ewúrẹ́ yó bàá dùbúlẹ̀ a bẹ ilẹ̀ ibẹ̀ wò.*
Inspector of the ground inspects the ground; if a goat wishes to lie down, it first inspects the ground. (Look well at the lay of the land before engaging in any new venture.)

1806. *Ọbọ ni yo para è.*
The monkey will be its own death. (Fools will bring their own undoing upon themselves.)[78]

1807. *Òdaràn eyẹ tí ńmusàn.*
Habitual criminal bird eats oranges. (Ad-

dressed to any person whose actions are likely to lead to some disaster.)

1808. *Ọ̀dárayá tí ńfi ẹ̀gbẹ́ na igi.*
Sprightly person hurls himself sidewise against a tree. (Said of a too-cheerful person whose excess energy is getting on others' nerves.)

1809. *Ọdẹ a-fi-fìlà-pa-erin: ojọ́ kan ni òkìkí-i rẹ̀ ḿmọ.*
The hunter who would kill elephants with his cap: his fame lasts only one day. (Whoever promises to do the impossible enjoys fame only as long as it takes for the impossibility to be manifest.)

1810. *Ọ̀gá-a má fi ẹsẹ̀ yí ẹrẹ̀, gbogbo ara ní ńfi yí i.*
The never-soil-your-foot-with-mud dandy eventually soils his whole body. (Too much squeamishness is its own undoing.)

1811. *Ọ̀gán ìmàdò ò ṣéé kò lójú.*
A full-grown warthog is not something to confront. (One would be wise to avoid dangerous people.)

1812. *Ògèdè ḿbàjẹ́; a ní ó ńpọ́n.*
The banana is rotting; people say it is ripening. (It does not help to rationalize a brat's behavior with silly explanations.)

1813. *Ògò ńgbé ògo rù.*
A fool carries a cudgel around. (A person is cultivating the means to his or her own ruin.)

1814. *Ògbágbá wọlẹ̀, ó ku àtiyọ.*
The iron stake has been driven into the ground; the problem now is how to pull it out. (Some ventures that are easy at the start prove mightily intractable down the line.)

1815. *Ọgbọ́n àgbọ́njù ní ńpa òdù òyà.*
It is excessive cunning that kills the mature

---

77. Apart from its noisiness, it is not clear why the introduction of a *gángan* drum (the talking drum) into town would be disastrous. One suggestion is that the bearer carries the drum on his head to signal sorrow.

78. The Yoruba use the word *ọbọ*, literally "monkey," to designate fools.

cane rat. (Too much cleverness brings trouble.)

1816. Ogbọ́n àgbọ́njù ní ńsọ ẹni diwin; bí
oògún bá pọ̀ lápọ̀jù a sọni di wèrè; bóbìnrín
bá gbọ́n àgbọ́njù, pẹ́npẹ́ lasọ ọkọ è ńmọ.
Excessive cleverness turns one into a phantom; too much magical charm turns the owner into an imbecile; if a woman is too cunning, her husband's clothes wind up ill-fitting. (People who are too cunning are headed for trouble; a man who marries too cunning a woman is headed for trouble.)

1817. Ogbọ́n ọdúnnìí, wèrè èmíì.
Today's wisdom, next year's madness. (What seems wise now may appear like lunacy in hindsight.)

1818. Ogbọ́n pẹ̀lú-u sùúrù la fi ńmú erin
wọ̀lú.
It is with cunning and patience that one brings an elephant into town. (The most difficult tasks can be accomplished with wisdom and patience.)

1819. Ojọ́ tí a ó bàá nù, gágá lara ńyáni.
The day one is destined to be lost one is never able to contain one's excitement. (Disaster attends overenthusiasm.)

1820. Ojọ́ tí a to ọkà a ò to ti èkúté mọ́ ọ.
The day one arranged the corn in the granary, one did not think in terms of the rat. (One hardly ever plans for trouble.)

1821. Ojọ́ tí àgbè síṣe-é bá di kíyèsílẹ̀, ká síwọ́
oko ríro.
The day farming entails being careful not to hurt the soil, one should stop farming. (If the basic condition for a trade is interdicted, one should no longer engage in that trade.)

1822. Ojọ́ tí elétutu-ú bá máa fọ̀, ìjàm̀pere kì í
rìn.
On the day the white flying ants wish to swarm, the worms that prey on them keep still. (Only cunning will deliver one's prey into one's hands.)

1823. Òkánjúwà àgbè tí ńgbin òwú sóko
àkùrọ̀.
[It is] an insatiable farmer who plants cotton on a farm by the stream. (Greed sometimes makes people work against their own interests.)[79]

1824. Òkánjúwà baba àrùn.
Covetousness, father of all diseases. (There is no disease like greed.)

1825. Òkánjúwà baba olè; àwòrò̀nṣoṣò-ó wo
ohun olóhun má ṣèéjú.
Covetousness, father of thievery; bug-eyed greedy person stares at another person's property without blinking. (Covetousness leads to stealing.)

1826. Òkánjúwà èèyàn-án dé àwùjọ, ó wòkè
yàn-yàn-àn-yàn.
The covetous person arrives in a gathering, and his eyes dart about restlessly. (The covetous person is always on the lookout for something.)

1827. Òkánjúwà kì í mu ẹ̀jẹ̀ ẹlòmíràn; ẹ̀jẹ̀ ara
ẹ̀ náà ní ńmu.
The greedy person does not drink other people's blood; he drinks only his own. (Greed recoils on the greedy.)

1828. Òkánjúwà ò ṣéé fi wá nǹkan.
Impatient envy is not a good state in which

---

79. Cotton will not thrive in too wet a condition, but the avaricious farmer thinks the more moisture, the better the yield.

to seek anything. (One should be patient in seeking one's fortune.)

1829. Ọ̀kánjúwà ológbò tó jókòó sẹ́nu ọ̀nà: ṣé eku eléku ló fẹ́ẹ́ pa jẹ?
The insatiable cat that sits in the doorway: does it want to kill cats in another house? (Greedy people are never satisfied with what they have.)[80]

1830. Ọ̀kánjúwà Onísàngó ní ńsọ ọmọ-ọ rẹ̀ ní Bámgbóṣé; ìwọ̀n oṣé tí a lè gbé là ńgbé.
It is an insatiable Ṣango priest who names his son Bámgbóṣé; one should procure for oneself a ritual rod one can carry.[81] (Avoid avarice.)

1831. Ọ̀kánjúwà pẹ̀lú olè, déédé ni wọ́n jẹ́.
Covetousness and thievery are similar to each other. (Covetousness is as bad as stealing.)

1832. Ọ̀kánjúwà-á bu òkèlè, ojú ẹ̀-ẹ́ lami.
A greedy person takes a morsel of food, and tears gush from his eyes. (Greed has its pains also.)[82]

1833. Ọ̀kánjúwà-á pín ẹgbàafà nínú ẹgbàaje; ó ní kí wọ́n pín ẹgbàá kan tó kù, bóyá igbiwó tún lè kan òun.
The insatiable person receives 12,000 cowries out of 14,000; he asks that the remaining 2,000 be shared, [so] perhaps 200 of them will come to him. (Greed knows no limits.)

---

80. The cat in the doorway is not paying attention to the mice inside the house; its attention is directed outside.

81. Oṣé is the ritual rod that Ṣango priests carry; it is reputed to have the power to invoke lightning. The name Bámgbóṣé means "Help me carry a ritual rod."

82. The morsel is evidently too big for him to swallow without pain or effort.

1834. Ọ̀kẹ́rẹ́ gorí ìrókò, ojú ọdẹ dá.
The squirrel scrambles up the ìrókò tree; the fire in the hunter's eyes is doused. (When affairs have gone out of one's control, one should cease worrying.)[83]

1835. Ọkọ̀ ńjò, ọkọ̀ ńjò! Ìgbà tó bá rì, kò parí ná?
The boat is leaking, the boat is leaking! After it sinks, won't matters end? (There is little one can do about a problem whose outcome is inevitable.)

1836. Ọ̀kòòkan lọwọ̀ ńyo.
Broomstraws drop off one by one. (Huge problems usually build up gradually.)

1837. Ọkùnrin tó fẹ́ òjòwú méjì sílé ò rẹni fi sọ́lé.
A man who marries two jealous women has no one to tend his home in his absence. (Jealousy is a terrible quality in a spouse.)

1838. Ọ̀kùn-ún mọ̀nà tẹ́lẹ̀ kójú ẹ̀ tó fọ́.
The millipede knew the way before it went blind. (The old knew how to live before they became frail.)

1839. "Ọ̀la ni mò ńlọ," tí ńfi koto ṣe àmù.
"Tomorrow I take my leave" uses a shallow pot as his water jar. (Shortsighted people make little provision for the future.)

1840. "Ọlá ò jẹ́ kí nríran"; ọmọ Èwí Adó tí ńtanná rìn lọ́sàn-án.
"Greatness won't let me see": the son of the Èwí, king of Adó, lights a lamp to walk with in broad daylight. (One should not allow one's good fortune to go to one's head.)

1841. Ọ̀làjà ní ńfi orí gbọgbẹ́.
It is the person who separates two fighters

---

83. It is taboo for hunters to shoot at an ìrókò tree.

who gets gashed on the head. (The peace-maker is likely to suffer for his pains.)

1842. Ọlọ́dẹ kì í torí atẹ́gùn yìnbọn.
A hunter does not fire off his gun because of the wind. (One should be deliberate and attentive in pursuing one's profession.)

1843. Ọlọ́gbọ́n bẹ̀ẹrẹ-ẹ́ pète ìgárá.
The excessively cunning person is trying his hand at stealing. (Too much cunning is like thievery.)

1844. Ọmọ adìẹ fò, a ní "Ẹran lọ àkẹ́ẹ̀!"
A chick flies up, and we exclaim, "A game animal has escaped, alas!" (Do not blow matters out of all credible proportion.)

1845. Ọmọ inú ayò ò ṣéé bá bínú.
The seeds in an ayò game are not things to be angry at. (One should not blame one's misfortune on innocent people.)

1846. Ọmọ orogún ẹ-ẹ́ kú, o ní ẹni rí ẹ lọ́run ò puró; bí tìẹ bá kú ńkọ́?
The child of your rival wife dies, and you say the person who saw you in heaven did not lie; what if your own child dies? (One should not go overboard in sharing other people's sorrow.)

1847. Ọmọdé bú ìrókò, ó bojú wẹ̀hìn; òòjọ́ ni ńjà?
A child insults an ìrókò tree and glances back apprehensively; does it take revenge immediately?[84] (The fact that there has been no repercussion for a misdeed does not mean one is home free; repercussions may be delayed. Compare 658.)

1848. Ọmọdé jí ti ojú orun wá, ó ní "Àkàrà kéjìkéjì"; wọ́n ti ńmú u kẹ́ẹ̀ kó tó jí, ì ká ká níkẹ̀?
A child wakes from sleep and says in code, "Bean fritters two-by-two." Had the others been taking them thus before he woke, would any have been left?[85] (Never misuse what those before you made available to you by their wise husbandry. Compare 1089.)

1849. Ọmọrí odó pani lọ́tọ̀, ká tó wí pé ká kùn ún lóògùn.
A pestle is a lethal weapon in itself, let alone after rubbing poison on it. (Overkill is pointless; if a situation is dangerous enough as it is, one should not aggravate it by acting provocatively.)

1850. Ọmùtí ò mu agbè já.
The drunkard does not drink the gourd through. (There is a limit to the pleasure a drunk can get from a bottle.)

1851. Ọ̀nà ẹ̀búrú dá ọwọ́ olúwa-a rẹ̀ tẹlẹ̀.
A shortcut causes a person to land on his palms. (There are perils to taking paths one is not familiar with.)

1852. Ọ̀nà ìgbàlẹ̀ a máa já sọ́run.
The road to the secret grove of the egúngún cult may lead to heaven. (People who do the forbidden may pay dearly for their temerity.)

1853. Ọ̀nà là ńsì mọ̀nà; bí a ò bá ṣubú, a kì í mọ ẹrù-ú dì.
It is by missing one's way that one learns the way; if one does not fall, one does not learn

---

84. The ìrókò tree is believed to house powerful spirits; anyone who insults it is foolhardy.

85. The child's real meaning is Àkàrà méjì-méjì ("Bean fritters two at a time"), and the rejoinder is Wọ́n ti ńmu bẹ́ẹ̀ kó tó jí ì bá bá nílẹ̀? ("Had people been grabbing them like that, would he have found any left?"). The child is using the sort of scrambled speech known as ẹnà.

how to tie one's load properly.[86] (Errors and failures are opportunities to learn.)

1854. Ọnà ni yó mùú olè; ahéré ni yó mùú olóko.
The road will eventually expose the thief; the farm hut will eventually expose the farmer. (When the habitual wrongdoer comes to grief, it will be in the course of his wrong-doing.)

1855. Ọnà ọfun, ọnà ọrun: méjèèjì bákannáà ni wọ́n rí.
The pathway of the throat, the pathway to heaven: the two are very much alike. (One's throat may lead to one's death.)

1856. Ọpá àgbéléjìká, a-tẹ̀hìn-lójú.
The walking stick that is carried on the shoulder has its eye pointed backward. (Said of people who pay no attention to their future.)

1857. Ọpọ̀ oògùn ní ńru ọmọ gàle-gàle.
It is a great deal of medicine that possesses a child and robs it of all self-control. (A person who lacks moderation is like someone overpowered by bad medicine.)

1858. Ọpọlọ́ lejò ńbùjẹ, tí à ńwí pé ilẹ̀-ẹ́ rorò?
Is it because a snake is biting a toad that one says the earth portends disaster? (Do not make too much of insignificant events.)

1859. Ọ̀ràn kì í yẹ lórí alábaun.
The responsibility for trouble never fails to fall on the head of the tortoise. (Said of people who are invariably the source of problems.)[87]

1860. Ọ̀ràn ńlá-ńlá ní ḿbá àpá; ọ̀ràn ṣékú-ṣékú ní ḿbá osè.
Only huge problems befall the mahogany-bean tree; only minor problems befall the baobab tree. (Different people have different levels of vulnerability.)

1861. Ọ̀ràn ò dun gbọ̀ọ̀rọ̀; a dá a láàárọ̀, ó yọ lálẹ́.
Problems have hardly any effect at all on the pumpkin shoot; broken off in the morning, it reappears the following night. (Said of people who are unimpressed by correction or punishment.)

1862. Ọ̀ràn ọ̀gèdè ò tó ohun tí à ńyọ àdá sí.
The problem posed by the banana tree is nothing that calls for a machete. (Do not make too much of a minor crisis.)[88]

1863. Ọ̀ràn ọkà-á ní ìba; ayé ní ọ̀ṣùwọ̀n.
A matter pertaining to corn has a limit; life has its measure. (To everything there is a proper limit.)

1864. Ọ̀rọ̀ lọmọ etí ńjẹ.
Words are what the child of the ear eats. (People who misbehave must endure tongue lashing.)[89]

1865. Ọ̀rọ̀ ò pọ̀, àkàwé-e rẹ̀ ló pọ̀.
The matter in question is not overwhelm-ing; it is the elaboration of it that is almost forbidding. (Creating a problem is easy; explaining it is not quite as easy.)

1866. Ọ̀rọ̀ púpọ̀ ò kún agbọ̀n; irọ́ ní ḿmú wá.
A lot of words will not fill a basket; they will only lead to lies. (Brevity is wise in discussions; wordiness leads to invention.)

---

86. The second part is used as a proverb by itself.
87. This proverb is based on the fact that *alábaun* (or *àjàpá*) the Tortoise is the Yoruba trickster figure.

88. The trunk of the banana plant is so soft that it does not take much effort to cut it down.
89. *Ọmọ etí,* literally "the child of the ear," refers here to the inner ear.

1867. *Ọ̀rọ̀ tí a dì ní gbòdògì: bo déwée kókò yó fàya.*
A matter that is wrapped in *gbòdògì* leaves will, if wrapped in coco-yam leaves, rip them to tatters. (If delicate matters are handled carelessly, the result will be the opposite of what was desired.)[90]

1868. *Ọ̀rọ̀ tí ò ní ohùn fífọ, dídáké ló yẹ ẹ́.*
A matter that does not have a means to voice itself had better be silent. (Matters that should not be mentioned should be left unbroached.)

1869. *Ọ̀ṣọ́ oníbùjé ò pé isán; ọ̀ṣọ́ onínàbì ò ju ọdún lọ.*
The beauty bestowed by tattooing with the juice of the *bùjé* plant does not last nine days; a prostitute's beauty does not last more than a year. (Fast living plays havoc with people's looks.)

1870. *Ọ̀tọ̀ọ̀tọ̀ là ńtẹ erè; ọ̀tọ̀ọ̀tọ̀ là ńtẹ eruku.*
One step after the other is the manner to walk through mire; one step after the other is how one walks through dust. (With great care, one can extricate oneself safely from any problem. Compare 1189.)

1871. *Ọ̀wọ́n yúnlé, ọ̀pọ̀-ọ́ yúnjà.*
Expensive commodities come to the home; inexpensive ones go to the market. (If one overprices one's goods, one will find no takers.)

1872. *Ọwọ́-ọ baba lẹ wò, ẹ ò wo esẹ̀-ẹ baba.*
Your eyes are on the patriarch's hand, but they ignore his feet.[91] (People who do not pay attention to details are likely to go astray.)

P

1873. *Pala-pálà kì í ṣe ẹran àjẹgbé; ẹ ṣáà máa mu àgúnmu.*
Stockfish is not a meat one eats without repercussions; keep on drinking herbal remedies. (One pays for one's indiscretions by and by.)

1874. *Pápá tó ní òun ó jòó wọ odò, ọ̀rọ̀ ló fẹ́ẹ gbọ́.*
The grassland that proposes to burn into the river is asking for a lecture.[92] (Abstain from actions that will provoke others' ire.)

1875. *Paramólẹ̀-ẹ́ kọ̀ ọ̀ràn àfojúdi.*
The serpent refuses to be trifled with. (Certain situations are not to be taken lightly, lest they result in painful repercussions.)

1876. *Pẹ̀lẹ́-pẹ̀lẹ́ lejò-ó fi ńgun àgbọn.*
It is very carefully and patiently that a snake climbs the coconut palm. (Dangerous and difficult tasks should be attempted with care and patience.)

1877. *Pẹ̀tẹ̀pẹ́tẹ̀ ọ̀rọ̀, a-ta-síni-lára-má-wọ̀n-ọ́n.*
The soiling caused by speech stains a person and cannot be removed. (Injury once spoken cannot be recalled. Compare 550.)

1878. *Pípé ni yó pẹ̀ẹ, agbọn á bo adìẹ.*
It may take long, but the coop will eventu-

---

90. *Gbòdògì* leaves are used for wrapping kola nuts and are therefore well regarded; coco-yam leaves are for all-purpose wrapping.

91. The underlying story is that a man entertaining a guest sent his son out to buy a goat to kill for the guest's dinner. He indicated the size of the goat by holding his hand at the midpoint of his thigh, but at the same time he lifted his other foot just slightly above the ground. The son returned with a rather small goat, and the guest wondered why he did not pay attention to his father's instructions. The son replied with proverb.

92. If the bush were to burn into the river, there would be a hissing sound when the water put the fire out.

ally cover the chicken. (One may put it off a while, but one cannot avoid one's fate. Compare 1878–84, all with the same beginning.)

1879. *Pípé ni yó pèé, akólòlò á pe baba.*
It may take long, but the stammerer will eventually manage to say "Papa." (With perseverance the most difficult task will be accomplished.)

1880. *Pípé ni yó pèé, akòpe yó wàá sílè.*
It may take a while, but the palm-wine tapster will descend from atop the palm tree. (With patience, what one desires will eventually happen.)

1881. *Pípé ni yó pèé, amòòkùn yó jàáde nínú odò.*
It may take a while, but the underwater swimmer will eventually surface. (If one is patient, what is bound to happen will eventually happen.)

1882. *Pípé ni yó pèé, èké ò mú rá.*
It may take a while, but the deceitful person will not be undiscovered. (Truth will unfailingly triumph in the end.)

1883. *Pípé ni yó pèé, ení lo sódò á bò wálé.*
It may take a while, but the person who went to the stream will return home. (There is no journey that does not end sometime.)

1884. *Pípé ni yó pèé, Òrúnmìlà yó je àgbàdo dandan.*
It may take a while, but Òrúnmìlà will surely eat corn. (What one deserves will unfailingly come one's way in the end.)

R

1885. *Rò ó kóo tó se é; ó sàn ju kóo sé kóo tó rò ó.*
Think it through before you do it; that is better than doing it before you think it through. (Plan ahead.)

1886. *Rora dì, ká lè bá o sá.*
Pack judiciously that we may accompany you while you escape. (A person who wants other people's help must lighten his or her baggage.)

S

1887. *Sà á bí olóògùn-ún ti wí.*
Invoke it exactly as the maker of the charm instructed. (Always follow instructions, and do not presume to know better than your instructor.)

1888. *Sùúrù loògùn ayé.*
Patience is the talisman for living. (Patience solves all problems.)

1889. *Sùúrù ò lópin.*
There is no end to the need for patience. (One must never tire of exercising patience.)

1890. *Sùúrù-ú lérè.*
Patience has its profits. (Patience is a useful quality to cultivate.)

Ṣ

1891. *Sàngbákó ró, a ní kò róo re, Sàngbàkù-ú gbè é lésè.*
Sàngbákó makes a sound and we say the sound is foul, and then Sàngbàkù lends its voice in its support. (Do not choose to do things that others before you have been condemned for doing.)

1892. *Se-ká-rí-mi, aláá tó so ègi mórùn.*
Exhibitionist: a dog owner who ties a sheep's mane around his own neck. (Do not go to

too great lengths to call people's attention to yourself.)[93]

1893. "Ṣé kí nfidí ẹ?" làfòmọ́ fi ńdi onílé.
"May I perch here awhile?" is the ruse by which the climber-parasite becomes a permanent resident. (Give people an inch, and they are likely to take several miles.)

1894. Ṣe-ǹ-ṣe dìwòfà, bó ṣe é yó derú-u wọn.
The habit that made a person a pawn, if the person persists in it, will make him or her a slave. (One should desist from pursuits that have proved unprofitable.)

1895. Ṣe-ǹ-ṣe ewúrẹ́ làgùntàn ńfiyè sí.
The habit of the goat is what the sheep pays attention to. (One would be wise to learn from the behavior and plight of fools.)

T

1896. "Ta á sí i" kì í báni wá ọfà.
"Shoot at it" does not help one find arrows. (People are ever eager to goad one to action but never to help one carry out the task.)

1897. Ta ní rán Abẹ́lù wọ ọkọ̀, tó ní ọkọ́ọ̀ ri òun?
Who sent Abẹlu into a boat, as a result of which action he says he was drowned? (People who get into trouble by their own actions should complain to no one.)

1898. "Tàná là ńjà lé lórí" ló pa Baálẹẹ Kòmòkan.
"It is yesterday's matter that we are fighting over" is what killed Chief Know-Nothing. (It is wise to let the past alone.)

1899. Tantabùlù, aṣòróówọ̀ bí ẹwù àṣejù.
An unbecoming thing is as unpleasant to

wear as the garment of disgrace. (Disgrace is not a pleasant thing to live with.)

1900. Tìjà tìjà ní ńṣe ará Ọ̀pọ́ndá.
Incessant proneness to fighting is the affliction of Ọ̀pọ́ndá people. (Said of people who are always out for a fight.)

1901. Tòsán tòsán ní ńpọ́n ìtalẹ̀ lójú; bílẹ̀-ẹ́ bá sú yó di olóńje.
It is the persistence of daylight that imposes suffering on the mud-floor worm; when night falls, it will find food. (Patience will bring what one lacks.)

W

1902. Wàrà ò sí lónìí, wàrà-á wà lóla.
No cheese today, but there will be cheese tomorrow. (Today's want will be followed by tomorrow's plenty.)

1903. Wẹ́rẹ́ wẹ́rẹ́ nikán ńjẹlé.
Slowly, slowly is the manner in which termites consume a house. (Inconspicuous and imperceptible problems in time become huge disasters.)

1904. Wíwò-ó tó ìran.
Watching is enough for a spectacle. (One would do well just to watch spectacles and avoid becoming part of them.)

1905. "Wó ilé ẹ kí mbá ọ kọ": ẹrù ikán kan ní ńpa fúnni.
"Demolish your house and I will help you rebuild it": he will give one only one bundle of thatching grass. (Never trust people who goad you into trouble with promises of help down the road.)

1906. Wòbìà-á yó tán, ó pe ẹgbẹ́ ẹ̀ wá.
The greedy person fed to satiation, and he summons his friends. (The freeloader

---

93. Ègi is a ram's mane used as an ornamental collar around a dog's neck.

always seeks opportunities to take as much as possible from his or her benefactor.)

1907. *Wọ́n ní, "Ìbàrìbá, ọmọ ẹ-ẹ́ jalè." Ó ní "A gbọ́ tolè tó jà; èwo lokùn ọrùn-un è?"*
People said, "Ìbàrìbá person, your child stole something." She responded, "That he stole something I can understand, but I cannot understand the rope around his neck." (Punishment should fit the offense, not be disproportionate.)

1908. *Wọ́n purọ́ fún ọ, o ò gbà; o lè dé ìdí òótọ́?*
People lie to you and you do not accept the lie; can you ever know what the truth is? (Since one can seldom be sure what the truth is, one would save oneself a great deal of grief by not always insisting on it.)

1909. *Wọ́n torí ajá ńlóṣòó lọ fowó ròbọ.*
Because the dog sits on its haunches, they went and spent their money on purchasing a monkey. (One should not pass up something useful for something useless simply because the latter looks better.)

Y

1910. *Yíyọ́ ẹkùn, tojo kọ́; ohun tí yó jẹ ní ńwá.*
The leopard's stealthy gait is not a result of cowardice; it is simply stalking a prey. (Do not mistake people's gentle nature for spinelessness.)

1911. *Yọkọlú-yọkọlú, kò ha tán bí? Ìyàwó gbọ́kọ sánlè, ọkọ́ yọké.*
All your strutting and bragging, where is it now? The wife threw the husband down so hard that he grew a hump on his back. (Said of braggarts who have been taken down a few notches.)

On perseverance, industry, resilience, self-confidence, self-reliance, resourcefulness, daring, fortitude, and invulnerability

A

1912. *A hán ìkokò lọ́wọ́ ọ̀tún, a hán ìkokò lẹ́sẹ̀ òsì; ó ku ẹni tí yó kò ó lójú.*
We lop off the hyena's right forelimb; we lop off the hyena's left hind limb; the question is, who will face it now? (Inflicting such injuries on the hyena is no victory; it only makes the animal more dangerous.)

1913. *A kì í dá ẹ̀rù okó ńlá ba arúgbó.*
One should not attempt to scare an old [woman] with a huge penis. (A person who has seen everything is not easily frightened. Compare 2273.)

1914. *A kì í dùbúlẹ̀ ṣubú.*
One does not fall from a prone position. (Hunger cannot make one faint and fall if one goes to sleep.)

1915. *A kì í fi ojoojúmọ́ rí olè jà kó dà bí-i tọwọ́ ẹni.*
One is never so fortunate at daily thievery that it matches owning one's own things. (Self-sufficiency is far better than fortunate opportunism.)

1916. *A kì í fi ojú olójú sòwò ká jèrè.*
One never trades with other people's eyes and profit. (There is nothing like attending to one's business oneself.)

1917. *A kì í fi ojúbọ́rọ́ gba ọmọ lọ́wọ́ èkùrọ́.*
One does not easily or casually take the

child from the palm nut.[1] (It takes effort to accomplish a good end.)

1918. *A kì í gbọ́ "gbì" ìràwé.*
One does not hear the "thud" of a falling leaf.[2] (Incantatory assertion that an accident will not befall the subject.)

1919. *A kì í mọ ibi tí à ńlọ kí ọrùn ó wọ ẹni.*
One does not, despite knowing where one is going, suffer a constricted neck from one's heavy load. (If one knows the size of the task, one should regulate one's effort accordingly.)

1920. *A kì í sọ pé ojà-á nígbà; bó bá nígbà, kíníse tí wọ́n tún ńná a?*
One does not say there is a time for the market; if it were so, why would people continuously patronize it? (Any time is a good time to trade.)

1921. *A kì í ṣe òjẹ̀ ṣe ojú tì mí; konko lojú alágbe.*
One does not carry the *òjẹ̀* masquerade and yet affect bashfulness; the mendicant's eyes must always be like flint.[3] (One must assume the attitude one's trade demands.)

---

1. The "child" in this case is the soft nut in the shell.
2. It is not in the nature of leaves to crash.
3. The *òjẹ̀* masquerader engages mainly in begging for gifts.

1922. *A kì í ṣe òtè eranko gán-ń-gán; bí a bá he ìgbín àdá là ńnà á.*
One does not conduct one's feud with an animal in a halfhearted manner; if one finds a snail, one hits it with a machete. (Give your all to every enterprise you embark upon.)

1923. *A kì í walè fún adìẹ jẹ.*
One does not scratch the ground for the chicken to find food. (Each person is responsible for his or her own welfare.)

1924. *À ńpa èkukù, èkukù ńrúwé; à ńyan nínú aṣero, aṣero ńdàgbà; à ńkébòsí Ògún, ara Ògún ńle.*
The more one weeds *èkukù*, the more it sprouts leaves; the more one tramples *aṣero*, the more it grows; the more one rails against Ògún, the more he thrives. (Because the two plants are hardy and virtually indestructible, and Ògún is the formidable god of metals and war, the proverb bespeaks resilience and invulnerability. Compare the following entry.)

1925. *À ńpòyì ká apá, apá ò ká apá; à ńpòyì ká oṣè, apá ò ká oṣè; à ńpòyì ká kànga, kò ṣé bínú kó sí.*
We make circles around the mahogany-bean tree, but it is too much to handle; we make circles around the baobab tree, but it is too much to handle; we makes circles around the well, but it is nothing to jump into in anger.[4] (The three items listed are formidable in their different ways and have nothing to fear from people. See the previous entry.)

1926. *"A ò mòyí Olórun yó ṣe" kò jẹ ká bínú kú.*
"We know not what God will do" keeps one from committing suicide. (Often it is hope that keeps people going.)

1927. *A pa ẹmọ́ lóko ilá, a jù ú sí òkẹ́ ìlasa; ilé ẹmọ́ lẹmọ́ lo.*
A giant rat is killed on an okra farm and thrown into a sack containing okra leaves; the giant rat has arrived at its home. (The resourceful person will find a way to adapt to any situation.)

1928. *Ààrẹ àgòrò tó bá gbójú, tòun tolúwa-a rè lẹgbéra.*
A subordinate military officer who is audacious is the equal of his superior. (Audaciousness will get one one's way.)

1929. *Abẹ́rẹ́ á lọ kí ònà okùn tó dí.*
The needle will pass before the way of the thread is blocked. (Unlike the thread's, the passage of the needle through the cloth is ever smooth.)

1930. *Abèwè ńwá òtá fúnra è.*
He who summons others to render him communal help seeks enemies.[5] (It is best to be self-sufficient.)

1931. *Abiyamọ òtá àgàn; ẹní ńṣiṣẹ́ òtá òlẹ.*
Nursing mother, enemy of the barren woman; working person, enemy of the idler. (The mother incurs the envy of a barren woman; the hard worker incurs the hatred of the idler.)

1932. *Aboyún bí, ìhá tù ú.*
The pregnant woman delivered; her sides

---

4. There is a play on the word *apá*, which is the name of a tree, *Afzelia africana* (Ceasalpinaceae; see Abraham 57), and the word for "arm." The expression *apá ká a*, "the arms can enfold it," means that one can deal with it. Both *apá* (the tree) and *oṣè* (baobab) are reputed to be inhabited by powerful spirits and to be favored as venues for witches' covens.

5. *Òwè* was a traditional means of assuring a large workforce for large projects: people pooled their resources to help a colleague in need on his farm. The custom was to provide such help when asked, but that did not obviate secret grumblings.

are much eased. (Relief comes in time to the persevering sufferer.)

1933. *Àdán tó sùn sídìí ọsàn ò rí he, ámbọ̀sì oódẹ tó ní òún jí dé.*
Bat, who slept by the orange tree, found no orange to pick, let alone the parrot which said it came over very early at dawn. (The more persistent person will surely be rewarded before the less persistent.)

1934. *Adékànmbí ò du oyè; ó bèèrè ni.*
Adékànmbí is not contesting a title; he is merely asking a question.[6] (One should not be coy in demanding one's rights.)

1935. *Adùn ní ńgbẹ̀hìn ewúro.*
The aftertaste of the bitterleaf is sweet. (Sweetness and pleasure come after exertion.)[7]

1936. *Adùn-ún tán lára aṣọ ogóje; a nà án han ẹni méje; a bẹ̀ ẹ́ wò a rí iná méje; ó di ọjọ́ keje ó fàya.*
One's delight in a cloth costing 140 cowries is over; one spreads it out to show to seven people, one finds seven lice, and on the seventh day it is torn.[8] (One gets what one pays for.)

---

6. The proverb is based on a deliberate misinterpretation of the name, which is a contraction of the sentence *Adé kàn mí bí*, meaning, "It is my turn to give birth to a person destined to wear a crown." The proverb takes the name to be a contraction of the sentence *Adé kàn mí bí?* in which *bí* is taken to be not the verb "to give birth to" but the interrogatory "is it that?" In many instances, succession to Yoruba chieftaincies is contested by many aspirants.

7. *Ewúro*, bitterleaf, one of the most popular stew vegetables, is very bitter to the taste; all its juice must be squeezed out before it is cooked. Then, although it is still bitter at first taste, its aftertaste is quite pleasant.

8. The proverb plays on the number seven. *Ogóje* is a contraction of *Ogún méje*, seven twenties, or 140; 140 cowries represent an inconsiderable amount in traditional monetary terms.

1937. *A-fàkàrà-jẹkọ́ ò mọ iyì ọbẹ̀.*
He-who-eats-corn-meal-with-bean-fritters does not know the virtues of stew. (Whoever leads a sheltered life misses out on some great experiences.)

1938. *Aféfé kì í fẹ́ kí omi inú àgbọn dànù.*
The wind does not blow against the liquid inside a coconut and cause it to spill. (Certain people are not susceptible to certain disasters.)

1939. *Àfejútoto ò mọ ọkùnrin.*
Glaring wildly does not bespeak manliness. (Action is more persuasive than appearance.)

1940. *Àfẹ́ká là ńfẹ́ iná.*
Blowing from all directions is how one blows at a fire [to kindle it]. (One should apply one's best effort to any task.)

1941. *Agẹmọ ò ṣé-é jẹ lẹ́nu.*
The chameleon is not a thing to eat in one's mouth. (Certain propositions are beyond the pale.)

1942. *Àgùdà ò jẹ lábẹ́-ẹ Gẹ̀ẹ́sì.*
The Catholic missionary is not in the pay of the British administration. (An assertion of nondependence on a supposedly higher authority.)

1943. *Àgbà tí kò tó ọmọdé-é rán níṣẹ́ ní ńsọ pé kó bu omi wá ká jọ mu.*
It is an elder who lacks the authority to send a child on an errand who tells the child to go fetch water so they can drink it together. (One who is sure of his or her authority does not need to sweeten orders with incentives. Compare 2104.)

1944. *Àgbàbọ́ ò di tẹni.*
A foster child does not become one's own child. (There is nothing like having one's own.)

1945. *Àgbàbọ̀-ọ ṣòkòtò, bí kò fúnni lẹ́sẹ̀ a ṣoni; rẹ́mú-rẹ́mú ni ohun ẹni ṁbáni mu.*
Borrowed trousers, if they are not too tight around the legs, will be too loose; one's own things fit one exactly. (Borrowed articles are never like one's own.)

1946. *Àgbàká lèéfí ṅgba igbó.*
It is completely that smoke fills the forest. (Whatever is worth doing is worth doing diligently and thoroughly. Compare 1950 and the following entry.)

1947. *Àgbàká lẹsẹ̀ ṅgba ọ̀nà.*
It is completely that the feet take over a path. (Indulge not in half measures. Compare the preceding entry and 1950.)

1948. *Àgbaṅgbá ṣe bẹ́ẹ̀, ó làwo lórí san-san.*
Despite all difficulties, the animal *àgbaṅgbá* sprouts prominent horns on its head. (Perseverance overcomes all difficulties.)

1949. *Àgbàrá kọ́ ni yó gbèé omi lọ.*
It is not the flood that will make away with the river. (The upstart cannot prevail against the well-established person.)

1950. *Àgbàtán ni gẹ̀gẹ̀ ṅgba ọ̀fun.*
It is completely that goiter takes over the neck. (One cannot stop matters from running their course. Compare 1946 and 1947.)

1951. *Àgbẹ̀ gbóko róṣù.*
A farmer remains on the farm and sees the moon. (The conscientious farmer spends long periods on the farm; persistence is the key to success.)

1952. *Àgbinsínú legbin ṅgbin; àkùnsínú lekùn ṅkùn; hùn hùn hùn ẹlẹ́dẹ̀ inú ẹlẹ́dẹ̀ ní ṅgbé.*
Groaning internally is how an antelope groans; rumbling internally is how a leopard rumbles; the grunts of a pig stay inside the pig. (People may grumble, but they dare not voice their complaints openly.)

1953. *Agbójúlógún fi ara-a rẹ̀ fọ́sì ta.*
He-who-places-his-hopes-on-inheritance delivers himself to destitution. (One should secure one's own living.)

1954. *Àgbólà ni tàgbọ̀nrín; ọjọ́ tí àgbọ̀nrín bá gbó ni ọjọ́ ikú-u rẹ̀ ṅyẹ̀.*
Baying-and-surviving is the fate of the deer; whenever a deer bays, on that day its death is averted. (Every reverse portends good fortune in the end.)

1955. *Àìdúró là ṅpè níjó.*
Not standing still is what is described as dancing. (Continuous striving deserves praise, whatever the outcome.)

1956. *Àìtó ehín-ín ká ni à ṅfọwọ́ bò ó.*
It is not-having-attained-the-age-for-losing-one's-teeth that makes one cover [the mouth] with one's hand. (One should not be reticent in asserting oneself. Compare 2455.)

1957. *Ajá ilé ò mọdẹ-ẹ́ ṣe.*
A domesticated dog does not know how to hunt. (Pampering kills initiative.)

1958. *Àjà kì í jìn mọ́ ológbò lẹ́sẹ̀.*
The snare does not snare a cat's paw. (Some people are immune to certain perils.)

1959. *Ajá tó máa rún ọkà á láyà; ológbò to máa jẹ àkèré á ki ojú bọ omi.*
A dog that will chew dried corn must be brave; a cat that will eat a frog will dip its face in water.[9] (It takes a great effort to accomplish a great feat.)

---

9. Dogs' teeth are not made for chewing corn; a dog that will chew corn must, therefore, have fortitude. Likewise, a cat with a taste for frogs must pay the price.

1960. *Ajá wéré-wéré ní ńpa ikún.*
It is an agile dog that kills a squirrel. (The world belongs to the quick.)

1961. *Ajá wo ẹyẹ láwòmójú.*
The dog looks at birds with eyes full of disdain. (Against adversaries beyond one's powers, one must be satisfied with futile gestures.)

1962. *Ajé sọ ọmọ nù bí òkò.*
Wealth throws a person away like a stone. (The search for wealth takes one into distant lands.)

1963. *Àjẹgbé nigún ńjẹbọ.*
Eating without adverse effects is the vulture's way of consuming sacrificial offerings. (Some people can engage in daring and dangerous behavior with impunity.)

1964. *Ajìnfín, má ta ojú ilé; ọ̀pọ̀lọ̀ jìnfín má ta ojú àtijáde.*
You who have fallen into the dungeon, do not be impatient to arrive home; when the toad drops into a pit, it cannot be impatient to get out. (Certain predicaments one does not get out of in a hurry.)

1965. *A-jókò-ó-kunkun ò jẹ́ kí a-jókòó-jẹ́jẹ́ ó jókòo.*
The sit-tight person denies the tentative sitter a place. (The meek will not inherit the earth.)

1966. *Àjùmọ̀bí ò kan ti àrùn; kí alápá mú apá-a rẹ̀ kó le.*
Familial obligations do not extend to diseases; let each person look well to his or her arms. (Relatives will not bear your disease for you.)

1967. *A-ká-ìgbá-tà-á náwó ikú.*
He-who-plucks-the-African-locust-bean-tree-seeds-to-sell spends death's money.

(Whoever engages in a dangerous venture more than earns his or her pay.)

1968. *Àkànṣe lofà ìmàdò; jagan oró ò ran èse.*
The arrow for a warthog is a major project; an ordinary poison has no effect on the cat. (Certain tasks call for deliberate and extraordinary efforts.)

1969. *Àkèekèé ní òún kúrò ní kòkòrò-o kí nìyí?*
Scorpion says that its status transcends what-type-of-insect-is-this? (Stature and importance are not always commensurate; some people should not be underestimated.)

1970. *Àkèekèé rìn tapó-tapó.*
The scorpion travels accompanied by venom. (The stalwart is never unprepared to answer a call.)

1971. *Akíkanjú-kankan, ogun ní ńlọ; abù-wàwà, ọjà ní ńná; àkànní òbúkọ, bó bá tòṣì a máa rí jẹ.*
For the exceptionally brave person the proper profession is warring; for the gregarious person, trading; the illustrious he-goat, even when it is poor, finds enough to eat. (Proper application of one's talent makes one prosper.)

1972. *Àkótán ni gègè ńkó òfun.*
It is completely that goiter takes over the throat. (Calamities give no quarter. This is the same as 1950.)

1973. *Àkùkọ-ó kọ, ọ̀lẹ́ pòṣé.*
The cock crows, and the lazy person hisses. (The coming of the morning is an annoyance to the lazy person.)

1974. *Alágẹmọ-ó ti bímọ-ọ rẹ̀ ná; àìmọ̀-ójó kù sówó-ọ rẹ̀.*
The chameleon has given birth to its young; inability to dance is the responsibility of the

child. (A parent has done his or her part by having a child; the child's fortunes are the child's responsibility.)

1975. *Alágbàró ò yege; aláṣọ á gbà á bó dòla.*
She who borrows a wrapper skirt to wear is not home free; the owner of the cloth will take it back tomorrow. (There is nothing like having one's own.)

1976. *Alákataṁpò ojú ò lè ta ẹran pa.*
A person with crossbows in his eyes cannot kill an animal. (Even the most vicious of looks cannot kill.)

1977. *Aláṅgbá tó já látorí ìrókò tí kò fẹsẹ̀ ṣé, ó ní bénìkan ò yìn un òun ó yinra òun.*
The lizard that fell from atop the *ìrókò* tree without breaking its limbs says if no one admires his feat, he will do the admiring himself. (One should be self-confident enough not to need validation by others.)

1978. *Alára ní ṅgbára-á ga; bádíẹ́ bá máa wọ̀ọ̀dẹ̀ a bẹ̀rẹ̀.*
It is the owner of the body that elevates the body; when a chicken wishes to enter the porch, it stoops. (One should sound one's own trumpet and not be unduly humble.)

1979. *A-lèjà-má-lè-jà-pé: ẹlẹgbẹ́ ojo.*
He-who-can-fight-but-cannot-fight-for-long: the equal of a coward. (Ability to start a fight is nothing like the ability to see it through.)

1980. *Àlejò orí ni kókó.*
The lump is only the head's visitor. (One should learn to live with afflictions.)

1981. *Apá lará; ìgbọ̀nwọ́ niyèkan.*
One's arms are one's relatives; one's elbows are one's siblings by the same mother. (Even more reliable than one's relatives and siblings are one's own resources.)

1982. *Àpáàdì-í gbóko kò rà.*
The potsherd lives on the farm but does not decay. (Resilience is a fortunate quality to have.)

1983. *Àpagbé lOrò ṅpagi.*
Killing-without-recourse is Orò's way of killing trees. (When unanswerable disaster befalls a person, there is neither recourse nor response.)

1984. *Apárí ní ṅfojú di abẹ.*
It is a bald person who may be disdainful of the razor. (The bald person has no use for razors. Compare 1345.)

1985. *Apééjẹ kì í jẹ ìbàjé.*
A person who waits patiently for a long time before eating will not eat unwholesome food. (Those who are patient will have the best of things.)

1986. *Àpọntán kò wí pé kí odò má sun.*
Scooping a spring dry does not stop more water from collecting. (If one's resources are limitless, some use will not exhaust them.)

1987. *Ara kì í wúwo kí alára má lè gbe.*
A body cannot be too heavy for the owner to lift. (Whatever others might feel, a person is never put off by himself or his own habits. See 2096.)

1988. *Ara-à mí gba òtútù, ó gba ònini.*
My body can endure chills and can endure coldness. (I am long-suffering.)

1989. *Àràbà ńlá fojú di àáké.*
The huge silk-cotton tree belittles the axe. (It takes a mighty person to defy a powerful force.)

1990. *Àríṣe làríkà.*
Having an opportunity to act is also having an opportunity to tell stories. (Whoever

accomplishes something worthwhile has a story to tell.)

1991. *Ariwo àjìjà ní ńdọ́run.*
It is only the noise of the whirlwind that reaches heaven. (One's enemies may be clamorous, but all they are capable of is noise.)

1992. *Àro-ó pẹ́ lóko, kò tún mọ ìlù-ú lù.*
Àro stayed so long on the farm that he forgot how to beat the drum. (If one neglects one's specialty long enough, one becomes incompetent at it.)[10]

1993. *Asúrétete ní ńwojú ojọ́.*
It is the person in a hurry who studies the complexion of the day. (When one has important tasks at hand, one pays particular attention to impinging conditions.)

1994. *Àṣá ò gbádìẹ níkòkò; gbangba làṣá ńgbádìẹ.*
The kite does not snatch chicks in secret; it snatches them openly. (What one dare do, one does openly. Compare 1956.)

1995. *Àṣá ò lè balẹ̀ kó gbéwúrẹ́.*
The kite cannot swoop down and carry off a goat. (Whoever attempts the impossible deceives himself or herself.)

1996. *Àṣá wo ahun títí; àwòdí wo ahun títí; idì baba àṣá, kí ló lè fi ahun ṣe?*
The kite looks long at the tortoise; the eagle looks long at the tortoise; what can the hawk, father of the kite, do to the tortoise?[11]

(When the prey's defenses are impenetrable, the predator can only glare. See the next entry.)

1997. *Àṣá wo ìgbín kòrò̀; ìkaraun-un rẹ̀ ò jẹ́ kó gbé e.*
The kite looks slyly at the snail, but its shell stops the bird from snatching it. (This is a more mundane version of the previous entry. See also 132.)

1998. *Àṣá wòbọ kò rọ́wọ́ gbé e.*
The kite watches the monkey but has no hands to carry it off. (A monkey is no prey to a kite.)

1999. *Àṣírí ìkokò, ajá kọ́ ni yó tùú u.*
The secrets of the hyena's being will not be revealed through the actions of the dog. (The stalwart's comeuppance will not happen at the hands of a no-account person.)

2000. *Àtẹ́lẹwọ́ ẹni kì í tanni.*
One's palm does not deceive one. (One's trust is best placed in one's own resources.)

2001. *Àyè kì í há adìẹ kó má dèé ìdí àba-a rẹ̀.*
The space is never so tight that a chicken will not be able to reach its incubating nest. (No obstacle should keep one from one's duty.)

B

2002. *Bí a bá ńpa èpo oṣè, ṣe ní ḿmáaá sanra sí i.*
The more one peels the bark of the baobab, the fatter it becomes. (The more a certain person is misused, the more successful he or she becomes.)

---

10. *Àro* is one of the titles of the secret order of *Ògbóni;* the proverb suggests that the member, from lack of practice, has forgotten the funerary rites of the order.

11. The words *àṣá, idì,* and *àwódì* signify the same bird for the purposes of this proverb; the availability of different designations for the same subject makes

---

possible the lexical shifts that constitute one of the characteristic elements of Yoruba poetry.

2003. *Bí a kò bá jìyà tó kún agbọ̀n; a ò lè jẹ oore tó kún ahá.*
If one does not experience enough suffering to fill a basket, one cannot enjoy enough good to fill a cup. (Suffering precedes pleasures.)

2004. *Bí a kò bá ṣe bí ẹlẹ́dẹ̀ lọ́nà Ìkòròdú, a ò lè ṣe bí Adégbọrọ̀ lójà ọba.*
If one does not act like a pig on the way to Ikòròdú, one cannot act like Adégbọrọ̀ at the king's market.[12] (Before one can live in luxury, one must soil one's hands with work.)

2005. *Bí ebí bá ńpa ọ̀lẹ, à jẹ́ kó kú.*
If a lazy person is suffering from hunger, he or she should be left to die. (Shiftless people deserve no sympathy.)

2006. *Bí ẹkẹ́-ẹ tálákà ò tó lówùúrọ̀, á tó lálẹ́.*
If a poor person's forked stake is not long enough in the morning, it will be long enough at night.[13] (The things one rejects when the choice is abundant will become acceptable when there is no choice.)

2007. *Bí ẹnìkan ò kíni "Kú-ù-jokòó," kíkí Ọlọ́run-ún ju ti igba èèyàn lọ.*
If a person does not extend greetings to you, God's greetings are worth more than those of two hundred people. (Being snubbed by people matters nothing, as long as God does not snub you.)

2008. *Bí ẹrú yó bàá jẹ ìfun, ibi èdọ̀ ní-í tí ḿbẹ̀rẹ̀.*
A slave that would eat intestines must begin with the liver. (One must endure unpleasantness before achieving one's ends.)

2009. *Bí èyá bá dẹkùn, ẹran ní ńpajẹ.*
When the cub becomes a grown leopard, it kills animals for food. (When the child becomes an adult, he adopts adult ways.)

2010. *Bí ìbí bá tẹ̀, bí ìbí bá wó, oníkálukú a máa ṣe baba nílé ara-a rẹ̀.*
If the pedigree is bent, if the pedigree is crooked, each person will play the father in his own home. (In difficult times, each person has the solace and security of his own home.)

2011. *Bí ilẹ̀-ẹ́ bá mọ́, ojú orun lọ̀lẹ ńwà.*
When day breaks, the lazy person will still be asleep. (Lazy people will not rouse themselves to do an honest day's work.)

2012. *Bí iná kò bá tán láṣọ, èjẹ̀ kì í tán léèékánná.*
If lice are not completely gone from one's clothing, one's nails will not be free of blood. (If the causes of one's problems are not removed, the problems will persist.)

2013. *Bí ìṣẹ́ bá ńṣẹ ọ̀dọ́ láṣèèjù, kó lọ sígbó erin: bó bá pa erin ìṣẹ́-ẹ rẹ̀ a tán; bí erín bá pá a, ìṣẹ́-ẹ rẹ̀ a tán.*
If a youth is in the grip of excessive privation, he should go after an elephant: if he kills an elephant, his privation will be over; if an elephant kills him, his privation will be over. (People in desperate straits should resort to desperate remedies; whatever the outcome, they will be no worse off than before.)

2014. *Bí iwájú ò bá ṣeé lọ sí, ẹ̀hìn a ṣeé padà sí.*
If one cannot go forward, one will be able to retreat. (If a goal proves impossible of achievement, one can at least abandon it.)

---

12. Ìkòròdú is a town a few miles from Lagos (the reference is to a farm on the way to the town). The name Adégbọrọ̀ means "The crown[ed head] receives riches."

13. Ẹkẹ́ is a forked pole used as a support while building a house.

2015. *Bí màlúù-ú tó màlúù, ọ̀pá kan ni Fúlàní fi ńdà wọ́n.*
However numerous the cattle might be, it is with only one staff that the Fulbe man herds them. (The good worker needs no elaborate tools.)

2016. *"Bí mo lè kú ma kú" lọmọkùrín fi ńlágbára; "Ng ò lè wáá kú" lọmọkùnrín fi ńlẹ.*
"If I must die, let me die" is what makes a man strong; "I simply will not court death" is what makes a man lazy or cowardly. (Daring makes the man; caution unmakes the man.)

2017. *Bí ó pẹ́ títí, akólòlò á pe baba.*
However long it may take, the stammerer will eventually say, "Father." (With perseverance, the most difficult task will eventually be accomplished.)

2018. *Bí ó pẹ́ títí, àlejò á di onílé.*
In time, a sojourner becomes a native. (Persistence leads to success.)

2019. *Bí ó ti wuni là ńṣe ìmàle ẹni; bó wu Lèmámù a felẹ́dẹ̀ jẹ sàdrì.*
One practices one's Islam as one pleases; if the imam wishes, he may break his fast with pork. (One lives one's life as one sees fit.)

2020. *Bí Ògún ẹní bá dánilójú, à fi gbárí.*
If one is sure of one's Ògún cult object, one taps one's head with it. (If one is sure of one's position, one confidently swears by anything. Compare 1436.)

2021. *Bí ojú kò pọ́nni bí osùn, a kì í he ohun pupa bí idẹ.*
If one's eyes do not become as red as camwood stain, one does not come by something as red as brass. (Unless one endures some hardship, one does not reap great benefits.)

2022. *Bí ojú owó ẹni ò yóni, ènì ò lè yóni.*
If what one bought for money does not fill one, neither will a little extra thrown into the bargain. (A person who cannot survive on his main occupation cannot survive on his sideline.)

2023. *Bí ojúmọ́ mọ́ lékèélékèé a yalé ẹléfun, agbe a yalé aláró, àlùkò a yalé olósùn.*
When day dawns, the cattle egret makes for the home of the dealer in chalk; the blue touraco heads for the home of the indigo dealer; the purple *àlúkò* bird seeks out the dealer in camwood resin. (Diligent people never dally in pursuing their trade.)

2024. *Bí ọwọ́ kò sin ilẹ̀, tí kò sin ẹnu, ayo ní ńjẹ́.*
If the hand does not cease going down and going to the mouth, satiation results. (If one keeps at a task, it will eventually be accomplished.)

2025. *Bí Ṣàngó bá ńpa àràbà, tó ńpa ìrókò, bíi tigi ńlá kọ́.*
Even though Ṣango kills the silk-cotton tree and kills the *ìrókò* tree, no such fate can befall the huge tree. (A boast that the person being referred to is mightier than even the mightiest other person around.)

D

2026. *Dàńdógó kì í ṣe èwù ọmọdé.*
Dàńdogo is not a garment for the young. (Certain feats are beyond certain people. Compare 1460.)

2027. *Dídán là ńdán òràn wò; bí olówó ẹní kú, à lọ ṣúpó.*
One should give everything a try; if one's owner dies, one goes to claim his wife. (One should attempt even the impossible.)

2028. *Dídán lẹyẹlẹ ńdán kú.*
A perpetually shining appearance is what characterizes the pigeon even until death. (Either an observation that a person's reputation cannot be tarnished or a wish that it never become tarnished.)

2029. *Díẹ̀-díẹ̀ leku ńjawọ.*
It is bit by bit that rats eat leather. (With slow and steady application, even a difficult task will be done. See the following two entries.)

2030. *Díẹ̀-díẹ̀ lẹyẹ ńmu ọsàn.*
It is bit by bit that a bird eats an orange. (Easy does it. See the preceding and following entries.)

2031. *Díẹ̀-díẹ̀ ní ńtánṣẹ́.*
Gradual efforts complete a task. (The biggest task is accomplished with gradual and steady attention. See the previous two entries.)

2032. *Dùndún fọ̀ràn gbogbo sàpamọ́ra.*
The talking drum endures all matters without complaint.[14] (It is best to be stoically resilient.)

E

2033. *Ebẹ̀ kan ṣoṣo àkùrọ́ kúrò ní "Mo fẹ́rẹ̀ẹ́ síwọ́."*
A single heap on the farm does not warrant "I am just about done." (The first step is not nearly the completion of a long journey.)

2034. *Ebi ni yó kọ̀ọ́ wèrè lọ́gbọ́n.*
It is hunger that will force sense into the imbecile. (Even an imbecile must heed hunger.)

2035. *Ebí ńpa ejò, ahún ńyan.*
The snake is hungry, and the tortoise saunters by. (If one is invulnerable, one may strut.)

2036. *Ebi ò jẹ́ ká pa ọwó mọ́; ebí ṣẹnú papala.*
Hunger keeps one from folding one's hands; hunger causes the mouth [or cheeks] to shrink. (One must work in order to eat.)

2037. *Èdì kì í mú ọjọ́ kó má là.*
No charm can act upon the day and keep it from dawning. (What is inevitable will come to pass, willy-nilly.)

2038. *Èébú kì í so.*
Insults do not attach to one's body like pods. (Insult ignored is insult defused.)

2039. *Eégún tí ńjẹ orí ẹṣin, orí àgbò ò lè kò ó láyà.*
The masquerader who is accustomed to eating horse heads will not be daunted by ram heads. (A person who has faced down serious challenges will not be defeated by a slight inconvenience. Compare 2272 and 2273.)

2040. *Èèwọ̀ ni tọwọ̀; a kì í figi ọwọ̀ dáná.*
As far as the broom is concerned, it is taboo; one does not make kindling of broomsticks. (Come what may, a threatening or threatened disaster will not happen.)

2041. *Èèyàn ìbáà kúrú, ìbáà búrẹ́wà, gbèsè ò sí, ìtìjú ò sí.*
Whether a person be short or ugly, if there is no debt, there can be no disgrace. (As long as one is debt-free, other details of one's personal circumstances are of little consequence.)

---

14. A reference to the cords, bells, and bands tied around the drum, as well as to the beating it takes from the stick used in playing it.

2042. *Èkó ilá gba ara è lówó òbe.*
Okro that has gone fibrous has delivered itself from the knife. (At some point, one outgrows some dangers.)

2043. *Èmìnrin ńjęni, ò tó ìyà.*
Being bothered by sandflies is no misfortune. (Whatever one's problems, they can always be worse.)

2044. *Èpè ìbínú ò pa odì.*
An angry curse does not kill an enemy. (One gets only psychological satisfaction from cursing one's enemy.)

2045. *Èpè ìlasa kì í ja àgbònrín.*
The curses of okro leaves do not affect the deer.[15] (One cannot be at risk for what one cannot help doing.)

2046. *Èpò ìbúlè kì í pa iré.*
Creeping weeds cannot kill the silk-rubber tree. (A puny person is no threat to a mighty person.)

2047. *Erín jè jè jè kò fowó kó asá; efòn-ón jè jè jè kò ki esè wo pòòlò; eye kékèké ńfò lókè won ò forí gbági.*
The elephant forages a long time without cutting its hand on a spear; the buffalo forages a long time without falling into a trap; numerous small birds fly across the sky without colliding with trees. (Despite the ubiquitousness of danger, one can be safe.)

2048. *Èsì ò róba dádé; Ògúnsosé ò róòrùn wèwù èjè; òdòdó ò róòrùn pón; ilé omo lomó ti pón wá.*
Error does not await the king before it dons a crown; Ogunsose[16] does not wait for the sun before it dons a bloody cloak; the flower does not wait for the sun before it brightens; brightness comes with the child from its house. (Native genius needs no external cultivation.)

2049. *Esinsín ńpontí; ekòló ńsú òlèlè; kantí-kantí ní ká wá nkan dí agbè lénu kí nkankan má kòó sí i.*
The fly is procuring wine while the worm is cooking bean meal, and the sugar fly asks them to find something to cork the gourd so nothing will enter into it. (The idler seeks to find more work for those already fully and usefully employed.)

2050. *Esú je oko tán esú lo; esú lo Wata, ilé-e rè.*
The locusts are done feeding; the locusts have departed; the locusts have gone to Wata, their home. (When one's task is completed, one returns to one's home. Or, the marauder has done his damage and has gone back where he came from.)

2051. *Ewu iná kì í pa àwòdì.*
The African black kite is never killed in a brushfire emergency.[17] (The bird is beyond any harm the fire might do.)

2052. *Ewúré ńsodún; àgùtán gbàlù séhìn; òbúko-ó ní ká sin òun lo sílé àna òun.*
The goat is celebrating an event; the sheep is in a procession with drums; and the he-goat asks to be accompanied to its in-law's home. (A person who has made no investment should not expect to reap the benefits of the venture.)

2053. *Ewúré ò lè rí ewé odán òkè fi se nnkan.*
A goat can in no wise take the fig tree's leaves aloft for any purpose. (Certain people

---

15. Okro is the favorite food of deer; for that reason, if okro curses deer, the curse is in vain.

16. The name means "Ògún [the god of iron] has caused a disaster."

17. This statement is used in the context of an incantation to ward off all disaster.

are beyond the reach of other people's machinations.)

2054. *Ewúro ò fi tojo korò.*
The bitterleaf did not become bitter as a result of cowardice. (One does what one must, regardless of the actions or wishes of others.)

Ẹ

2055. *Ẹbọ jíjẹ kì í pa igún.*
The consumption of sacrificial offerings will not kill the vulture. (One cannot be hurt by one's natural calling.)

2056. *Ẹgbẹ̀rún eèrà ò lè gbé súgà; wọ́n ó kàn tò yí i ká lásán ni.*
A thousand ants cannot lift [a cube of] sugar; they can only mill around it in vain. (Some tasks are beyond certain people.)

2057. *Ẹgbẹ̀rún ẹja ò lè dẹ́rù pa odò.*
A thousand fishes will not overload a river. (It is futile to attempt to overwhelm an invincible person.)

2058. *Ẹ̀hìn ológbò kì í balẹ̀.*
A cat's back never touches the ground. (One's opponent in a fight will never succeed in throwing one.)[18]

2059. *Ẹjọ́ ẹléjọ́, lóyà ńrò ó, ámbọ̀ntorí ẹjọ́ ara-a rè.*
The lawyer argues other people's cases, much more his own. (One who is conscientious on behalf of others can be expected

to be even more conscientious on his or her own behalf.)

2060. *Ẹlémùn-ún ò mú eégún.*
An apprehender does not apprehend a masquerader. (Certain people are beyond anyone's control.)

2061. *Ẹ̀lukú tí kò ní èlè legbẹ́-ẹ rẹ̀ ńsá pa.*
It is the *Ẹ̀lukú* masquerader without a machete that is hacked to death by his colleagues.[19] (Whoever goes into a contest less prepared than his or her adversary is in for trouble.)

2062. *Ẹ̀lúlùú ní kàkà kí òun má dun ọbẹ̀, òun á rúnwọ rúnsẹ̀ sí i.*
The lark-heeled cuckoo vows that rather than not being delicious in the stew, it will crush its arms and legs in pursuit of that end. (One vows that even up to the cost of one's life, one will give everything one has to achieve an end.)

2063. *Ẹni bá ńjẹ òbúkọ tó gbójú, yó jẹ àgùtàn tó yòwo.*
Whoever is used to eating full-grown he-goats will eat lambs that have sprouted horns. (A person known for daring deeds can always be expected to defy custom; one cannot cure people of ingrained habits.)

2064. *Ẹni bá ńsisẹ́ kì í sọlẹ; bórí bá túnnisẹ a kì í tẹ́ bọ̀rọ̀.*
Whoever has a job should not malinger; if Providence smiles, one can hardly fail. (Diligence in one's pursuit will certainly result in prosperity. Compare 1517.)

2065. *Ẹni bá yẹ ọ̀nà Ìjẹ̀bú tì ni yó yẹ́ ẹ tán.*
The same person who weeds the road to

---

18. This is a reference to the cat's ability to right itself and land on its feet, however much one tries to drop it on its back. The saying is most often used by wrestlers as an incantation to prevent their opponents from throwing them.

19. *Ẹ̀lukú* or *Àlukú* is a fearsome masquerader, one of whose props is a machete supposedly used indiscriminately as a weapon.

Ìjèbú without carrying off the weeds will eventually remove them. (The shirker will sooner or later be forced to do his or her duty; one should do a thing efficiently, not halfheartedly.)[20]

2066. Eni èèyàn ò kí kó yò; ẹni Olórun ò kí kó sóra.
Whoever is shunned by people should rejoice; whoever is shunned by God should look out. (God's favor is preferable to that of other people.)

2067. Ẹní gbani láya ò ní kírú ẹni má rà.
The person who takes one's wife cannot stop one's locust-bean seeds from fermenting. (A person who injures you cannot stop you from pursuing your destiny.)[21]

2068. Ẹní máa jẹ oyin inú àpáta kìí wo ẹnu àáké.
Whoever will eat the honey in a rock does not worry about the edge of the axe. (One should be prepared to make the sacrifices necessary to achieve a worthy goal.)

2069. Ẹní máa jẹun kunkun a tìlèkùn kunkun.
Whoever wishes to eat heartily must lock his door firmly. (To prevent intrusion into one's affairs, one should keep them well guarded.)

2070. Ẹní máa rí àtisùn akàn á pé létí isà.
Whoever wishes to see a crab go to sleep will stay long by its hole. (Whoever seeks the

impossible will wait forever.[22] See also the following entry.)

2071. Ẹní máa rí àtisùn-un pépéyẹ á jẹ gbèsè àdín.
Whoever wishes to see ducks go to sleep will go into debt paying for [fuel] oil. (Whoever awaits the impossible will wait forever.[23] Compare the preceding entry.)

2072. Ẹni òlé pa-á re òrun òsì; ẹni isẹ́ pa-á re òrun èyẹ.
Whoever dies from poverty dies a miserable death; whoever dies from work dies a noble death. (Better to die on one's feet than to give in to reverses.)

2073. Ẹni tí à mbọ́ ò mọ̀ pé ìyàn-án mú.
A person fed by others is never aware that there is famine. (A person who has no responsibilities does not appreciate the efforts of those who do.)

2074. Ẹni tí eégún mlé kó máa rójú; bó ti mrẹ ará ayé, bẹ̀ẹ́ ní mrẹ ará òrun.
The person being chased by a masquerader should persevere; just as an earthling tires, so does the being from heaven.[24] (Perseverance solves all problems.)

2075. Ẹni tí isẹ́ mpa-á yá ju ẹni tí ìsẹ́ mpa.
A person dying fom overwork is better than a person dying of destitution. (Better to succumb to overwork or occupational hazards than to succumb to poverty.)

---

20. The proverb is probably based on the commercial importance of the road, which ensures the keen interest of the authorities (of Ibadan presumably) in seeing that whoever is responsible for keeping it open and clean does so efficiently.

21. Irú is the fermented condiment derived from the seeds of the locust-bean tree. The suggestion seems to be that the man deprived of a wife can still cook his stew, since his irú can still ferment even in the absence of a wife (who would normally cook the stew).

22. The proverb is based on the fact that crabs' eyes never close, because they have no lids.

23. This proverb is based on the supposition that ducks never sleep. Àdín is oil made from palm kernels, used to fuel lamps and as a body lotion.

24. Because eégún (masqueraders) are believed to be reincarnated dead ancestors, they are thus ará òrun, "heavenly beings." Some chase people and belabor them with whips.

2076. Ẹni tí kíkí-i rẹ̀ ò yóni, àìkí-i rẹ̀ ò lè pani lébi.

A person whose greetings do not fill one's stomach cannot cause one to starve by with-holding the greetings. (A person whose benevolence has little effect on one's fortune cannot affect one with malevolence. Compare 5033.)

2077. Ẹni tí ńgbẹ́lẹ̀ ní ńsìnkú; ẹni tí ńsunkún ariwo ló ńpa.

The person digging a grave is the one performing his or her funerary duties; the person crying is merely making a noise. (Tangible help is better than useless sympathetic gestures.)

2078. Ẹni tí ó bá ní ìtara ló ní àtètèbá.

It is the industrious person who wins the spoils. (Industry ensures success.)[25]

2079. Ẹni tó bá ńjẹ lábẹ-ẹ Jégédé ló ńpè é nÍgi Àràbà.

Only those whose livelihood depends on Jẹgẹdẹ call him a silk-cotton tree.[26] (Only those beholden to a person are compelled to flatter him or her.)

2080. Ẹni tí ó bá pé lẹ́hìn ni à ńyọ́ omi ọbẹ̀ dè.

Those who arrive late are the ones who find the watery residue of the stew awaiting them. (Timeliness earns one the best choice, tardiness the worst.)

2081. Ẹni tí ó bá wo ojú ìyàwó ní ńmọ̀ pé ìyàwó ńsunkún.

Only a person who looks at the bride's face knows that the bride is crying. (It is futile to seek sympathy when no one is paying attention.)[27]

2082. Ẹni tí ó bẹ Ìgè Àdùbí níṣẹ́, ara-a rẹ̀ ló bẹ̀; Ìgè Àdùbí ò níí jẹ, bẹ̀ẹ̀ni kò níí kọ̀.

Whoever assigns a task to Ìgè Àdùbí assigns it to himself or herself; Ìgè Àdùbí will neither agree to do the task nor will he refuse.[28] (One should expect little from a spoiled child.)

2083. Ẹni tí ó fò sókè-é bẹ́ ijó lórí.

Whoever leaps up decapitates dance. (Nothing more can be expected from a person who has given the ultimate effort.)[29]

2084. Ẹni tí ó forí sọlẹ̀-ẹ gbìyànjú ikú.

Whoever dives headfirst to the ground has made a creditable attempt at suicide. (One should acknowledge people's sincere efforts.)

2085. Ẹni tí ó gbálẹ̀ ni ilẹ̀ ńmọ́ fún.

It is for the person who sweeps the floor that the floor is clean. (Those who exert themselves are the ones who reap rewards.)[30]

2086. Ẹni tí ó gbin ọrún èbù tó pè é nígba, tó bá jẹ ogọ́rùn-ún òtítọ́ tán, á wá jẹ ogọ́rùn-ún iró.

25. Ìtara (industry or sharpness) is equated here with àtètèbá, a charm ensuring that the user will be the first to come upon a valuable thing.

26. Àràbà, the silk-cotton tree—Ceiba pentandra (Bombaceae)—is the largest African tree (see Abraham 61–62), while the sound of the name Jégédé suggests someone of insubstantial physical stature.

27. Traditionally, brides cried, as a matter of form, on their departure for their future homes; onlookers made light of these supposedly crocodile tears.

28. Ìgè is the name usually given to a child born feet first, and Àdùbí means someone everyone would like to have given birth to. The suggestion is that the child so named is excessively pampered and can therefore get away with anything.

29. A dancing leap is regarded as the supreme figure in dance.

30. The expression Ilè-ẹ́ mọ́ means both "the floor is clean" and "morning has broken." The proverb thus also carries the suggestion that a new day, supposedly an auspicious day, dawns for those who sweep the floor, especially since sweeping is one of the first orders of duty for conscientious housekeepers every morning.

The person who plants a hundred yam seedlings and says he planted two hundred, after he has eaten a hundred truths, will come to eat a hundred lies. (A person who overstates his investment will still not earn more than the investment can generate.)

2087. Ẹni tí ó pa méfà lógun Ọla: wọ́n ní "Háà, hà, háà!" Ó ní kí wọ́n gbé ọpọ́n ayò wá, ó tún pa méfà; ó ní bí ojú kò tó tẹ̀gi, ojú kò tó tilé?
The man who [claimed to have] killed six people during the Ọla war: people exclaimed in disbelief, "Ha, ha, ha!" He asked them to bring an *ayò* board, and he won six games. He said, if there were no witnesses for what happened in the secluded forest, aren't there witnesses for what happens in the house? (One may not believe what one was not witness to, but what one sees, one must believe; seeing is believing.)[31]

2088. Ẹni tí ọ̀ṣọ́ bá wù kó ṣòwò; ẹni ajé yalé-e rẹ̀ ló gbọ́n.
Whoever likes fineries should engage in a trade; it is the person blessed by riches who is wise. (Good things come only to the industrious.)

2089. Ẹní yára lÒgún ńgbè.
Ògún is on the side of the swift. (The swift are justified in taking advantage of the tardy.)

2090. Ẹnú dùn-ún ròfọ́; agada ọwọ́ dùn-ún ṣánko.
The mouth cooks vegetable stew most expertly; the hand emulating a machete cuts

a field most effortlessly. (A person's mouth may boast of anything, and his or her hand may claim to be able to do anything until put to the test.)

2091. Ẹnu iṣẹ́ ẹni ni a ti ńmọ ẹni lọ́lẹ.
It is at one's occupation that one proves oneself an idler. (One reveals one's mettle at one's place of employment.)

2092. Ẹnu òfifo kì í dún yànmù-yànmù.
Empty mouths do not make chewing noises. (If one has not filled others' mouths with food, one cannot expect them to be full of one's praise.)

2093. Ẹ̀rù kì í ba igbó, bẹ́ẹ̀ni kì í ba odò; ẹ̀rù kì í ba ọlọ lójú ata.
The forest knows no fear, and neither does the river know fear; the grindstone never shows fear in the face of pepper. (A worthy person should not give way to fear.)

2094. Ẹ̀rù kì í ba orí kó sá wọnú.
The head is never so frightened that it disappears into the shoulder. (One should be brave enough to meet one's fate.)

2095. Ẹ̀rù ogun kì í ba jagun-jagun.
Fear of battle never afflicts a warrior. (One should be bold in pursuing one's goals.)

2096. Ẹsẹ̀ kì í wúwo kí ẹlẹ́sẹ̀ má lè gbé e.
The feet are never so heavy that the owner cannot lift them. (Each person must live with his or her own peculiarities. Compare 1987.)

2097. Ẹsin kì í dani kí á má tún gùn ún.
Do not refrain from mounting a horse that has thrown you. (A failure should not stop you from making further attempts.)

2098. Ẹsin kì í já kó já èkejì-i rẹ̀.
A horse does not get loose and stop to free

31. The humor, even the wit, of this proverb resides, more than in anything else, in the play on *pa*, which in the context of an *ayò* game means "to win" but in the context of a war means "to kill." The stalwart in question settles the argument about whether he could have killed six people in a war by winning six *ayò* games.

its companion. (Each person must look to his or her own salvation.)

2099. *Èsò èsò ni ìgbín fi ńgbà gun igi.*
Slowly, slowly is the way a snail climbs a tree. (With dogged persistence, one accomplishes the most difficult of tasks.)

2100. *Ètè bá òle.*
Disgrace comes upon the shiftless. (Disgrace attends shiftlessness.)

2101. *Eye ò so fún eye pé òkò ńbò.*
A bird does not tell a bird that a stone is on its way. (Each person looks out for his or her own safety.)

F

2102. *Fi gògò sílè fún òdáwé; fi oko sílè fún onílara.*
Leave the hooked stick alone for the leaf plucker; leave the husband alone for the jealous woman. (One should simply shun persons who will not share what they have.)

2103. *Fífé la fé èfó tí à ńpè-é ní òré èko; ti ilé oge-é tó oge-é je.*
It is only because one loves spinach that one calls it a friend of corn loaf; what the dandy has at home is enough food for him or her. (That one delights in another person's company is not to say that one cannot do without it. Compare 3374.)

2104. *"Fó èko ká jo mu ú," kò tó okolóbìnrin-ín se ni.*
"Prepare the corn pap and let us eat it together" is an indication that the speaker lacks what it takes to be a husband. (One should not be tentative in exercising one's authority. Compare 1943.)

Gb

2105. *Gbèdó-gbèdó kan ò lè fi ògèdè se nnkan.*
No carver of mortars can do a thing to the banana stem. (Certain people and certain objects have nothing to fear from certain types of adversaries.)

I

2106. *Ìbèrù ejò ò jé ká te omo ejò mólè.*
Fear of the snake keeps one from stepping on the young of the snake. (One usually benefits from the stature or position of one's parents or protector.)

2107. *Ibi gbogbo ní ńro àdàbà lórùn.*
Every place is hospitable and comfortable for the dove. (Said to mean that no circumstance will be beyond one's ability to cope.)[32]

2108. *Ibi gbogbo nilè òwò.*
Every place deserves to be treated with respect and reverence. (Decorous behavior is not for certain occasions only.)

2109. *Ibi tí a ní kí gbégbé má gbèè, ibè ní ńgbé.*
The spot one cautions the *gbégbé* plant not to inhabit, there it will surely inhabit. (One will fulfill one's destiny, whatever others might do to prevent it. Compare the following entry.)

2110. *Ibi tí a ní kí tètè má tè, ibè ní ńtè.*
Wherever one orders wild spinach not to step, there it will surely trample.[33] (The des-

---

32. It is also used in the context of a prayer to wish that wherever the addressee goes, he or she will always find ease and comfort.

33. The proverb is often used in a sort of incantation or prayer to wish (or assert) that a person will

tinies of certain people defy manipulation by adversaries. Compare the preceding entry.)

2111. *Ibo ni imú wà sẹ́nu? Ibo ni Làńlátẹ̀-ẹ́ wà sí Èrúwà?*
How much distance exists between the nose and the mouth? How much distance exists between Làńlátẹ̀ and Èrúwà? (One should not make a fuss over running an errand that is not a great imposition.)[34]

2112. *Idà kì í lọ kídà má bọ̀.*
The sword never departs without returning. (Said in the context of a prayer that a person departing on a journey might return safely.)

2113. *Ìdẹra ò kan àgbà.*
Ease has nothing to do with age. (Industry pays off more surely than longevity.)

2114. *Igi kì í dá lóko kó pa ará ilé.*
A tree does not snap in the forest and kill a person at home. (Disaster cannot befall a person who is not in an exposed position.)

2115. *Igúnnugún pa guuru mádìẹ; kò leè gbe.*
The vulture rushes at the chicken, but it cannot carry it off. (One should not attempt what one knows one cannot accomplish.)

2116. *Igba esinsin kì í dènà de ọwọ̀.*
Two hundred flies will not lie in ambush for a broom.[35] (Despite their number, one's adversaries are no match for one. Compare the next entry.)

2117. *Igba ẹranko kì í dènà de ẹkùn.*
Two hundred animals will not lie in ambush for a leopard. (Exercise prudence and recognize an adversary that is more than your match. Compare the preceding entry.)

2118. *Ìgbà yí làárọ̀? Arúgbó ńkogba.*
Is it just morning now? The old man is striving to make two hundred heaps a day. (The efforts that would have been commendable if timely are now worthless.)

2119. *Ìgbà yí làárọ̀? Arúgbó ńṣoge.*
Is it just morning now? The old person is grooming himself or herself. (Never wait until it is too late before you look to your well-being.)

2120. *Ìgbé a gbé ìyàwó kò ṣéé gbé owó.*
The strategy one adopts in acquiring a wife will not do with regard to money. (What suffices in one situation may not be applicable in another.)

2121. *Igbe kí-ni-ngó-jẹ-sùn ní ḿpọ̀lẹ.*
The cry "What shall I eat for supper?" is what kills the lazy person. (The lazy person would rather put effort into lamenting his or her fate than into gainful employment.)

2122. *Ìgbín kì í tẹnu mógi kó má gùn ún.*
The snail will not fasten onto a tree and fail to climb it. (Once one takes on a job, one should see it through.)

2123. *Ìgbín kọ mímì ejò.*
The snail rejects the fate of being swallowed by a snake. (There are some perils to which one is immune.)

2124. *Ìjà ò mọ ègbọ́n, ó sọ àbúrò dakin.*
Fighting knows not who is the elder; it makes a hero of the younger. (In certain situations, prowess is more important than age. Compare 2320.)

---

never be vulnerable to his or her enemies. The verb *tẹ̀* means "to step" as on a spot; it is used here in a play on words, because the name for wild spinach seems to be a reduplication of the verb.

34. Làńlátẹ̀ and Èrúwà are neighboring villages in the Ibadan orbit. The proverb suggests that since they are as close together as the mouth and the nose, a person sent on an errand from one to the other should not complain.

35. A broom is a favorite weapon for killing flies.

2125. Ìje òun oore ní ḿmú ọmọ ṣiṣẹ́.
Competition and reward are the induce-
ments for a child to work hard. (It is the
wish to at least keep up with others or the
hope for a reward that makes one work
hard.)

2126. Ìjèṣà ò nìídì ìṣáná; ilé lọmọ Ọwá ti
ńfọnná lọ sóko.
The Ìjèṣà [person] does not need matches; it
is from the home that the scion of Ọwa takes
burning faggots to the farm. (Said to assert
self-sufficiency, that one does not need the
aid of other people.)[36]

2127. Ìjẹkújẹ kì í pa ahanrandi.
Careless eating does not kill the worm *ahanrandi*. (One can do what one pleases without
fear of repercussion.)

2128. Ikán ò lè rí ṣe lára ìgànná.
The termite can have no adverse effect on
a wall. (Certain things are invulnerable to
certain disasters.)

2129. Ìkọ́ kì í kọ́ ejò lẹ́sẹ̀.
A snare never catches a snake in the leg.
(One will remain invulnerable to any dan-
ger.)[37]

2130. Ikọ̀ tí ò mọ iṣẹ́-ẹ jẹ́ ní ńjẹ ẹ lẹ́èmejèè.
It is the messenger who does not know how
to deliver a message properly that delivers
it seven times over. (Incompetence imposes
additional burdens on a person.)

2131. Ìkòkò tí yó jẹ ata, ìdí ẹ̀ á gbóná.
The pot that wishes to eat pepper [stew] will

first endure a scalded bottom. (Good things
come only after great labor or suffering.)

2132. Ilá kì í ga ju akórè lọ kó má tẹ̀ ẹ́ ká.
The okro plant is never so much taller than
the harvester that he or she cannot bend it
to harvest. (The conscientious worker will
always find the means to complete the task.)

2133. Ilé tí a tó lọ sùn lọ́sàn-án, a kì í tó òru lọ
sùn ún.
A house one has the right to sleep in during
the day, one does not wait for the cover of
night to go sleep in it. (One should not be
coy about doing what one has the right to
do. Compare the following entry.)

2134. Ilé tí a tóó kun, a kì í bo ìtùfù-u rẹ̀.
A house one is in a position to burn, one
does not conceal the torch to set it ablaze.
(One need not be coy in doing what one has
the authority or standing to do. Compare
the preceding entry.)

2135. Ìlẹ̀kẹ̀ ọpọ̀lọ́ ò yí olè lójú.
Frogs' eggs do not attract the attention of
the thief. (If one has nothing for others to
covet, one is safe from envy.)

2136. Ìlẹ̀kẹ̀-ẹ́ gbé orí àtẹ wu ọ̀le.
Beads remain on the display tray and from
there attract the admiration of the feckless
person. (The feckless person can admire
desirable things but will not have the means
to purchase them.)

2137. Ìlérí adìẹ, asán ni lójú àwòdì.
The chicken's boasts are unavailing before
the kite. (The puny person who threatens a
formidable person fools himself or herself.)

2138. Ìlọrin ò lóòṣà; ẹnu lòóṣà Ìlọrin.
The Ìlọrin person has no god; his or her
mouth is his or her god. (The person under
reference is all mouth and no substance.)

---

36. Before the white man came with his matches,
people knew how to make fire. This is obviously a proverb coined in Iléṣà, home of the Ìjèṣà, whose king is
the Ọwá. The *nídìí* (*ní ìdí*) translates literally as "have a
reason for," but it is a play on the English "need."

37. This is used in the context of prayers.

2139. *Ìmúmúnàá abìdí sembé-sembé; ìmúmú-nàá ò dáná rí, tiná-tiná ní mbá kiri.*
Firefly with its rear ablaze: the firefly has never kindled a fire but carries fire with it wherever it goes. (Said of people who want results without making any effort.)

2140. *Iná kì í jó kí ògiri sá.*
Fire does not rage and cause a wall to flee. (Certain entities are invulnerable to certain dangers.)

2141. *Iná kì í jó kó wolé akàn.*
A fire does not rage and enter the home of the crab. (An incantatory observation invoking immunity for a person from some danger.)

2142. *Ìpa à mpose ara ló fi nsan.*
Our attempt to kill the *ose* tree only makes it fatter. (Some people prosper in spite of their enemies' machinations.)

2143. *Ìpèta lose àpón.*
The sap of the violet tree is what the bachelor uses for soap. (A person who lacks the means to provide properly for himself or herself must be resourceful at making do.)

2144. *Ìpilè orò-ó légbin.*
The beginning of wealth is chock-full of filth. (Success comes after great effort and much headache. This is a variant of 2155.)

2145. *Ìpónjú àgbè ò ju odún kan.*
A farmer's suffering will not last longer than a year. (Every reversal has its end.)[38]

2146. *Ìpónjú lomodé fi nkóFá, ìgbèhìn-in rè a deni.*
A child's learning of Ifá is full of privations, but the outcome is a life of ease. (The ease that comes in the end makes up for the effort to achieve one's goal.)

2147. *Ire tí owó-ò mi ò tó, ma fi gòngò fà á.*
The good my hand cannot reach, I will pull down with a hooked stick. (I will spare no effort in pursuit of my goals.)

2148. *Ìrèké ti ládùn látòrun.*
The sugarcane came with its sweetness from heaven. (An illustrious person's qualities are native, not conferred by admirers.)[39]

2149. *Ìríkúrìí kì í fó ojú.*
Evil sights do not make the eyes go blind. (There is nothing in the offing that one cannot withstand.)

2150. *Irínwó efòn, egbèrin ìwo; ogún-un Fúlàní, ójì-i bàtà: Ògídíolú ò wèhìn tó fi lé Adalo lùgbé.*
Four hundred buffaloes with eight hundred horns; twenty Fulbe men and forty shoes: Ògídíolú did not look back until he had chased Adalo into the bush. (Comment on a formidable man who does not flinch before any enemy.)

2151. *Ìròjú baba òle.*
Shirking work [is the] father of laziness. (The person who will not work is worse than a lazy person.)

2152. *Ìrókò o-nígun-mérìn-dín-lógún ò tó erin-ín gbémì, ámbòntorí ìtóò a-lára-bóró-bóró.*
An *ìrókò* stick with sixteen edges is nothing for an elephant to swallow, much less the melon fruit with a smooth body. (A person not defeated by a formidable obstacle will certainly not be stopped by a minor irritant.)

---

38. The annual ripening of the harvest will end the suffering.

39. The formulation applies to the sugarcane plant the belief that heaven is where all things were created.

2153. Ìrònú ìkokò ní yó pa ajá.
Worrying about the wolf is what will kill the dog. (Some people are already vanquished by the mere anticipation of a struggle.)

2154. Ìrójú ni ohun gbogbo; ojoojúmọ́ ní ńreni.
Perseverance is everything; one gets tired daily. (One should not fold up in the face of the first trial. Compare 2172.)

2155. Ìsàlẹ̀ ọrò-ọ́ légbin.
The dregs of wealth are filthy. (Wealth comes only after one has endured a great deal of rubbish. This is a variant of 2144.)

2156. Isán ńbójú, ìtàlá ńwẹsẹ̀.
Nine days wash the face, thirteen days wash the feet. (Said of a person who takes an eternity to do simple things.)

2157. Iṣẹ́ ajé le, ó tó ọpa.
Gainful employment is tough, as tough as a supple pole. (Gainful work is not easy.)[40]

2158. Ìṣẹ́ kì í ṣe ohun àmúṣeré; ìyà kì í ṣe ohun àmúṣàwàdà.
Destitution is not something to treat with levity; mysery is nothing to joke about. (One should not trifle with one's problems.)

2159. Iṣẹ́ loògùn ìṣẹ́.
Work is the antidote for destitution. (One must work in order to better one's condition.)

2160. Ìṣẹ́ ní òun ó kòówó; ìyà-á ní òun ó singbà; réderède-é ní òun ó ṣe onígbòwó: ta ní jẹ́ rere nínú-u wọn?
Destitution proposes to trade its services for money; suffering proposes to pawn itself for money; wretchedness proposes to stand surety for them: which of them has anything going for it? (In a community of losers no one person can be expected to turn the situation around.)

2161. Ìṣẹ́ ńṣẹ ọ ò ńrojú; ta ni yó fún-ún ọ ni oògùn-un rẹ̀?
Destitution grips you and you sit scowling; who will give you the antidote? (One should take practical steps to solve one's problem rather than sit around moping.)

2162. Ìṣẹ́ ò gbékún, ebí jàre òle.
Destitution does not yield to tears; hunger has a claim on the shiftless. (One does not end destitution by simple lamentation; whoever does not work is a fair victim to hunger.)

2163. Ìṣẹ́ ògerò lòlé mò-ọ́ ṣe; kò jẹ́ wá iṣẹ́ agbára.
The lazy person knows how to do only things that call for little effort; he or she never seeks out work that demands strength. (Said of those who always look for the easiest way out of a dilemma.)

2164. Ìṣẹ́ tó ṣẹ ọmọ lógún ọdún, ìyà tó jẹ ọmọ lógbọ̀n oṣù, bí kò pa ọmọ, a sì léhìn ọmọ.
The poverty that has plagued a child for twenty years, the suffering that has been the fate of a child for thirty months, if it does not kill the child should leave the child in peace. (Perseverance puts an eventual end to all suffering.)

2165. Iṣẹ́-ajé-ò-gbé-bòji, ọmọ è Òjíkùtù.
Gainful-work-does-not-keep-to-the-shade; his or her child is named First-up-at-dawn. (Success in life calls for self-sacrifice.)

2166. Iṣu àtẹnumọ́ kì í jóná; òkà àtẹnumọ́ kì í mẹrẹ; àwòdì kì í gbé adìẹ à-tẹnu-kunkun-mọ́.
The yam one does not stop speaking about

---

40. Ọpa, translated here as "supple pole," can also refer to a masquerade in the Ìjẹ̀bú area; carrying it is no easy task either.

will not get burned; the corn meal one speaks constantly about does not become too well done; a chicken that is the subject of constant caution does not get snatched up by a hawk. (Anything that is the subject of constant attention will not be ruined.)

2167. *Iṣu eni kì í fini pe ọmọdé kó má ta.*
One's yam will not, because one is only a youth, refuse to grow to maturity. (Even a youth can accomplish much if he or she makes an effort.)

2168. *Iṣú wà lọ́wọ́ ẹ; ọ̀bẹ́ wà lọ́wọ́ ẹ.*
The yam is in your hand, and the knife is in your hand. (Said to encourage one to do what he or she has to do without further delay, especially when all requisite conditions have been met.)

2169. *Ìwà ọlẹ ḿba ọlẹ lérù; ọlẹ́ pàdánù, ó ní aráyé ò fẹ́ràn òun.*
The lazy person's character fills him or her with fear; the lazy person loses all and complains that the world hates him or her. (Each person is more the architect of his or her own fortune than the victim of others' machinations.)

2170. *Ìwòyí èṣí ewùrà-a baba-à mí ti ta: ìrègún rere ò sí níbẹ̀.*
"By this time last year my father's water-yam had grown huge": that is nothing good to reminisce about. (One should look to the present instead of dwelling on past achievements, and others' at that.)

2171. *Ìyà tó ńje ọlẹ ò kéré: a-lápá-má-ṣiṣẹ́.*
The malaise that afflicts the lazy person is not trifling: [it is] one-who-has-arms-that-will-not-work. (Laziness is a great affliction.)

2172. *Ìyànjú là ńgbà; bí a ò gbìyànjú bí ọlẹ là ńrí; ojoojúmọ́ ní ńrẹni.*

One simply makes an effort; if one does not make an effort one seems like a shiftless person; one copes with weariness daily. (In spite of weariness, one must still make a decent effort at one's calling. Compare 2154.)

2173. *Ìyáwọ́, ìyásẹ̀ lajá fi ńpa ehoro; wàrà-wàrà lẹkùn ńgùn.*
Nimble hands and nimble feet make it possible for a dog to kill a rabbit; the leopard attacks its prey with lightning speed. (One should be brisk about what one has to do.)

J

2174. *Jagajìgì ò mọ ogun; ogun ńpa elégbèje àdó.*
Loading the body down with charms has no effect in a war; war kills even the person carrying 1,400 juju gourdlets. (One should trust in one's arms rather than in one's charms.)

K

2175. *Kàkà kí ilẹ̀ kú, ṣíṣá ni yó ṣàá.*
Rather than die, the earth will only become bare. (One may be inconvenienced by one's enemies' machinations, but one will not be destroyed by them.)

2176. *Kí á gbé ọkọ́ so sájà ká pète ìmẹ́lẹ́, ojúgun-ún yó tán ó fikùn séhìn.*
Hiding the hoe in the loft and contriving to shirk work, the shin ate its fill and developed a stomach at its back. (Said of people who shirk work but eagerly partake of the rewards.)

2177. *Kí á ránni níṣẹ́ ò tó ká mọ̀ ó jé.*
To be sent on an errand is nothing compared to knowing how to carry it out. (The good servant is the one who can perform his or her tasks well.)

2178. *Kí a re odò ká sùn; kí ni ará ilé yó mu?*
If we go to the river and sleep there, what will the people left at home drink? (We must not fail those who depend on us.)

2179. *Kí á tó bí ọmọdé, ẹnìkan là mbá ṣeré.*
Before the child was born, one had someone as a playmate. (Message to someone that before he or she came around, one got along rather well and would do so again if that person were to disappear from the scene. Compare 2187 and 2242.)

2180. *Kí eégún tó dé lAlágbaà-á ti nfọlẹ̀lẹ̀ jẹ̀kọ.*
Long before the arrival of masqueraders the Alágbaà had been eating corn meal with steamed bean loaves. (One got on very well before the other person happened on the scene.)[41]

2181. *Kì í kan ẹni ká yẹrí.*
When a duty is one's turn, one does not duck it. (One must step up and carry out one's responsibility when the time comes.)

2182. *Kì í rẹ òòrẹ̀ kó rẹ sinsin ìdí ẹ̀.*
The porcupine may tire, but never the quills at its rear. (One can never be so tired that one will leave oneself defenseless.)

2183. *Kì í tán nígbá osùn ká má rìí fi pa ọmọ lára.*
The calabash of camwood is never so empty that one does not find enough in it to rub on a baby. (One may lack many things but never the means to fulfill one's obligations. Compare 1659 and 4617.)

2184. *Kí ni eégún nwò tí kò fi òwúrọ̀ jó?*
What was the masquerader looking at that he did not take advantage of the morning to dance? (One should not dawdle but rather do things at the most opportune moment.)[42]

2185. *Kí ní mbẹ nínú isà tí yó ba òkú lẹ́rù?*
What is there in the grave to frighten a corpse? (There is nothing in the offing that one cannot cope with.)

2186. *Kí ni ọmọ eye ó ṣe fún ìyá ẹ̀ ju pé kó dàgbà kó fò lọ?*
What will a nestling do for its mother other than become mature and fly away? (People who are powerless to help one cannot hurt one by witholding their support.)

2187. *Kí òyìnbó tó dé la ti nwọ aṣọ.*
Long before the white man came, we were wearing clothes. (One got along pretty well before a certain person came on the scene. Compare 2179 and 2242.)

2188. *Kíkú ajá, ng kò ní omitooro è-ẹ́ lá; àìkú ẹ̀ ng kò ní pè é rán níṣẹ́.*
When the dog dies, I will not lick the stew made with it; alive, I will not send it on an errand. (One has absolutely no use for the person at whom the proverb is directed. This is a variant of 169.)

2189. *Kìnìún ò níí sàgbákò ẹkùn.*
A lion does not face peril from a leopard. (The stronger person has nothing to fear from the weaker.)

2190. *Kò ka ikú, àdàbà sùú-sùú tí njẹ̀ láàrin àsá.*
It fears not death, the pigeon that forages among hawks. (Said of people who habitually court danger.)

---

41. *Alágbaà* is the title of the chief of the *eégún* (masqueraders), who are supposed to be partial to ọ̀lẹ̀lẹ̀ (steamed bean loaf).

42. As the day wears on and the sun beats down, the masquerader's shroud would become uncomfortably hot and strenuous exertions that much more of a trial.

2191. *Kò sí alápatà tí ńpa igún.*
There is no butcher who slaughters the vulture for sale. (Certain actions are forbidden. Or, one is beyond the power of one's enemies.)

2192. *Kò sí bí igbó ṣe lè ta kókó tó, erin òò kojá.*
No matter how knotty the bush might be, the elephant will find a way through it. (No obstacle can stop a resourceful and formidable person. Compare 1504.)

2193. *Kò sí èrè nínú-u "Gba owó kà."*
There is no profit in "Take this money and count it [for me]." (One cannot depend on profiting from others' industry.)

2194. *Kò sí ewu lóko, àfi gìrì àparò.*
There is no danger on the farm except for the sudden noise of partridges taking to the air. (An incantatory wish that all dangers will stay well away from oneself or some subject of one's wishes.)

2195. *Kò sí ẹni tí Ọlórun ò ṣe fún, àfi ẹni tó bá ní tòun ò tó.*
There is no one to whom God has not been generous, only those who will say he has not been generous enough. (Everyone has something to be thankful for.)

2196. *Kò sí ibi tí kò gba ọgọ̀; ọle layé ò gbà.*
There is no place where a fool is not welcome; the world rejects only shiftless people. (People may be foolish, but they had better not be shiftless.)

2197. *Kò sí ibi tí owó-ọjà erin ò tó.*
There is no place an elephant's trunk cannot reach. (There is no place beyond a person's reach or influence.)

2198. *Kò sí ikú tí kò rọ adìẹ lórùn.*
There is no manner of death that is incon-

venient for the chicken. (One is game for whatever propositions another might make.)

2199. *Kò sí ohun tí ńti òkè bọ̀ tí ilẹ̀ ò gbà.*
There is nothing dropping from above that the earth cannot withstand. (There is no eventuality that one cannot cope with.)

2200. *Kò sí oúnjẹ tí ḿmú ara lókun bí èyí tí a jẹ sẹ́nu ẹni lọ.*
There is no food that nourishes one's body like what one puts in one's own mouth. (The only thing one can be sure of is what one has in one's possession.)

2201. *Kó wó, kó wó, àràbà ò wó; ojú tìrókò.*
"May it crash! May it crash!" The silk-cotton tree does not crash; the ìrókò tree is shamed.[43] (The person whose enemies have been wishing and expecting him or her to fail has not failed; the enemies are shamed.)

2202. *Kọ̀nkọ̀sọ̀-ọ́ ní bí a ti ṣe òun tó yìí, òún sì ńku èlùbọ́.*
The sieve says despite all that has been done to it, it still manages to sift yam flour.[44] (Despite all vicissitudes placed in one's path, one was still able to do what was expected.)

2203. *Kùtù-kùtù kì í jíni lẹ́ẹ̀mejì; kùtù-kùtù ní ńjẹ́ òwúrọ̀; biri ní ńjẹ́ alẹ́.*
Early dawn does not wake one twice; early dawn is the morning; deep darkness is night. (The morning comes only once; whoever wastes it will discover too late that night has fallen.)

---

43. Both trees are huge, and there is supposedly some rivalry between them.

44. The sieve's complaint would be either that it is incessantly agitated or that it has been made full of holes.

L

2204. *Labẹ́-labẹ́ ò bá tìjà wá odò; kanna-kánná ò bá ti ẹ̀kọ wá oko.*
The *labẹ́labẹ́* plant[45] did not come to the river looking for a fight; the crow did not come to the farm in search of corn gruel. (One may be minding one's business when one is provoked but should nevertheless be prepared to respond. The next entry is a version of the same proverb.)

2205. *Labẹ́-labẹ́ ò bẹ̀rù ìjà.*
The *labẹ́labẹ́* plant is not afraid of a fight. (One is prepared for whatever trouble might come one's way. See the previous entry.)

2206. *Lékèélékèé gbàràdá, ó gba tẹlòmíràn mọ.*
The cattle egret borrows wonders to perform and performs enough for itself and others. (Said of people who have done far more than anyone expected of them.)

2207. *Lójú-lójú là ńwo ẹni tí a óò kéwì fún.*
It is directly in the eyes that one looks at the subject of the praise poem one is performing. (One should squarely face the person with whom one has business.)

M

2208. *"Má kojá mi Olùgbàlà" kì í ṣe orin à-kúnlẹ̀-kọ.*
"Pass me not by, dear Redeemer" is not a song one sings on one's knees. (The Redeemer helps only those who make an effort on their own behalf.)

2209. *Máà gbíyè lógún; ti owó ẹni ní ńtóni.*
Place not your hopes in inheritance; the

product of one's hand labor is what sustains one. (Whoever trusts in inheritance courts disaster.)

2210. *Màrìwò ò wí fúnra wọn tẹ́lẹ̀ tí wọ́n fi ńyọ.*
Palm fronds do not consult with one another before they sprout. (Each person is responsible for his or her own decisions.)

2211. *Màrìwò ò wojú ẹnìkan, àfi Ọlọ́run.*
Palm fronds look up to no one except God. (One's trust is in God only.)

2212. *Mo di arúgbó ọdẹ tí ńtu olú, mo di àgbàlagbà ọdẹ tí ńwa ògòngò láàtàn; mo di ògbólógbòó akítì tí ńgba ìbọn lọ́wọ́ ọdẹ.*
I have become an aged hunter reduced to gathering mushrooms; I have become an old hunter good only for digging palm weevils; I have become an aged monkey that snatches the gun from the hunter's grip. (A helpless person pushed to the wall will somehow find the means to put up a fight.)

2213. *"Mo kúgbé" lehoro ńdún lóko; "Mo mówó rá" làparò ńdún lábà-a bàbà.*
"I have perished!" is the cry of the hare in the bush; "I have destroyed things worth a lot of money!" is the cry of the partridge in the guinea-corn field. (A worthless person can also be counted upon to destroy things of value.)

2214. *"Mo ṣe é tán" ló níyì; a kì í dúpẹ́ aláṣekù.*
"I have completed the job" is what deserves praise; one does not thank people who leave a job only half done. (Whatever one embarks upon, one should see it through.)

2215. *Múlele múlèle: ilá tí ò mú lele ò léè so; ikàn tí ò mú lele ò léè wẹwù ẹ̀jẹ̀.*
High potency upon high potency: the okro that lacks high potency cannot fruit; the

---

45. A sharp prickly plant found near rivers. It is presumed to be ever ready to attack.

bitter tomato that lacks high potency cannot achieve the blood-red complexion.
(Sharpness is a requisite quality for success.)

N

2216. "Ng ó lọ, ng ó lọ!" lobìnrín fi ńdérù ba
ọkùnrin; "Bóo lè lọ o lọ" lọkùnrín fi ńdérù ba
obìnrin.
"I will leave you, I will leave you!" is the
threat a woman flings at a man. "If you have
a mind to leave, go ahead and leave!" is the
retort a man throws at a woman. (Every person in a relationship has something he or
she can hold over the others.)

2217. Ní inú ègún, ní inú-u gọ̀gọ̀, ọmọ ayò a
ṣara bòró.
In the midst of thorns, in the midst of
crooked twigs, the ayò seeds remain smooth.
(A person who will thrive will do so in spite
of adversities.)

2218. Ní inú òfìì àti òláà, ọmọ páńdọ̀rọ̀ ńgbó.
Despite being blown hither and thither in
the gale, the fruits of the sausage tree survive
to maturity. (Some people will thrive despite
adversities.)

2219. Ní inú òwú la ti ṁbù sèní òwú.
It is out of one's stock of cotton that one
takes some for makeweight. (It is to one's
treasury that one resorts for investments to
build the treasury further.)

2220. Ní ọjọ́ eré nìyà ńdun ọ̀lẹ; kàkà kó wọlé
kó jáde a fọwọ́ rọ igi, a pòṣé sàrà.
It is on the day of festivities that the lazy person is miserable; instead of going inside his
room and emerging again [in other words,
fetching gifts for the revelers], he leans his
arms against a tree and hisses incessantly.
(Shiftless people eventually reap the disgrace

of their laziness when they are unable to do
what is socially expected of them. Compare
2341.)

2221. Ní teere, ní tèèrè, Ṣàngó ṣe bẹ́ẹ̀ ó jó
wọjà.
Erratically, with almost imperceptible forward movement, just so Ṣango danced until
he was at the market. (If unimpeded or
unattended to, a seemingly negligible development will eventually assume proportions
one cannot ignore.)[46]

O

2222. Ò báà kúrú, ò báà párí, gbèsè ò sí, èsín
ò sí; onígbèsè ló lè fini sèsín.
One may be diminutive, and one may be
bald, but without debt one has not earned
ridicule; only one's creditor has grounds
to poke fun. (However much one might be
devoid of accomplishments, as long as one
stays out of debt, one's dignity is intact.)

2223. Ó di ọjọ́ tí àkàrà ìyá kùtà ká tó mọ ọmọ
tó lè jẹkọ.
It is only on the day when the mother's bean
fritters do not sell that one knows which
child can consume large quantities of corn
meal.[47] (One knows the good worker not at
the time of boasting but when there is work
to be done.)

2224. Ó gbọ́ tiyán sògìrì mọ́dìí; ó gbọ́ toko sọ
àdá nù.
On hearing about pounded yam he girded
himself with cooked melon seeds for stew

---

46. The proverb refers to the sometimes sedate,
sometimes erratic dancing of the cultists of the god
Ṣango.

47. Àkàrà and èkọ are meals that most often go
together.

seasoning; on hearing about farm work he threw his cutlass away. (The lazy person will eagerly heed the summons to eat but not to work.)

2225. *O kò gun ẹṣin lọ́sàn-án, o ò gun èèyàn lóru, o ò du nǹkan kàrà-kàrà; báwo lo ṣe lè ní káyé má fọ́ọ́?*
You do not ride a horse by day; you do not ride people by night; and you do not make great exertions to achieve any goal. How could you have a say in saving the world from disaster? (A person who makes no effort cannot affect human affairs.)

2226. *O kò ṣá igi lógbé, o ò sọ ògùrọ̀ lófà, o dédìí ọpẹ o gbẹ́nu sókè ò ńretí; ọ̀fẹ́ ní ńro?*
You did not slash the trunk with a cutlass; you did not shoot an arrow at the top of the palm-wine-producing palm tree; you come to the foot of the palm tree and raise your open mouth. Does it drip all by itself? (Said of people who expect to reap benefits where they have not made any effort.)

2227. *"Ó kù díẹ̀ kí nwí": ojo ní ńsọni da.*
"I was just on the verge of speaking my mind": it only makes one into a coward. (One should either engage or refrain from making excuses.)

2228. *Ó ní ibi tí ó ńdé, itọ́-dídámì nínú ààwẹ̀.*
It goes some way [in assuaging hunger], saliva swallowing during a fast. (Every little effort helps.)

2229. *O ní kí o gbó ogbó Olúàṣọ; o lè jìyà bí Olúàṣọ?*
You pray to live as long as Olúàṣọ, but can you endure the trials of Olúàṣọ?[48] (Who-

ever wishes for the sort of glory another person enjoys must also be willing to endure whatever tribulations that person has endured.)

2230. *Ó pa obì, ó yọ abidún-un rẹ̀.*
He split the kola-nut pod open and also removed the bad among the seeds. (Said of a person who has fulfilled an obligation to the utmost.)

2231. *Obìnrin téẹ́rẹ́ yẹ ọkọ è níjọ́ ijó, obìnrin gìdìgbá yẹ ọkọ è níjọ́ èbù; bó bá ru ogórùn-ún èbù tán a kó kébé-kébé níwájú ọkọ.*
A slender woman is the joy of her husband on a day of dancing, but a hefty woman is her husband's joy on the day of yams quartered for planting; after she has toted a hundred yam pieces, she walks smartly [toward the farm] ahead of her husband. (Good looks are not all that make a good wife.)

2232. *Obìnrin tí yó fẹẹ́ alágbára, ọkàn kan ní ḿmú.*
A woman who would marry a formidable man must have an unwavering mind. (Once one has made a decision on an important matter, one should remain resolute.)

2233. *Òbúrẹ́wà ẹni, tòrìṣà ni; àìraṣọlò, tolúwarè ni.*
A person's ugliness is the god's doing; the person's lack of clothing is his or her own fault. (One must take responsibility for some conditions, but cannot be blamed for others.)

2234. *Odíderé kì í kú sóko iwáje.*
The parrot never dies in the grazing field. (A prayer that just as the parrot always returns home from grazing, the subject of the prayer will return safely from a business venture away from home.)

---

48. Olúàṣọ was a king (Aláàfin) of Ọ̀yọ́ reputed to have lived for 320 years and to have sired 1,460 children (Johnson 158).

2235. *Odò kì í kún bo eja lójú.*
A river does not so swell as to be over the head of the fish. (A statement that an adversary at his most powerful can never pose a threat.)

2236. *Odò tí a bá mọ orísun è kì í gbéni lọ.*
A river whose source one knows does not carry one away. (A person whose beginning one knows cannot pose a great threat.)

2237. *Odó tó bá tojú eni kún kì í gbéni lọ.*
A river that swells in one's presence does not carry one away. (A danger that one sees in the making can be avoided. Compare 1723.)

2238. *Ogun kì í jà kó wọlé Aséyìn.*
War does not rage and destroy the home of the Aséyìn.[49] (Certain personages are beyond the reach of misfortune.)

2239. *Ogun kì í rí èhìn ogun.*
An army does not see the rear of an(other) army. (One should face one's adversary squarely.)

2240. *Ogún ọdún tí ebí ti ńpa ògà, ìrìn-in fààjì ò padà lésè-ẹ rè.*
In all the twenty years that the chameleon has been in the throes of hunger, its dignified gait has not deserted it. (The dignified person never allows himself or herself to be ruffled by adversity.)

2241. *Ògbógbó àwọn ní ńbi ajáko.*
It is a mighty net that can trip the civet cat. (It takes extraordinary efforts or capabilities to accomplish extraordinary tasks.)

2242. *Ohun kan ladìe ńje kágbàdo tó dé.*
The chicken had something to eat before there was corn. (A statement that one does

not depend on somebody else, since one survived before his or her arrival. Compare 2187.)

2243. *Ohun tí a bá gbìn la ó kàá.*
What one plants is what one reaps. (Every action has its proper reward. Compare the following entry.)

2244. *Ohun tí a bá gbìn séhìn la ó padà bá.*
Whatever one sows behind one is what one will return to find. (One reaps whatever one sows. Compare the preceding entry.)

2245. *Ohun tí a fún èsó sọ ni èsọ ńsọ.*
Whatever one hands to a warrior to look after is what he looks after. (One should concentrate on the duty entrusted to one.)

2246. *Ohun títán lọdún eégún.*
The annual *egúngún* festival is not endless. (Every condition ends sometime. Sometimes the proverb is rendered *Ohun títán leégún ọdún*, meaning, "The outing of the annual *egúgún* is something that has an end.")

2247. *Ohun tó se ìjímèrè tó fi gungi ègè: bí kò bá rí ohun tó jù béè lọ kò ní sòkalè.*
Whatever it was that sent the brown monkey climbing to the top of the thorny acacia tree, unless it sees something even more terrifying, it will not climb down. (It takes a threatened catastrophe to make one look kindly on minor inconveniences.)

2248. *Ohun tó se ìwòfà tí kò fi wá sóko olówó, bójú bá kan ojú yó sọ fún olówó-o rè.*
Whatever caused the pawned worker to stay away from the creditor's farm, when the two come face to face, he or she will have some explaining to do. (Whoever shirks his or her duty will eventually have to explain why.)

2249. *Òjiji ò bèrù òfin.*
The shadow has no fear of the gully. (One has no need to fear a harmless adversary.)

---

49. Aséyìn is the title of the chief of Ìséyìn, a town north of Ọyọ́.

2250. Òjìjí ṣe légé-légé má wòó.
The shadow lacks substance but it never crashes. (Apparent fragility may mask real resilience.)

2251. Òjò ìbá rò, kí ladétè ìbá gbìn? Ọwọ́ adétè ò ká eyo àgbàdo mẹ́wàà.
Were it to rain, what would the leper have planted? A leper's palm cannot scoop ten grains of corn. (Said of people who blame their deficiencies on flaws in Nature.)

2252. Òjó jìyà gbé; alágbára-á bú u, ó gun àjà; a tọ̀ ọ́.
Òjó is victimized without recourse; a bully insults him, he goes to hide in the rafters, and his nemesis follows him there. (Said of poeple who are powerless to stop being victimized.)

2253. Òjò pamí, òjò pa ère-è mi; òjò ò pa ẹwà ara-à mi dànù.
The rain may beat me, and the rain may beat my statue; the rain cannot wash away my good looks. (Adversity will not get the better of me.)

2254. Òjòjò ọle ò tán bọ̀rọ̀; ọlẹ́ bà á tì ó dáná orí.
A lazy person's illness is not soon over; the lazy person finds no way out and prepares a fire to warm his head.[50] (A lazy person will use every excuse to avoid any obligation, and when he cannot avoid it, his fulfillment of it is always pitiable.)

2255. Òjò-ó pa alágùn-úndì, àgúndìí domi; ìyàwó ńretí àgúndì, ọkọ sùn sóko.

---

50. The point of lighting a fire to warm his head is obscure. Another possibility, dáná ori, "offer a feast of corn meal," would suggest a laughable endeavor, since ori (ẹkọ) is not a particularly popular meal. A third possibility, equally problematic, is dáná òrí, "make fire using shea butter as fuel," or "make fire for shea butter."

Rain beats the man carrying pounded yams wrapped in leaves, and the pounded yams become waterlogged; the wife awaits the pounded yams; the husband sleeps on the farm. (When one fails to deliver on a promise, one is hardly able to show one's face before those one has betrayed.)

2256. Òjò-ó pa odíde àlùkò ńyọ̀, àlùkò-ó rò pé ìkó bàjẹ́; òjó mú ìkó wọso.
Rain beats the parrot and the touraco rejoices, thinking that the parrot's tail feather is ruined; the rain only makes the tail feather brighter. (The occurrence one's adversaries hoped would destroy one only improved one's fortunes.)

2257. Òjò-ó ponmi fún ọle, kò ṣégi fún ọle.
The rain provides water for the lazy person, but it does not fetch firewood for the lazy person. (Parasites can have only so much done for them, never everything.)

2258. Ojú abanijẹ́ pọ́n, kò lè tan fìtílà.
The detractor's eyes glow red, but they cannot light a lamp. (A detractor's slanderous efforts are in vain.)

2259. "Ojú àna-à mi ò sunwọn"; kò ju kó gba ọmọ è lọ.
"The look on my parent-in-law's face is baleful"; the worst he or she can do is take his or her daughter back. (There is a limit to which a benefactor's withdrawal of his or her beneficence can hurt one.)

2260. Ojú kì í pọ́n iṣin ká má bàá wóró nínú è.
The Akee apple is never so blighted that one does not find a seed in it. (Whatever befalls, one will be left with some residual property.)

2261. Ojú kì í pọ́n iṣin kó má là.
The Akee apple is never so blighted that it does not eventually split open. (Whatever

misfortune might befall, one would be able to do those things that are second nature.)

2262. *Ojú là ńrọ́; ọgọ́ sọro-ó ṣe.*
One only tries one's best; heroic deeds do not come easy. (One's best is enough. Compare 2172.)

2263. *Ojú lakàn-án fi ńṣọ́ orí.*
The crab watches after its head with its eyes. (One should have one's eyes open to protect one's interests.)

2264. *Ojú mẹ́wàá kò jọ ojú ẹni.*
Ten eyes are not like one's own. (Seeing something oneself is far better than hearing a report of it from ten people. Compare 2267.)

2265. *"Ojú ò fẹ́rakù" tí ńta ajá ẹ lọ́kòó; ó fowó ṣíyán jẹ.*
"We might see each other again" sold his dog for 20 cowries and spent the money on pounded yams to eat.[51] (A footloose person will part with valuables for little or nothing.)

2266. *Ojú olójú kì í gba òràn fúnni wò.*
Other people's eyes will not look after matters for you. (No one else will take care of your affairs. Compare 2264 and the following entry.)

2267. *Ojú olójú ò jọ ojú ẹni; a-sọ̀ràn-deni ò wọ́pọ̀.*
Other people's eyes are nothing like one's own; minders of other people's business are few. (No one can look after one's affairs as one would oneself. Compare the foregoing entry and 2264.)

2268. *Ojú pọ́n koko má fọọ́; ọ̀gẹ̀dẹ̀ pọ́n koko má rọ̀; òràn fini dùgbẹ̀-dùgbẹ̀ yunni nù; òràn tí ńfinni ò leè pani.*
The eyes go red but do not go blind; the banana goes brilliant yellow but does not rot; a problem rattles one to the foundations and lets one go; a problem that rattles one will not kill one. (Every problem soon comes to an end in time.)

2269. *Ojú rẹ́gbin kò fọ́, a-jọ̀pọ̀-ìyà-má-rù.*
The eye looks on a filthy sight and does not go blind, [like] one who sustains a succession of sufferings without wasting away. (With resilience one will overcome all problems.)

2270. *Ojú ti kókó, ojú ti eéwo; ojú ti aáràgbá ìdí pẹ̀lú.*
The lump that attacks the head is shamed, the boil is shamed, and the hardened tissue on the buttocks is shamed also. (An assertion of defiance in the face of adversity.)

2271. *Ojú tí ńpọ́n awo àpọ́nkú kó; ìyà tí ńjẹ awo àjẹlà; iṣẹ́ tí ńṣẹ awo à-ṣẹ́-ṣẹ́-obì-jẹ ni.*
The suffering that the *babaláwo* is experiencing is not something that leads to death; the hard time that the *babaláwo* is going through is one that leads to riches; the vicissitudes that now befall the *babaláwo* leave room for taking a bite of kola nut.[52] (One's present troubles will lead to even better times.)

2272. *Ojú tó ti rí gbẹ̀lẹ̀dẹ́ ti rópin ìran.*
The eyes that have seen *gbẹ̀lẹ̀dẹ́* have seen the ultimate in sights.[53] (Having passed the

---

51. *Ojú ò fẹ́rakù* is an expression people use on parting; it means, literally, "Our eyes are not giving up the sight of one another."

52. *Babaláwo,* literally "father of mysteries," is the title of the priests of Ifá, who are diviners, healers, and general-purpose medicine men.

53. *Gbẹ̀lẹ̀dẹ́* is probably a corruption of Gẹ̀lẹ̀dẹ́, a women's secret cult, since there is no such word as *gbẹ̀lẹ̀dẹ̀,* as far as I know, in current Yoruba.

ultimate test, one will have little difficulty with lesser ones. Compare the next entry and 2039.)

2273. *Ojú tó ti rókun ò níí rộsà kó bèrù.*
The eyes that have seen the ocean will not tremble at the sight of the lagoon. (Once one has survived a grave peril, small inconveniences will not be unduly impressive. Compare the previous entry.)

2274. *Ojúmộ kì í mộ kí ọwộ má yùn-ún ẹnu.*
Never a day dawns that the hand does not make a trip to the mouth. (Certain obligations are unavoidable.)

2275. *Ojúoró ní ńlékè omi; òṣíbàtà ní ńlékè odò.*
The water lettuce always winds up on the surface of the water; the waterlily always winds up on the surface of the stream. (Just as those plants remain on top of their habitats, so one will remain triumphant over one's adversaries.)[54]

2276. *Òkè lẹyẹ ńfohùn.*
It is from aloft that the bird sounds off. (It is time for one to rise up.)

2277. *Òkè méjì kì í bínú ẹni; bí a bá gun òkan, à sì máa rọ òkan.*
One cannot be bedeviled by two hills; if one ascends a hill, one descends a hill. (Every hill one must climb has a descent on the other side.)

2278. *Òkété fijà séhìn; ó dộjà tán ó káwộ léri.*
The giant bush rat turns its back at the place where it has a quarrel; after getting to the market it clamps its hands on its head.[55] (The moment and the place to act

are when and where the matter is taking place, not when all is over and everybody has dispersed.)

2279. *Òkìkí ajá kì í pa oṣù.*
A dog's howling will not kill the moon. (The threats of ineffectual enemies amount to nothing.)

2280. *Òkìkí ò poṣù; ariwo ò pagún; ibi ẹ rí ẹ kíbòsí-ì mi lọ.*
Being widely reputed does not kill the moon; being noised about does not kill the vulture; wherever you please, make a noise about me. (A statement that one is not bothered by people who spread stories about one.)

2281. *Oko etílé ladìẹ lè ro.*
The chicken is good at cultivating only the soil close by the home. (Said of people who boast when in the safety of their rooms but can do nothing once outside.)

2282. *Òkò kan igi; òkò padà séhìn kí o rebi o ti wá.*
Stone, hit a tree; stone, retrace your steps and return to whence you came. (Something of an incantation to send evil wishes back toward those who sent them.)

2283. *Òkú ò moye à ńràgò.*
The corpse does not know the cost of the shroud. (The person who does not have to pay the bills does not care how expensive the things he wastes are.)

2284. *Òkú ọdún mẹta-á kúrò ní àlejò-o sàréè.*
A three-year-old corpse is no longer a new-

---

54. *Ojú oró* is *Pistia stratiotes* (Arcideae), and *òṣíbàtà* is *Nymphaea lotus* (Abraham 463, 491).

55. The fight here refers to the circumstances in

which the bush rat is captured. After hunters kill a giant bush rat, they gut it and affix it to a stake that runs the length of its body, through the head, and, finally, through the forelimbs, which are clasped together above the rodent's head. A common gesture people visited by misfortune use is clamping their head in their hands.

comer to the grave. (In time, a sojourner becomes a native.)

2285. *Òkú òlẹ ò ní pósí.*
A lazy person's corpse does not merit a coffin. (One does not receive in death a treatment one's life has not earned. Or, one reaps what one sows.)

2286. *Olójú kì í fojú ẹ̀ sílẹ̀ kí tàlùbọ́ kó wọ̀ ọ́.*
The owner of the eyes will not neglect them and watch foreign matter lodge in them. (One does not simply look on as one's interests are jeopardized.)

2287. *Olówó kì í fi owó ẹ̀ fún abọ̀ṣì na.*
The rich person will not give his or her money to a poor person to spend. (Generosity has its limits.)

2288. *Olówó mọ òwò.*
The rich person is an expert at trading. (Success comes from expertise.)

2289. *Olúmọ Ègbá ò ṣéé gbé.*
The Olúmọ of the Ègbá territory is impossible to carry.[56] (Some tasks are absolutely impossible.)

2290. *Omi adágún ò lè gbé màlúù lọ.*
A stagnant pool cannot carry off a cow. (Some adverse situations are annoyances only and pose no danger.)

2291. *Omi ló dànù, agbè ò fọ́.*
It is the water that is spilled; the water gourd is not broken. (A proverb usually used to console parents who have lost a child: the child is likened to the water, and the mother to the vessel.)

2292. *Omi ńbẹ látọ́.*
There is water in the long-necked calabash.

(One has resources that others may not know about.)

2293. *Omi ṣẹ̀lẹ̀rú ò mu akèrègbè.*
The water from a new spring will not cover a gourd to the top. (An upstart cannot defeat a veteran.)

2294. *Omí wọ́ yanrìn gbẹrẹrẹ, bẹ̀ẹ̀ni omi ò lọ́wọ́, omi ò lẹ́sẹ̀.*
Water drags the sand about, and yet water lacks hands and lacks legs. (One may not have a great deal but can nevertheless perform wonders.)

2295. *"Oní ló ńmọ," ìjà òlẹ.*
"It will all end sometime today": a lazy person's motto in a fight. (The idler or shirker forced to perform some task is always eager for the day's end.)

2296. *Òní, "Mò ńlọ"; ọla, "Mò ńlọ," kò jẹ́ kí àlejò gbin awùsá.*
Today "I am leaving" and tomorrow "I am leaving" prevents the sojourner from planting *awùsá.* (Constant awareness of one's sojourner status prevents one from engaging in long-term projects or establishing roots in a place.)[57]

2297. *Òní òwè, ọla àro: iṣẹ́ oníṣẹ́ ò jẹ́ ká ráàyè ṣe tẹni.*
Today, a communal project; tomorrow, group work on a somebody's farm: other people's work prevents one from doing one's own. (Too many communal responsibilities take one from one's own affairs.)[58]

2298. *Oníbàjẹ́ ò lódó; ẹnu gbogbo lodó-o wọn.*
Detractors of others have no pestles; their

---

56. Olúmọ is an imposing inselberg near Abẹ́òkúta.

57. *Awùsá* is the creeper that yields fruits known locally as wallnuts.

58. *Òwè* and *àro* are both names for the traditional arrangements through which a group of people take turns working together on one another's projects.

mouths are their pestles. (Detractors have no weapons other than their mouths.)

2299. *Oníbànà ní ńtójú òrombó; onídẹ ní ńtójú awẹdẹ.*
It is he who has copper ornaments who must procure oranges; whoever has brass ornaments must procure the herb *awẹdẹ*. (Each person must see to procuring whatever he or she needs.)[59]

2300. *Onígbèsè èèyàn-án ti kú; a ò tíì sìnkú ẹ ni.*
The habitual debtor is already dead, except that he has not yet been buried. (Someone always in debt is no better than a dead person.)

2301. *OníṢàngó ò mẹni tí òún ńwà lóògì dànù.*
The Ṣango worshiper knows not whose ground corn he is spilling. (One does not care who is affected by one's actions.)

2302. *Oníṣe kì í fiṣe è sílẹ̀ re ibi; ó ńre àjò ó mú iṣe è lówó gírígírí.*
The owner of a habit will not go on a journey and leave his habit at home; when he goes, he takes his habit along with him. (One cannot escape from one's character.)

2303. *Oníṣòwó wà lóòrùn; náwónáwó wà níbòji.*
The person who does the trading is in the sun; the person who spends the money is in the shade. (A criticism of people who expend no effort but take advantage of other people's exertions. Compare 2317.)

2304. *Oníṣú fiṣu ẹ se èbẹ; ojú ti atèèpojẹ.*
The owner of the yams makes yam pottage out of the yams; the person who eats the yam scrapings off the peels is shamed.[60] (The parasite is shamed when the host finds a way to shut him out.)

2305. *Oògùn kì í gbé inú àdó jẹ.*
A magical charm does not work from within its gourdlet. (One cannot expect any benefit from one's resources without deploying them.)

2306. *Oòrùn ò kan àtàrí, ọwó ò dá.*
The sun has not risen directly above the head; working hands cannot cease their toil. (The day is for working.)

2307. *Oòrùn ò pa ó, òjò ò pa ó, o ní ò ńsiṣẹ ajé.*
The sun does not beat you; the rain does not beat you; yet you say you are engaged in a gainful pursuit. (Profitable labor is seldom pleasurable.)

2308. *Orí adẹtù ńpète àrán; orí adáràn-án ńpète àtijọba.*
The head that wears a cloth cap strives to wear a velvet cap; the one that wears a velvet cap strives to become a king. (Everyone hopes for a better tomorrow.)

2309. *Orí iṣẹ́ laago ńkú lé.*
It is while at work that a clock dies. (A vow never to stop working until death.)

2310. *Orí kì í tóbi kólórí má lè gbé e.*
A head is never so heavy that the owner cannot carry it. (One should always be capable of taking care of one's affairs.)

2311. *Orí ńlá kì í pá tán.*
A huge head does not go completely bald.

---

59. The proverb refers to the materials needed for cleaning the metals.

60. In the preparation of *èbẹ* (or *àṣáró*) no yam remnant is left on the peels for a parasite to take advantage of; roasting and later peeling yams, on the other hand, for example, would leave something for such a parasite.

(The more one has in abundance, the more cushion one has against reverses.)

2312. *Orí olórí kì í báni gbérù.*
Other people's heads will not carry one's load. (Each person must bear his own burden.)

2313. *Òrìsà tí ńgbòle ò sí; apá eni ní ńgbeni.*
No god comes to the aid of shiftless people; only their arms aid them. (One's well-being is in the muscular strength of one's arms.)

2314. *Oríta méta ò konnú ebo.*
A crossroads where three roads meet is not afraid of sacrificial offerings. (One does not fear any eventuality.)[61]

2315. *Òru ni ìnàhìn àgbè.*
Nighttime is a farmer's time to stretch the back. (As long as the day lasts, there will be work to do.)

2316. *Òsìsé lòtá òle.*
The industrious person is the enemy of the shiftless person. (People with flaws hate those who might show them up.)

2317. *Òsìsé wà lóòrùn; ení máa jé wà níbòji.*
The laborer is in the sun; the person who will reap the fruit is in the shade. (Quite often those who do the work are not the ones who gain the benefits of the labor. This is a variant of 2303.)

2318. *Osù méta lebi ńpàgbè.*
The farmer's hunger lasts only three months.[62] (The hardship an industrious person experiences does not last long.)

2319. *Òwò àdá kì í pa àdá; òwò okó kì í yo okó lénu.*
A machete's trade does not kill the machete; a hoe's trade does not cause problems for the hoe. (A person's forte does not constitute a problem for him or her.)

2320. *Owó ò mo ègbón, ó so àbúrò dàgbà.*
Wealth does not know who is the elder; it makes a senior of the younger person. (Success does not depend on age or maturity. Compare 2124.)

2321. *Owó ò níran àfi eni tí kò bá sisé.*
Money has no lineage, except for the person who will not work. (Money does not restrict itself to certain families; only the shiftless are shunned by money.)

2322. *Owó olówó leégún ńná.*
Other people's money is what the masquerader spends. (The parasitic person always relies on other people's largesse.)

2323. *Òwò tí a bá máa se àselà, a kì í rí àpá è lára eni.*
The trade that one will pursue and that will make one prosper does not leave scars. (A pursuit that is destined to make one prosperous will not cause unbearable hardship.)

2324. *Òwò tí a fowó rà, owó la fi ńpa.*
Merchandise that one buys with money, one earns money for. (One does not give away merchandise for which one paid money. Compare 2337.)

2325. *Òwò tí a ó se là ńtójú; Òjí fabe hora.*
The trade one will pursue is the one one protects; Òjí scratches his body with a razor. (The gadgets people favor give away their trade.)

2326. *Òyìnbó baba ònájà; ajé baba téní-téní.*
The white man is the past master of trading; money is the guarantee of fashionableness.

---

61. The favorite spots for leaving sacrifices are crossroads, especially the confluence of three roads.
62. The period between harvests (of one crop or another) is seldom more than three months.

(Without money one cannot be fashion-able.)

2327. *Òyìnbó ta ọjà ta orúkọ; Ègún tajà ta èdìdì.*
The white man sells merchandise with the name brand still attached; the Ègún person sells cloth still in its bundle. (One deals with matters wholesale, as it were, not retail.)

Ọ

2328. *Ọba tó fi iyùn bọlè, ọba tó wú u, àwọn méjèèjì la ó máa sọ orúkọ-ọ wọn.*
The king who buries coral beads, the king who digs them up: both will have their names remembered by posterity. (Whoever performs an unprecedented feat, whatever it might be, will be remembered by posterity. The following entry is a variant.)

2329. *Ọba tó sọ ẹgàn di erùfù, ọba tó sọ erùfù dẹgàn: àwọn méjèèjì la ó máa sọ orúkọ-ọ wọn.*
The king who turned a forest into a sandy plain, the king who turned a sandy plain into a forest: both their names will be re-membered by posterity. (Whoever performs a great feat will be remembered. See the previous entry.)

2330. *Ọbè tó dùn, owó ló pa á.*
A delicious stew was procured with money. (Nothing good happens without money.)

2331. *Ọbè-ẹ tutù tán, a dawọ́ bù ú lá.*
The stew having cooled, one hollows one's palm to eat it. (When the back of a difficult task has been broken, people are eager to tackle it.)

2332. *Òdájú ló bí owó; ìtìjú ló bí gbèsè.*
It is brazenness that gives birth to wealth; it is excessive reticence that gives birth to poverty. (Nothing succeeds without some audaciousness.)

2333. *Ọdọodún làgbè ńníyì.*
It is every year that the farmer receives praise. (Statement or prayer that some person will receive perennial praise, just as the annual harvest brings praise to the farmer.)

2334. *Ọdúnníì ọdẹ́ pa erin; èèmíràn ọdẹ́ pa efòn, ọdún méfà ọdẹ́ pa òló; ọlá ńrewájú, tàbí ọlá ńrèhìn?*
This year the hunter kills an elephant; the next year the hunter kills a buffalo; two years hence the hunter kills a grass mouse: is his glory increasing or decreasing? (One should always strive for greater accomplishments, not lesser.)

2335. *Ògèdè dúdú ò sẹ́ẹ bùsán; ọmọ burúkú ò sẹ́ẹ lù pa.*
An unripe plaintain is not something to eat; a useless child is not something to beat to death. (Certain problems one simply has to live with.)

2336. *Ogbọ́n òyìnbó ti ojú òkun là wá; aṣọ kí ni ó borí akẹsẹ?*
The white man's wisdom shines even across the seas; what cloth, though, is better than *akẹsẹ* cloth?[63] (Despite the appeal of foreign goods, local wares are preferable.)

2337. *Ọjà tí a fowó rà, owó la fi ńpa.*
One makes money from goods one pur-chased with money. (Do not make gifts of commodities purchased for trade. Compare 2324.)

2338. *Ò-jẹ-wòmù-wòmù-kú-wòmù-wòmù lorúkọ tí àpà ńjẹ.*
One-who-eats-recklessly-and-dies-recklessly

---

63. *Akẹsẹ* is local yellow cotton cloth.

is the name one calls a wasteful person. (Wasteful people will never learn the value of things.)

2339. *Ojó a bá kó òle là ńkó inú ríró.*
The day one learns laziness is the day one should learn how to endure a painfully empty stomach. (The lazy person should not expect to be fed by others.)

2340. *Ojó a bá rí ibí nìbí ńwolè.*
The day one sees the afterbirth is the day it enters the earth. (Once one perceives a threat, one can deal decisively with it.)

2341. *Ojó eré lòràn ńdun òle.*
It is on the day of relaxation that the lazy person experiences regret. (People who did not save for a rainy day will be sorry when those who did save enjoy the benefits of their foresight. Compare 2220.)

2342. *Ojó tí a dóko là ńjìjà ilè.*
The day one gets to the farm is the day one fights over boundaries. (Do not procrastinate.)

2343. *Ojó tí a ńkósé là ńkó ìyára.*
The day one learns a trade is the day one learns to be quick at it. (Whatever one does should be done thoroughly and expertly.)

2344. *Òkàràkàrà ńké, enu è ńbéjè; ó ní bí enu òún ya dé ìpàkó, oun ó sàáà máa wí tòun.*
Òkàràkàrà is calling and blood drips from its beak; it says even if its mouth tears to the occiput, it will continue its calling.[64] (As long as a serious problem persists, one should not stop calling for help.)

2345. *Òlé bà á tì, ó kó sílé Ifá.*
The lazy person fails at everything, where-

upon he becomes an Ifá acolyte.[65] (The lazy person finds easy tasks to do. The following entry is a variant.)

2346. *Òlé bà á tì, ó kó sílé-e kéú.*
The lazy person fails at everything, whereupon he goes to a Koranic school.[66] (The lazy person always seeks out the easiest employment. Compare the previous entry.)

2347. *Òle, baba àrùn.*
Laziness, father of all diseases. (Laziness is worse than any disease.)

2348. *Òle èèyàn ò rí ayé wá.*
A lazy person has found no world to come to. (The lot of a lazy person in this world is misery.)

2349. *Òlé fé àrùn kù, ó bú pùrù sékún.*
[If] the lazy person cannot find a disease to contract, he bursts into tears. (A lazy person would rather catch a disease than submit to work.)

2350. *Òlé fi òràn gbogbo se "hòo."*
The lazy person replies "yes" to all propositions. (You will get no argument from a lazy person.)

2351. *Òlé jogún ìbànújé, ó ní òún jogún ìran òun.*
The lazy person inherits unhappiness; he says he has inherited the fate of his lineage. (The lazy person has himself to blame, not his destiny.)

2352. *Òlé jogún ìbáwí.*
The lazy person inherits recriminations. (The lazy person is a tempting scapegoat.)

---

64. Òkàràkàrà is an obscure name for a kind of animal that makes loud noises.

65. The chief task of the Ifá pupil is to memorize the huge texts associated with it.

66. Pupils in Koranic schools recite the Koran all day, a supposedly easy task.

2353. Ọ̀lẹ́ kákò, ó di ọ̀jọ̀jọ̀.
The lazy person curls up, and his condition becomes a serious ailment. (The simplest tasks become impossible undertakings for the lazy person.)

2354. Ọ̀lẹ́ kún àárẹ̀ lọ́wọ́.
Laziness lends weariness a hand. (Laziness is often a contributor to weariness.)

2355. Ọ̀lẹ́ mọ ẹ̀èwọ̀ ìjà: ó ní bàbá òún ní kóun má jà lọ́nà oko.
The coward knows the preventive for fighting: he says his father has ordered him not to fight on the way to the farm. (The coward will use every excuse to get out of a fight.)

2356. Ọ̀lẹ́ ní ọjọ́ tí ikú bá pa òun, inú òhun á dùn. Ikú ní òun ó jẹ́ẹ́ kí ojú ẹ̀ rí màbo.
The lazy person says on the day he dies, he will be happy. Death says he will visit him [the lazy person] with suffering that is out of this world. (There is no way for the lazy person to avoid suffering. The following entry is a variant.)

2357. Ọ̀lẹ́ ní ọjọ́ tí òún bá kú òun ó yọ̀; ohun tí ojú òlẹ́ máa rí kó tó kú ńkọ́?
The coward says he will rejoice on the day he dies, but what about the woes he will experience before he dies? (Death may offer the coward a respite, but he will suffer before death comes. Compare the preceding entry.)

2358. Ọ̀lẹ o yẹẹ́ ní lọ́mọ.
A lazy person is not something one wants as a child. (Who wants a lazy child?)

2359. Ọ̀lẹ́ wáṣẹ́ rírọ̀ ṣe.
The lazy person seeks out an easy task to do. (Trust the lazy person to find the easiest tasks.)

2360. Ọlọgbọ́n kì í kú sóko ọ̀lẹ; bí ọlọgbọ́n bá kú sóko ọ̀lẹ, ọ̀ràn náà-á nídìí.
The wise will not die on a farm for the lazy; if a wise person dies on a farm for the lazy, there must be some explanation. (The resourceful person will always find a way out of a predicament.)

2361. Ọlọ́mú dá ọmú ìyá ẹ̀ gbé.
Each child must lift its mother's breast by itself. (Every person to his or her own resources.)

2362. Ọlọ́run yó pèsè; kì í ṣe bí èṣè oríta.
The Lord will give alms, but not the sort one comes upon at crossroads. (One wishes for good gifts from God, not just any sort of leavings.)

2363. Ọmọ tí yó jẹ́ẹ́ àṣàmú, kékeré ní ńtií ṣenu sámú-ṣámú.
A person who will become exemplary begins showing precociousness from childhood. (Childhood shows the adult.)

2364. Ọmọ tó káwọ́ sókè ló fẹ́ ká gbé òun.
It is the child who raises its arms that induces people to lift it. (If you want people to come to your aid, first lift a finger on your own behalf. Compare the next entry.)

2365. Ọmọ tó ṣípá fúnni là ńgbé jó.
It is the child who lifts its arms that one picks up and dances with. (One makes friends with people who offer friendship. Compare the preceding entry.)

2366. Ọmọdé ò mọ ibi tí à ńpọn òun rè.
A child does not know where the person who carries it on her back is headed. (People who depend on others do not know what those others have in mind for them.)

2367. Ọ̀mu ní ńgbé ọmu mì.
It is drunkenness that swallows [or drowns] a champion drinker. (Only an intrepid con-

testant can match another intrepid contestant.)

2368. Ọnà kì í dí mọ́ aládàà.
The path does not close on a man carrying a machete. (No problem is insoluble for a resourceful person.)

2369. Ọ̀ràn búburú kì í bá ikún nílé.
An evil event never finds the squirrel at home. (A statement that one will never be around when disaster occurs.)

2370. Ọ̀ràn fini dùgbẹ̀-dùgbẹ̀ yinni nù; ọ̀ràn fini dùgbẹ̀-dùgbẹ̀ bí ẹnipé kò ní í tán; ọ̀ràn ńbọ̀ wá tán; ojú á telégàn, a sì ti ẹni tí ńyọnusọ.
A problem shakes one up vigorously and lets one go; a problem shakes one up vigorously as though it will never end; the trouble will end, deflating the ill wishers and also those who will not mind their own business. (However terrible one's problems, they will cease and leave one in better shape than one's enemies would like.)

2371. Ọ̀rùn kì í wọ òsùká; ẹlérù lọrùn ńwọ̀.
The pad placed on the head to soften the friction of the load on the head does not suffer from the weight; the person carrying the load is the one whose neck suffers under the weight. (Commiserators and people lending a hand do not suffer the troubled person's pain; the troubled person is the one who bears it all.)

2372. Ọwọ́ atégùn ò ká gẹdú.
The wind is no match for timber. (Even powerful forces come up against objects they cannot move.)

2373. Ọwọ́ ẹni la fi ńtú ìwà ara ẹni ṣe.
One's own hands are what one uses to mend one's fortune. (Each person's fortune is in his or her own hands.)

2374. Ọwọ́ ẹni ni yó yòóni.
One hands are what feed one to satiation. (Your hands are your best resources.)

2375. Ọwọ́ ní ńtún ara ṣe.
The hands are the agents for grooming the body. (One's well-being is in one's hands.)

2376. Ọwọ́ tó dilẹ̀ là ńfi lérán.
It is on an idle hand that one rests one's chin. (It is when one has nothing to do that one engages in mischief.)

2377. Oyé ni yó kìlọ̀ fún onítòbí.
It is the harmattan that will teach the person who has only a loincloth a lesson. (People who do not provide for the rainy day will pay when the storm does come.)

P

2378. Pa á ní ńjẹ́ ogbé, tiiri ní ńje ọfà; bí a bá ta á ṣe là ńwá a; bí a ò bá wá a a dẹran ìdin.
A sharp report is what accompanies a machete wound; a flying motion is the characteristic of an arrow; if you hit your prey, you should go in search of it; if not, it becomes meat for maggots. (Always follow through in your pursuits.)

2379. Páńdòrò-ó já, ará rọ ìyá ẹ̀.
The fruit of the sausage tree drops, [and] its mother knows relief. (Relief is sweet after one's burden has been lifted.)

2380. Pà-pà lójú lẹ́ẹ̀kínní, pà-pà lójú lẹ́ẹ̀kejì: bójú náà ò bá fọ́, bàì-bàì ní ńdà.
A blow to the eye the first time and a blow to the eye a second time: if the eye does not go blind, it will see only dimly. (Continual attacks will eventually leave their mark on the victim.)

Ṣ

2381. *Ṣàngó ò lè pa igi ńlá.*
Ṣango cannot destroy a huge tree. (The substantial and well-established peron is better able to withstand adversity than weaklings.)

2382. *Ṣe kóo ní; àbá ò di tẹni; èèyàn ò ṣoògùn ọrò.*
Work in order to have; intentions do not become possessions; no one makes money by magic. (Labor, not idle thought, produces wealth.)

2383. *Ṣiṣe-é rorò, jíje òfé.*
Working is difficult; one would rather freeload. (Few people enjoy labor; all would like to live the good life for free.)

2384. *Ṣòkòtò gbọọrọ ò dọlà; abíni lÉkòó ò dowó.*
Long trousers do not amount to wealth; being born in Lagos does not ensure riches. (Wealth does not come from dressing well or living in a big city.)

2385. *Ṣòkòtò tí ńṣiṣẹ́ àrán, oko ní ńgbé.*
The pants that do the work that purchases the velvet fabric stay on the farm. (The real workers and producers of wealth are likely to be less in the public eye than their beneficiaries.)

T

2386. *Tàkúté tí yó pa Aláginjù á pẹ́ lóko kí wọ́n tó gbé e wálé.*
The snare that will capture the lord of the wilderness will stay long in the bush before returning home. (Whoever attempts the impossible is in for long frustration.)

2387. *Tàpò-tàpò là ńyọ jìgá; tewé-tewé là ńyan èkọ.*

With their sac and all is how to remove chiggers; with its wrapping-leaves is the way to buy corn meal. (One must do things thoroughly, not by halves.)

2388. *Tètè ègún ti lómi tẹ́lẹ̀ kójò tó rọ̀ sí i.*
The prickly spinach was succulent before the rain fell on it. (A statement that one does not depend on largesse from other people.)

2389. *Títa ríro là ńkọlà, bó bá jinná a di tẹni.*
Facial scarification causes with a great deal of pain; when it heals, its beauty becomes one's pride. (Good things come with some pain.)

2390. *Tojú tìyẹ́ làparò-ó fi ńríran.*
It is with both its eyes and its feathers that the partridge sees. (A statement that someone is all eyes.)

2391. *Tòsán tòru, imú ò gbélè; bó bá dákẹ́, a jẹ́ pé ó pin.*
Day or night, the nose does not rest; if it stops, that means the end. (Some things are so reliable that they never fail.)

W

2392. *Wàhálà ló bí ìrọra; òṣì ló bí wàhálà.*
Struggle gives birth to ease; destitution gives birth to struggle. (He who exerts himself will find ease in the end; he who avoids exertions is doomed to struggle in the end.)

2393. *Wèrè èèyàn ní ńru erù wòran; ẹní ru erù wòran ni wèrè èèyàn ńwò.*
Only an imbecile carries a heavy load and stops to watch a spectacle; such a heavily laden spectacle watcher is the sort of spectacle that attracts the attention of imbeciles. (Only a fool neglects pressing duties to dawdle.)

2394. *Wèrèpè ò níbìkan àgbámú; gbogbo ara ní ńfi-í jóni.*
The cow-itch offers no place to be handled; it stings with its whole body.[67] (Said of problems that present no visible means of solution, or people who show no visible signs of vulnerability.)

2395. *Wíwè là ńwè ká tó jàre oyé.*
Only by taking a cold shower can one shake off the chill of the harmattan. (The solution to a problem may require some initial unpleasantness.)

2396. *Wón ní, "Àparò aso eé se pón báyìí?" Ó ní ìgbà wo laso òun ò níí pón? Kóun tó ko igba láàárò, kóun tó ho ilè kùrè-kùrè lábùsùndájí. Ìgbà wo lòun ó ràáàyè foso?*
People asked the partridge, "Why is your clothing so dirty?" He responded, "Why would my clothing not be dirty? Given the time it takes me to make a hundred heaps in the morning, and the time I need to scratch the ground at dawn, what time is left for me to wash my clothes?" (The shiftless can always find excuses to explain their predicament. Compare 2616.)

Y

2397. *"Yán sí i, yán sí i" ní ńpa alákàrà lérìn-ín.*
"Sell more to me, sell more to me" is what brings smiles to the face of the bean-fritters seller. (Good fortune always makes people happy.)

2398. *Yànmù-yanmu là ńjògèdè.*
Gracelessly is the way one eats bananas. (Certain activities do not permit gracefulness.)

2399. *Yànmùyánmú ńse fújà láìlápa.*
The mosquito brags despite its lack of arms. (Insignificant pests can still be the source of considerable annoyance.)

2400. *Yí mi sébè, kí nyí o sí póró oko.*
Throw me on the heaps, and I will throw you into the furrows. (To whatever attack you mount against me, I will respond in kind.)

---

67. *Wèrèpè* (cow-itch) is *Mucuna flaggelipes* (Papilonaceae), a creeper whose seed pods are covered with fine stinging hairs. If one's skin comes in contact with the dry pods, the hairs attach to the skin, causing almost unbearable irritation — worse than poison ivy.

On consistency, honesty, openness, plain speaking, and reliability

A

2401. *A kì í pè é lẹ́rú, ká pè é lóbí.*
One does not call it a slave and also call it a child of the house. (One must be clear about one's attitude toward a thing or person; ambivalence causes trouble.)

2402. *A kì í pè é lẹ́rù ká pè é lọ́ṣọ̀ọ́.*
One does not call it a burden and also call it an adornment. (An event is either a boon or a disaster, never both.)

2403. *A kì í rí ẹsin ní ìso.*
One does not find a horse on tether. (Too easy and too convenient a find suggests stealing.)

2404. *A kì í rí i ká tún sọ pé a ò ri mọ́.*
One does not see a thing and then say one does not see it. (Always stand by your word.)

2405. *A kì í ró aṣọ ajé sídìí ká dájọ́ òdodo lẹ́bi.*
One does not wear the ritual loincloth for presiding over a trial-by-ordeal and judge the righteous guilty. (One must not violate the oath one is sworn to observe.)

2406. *A kì í so ẹran mẹ́ran kó kàn án pa.*
One does not tie a goat with another goat and keep one from butting the other to death. (One must not injure a person committed to one's protection.)

2407. *A kì í sọ̀rọ̀ ìkọ̀kọ̀ kó má diyàn ní gba-n-gba.*
One does not conspire in secret without having the matter eventually cause a public argument. (Whatever is done in secret soon becomes exposed.)

2408. *A kì í ṣe ẹléjọ́ ní "Ngbọ́?"*
One does not ask the main litigant, "How about it?" (Do not expect impartial witnessing from an interested party.)

2409. *Àbàtá pani; àbàtá pani; ká sá sọ pé odò-ó gbéni lọ.*
He died in the mire, he died in the mire; let us simply say that the person drowned. (One should prefer plain talk to euphemisms.)

2410. *Àbẹ̀tẹ́lẹ̀ ní ńfọ́jú onídàájọ́.*
It is bribery that blinds a judge. (Bribery beclouds judgment.)

2411. *Adánu tí ńjẹ ilá: ó ní "Ẹ ò rí ilẹ̀ báyìí?"*
Cleft-lipped person eating okro complains, "Can you believe what a mess the floor is?" (The culprit complains about a condition as though he or she had nothing to do with it.)[1]

2412. *Àdàpè olè ní ńjẹ́ àfọwọ́rá.*
It is simply a euphemism for theft to say *àfọwọ́rá* [literally, causing to disappear

---

1. Okro, because of its sliminess, is difficult enough for a person with no labial deformity to eat.

through the operations of the hand]. (The use of a euphemism does not change the nature of a thing. See the following entry and 2422.)

2413. Àdàpè olè ní ńjé "ọmọ-ọ̀ mi ńféwọ́."
It is a euphemistic description of stealing to say, "My child's hands are uncontrollably nimble." (One should face facts and not skirt them. Compare the preceding entry.)

2414. Àdàpè ọ̀rọ̀ ò jé ká mọ ìtumọ̀ orúkọ.
Riddling makes it impossible for one to know the meanings of names. (Circuitous talk can lead to confusion.)[2]

2415. Adétèé sọ̀rọ̀ méjì, o fikan purọ́; ó ní nígbàtí òún lu ọmọ òun lábàrá, òún ja léèékánná pàtì.
The leper said two things, one of them being a lie; he said after he had struck his child with his palm, he also pinched him severely with his fingernails. (One fools only oneself when one claims to have done the impossible.)

2416. A-dógbọ́n-pàgùntàn-je Ìlárá, ó ní ojú ẹ̀ ṁba òun lérù.
Person-who-schemes-to-kill-a-sheep-to-eat, native of Ìlárá, says that he is afraid of its eyes. (One should avoid dissembling. Compare 2446.)

2417. Afaségbèjò ńtan ara-a rè jẹ.
He who would collect rainwater in a sieve deceives himself. (The shiftless person hurts himself more than others.)

2418. Afatarénilójú, alè-e baále.
One-who-smears-one's-eyes-with-pepper: one's husband's concubine. (The illicit lover of a woman's husband is no friend of hers.)

2419. Afénilóbìnrin ò ro ire síni.
He-who-has-an-affair-with-one's-wife harbors no good will toward one. (One knows one's friends by their behavior.)

2420. Afikòkòjalè, bí ọba ayé ò rí ọ; tòrún rí ọ.
You-who-steal-in-secret, if an earthly king does not see you, the heavenly king sees you. (Nothing is hidden from God.)

2421. Afójú àjànàkú, kò mọ igi, kò mọ èèyàn.
A blind elephant does not know a man from a tree. (Fate is no respecter of persons.)

2422. Àfowọ́rá ní ńjẹ́ olè.
Employing-the-hands-to-make-things-disappear is called stealing. (Euphemistic circumlocution does not relieve a crime of its true nature. Compare 2412.)

2423. Agada ò morí alágbèdẹ.
The sword cannot tell the smith's head from others. (Natural justice does not play favorites.)

2424. Àgbàdo kì í ṣe èèyàn; ta ní ńrí ọmọ léhìn eèsún.
The maize plant is not human; whoever saw children on the back of elephant grass? (One should not overestimate the value of things.)[3]

---

2. People are likely to be cryptic in naming their children. The Yoruba give names that indicate the circumstances of the family, comment on the hopes of the family, or otherwise express its chief concerns at the time of the birth. Usually, of course, only those who are intimate with the family understand the full import of such names, because they are not always explicit.

---

3. When the maize plant develops fruits the Yoruba say Ó yọ ọmọ, "It is carrying a child." The literal expression does not, however, mean that the people believe the plant is human. Elephant grass is almost identical to maize in size and looks, even though it bears no fruit.

2425. *Àgbàká lodi ńgba ìlú.*
It is completely that a fortification wall encircles a town. (Brook no half measures.)

2426. *Àgbàká nigbà ńgba òpẹ.*
It is completely that the climbing rope encircles the palm tree. (What is worth doing at all is worth doing well; there will be no obstacle in the way of one's ventures.)[4]

2427. *Àgbẹ̀ gbóko rósù.*
A farmer stays on the farm and sees the moon. (The conscientious farmer spends long periods on the farm; persistence is the key to success.)

2428. *A-gbéjó-ẹnìkan-dájó, òsìkà èèyàn.*
He-who-decides-a-case-after-hearing-only-one-side [is] the dean of wicked persons. (Justice requires considering both sides of a case.)

2429. *Àgbọ́ìgbọ́tán Ègùn, ìjà ní ńdá sílẹ̀.*
Imperfect understanding of Ègùn [a language spoken to the west of Yoruba] brings nothing but dissension. (Half-knowledge is a bad thing.)

2430. *Àì-fẹ́-àlejòó-ṣe là ńwí pé "Ọ̀rẹ́ òrẹ́-ẹ̀ mí dé"; ká sáà ti wí pé, "Ọ̀rẹ́-ẹ̀ mí dé."*
Reluctance-to-extend-hospitality makes one say, "My friend's friend has arrived"; one should simply say, "My friend has arrived." (If one's friend's friend is one's friend, one should not stress that the friend is once removed; one should avoid doubletalk.)

2431. *Àìfẹsọ̀ké ìbòsí ni kò sẹ́é gbè.*
It is an alarm that is raised without moderation that finds no helpers. (If the person who raises an alarm puts people off by his

or her methods, they will not come to his or her aid.)

2432. *Ajá ní òun ìba má dèé oko rí òun ìbá sọ pé òrun ni wọ́n ti ńkálá wá.*
The dog says that if it had never been to a farm, it would have thought that okra came from heaven. (People are inclined to hoodwink the innocent or the ignorant.)

2433. *Ajá ti erée rẹ̀ẹ́ bá dánilójú là ńdẹ sí ehoro.*
It is a dog in whose speed one has faith that one sics on a hare. (One entrusts important tasks only to those one can trust. This is a variant of 726 and 729.)

2434. *Ajá tí ò létí ò sẹ́é dègbé.*
A dog without ears is no good for stalking prey. (A person who cannot be instructed is useless.)

2435. *Àjàlá, ta ní nà ọ́? Ìwọ náà kọ́ un?*
Àjàlá, who whipped you? It is none other than you, isn't it? (An evildoer is often also a dissembler.)

2436. *Àjànàkú kúro ni "A rí ńkan firí"; bí a bá rérin ká wí.*
The elephant is more than something of which one says, "I caught a fleeting glimpse of something"; if one saw an elephant, one should say so. (Don't hedge when discussing the obvious.)

2437. *A-jí-má-jẹ-ńkan, a-fàkàṣù-méfà-ṣoògùn-aràn.*
He-who-wakes-in-the-morning-and-eats-nothing; he-[who-]makes-a-wormer-of-six-loaves. (The deceitful person deceives himself.)[5]

---

4. *Igbà*, a thick rope made by braiding strips of palm bark, is used by palm-wine tappers to help them climb palm trees, much as lumberjacks use ropes.

5. A person who says his condition forbids eating but eats six loaves as a means of expelling worms is inconsistent and deceives no one.

2438. *Àjò àìwuniíyún là ńdÍfá sí.*
It is about a journey one does not want to make that one consults the oracle. (Where there is no desire, excuses are easy to find.)

2439. *A-kápò-má-ṣọdẹ: òtá ẹranko, òtá èèyàn.*
He-who-carries-a-hunting-bag-but-does-not-hunt: enemy alike of man and beast. (Be not a dog in the manger.)

2440. *Àkàsò faratilè faratilè; bí ẹni tí a fẹhìntì ó bàá yẹni a wí fúnni.*
A ladder rests on the ground and leans on the house; if the person one leans on must remove his support, he should give warning. (A person one trusts should be completely trustworthy.)

2441. *Akíni ńjé akíni; afinihàn ńjé afinihàn; èwo ni "Ọ kú, ará Ìjàyè!" lójúde Ògúnmọ́lá?*
A person who will greet one should greet one, and a person who will betray one should do so; what is the meaning of "Hello, Ìjàyè person!" before Ògúnmọ́lá's house?[6] (One should not do evil to others in the guise of being good to them.)

2442. *Ako asín kì í gbọ́ ohùn ọmọ-ọ rẹ̀ kó dúró; abiyamọ kì í gbọ́ ẹkún ọmọ-ọ rẹ̀ kó má tara sàsà.*
A male *asín* rat does not hear the cry of its young and remain still; a nursing mother does not hear the cry of her baby without responding anxiously. (One must take one's chief responsibilities seriously.)

2443. *Alákatampò ò mọ irú ẹran.*
The user of a crossbow does not know what sort of game he shoots at. (Some people lack a sense of discrimination. See the next entry.)

2444. *Alápatà ò mọ irú ẹran.*
The butcher does not know what the animal is. (A butcher is indifferent to the type of animal he butchers. See the foregoing entry.)

2445. *Amòrànbini Òyọ́, bí o bá gbé kete lérí, wọn a ní oko lò ńlọ tàbí odò.*
People-who-know-the-answer-yet-ask-the-question, natives of Òyọ́: if they see you carrying a water pot, they ask whether you are on your way to the farm or the stream. (If the answer is plain to see, one does not ask the question.)

2446. *Apajájẹ-ẹ́ ní ẹ̀rù adìẹ ńba òun.*
The-person-who-kills-and-eats-dogs claims to be afraid of chickens. (A hardened criminal pretends to have scruples about mere peccadilloes. Compare 2416.)

2447. *Apani kì í jẹ́ ká mú idà kojá nípàkọ́ òun.*
A murderer never permits the passage of a sword behind his skull. (The criminal is ever suspicious of other people's intentions.)

2448. *Àpèjúwe lalágbèdẹ ńrọ.*
The blacksmith manufactures from a description. (Unless a person speaks his or her mind, others cannot know what the person has in it.)

2449. *Ará Ìbàdàn kì í ságun; à ó rìn sẹ́hìn ni wọ́n ńwí.*
Ibadan people do not run from war; what they say is, "We will fall back a little." (There are ways of avoiding battle without seeming to do so.)

2450. *Arítẹnimòọ́wí, ó fi àpáàdì ràbàtà bo tirẹ̀ mọ́lè.*
He-who-eagerly-speaks-of-one's-problems covers his own with a huge potsherd. (People will talk about others' problems while carefully hiding their own.)

---

6. During the internecine Yoruba wars of the nineteenth century, Ògúnmọ́lá led Ibadan's forces in their war with Ìjàyè.

2451. Àrókanlẹ̀ lasọ ayaba; àwàkanlẹ̀ ni ti yàrà.
Wrapping-from-waist-to-the-floor is the style of the queen's wrapper; digging-down-to-the-deepest-bottom is the requirement of yàrà, the dry moat. (Whatever one has to do, one must be thorough and not satsified with half measures.)

2452. Arúgbó oǹdágbèsè, ó ní mélòó ni òun ó dùúró san níbè?
The old person who incurs debt says, how much of it will he be around to repay? (A person whose days are numbered can afford to take on long-term obligations.)

2453. Asárélówó ḿbẹ lónà ogun; Apòsẹ̀sẹ̀ ḿbẹ lónà èrò; Bó-pẹ́-títí-ng-ó-là ḿbẹ lábà, ó ńjẹ èsun isu.
He-who-hurries-after-riches is on his way to battle; He-who-has-in-abundance is off on his travels; By-and-by-"I-will-be-rich" is back in his hut, eating roasted yams. (Wealth comes to those who exert themselves, not to those who wait for it to find them.)

2454. Àsòròàìlàdí ló pa Elempe ìsáájú tó ní igbá wúwo ju àwo.
Speaking-without-explaining killed the first Elempe who said that calabash was heavier than china. (Excessive economy in speech leads to obscurity.)[7]

2455. Àsá ò gbádìẹ níkòkò; gba-n-gba làsá ńgbádìẹ.
The kite does not snatch chicks in secret; it snatches them openly. (What one dares to do, one does openly. Compare 1956.)

2456. Aseburúkú tẹsẹ̀ mọ́nà.
The evildoer makes a brisk exit. (The evildoer would not wait for his nature to catch up with him.)

2457. A-sòtún-sòsì-má-ba-ibìkan-jé, irọ́ la ó bàá níbè.
One-who-is-tight-with-the-right-and-tight-with-the-left-without-alienating-either: what one will find in that characterization is a lie. (There is no way to support both sides of a quarrel without betraying one side.)

2458. Àwárí lobìnrin ńwá nǹkan ọbè.
Seeking-until-finding is how a woman looks for ingredients for stew. (The dutiful person does not permit difficulties to keep her from accomplishing her duty.)

2459. Àwíyé ní ḿmú òràn yéni; òọ́dúnrún okùn la fi ńsin egbèta; bí a ò bá là á, kì í yéni.
Explicitness makes matters clear; it takes 300 strings to string 600; unless one explains it, no one understands. (Too much economy in speech leads to confusion.)[8]

2460. Àwíyé nIfẹ̀ ńfọ; gba-n-gba lOrò ńpẹran.
Explicitly is the way Ifẹ speaks; it is openly that Orò kills animals.[9] (Whatever one has to say, one should say without mincing words.)

2461. Àyè kì í há adìẹ kó má dèé ìdí àba-a rẹ̀.
The space is never so tight that a chicken will not be able to reach its incubating nest. (No obstacle should keep one from one's duty.)

---

7. The reference is to a certain character who came to grief by asserting the point without explaining that he was comparing a full calabash with an empty china plate.

8. The message is that it takes a string costing 300 cowries in the old currency to string 600 cowries.

9. The references are to the oracle at Ifẹ and to a religious mystery of the people that is audacious in claiming its victims.

B

2462. *Bí a bá ká okó mọ́ obìnrin nídìí á ní kùkú ni.*
If one catches a penis in a woman's vagina, she will argue that it is only a corncob. (Trust a woman to deny even the obvious.)

2463. *Bí a bá ńyọ́lẹ̀ dà, ohun abẹ́nú a máa yọ́ni ṣe.*
If one engages secretly in treachery, secret disasters come. (Crimes committed in secret do not go unrequited.)

2464. *Bí abẹ́rẹ́ bí abẹ́rẹ́ lèèyàn ńṣèké; ojọ́ tó bá tóbi tó okọ́ tí a fi ńroko ní ńpani.*
Like a needle, like a needle, one compiles falsehood; the day it is as big as the hoe one uses on a farm, that is the day it kills one. (Small falsehoods eventually grow into a habit powerful enough to kill.)

2465. *Bí ẹnú bá jẹ, ojú á tì.*
If the mouth has eaten, the eyes shut down. (If one has received some favor from a person, one's eyes will be closed to the person's faults.)

2466. *Bí ìgbín ńfà, ìkaraun a tẹ̀lé e.*
When the snail crawls, its shell follows. (The dependent person always sticks close to his or her support.)

2467. *Bí ìkà-á bá ńrojọ́, ìkà kọ́ ni yó da.*
If the wicked person states a case, it is not the wicked person who will judge it. (The wicked will not prevail in the face of impartial judges.)

2468. *Bí o fínú ṣìkà tí o fọde ṣòótọ́, ọba sẹ́ríkí á rín ọ rín ọ.*
If you hide wickedness inside you while displaying a kindly disposition, God above will laugh hard at you. (No secret act of wickedness is concealed from God.)

2469. *Bí o ní ọ̀pọ̀ oògùn, tí o ní èké, kò níí jé; orí ẹní jé ó ju ewé lọ; ìpín jà ó ju oògùn lọ.*
If you have a great deal of medicine and you are false, it will not work; one's head works better than any herb; one's destiny is far more effective than any medicine. (Evil intentions make one's medicine ineffective; the best hope lies in one's head and one's destiny.)[10]

2470. *Bí o rí i, wà pé o ò rí; okọ́ fún ọ lówó, àlé gbà á ná.*
If you saw it, you would say you did not; your husband gave you money and your lover spends it. (An unfaithful woman deserves no trust.)

2471. *Bí ó ti wù kó pẹ́ tó, olóòótọ́ ò níí sùn sípò ìkà.*
However long it takes, a truthful person will not wind up in the bed made for the wicked. (Whatever happens in the short run, in the long run the truthful person will be vindicated.)

2472. *Bí obìnrín bá máa dán èké wò, a da aṣọ dúdú bora.*
When a woman wishes to engage in mischief, she wears dark clothing. (A woman's furtiveness portends mischief.)

2473. *Bí ojú bá sé ojú; kí ohùn má yẹ ohùn.*
If eyes no longer see eyes, let the voice not miss the voice. (Though separated by distances, people should keep agreements they made.)

2474. *Bí olókùnrùn yó bàá kú, kó má purọ́ mọ́ àlapà; omitooro kì í korò.*
If an invalid is approaching death, he should not lie about the melon-seed loaf; stew is never bitter. (If one must make excuses for

---

10. For the Yoruba, *orí* (literally, "head") is the guardian of one's destiny.

one's flaws, one should make them plausible.)

2475. *Bí òru bí òru ní ńṣe alásọdúdú.*
Longing for nighttime, longing for nighttime is the tendency of the person in dark clothing. (A person engaged in secret business is always secretive.)

2476. *Bí ọgbọ́n bá tán nínú, a tún òmíràn dá.*
When an elder has exhausted all his wisdom, he turns to another's wisdom. (An elder is never at a loss for what to do.)

2477. *Bí ọmọdé bá mọ igbá-di-ogóje, kò lè mọ èrò-kò-wájà.*
If a youth knows two-hundred-becomes-one-hundred-forty, he cannot know traders-refuse-to-come-to-the-market. (A person who knows how to cheat those who deal with him will not know how to win them back when they refuse to deal with him.)

2478. *Bí ọmọdé bá ri oyin, a ju àkàrà nù.*
When a child sees honey, he throws away bean fritters. (The inconstant person's concern is limited to the latest attraction.)

D

2479. *Dúkìa tí a fi èrú kójọ kò mú ká dolówó.*
The treasure one gathers by foul means will not make one rich. (Wealth garnered unfairly does not last.)

E

2480. *"Ebí ńpa mí" ò ṣéé fífé wí.*
"I am hungry" is not a message that whistling can convey. (A person in need of help must not be coy or cryptic in asking for it.)

2481. *Eegun tí a bá so mọ́ ajá lọ́rùn, kì í ṣán an.*

A dog does not eat a bone tied to its neck. (One may not take advantage of a person or thing entrusted to one's care.)

2482. *Èké Ìbídùn, tí ńkí eégún "Kú àtijọ́."*
[It is a] lying Ìbídùn who greets a masquerader with "It's been quite a while!" (The subject of the comment [here named Ìbídùn] is prone to telling blatant lies.[11] Compare 3380.)

2483. *Èké lojú ó tì bó dọ̀la.*
The devious will reap shame in the future. (Wickedness will receive its just deserts in due time.)

2484. *Èké mọ ilé-e rẹ̀ ó wó; ọ̀dàlẹ̀ mọ tirẹ̀ ó bì dànù.*
The devious person builds a house, and it collapses; the treacherous person builds one, and it tumbles in ruins. (Evil people will not profit from their enterprises.)

2485. *Elékèé lèké ńyé; oun a bá ṣe ní ńyéni.*
Only a devious person knows what he or she is about; each person alone is privy to what he or she has done. (One can never be sure about a devious person. See also 4516.)

2486. *Eléwe-é ní iyènú; àìní mọ ìwà-á hù.*
A person who has children must be responsible; one who does not must know how to behave. (One should live up to one's responsibilities.)

2487. *Èlùbọ́ lo wáá rà; ọmọ ẹrán ṣe dénú igbá?*
You came to buy yam flour; how did a kid find its way into your calabash? (The alibi

---

11. Ìbídùn is a woman's name, and women are forbidden to confront masqueraders. Moreover, no one, male or female, is supposed to know the identity of the carrier of the masquerade except for the initiates of the *eégún* (*egúngún*) cult, usually men.

offered by a culprit [subject of the proverb] is full of holes.)

2488. *Èrò ò kí baálè, baálé ló ńkí.*
The guest does not pay homage to the chief, only to the host. (One's first obligation is to one's immediate benefactor, not to a remote authority, however great.)

2489. *Eṣinsín ńje Jagùnnà Àró ò gbó, Ọdòfin ò mò; ṣùgbón nígbàtí Jagùnnà ńje eṣinṣin Àró gbó, Ọdòfin-ín mò.*
When flies were eating [biting] the *Jagùnnà*, *Àró* heard nothing of it, and the *Ọdòfin* knew nothing of it; but when the *Jagùnnà* began to eat flies, *Àró* heard, and the *Ọdòfin* knew.[12] (People pay no attention to a victim's complaints but are quick to fault one who takes revenge.)

2490. *Etí, gbó èkejì kí o tó dájó.*
Ear, hear the other side before passing judgment. (One should not form an opinion after hearing only one side of an argument.)

2491. *Etí tó gbó àlọ ni yó gbòọ àbò.*
The same ears that heard about the departure will hear about the return. (Whoever is privy to the genesis of an affair will [must] be privy to its conclusion.)

2492. *Ewúrẹ́ ní òun ò mọlé odì; eni òún bá ṣè kó bi òun.*
The goat says it does not set aside any house as an enemy's; whoever it has offended should ask it why. (One wants no enemies; if one has offended anyone, that person should ask why.)

E

2493. *Ẹ̀èmejì letí ọlójà ńgbórò.*
The ears of the king hear everything twice. (Whoever will judge a case must hear it twice from both sides of the dispute.)

2494. *Egẹ́ ò ṣákìí; ẹní bá bọ́ sábẹ́-ẹ rẹ̀, a pa á kú pátá-pátá.*
The *egẹ́* trap never misses; whatever passes beneath it, it strikes dead.[13] (A certain person, or thing, can be relied upon to do what is expected of him, her, or it.)

2495. *Egbètàlá: bí a ò bá là á, kì í yéni.*
Egbètàlá: if one does not explain it, no one understands what it means. (Ambiguous statements result in confusion.)[14]

2496. *E-kòì-fẹ́-mi-kù, tó ta ajá-a rẹ̀ lókòó.*
You-have-not-seen-the-last-of-me, who sold his dog for 20 cowries. (A person duped without his or her knowledge will be back for redress once the fact dawns on him or her.)

2497. *Ẹ̀là lọrọ̀; bí a ò bá là á rírú ní ńrú.*
Statements must be clarified; if they are not, they become muddy. (Compare the following entry.)

2498. *Ẹ̀là lọrọ̀; bóbìnrín bá jókòó a laṣọ bòbò.*
Statements must always be clarified; when a woman sits, she covers her genitals with her wrapper.[15] (One must always be clear in

---

13. *Egẹ́* is a trap made of sharp spikes, designed to impale from above whatever trips it.

14. The word *egbètàlá* could be a contraction of either *igba métàlá* (2,600) or *ẹgbàá métàlá* (26,000).

15. The second part about a woman's genitals is gratuitous flippancy; it takes advantage of the syllable *là* (in *Ẹ̀là*), which means "clarify" and also denotes the action of passing one's loincloth between one's thighs so as to cover the genitalia.

---

12. *Jagùnnà*, *Àró*, and *Ọdòfin* are all chieftaincy titles.

one's speeches or intentions. This is a variant of the preceding entry.)

2499. *Ẹlẹ́rìí ní ńyanjú ẹjọ́; ẹlẹ́rìí kì í ṣe elégbè.*
It is a witness that clears up a case; a witness is not a partisan. (People called to bear witness in a case should be impartial.)

2500. *Ẹni a kò fẹ́ nilé-e rẹ̀ ńjìnna lójú ẹni.*
It is a person one does not love whose house is distant in one's estimation. (One can always find an excuse for not doing what one does not wish to do.)

2501. *Ẹní bá sùn là ńjí, a kì í jí apirọrọ.*
One wakes only those that sleep, not those pretending to sleep. (Deal with people who are in earnest, not with gamesters.)

2502. *Ẹní gbé àrùn pamọ́ kojá ore oníṣègùn.*
Whoever conceals a disease is beyond help from a doctor. (People in need of help should not conceal the fact.)

2503. *Ẹni tí a nà ní kùmmọ̀ méfà, tó ní òkan ṣoṣo ló ba òun, níbo nìyókùú sọnù sí?*
[If] a person is hit six times with a club and says only one blow landed, where did the other blows disappear? (A person who tries to minimize obvious misfortune deceives no one.)

2504. *Ẹni tí ó bá máa jẹ́ Ọ̀ṣákálá a jẹ́ Ọ̀ṣákálá; ẹni tó bá máa jẹ́ Òṣokolo a jẹ́ Òṣokolo; ẹwo ni Ọ̀ṣákálá-ṣokolo?*
Whoever wants to be known as Ọ̀ṣákálá should be known as Ọ̀ṣákálá; whoever wants to be known as Òṣokolo should be known as Òṣokolo; what is the meaning of Ọ̀ṣákálá-ṣokolo? (One should make up one's mind to be one way or the other and not keep straddling fences.)

2505. *Ẹni tí ó bá mọ ìṣe òkùnkùn, kó má dàá òṣùpá lóró; ohun a ṣe ní ńmúni-í rìnde òru; òkùnkùn ò yẹ ọmọ èèyàn.*
Whoever knows what darkness can do must not antagonize the moon, [since] one's actions [sometimes] send one abroad at night; roaming around in the dark is not a becoming habit. (It is best to cultivate those forces that might serve one well in the future.)

2506. *Ẹni tí ó fẹ́ẹ́ kúure, kó hùwà rere.*
Whoever wishes to die a decent death, let him or her live decently. (As one lives, so one dies, and so one is remembered.)

2507. *Ẹni tí ó gbépo lájà ò jalè bí ẹni tó gbà á sílẹ̀ fún un.*
The person who removes oil from the rafter is less a thief than the person who helps him set it on the floor. (The abettor is more a culprit than the perpetrator.)

2508. *Ẹni tí ó gbọ́n tó ńpurọ́; ẹni tó mòràn tó ńṣèké; ẹni tó mò pé nnkan ò sí tó ńtọrọ; ẹwo ló sàn nínú àwọn métẹ̀ẹ̀ta?*
The person who is wise and yet lies, the person who knows the truth and yet dissembles, the person who knows one has nothing and yet asks for something: which is any good among the three? (The liar, the dissembler, and the one who would embarrass you are all equally evil.)

2509. *Ẹni tí ó sá là ńlé.*
People chase only those who flee. (Those who act as though they are guilty are presumed to be guilty.)

2510. *Ẹni tí ó sùn tó ní òún kú, tó bá jí, ta ni yó wìí fún?*
The person who is asleep but spreads the word that he or she is dead, when he or she awakens, whom will he or she tell? (If one

paints oneself into a corner, one is truly stuck.)

2511. Ẹni tí ó ṣe ojú kò da bí ẹni tó ṣe èhìn.
The person who honors one in one's presence is nothing like the person who honors one in one's absence. (It is what people say of you or do on your behalf in your absence that matters.)

2512. Ẹnìkan kì í yọ̀ kí ilẹ̀ ó ṣẹ́.
When a person slips, the earth may not deny responsibility or knowledge. (For whatever one does, one should be willing to accept responsibility.)

2513. Ẹnu òpùrọ́ kì í sẹ̀jẹ̀.
The liar's mouth does not bleed. (Lies have no telltale labels attached.)

2514. Ẹnu-u rẹ̀ ní ńdá igba, tí ńdá ọ̀ọ́dúnrún.
His or her mouth is the same one that proposes two hundred and proposes three hundred. (An unreliable person's mouth is ever running, and what comes out of it is not to be trusted.)

2515. Ẹran tí a kì í jẹ, a kì í fi ehín pín in.
Meat that one does not eat, one does not bite into with one's teeth. (One should be unequivocal in one's commitments or avoidances.)

2516. Ètàn kì í ṣe ogbọ́n.
Deceit is no wisdom. (Deceit is not a reliable strategy to count on.)

2517. Ẹ̀wà yí kò dùn, ẹ̀wà yí kò dùn, àáṣó ìpàkọ́ ḿmì tìtì.
These beans are not delicious, these beans are not delicious, yet the coiffure at the occiput is shaking vigorously. (A person's actions toward a person or thing belie his or her detracting comments; if one claims to dislike something or someone, one's actions should not say the opposite. Compare 2590.)

2518. Ẹyẹlé ní òun ò lè bá olúwa òun jẹ, kí òun bá a mu, kí ó di ojọ́ ikú-u rẹ̀ kí òun yẹrí.
The pigeon says it cannot share its owner's food and drink, and then, when the day of his death arrives, ducks its head. (If one shares the good times with a person, one should be prepared to share the bad times also.)

F

2519. Fi inú ṣìkà, fi òde ṣòótọ́; ẹni tí ḿbini kò níí sàì bini.
Hide wickedness in you and affect a benevolent comportment; the one who calls people to account will not forget. (God sees all hidden acts of wickedness and metes out punishment to their perpetrators.)

Gb

2520. Gba-n-gba là ńṣe gbàǹgbà; bẹ́sín bá kú, ìta gbangba là ńsin í sí.
One performs one's great feats in the open; if a horse dies, one buries it in a wide-open space. (One should not attempt to keep weighty matters under wraps.)

2521. Gba-n-gba làsá ńta.
The hawk always spreads its wings to the fullest. (Whatever one has in mind, one should lay it out fully in the open.)

2522. Gba-n-gba lÒgèdè̀ǹgbé ńṣawo.
Ògèdèǹgbé always performs his rituals in the open. (A great person need not hesitate to do whatever he or she has a mind to do.)[16]

---

16. Ògèdèǹgbé was a late-nineteenth-century Ìjẹ̀sà warrior during the internecine Yoruba wars of the period.

2523. *Gbogbo wa la fòkété san ọgófà; ìgbà tí*
òkété ó fi di ogóje, ojú-u gbogbo wa ni yó ṣe.
We all agreed on 120 cowries as the value of
the bush rat; when the value changes to 140,
we must all know about it. (No subgroup
has the right to alter in secret the decisions
the whole group has arrived at.)[17]

I

2524. *Ìbáà tínrín, okùn òtítọ́ kì í já; bí irọ́ tó*
ìrókò, wíwó ní ńwó.
Even if it is flimsy, the thread of truth never
snaps; even though a lie might have the girth
of an *ìrókò* tree, it inevitably crashes. (Truth
will inevitably triumph over lies.)

2525. *Ibi tí a ti na ọmọ ọba là ḿbèrè, a kì í*
bèrè ibi tí ọmọ ọbá ti pọ́n légbèẹ́.
What one should ask is where the prince
was attacked and flogged; one does not ask
where the prince got the welts on his side.
(When matters require urgent attention, one
should not speak in riddles or prevaricate.)

2526. *Igbó kannáà lọde ńdẹ.*
It is in the same forest that a hunter hunts
[or all hunters hunt]. (One should stick to
that which one knows. Or, the manners and
behaviors of members of a fraternity should
be consistent and uniform.)

2527. *Ìjòkó là ḿbá eèbà.*
The oil pot is ever found in a sitting position. (The constancy of the pot is worth
emulating.)

2528. *Ìkòkò kì í ṣelé ìgbín; ṣe ló dè ìgbín mọ́lẹ̀.*
The pot is no shelter for the snail; all it does

is trap the snail. (One should not try to
pass off as a favor an injury one is causing a
person.)

2529. *Ilé ahun ò gba ahun; òdèdè ahun ò*
gbàlejò; ahún kọ́lé ẹ̀ tán ó yọ òdèdè níbàdí.
The tortoise's house is not large enough for
it; the tortoise's porch is not large enough
to receive visitors; the tortoise built its
house and adds a porch at the rear. (The
miser never has enough to share with
others.)[18]

2530. *Ìlú tí a bá rè là ḿbá pé.*
The citizens one goes abroad with are those
in whose ranks one remains. (One should
not desert one's colleagues midway through
an enterprise.)

2531. *Ìmàlé gbààwẹ̀ ó lóun ò gbétọ́ mì; ta ní*
ńṣe ẹlẹ́rìí fún un?
The Muslim fasts and swears he did not
swallow his saliva; who is to corroborate his
story? (There is no point is paying attention
to a claim that cannot be verified.)

2532. *Ìmàlé sọ̀rọ̀ òjó kù, ó ní Ọlọ́run-ún jẹ́rìí*
òun.
The Muslim says something and thunder
rumbles; he says the Almighty is corrobo-
rating his statement. (Said of someone who
claims a neutral occurrence as evidence
support for his or her position.)

2533. *Ìmùlẹ̀ ò gbọdọ̀ tan ara wọn jẹ; ìmọ̀*
ẹnìkan ò yàn.
Those who enter into a covenant must not
betray one another; one person's counsel is
not enough by itself. (One must not break
covenants.)

---

17. The amounts stated here were considerable before the English colonizers imposed their own currency
and also a conversion rate that drastically devalued
people's wealth.

18. *Ahun,* the tortoise, is a designation also applied
to miserly people. The "porch" is the overhang of the
shell above the tortoise's tail.

2534. *Ìpépérè ìgò méje; bí kò bá pé méje ara kì í gbà á.*
Seven trifling bottles; fewer than seven and one cannot endure the thought. (If a matter is really of no importance, one should not dwell on it.)

2535. *Iró ni "Má jèénìkan ó gbó"; òótó ni "Eni o rí o bi."*
"Breathe not a word of it to anyone" denotes a lie; "Ask anyone you please" indicates the truth. (It is a only a lie that one wants no witness to; one will gladly proclaim the truth.)

2536. *Ìrókò tó bá gbàbòdè, bíbé ni.*
Whichever *ìrókò* tree becomes involved in treachery gets felled. (Whoever engages in treachery will be destroyed, no matter his or her status.)

J

2537. *"Jé kí nfìdí hé e."-é gbàjòkó; àfòmó di onílé.*
"Permit me to perch by you" takes the whole seat; the parasite becomes the host. (Said of people who take over by wiles what belongs to others.)

K

2538. *Kí a baà lè pé níbè, abuké ní bí òun bá kú, kí wón ti èhìn tú ìfun òun.*
Just to delay people deliberately, the hump-back says when he dies his intestines should be removed from the back. (Said of people resorting to transparent delaying tactics.)

2539. *Kí á gà, kí á gò, èdè ni ò yédè.*
Sitting and refusing to budge from one's position results from lack of communica-

tion. (It is when people fail to compromise that problems defy solution.)

2540. *Kí á rí ká rà, ká rà ká má san: à-rà-àì-san èkejì olè.*
To see and buy, to buy and not pay: buying without paying [is] the twin of stealing. (One should pay for whatever one buys. Compare the following entry.)

2541. *Kí olówó wá, kí aláwìn wá; à-rà-àì-san ni ò sunwòn.*
Let the purchaser with cash come, and let the purchaser on credit come; only buying without [eventually] paying is bad. (What is important is not so much when but that one fulfill one's obligation. Compare the preceding entry.)

2542. *"Kò dùn mí, kò dùn mí"; àgbàlagbà ńbú opa léèmefà nítorí iyán àná.*
"I am not upset, I am not upset!" Yet a grown man swears angrily six times because of last night's pounded yam. (A person's protestation of indifference is belied by agitated behavior.)

2543. *Kò jo agbe kò jo olè tí ńsúfèé yàgbàdo; bí kò bá bá mi a di olè; bó bá bá mi a di onílé.*
It-is-not-begging-and-it-is-not-stealing who whistles as he harvests corn ears: if he does not come upon me, it becomes stealing; if he comes upon me, it becomes [the action of] a member of the household. (Said of a person who secretively takes something from a relative instead of asking openly for it.)[19]

---

19. The idea is that the person goes secretively to a relative's farm to harvest some corn and whistles while doing so in order to give the impression that he or she is carefree because not doing anything wrong. If the owner of the farm does not come upon the person, then the action goes down as stealing; if the farmer does come, the person will claim the rights of a relative.

2544. *Kò sí ohun tí a ò lè fi òru ṣe; ẹrù òsán là ḿbà.*
There is nothing one cannot do in the dead of night; the light of day alone is what one fears. (The cover of darkness is a perfect protection for any sort of enterprise.)

2545. *Kò ṣeku kò ṣeyẹ ò jẹ́ kí àjàò sanwó òde.*
Being neither a rat nor a bird keeps *àjàò* (a birdlike animal) from having to pay poll tax. (It is impossible to be really sure of a person who will not commit to any side in a dispute.)

M

2546. *Má sèẹ́ kí òràn má pò.*
Do not deny your responsibility; that way the problem will be minimized. (Refusing to accept one's responsibility only aggravates one's difficulties.)

2547. *"Mo kò ó" kì í ṣe àìní àpèjúwe.*
"I met him" is an incomplete statement without further elaboration. (One should say enough to make one's message understood.)

N

2548. *Nì palaba, ní wonko, ẹrẹkẹ́ á sèkan.*
Either sunken or swollen, the cheeks will be one or the other. (If one is not one way, one must be the other way; one cannot be no way at all.)

2549. *Nígbàti ọwọ́ ò tẹ ìjàdù là ńní kò sí ohun tí à ńjẹ tí kì í tán.*
It is when one has come up empty in a scramble for food that one says there is nothing one eats that is not finished sooner or later. (An affectation of indifference is often disguised disappointment.)

O

2550. *"Ó fò sókè ó pẹ́ títí," irọ́ ló ńpa.*
"He jumped up and stayed aloft almost forever": that is a lie. (One should control the urge to exaggerate.)

2551. *Ó jọ gàtè, kò jọ gàtè, ó fẹsẹ̀ méjèèjì tiro rìn.*
It may seem like staggering, and it may not seem like staggering, but he is tipping forward on tiptoes. (A euphemism does not make an action anything other than what it is.)

2552. *O kò pọ̀ ọ́, béẹ̀ni o ò gbé e mì.*
You do not spit it out, and yet you do not swallow it. (Said of a person who will neither accept nor reject a proposition.)

2553. *"Ó mọ́ mi lọ́wọ́" ní ńdi olè.*
"It is an exact fit for my hand" leads to thievery. (One should not grow too attached to other people's possessions.)

2554. *O mú oori lọ́wọ́ ọ̀tún, o mú kùùmọ̀ lọ́wọ́ òsì, o ní kí Orímáfọ́ọ̀ wá gba oúnjẹ.*
You hold corn loaf in your right hand and hold a cudgel in your left hand, and you call to Orímáfọ́ọ̀ to come take the food from you. (If one wishes to entice a person, one should not adopt a threatening posture.)[20]

2555. *Ó ńṣe apá kúlú-kúlú bí ẹni ká gbé e jó, ó sì ńṣenu hàmù-hàmù bí èyí tí yó gbèéni mì.*
It wiggles its arms as though it would have one dance with it, and yet it is working its mouth as though it would swallow one. (Said of a person who mixes friendly gestures with threatening ones.)

2556. *Ó pẹ́ títí ni "A-bẹnu-bí-ẹnu-òbo"; ká sá sọ pé, "Ìwọ Lámọnrín, òbo ni ọ́."*

---

20. *Orímáfọ́ọ̀* means "Let not the skull crack."

It is mere circumlocution to say, "A person has a mouth like a fool's"; one should rather say, "You, so-and-so, you are a fool." (Be confident enough to speak without hedging.)

2557. *Ó ta ọfà sókè, ó ṣí odó borí.*
He shot an arrow toward the sky and covered his head with a mortar. (Said of a person who causes problems and goes into hiding, leaving others to suffer the consequences.)

2558. *Obì-í bọ́ lọ́wọ́ alákẹdun ó ní òún fún ará ilẹ̀; bí kò fún ará ilẹ̀, yó sọkalẹ̀ wá mú u?*
Kola nut drops from the grip of a monkey, which says it makes a gift of the nut to ground dwellers; if it does not make a gift of it to ground dwellers, would it come down to fetch it? (One can tell when necessity is being disguised as virtue.)

2559. *Obìnrin abàlèméfà: àlè méfà ò mọ ara wọn.*
A woman who has six lovers: the six lovers never know about one another. (Women are past mistresses of deceit.)

2560. *Obìnrín bímọ fúnni kò pé kó má pani; obìnrin ò bímọ fúnni kò pé kó má pani.*
That a woman has had your child does not mean she cannot kill you; that a woman has not had your child does not mean she may not kill you. (Intimacy is no protection against a woman.)

2561. *Obìnrín pẹ́ lọ́jà ó fìgbójú wọlé.*
A woman who tarried too long at the market returns home with a brazen face. (An offender will try to ward off criticism by first going on the offensive.)

2562. *Obìnrín re ilé àlè, ó fi ilé ìyá ẹ̀ tan ọkọ jẹ.*
A woman goes to her lover's house and uses

her mother's home to deceive her husband. (Legitimate pursuits ofen serve as cover for illegitimate ones.)

2563. *Odídẹrẹ́ ẹyẹ òkun, àlùkò ẹyẹ ọ̀sà; bí a bá jẹun gbé, ká má jẹ́ẹ̀ún gbé.*
The parrot is a bird of the sea, and the kingfisher a bird of the lagoon; even though we may forget that we once partook of the food, let us never forget what we covenanted. (However far we may roam, and however long, we should never forget promises made.)

2564. *Òfiífií là ńrí, a ò rí òkodoro; òkodoro ṁbọ̀, baba gba-n-gba.*
All we see is shadows, not clarity; but clarity will come, father of all openness. (The truth may be long hidden, but in the end it will emerge into the open.)

2565. *Ògèdèṁgbé iró kì í dáni síyẹ̀wù; gba-n-gba ní ńdáni sí.*
An audacious lie does not trip one in one's closet; it exposes one in a public place. (One's transgressions are likely to catch up with one in the most embarrassing circumstances.)

2566. *Ohun tí a ò fẹ́ kéèyàn ó mọ̀ là ńṣe lábẹ́lẹ̀.*
It is what one wishes to keep a secret that one does in private. (One who has nothing to hide should not do things in secret.)

2567. *Ojo díẹ̀, akin díẹ̀; ìyà ní ńkó jẹni.*
A little cowardice [or] a little bravery: all it brings one is trouble. (One should decide whether one will be bold or cowardly; inconsistency in such matters results in suffering.)

2568. *Òjò ògànjọ́ ò pa ẹni rere; bí kò pa jalè-jalè a pa yíde-yíde.*
A midnight rain does not beat a decent person; if the person it beats is not a habitual

thief, he or she will be a habitual [night] wanderer. (Honest people are seldom caught in compromising positions.)

2569. *Ojú gba-n-gba là ńta awọ gbà-ǹ-gbà.*
It is out in the open that one spreads a huge skin. (A matter that is of great consequence to all should be discussed in the presence of all.)

2570. *Ojú kì í fẹ́nikù kó hu ibi.*
The eyes do not, because they do not see one, engage in evil against one. (Never take advantage of people's absence to do them ill.)

2571. *Ojú lobìnrín mọ̀.*
Women know only the face. (The only time one can rely on women is when one is present.)

2572. *Ojú lọ̀rọ̀-ọ́ wà.*
Discourse is in the eyes. (Look the person with whom one is holding a dialogue in the eyes.)

2573. *Ojú olóbì la ti ńjèrè obì.*
It is in the presence and with the knowledge of the kola-nut seller that one receives a gratuitous addition to one's purchase.[21] (If one has a right to something, one should not take it surreptitiously.)

2574. *Ojú tó ti mọni rí kì í wípé òun ò mọni mọ́.*
The eyes that used to recognize us cannot say they no longer recognize us. (Whatever happens, one should not refuse to acknowledge one's friends.)

2575. *Òkété, báyìí nìwà ẹ: o báFá mulẹ̀ o daFá.*

So, giant bush rat, such is your character: you made a pact with Ifá and you betrayed Ifá. (An address to a person whom you trusted but who has betrayed you.)[22]

2576. *Òkété ní ọjọ́ gbogbo lòún mọ̀, òun ò mọ ọjọ́ mìíràn.*
The large bush rat says it knows every day but not some other day. (If one makes a promise, it should be firm and definite, not vague.)

2577. *Òkóbó kì í bímọ sítòsí.*
The eunuch never has children close by. (The person who has something to hide will always offer outlandish explanations.)[23]

2578. *Olófòófó ò gbẹ́gbàá; ibi ọpẹ́ ní ḿmọ.*
The tattler does not earn six pence; thanks are all he gets. (Tattling is not a profitable or appreciated habit.)

2579. *Olóòótọ́ ìlú nìkà ìlú.*
The honest person in a town is the ogre of the town. (Honesty seldom makes one popular.)

2580. *Olóòótọ́ kì í sùn sípò ìkà.*
The honest person will not sleep in the place prepared for the wicked person. (The honest person will in the end be vindicated.)

2581. *Òṅrorò lègbọ́n òfófó.*
Lack of compassion is the elder of back-biting. (A person who lacks compassion will think nothing of spreading false news about others.)

---

21. Sellers often gave purchasers some extra as a sweetener, or gratuity.

22. Giant bush rats love palm kernels, and these are also used in Ifá divination; the rat is apparently raiding Ifá's preserve when it gathers them.

23. In a bid to conceal his calamity the eunuch will always claim that he has fathered several children but that they live far, far away.

2582. *"Orí jẹ́ kí mpé méjì" obìnrin ò dénú.*
"May my head grant that I have a partner"
as a woman's prayer is not sincere. (People
often pay lip service to concepts they do not
believe in.)[24]

2583. *Òtítọ́ dójà ó kùtà; owó lọ́wọ́ là ńra èké.*
Truth arrives at the market but finds no
buyer; it is with ready cash, though, that
people buy falsehood. (People appreciate
falsehood more than truthfulness.)

2584. *Òtítọ́ kì í kú ká fi irọ́ joba.*
The truth does not die to be replaced as king
by the lie. (The lie cannot match the truth in
esteem.)

2585. *Òtítọ́ kì í sìnà; irọ́ ní ńforí gbogbé.*
Truth never goes awry; it is falsehood
that earns a gash on the head. (Truth will
not bring misfortune; falsehood leads to
trouble.)

2586. *Òtítọ́ korò; bí omi tooro nirọ́ rí.*
Truth is bitter; falsehood is like meat stew.
(It is more difficult to be truthful than to
lie.)

2587. *Òtítọ́ lolórí ìwà.*
Truthfulness is the chief of attributes. (There
is no better attribute than truthfulness.)

2588. *Òtítọ́ ní ńtú ẹrù ìkà palẹ̀.*
It is truth that unpacks the load of the
wicked for all to see. (Truth will triumph
over the wicked.)

2589. *Owó lobìnrín mọ̀.*
Women care only about money. (Whatever
women do, they do only for money.)

---

24. The reference is to a woman's co-wife.

Ọ

2590. *Ọbẹ̀-ẹ́ dùn, ọbẹ̀ ò dùn, iyán tán nígbá.*
The stew is delicious, the stew is not delicious; the pounded-yam meal is completely
gone from the dish. (Said of people who
complain about something yet will not let
go of it. Compare 2517.)

2591. *Òkánkán là ńṣe ibí; ikòkò là ńṣe ìmùlẹ̀;
bí a tójú ìmùlẹ̀ tán, ká tójú ibí pẹ̀lú; bí a bá
kú ará ẹni ní ńsinni.*
One conducts affairs with one's kin with
forthrightness; one enters into covenants
[with nonrelatives] in secret; as one attends
to one's secret compacts, one should also
attend to affairs with one's kin; on the day
one dies, it is one's kin who attend to the
funeral. (Never neglect your relatives in
favor of others.)

2592. *Ọmòrán bèèrè òràn wò; Àjàpá ní, "Ẹni
tí wọ́n pa lánàá, kàà kú tán?"*
The sage asks for information; Àjàpá the
trickster asks, "About the person who was
killed yesterday, is he already dead?" (If you
know the answer to a question already, don't
ask it.)

2593. *Ònà irọ́ kì í pẹ́ẹ́ pin.*
The path of deceit soon ends. (Deceit is soon
exposed.)

2594. *"Òràn yí ò dùn mí": èèkanṣoṣo là ńwí i.*
"This matter does not hurt me": stating it
only once suffices. (If one is indifferent to
something, it should not dominate one's
conversations.)

2595. *Òrò ìkòkò, ní gba-n-gba ní ńbò.*
Secret matters have open exposure as their
ultimate destination. (Whatever is done in
secret will eventually be brought to light.)

2596. *Òrò ò pariwo.*
The matter in question does not make a

noise. (The matter under discussion poses little problem.)

2597. Ọ̀tá ẹni kì í pòdù òyà.
One's enemy never kills a huge cane rat. (One is always tempted to minimize the accomplishments of one's enemies.)

P

2598. Pàkìtí ṣe bí òkú wọlú; labalábá ṣe bí eye jáko.
The coarse mat enters the town like a corpse; the butterfly enters the bush like a bird.[25] (Said of people who appear to be what they are not.)

2599. Pátá-pátá là ńfójú, kùmbò-kumbo là ńdẹ́tẹ̀; ojú à-fọ́-ì-fọ́-tán ìjà ní ńdá sílẹ̀.
One's blindness should be absolute, and one's leprosy should pervade the whole body; half-blindness only brings dissension. (One's condition should be definite, not ambiguous or undetermined. See also the next entry.)

2600. Pátá-pátá leégún ńfaso borí.
It is completely that the masquerader covers his head with his shroud. (One must be thoroughgoing in whatever one does. Compare the preceding entry.)

2601. Pẹ̀hìndà kí o ríṣe èké, fara pamọ́ kí o rí bí aṣeni ti ńṣo.
Turn your back, and you will discover how the deceitful person behaves; hide, and you will find out what the detractor is saying. (If one could surprise them, one would discover the true nature of one's enemies.)

25. Corpses are carried on the head when being brought home from the farm or some other place; mats are also usually wrapped up and carried on the head.

2602. Pípọn niyì idẹ; èjẹ́ niyì oògun.
Redness is the glory of brass; efficaciousness is the glory of medicine. (Truth to one's nature and fulfillment of one's obligations are the determinants of one's worth.)

2603. Pòngbà-pongba là ńbá odi.
Firmly planted and unshakable is the way one finds the city fortification. (An injunction to be firm and unshakable.)

2604. Puro kóo níyì; bí a bá jáni tán, ètẹ́ ní ńdà.
Lie and become renowned; once you have been found out, the result is disgrace. (The glory that results from deceit does not last.)

R

2605. Rìkíṣí pa wọ́n pò wọ́n dọ̀rẹ́; kò lójó kò lósù òrẹ́ bàjẹ́.
Intrigue brought them together and they became friends; it did not take days, let alone months, before the friendship ended. (People united in friendship by intrigue soon become enemies.)

2606. Rìkíṣí pin, alábòsí lọ.
When the intrigue is terminated, the devious person takes his leave. (When the intrigue is exposed, the career of the devious person is over.)

S

2607. Sàráà baba ẹbọ.
Alms are the ultimate sacrifice. (It is blessed to give alms.)

Ṣ

2608. Ṣìgìdì ò lẹ́nu fọhùn; iró ńpuró fúnrọ́.
The earthen idol has no mouth to speak; lies

are lying to lies.[26] (One should not be fooled by people who, for example, offer to reveal one's future.)

2609. *Ṣìgìdì tí ò sọ̀rọ̀, a ò mẹni tí ńgbè.*
[Since] the earthen idol does not speak, no one knows whose side it is on. (No one can ascribe any position to a person who is cagey.)

T

2610. *Ta là bá rí báwí bí ẹní fọmọ fọ́kọ lóru, tí ò jẹ́ kílẹ̀ mọ́?*
Whom should one blame, if not the person who delivered a child to a husband in the middle of the night without waiting until daylight? (The person to blame in the event of a preventable problem is the one whose thoughtless action causes it.)

2611. *Ta la domi sí lára? Ta lòrìṣà ńgùn?*
Who is the one on whom water was poured? Who is the one being mounted by the god? (The person receiving all the attention cannot pretend not to be the one in need of attention.)

2612. *Ta lẹsinsin ìbá gbè bí kò ṣe elégbò?*
Who else will the flies flock after if not the person with open sores? (Opportunistic people can be expected to stick with those who offer them the most benefits.)

2613. *Ta ló dè ọ́ tí ò ńkakọ?*
Who has tied you down and thus forced you to confess your guilt? (Said to stop the mouths of people who protest too much as a result of a guilty conscience.)

2614. *Ta ní ńṣoògùn lódò tí lábẹ-lábẹ ò gbọ́?*
Who is concocting a medicine by the river about which the *lábẹlábẹ* plant is ignorant? (Trying to keep someone in the dark about a matter is futile.)[27]

W

2615. *"Wá jẹun." "Ng ò jẹ." Ó fọgọ́rùn-ún òkèlè tọ́ ọbẹ̀ wò.*
"Come join me at my meal." "Thank you, but no." Still he eats a hundred mouthfuls, just to taste the stew. (If you intend to decline an invitation, match your action to your words.)

2616. *Wọ́n ní, "Àwòko, o bú ọba." Ó ní ìgbà wo lòún ráàye bú ọba, kóun tó kọ igba lówùúrọ̀, igba lọ́sàn-án, igba lálẹ́, kóun tó fi àyìndà-yindà lù ú?*
They said, "Mockingbird, you are accused of insulting the king." It asked, when would it have time to insult the king, seeing that it must sing two hundred songs in the morning, two hundred in the afternoon, and two hundred at night, mixing it all up with some frolicsome notes? (The person in trouble will resort to ludicrous alibis to escape punishment. Compare 2396.)

2617. *Wọ́n ní kárúgbó gba ọmọ pọ̀n, ó ní ṣe bí wọ́n mọ̀ pé òun ò léhín; wọ́n ní kó pa ọmọ jẹ ni?*
The old woman is asked to carry a child on her back, and she says but they know she has no teeth; was she asked to eat the child? (Said of people whose comment on a proposition is wildly irrelevant.)

---

26. The proverb refers to the use of earthen idols as divination mediums.

27. The plant is presumably an ingredient in the medicine anyway.

On consideration, kindness,
and thoughtfulness

A

2618. *A kì í dùbúlẹ̀ ṣubú.*
One does not fall from a prone position.
(Hunger cannot make one faint and fall if
one goes to sleep.)

2619. *A kì í fi àìmọ̀nà dá pàdé-m̀-pàdé.*
One does not play the rendezvous game
without knowing one's way. (One should
not enter into competition handicapped by
ignorance.)

2620. *Abúni ò tó abẹ̀rín; bẹ́ẹ̀ni abẹ̀rín ò mọ
ẹ̀hìn ọ̀la.*
The person who insults one is not as bad as
the person who derides one; yet the person
who derides one does not know what the
future may bring. (Fortunes and circumstances may be reversed in time.)

2621. *Adìẹ yẹ̀gẹ̀; a ṣe bí ó ṣubú.*
The chicken lists to one side; we think it has
fallen. (Never be too quick to celebrate the
demise of a nemesis.)

2622. *Àfẹ́ẹ̀rí kan ò ju ká rí igbó ńlá bọ́ sí lọ;
ẹbọ kan ò ju ọ̀pọ̀ èèyàn lọ; "Òrìṣá gbé mi lé
àtète" kan ò ju orí ẹṣin lọ.*
There is no disappearing trick better than
the availability of a dense forest to disappear
into; there is no sacrifice more efficacious
than having many people on one's side;
there is no "The gods have elevated me" that
is higher than the back of a horse. (Practical
and realistic moves are more reliable than
mysterious expectations.)

2623. *A-fi-tirẹ̀-sílẹ̀-gbọ́-tẹniẹléni: Ọlọ́run ní
ḿba gbọ́ tirẹ̀.*
He-who-neglects-his-affairs-to-care-for-
others'-affairs: it is God that takes care of his
affairs. (God takes care of the benevolent.)

2624. *Àgbà ṣoore má wo bẹ̀.*
Elder, do a favor and remove your eyes from
it. (Do not advertise your acts of kindness or
pointedly await acknowledgment of them.)

2625. *Àgbò ò ṣéé mú; ọ̀dá ò ṣéé mú; ohun
gbogbo ní ńtóbi lójú ahun.*
A ram is too much to give; a gelded animal
is too much to give; everything is excessive
in the sight of a miser. (Expect no favor
from a miser.)

2626. *Àì-fi-ǹ-kan-pe-ǹ-kan ní ḿba ǹ-kan jẹ́.*
It is failure-to-count-anything-as-significant
that ruins things. (Minimizing problems
results in disaster.)

2627. *Àìmète, àìmèrò, lọmọ ìyá méfà-á fi ńkú
sóko egbàafà.*
Lack of resourcefulness and lack of thoughtfulness cause six siblings to die as pawns for
only 12,000 cowries. (Pooling resources and
wisdom ensures better results than going it
alone.)[1]

---

1. If the children had known how to plan and pool
their resources, they could have redeemed themselves;
the amount in question is insubstantial. It was usual in
traditional Yoruba society for a person to pawn himself

2628. *Àjégbà ni ti kòǹkò.*
Croaking-in-relays is the mark of frogs. (It is in the nature of sheep to follow and to lack initiative.)

2629. *Akéyinje ò mò pé ìdí ńro adìe.*
The person who gathers eggs to eat does not know that the chicken's orifice hurts. (One should never be so preoccupied with one's own pleasures that one does not care what they cost others.)

2630. *A-lágbára-má-mèrò, baba òlé.*
He-who-has-strength-but-lacks-diecretion [is the] father of laziness. (A powerful but thoughtless person is worse than the laziest person.)

2631. *A-láì-mète-mèrò oko tó fi adìe ìyàwó bo orí ìyálé; bí baálé bá jé ìkà, èwo ni tòrìsà?*
The shiftless, thoughtless husband makes the junior wife's chicken a sacrifice to the senior wife's head; if the husband is wicked, what about the god? (God will not accept offerings or prayers tainted with wickedness.)

2632. *Aláràje ò mo odún; a-bisu-úta-bí-igi.*
He who purchases the food he eats cares not what the season is; his yams always flourish like trees. (The consumer does not know what the producer goes through.)

2633. *Arúgbó soge rí; àkísà-á lògbà rí.*
The old person was once a dandy; the rag was once in fashion. (Those who are favored should remember that times and circumstances do change.)

2634. *Àse Òyó kì í ró "Gbà," àfi "Múwá."*
The order from Òyó never sounds *Gbà* [meaning "Take!"], only *Múwá* [meaning "Bring"]. (It is good to give as well as to receive.)[2]

2635. *Àsírí-i náwó-náwó kì í tú lójú ahun.*
The big spender is never disgraced in the presence of the miser. (The free spender will always be honored in the community.)

2636. *Asiwèrè ló bí ìyá òbo.*
It was an imbecile that gave birth to the mother of the monkey. (The fool belongs in the same lineage as the imbecile.)

2637. *A-ti-ara-eni-roni, ajá ode.*
A-creature-that-applies-another's-circumstances-to-itself: a hunter's dog. (The hunter's dog would do well to place itself in the shoes of the animals it hunts.)

2638. *Ayídóborí tafà sókè: ojú Olúwaá tó won.*
Those who cover their heads with mortars and shoot arrows into the sky: God's eyes encompass them all. (God sees all acts of selfishness and wickedness toward others.)

B

2639. *Bámijókòó làbíkú ńjé; eni tí ò bímo rí ò gbodò so Omóláriwo.*
Bámijókòó [Sit-with-me] is the name one gives an *àbíkú*; a person who has never had a child does not name a child Omóláriwo. (A reference to the crying that accompanies the death of an *àbíkú*.)[3]

2640. *Bí a bá gé igi nígbó, ká fi òràn ro ara eni wò.*

---

or a willing relative for a certain amount; as soon as the amount was repaid, the pawn was redeemed.

2. This is obviously the sentiment of Òyó's vassal towns, which have to send tributes periodically.

3. *Àbíkú* ("One born to die") is the name given to children believed to plague certain women by entering into them to be born, only to die prematurely, and then repeating the process several times.

When one fells a tree in the forest, one should apply the matter to oneself. (Whenever one does something to another, one should put oneself in that person's shoes.)

2641. *Bí a bá rí òkú ìkà nílẹ̀, tí a fi ẹsẹ̀ ta á; ìkà-á di méjì.*
If one sees the corpse of a wicked person on the ground and one kicks it, there are then two wicked people. (If one returns evil for evil, one joins the ranks of the evil.)

2642. *Bí o ṣe rere yó yọ sí ọ lára; bí o kò ṣe rere yó yọ sílẹ̀.*
If your deeds are good, the benefits return to you; if your deeds are not good, they will be apparent to all. (Neither good nor evil goes for nought.)

2643. *Bí ó ti ńdun ọmọ eye, bẹ̀ẹ̀ ló ńdun ọmọ èèyàn.*
As the young of birds know pain, so do the young of humans. (Others feel hurt, just as we do.)

E

2644. *"Èrò tètè jí;" "Èrò jẹ́ ilẹ̀ ó mọ́": tèrò là ńrò.*
"Traveler, get up early"; "Traveler, wait until light": it's all out of solicitousness for the traveler's welfare. (Good intention does not guarantee good reception; the person of whose welfare one is being solicitous may resent one's attention.)

Ẹ

2645. *Ẹ ní ká má tafà; kí ni a ó fi lé ogun? Kànnà-kànnà la fi lé Boko.*
You forbid us to shoot arrows, so with what shall we repel invaders? In the past the Boko were repelled with catapults. (It is unhelpful

to deprive people of the tools they need for what they must do.)

2646. *Ẹní fowó lògbà ló káyé já.*
It is the person who uses his or her money to enjoy life who lives well. (Money is to be used to enjoy life.)

2647. *Ẹní lówó kó ṣe bí ọba; àrà wo lahún fẹ́ẹ́ fi owó dá?*
Whoever has riches should act like a king; what kind of feat can a miser perform with money? (The best thing to do with wealth is use it to live well.)

2648. *Ẹní mọ owó-ó lò lowó ńbá gbé.*
It is the person who knows how to use wealth that wealth attaches to. (Wealth follows only those who know how to use it.)

2649. *Ẹni tí a ṣe lóore tí kò dúpẹ́, bí ọlọ́ṣà-á kóni lẹ́rù ni.*
A person for whom one does a favor but who shows no gratitude is like a robber who has stolen one's goods. (Ingratitude is comparable to robbery.)

2650. *Ẹni tí ó bá máa bímọ á yọ̀ fọ́lọ́mọ.*
Whoever would have children of her own must rejoice with those who already have. (Those who seek good fortune must not begrudge those who are already fortunate.)

2651. *Ẹni tí ó bèèrè ọ̀rọ̀ ló fẹ́ ìdí-i rẹ̀ ẹgbó.*
Whoever asks about a matter genuinely wishes to know its causes. (If a person asks for help with a problem, one should appreciate the gesture and comply.)

2652. *Ẹni tí ó gòkè, kó fa òré-ẹ rẹ̀ lọ́wọ́; ẹni tó rí jẹ, kó fún òrẹ́-ẹ rẹ̀ jẹ.*
Whoever has reached the top, let him or her pull a friend by the hand; whoever has food to eat, let him or her share it with a friend.

(If one has succeeded, one should give aid to those still struggling.)

2653. *Ẹni tí ó so ìlẹ̀kẹ̀-ẹ́ parí ọ̀ṣọ́; ẹni tó fúnni lọ́mọ-ọ́ parí oore.*
The person who adorns herself with beads has done the ultimate in self-beautifying; the person who gives one a child [in marriage] has done the ultimate in favor. (There are certain gestures that cannot be surpassed. Compare 4955.)

2654. *Ẹni tí ó ṣe ìbàjé èèyàn-án ṣe ìbàjé ara-a rè.*
Whoever defames others defames himself or herself. (The evil one does to others reflects on oneself. Compare 2656.)

2655. *Ẹyẹlé fi èsín-in rẹ̀ pamọ́, ó ńṣe èsín adìẹ.*
The pigeon hides its own disgrace and goes ridiculing the chicken. (A person full of flaws insists on finding fault with others.)

I

2656. *Ìbàjé iṣu nìbàjé ọbẹ; ẹni tó ṣe ìbàjé èèyàn-án ṣe ìbàjé ara è.*
The blemish of the yam is the blemish of the knife; whoever besmirches other people's names besmirches his or her own. (How one treats others reflects more on oneself than on the others. Compare 2654.)[4]

2657. *Igbá olóore kì í fọ́; àwo olóore kì í fàya; towó tọmọ ní ńya ilé olóore.*
The calabash of a kindhearted person never breaks; the china plate of a kindhearted person never cracks; both riches and children ever converge in the home of a kindhearted

person. (Good always attends those who are good. The following entry is a variant. Compare also 2659.)

2658. *Igbá onípẹ̀lẹ́ kì í fọ́; àwo onípẹ̀lẹ́ kì í fàya.*
The calabash belonging to a patient person never breaks; the china plate belonging to a patient person never cracks. (Patient people never come to grief. This is a variant of the preceding entry, and compare the next entry.)

2659. *Ilé olóore kì í wó tán; tìkà kì í wó kù.*
The home of a kindhearted person never collapses completely; the home of a wicked person always collapses, leaving nothing standing. (Good will attract good, and evil will attract evil. Compare the two preceding entries.)

2660. *Ilé ọ̀sọnú àyàyó; ta ní jẹ́ yalé ahun-káhun?*
To visit the home of a generous person is to be plied with food aplenty; who would think of visiting a miser? (One's generosity or miserliness makes one friends or loses one friends.)

2661. *Inú búburú, oògùn òṣì.*
Ill will [is the] medicine that ensures misfortune. (Misfortune will surely attend a person who harbors ill will toward others.)

2662. *Inúure kì í pani, wàhálà ní ńkọ́ báni.*
Good will toward others does not kill; it only gets one into trouble. (One should be wary of kindness to others. But compare the previous entry.)

2663. *"Iyán dára, ọbẹ̀-ẹ́ dùn" ló pa Akíndélé lóko Ìgbájo; "Òrìṣà, nkò fún ọ ní èdì jẹ" ló pa abọrìṣà Ìkirè.*
"The pounded yam is good and the stew is delicious" killed Akíndélé on his farm

---

4. The idea is that if one peels a yam with a knife and streaks show on the yam, the flaw is the knife's, not the yam's.

at Ìgbájọ; "God, I will not give you some food to eat" is what killed the priest at Ìkiré. (Closed-fistedness and stinginess bring people nothing but misfortune.)[5]

2664. *Ìyàwó jẹ ọkà jẹ igbá.*
The wife ate the yam-flour meal and ate the calabash with it. (One should show consideration and exercise care in using others' property.)

K

2665. *Kí á ṣá a ṣá a, kí á gbọ̀n ọ́n gbọ̀n ọ́n; ká fi oko eéran sílẹ̀ ló dá eéran lára.*
One may slash at it and slash at it, and one may shake the sand from its roots forever, but nothing affects the *eéran* grass like being abandoned. (The best treatment for a recalcitrant person is to shun him or her.)

2666. *"Kiní yìí ò pọ̀; ng ò lè fún ọ níbẹ̀": olúwàrè ahun ni.*
"This thing is not plentiful; I cannot give you any of it": the person is a miser. (However little one has, one should be willing to spare some for others. Compare the following entry.)

2667. *"Kiní yìí tí o fún mi ò pọ̀": ahun ní ńjẹ́ bẹ́ẹ̀.*
"This thing that you have given me is not plentiful": that statement indicates a greedy person. (One should not be too demanding of one's benefactors. Compare the previous entry.)

2668. *Kò mú ti ọwọ́ ẹ wá ò gba tọwọ́ ẹni.*
He-will-not-bring-what-he-has will not

have what one has. (A person who will not share what he or she has will not have a share of others' possessions either.)

2669. *Kò sí kò sí; bẹ́ẹ̀ni ọmọ wọn ńyó.*
"We have nothing, we have nothing!" Yet their children always have full stomachs. (Said of people who are too tightfisted to help others.)

2670. *Kò tó ǹkan ní ńsọni dahun.*
"There is not much of it" is what turns one into a miser. (Only a miser does not have enough to share with others.)

M

2671. *"Má bàá mi jẹ ìdùn," ẹran ní ńlé lọ.*
"Do not share in my delicious meal" chases away the animal. (The selfish person would rather ward off good fortune than allow others to share it.)[6]

2672. *"Má fẹ́ẹ́ ọwọ́-ọ̀ mi kù" tí ńyan gúgúrú fún eégún; eégún nàáà ní "Má fẹ́ẹ́ ọwọ́-ọ̀ mi kù"; ó fún un ní ọmọlángidi.*
"Just so you won't find my hand empty" roasted popcorn for the masquerader; the masquerader responded, "Just so you won't find my hands empty" and gave him a wooden doll. (Stinginess will not win generosity in return.)[7]

2673. *Ǹbá-lówó-ǹbá-se-òlèlè-fún-Agón: ìjímèrè kì í jẹ oko ẹ̀ kó sọ̀.*

---

5. Presumably, Akíndélé would not share the pounded yam and stew because they were delicious, and the priest kept for himself all the things meant for sacrifice to the god.

6. The reference is to a hunter who would rather scare away game he cannot kill than give another hunter the opportunity of killing it.

7. Masqueraders, who are supposed to be the embodiment of ancestors, are credited with the power to grant boons—including children—to supplicants. A person who makes lame excuses while offering inadequate gifts *to* the masquerader will hear lame excuses and receive worthless boons *from* the masquerader.

Had I money, I would cook bean meal for the Agọ́n masquerader; the brown monkey's raiding of his farm never elicits a complaint from him. (One should acknowledge and reciprocate favors done one by others.)[8]

2674. *"Mú wá, mú wá" lapá eyelé ńké.*
"Bring! Bring!" is the sound of the pigeon's wings. (Some people know only how to take, never how to give.)[9]

N

2675. *Náwó-náwó kì í sàpà.*
The big spender is not a prodigal. (There is nothing wrong with spending one's money.)

O

2676. *O jẹbẹ, o mubẹ, o babẹ jẹ́.*
There you ate, there you drank, and there you fouled. (Don't besmirch a place that has been good to you.)

2677. *"O kú iṣẹ́" ò lè bí aráyé nínú.*
"Greetings to you at work" cannot invite people's anger. (A courteous act does not expose one to trouble.)

2678. *"Ó kún mi lójú," èkọ Arogun; òkan ṣoṣo ni mo rà, igba ènì ló fi sí i.*
"Its impression on me is tremendous": such is Arogun's corn meal; I bought only one, but she gave me two hundred as makeweight [or extra measure]. (Said of people who have gone well beyond the call of duty.)

2679. *Obì kékeré kọjá òkúta ńlá.*
A small kola nut is superior to a large stone. (A small gift is better than none at all.)

2680. *Obìnrin tó bímọ tó bí olómitútù, wàhálà ọkọ è-é dínkù; kò ní já ewé mọ́, bẹ̀ẹ̀ni kò ní wa egbò.*
A woman who bears a child that requires only cold water for all cures has saved her husband much worry; he will never again go searching for medicinal leaves, nor will he go digging roots. (A considerate woman is the joy of her husband.)

2681. *Obínrin-ín bímọ fún ọ o ní o ò rínú è; o fẹ́ẹ́ kó o nífun ni?*
A woman has a child by you, and you still say you do not see her inside [know her mind]; would you have her expose her intestines? (People's actions are enough, without accompanying words, to prove the extent of their commitment.)

2682. *Ògún ò rọ ike; àgbèdẹ ò rọ bàtà; oko ò ṣòro-ó rọ, àgbèdẹ ò pa ọkọ́ tà.*
Ògún [god of metals] does not fashion ivory; the blacksmith does not make shoes; were farming not a difficult pursuit, the blacksmith would not manufacture hoes for sale. (One should appreciate people for their efforts and not belittle their accomplishments.)

2683. *Ohun tí ńbá ahun náwó è ńbẹ lápò-o è.*
What will help a miser spend his money is right there in his or her pocket. (The person who does not willingly share what he or she has will somehow find himself or herself being deprived of it.)

2684. *Òjò pa ewé-e kòkò; bó lè ya kó ya.*
The rain beats the coco-yam leaf; if it will tear, let it tear. (When one has no invest-

---

8. The *egúngún* (masqueraders) are believed to favor *ọlèlè*, seasoned and steamed ground beans. Agọ́n is the masquerader charged with executing witches.

9. The bird's wings in flight are supposed to make a sound like *Mú wá, mú wá!* ("Bring, Bring").

ment in a property, one is likely to be careless in using it. Also, one will do what one
pleases, and damn the consequences.)

2685. *Ojú la rí là ńkọrin òkú, òkú ò forin sáyé
kó tó lọ.*
It is out of regard for onlookers that one
sings in praise of the dead; the dead did not
prescribe a song before departing this life.
(One does certain things out of a sense of
propriety, not because one must.)

2686. *Ojú ní ńrójú sàànú.*
Eyes are what look on eyes and fill with
kindness. (When the eyes actually see suffering, they cannot avoid compassion.)

2687. *Ojú ọba ayé ló fọ́; tọ̀rún là kedere, ó
ńwo aṣebi.*
Only the king of this earth is blind; that of
heaven is wide-eyed, watching evildoers.
(God sees all acts of wickedness that may be
hidden from earthly authorities.)

2688. *Òkulú ní ta ni òun ó ro tòun fún? Ta ní
wá ro tiẹ̀ fun Òkulu?*
Òkulu asks with whom should he lodge his
complaint? Did anybody lodge his complaint
with Òkulu? (If one has been unhelpful to
others, one should not expect any help from
them.)

2689. *Onígẹ̀gẹ̀ ìsáju ba tìkẹhìn jẹ́.*
The goitered person going in front ruins the
fortunes of the one coming behind. (A person's misdeeds compromise those coming
after him.)

2690. *Oore kì í gbé; ìkà kì í dànù; à-ṣoore-
jindò ní mmúni pàdánù oore.*
A good deed does not go for nought; a
wicked deed is never lost; drowning while
doing a favor is what makes the good person
lose out on the rewards for his goodness.

(Every kindness, like every wickedness, is
rewarded; one should be prudent, though,
in doing favors.)

2691. *Oore tí a ṣe fádìẹ ò gbé; bó pẹ́ títí a ṣomi
tooro síni lẹ́nu.*
The favor that one does a chicken is not
for nought; in due course it will make stew
to delight one's mouth. (There will always
be a return for whatever favor one does for
others.)

2692. *Òrẹ́hìn ní ńṣe ọmọ òkú pẹ̀lẹ́; ta ní jẹ́ ṣe
ọmọ Ègùn lóore?*
Only a person who thinks of the future commiserates with an orphan; otherwise, who
would show kindness to an Ègùn person?
(Only the knowledge that one never knows
the future makes one show kindness to
people who do not appreciate goodness.)[10]

2693. *Òṣónú ò bí èjìrẹ́; onínúure ní ḿbí ẹdun.*
An ill-natured woman will not give birth to
twins; only good-natured people give birth
to twins. (Only good people are fortunate
enough to have twins.)[11]

2694. *Owó ló ńpe ìná owó.*
Money is what calls for spending money.
(The availability of money creates the need
to spend it.)

Ọ

2695. *Ògá Ìwátà, eṣú ò mọ olóòótọ́; eṣú dé,
eṣú jẹ oko olóore.*
Big shot of Ìwátà town; the locusts do not
know who is honest; the locusts arrive and

---

10. Another example of the Ègùn, a branch of the
Yoruba, suffering a good deal of detraction.
11. Ẹdun is the colobus monkey, but the Yoruba,
who greatly favor twins, associate them with the animal.

the locusts eat up the good person's farm. (Vandals care not which property belongs to good people and which to bad people.)[12]

2696. Ọmùtí kì í ṣàpà; owó ẹ̀ ló ńná.
The drunkard is not a prodigal; it is his money that he is spending. (One can spend one's money as one wishes.)

2697. Ọ̀ràn-an-yàn ò sí nínúu iyánrán.
There is no compulsion in voluntary work. (Volunteering is not an obligation.)

2698. Ọtí gbélé ahun ó kan.
Wine stays in the home of the miser until it goes sour. (The miser would rather see things go bad than share them.)

2699. Ọ̀tọ̀ niṣẹ́ olókùnrùn.
The assignment for an invalid must be different from everybody else's. (People should be employed only according to their capabilities.)

2700. Ọwọ́ híhá àhájù ní ńdínà ire mọ́ni.
Excessive stinginess is what slams the door of fortune in one's face. (Miserliness will divert good fortune away from the miser.)

P

2701. Pègàn-pègàn-án bọ́ sóde kò ní láárí; ẹni tí ò rówó ṣe fújà ní ńpẹ̀gàn ẹni.
He who derides others steps outside and does not amount to much; it is he who has no basis for bragging that derides others. (People who belittle others are themselves worthless.)

Ṣ

2702. Ṣe sílẹ̀: ẹrù-u rẹ̀ kì í pé níbodè.
He who extends kindness beforehand: his goods will not stay long at the frontier. (The generous person will always find helpers to ease his passage.)[13]

2703. Ṣègàn-ṣègàn ò láṣọ méjì; pé-ń-pé laṣọ abúni ḿmọ.
The detractor of others does not possess a change of clothing; the garment of the insulter of people is always skimpy. (People who make a habit of cutting others down never prosper either.)

2704. Ṣìkà-ṣìkà-á fi díẹ̀ ṣe ara ẹ̀.
The wicked person does a little wickedness to himself or herself. (Wickedness has some adverse effect on the perpetrator.)

2705. Ṣìkà-ṣìkà-á gbàgbé àjọbí, adánilóró gbàgbé ọ̀la.
The wicked forget kinship; the person who hurts others forgets tomorrow. (People who inflict injury on others forget that the gods of kinship will inflict punishment on them and that they themselves may be at the receiving end in the future.)

2706. Ṣìkà-ṣìkà ò jẹ́ pe ara ẹ̀ níkà.
The wicked person will never describe himself as wicked. (The wicked always strive to appear as decent, kind people.)

T

2707. Tewé tegbò ní ńṣàánú àfòmọ́.
Both the leaf and the root take pity on the climbing parasite. (A plea for consideration

---

12. Ìwà tà (ìwà-á tà) means "Character pays": some irony there.

13. The reference is to traveling traders and tariff collectors.

from all and sundry. Compare the following two entries.)

2708. *Tigi tòpè ní ńsàánú àfòmó.*
Both trees and palms take pity on the climbing plant. (A plea for mercy from all and sundry. Compare the preceding and following entries.)

2709. *Tigi tòpè ní ńsàánú ìyèré lóko.*
Both trees and palms extend kindness to the African black pepper plant. (A plea for kind-ness from others. Compare the preceding two entries.)

2710. *Tìkà toore, òkan kì í gbé.*
Wickedness or kindness, neither goes for nought. (Wickedness and kindness will be rewarded unfailingly.)

2711. *Tútù ní ńtẹnu eja wá.*
Only coolness come out of the fish's mouth. (Permit your mouth to say only soothing things.)

TWO

The Fortunate Person
(or The Good Life)

On good name (good repute)

A

2712. *Àì-lóbìnrin kò ṣé-é dákẹ́ lásán; ó tó ká pe gbogbo ayé kó báni gbọ́ ọ̀rọ̀ náà.*
Not-having-a-woman is not a problem to keep secret; it merits appealing to the whole world to intervene in the matter. (A man without a woman needs drastic measures to resolve his problem.)

2713. *Àkẹ́bàjẹ́, ọmọ àgan-án-dáríjọ-bí.*
Spoiled rotten, child-collectively-mothered-by-barren-women. (Infertile women make poor mothers.)

2714. *Àkéjù tí ṁba ọmọ olówó jẹ́.*
Excessive pampering ruins the child of a wealthy person. (Children of wealthy parents are likely to be spoiled with too much pampering.)

2715. *Aṣèbàjẹ́ ṁwá ẹni rere kúnra.*
The evildoer seeks good people to associate with. (Evil people always seek the company of good people to burnish their image.)

2716. *Àwòdì òkè ò mọ̀ pé ará ilẹ̀ ṁwo òun.*
The hawk in the sky does not know that ground dwellers are watching it. (One may be unaware, but one's machinations are not hidden.)

B

2717. *Bí eégún bá jóore, orí a yá atọ́kùn-un rẹ̀.*
If a masquerader dances well, his attendant is filled with pride. (The accomplishments of one's relatives make one proud. This is a variant of the following entry.)

2718. *Bí eégún ẹní bá jóore, orí a yáni.*
If one's masquerader dances well, one is proud. (The accomplishments of one's relatives give one cause for pride. Compare the preceding entry.)

2719. *Bíbí ire ò ṣé-é fowó rà.*
A good pedigree is not something one can buy with money. (Money cannot improve the circumstances of one's birth.)

D

2720. *Dídùn dídùn nílé olóyin; kíkorò nílé agbọ́n.*
Sweetness is the constant characteristic of the honey seller's home; bitterness is the permanent characteristic of the wasp's home. (The good person will always be attended by goodness, the wicked person by wickedness.)

E

2721. *Èèyàn-án dára ó ku ìwà; ilé dára ó ku ìgbé.*
A person may be attractive, but character still matters; a home may be gorgeous, but what matters is its livability. (Looks are not everything.)

2722. *Èèyàn-án rìn, òjìjí tè lé e; kò ṣé-é mú, kò ṣé-é jù sápò.*
A person walks along, and his or her shadow follows; it cannot be grabbed, and it cannot be slipped into the pocket. (No one can hide his or her character.)

2723. *Ehín funfun lèṣó èrín; ìwà rere lèṣó èèyàn.*
The adornment of a smile is white teeth; the adornment of a person is good character. (Good character is more valuable than good looks. Compare 4991.)

2724. *Ehín òkánkán obìnrín kán; olórí ẹwà-á lo.*
A woman's front teeth break; the mainstay of [her] beauty is demolished. (When one's main asset is gone, one is as good as finished.)

2725. *Èjì Ogbè ni baba Ifá.*
Èjì Ogbè is the father figure in Ifá. (The subject of this comment is thought to be without peer in its category.)[1]

2726. *Èké kú, a gbélè ó kan òkúta.*
The devious person dies, and while digging his or her grave one strikes a rock. (Even the earth bears witness against the wicked.)

2727. *Èké ṣíṣe ò ní ká má lòówó; ìkà ṣíṣe ò ní ká má dàgbà; ṣùgbón ojó àtisùn lebọ.*
Being devious does not prevent one from prospering; being evil does not prevent one from living long; but it is one's dying day that one needs to worry about. (The devious and the evil may prosper and live long, but their end will be terrible.)

2728. *Epo kì í té; iyò kì í té.*
Palm oil never goes stale; salt never goes stale. (Certain things never go out of season or favor. Also, this is a prayer that a person may never be disgraced.)

2729. *Èṣù ò níwà, a kólé-e rè síta.*
Èṣù lacks good character; therefore, his house is built outdoors.[2] (Whoever lacks social graces deserves to be ostracized.)

Ẹ

2730. *Egbàá òbùn ò tó òkan ṣoṣo ògá.*
Two hundred filthy persons are no match for one person of good repute. (One decent individual is worth more than two hundred tasteless people.)

2731. *Èhìn ò sunwòn: ajá mú awọ ẹkùn té sùn.*
The end is inauspicious: a dog sleeps on the hide of a leopard. (The way one is remembered after death is a good indication of whether or not one lived and died well.)

2732. *Ẹní bá ṣè jalè léèkan, bó bá fàràn ogún òké bora, aṣọ olè ló wò.*
Whoever stole once, if he or she later drapes himself or herself in expensive velvet cloth, is draped in stolen goods. (A reputation once ruined is impossible to mend.)

2733. *Ẹní bú ẹsin lóbùn-ún jàre ẹsin: ẹsin ò bójú lálé; kò wesè lówùúrò; pètè-pétè èṣí ńbẹ látèélesè-e ẹsin.*
Whoever calls the horse filthy is justified: the horse does not rinse its face at night; the horse does not wash its feet at night; there is year-old caked mud on the hooves of the horse. (If one does not look well to one's behavior, one deserves the contempt of others.)

2734. *Ẹní fi ẹnu ra iyì, ètè è ńbò.*
The disgrace of the person who bought

---

1. In Ifá, the elaborate Yoruba system of divination, Èjì Ogbè is the first and most important of the sixteen main chapters.

2. The reference is to the practice of erecting outdoors the images of Èṣù, the rascally Yoruba god.

glory with his or her mouth is near at hand. (Undeserved glory is soon exposed.)

2735. *Ẹní mọ ẹni ò dàbí ẹni a mọ̀.*
A person who knows one is not like a person one knows. (One can vouch for the character of a person one knows, not of a person who knows one.)

2736. *Ẹni rere kì í kú sípò ìkà.*
A good person does not die the death of an evil person. (Each person will be recompensed according to his or her character.)

2737. *Ẹni tí a bí nílé ogbọ́n, tí a wò nílé ìmọ̀ràn, ogbọ́n ni kò níí gbọ́n ni, tàbí ìmọ̀ràn ni kò níí mọ̀?*
A person who is born in the house of wisdom and reared in the house of discernment, will he or she lack wisdom or be without discernment? (A person carries the marks of his or her pedigree and upbringing. See 3476.)

2738. *Ẹni tó bá ìwà búburú wá sáyé, tòun tòkùn àjàrà ní ńlọ sọ́run.*
Whoever comes into this world accompanied by bad character goes back to heaven by means of a vine. (Bad character will be the undoing of its owner.)[3]

2739. *Ẹni tó lórí rere tí kò níwà, ìwà-a rẹ̀ ni yó ba orí-i rẹ̀ jẹ́.*
A person who is blessed with good fortune but lacks good character: his character will ruin his or her good fortune. (Evil character ruins good destiny.)

2740. *Ẹni tó lówó tí kò níwà, owó olówó ló ní.*
The person who has riches but lacks good character has other people's riches. (A rich person without good character soon loses his or her riches to others.)

2741. *Ẹni tó pẹ́ lóko ọpẹ ló ní ká dá àbá-kábàá.*
The person who stayed too long on the palm-wine farm is the one who encouraged all sorts of speculation about what he was up to. (If one's behavior is devious, people are justified in wondering about one's character.)

2742. *Ẹsẹ̀ igúnnugún tí ńba obẹ̀ jẹ́.*
The legs of vultures, which ruin the stew. (An abomination [is] like the legs of a vulture in a stew.)

2743. *Ẹsẹ̀-ẹ́ pọ̀ léhìn-in kòrikò.*
There is a multitude of feet in the wake of the wolf. (An illustrious person attracts a great following.)

I

2744. *Ikú yá ju èsín.*
Death is preferable to disgrace. (One should die rather than besmirch one's name.)

2745. *Ilé dára ó ku ẹkẹ́; èèyàn-án dára ó ku ìwà.*
The house is beautiful but for its pillars; a person is handsome, but what of character? (Bad character nullifies any charm a person might have.)

2746. *Ilé kan-án wà lÓyọ̀ọ́ nígbà àtijọ́ tí à ńpè ní Àkîìjẹ́; òyìnbó kú níbẹ̀.*
There was a house in Ọ̀yọ́ in ancient times called One-that-does-not-acknowledge-greetings; a white man died there. (Comment on ill-mannered people who do not respond to greetings.)[4]

2747. *"Ìṣe ẹ̀ ni" ò jẹ́ ká mọ ikú àbíkú.*
"That is his or her habit" keeps one from

---

3. The idea of the vine is that the bad person may well be liable to hang.

4. The proverb associates this bad habit with Europeans and suggests that those who do not greet others are like dead people.

knowing when an *àbíkú* is really dying. (One who cries "wolf" too many times will attract no one in times of real trouble. See note 6 at 3488 and compare 3627.)

2748. *Ìwà kì í fi oníwà sílè.*
Character will not forsake its owner. (One cannot shed one's character.)

2749. *Ìwà lèsìn.*
Character is worship. (One's worship and prayers are only as efficacious as one's character is good.)

2750. *Ìwà lewà.*
Character is beauty. (A person is as beautiful as his or her character is good.)

2751. *Ìwà lòrìsà; bí a ti hù ú sí ní ńgbeni sí.*
Character is a god; just as one lives it, so it succors one. (One's fortune depends on one's character.)

2752. *Ìwà rere lèsó èèyàn; ehín funfun lèsó èrín.*
Good character is a person's [best] adornment; white teeth are the adornment of a smile. (A person's most desirable trait is good character, just as a smile's best aspect is white teeth.)

2753. *Ìwàniyì, alágbède Ifòkò; wón fún un nírin, ó lájá gbé e je; ajá a máa je irin bí?*
Ìwàniyì [Good character brings good regard], blacksmith of Ifòkò quarters [in Ibadan], was given an iron rod, and he claimed a dog ate it up; do dogs eat iron? (If you wish others to think well of you, you must be reliable and trustworthy.)

K

2754. *Ká ròhìn eni ò tó ká bá eni béè.*
To have people say good things about one

is nothing like being found to vindicate the report. (One's real character is more important than what others say.)

2755. *"Kítìjú pa mí": ààre èpè ni.*
"May I die of shame": that is the chief of all curses. (No fate is worse than disgrace.)

2756. *Kò sí omo nínú omo Lébé; òkú ní ńgbé òkú pòn.*
There is no child worthy of the name among the children of Lébé [the acrobatic masquerader], only dead people carrying dead people on their backs. (Said as a dismissive statement about worthless, ill-behaved children.)[5]

M

2757. *Màá-se-é-màá-lo obìnrin, ojú-u pópó lòrìsà-a rè ńgbé.*
I-will-do-as-I-wish-and-go-my-way woman: the memorial shrine to her goddess belongs by the roadside. (A wife who cares not about her character is not worth keeping.)

2758. *Méjì là ńwé èèyàn; bí ò se yíyìn a se bíbú.*
There are two ways of speaking about people; if it is not in praise, it will be in castigation. (One has either a good reputation or bad, never neutral.)

2759. *"Mo bí, mo bí" kì í se omo rere.*
"I have just had a baby; I have just had a baby!" does not make for good breeding. (Frequent births are less desirable than painstaking child rearing.)

---

5. The masqueraders, supposed to be the incarnated spirits of the dead, actually have only props made to look like children on their backs.

O

2760. *Ó di orí ẹni ó bàjẹ́, àì-mọ̀wà-á-hù ni.*
[If] all was ruined during one's watch, that spells a defect in character. (A person of good character will not be responsible for social disasters.)

2761. *Obìnrin tí kò níwà, ìyá ẹ̀ ní m̀bá ṣorogún.*
A woman without good character will have only her mother as co-wife. (A woman without good character is unlikely to find a husband.)

2762. *Obínrin tó bímọ tí ò gbọ́n fabẹ́ jóná.*
A woman who gives birth to a child that lacks wisdom only singed her genitals. (A child who grows up lacking wisdom is the bane of his or her mother.)

2763. *Òbúkọ-ó dé, òórùn-ún dé.*
The he-goat has arrived; stink has arrived. (When evil people arrive at a gathering, dissension ensues.)

2764. *Odò gbẹ má gbẹ́ orúkọ.*
Rivers dry up but not their names. (One's deeds will survive one.)

2765. *Ojú ìkà la ti ńfi ọmọ olóore jọba.*
It is in the presence of the wicked person that the son of the good person is crowned king. (The wicked will live long enough to see the good prosper.)

2766. *Olè kì í gbọ́ orúkọ ẹ̀ kó dúró.*
A thief does not hear his name and stand in place. (A person who has something to hide is always worried about being exposed.)

2767. *Oníwàpẹ̀lẹ́: a-báni-gbé-tuni-lára.*
A mild-mannered person [is] one with whom cohabitation envelops one in ease. (A mild-mannered person is a joy to live with.)

2768. *Òrìṣà nìwà; bí a ti hù ú ló ṣe ńgbeni.*
Character is a god; it aids one according to how one uses it. (One's character determines one's fortune.)

2769. *Orúkọ ẹni ní ńjẹ́rìí ẹni lókèèrè.*
One's name is one's most effective advocate abroad. (Your reputation determines what people who do not know you go by.)

2770. *Orúkọ lègbọn oyè.*
A name is the elder of a chieftaincy title. (A good name is better than an important position.)

2771. *Orúkọ ńroni; àpèjà ńroni.*
One's name affects one's character; one's war name determines how one behaves. (People are influenced by their names.[6] Compare the following entry.)

2772. *Orúkọ tí a sọ ọmọ ní m̀mọ́mọ lára.*
It is the name a child is given that sticks to the child. (People behave later in life the way they were brought up. Compare the foregoing proverb.)

2773. *Òyìnbó ńlọ ó ṣu sága.*
The white man takes his leave; he shits on the chair. (Said of persons who leave a mess of problems behind when they depart a place.)

Ọ

2774. *Ọmọ́ tán lára ọmọ tí ńjẹ eérú.*
There is no longer anything worth calling a child in a child that eats ashes. (A youth whose habits are filthy and bestial is worthless.)

---

6. This is a Yoruba belief.

P

2775. *Pála-pàla nilé ìgbín, igbó rere nilé ahun.*
The home of the snail is ever disorganized, but the home of the tortoise is a tidy bush. (One can always expect to find certain people in an orderly state.)

S

2776. *Sán òbẹ sùn, fi apó rọrí; ìwà ọmọ ní ḿmú ọmọ jẹ òkígbẹ́.*
Tie a knife on you before you sleep; use a quiver as your pillow: your character forces you to resort to charms for rendering cutlasses harmless against your flesh. (People whose characters are evil have good reason to fear attack from others.)

T

2777. *TẸ̀gbá tẸ̀sà ló mọ Láfi lágẹmọ; gbogbo ayé ló mọ Tẹlẹ̀mú lólè.*
Both the Ẹ̀gbá and the Ẹ̀sà people know that Láfi is like the chameleon; the whole world knows Tẹlẹ̀mú as a thief. (Said of a person whose bad character is common knowledge.)[7]

2778. *Tìwà tìwà là ńràjò.*
It is in the company of one's character that one goes on a journey. (No one leaves his or her character at home when venturing abroad.)

Y

2779. *Yíyẹ ní ńyẹ ẹyẹlé; dídẹ̀ ní ńdẹ àdàbà lọ́rùn.*
The fate of the pigeon is always to enjoy good report; the fate of the dove is always to be at peace. (A way of wishing people peace and good regard.)

---

7. Ẹ̀gbá and Ẹ̀sà people are from two locations in Yorubaland; Láfi and Tẹlẹ̀mú are persons from those places whose poor reputations are widely known.

On health

2780. *Akíríboto kì í lójú awẹ́; ẹ̀là ìlẹ̀kẹ̀ kì í lójú àtokùnbọ̀.*
One-piece kola nut has no cleavage lines; a split bead has no string hole. (A defective thing or person is not as well off as a whole thing or person.)

2781. *Àlàáfíà baba ẹṣọ́; ojúrírí baba ara líle.*
Well-being, father of commanding presence; peace of mind, father of well-being. (Without well-being there is no good impression; without peace of mind there is no well-being.)

2782. *Àlàáfíà baba ọ̀rẹ́.*
Well-being, father of friendship. (Nothing conduces to friendship like well-being.)

2783. *Anìkànrìn ejò là ńfàdá pa.*
It is a snake that travels alone that one kills with a machete. (The lone traveler is vulnerable to opportunistic attacks. Compare 2802.)

2784. *Ara líle loògùn ọrọ̀.*
A healthy body is the medicine for wealth. (Health is wealth.)

2785. *Aràrá kì í yin Ọlọ́run, àfi bó bá ráro tí ńrákò.*
A dwarf does not show gratitude to God until he sees a crawling cripple. (Until seeing people who are worse off, one does not appreciate one's own good fortune.)

2786. *Aṣunú ò mọ̀-ọ́ láyọ̀; ó dìgbà tó bá rí ẹni tí kò lè ṣu.*
The person who has diarrhea does not know his or her good fortune until seeing someone who cannot relieve himself or herself. (Until seeing others who are worse off, one makes too much of one's misfortune.)

2787. *Bírí lolongo ńyí; a kì í bá òkùnrùn ẹyẹ lórí ìtẹ́.*
The orange waxbill is always sprightly; one never finds an invalid bird in a nest. (The person addressed is ever healthy or will ever be healthy.)

2788. *Lékèé-lékèé ẹyẹ ìmàle; bó bá ṣí lórí ọ̀pọ̀tọ́ a bà sórí òròmbó, a máa fi gbogbo ara kó ewú eléwú kiri.*
Cattle egret, Muslim of a bird; if it flies off the fig tree, it alights on the orange tree, carrying on its whole body gray hair gathered from sundry sources. (Said of irrepressible and sprightly older people.)[1]

---

1. The egret is described here as a Muslim bird because it is all white, just as Muslims favor all-white garments. The whiteness also suggests graying hair.

O

2789. *Ohun à ńjẹ kọ́ là ńtà.*
What one eats is not what one sells. (One should satisfy one's needs before thinking about disposing of the excess.)

2790. *Olókùnrùn ẹ̀ṣọ́ kì í ru ẹkù; kí alára tún ara mú.*
A sickly warrior does not carry rope snares; everyone should prepare properly for the task at hand. (People who have important duties to perform should gird up their loins accordingly.)

On happiness and success

A

2791. *A kì í léni ní Mọsàn ká mu ìgán.*
One does not have people at Mọsàn and yet eat deformed sour oranges. (There should be some benefit to having connections.)[1]

2792. *A kì í nìkan gbé agán kẹ́sẹ̀-ẹ rẹ̀ má wọ́ọ́lẹ̀.*
One does not carry a masquerader's shroud by oneself and succeed in keeping its train off the ground. (One can succeed in certain ventures only with the aid of others.)

2793. *A kì í nìkan jayé.*
One does not enjoy life alone. (A person without other people is nothing.)

2794. *Abẹ́rẹ́ kì í nù tòun tòwú nídìí.*
A needle is never lost with a thread in its eye. (As the thread will reveal where the needle is, a person with relatives will always have people interested in his or her fate.)

2795. *Abímitán ò da nǹkan; ara la fi ńré.*
"I am well born" guarantees nothing; all it permits is flaunting. (It is personal qualities, not birth, that determine one's fortune.)

2796. *Abiyamọ, a-bẹ̀hìn-jíjà.*
Nursing mother with a fighting back. (The child she carries fights, and fights for her.

People who have family thereby have defenders.)[2]

2797. *Àgbà ò lówó a ní kò gbọ́n; olówó ńṣe bí ọba lóko.*
An elderly man has no money, and we say he lacks wisdom; the rich man is like a king on his farm. (Money is everything.)

2798. *Àgbà tí ńfọ̀ ní káà láìlówólọ́wọ́, akọ ajá ní ńgbó.*
An elder sounding off in the back yard without money in his possession is like a barking male dog. (Money makes the person.)

2799. *Àgbájọ ọwọ́ la fi ńsọ àyà.*
It is with bunched fingers that one strikes one's chest. (One assembles all one's resources in preparation for a struggle.)[3]

2800. *Àgbàtọ́ ò jọ obí; ọmọ-ọlọ́mọ ò jọ tẹni.*
A foster child is not like a child one gave birth to; other people's children are not the same as one's own. (There is no substitute for one's own possession. Compare 704.)

---

1. The place-name Mọsàn literally means "Eat oranges" (*mu ọsàn*), an indication that the place is the home of orange groves.

2. There is a double entendre in the proverb. Because mothers customarily carry their babies on their backs, the saying could refer to the restlessness of a child thus carried, which would trouble the mother. On the other hand, because children presumably survive their parents, the saying would indicate that a mother has someone who will look out for her and survive her.

3. The proverb refers to the practice of striking one's chest with a fist in making a vow.

2801. *Agbòràndùn bí ìyá ò sí; ẹni tó ní baba ló tó ara-á ré.*
There is no commiserator like one's mother; only those who have fathers dare to be impudent. (With the backing of a powerful patron, one can attempt anything.)

2802. *Àìkọ́wọ̀ọ́rìn ejò lọ́mọ aráyé fi ńfàdá pa wọ́n.*
The failure-to-travel-in-groups habit of snakes makes it easy for humans to kill them with machetes. (Those who hang together will not hang separately. Compare 2783.)

2803. *Àìlẹ́bíyéye làìní aáwọ̀ lọ́rùn.*
Not-having-numerous-relatives explains not having quarrels to attend to. (Many relatives make many quarrels.)

2804. *Àìlówó lòrẹ́ ò sí; bí a bá lówó lọ́wọ́, tajá teran ní ńbáni tan.*
Lack of money is lack of friends; if you have money at your disposal, every dog and every goat will claim to be related to you. (Money makes the person, socially.)

2805. *Àìlówólọ́wọ́ kì í sàìsàn; àìníṣẹ́ lòràn.*
Lack of money is no disease; it is lack of work that is a disaster. (As long as one has a job, one has hope.)

2806. *Àìmọ èèyàn lọjà ò tà.*
It is not-knowing-people that makes one unable to sell one's wares. (To know people is to be a successful trader.)

2807. *Àìsí ẹnìkẹta ni ẹni méjì-í fi ńja àjàkú.*
It is the absence of a third person that makes it possible for two people to fight to the death. (Communal living minimizes the effects of personal conflicts.)

2808. *Ajá kì í kọ "Wá gbà; wá gbà."* A dog does not turn a deaf ear to "Come take; come take." (One should never reject generosity.)

2809. *Ajá tó léni léhìn á pọbọ; èèyàn tó léni léhìn á jàre ejó.*
A dog that has people behind it will kill a monkey; a person with people behind him will win lawsuits. (With people behind one, one can accomplish the impossible.)

2810. *Ajániláyà bí àì-lówó-lọ́wọ́, àìlówó baba ìjayà, owó ní ńtúniṣe.*
Frightful-thing-like-lack-of-ready-money, lack-of-money [is] father of frights; it is money that repairs a person's fortunes. (Lack of money is a frightful condition.)

2811. *Ajé nìyá ògo.*
Wealth is the mother of glory. (Money makes all things possible.)

2812. *Ajé tún ọmọ bí.*
Wealth brings rebirth. (However one was born, wealth makes one over.)

2813. *Àjòjì ò réni jẹ́rìí-i rẹ̀.*
The stranger has no one to bear witness for him or her. (A stranger cannot hope for vindication against an indigene.)

2814. *Àjọrìn ní ńyẹ èrò.*
Traveling in company best suits the wayfarer. (There is glory in numbers.)

2815. *Àkọ́bí ẹni ní ńrọni.*
It is one's firstborn that is one's support. (One's heir is also one's security in old age.)

2816. *A-kọrin-láì-lélégbè, bí ẹni lu agogo lásán.*
He-who-sings-and-lacks-a-supporting-chorus [is] the same as one who merely beats a gong. (A chorus enhances a solo performance.)

2817. *Aláàyan ní ńjẹun ogun.*
It is the industrious person who enjoys the booty of war. (To the valiant belong the spoils.)

2818. *Alágemo ò réni wá wòran òun; ẹní bá gbọ́ ṣẹ́ṣẹ́, èèyàn ní nsáré.*
The chameleon has no audience to watch it; if one hears footsteps, it is people that are running. (People should know the limits of their capability and act accordingly.)

2819. *Ará ilé ẹni ò ṣeun; èèyàn ẹni ò sunwọ̀n; a ò lè fi wé àlejò lásán.*
The members of one's household have not done well by one; one's relatives are not good-natured; yet one cannot liken them to mere strangers. (Whatever one may have against one's own people, they are still preferable to strangers.)

2820. *Àtàmpàkò ni oníkìmí ìka; baba ọmọ-ọ́ kú ọmọ-ọ́ deyọ.*
The thumb is the pillar among fingers; a father dies and the children are disunited. (As thumb to fingers, so is a father to his children: remove the one and the others are dispersed. This is a variant of the next entry.)

2821. *Àtàmpàkò ò sí ìká dẹ̀tú; baba ọmọ́ kú ọmọ́ deyọ.*
The thumb is missing and the fingers become unbunched; the father dies and the children become individuals. (Without the thumb, the fingers cannot be bunched; without a father the children are dispersed. See also the preceding entry.)

2822. *Àtàrí ni ò jẹ́ kóòrùn ó pa àgbọ̀n ìsàlẹ̀.*
It is the skull that keeps the sun off the chin below. (As the chin is beholden to the skull, one is beholden to one's benefactor.)

2823. *Àtẹ́wọ́ lará; ìgbònwọ́ niyèkan.*
One's palms are one's relatives; one's elbows are one's siblings of the same mother. (The most reliable things are one's own resources.)

B

2824. *Bí a bá mú iná kúrò lóko, àfi àgbẹ̀ tí yó jògèdè; bí a bá mú ti Ìbíkúnlé Olókè kúrò, Balógun Ògbóríẹfọ̀n, à di agírase.*
If one removed fire from the farm, only farmers satisfied with a diet of bananas would be unconcerned; but for Ìbíkúnlé Olókè, General Ògbórí Efọ̀n, we could achieve nothing. (Deprived of their founts of power, people are ineffective.)[4]

2825. *Bí a bá ní ogún ẹrú, tí a ní ìwọ̀fà ọgbọ̀n; ọmọ lèrè ẹni.*
If one owns twenty slaves and thirty pawns, children are still one's profit. (Children are preferable to slaves or pawns.)[5]

2826. *Bí a kò bá ní ohun àgbà, bí ewe là ńrí.*
If one does not have the accouterments of elders, one seems a mere youth. (An elder is not an elder without the means to be one.)

2827. *Bí a kò bá réni fẹ̀hìntì bí òlẹ là ńrí; bí a kò bá réni gbójúlé, à tẹra mọ́ṣẹ́ eni.*
With no one to lean on, one seems a lazy person; with no one to rely on, one faces one's duties with devotion. (The person with powerful support seems better than his or her peers; lacking such support, one should redouble one's efforts.)

2828. *Bí a kò lówó, à léèyàn; bí a kò lééyàn à lóhùn rere lẹ́nu.*
If one lacks money, one should have people; if one lacks people, one should be pleasant in one's speech. (If you lack a social asset, make up for it in other ways. Compare 2961.)

---

4. The person named was a famous and illustrious Ibadan war chieftain of the nineteenth century.

5. The construction reflects the conception of the world as a market from which people eventually return to the home whence they came.

2829. *Bí ebí bá kúrò nínú ìṣé, ìṣé bùṣe.*
If hunger is removed from poverty, poverty comes to an end. (Whoever has food to eat is not poor.)

2830. *Bí eégún ò bá mọ Òdèré, tí kò mọ́ Àṣàké, atọ́kùn-ún rẹ̀ ní ńwi.*
If a masquerader cannot recognize Òdèré and cannot recognize Àṣàké, his attendant has to tell him. (One's aides are there to make up for one's deficiencies.)

2831. *Bí eégún yó lọ, a di ìròjú fún atọ́kùn.*
When the time comes for the masquerader to depart, the attendant begins to grieve. (One is saddened at losing one's benefactor and patron.)

2832. *Bí ẹni ńlá ò bá tán, òràn ńlá ò lè pani.*
If there is no scarcity of great people, a great problem cannot kill one. (As long as one has powerful patrons, difficult problems will not defeat one.)

2833. *Bí ìbí ò tẹ̀, bí ìbí ò wọ́, ẹni tí a bá níwájú tó baba-á ṣe fúnni.*
If the pedigree is not bent, if the pedigree is not crooked, the person ahead of one is enough to play the role of father. (Unless there is dissension in the family, the elders in it exercise responsibility over the youth.)

2834. *Bí ìtì ò wó, ọwọ́ kì í ba ìṣépé.*
If the trunk does not fall, the twigs are not endangered. (One is safe as long as one's protector is around.)

2835. *Bí ìyá ò sí, ta ní jẹ́ ṣe ọmọ ọlọ́mọ lóore?*
If there is no mother, who would show kindness to another person's child? (A child can look only to its mother for protection.)

2836. *Bí ìyàwó ọ̀lẹ́ bá dàgbà, olówó ni yó gbé e.*
When the woman betrothed to a lazy person

matures, the rich man marries her. (The idle will be left empty-handed.)

2837. *Bí kò bá sí owó, baba ẹnìkan ò ju baba ẹnìkan lọ.*
In the absence of money, one person's father is no greater than another person's father. (Money determines status.)

2838. *Bí kò sí igi léhìn ọgbà ọgbà á wó; bí kò sí ako nínú-u bàtá bàtá ò níí le.*
Without a post behind the fence, the fence will collapse; without masculine forces in *bàtá* drumming, the music is not gripping. (Without his or her main support, a person is nothing.)

2839. *Bí kò sí tọmú tí ńbẹ láyà obìnrin, tí kò sí ìlèkè tí ńbẹ nídìí àgbèrè, òrẹ́-ẹ̀ mí dára díẹ̀ ju obìnrin lọ.*
Except for the breasts on the chest of a woman, and the beads around the waist of the woman who sleeps around, my friend is somewhat more attractive than a woman. (But for feminine sexual organs, a male friend is preferable to a female.)[6]

2840. *Bí kò sí towó, kí la ó fowò ṣe?*
Were it not for the matter of money, what would one want with trading? (The need for money gets one into a trade.)

2841. *Bí kò sí tỌya, ogun a ti kó Irá, bí kò sí tOlúfọ́n, ogun a ti kó Ifọ́n lọ.*
But for the goddess Ọya, Irá would have been sacked in a war; but for the god Olúfọ́n, Ifọ́n would have been destroyed. (Thanks to one's protector, one survives.)

2842. *Bí ó ku òní ku òla kí òùngbẹ pa awọ́n-rínwọ́n, òjò yó rò.*
If it is only a matter of days before the iguana dies of thirst, rain will fall. (For

6. This is one proverb that only men would use.

those the gods favor, rescue will come before disaster. See the next entry also.)

2843. *Bí ó ku òní ku òlá kí ọmọ olódò-ó kú fún òùngbẹ, ọ̀sọ̀rọ̀ òjò á rọ̀.*
If it is only a matter of days before the child of the river goddess dies of thirst, a torrential rain will fall. (The favored of the gods will always be rescued before disaster falls. See the previous entry.)

2844. *Bí ojú kò bá ti Ẹ̀hìn Ìgbẹ̀tì, ojú ò níí ti Èkó.*
If Ẹ̀hìn Ìgbẹ̀tì is not disgraced, Lagos will not be disgraced. (As long as one's defenses hold, one will be secure.)[7]

2845. *Bí òkété bá dàgbà, ọmú ọmọ-ọ rẹ̀ ní ḿmu.*
When the giant rat becomes old, it sucks from its child's breast. (In one's old age, one depends on one's children.)

2846. *Bí olówó sọ̀rọ̀, tó sèké, ajé a ní kò puró.*
If a rich person speaks and lies, money will say he or she has not lied. (A rich person can get away with any lie.)

2847. *Bí òtútù ńpa ìwòfà wọn a ní ó kó ìsẹ-e rẹ̀ dé; bí ó ńpa olówó wọn a ní kó rójú kó ata sẹ́nu.*
When the pawn has a fever, people say he is up to his usual tricks; when the owner is thus afflicted, they urge him to make an effort to eat. (The poor cannot expect the consideration the rich enjoy.)

2848. *Bí owó bá sì nínú ọ̀rọ̀, a súni pa.*
If money is removed from a matter, it bores one to death. (Money gives weight to matters.)

---

7. Ẹ̀hìn Ìgbẹ̀tì was important as a defensive buffer for Lagos.

2849. *Bíọ́-bíọ́ tí apó ńdá, ọràn ló gbójúlé.*
The quiver's boasting is due to its confidence in the backing of the bow. (A person who is sure of his backers can boast as much as he likes.)

2850. *Bòròkìnní ju olórò lọ.*
The popular rich man is superior to the merely wealthy. (To be well regarded is better than to be rich.)

I

2851. *Ìbí-ì rẹ-ẹ́ sẹ̀ nù ò ńyọ̀; o ò mọ̀ pé irú ẹ ló ńrá.*
Your pregnancy aborts and you rejoice; you are not aware that it is your kind that is perishing. (What in the short run is a boon might turn out in the long run to be a disaster.)

2852. *Ire kì í dé ká má gbọ̀ọ́ ohùn-un gudu-gudu.*
Good fortune does not arrive without being trailed by the sound of the *gudugudu* drum. (Good fortune must be greeted with rejoicing.)

O

2853. *Òwúsúwusù-ú mú ojú òrun bàjé; gùdè-gùdè ò jẹ́ kóòrùn ó ràn.*
The fog besmirches the face of the sky; the clouds keep the sun from shining. (An unfortunate matter keeps happiness or cheerfulness at bay.)

T

2854. *Títù là ḿbá Olúwẹri.*
Ever cool is how one finds Olúwẹri. (May

calmness and peace ever attend a certain
person's affairs.)[8]

W

2855. *Wè níwòn; ajé ní ńwẹni.*
Limit how often you take a bath; it is wealth
that grooms a person. (Wealth beautifies
more efficiently than a lot of grooming.)

---

8. This is a prayer, an incantation. Olúwẹri is
presumably a river or spring that is always cool.

On children and elders

2856. *A kì í délé ayò ká má bàá ọmọ.*
One never arrives at the home of the *ayò* game without finding children. (A prayer for a blessing of children in abundance.)

2857. *Àgbà ló tó Orò-ó lọ̀; ọba ló tó ehín erin-ín fun.*
Only a [male] elder is qualified to invoke Orò; only a king is qualified to blow a horn carved out of elephant tusk. (Certain tasks are for august people only.)

2858. *Àgbà mẹ́ta kì í ṣi èkùlù pè; bí ọkán bá ni "ekulu," èkejì a ní "ekùlù," èkẹta a ní "èkùlù."*
Three elders will not mispronounce *èkùlù*; if the first says, *"ekulu,"* the second will say, *"ekùlù,"* but the third will say, *"èkùlù."*[1] (Three heads are better than one.)

2859. *Àgbà mẹ́ta ní ṁmọ ìdí ẹẹ́ta.*
It takes three elders to know the mystery behind three. (It takes the pooled wisdom of many elders to resolve deep matters.)

2860. *Àgbà ní ńgbà.*
It is an elder that accepts. (Certain privileges, and obligations, attach to age.)[2]

2861. *Àgbà ní ńjẹ orí àdán; ọmọdé ní ńjẹ orí eyekéye.*
It is an elder who eats bats' heads; youths eat the heads of ordinary birds. (Only elders can confront extraordinary eventualities.)[3]

2862. *Àgbà ní ńjẹ ọkàn; ọmọdé ní ńjẹ ara ẹran.*
Only elders eat the heart; the youth eat the flesh. (Each station has its particular obligations.)[4]

2863. *Àgbà ní ńkọ́ àpò àgbà.*
Only an elder may hang the satchel of an elder [on his shoulder]. (Certain privileges are restricted to elders.)

2864. *Àgbà ò sí ìlú bàjé; baálé ilé kú ilé dahoro.*
Without elders a town is ruined; the patriarch of the compound dies, and the household becomes an empty shell. (Elders hold a community together.)

2865. *Bí a kò kú, a ó jẹ ẹran tó tó erin.*
If one does not die, one will eat as much as

---

1. *Èkùlù* is another name for *ẹtu*, a kind of duiker.
2. The proverb is based on a play on the syllable *gbà*. By itself it means "accept" (a proposition) or "take" ("receive"). Since Yoruba forms nouns from verbs by attaching certain initial vowels to them, in this case the vowel *à*, the word *àgbà (à-gbà)*, which means "elder," is construed to mean "someone who takes or accepts" (*a-gbà*).

3. Birds' heads are not usually eaten. Bats are never used as food, let alone their heads. Bats' heads would be eaten only as part of a mystery or cult.
4. The heart of an animal is supposed to be more desirable food than the flesh.

an elephant's meat. (Whoever has life has things to accomplish.)

2866. *Bí a kò kú, ìṣe ò tán.*
If one does not die, one's accomplishments are not over. (As long as one has life, one has feats to accomplish.)

2867. *Bí orí pẹ́ nílẹ̀, á di ire.*
If a head remains long on earth, it becomes fortunate. (If one lives long enough, one will prosper.)

2868. *Bí ọmọdé ò kú, àgbà ní ńdà.*
If a youth does not die, he becomes an elder. (In time even a youth assumes the mantle of an elder.)

I

2869. *Iná kú feérú bojú; ògèdè kú fọmọ ẹ̀ rópò; olóyè-é kú fọyè sílẹ̀ lọ.*
The fire dies and covers its face with ashes; the banana tree dies and replaces itself with an offshoot; a chief dies and leaves his title behind. (When a person dies, survivors inherit his or her place and property.)

2870. *Ìyàwó dùn-ún gbé; ọmọ dùn-ún kó jáde.*
Marriage is a pleasurable activity, and so is christening a child. (Marrying and christening are pleasures.)

K

2871. *Kí ni à bá fowó rà tó lè kojá ọmọ?*
What can one use one's money to buy that would be more precious than children? (Nothing is more precious than children.)

L

2872. *Lílé lọmọ ayò ńlé.*
Increasing is the way of the *ayò* game's counters. (An incantatory prayer that a person's fortunes will always increase.)[5]

O

2873. *Obìnrin tó jí ní kùtùkùtù tó ní Ọlọ́run ni yó mọ oye ọmọ òun, ó gbégbá ìrégbè.*
A woman who at the dawn of her life vows that only God will know how many children she will bear has placed a load of trouble on her own head. (Children are not an unmixed blessing for women.)

Ọ

2874. *Ọjọ́ tí a bá kú, ọwọ́ ò gba okòó; ọmọ ẹni ní ńjogún ẹni.*
The day one dies one's hand cannot hold a coin; one's children inherit one's property. (One cannot take earthly possessions into the grave but must leave them to one's survivors.)

2875. *Ọlọ́mọ́ kúrò ní "Kí lo bí?"*
A person who has a child is not a person who can be asked, "What did you sire?" (A child is a child; whoever has one cannot be taunted with childlessness.)

2876. *Ọlọ́mọ́ là.*
The person who has children has prospered. (Having children is the best kind of prosperity.)

2877. *Ọmọ bẹẹrẹ, òsì bẹẹrẹ.*
A multitude of children, a multitude of

---

5. The proverb refers to the fact that when an *ayò* player takes his turn, he adds counters to the ones already in each of several holes.

misery. (Children are desirable, but not in excess.)

2878. Ọmọ ẹni kì í di méjì kínu kanni.
One's mind does not become sour because one has had a second child. (People always rejoice at having children.)

2879. Ọmọ ẹni là ḿbí; ẹrú ẹni là ńrà lójà.
One gives birth to one's children; one buys one's slave in the market. (No one can buy children in the market.)

2880. Ọmọ kì í nù bí ẹranko.
A child does not become lost like an animal. (One must place great value on one's children. Compare 2884.)

2881. Ọmọ́ mọ ìyá ẹ̀; talágbàtọ́ nìyà.
A child knows its mother; the foster mother's lot is misery. (A child will never treasure a foster mother as much as a natural mother.)

2882. Ọmọ ò láyọ̀lé; ẹni ọmọ́ sin ló bímọ.
Children are not to be rejoiced over; only those whose children bury them really have children. (The most valuable service one may expect from one's children is that they attend to one's funeral.)

2883. Ọmọ olọ́mọ-ọ́ ṣòro-ó pè rán nísẹ́.
Another person's child is not easy to send on an errand. (There is nothing like having one's own children.)

2884. "Ọmọ-ò mí kú" yá ju "Ọmọ̀ò mí nù" lọ.
"My child is dead" is far better than "My child is lost." (One may lose a child to death, but it is unspeakable parental irresponsibility simply to lose a child. Compare 2880.)

2885. Ọ̀rọ̀ tí aboyún bá sọ, ẹni méjì ló sọ ọ́.
Whatever a pregnant woman says is said by two people. (A pregnant woman's words should not be taken lightly.)

T

2886. Tọmọ tó máa kú, tọmọ tó máa yè, ká yọ́ fọ́lómọ.
Whether the child will survive or not, let us rejoice with a person who has a baby. (Childbirth is always an occasion for joy.)

On material wealth

A

2887. *A kì í fi eku kan rẹ ọmọ méji.*
One does not placate two children with one rat. (An otherwise sufficient commodity divided too many ways satisfies no one.)

2888. *A kì í fi èjè dúdú sínú tutọ́ funfun jáde.*
One does not leave red blood inside and spit out white saliva. (Never let people think you love them when in fact you wish them ill.)

2889. *A kì í láhun níyì.*
One cannot be both stingy and respected. (Only generosity earns respect.)

2890. *Àìsí owó là ńpa ọ̀ọ́dúnrún mọ́; kí ni irínwó baba ìgbiwó tó-ó ṣe?*
It is lack of money that makes one hoard 300 cowries; what can 400 cowries, the father of 200 cowries, accomplish? (Those who have little make too much of little things. See also the following entry.)

2891. *Àìsí owó là ńtìlẹ̀kùn mọ́ ọ̀ọ́dúnrún; kí ni irínwó baba ìgbiwó tó-ó ṣe?*
It is lack of money that makes one keep 300 cowries under lock; what can 400 cowries, father of 200 cowries, accomplish? (The import is the same as that of the preceding entry. See also 119.)

2892. *Àìsí owó ni, "Jẹ́ kílẹ̀ ó mọ́"; ajé kì í gbowó ká ní ó dòla.*
It is lack of money that makes one say, "Wait until morning"; if the terms are agreeable, one does not wait until morning. (Lack of money makes one temporize even when the market is in one's favor.)

2893. *Àjẹ́kù là ńmayo.*
Leaving remnants is the indicator of satiation. (How one lives will show how well off one is.)

2894. *Ajé-ṣàlúgà! Ó fi ẹni iwájú sílẹ̀ ṣe ẹni èhìn ní pẹ̀lẹ́.*
Almighty wealth! It skips over the person in front to offer salutations to the person behind. (Wealth is no respecter of age.)

2895. *Ajíjìfà ní ńní tìtì ìpàkọ́.*
It is a person who wakes to free booty that develops an overhanging nape. (Those who labor for their food are not plagued with obesity.)

2896. *Àkẹ̀hìnsí ọlá ò sunwọ̀n.*
The reverse side of greatness is unattractive. (A fall from greatness, or turning one's back on greatness, is unfortunate.)

2897. *Àkísà-á ba ẹni rere jẹ́.*
Rags demean illustrious people. (A ragged attire overrides innate qualities.)

2898. *Akọ ebi tí ńdi òjòjò.*
Masculine hunger, one that becomes an illness.[1] (When hunger is extreme, it becomes an illness.)

2899. *A-kó-èésú-má-dàá, ẹrùngbà olè.*
He-who-collects-the-pool-in-turn-but-

---

1. In Yoruba usage, describing something as masculine is stating that it is the most formidable of its kind.

does-not-make-a-contribution: same as a thief. (Reaping without sowing is akin to stealing.)[2]

2900. *A-pèèpò-léhìn-àgbà, àgbà ḿbọ̀ wá.*
You-who-clear-the-weeds-behind-an-elder, your old age approaches. (Those who do favors for old people should be reminded that they too will some day grow old.)

2901. *Àrùn tí ńjẹ́ nárun ò sí; ebi ní ḿmú ara-á yi.*
There is no sickness called nettle rash; it is hunger that makes one develop welts. (Hunger is a disease not to be belittled.)

2902. *Àṣírí ẹ̀kọ kì í tú lójú ewé.*
The secrets of corn meal's being will not be exposed in the presence of leaves. (As long as one has champions, one will not be disgraced.)

2903. *Àtètèdáyé ò kan tàgbà; orí ẹni ní ńgbéni ga.*
Primogeniture has nothing to do with elderliness; it is the head that elevates one. (Age is no guarantee of status. Compare the following entry.)

2904. *Àtètèdáyé ò kan tọrọ̀; Ọlọ́run ní ńṣe orí owó.*
Primogeniture has nothing to do with wealth; God assigns wealth to heads.[3] (Age is no guarantee of wealth.)

B

2905. *Bí a bá lówó lọ́wọ́ tó tó ti ṣèkèrè, ìwà rere ni nǹkan.*
Even if one has as much money as the

beaded gourd, it is good character that matters.[4] (Character is more important than wealth.)

2906. *Bí mo lọ léhìnkùlé Olúgbọ́n, Olúgbọ́n á mọ̀ pé mo lọ léhìnkùlé òun; bí mo lọ léhìnkùlé Arẹsà, Arẹsà á mọ̀ pé mo lọ léhìnkùlé òun; bí mo lọ́ léhìnkùlé Oníkòyí Màgbó, yó mọ̀ pé mo lọ léhìnkùlé òun.*
If I pass behind the house of the *Olúgbọ́n,* the *Olúgbọ́n* will know that I have passed behind his house; if I pass behind the house of the *Arẹsà,* the *Arẹsà* will know that I have passed behind his house; if I pass behind the house of the *Oníkòyí Màgbó,* he will know that I have passed behind his house.[5] (My fame is such that my presence is loudly proclaimed.)

2907. *Bí òtútù ńpa ọ̀lẹ à jẹ́ kó kú; kíkú tàìkú ọ̀lẹ ò ṣe nǹkan fúnni.*
If a lazy person has a fever, one lets him die; neither a live nor a dead lazy person does anything for one. (A lazy person is not worth troubling over.)

2908. *Bóomọ́ yọ láàrin bàbà.*
Red corn shows amid guinea corn. (A good person sticks out among bad people.)

E

2909. *Èkó ò dùn lójú ẹni tí ò lówó lọ́wọ́.*
The city of Lagos offers no pleasures in the view of a penniless person. (Without money, one is shut out of many pleasures.)

---

2. *Èésú (èsúsú)* is a mutual organization whose members regularly contribute money to a pool from which each member in turn withdraws the total sum.

3. Again, *orí* (head) here refers to destiny.

4. *Ṣèkèrè* is a gourd that has beads or cowrie shells, the currency before colonization, strung around it and that is used as a musical instrument.

5. The three titles are those of renowned Yoruba chiefs.

E

2910. Ẹni ajé ya ilé-e rẹ̀ ló gbọ́n.
It is the person whose home riches have
found that is wise. (Whoever has prospered
may boast that he or she is wise.)

2911. Ẹni Ọlọ́run-ún dá ò ṣé-é farawé.
The person fashioned by God is not one to
emulate. (It is unwise to emulate people who
have means that do you not have.)[6]

I

2912. Ìṣẹ́ aago kì í ṣé òyìnbó.
The dearth of watches does not afflict the
white man. (One never lacks a thing for
which one is the source.[7] See also the following three entries.)

2913. Ìṣẹ́ agbádá kì í ṣé ìmàle.
The dearth of agbádá [the traditional Yoruba garment] never afflicts the Muslim.[8]
(A person is never short of something that
characterizes him. Compare the preceding
entry and the following two.)

2914. Ìṣẹ́-ẹ bàtà kì í ṣé òyìnbó.
The dearth of shoes never afflicts the white
man. (This is a variant of 2912. Compare
also the preceding and following entries.)

2915. Ìṣẹ́ owó kì í ṣé Dàda, Dàda olówó eyo.
The dearth of money never afflicts Dàda,
Dàda who is blessed with coins.[9] (One will

___

6. Ẹni Ọlọ́run-ún dá, translated literally as "a person
fashioned by God," actually means a person who is
under God's constant protection.

7. This proverb and its variant are based on the fact
that the white man introduced the watch to Yorubaland
and is never seen without shoes.

8. The agbádá is the characteristic attire of the
Muslim.

9. Dàda is the name automatically given to a child

___

never lack whatever is part of one's essence.
Compare the preceding three entries.)

2916. Ìṣẹ́ ò mú ọkọláyà kó má ran ọmọ;
akúṣẹ̀ẹ́ kì í ní ará.
Destitution does not afflict the husband
and spare his children; the poverty-ridden
person does not have relatives. (The destitution of the head of the household affects
all members of the household; on the other
hand, the poor person does not have many
friends.)

N

2917. Náwó-náwó ò ná sègi; òtòṣì ò ná erèé
dàgbà; Ìràtà tí ńṣégi tà nínú ìgbé: owó ni
gbogbo wọ́n jọ ńná.
The big spender does not use beads for
money; the poor person did not grow up
spending peas; the person who gathers firewood from the forest for sale: all of them
spend money. (Rich or poor, no one can do
without money.)

O

2918. Òde ò sú aláṣọ-ọ́ lọ.
Public functions do not faze a person with
many clothes. (No eventuality can overwhelm a person with abundant resources.)

2919. Òkú tó bá láṣọ, Ifẹ̀ ní ńsin ín.
A dead person who owns a wealth of clothes
is buried by Ifẹ̀ itself. (The community itself
sees to the funeral of an illustrious person;
the problems of a popular person arouse the
concern of everyone.)

___

born with an abundance of curly hair; the curls, being
likened to the traditional currency of cowrie shells,
are sometimes referred to as owó (money), and people
customarily offer coins to such children.

2920. *Olówó lará mò; ará ò mọ ìṣẹ́; èrò tí ò lówó, ará fa ìwé ẹ̀ ya.*
Kin acknowledges only the rich; no kin claims a poverty-ridden person; the wayfarer who has no money for kin rips up his papers.[10] (Everybody associates with a rich person, but nobody knows a poor person.)

2921. *Olówó layé mò.*
Humankind knows only the rich. (The poor do not count in this world.)

2922. *Olówó lọba lÉkòó.*
The rich man is king in Lagos. (Lagos is an ideal playground for the rich.)

2923. *Olówó sòkè dilẹ̀.*
The rich person turns a hill into a plain. (Nothing is beyond a rich person, not even drastically altering the face of Nature.)

2924. *Òrìṣà bí ajé ò sí; ajé ní ńgbéni ga.*
There is no god like money; it is money that makes people great. (Money can accomplish anything.)

2925. *Òṣì ní ńjẹ́ "Ta ní mọ̀ ọ́ rí?" Owó ní ńjẹ́ "Mo bá ọ tan."*
Poverty is what explains "Who knows you?" Wealth explains, "I am related to you." (No one knows a poor person, but everybody claims kinship to a rich person.)

2926. *Owó ilé yọ, gbèsè ńbínú.*
The household money makes its appearance, and debt becomes angry. (One's enemies are never happy to see one escape misfortune.)

2927. *Owó-là-ńró: tòbí Àlàbá.*
Money-is-what-we-are wearing: Àlàbá's knickers. (Said of a person who is so wealthy

that even his clothing is virtually all money.)[11]

2928. *Owó lẹ̀gbọ́n; ọmọ làbúrò.*
Money is the elder sibling; a child is the younger sibling. (Having wealth makes having children easier.)

2929. *Owó ló wọ́n, ìyàwó ò wọ́n.*
Only money is hard to come by; a wife is not hard to come by. (If one has money, finding a wife is a simple matter.)

2930. *Owó lorí ọ̀ràn; bówó bá dénú ọ̀ràn, yíyọ ní ńyọ.*
Money is the head of any problem; when money is introduced into a problem, its solution results. (Money solves all problems.)[12]

2931. *Owó lojà.*
Money is trade. (There is no trading in the absence of money:)

2932. *Owó ní nígbà tí òun ò sí nílé, ta ní ńdámọ̀ràn léhìn òun?*
Money asked, when it was not at home, who dared to make plans in its absence? (Without money, all plans are useless.)

2933. *Owó ò sí, èèyàn ò sunwọ̀n.*
[If] money is lacking, a person is unattractive. (Wealth is beauty.)

2934. *Owó òtòsì ní ńgbé òkè ẹrù; tolówó a máa gbé ìsàlẹ̀ igbá.*
It is a poor man's money that stays at the top

---

10. The expression "to rip up one's papers" means to ruin one's fortunes.

11. The concept is that the knickers (or male skirt) of the obviously real person named in the proverb, Àlàbá, is made of money or material as valuable as money.

12. The proverb is based on the Yoruba phrase *yọ orí*, literally meaning "pull the head out," an idiom for "solve."

of the load; the rich person's money rests
at the bottom of the calabash. (A poor man
wants to be able easily to see and reach his
money, but the rich person can afford to be
more carefree.)

2935. *Owó yẹ ilé, Ògún yẹ odò.*
Money fits a home quite well; Ògún is at
home by the river. (Money is a desirable
thing in a home.)

Ọ

2936. *Ọbẹ̀ làwọ̀.*
Stew is complexion. (What one eats determines one's well-being.)

2937. *Ọbẹ̀ lọmú àgbà.*
Stew is the breast milk of adults. (Adults
have their own nourishment, even if it differs from children's.)

2938. *Ọjà tí ò tà, owó ló ńwá.*
Goods that will not sell are only in need of
money. (All things are possible if there is
money.)

2939. *Ọmọ ewà kan ò sí; ọmọ aṣọ ní ńbẹ.*
There is no such thing as a child that is a
creation of beauty, but there is something
like a child that is a creation of clothing.
(Clothing, rather than facial beauty, determines the impression one makes on others.)

2940. *Ọnà ọlá pọ̀.*
The approaches to wealth are plentiful; also,
the responsibilities of affluence are plentiful. (There are many different approaches
to wealth. And the more one has, the more
responsibilities one must shoulder.)[13]

2941. *Ọ̀pọ̀ irú kì í ba ọbẹ̀ jẹ́.*
A surfeit of locust-bean seasoning does not
ruin a stew. (One cannot have too much of a
good thing.)

2942. *Ọ̀ràn gbogbo, lórí-i ṣílẹ̀ ní ńdá sí.*
All matters resolve themselves around a
shilling.[14] (Money solves all problems.)

2943. *Ọ̀ràn tí ẹgbà-á wò, ó kúrò láwàdà.*
A problem complicated by as much money
as 2,000 cowries is no longer a joking
matter. (Matters that involve significant
amounts of money are not to be trifled
with.)

T

2944. *Ta la gbé gẹṣin tí kò sèpàkọ́ lùkẹ?*
Who would be placed on the horse and
not cock his head haughtily? (One should
forgive the arrogance of fortunate people.)

2945. *Tí alágbádá ó fi kú, yíyan ni yó máa
yan.*
Until the time the owner of elaborate garments dies, he will keep strutting. (One
should not be bashful about displaying one's
wealth.)

W

2946. *Wọ́n ṣe bí òtòṣì ò gbọ́n bí ọlọ́rọ̀; wọ́n ní
ì bá gbọ́n ì bá lówó lọ́wọ́.*
People think the poor person lacks the wisdom the wealthy person has; they say if one
had wisdom, one would be rich. (It is folly
to equate wealth with wisdom.)

---

13. Most often used as a comment on people who
have too much on their minds to pay attention to
routine expectations.

14. This proverb came into being when Nigeria still
used British currency.

On longevity

A

2947. *Agẹmọ kì í kú ní kékeré.*
The chameleon does not die young.
(A prayer for longevity.)[1]

Ẹ

2948. *Ẹmí gígùn lèrè ayé.*
Longevity is the reward of living. (Longevity is most to be desired by all. This is a variant of 2953.)

2949. *Ẹmí gígùn ní ńsànyà.*
It is longevity that makes up for suffering. (Longevity makes all suffering worthwhile.)

K

2950. *Kí èèmọ̀ ó mọ ní Ìbèṣè, kó má ṣe dé Ìjánà.*
May the disaster stop at Ìbèṣè and not get to Ìjánà. (May trouble stop before it reaches our frontier.)[2]

Ọ

2951. *Ọ̀dọ́mọdé kì í mọ oríkì ìpọ̀nrí è.*
A child never knows the praise name of his guardian spirit.[3] (Only age brings deep knowledge of how the world goes.)

2952. *Ojó alé là ńtọrọ.*
It is nighttime [i.e., old age] that one should pray for. (Old age is everybody's desire.)

P

2953. *Pípẹ́ láyé lèrè ayé.*
Longevity is the profit of living. (Longevity is the reward for having lived a good life. This is a variant of 2948.)

---

1. The chameleon's slow, deliberate gait suggests advanced age.

2. Ìbèṣè and Ìjánnà, neighboring Yoruba towns, were destroyed during the Yoruba wars of the nineteenth century.

3. *Oríkì* is a panegyric, either a short "praise name" for an individual or a long "praise poem," often recited (performed) in honor of important persons or, on state occasions, of kings.

On wealth in people (popularity)

A

2954. *Àfòmọ́ ò légbò; igi gbogbo ní ḿbá tan.*
The climbing plant has no roots; it claims relationship with every tree. (A feckless person is ever in search of benefactors.)

B

2955. *Bí ilé kan ilé, tí ọ̀dẹ̀dẹ̀-ẹ́ kan ọ̀dẹ̀dẹ̀, bí a kò fẹ́ni níbẹ̀, a ò tó abẹ́rẹ́.*
If houses adjoin and living rooms abut, if one is not wanted there, one is not worth so much as a needle. (Being neighbors amounts to nothing if there is no mutual regard.)

E

2956. *Elègbè [or elégbè] ní ḿmú orin dùn.*
It takes a chorus to make a song melodious. (It is good to have backers.)

2957. *Eṣinṣin tí ḿbá ọdẹ rìn á mu ẹ̀jẹ̀ yó.*
A fly that keeps a hunter company will drink blood to its fill. (The fortunes and misfortunes of one's associates will surely rub off on one.)

2958. *Etí-i baba nílé, etí-i baba lóko, èèyàn ní ńjẹ́ bẹ́ẹ̀.*
"Father's ears encompass the house, father's ears reach to the farm" spells "people." (A person who is privy to what goes on everywhere has people everywhere. Compare 2960.)

Ẹ

2959. *Ẹ̀mí àbàtà ní ḿmú odò ṣàn; ọlá-a baba ní ḿmú ọmọ yan.*
It is due to the life in the marshes that the river flows; it is owing to the greatness of the father that the son struts about. (The successful person has some backing that must be acknowledged.)

2960. *Ẹni tí a bú léhìn tó gbọ́, a-betí-í-lu-lára-bí-ajere.*
A person who is insulted in absentia but hears about the insult anyway: his or her entire body is all ears, as a sieve is all holes. (If one cannot be everywhere, one should make sure one has people everywhere. Compare 2958.)

2961. *Ẹni tí kò lówó a léèyàn; ẹni tí kò léèyàn a láápọn.*
A person who lacks money should have people; a person who lacks people should be gregarious. (Good connections can make up for lack of money; but if one also lacks good connections, one had better be gregarious or personable. See 2828.)

2962. *Ẹni tí kò ní adèsò kì í pàtẹ.*
A person who has no one to watch a stall should not display his or her wares there. (If one lacks helpers, one should be judicious in the extent of one's undertakings.)

2963. *Ẹni tí kò ní "Ẹ bá mi pè é!" kì í dákú.*
A person who does not have "Help me revive him!" does not faint. (If one does not

have a champion, one should stay out of trouble.)

2964. Ẹni tí kò ní igi obì kì í léso.
Whoever does not have a kola-nut tree cannot have its fruits. (Unless one owns the means of production, one cannot claim the product.)[1]

2965. Ẹni tó fi ilé sílẹ̀-ẹ́ sọ àpò ìyà kọ́; ẹni tí ó sọ ọkọ́ nù-ú kọ́ àpò ebi.
Whoever moves away from home drapes the satchel of suffering on his or her shoulder; whoever loses a hoe drapes the satchel of hunger. (To move from one's home is to expose oneself to hardship; to lose the means of making a living is to expose oneself to hunger.)

F

2966. Fóró-fóró imú ìyàwó, ó sàn ju yàrá òfifo lọ.
A bride with a gaping nose is better than an empty bedroom. (To have something blemished is much better than to have nothing at all.)

I

2967. Ìdí ìyá là ḿpọ̀n sí.
It is on the mother's waist that a child rests. (One should know where one's succor lies.)[2]

2968. Igbó rúrú níwájú ọlọ́dẹ, èèyàn sùsù léhìn ọlọ̀tẹ̀.

Dense forest behind the hunter; teeming crowd in the wake of a schemer. (Just as a hunter does not run out of forest and a schemer never runs out of co-plotters, so one will not run out of backers.)

2969. Ìhín ilé, ọ̀hún ilé; òjò kì í rọ̀ kó pa ọmọ adìẹ.
Here a home, there a home; the rain does not fall and drench a chick. (One should not submit to suffering when relief is everywhere around.)

2970. Ikú tí kò níí pani ní ńgbé aláwo rere koni.
It is the death that has no intention of killing one that brings an expert diviner man one's way. (One should be grateful if one has people to warn one about impending dangers.)

2971. Ìlẹ̀kùn tí kò ní alùgbàgbà, kó jókòó è jẹ́jẹ́; ẹni tí ò ní baba kì í jìjà ẹbi.
A door without a knocker should keep its peace; a fatherless child does not fight an unjust fight. (People who have no strong backing should not court trouble.)

2972. Ìràwọ̀ sán sán sán, a-lọ́mọ-lẹ́hìn-bí-òsùpá.
Brilliantly twinkling star, with a multitude of followers like the moon. (Comment on an illustrious person who has a huge following.)

2973. Ìyàwó dùn lọ́sìngín.
Marriage is pleasant when it is new. (No pleasure compares to that of a honeymoon.)

---

1. This proverb is usually employed to state that a man not married to a woman may not claim her children as his.
2. This is a reference to the Yoruba women's practice of carrying their children mounted on their backs, so that the mother's waist supports the child.

J

2974. Jòjò àgbò ní ḿmú àgbò níyì; ọlá-a baba ní ḿmú ọmọ yan.
It is the ram's dewlap that lends it dignity;

it is the father's greatness that gives the son reason to strut. (One who has good grounds for doing so may walk proudly.)

K

2975. *Ká jà ká re Ọ̀yọ́, ká mọ ẹni tó lọba.*
Let us quarrel and go to Ọ̀yọ́, and we will see on whose side the king is. (Boast that one would have the powers-that-be on one's side in any quarrel.)

2976. *Ká rìn ká pọ̀, yíyẹ ní ńyẹni [bí-i tọnà ọ̀run kọ́].*
Traveling in the company of others shows people in a good light [but not if the journey is to heaven]. (People are best in association with others, and not as loners.)[3]

2977. *Ká ríni lókèèrè ká ṣàríyá, ó yóni ó ju oúnjẹ lọ.*
To see one from afar and greet one cheerfully satisfies far better than food ever could. (Fellowship is far better than material gifts.)

2978. *Ká síni létí ò jẹ́ kágbà ó ṣìṣe láàrin ilé.*
Being quietly advised keeps an elder from committing a blunder within his household. (Even elders will do well to heed advice.)

2979. *Kàkà kí gbajúmọ̀ ó jẹ ọ̀pọlọ́, ẹni tí yó pa kọ̀nkọ̀ fun yó jàáde.*
Rather than the popular person finding himself reduced to eating a toad, someone will emerge to kill a frog for him. (The well-regarded person will always have people to come to his or her aid in times of need.)

2980. *Kì í burú burú kó má ku ẹnikan mọ́ni; ẹni tí yó kù la ò mọ̀.*

One's fortune never turns so bad that one is left with no one; whom one will be left with is what one does not know. (One never knows, until trouble comes, who among one's friends is faithful.)

2981. *Kò sí ohun tó dàbí-i ká wáni wálé.*
There is nothing that compares with being visited at home. (It is a great honor to be visited in one's home.)

L

2982. *Lára èèyàn lowó wà.*
Riches are inseparable from people. (Whoever has people around him is rich indeed.)

O

2983. *Orí olókìkí ò jẹ́ asán; wọ́n ńkígbe ẹ̀ nílé, wọ́n ńkígbe ẹ̀ lógun.*
The lot of a valorous person is not simple; he is called upon at home, and he is called upon in battle. (A great person is subject to demands from all sides.)

2984. *Oṣùpá gbókè mỌ̀yọ́; ọbá gbélé mọ ará oko.*
The moon remains on the firmament and knows all about Ọ̀yọ́; the king remains at home but knows all about the farm dweller. (An influential person does not have to be present at a place to know what goes on there. Compare 2958.)

2985. *Owó fífún ò tó èèyàn.*
A gift of money is not equal in value to a [gift of a] person. (Human presence or company is worth more than money.)

2986. *Owó kan ò ró ṣẹkẹ; èèyàn mẹ́ta ò dúró ní méjì méjì.*
A solitary coin does not clink; three people

---

3. The tag about the journey to heaven was not originally part of the proverb but is in fact a cynical rejoinder to the original observation.

cannot stand in twos. (One cannot make
sufficiency out of deficiency.)

Ọ

2987. *Ọlọ́rò-ọ́ kú, ẹ̀hìn-in rẹ̀-ẹ́ kún.*
The wealthy person dies and his wake is
congested. (A wealthy person has many
mourners.)

T

2988. *Ta ló lè ṣe bí atọ́kùn fún eégún?*
Who can play the role of the guide for a
masquerader? (No one can replace a devoted
benefactor.)[4]

W

2989. *Wèrèpè-é gba ara ẹ̀ gba igi oko.*
The cow-itch protects itself and protects
other trees in the forest. (Closeness to a
powerful person is good protection.)

---

4. The *atọ́kùn* is the ever vigilant attendant who
ensures that the masquerader, with his vision limited
and movements often restricted by his costume, does
not get into difficulties.

THREE

Relationships

On relationships with the divine and the supernatural

2990. *A kì í ba Ọlọrun ṣòwò ká pàdánù.*
One does not trade with God and come up
a loser. (Any venture that takes God into
account will surely prosper.)

2991. *A kọlé bíríkótó, a ní kí òrìṣà gbà á; bí kò
bá gbà á, kó lọ sígbèẹ kó lọ sá ẹké, kó lọ sọdàn
lọ họ okùn, kó mọ bí agara-á ti ńdáni.*
We build a modest shrine and implore the
god to accept it; if he does not accept it, let
him go into the forest to cut stakes, let him
go into the grassland for vines, so that he
might appreciate the pains we have taken.
(A god must not be too demanding of his
worshipers, for if pushed too far they will
rebel.)

2992. *Àkèré ńgbọ tọmọ ẹja lódò.*
The frog pays attention to the doings of little
fishes in the river. (One must be attentive to
those beholden to one.)[1]

2993. *Àtidádé Olókun ò sẹ̀hìn òkun; àtidádé
Ọlọ́sà ò sẹ̀hìn ọ̀sà; àti dádée kìnnìún ò sẹ̀hìn
Olúigbó.*
The crowning of the Olókun, goddess of
the sea, will not be in the absence of the
sea; the crowning of the Ọlọ́sà, goddess of
the lagoon, will not be in the absence of the
lagoon; the crowning of the lion will not
be in the absence of the deity of the for-
ests. (Nothing can be accomplished without
God's help.)

2994. *Àtisùn èdá ò sẹ̀hìn Olódùmarè.*
A human being's dying is not hidden from
the Creator. (Only God determines the time
of a person's death.)

2995. *Ayé ò fẹ́ ká rẹrù ká sò; orí ẹni ní ńsọni.*
The world would not wish to see one set
down one's heavy burden; only one's head
relieves one of the burden. (One cannot
count on the good will of the world; one can
count only on one's protective spirit.)

2996. *Bí alàgbà-á bá júbà fÓlúwa, ọ̀nà á là.*
If the elder pays homage to God, the path
opens. (Nothing is possible without God,
and nothing is impossible with God.)

2997. *Eégún ṣé-é jó; òòsà-á ṣé-é jó; ti
Olódùmarè-é yàtọ̀.*
A masquerader can be set alight; a god [or
idol] can be set alight; God, though, is a different matter. (Only God is beyond peril at
the hands of humans.)

---

1. Since the frog shares a habitat with the fishes, it
cannot help being attentive to their doings. This saying
is often used by Christians as a justification for paying
attention to the wishes of God.

E

2998. Ẹni tó bá fojú àná wòkú, ẹbọra á bọ́ ọ láṣọ.
Whoever looks at the dead with yesterday's eyes will be undone by the spirits. (Never deal with newly powerful people as you did before they became powerful.)[2]

I

2999. Igba ẹkẹ́ ní ńfọwọ́ tilé; igba alámù ní ńfọwọ́ ti ògiri; Olú-fọwọ́-tì ni Ṣàngó; gbogbo ayé ní ńfọwọ́ ti ọba.
Two hundred poles hold up a house; two hundred lizards support a wall with their hands; Chief-lends-support is Ṣango's name; the whole world lends support to the king. (Used in the context of prayer or incantation to invoke the support of the powers that control the universe.)

K

3000. Kàkà kí ebí pa ọmọ awo kú, ìpèsè ni yó yòó o.
Rather than the child of the priest dying of hunger, he or she will feed to satisfaction on goods provided for sacrifice. (Providence will not permit the referent to suffer want.)

3001. Kò sí òrìṣà tí kò ní ìgbẹ́.
There is no òrìṣà [god] that does not have a bush.[3] (Every god provides some benefit for its worshipers.)

3002. Kọ̀lọ̀kọ̀lọ̀ ìbá kú, adìẹ ò sunkún; kọ̀lọ̀kọ̀lọ̀ ò gba adìẹ sìn.
Were the fox to die, the chicken would not shed a tear; the fox never fostered a chick. (One does not mourn an enemy's disaster.)

M

3003. Màlúù tí ò nírù, Ọlọ́run ní ńbá a lésinsin.
A cow that has no tail can count on God to help it chase flies away. (There is always some help for even the most helpless person.)

3004. Múni-múni ò lè mú Olódùmarè.
The professional arrester cannot arrest the Almighty. (God is beyond human punishment.)

N

3005. "Ng ò níí sin Olúwa, ng ò níí sin Ànábì"; ohun tí olúwarè ó sìn ò níí tó èkùró.
"I will not worship God, and I will not worship Allah"; what such a person will worship will not be so large as a palm kernel. (A person who is too picky will wind up having no pick at all.)

3006. Nítorí Ọlọ́run nìmàlè fi ńjẹ mọ́sà.
It is in deference to God that the Muslim eats fried corn cake. (Necessity obliges one to do things one would not do otherwise.)

O

3007. Ohun tí babá ṣe sílẹ̀ nìrègún ọmọ.
What the father provided is what the children inherit. (Children benefit from the industry of their father.)

---

2. Because the dead are believed to assume supernatural powers in their new status as spirits, any human who approaches them as he or she did when they were alive courts disaster.

3. Ìgbẹ́ (bush) here refers to the medicinal herbs that are associated with an òrìṣà and whose properties are known to that god's devotees.

3008. *Ojú ilẹ̀ la ṣe dá a tí a ṣe rú u; bí ẹbọ bá máa jẹ́ kí ilẹ̀ ó jẹ́rìí.*
It is in the presence of Earth that one consulted the oracle and offered the prescribed sacrifice; if the sacrifice will yield the promised result, let Earth bear witness. (The Earth will monitor and enforce oaths sworn in her presence.)

3009. *Òkùtù ọpẹ kì í wo ojú ẹlòmíràn bí kò ṣe ojú Ọlọ́run.*
Young palm leaves do not raise their eyes to anyone other than God. (All affairs are best left to God.)

3010. *Oore wo lòrìṣá ṣe fún abuké tó sọ ọmọ ẹ̀ ní Òrìṣá-gbè-mí?*
What favor have the gods granted the humpback who names his child Òrìṣágbèmí [The gods have come to my aid]? (There is no point in offering gratitude in a direction from which no help has come.)

3011. *Òrìṣà, bí o ò le gbè mí, ṣe mí bí o ti bá mi.*
God, if you will not save me, leave me as you found me! (If the person one looks to for help does not help, he or she at least should not leave one worse off than before.)

3012. *Òrìṣà ní ńpeni wá jẹ okà; a kì í gbọ́ ọwọ́ orógùn lẹ́hìnkùlé.*
It is the gods that summon one to come eat yam-flour meal; one does not hear the sound of the stirring stick from the back yard. (If one chances on good fortune, one should give thanks to the gods.)

3013. *Òrìṣà tí a ké, ké, ké, tí kò gbọ́, tí a gè, gè, gè, tí kò gbà; ojú-u pópó ní ńgbé.*
The god that one praises, praises, and praises but who does not listen, that one worships, worships, and worships but who refuses to heed, ends up in the streets. (If a supposed savior consistently fails you, discard it and find yourself another.)

Ọ

3014. *Ọlọ́run la kì í sú.*
Only God never gets fed up with us. (Unlike people, God is infinitely patient.)

3015. *Ọlọ́run ní ńṣèdájọ́ a-fehín-pínran.*
Only God can render justice to the person who uses his teeth to share out meat. (God alone sees, and can reward, what people do in secret.)

T

3016. *Ta ni tàkúté Olúwa ò leè mú?*
Who is beyond being caught in God's trap? (No one is beyond God's judgment.)

3017. *Tinú tẹ̀hìn ni labalábá fi ńyin Ọlọ́run.*
It is with both its belly and its back that the butterfly praises the Lord. (One should glorify God with all one has.)

On relationships with the family

A

3018. *A kì í dúró nílùú ká fara hẹ.*
One does not stay for long in a town and remain uninvolved. (One must live as a part of one's community.)

3019. *A kì í mọ alájá ká nà á lópa.*
One does not know a dog's owner and yet rain blows on it with a rod. (One's regard for a person should extend to that person's interests. Compare the two following entries.)

3020. *A kì í mọ alájá ká pè é ní títà.*
One does not know the owner of a dog and yet announce that it is for sale. (One should safeguard the interests of those one knows, even in their absence. Compare the preceding and following entries.)

3021. *A kì í mọ alájá ká pé kẹ́kùn ó pa á jẹ.*
One does not know the owner of a dog and yet wish that a leopard would eat it. (One should invoke no ill on things dear to people one knows. Compare the preceding two entries.)

3022. *A kì í sọ pé ó di ojọ́ tí a bá bímọ ká tó sọ ọmọ níkòó.*
One does not say it will not be until one has fathered a child that one raps a child on the head with one's knuckles. (Every adult shares the responsibility for disciplining all children, not only his or her own.)

3023. *Abánigúnwà ní ḿmọ ìjagun ẹni.*
It is he who shares one's throne that knows one's strategy in battle. (Only soulmates know each other's minds. Compare the next entry.)

3024. *Abánigbé ní ḿmọ ìṣe ẹni.*
Whoever one lives with knows one's habits. (The public image is not reliable. Compare the preceding entry and 3400.)

3025. *A-bánigbé-má-mọ̀wà-ẹni, ọ̀tá ẹni ni.*
He-who-lives-with-one-without-knowing-one's-habits: he is one's enemy. (A housemate who does not know one's ways cannot be trusted.)

3026. *Abíni ò tó atọ́ni.*
The parent is no match for the rearer. (Raising a child is more important than giving birth to a child.)

3027. *Àdábọwọ́ lọrẹ́; baba ọmọ ní ńfi ọmọ fọ́kọ.*
A friend is like a glove; it is a child's father that gives her away to a husband. (Only the relationship sanctioned by the woman's father is legitimate.)[1]

3028. *A-dáko-má-gbin-ọkà-á ní òún dá ikún lára; bíkún ò bá rí jẹ lóko-o rẹ̀, áá rí jẹ lóko ẹlòmíràn.*

---

1. *Ọ̀rẹ́* in this instance means a male friend with whom a woman has relations before marriage: like a glove, he can be discarded. The man that the father recognizes as her husband is the person with whom she may have a lasting relationship.

He-who-prepares-a-farm-and-does-not-plant-corn says he is denying something to the squirrel; if squirrel finds nothing to eat on his farm, it will find something on another person's farm. (Obsessive attempts to injure others can and do backfire.)

3029. *Adámú ò lè wà nílé ká má gbọdọ̀ ṣe han-han.*
One does not stop saying *han-han* simply because there is a person with a nasal speech defect in the home. (There is a limit to the concessions one can make to those one lives with.)

3030. *Adárugudu adìẹ ní ńyé sí ìbọ̀wọ́.*
It is a troublemongering chicken that lays eggs in a glove. (A dependent's recklessness causes problems for his or her protector.)[2]

3031. *Àì-fojú-kan-ara-ẹni ò jẹ́ kí ọ̀tẹ̀ ó tán.*
Not-seeing-each-other-face-to-face perpetuates a conspiracy. (Lack of personal contact prevents the ending of a feud.)

3032. *Ajá tó ti ńríni yọ̀ kì í tún ríni gbó.*
A dog that once rejoiced on seeing one does not switch to barking on seeing one. (Radical changes in other people's attitude to one are developments not to be wished for.)

3033. *Àjànàkú yáwó tán kò singbà mọ́; erin-ín gbówó olówó wọgbó lọ.*
The elephant pawned itself for money but did not serve as promised; the elephant took others' money and disappeared into the bush. (The mighty person can get away with anything.)

3034. *Ajé ló mọ bí òun ó ti ṣe ọlọ́jà Odògbo, tí a pa ẹkìrì ká fi wójò, tó nìkan kun ún tà.*
Only the demon of prosperity knows what it will do with the chief of Odògbo; we killed a wild goat as an offering for rain, and he cut it for sale for himself. (A powerful person who betrays his trust must be left to the gods to deal with.)

3035. *Àjèjé ọwọ́ kan ò gbégbá karí.*
A single hand does not lift a calabash to the head [to be carried]. (It takes two hands to lift a heavy load. Cooperation is best.)

3036. *Ajèbimágbà ní ńkógun wòlú.*
It is he-who-is-guilty-but-refuses-to-accept-the-guilt that brings warfare into a town. (Refusal to accept one's guilt ruins communal harmony.)

3037. *Aládùúgbò ẹni ni ọmọ ìyá ẹni.*
One's neighbor is one's same-mother relative. (A neighbor is as close as any sibling.)

3038. *Aláìláyà ò lè gbé ilé ńlá; bí a bá láyà ihòrò ní ńsinnií lọ.*
A fainthearted person cannot live in a large house; if one has a lion heart, it leads one to the grave. (Whatever the inconvenience, one must learn to get along with people or else live as a hermit.)

3039. *Alájọbí ò sí mọ́, alájọgbé ló kù.*
Kin is no longer to be found; only cohabitors remain. (Kinship is no longer in fashion, only neighborliness.)

3040. *Ànìkànjẹ ayé kì í dùn; jíjọjẹ ní ńdára.*
Going through life by oneself is unpleasant; living life in company is pleasant. (Having riches is nothing like having people.)

3041. *Àńtètè, ó dá yànpọ̀n-yànpọ̀n sílẹ̀.*
The cricket sows confusion among others. (When people like the cricket depart a place, they leave dissension and confusion in their wake.)

---

2. The chicken will put its owner and the owner of the glove at loggerheads.

3042. *Àpésan kì í tú ìlú.*
Contributing to a common purse does not ruin a town. (A town that acts together stays together.)

3043. *Àpón yan ìyà ó ní òún yan ìyá; ta là bá kó isu méjì fún tí kò gúnyán konko fúnni?*
A bachelor chooses suffering but says he chose his mother; to what person would one give two yams but would not make pounded yam? (Whatever a mother can do for a man, a wife can do, and more.)

3044. *Ará òde ò moni lẹ́rú; ará ilé eni ní ńnawọ́ erú síni.*
Outsiders do not know that one is a slave; people of one's household are the ones who point one out as a slave. (If those of one's household do not dishonor one, outsiders will not.)

3045. *Aríjàmálàjà, òtá Olórun.*
One-who-sees-a-fight-and-does-not-try-to-stop-it: an enemy of God. (To fail to stop a fight is to offend God.)

3046. *Àrò méta kì í da obè nù.*
A trident cooking hearth does not spill stew. (Many hands ensure success.)

3047. *Àrùn tí ńse ogójì ní ńse òódúnrún; ohun tí ńse Abóyadé gbogbo olÓya ní ńse.*
The same disease that afflicts the forty afflicts the three hundred; whatever afflicts Abóyadé afflicts all devotees of Oya.[3] (Every member of a group shares in the collective fate and reputation of the group.)

3048. *Àsopò ní ńmú ewúrẹ́ wè.*
It is being-tied-together that forces goats to

take a bath. (If one must act in concert with others, one loses some freedom to do what one would rather do.)

3049. *Àtẹlẹwó finú sòkan; àtàmpàkó se tiè lótò.*
The palms of the hand have only one interior; the thumb separates itself from the rest. (A person who so wishes may refrain from going with the group.[4] Compare 3189.)

3050. *Àwáyó fara è gbodì.*
We-are-full makes enemies for himself. (A person who refuses favors on behalf of others makes enemies of those others.)

3051. *Awo ní ńgbe awo nígbònwó; bí awo ò bá gbe awo nígbònwó awo á té.*
Initiates of mysteries must rally round other initiates; if initiates do not rally round one another, they suffer disgrace. (Cooperation among group members protects their collective image.)

B

3052. *Bí a bá bu ìgbé lábùká, a ó rìí eran inú-u rè pa.*
If hunters encircle the bush, they will succeed in killing the animals therein. (If all available hands converge on a task, it will be accomplished.)

3053. *Bí a bá fa gbùùrù, gbùùrù a fagbó.*
If one pulls the vine, the vine pulls the bush. (If one goes after an offender, one becomes entangled with his or her patron.)

3054. *Bí a bá ńbú etù, orí a máa fó awó.*
If one insults the guinea fowl, the guinea

---

3. The name Abóyadé means "One who arrived with Oya," the Yoruba goddess of the river Niger. Born during the sabbath (the period of worship) of the river, the child is presumed to be a ward of the goddess.

4. The palms of one's hands are face to face when brought together.

fowl gets a headache. (When one hears one's close relative insulted, one feels insulted.[5] Compare 4555.)

3055. *Bí àṣá kò bá féé fé àṣá níràn, ojú-u sánmà-á tó-ó fò féyẹ láì fara gbúnra.*
If an eagle does not want to provoke an eagle, the sky is wide enough for birds to fly without bumping one another. (If one is spoiling for a fight, any excuse will do.)

3056. *Bí ayá bá gbó tokọ, wàhálàá tán.*
If a wife does the husband's bidding, all problems disappear. (Domestic bliss depends on the wife's complaisance.)[6]

3057. *Bí ejọ́ ò sunwọ̀n, ẹléjọ́ là ńfún dá.*
If a case is hopeless, one asks the owner to judge it. (If guilt is obvious, the guilty should be made to declare it.)

3058. *Bí ẹrú bá jọ ara-a wọn, à mọ̀ pé ilé kannáà ni wọ́n ti wá.*
If slaves resemble one another, one surmises that they came from the same household. (People who share similar traits deserve to be lumped together.)

3059. *Bí ìbágbé ò bá wò, ká yàgò fúnra.*
If cohabitation does not work, let us give each other some space. (If people cannot be friends or husband and wife, they should part amicably.)

3060. *Bí ilé kò dùn, bí ìgbé nìlú ńrí.*
If the home is not pleasant, the town seems like a jungle. (The tone of the town depends on the condition of the homes in it.)

3061. *Bí obìnrín bá di méjì, imú okọ a di odó, a ní wọn ò tún yí imú lu òun mọ́.*
When women number two, the husband's nose becomes a mortar; she [the first wife] says that he no longer rolls his nose in her direction. (The erstwhile favorite never takes kindly to being supplanted by a new favorite.)

3062. *Bí ojú bá ko ojú, àlà yó tòọ́ nídìí ìgbá.*
If eyes meet eyes, the boundary line will be straight at the base of the locust tree. (When all parties participate in dividing something among them, no one is cheated.)

3063. *Bí ọmọ ò jọ ṣòkòtò a jọ kíjìpá.*
If a child does not resemble the trousers, he should resemble the wrapper. (If a child does not take after his father, he should take after his mother.)

3064. *Bí ọmọdé bá ní aṣọ bí ìyá-a rè, kò ní èyí tí ìyá-a rè-ẹ́ fi pọ̀n ón.*
If a youth has a wrapper like her mother's, she does not have the one her mother used to bear her.[7] (However rich or great a person becomes, the person owes deference to his or her parents.)

3065. *Bí ọmọdé bá pa eku, a dá a jẹ, bó bá pa ẹyẹ, a dá a jẹ, ṣùgbọ́n ọjọ́ tó bá dáràn gòdògbà, a fà á wá sọ́dọ̀ ọ bàbá-a rè.*
When a youth kills a rat, he eats it alone; when he kills a bird, he eats it alone; but when he is in serious trouble, he drags it home to his father. (A youth does not remember his parents until he needs their help.)

---

5. The proverb works in Yoruba, where *ẹtù* and *awó* mean the same thing; the construction then permits the suggestion that they are two different (because of different names) but very similar entities.

6. The sexism is not accidental.

7. The wrapper referred to is the fabric that forms the lower piece of a Yoruba woman's attire. Nursing mothers wrap their children on their backs inside the cloth.

E

3066. Èèyàn bí ìyá ò sí; ta ní jẹ́ ṣe ọmọ-ọlọ́mọ
lóore?
There is no being like a mother; whoever did
another person's child a favor? (A mother is
the surest support a person can ever hope
for.)

3067. Ehín tó tayọ, wàhálà ẹnu ni.
A bucktooth is trouble for the mouth. (One
pays one way or another for one's shortcomings. Or, the shortcomings of one's
relatives spell problems for one also.)

3068. Èkó ilá gba ara-a rẹ̀ lọ́wọ́ ọbẹ̀: ilá táa
kókìkí ò so; gbọ̀ọ̀rọ̀ táa gbẹ́kẹ̀lé ò fà; ọmọ ìfẹ́
táa gbẹ́kẹ̀lé ò ṣe bí a ti rò.
Okro that goes to seed saves itself from
being stewed: the okro one boasted about
fails to fruit; the pumpkin one placed one's
hopes on sends out no trailers; the beloved
child one relied on fails to do as one hoped.
(One can hope for no rewards for one's pains
from an ungrateful child.)

3069. "Èyí wù mí kò wù ọ́" lọmọ ìyá méjì-í fi
ńjẹun lọ́tòọ̀tọ̀.
"This appeals to me but not to you" is the
reason why two children of the same mother
eat separately. (Even the closest of relatives
may differ in taste.)

Ẹ

3070. Ẹ̀ ńgbàdúrà kẹ́sin ilé kú; ẹ ò níí lẹ́sin
mìíràn níran yín mọ́.
You pray for the death of the household
horse; there will never be another horse in
your lineage. (Any household that wishes for
the destruction of its most illustrious member will never again be blessed with a worthy
member.)

3071. Ẹ̀ẹ̀tán lelégbè ẹyìn; ọmọ bíbí inú ẹni
lelégbè ẹni.
Young palm fruits are the support of ripe
ones; one's children are one's support. (In
their old age parents have their children to
lean on.)

3072. Ẹ̀là ìlẹ̀kẹ̀ ò lójú àtokùnbọ̀; alágbẹ̀dẹ ò
rójú ará.
A split bead lacks a hole for a thread; the
blacksmith has no time for relatives. (Some
occupations leave no room for the observance of courtesies.)

3073. Ẹlébí ò run orín gbooro.
A person with a large family does not chew a
long chewing stick. (If one has many dependents, there will be great demands on one's
resources.)[8]

3074. Ẹlébí ò sinmi; ẹni a bí ire ò ráyè.
A person with a large family does not rest; a
person of good birth has no time to himself
or herself. (Whoever has a large family or is
very popular has many obligations and great
demands on his or her time.)

3075. Ẹni a bí wọn bí kì í wù wọ́n; ẹni ẹléni ní
ńyá wọn lára.
Their blood relatives never find favor with
them; only strangers evoke their enthusiasm.
(People always appreciate what is remote
more than what is near at hand.)

3076. Ẹní bímọ ọ̀ràn ní ńpọ̀n ọ́n dàgbà.
Whoever mothers a problem child will bear
it on her back until it is weaned. (Oneself,
and no one else, bears the consequences of
one's own actions.)

3077. Ẹni tí yó kùú kì í la odó yáná.
A dying person does not split the mortar

---

8. Chewing sticks, the means for cleaning teeth, are
twigs or roots of certain plants. If a person has a long
one, relatives ask for pieces of it.

to kindle a fire to warm himself or herself. (However desperate one's circumstances, one should respect the interests of others.)

3078. Ẹni tó bá yọ ará ilé-e rẹ̀ lẹ́nu yó jogún òfo.
Whoever makes himself or herself a nuisance to those of his or her household inherits nothing. (It pays to look well to one's relations with one's family.)

F

3079. Fìlà lobìnrin, wọn kì í bá ọdẹ wọ ìtí.
Women are caps; they never accompany the hunter into the dense forest. (Women do not stick around when their men suffer reverses.)[9]

G

3080. Gángán ló báni tan; kò ṣéé fi ọbẹ rẹ́.
His relationship to one is very slight; even so it cannot be severed with a knife. (The most distant relative still deserves to be acknowledged and treated as such.)

I

3081. Ìfẹ́ ni kókó ìpàkọ́; a kì í fi aṣọ kọ́ o.
The knot at the occiput is something one tolerates out of love; one cannot hang clothes on it. (One does or endures certain things without expecting material benefits from them.)

3082. Ìgbà ò lè di ìgbà òyìnbó ká fi àbúrò ẹni ṣaya.
No matter to what extent the era has become

a white man's era, one cannot take one's own sister as a wife. (There are some values and habits that will survive the strongest foreign influences. Compare the next entry.)

3083. Ìgbà ò lè di ìgbà òyìnbó kọ́mọ ẹní sọnù ká má wàá a.
However strong the white man's influence, if one's child is lost, one will go searching for him or her. (A people's values must survive the strongest foreign influences. Compare the preceding entry.)

3084. Ikú òde ní ńpa ọmọdé fún ìyá ẹ̀.
It is death from outside that kills a child for his or her mother. (A child not properly instructed at home will learn a lesson from strangers outside the home.)

3085. Ìlasa ò sunwọ̀n; ta ló bí ilá?
Okro leaf is no good; who gave birth to the okro? (However great the offspring, he or she must yet acknowledge his or her parents.)

3086. Ilé là ńwò ká tó sọmọ lórúkọ.
One considers the home before giving a child [from it] a name. (A child's character is a good indication of the sort of home he or she comes from.)

3087. Ilé la ti ńkẹsọ̀ọ́ ròde.
One adorns oneself with finery in one's home before stepping outside. (One's character follows one from home into the world outside.)

3088. Ilé làbọ̀sinmi oko.
The home is where one returns for rest after the farm. (However long one wanders, one eventually returns home.)

3089. Ilé ni bòyí máa bò sí.
The home is the place the houseboy returns

---

9. A hunter's cap is likely to be knocked off his head by hanging branches when he enters a thick forest.

to in the end. (One may try, but one cannot escape one's destiny.)

3090. *Ilé ọkọ lobìnrín ti ńtún ìpín yàn.*
It is in the marital home that a woman's destiny is revised. (A woman's destiny begins anew when she goes to her husband's home.)

3091. *Ilénikúwà ẹran Àjàyí; Àyànmọ́-ìpín ẹran Olúgbòde.*
The-home-is-where-death-lurks, the name of Àjàyí's goat; One's-fate-is-set-at-one's-creation, the name of Olúgbòde's goat. (If one's home base is secure, one is safe from disaster; yet no one can avert his or her fate.)

3092. *Ilésanmí dùn ju oyè lọ.*
The-home-is-blissful-for-me is far better than a chieftaincy title. (It is better to have a peaceful home than to be a chief.)[10]

3093. *Ipin lójú, ikun nímú, ará ilé ẹní mọ̀dí è: àrùn lará ìta ńpè é.*
Eyes oozing matter, mucus in the nose: those of one's household know the cause, but strangers attribute them to disease. (Only those really close to a person know the real reasons for his or her condition.)

3094. *Iṣẹ́ àpọ́n ò lórí; tabiyamọ ló sàn díẹ̀.*
The bachelor's privations are to no purpose; those of a mother are somewhat better. (Suffering is tolerable as long as it is not purposeless.)

3095. *Iṣẹ́ ńbẹ lóko òkú tí a pè tí kò dáhùn.*
There is work to be done on the farm of the dead person, who is called but does not respond. (When a person becomes incapable of performing his or her duties, the relatives inherit the obligation to take them up.)

3096. *Iṣu kì í ta kó gbàgbé ewé; àgbàdo kì í yọmọ kó gbàgbé ìrùkèrè; kí ni ngó jẹ gbàgbé ọmọ-ọ̀ mi?*
The yam does not mature and forget the leaves; the corn does not ripen and forget the tassels; what would I eat that would make me forget my children? (However successful one might be, ones's children would still be uppermost in one's mind.)

3097. *Ìtàkùn ní ńṣe ikú pa ọ̀kéré; obìnrin ní ńṣe ikú pa ọkùnrin.*
Vines are the death of squirrels; women are the death of men. (As dangerous as vines are to the squirrels, so dangerous are women to men.)

3098. *Ìtàkùn tó so igbá, tó so agbè, ló so elégédé.*
The same vine that grew a calabash and grew a gourd also grew a pumpkin. (Said of people who are of the same stock but harbor enmity toward one another.)

3099. *Ìtàn ìnàkí lojú-u wa ò tó; bó ṣe tọ̀bọ ni, ojú-u wá tó díẹ̀ níbẹ̀.*
The story of the baboon is something we do not know anything about, but when it comes to the story of the monkey, we know something about it.[11] (One may be ignorant about the affairs of other households but can certainly speak to the affairs of one's own.)

3100. *Iwájú la ti ńjogún; ẹ̀hìn la ti ńṣàgbà.*
One inherits from one's front, and one sets an example at one's back. (Deriving benefits from one's elders, one is obligated to pass on some benefits to those who are younger.)

---

10. Ilésanmí is a common name that means "The home is blissful for me."

11. Monkeys are popular household pets, whereas baboons are not.

3101. *Ìyá là bá ní; ará ò ṣe nǹkan fúnni.*
One whould rather have a mother; relatives hardly do one any favor. (A mother is to be preferred over other kin.)

3102. *Ìyá ni wúrà, baba ni jígí; ọjọ́ ìyá kú ni wúrà-á bàjé; ọjọ́ tí babá kú ni jígí lọ.*
Mother is gold, father is glass; the day the mother dies is the day the gold is ruined; the day the father dies is the day the glass is gone. (One's parents are of great value, but the mother is more precious than the father.)

J

3103. *"Jọ mí jọ mí," òkú òǹrorò ní ńsọni dà.*
"Be just like me, be just like me!" makes one an intolerable tyrant. (One should allow others to be themselves.)

K

3104. *Kí adití baà gbọ́rọ̀ la ti ńsọ ọ́ lójú ọmọ ẹ̀.*
It is so that a deaf person might hear something that one says it in his or her child's presence. (One way of making one's opinion known to a person one cannot or dares not speak to is to say it in the hearing of someone close to that person.)

3105. *Kí ni a ó ṣe fún ọmọ àlè tí yó peni ní baba?*
What could one do for a bastard that would induce him or her to call one "father"? (A favor done for unworthy and ungrateful people is a favor done in vain.)

3106. *Kòbánitan ò jogún eni.*
He-[or-she]-is-not-related-to-one does not inherit from one. (Those one has nothing to do with have no rights in one's affairs.)

M

3107. *Má ṣe fìwà jọ mí; ọmọ olè lolè ńjọ.*
Do not take after me; a thief takes after a thief's offspring [or a thief's offspring takes after his parents]. (One should take after one's parents in character.)

3108. *Màlúù tó jẹ èbù ló ní ká na Fúlàní ní patiyẹ.*
The cow that ate yam pieces cut for planting is the cause for the whipping that the Fulbe man suffered.[12] (People are responsible for the misdeeds of those in their charge: *respondeat superior.*)

N

3109. *"Ng ó ṣe ìyá" ò lè jọ ìyá; "Ng ó ṣe baba" ò lè jọ baba; "Wòsọ̀ dè mí" ò lè jọ onísọ̀; ojú mẹ́wàá ò lè jọ ojú ẹni.*
"I will be like a father to you" does not compare to one's real father; "I will be a mother to you" is not the same as a real mother; "Watch the store for me" is not the same as the owner of the store; ten eyes are not like one's own. (A substitute is never as good as the real thing. Compare 3150.)

3110. *Nínù là ńnu ọmọ ẹyẹ dàgbà.*
Until it matures, the young bird is fed by having food placed in its mouth. (People have the responsibility to care for their dependents until they are able to care for themselves.)

O

3111. *Obìnrín délé ọkọ ó gbàgbé òrẹ́.*
On arriving at her marital home, a woman

---

12. The Fulbe man is the cowherd; Fulbe men are identified with cowherding.

forgets her suitors. (On leaving a stage in one's life, one should abandon the habits of that stage.)

3112. *Obínrin tí kòì lórogún ò tíì màrùn tí ńṣèun.*
A woman who does not yet have a co-wife does not yet know what disease she has. (Until one has enemies, one seldom knows one's flaws.)

3113. *Òde là ńṣàgbà, ilé kan bí ìbó; bó pé títí, àtilé àtòde ní ḿbọ̀ wáá kàn.*
When one is abroad, one acts the venerable sage, even though one's homestead is as sour as the sap of the *ìbó* plant; but sooner or later both the homestead and the outside become sour. (One cannot conceal one's secret shame forever.)

3114. *Odò kì í ṣàn kó gbàgbé ìsun.*
A river does not flow and forget its source. (However far you may roam, always remember where you came from.)

3115. *Ogún-mobí, ọmọ kòrikò; Ogbòn-mo-wò ọmọ Èrúwà; kàkà ká bí egbàá ọ̀bùn, ká bí ọ̀kanṣoṣo ọ̀bùn, ó kúkú yá.*
Twenty children I have, a hyena's litter; thirty children I raised, Èrúwà's brood; rather than two hundred ill-groomed brats, one would be better off with just one stupid child.[13] (The more children a person has, the more likely they all are to turn out bad.)

3116. *Òkò lọmọ: Ọlọ́run ní ńwí pé ká sọ ó síbi tó dára.*
A child is [like] a stone: only God's grace guides one to throw it to a propitious place. (It takes Providence to help one do right by one's children.)

---

13. Hyenas presumably have large litters, and the people of Èrúwà, an Ìbàràpá town, presumably have many children of doubtful character.

3117. *Òkú ọlọ́mọ kì í sun à-sùn-gbàgbé.*
The corpse of a person who left children behind does not forget itself in sleep. (An expression of the belief that dead people survived by young children will continue to care for them from their new abode.)

3118. *Oǹsìn ní ḿmọ ìwà.*
The servant is best placed to know [the master's] character. (Those dependent on you can best tell what sort of person you are.)

3119. *Orí kì í pọ̀ lójà ká má mọ tìyá ẹni.*
Heads are never so plentiful in the market-place that one does not recognize one's mother's. (One must always favor one's kin.)

3120. *Òrìṣà ilé ẹni kì í hunni.*
One's household god never turns on one. (One should always be able to count on succor, not betrayal, from one's own house-hold.)

3121. *Òrìṣà ò níkà; ará ilé ẹni ní ńroni pa.*
The gods are not wicked; it is people from one's household who kill one with defama-tion. (One's greatest enemies often come from one's own household.)

3122. *Orogún kì í jogún orogún.*
Co-wives do not inherit from co-wives. (People with distinct interests should keep them distinct.)

Ọ

3123. *"Ọba, èmi lẹrú ẹ; Baṣọ̀run, èmi lẹrú ẹ"; àtọba àti Baṣọ̀run, wọn ò mọ iye ẹrú tí wọn rà?*
"Oh King, I am your slave; Oh Chief Adviser of the king, I am your slave"; king and chief adviser, don't they know how many slaves they bought? (It is devious to manufacture

kinship to illustrious people; illustrious people know their own kin.)

3124. Ọkọ ẹni lodì ẹni.
One's husband is one's closest kin. (There should be no relationship more intimate than that between spouses.)

3125. Ọlá àbàtà ní ńmú odò-ó ṣàn; ọlá-a baba ní ńmú ọmọ yan.
It is the by the grace of the marshy land that a river flows; it is by the grace of the father that the son struts. (The person who has strong backers can afford to strut.)

3126. Ọlanfẹ ni baba ẹyẹ, iyùn ni baba ìlèkè; ẹni tí a bá fẹ́ ìyá è lọmọ è ńwunni.
The ọlanfẹ bird is the father of all birds; the coral bead is the father of all beads; it is the offspring of the person whose mother one loves that are attractive. (One's love for a woman affects one's feelings toward her children.)

3127. Ọmọ àlè, ilé ní ńtú.
A bastard does nothing but disrupt the household. (Illegitimate children ruin families.)

3128. Ọmọ́ bọ́ lọ́wọ́-ọ nínà, ó di à-wò-mójú.
[When] a child outgrows whipping, he becomes a person one looks at and rolls one's eyes in disgust. (When a child becomes an adult and still has not learned to behave well, one can only throw up one's hands in resignation.)

3129. Ọmọ ẹni ò sẹdí bẹbẹrẹ, ká sòlèkè mọ́ ọmọ ẹlòmíràn nídìí.
One does not, because one's child's waist is too fat, put waist beads around the waist of another person's child. (One always loves one's own children best, despite their flaws.)

3130. Ọmọ olúgelegele-é pa ìdí è mọ́ búúbú.
The olúgelegelé plant tidies up its base dili-

gently. (One should look well to one's family and home.)[14]

3131. Ọmọ olọ́mọ là ńpè ní Alébíowú; bó bá ṣe tẹni ni à pè é ní Ajíbọ́ládé.
It is another person's child that one names Alébíowú; one's own child one names Ajíbọ́ládé. (One always harbors a better opinion and a better expectation of one's own than of other people's.)[15]

3132. Ọmọ olọ́mọ là ńrán níṣẹẹ "dé tòru-tòru."
It is only another person's child that one sends on a return-unfailingly-even-after-nightfall errand. (One always feels more free to misuse other people's property than one's own.)

3133. Ọmọ olọ́mọ ní ńjẹ Abéégúndé.
Only other people's children are named Abéégúndé. (One chooses only the most appealing names for one's own children.)[16]

3134. Ọmọ olọ́mọ ní ńpa baba oníbaba.
It is another person's child that kills another person's father. (Both the perpetrator and the victim of an evil deed have relatives to whom they relate differently. People often do evil to other, unrelated, people.)

3135. Ọmọ tí ò ní ẹlẹrù yó bàjẹ́.
A child who fears no one will be rotten. (Any person who refuses to be disciplined is worth nothing.)

---

14. Olúgelegele is a creeping plant that spreads and kills off all undergrowth.

15. Alébíowú means "one who lies contentedly like festering jealousy"; Ajíbọ́ládé means "one who rises accompanied with prosperity." The two are to be pictured as in their characteristic morning poses.

16. Abéégúndé means "One who arrives during the annual eégún festival." Only those who belong to the cult may give such a name to their children; the sense of the proverb seems to be that those who do not belong to the cult may not give their own children such a name.

3136. Ọmọ tí ò níyàá kì í dégbò èhìn.
A motherless child should not get a sore on
his back. (Unless you have people to help
you out, do not get into trouble. Compare
1207.)

3137. Ọmọ tó bu ìyá è lẹ́hìn jẹ, ẹni tí yó pọ̀n ọ́n
á sìṣẹ́.
A child that bit its mother's back: whoever
will carry it on her back has her work cut
out for her. (Children who cannot be disciplined by their parents pose even greater
problems for their caretakers. See the following entry.)

3138. Ọmọ tó bu ìyá è lẹ́hìn jẹ, kò sí alágbàpọ̀n
tó jẹ́ pọ̀n ọ́n.
The child that bit its mother's back, no
surrogate carrier will carry on her back.
(Children that cannot be controlled by
their parents will not easily find caretakers.
Compare the preceding entry.)

3139. Ọmọ tó dára ti bàbá è ni; ọmọ burúkú
tìyá è ni.
A well-disciplined child is the father's child;
an ill-bred child is the mother's. (It is up to
the father to discipline the child; it is up to
the mother to see that the child accepts the
discipline.)

3140. Ọmọ tó ní kíyàá òun má sùn, òun náà ò
níí fojú kan orun.
A child that is determined to keep its
mother awake will itself not catch a glimpse
of sleep. (People intent on making trouble
for others will not themselves remain un-
troubled. Compare 1693.)

3141. "Ọmọ yìí ṣe gbọ́n báyìí?" Ó ní baba
nísàlè ni.
"How did this child come to be so wise?" It
is only because he has a father somewhere.
(A well-bred child is evidence of his father's
good influence.)

3142. Ọmọdé tó yá tọ́rọ́ lóde, owó ilé ló ná.
A child who borrows three pence on the
streets is actually spending household
money. (Members of the household will ultimately be held responsible for the actions of
the minors in the household.)

3143. Ọ̀ràn tó bá bá ojú á bá imú.
The trouble that befalls the eyes will also affect the nose. (Whatever afflicts those close
to one afflicts oneself also.)

3144. Ọ̀rẹ́ eni ní ḿbáni pilè ọ̀rọ̀, ará ilé eni ní
ḿbani kó o.
It is a friend that helps one lay the foundation of a venture; kinfolk help one carry
it to fruition. (Kin are more valuable than
friends.)

3145. Ọ̀ré kítí-kítí, iyèkan kàtà-kàtà: bọ́rèé
kítí-kítí bá kú, iyèkan kàtà-kàtà ní ńgbé e sin.
The closest of friends, the most distant of
relatives: when the closest friend dies, the
most distant relatives are the ones who arrange the funeral. (The closest friend is not
as important as even distant relatives.)

3146. Ọ̀rọ̀ àgbà, bí kò bá ta èdé, ogun ní ńta.
The word that issues out of the mouth of an
elder, if it does not hit at hunting, will hit at
war. (There is always considerable substance
and weight in what an elder says.)

3147. Ọ̀wọ́n èèyàn là ńpe ajá ní Ifádèyí.[17]
Only scarcity of human beings makes one
name a dog Ifádèyí. (Said to mean that
one would never have had anything to do
with the person referred to if any other
alternative had been available.)

---

17. The name means "Ifá, the Oracle god, has preserved this one," and it is usually given to children one
is grateful to the god for preserving.

Ṣ

3148. *Ṣe igbá ilé jéjé; a ò mọ ìwà tí toko yó hù.*
Handle the home calabash with care; no one knows how the farm calabash will behave. (Be good to the things and people you already have; you can never be sure what you might end up with if you were to trade them for new ones.)

T

3149. *Tímọ́-tímọ́ letí m̀mọ́ orí, tìmọ́-tìmọ́ lalámọ̀ ńgún amọ̀.*
Closely is the manner of the ear's attachment to the head; smoothly is the way the clay worker pounds his clay. (An admonition to people to remain intimate.)

W

3150. *"Wo ìsò dè mí" kì í jọ onísò; "Ng ó ṣe baba fún ọ" ò lè jọ baba.*
"Watch the stall for me" cannot be like the store owner; "I will be like a father to you" can never be like a father. (Where kinship is concerned, substitutes can never be like the real thing. Compare 3109.)

On relationships within the community

A

3151. *A kì í bá ẹni gbé ká má mọ ojú ẹni.*
One does not live with a person and yet not know how to deal with him or her. (To know a person well is to know that person's habits and tastes.)

3152. *A kì í bá ẹni tan ká tún fani nítan ya.*
One does not claim kinship with a person and yet split the person's thighs. (Sexual activities between blood relatives are taboo.)

3153. *A kì í bá ọmọ ẹni ṣeré kó doko egba.*
One does not play with one's child and then head for the bush of whips. (One should keep the play in playing and not turn it into a quarrel.)

3154. *A kì í tóó bánigbé ká má tòó òrò-ọ́ bánisọ.*
One does not qualify to live with a person without also qualifying to talk to the person. (Friends and relatives have every right to counsel with a person.)

3155. *A kì í yan àna ẹni lódì.*
One does not refuse to speak to one's family-in-law. (Certain obligations must never be neglected out of pique.)

3156. *Ààyè ọmọ là ńfẹ́; a kì í fẹ́ òkú ọmọ.*
One courts a live person; one does not court a dead person. (One should spare no effort to keep one's child alive.)

3157. *Adásínilórùn, obìnrin òdògọ: ẹlẹ́rú ńwá ẹrú è, ó ní kí wọ́n jẹ́ kí ọkọ òun ti oko dé ná.*
Person-who-involves-one-in-trouble, idiotic woman: a slave owner comes searching for his missing slave, and she says he should wait until her husband returns from the farm. (A loose mouth is a dangerous thing for the owner and his or her kin.)

3158. *Agbè ní ńjẹ ègbin omi; àgbàlagbà ní ńjẹ ìyà òrò.*
It is the gourd that inherits the dregs of water; it is the elder that inherits the unpleasantness of a dispute. (Every position carries its responsibilities.)[1]

3159. *Àjọ ni tìlú; ọba ló lagbo.*
The assembly is for the people; to the king belongs the crowd. (The populace may gather, but only the king can unite them.)[2]

3160. *Àkèekèe òjògán fidí jà; ará ilé ẹni-í fojúdini.*
The formidable scorpion fights with its tail; members of one's household belittle one. (Those most familiar with you are likely to show you disrespect. The scorpion's fighting with its tail, rather than its arms, is here

---

1. The sediment remains in the gourd after the water is gone; the elder must listen to the troubles of all and sundry.

2. *Àjọ* suggests a gathering of individuals for consultation; *agbo* suggests a coming-together for a ceremony or celebration in common.

construed as a sign of contempt for the adversary.)

3161. *Amúníbúni ẹran Ìbíyẹ; Ìbíyẹ-ẹ́ fójú òtún, ẹran-an rẹ̀-ẹ́ fó tòsì.*
A-creature-that-makes-one-insult-another-person, Ìbíyẹ's goat; Ìbíyẹ is blind in the right eye, and her goat is blind in the left.[3] (If the parent and the child share the same trait, one risks provoking the parent by remarking on the trait in the child.)

3162. *Aṣenilóde ò tó tílé; ilé ni wọ́n ti ńṣeni.*
The-enemy-outside is no match for the enemy at home; one is done in in one's own home. (The enemy at home is more formidable than the enemy abroad.)

3163. *Aṣiwèrè èèyàn ní ńkọ̀ṣẹ́ àbọ̀ ọjà.*
Only an imbecile refuses to run an errand he or she can do on the way from the market. (One should not refuse to do a favor that entails no hardship or inconvenience.)

3164. *Aṣusọ́nà ní ńfi ìyá-a rẹ̀ gbẹpẹ̀.*
A child who shits on the path brings down curses on its mother. (A child's behavior is a reflection on its mother; a child's misbehavior exposes its parents to castigation.)

B

3165. *Bàbá laláàbò; ìyá lonírànwọ́; orogún nikú.*
A father is a protector; a mother is a helper; a co-wife is death. (Two women who share the same husband are deadly enemies.)

3166. *Bí a bá wí pé kí ará ilé ẹni má lòówó, ará òdé ní ńyáni lófà.*

If one schemes so that one's relatives may not prosper, outsiders eventually receive one as a pawn. (One who works to ensure that one's people do not succeed becomes fair game for outsiders.)

3167. *Bí a kò bá fi oògùn pa ọmọ ìyá ẹni, ọmọ bàbá ẹni kì í sá fúnni.*
If one did not kill one's sibling by the same mother with poison, one's sibling by the same father does not flee. (If one has done nothing to encourage them to do so, one's close relatives will not avoid one.)

3168. *Bí a kò bá lè dijú kan ọmọ ẹni níkòó, ojú là ńlà sílẹ̀ tí wọ́n fi ńkàn án lọ́mọríodó lórí.*
If one cannot close one's eyes to rap one's child on the head, one will watch with wide-open eyes as others hit him on the head with a pestle. (If one will not discipline one's child, others will, and much more mercilessly.)

3169. *Bí a kò bá sọ fún ọmọdé pé èèyàn lọkọ ìyá-a rẹ̀, a ní ta ní ńwá gba ìyá òun lẹ́kọ jẹ lójoojúmọ́ yìí?*
If a child is not told that a certain person is its mother's husband, the child asks who this person is who comes everyday to take food from its mother. (Without knowing the relationship between two people, one cannot understand their actions.)

3170. *Bí àkùkọ́ bá kọ láyé, àwọn ẹgbẹ́ ẹ̀ á gbè é lọ́run.*
If a cock crows on earth, its peers respond in heaven. (A company always backs up its leader.)

3171. *Bí ará ilé ẹní bá ńjẹ kòkòrò tí kò sunwọn, tí a kò sọ fún un, hùrùhẹ̀rẹ̀-ẹ rẹ̀ ò níí jẹ́ ká sùn lóru.*
If a member of one's household is eating bad insects and is not cautioned, his or her hack-

3. If one angrily called an offending goat ẹran olójúkan (one-eyed goat), one could be accused of saying what the construction also means: "the goat of a one-eyed person."

ing cough will not permit one any sleep during the night. (If one does not counsel one's brother, one will share in his misfortune.)

3172. *Bí ẹni ẹní bá kú lókèèrè, à pẹta-a rẹ̀ wálé.*
If one's relative dies far away from home, the dead person's relic is sent home. (However far a person wanders, something of that person must eventually return home.)

3173. *Bí ikú ilé ò pani, tòde ò lè pani.*
If the death at home does not kill one, the death outside will not. (If one is secure at home, one will be secure abroad.)

3174. *Bí ó bá bá ojú, á bá imú pẹ̀lú.*
Whatever disaster befalls the eye will also befall the nose. (One shares in the fate of people close to one.)

3175. *Bí orí kan-án bá sunwọ̀n á ran igba.*
If a head is blessed with good fortune, it will affect a hundred others. (To be associated with success is to benefit from the success.)

3176. *Binisí-binisí: ọ̀tá ilé ò rí kòtò bini sí.*
Push-one-into, push-one-into: one's household enemy can find no ditch to push one into. (The enemy in your own home cannot openly hurt you.)

E

3177. *Èèyàn ẹni là ńfi ààyè ọmọ hàn; nígbà tó bá dòkú gbogbo ayé ní ńyorí-i rẹ̀.*
One presents one's live child only to one's kin; when it dies, the world makes itself scarce. (One shares good fortune only with those who will stand by in times of need.)

3178. *Egbò-ó kẹ̀, iná kẹ̀, ohùn èèyàn-án kẹ̀.*
The ulcer grows bigger, the fire glows redder, and one's voice grows hoarse. (The unrelent-

ing misbehavior of others necessitates one's continuous admonition.)

3179. *Èkúté ilé tó fàkò sílẹ̀ tó ńjọbẹ, tẹnu ẹni ló féé gbọ́.*
The house mouse that spares the sheath but eats the knife is bent on provoking one. (A person who deliberately provokes another is spoiling for a fight.)

3180. *Ẹní tere, èjì tere lojà-á fi ńkún.*
The first solitary person, then the second solitary person: thus is the market filled. (A collection of solitary individuals makes a multitude. See the next entry.)

3181. *Ẹní tere, èjì tere, ọ̀pọ̀ wọmù.*
The first solitary person, then the second solitary person, eventually a multitude. (This a variant of the preceding entry.)

3182. *Èpìpà ńpa ara-a rẹ̀ ó ní òun ńpa ajá.*
The hard tick is committing suicide but believes it is killing the dog. (The host's death is the parasite's also; one destroys oneself if one destroys one's only support. A vulnerable person who does not lie low invites disaster.)

Ẹ

3183. *Ẹni ẹlẹ́ni ní ńkọ́lé fún ikán.*
It is other people who build homes for the termite. (One may benefit from other people's labors.)

3184. *Ẹní ní ìlú ò dùn, kó kẹ̀rù kó gba oko lọ.*
Whoever says the town is not pleasant should pack his or her luggage and head for the bush. (Antisocial people deserve to live by themselves in the forest.)

3185. *Ẹni tó ba ọmọ ọlọ́mọ lórí jẹ́, òrìṣà inú ilé yó ba tirẹ̀ náà jẹ́.*

Whoever ruins the lot of an innocent person will have his own lot ruined by the god of the hearth. (The gods visit retribution on those who do evil to others.)

3186. *Ẹnìkan ní ńkésẹ̀ nílùú, tí a fi ńsọ wípé à ńlọ sílùú akésẹ̀.*
Only one person in a town has to have his or her leg amputated before people will say they are on their way to the amputee's town.[4] (One person's blight rubs off on all associated with him or her. Compare 3395.)

G

3187. *Gàmbàrí pa Fúlàní, kò léjọ́ ńnú.*
A Hausa person has killed a Fulani person; there is no case to answer. (If the offender and the offended are so close as to be virtual twins, it is as though there has been no offense.[5] Compare 4970.)

Gb

3188. *Gbódó rù mí kí ngbé àlàpà ru ọmọ-ọ̀ rẹ.*
Burden me with a mortar, and I will burden your child with a denuded wall. (A vow to pay like with like. Compare 3243.)

3189. *Gbogbo ìká fojú ṣe ọ̀kan, àtàmpàkò-ó ṣe tiẹ̀ lọ́tọ̀.*
All fingers face in one direction; the thumb alone goes its own way. (In a consensual assembly, there is the loner who must go it independently. Compare 3049.)

---

4. In Yoruba, *ìlú akésẹ̀* can mean either "amputee's town" or "amputees' town."
5. The Hausa and the Fulani (Fulbe) live in the northern parts of Nigeria and, as far as the Yoruba are concerned, are indistinguishable.

I

3190. *Ìbàdàn kì í gbe onílé bí àjèjì.*
The city Ibadan is never as hospitable to its natives as to strangers. (Said of people who are kinder to strangers than to their friends or relatives.)

3191. *Ifá ní ká jọ wò ó; mo ní ká jọ wò ó; ohun tí a bá jọ wò gígún ní ńgún.*
Ifá says we should mind it together; I say we should mind it together; whatever all mind together will come out just right. (When all people pool their resources, everything comes out right. This is a variant of 3203.)

3192. *Igi wọ́rọ́kú daná rú; èèyàn burúkú bàsè jẹ́.*
A crooked piece of wood scatters the fire; an evil person ruins a feast. (The presence of a contrary person in a group robs the group of any harmony.)

3193. *Igún pá lórí, kò kan alábẹ.*
The vulture's baldness has nothing to do with a barber. (Said of a certain person's troubles which are not of others' making.)

3194. *Igbó etílé òun ẹ̀gbin, àdàpọ̀ ọwọ̀ òun ìyà; yàrá à-jùmọ̀-gbé ìtalẹ̀ ni nínú.*
The forest close by the town is doomed to cope with filth; a trading partnership exposes one to suffering; a shared bedroom is a breeding ground for mud-earth-dwelling biting worms. (All relationships entail irritants and require some capacity for accommodation.)

3195. *Ìjà ló dé lorín dòwe.*
It is the breaking out of a quarrel that turns an innocent song into a satirical song. (Innocent gestures take on hostile aspects in a quarrel.)

3196. *Ìrírí ni ìkíni; ìkíni ni ìjẹ́ni.*
To see a person is to greet the person; to be
greeted is to respond. (The well-bred person
greets people when he or she sees them, and
the well-bred person responds to greetings.)

3197. *Ìwó nílé oódẹ, Ìbarà nílé àwòdì, a ti ńpe
ilé agánrán?*
Ìwó is the home of the gray parrot; Ìbarà is
the home of the kite; what does one call the
home of the scarlet-billed Senegal parrot?
(Comment about a person who comes from
no one knows where.)

3198. *Kí àdàbà sùú-sùú wí fú jẹdíẹdíẹ; kéyẹ ó
wí féyẹ.*
Let the pigeon talk to the woodpecker; let
bird speak to another bird. (Each person
should spread a matter under discussion to
as many ears as possible.)

3199. *Kò-gbélé-kò-gbọ́nà ní ńsìnkú àbíkú.*
He-does-not-live-in-the-home-and-he-
does-not-live-on-the-path is the one who
buries the *àbíkú.*
(The footloose stranger will always be called
upon to help do things no one else wants
to do.)

3200. *Kọ̀nkọ̀sọ̀ ò dá ku èlùbọ́.*
The sieve does not sift yam flour on its own.
(No individual is self-sufficient.)

3201. *Lójọ́ ikú ọ̀tà, gbogbo ọ̀tà ní ńpé jọ.*
On the day a merchant dies, all merchants
gather. (It is right and fitting to do one's
duty by one's comrades.)

3202. *"Má ta omi sí mi lára" kì í dé odò; "Má
fara kàn mí" kì í wá ọjà.*
"Do not splash water on me" should stay
away from the river; "Do not touch my person" should stay away from the market.
(People who would rather be alone should
avoid gathering places. Compare 3216.)

3203. *Mo ní "Àjọwò," wọ́n ní "Àjọwò"; ohun
tí a bá jọ wò gígún ní ńgún.*
I said, "Let us mind it together," and they
responded, "Let us mind it together"; whatever has everyone's attention and care comes
out straight. (Pooling resources ensures
success. This is a variant of 3191.)

3204. *"Mo ti wí?" "Bẹ́ẹ lo wí!" Ẹ̀ẹkannáà
làwọn méjèèjì ńgbẹnu sókè.*
"What did I say?" "So you said!" Both
mouths speak in unison. (Unanimous agreement leaves no room for dispute.)

3205. *"Ng ò lè jẹ ìjẹkújẹ̀" kì í gbé àwùjọ ọpọ̀
èèyàn.*
"I will not eat rubbish" does not live in a
crowd. (One must have a thick skin if one
wishes to be part of a crowd.)

3206. *"Ng ò níí fẹ́, ng ò níí gbà": ibi tó sùn sí
lánàá, kò níí sùn síbẹ̀ lónìí.*
"I will never agree, and I will never concede": wherever he slept last night, he will
not sleep there today. (A disagreeable person is not welcome company anywhere for
long.)

O

3207. *Ò ńwòmí, mò ńwò ọ́; ta ní ṣeun nínú-u wa?*
All you do is look at me, and all I do is look at you; which of us is any use to the other? (A person who does not lift a hand to help another deserves no help from that other in return.)

3208. *Ó pa wọ́n tán nínú ọmọ ataare; kí là bá tún fèèpo ẹ̀ ṣe?*
He has removed all the seeds from the alligator pepper; what now can one do with the shell? (Said of a person who has taken the best of some communal property, leaving others with little that is of any use.)

3209. *Ojú ẹni là ńbi aṣeni lóhun.*
It is in the presence of witnesses that one challenges the person who caused one injury. (One should make a point of exposing one's detractor or injurer to the public.)

3210. *Ojúlùmọ̀ ò níí jẹ́ ká na ìyá ọ̀gbà ẹni.*
The community will not let one flog the mother of one's comrade. (Communal sanctions prevent outrageous behavior. See the following proverb for comparison.)

3211. *Ojúlùmọ̀ ò níí jẹ́ káhun ó sun ìgbẹ́.*
The community will not let the miser sleep in the wild. (Even the antisocial person will benefit from communal solicitousness. Compare the preceding proverb.)

3212. *Òkò là ńsọ sígúnnugún níyà míràn; ibi a gbé mọgún la ti ńsẹgún lóore.*
It is with stone missiles that the vulture is greeted in foreign lands; only where the vulture is known does it receive favorable treatment. (Only where people know one's stature does one receive the respect one deserves.)

3213. *Onílù-ú ò fẹ́ kó tú; abánigbé ló ńṣe é bẹ̀ẹ̀.*
The native of the town does not wish it to break up; it is the doing of the sojourner. (People with no stake in a venture might wish to destroy; not so those with a stake in it.)

3214. *Orí kìí burú lọ́wọ̀ọ́.*
One head is never [individually] unfortunate in a large company. (Misfortune does not single out a person from among a group.)

3215. *"Òun ló mò" kì í mọ ní òun nìkan.*
"That is his business" never confines itself to him. (A matter that concerns one person inevitably comes to concern others also.)

3216. *Òyìnbó ò fáriwo, ó kọ́lé sígbó.*
The white man dislikes noise; therefore he built his house in the bush. (People who cannot put up with the habits of others will have to live in isolation.[6] Compare 3202.)

Ọ

3217. *Ọba ní ńgba a-láì-lárá.*
The king is the defense of the person who has no kin. (The king is the ultimate protector of his people.)

3218. *Ọbẹ̀ tó dànù, òfò onílé, òfò àlejò.*
The stew that spilled [is] a loss to the host and a loss to the visitor. (The destruction of anything valuable is a loss to everybody.)

3219. *Ọkọ́ kú, ọmọ ọba mẹ́ta-á pète; Ọbẹ̀ẹ́ mú epo, Lálá mú iyọ̀, Àjùwọ́n mú ata.*
The husband died, and three princesses

---

6. During the colonial period, Europeans lived in reservations well removed from African dwellings. Separated by a "sanitizing" buffer of forest, they thus lived in the bush as far as Africans were concerned.

made their contribution [to the feast]; Ọbẹ̀ brought palm oil, Lálá brought salt, and Àjùwọ́n brought pepper. (Said of people who are supposed to carry out a project but who cannot effectively coordinate their efforts.)[7]

3220. Ọlá adìẹ ni alámù-ú fi m̀mu omi nínú agada.
It is by the grace of the chicken that the lizard can drink out of a potsherd. (People may benefit from others' good fortune.)[8]

3221. Ọmọdé gbọ́n, Ààrẹ́ gbọ́n, la fi ńtẹ ilẹ̀ Ifẹ̀.
A youth is wise, and the chief is wise: that is the principle by which people go about at Ifẹ̀. (A youth's counsel is as worth entertaining as a chief's.)

3222. Ọmọdé ò jobì, àgbà ò joyè.
The youth does not eat kola nuts; the elder does not win the chieftaincy title. (If you do not cultivate others, even those lesser than yourself, then you cannot expect any consideration from them.)

3223. Ọpẹ tó darí, igbà-á kọ̀ ọ́.
The palm tree whose top is bent to the ground is rejected by the climbing rope. (If you pose no challenge, people won't expend any effort in dealing with you.)

3224. Ọ̀pọ̀ èèyàn kì í wọ Orò kí Orò gbé wọn.
A multitude of people cannot enter the Orò grove and be carried away by Orò. (There is strength and security in numbers.)

3225. Ọ̀pọ̀ èèyàn ní ńjẹ́ jànmáà.
It is a multitude of people that is called

a congregation. (No one person can be a multitude.)

3226. Ọ̀pọ̀ lẹṣú fi ya igi lóko.
It is by means of their numbers that locusts tear down a branch on the farm. (There is strength in numbers.)

3227. Ọ̀ràn hànnìyàn-hànnìyàn; ọ̀ràn hànnìyàn-hànnìyàn, èèyàn là ńfi hàn.
Terrible, terrible problems; terrible problems must be brought to people's attention. (Never keep your problems to yourself.)[9]

3228. Ọ̀ràn tó bá ṣe ojú ìlú ò fara sin.
Whatever happened in the presence of the whole town cannot be kept secret. (It is pointless to be secretive about something everybody already knows about.)

3229. Ọ̀run ńya bọ̀, kì í ṣọ̀ràn ẹnikan.
The sky falling down is not any one person's problem. (One should not be overly concerned at the threat of a danger that is general. See the following entry.)

3230. Ọ̀run ńya bọ̀, ò ńyẹrí; ìwọ nìkan ni?
The sky is falling and you are ducking your head; are you the only one [in danger]? (There is no sense in trying to avoid a danger that is general. See the previous entry.)

3231. Ọ̀sín mọ ìwẹ̀, inú m̀bí ẹyẹ oko.
The fish eagle knows how to swim; the other birds of the forest seethe with anger. (People are ever jealous of others' accomplishments.)

3232. Ọ̀tòòtò èyí lànà ìgbín? Ìpére-é kú o ò sunkún, ìlákòṣe-é kú o ò gbààwè, o bá ẹlétẹ lọ́nà o tẹ̀ ẹ́ ré, odò ńgbé ìsáwùrú lọ o ní "Dẹ̀ẹ̀, dẹ̀ẹ̀, máa rà"; ta ló ńṣe àna fún?
What sort of in-law are you to the snail? A

7. The three princesses were married to the dead man, but what they have brought will not suffice to make a feast.

8. The lizard drinks the water left out in a potsherd for the chicken.

9. The expression hánnìyàn (or, better, hàn-ń-yàn for han èèyàn) literally means "show people."

small snail dies and you do not cry; tiny snails die and you do not abstain from eating; you see the grasshopper on the path and you step on it; the stream is carrying rounded small snails away and you say "Float gently away!" To whom do you perform in-law obligations? (Said of people who display no fellow feeling with anyone.)

3233. *Òtùn ì bá pọ̀ tó Ìbàdàn, à-múró-yaró ni ò jé.*
Òtùn could have grown as populous as Ibadan but for the addiction of its people to vengeance. (Insistence on vengeance will disperse a community.)

3234. *Ọ̀tún wẹ òsì, òsì wẹ ọ̀tún lọwọ́ fi ḿmọ́.*
The right washing the left and the left washing the right is the way to get the hands clean. (Success in a venture depends on cooperation.)

3235. *Ọwọ́ epo layé ḿbáni lá, ayé kì í báni láwọ́ ẹ̀jẹ̀.*
The world will join one in licking fingers dripping with palm oil but not in licking fingers dripping with blood. (People will share your good fortune with you, but not your misfortune.)

3236. *Ọ̀wọ́ ni ọ̀wọ́ ikán, ọ̀pọ̀ ni ọ̀pọ̀ èèrùn.*
The orderliness is the orderliness of termites; the multiplicity is the multiplicity of the swarming brown ants. (Said in describing a great multitude attending an event.)

3237. *Ọwọ́ ọmọdé ò tó pẹpẹ, ọwọ́ àgbà ò wọ kèrègbè; iṣẹ́ tí àgbà-á bá bẹ ọmọdé kó máse kò ọ́; gbogbo wa la ní ohun tí a lè ṣe fúnra-a wa.*
The youth's hand cannot reach the rafters, and the elder's hand cannot enter the gourd; the youth should not refuse to run the errand on which the elder sends him or her; each one of us can do something for the other. (Everybody needs someone some-

time; therefore, one should not refuse to aid others, even those one thinks one will never need.)

3238. *Ọwọ́ púpọ̀ ni ńpa osùn.*
Many hands are required to rub camwood powder on the body. (Many hands cooperating ensure that a task is thoroughly done.)

3239. *Ọ̀yọ́ ò gbọ́ "Wòde," Ìjèsà ò gbọ́ "Wọdà," Ọ̀yọ́ gbọ́ "Wọdà" bí ẹní gbọ́Fá.*
Ọ̀yọ́ people do not understand "Wòde," Ìjèsà people do not understand "Wọ dà" ["Ìwọ dà?"]; Ọ̀yọ́ people understand "Wọ dà" as well as they understand Ifá. (What one person knows, another person does not know; together they can solve all their problems.)[10]

P

3240. *Pàǹlà àkàsù ní ḿbá gbọọrọ isu wá.*
A large loaf of corn meal is what comes of a big yam.[11] (The good that one does brings a recompense in kind in the future. Compare 3321.)

3241. *Pípé là ńpé gbọ́n, a kì í pé gọ̀.*
People assemble to seek wisdom collectively; people do not assemble in order to become stupid. (Consultation should lead to wisdom, not folly.)

S

3242. *Sòrò-sòrò-ọ́ wà, bẹ̀ẹ̀ ni ẹní máa gbọ́ ḿbẹ.*

---

10. *Wòde* in Ìjèsà would mean "Look outside." *Ìwọ dà?* in Ọ̀yọ́ would mean "Where are you?"

11. In plain language the statement is *Àkàsù pàǹlà ní ńmú isu gbọọrọ wá,* "A huge loaf of corn meal is what brings a long yam."

There is the loquacious person, and so
also there is the person willing to listen.
(If people are willing to talk, others will be
willing to listen.)

3245. *Túlùú-túlùú, ẹyẹ Elẹ́m̀pe.*
Town disperser, the Elẹ́m̀pe bird. (A person
who carries rumors from people to people
will cause dissension in the community.)

T

Y

3243. *Tẹ̀ mí ntẹ̀ ọ́, layé gbà.*
Step on me and I will step on you is what
life takes. (In life we must act toward others
as they act toward us. Compare 3188.)

3246. *Yánníbo-ó mú erèé rún; gbẹ̀gìrì-í ṣàn.*
Yánníbo chewed up the black-eyed peas;
the black-eyed-pea stew is watery. (Said of
people who ruin or deplete what was set
aside for the benefit of a whole group.)

3244. *Tijú fún mi kí ntijú fún ọ; ẹni tó tijú
fúnni là ńtijú fún.*
Behave with decorum toward me, and I
will behave with decorum toward you; only
those who approach one with decorum earn
decorum in return. (Act toward people the
way you would like them to act toward you.)

3247. *"Yó bàá ọ," kì í ba ẹnìkan mọ.*
"A pox on you!" does not limit its effect to
only one person. (Ill fortune invoked for
specific people affects others close to them.)

On relationships with elders

3248. *A kì í tẹ́ní fún ẹni ilé jókòó.*
One does not spread a mat for a member
of the household to sit on. (Acquaintances
should not insist on being waited upon like
strangers.)

3249. *A-bánise-mábàánise-mọ́: à bùṣà
fáláṣejù kété-kété.*
He-that-once-fraternized-with-one-but-
stops-doing-so: one would do well to give
such a person a wide berth. (A friend turned
enemy is a danger to be avoided.)

3250. *A-bániwọ́ràn-bá-ò-rídá; ó fúnni léyìí tí
kò wuni; ó pa ọmọ tún ọmọ rọ̀.*
He-who-helps-one-find-trouble-when-one-
has-none gives what one does not want; he
kills a child and returns to soothe the child.
(A person who involves one in difficulties
by his actions is no friend, however much
he might pretend to be. See the following
entry.)

3251. *A-bániwọ́ràn-bá-ò-rídá; ó yé kọ́ńdú-
kọ́ńdú séyin ẹléyin; ó di òkúta sẹrù ẹni tó
fúyẹ́.*
He-who-helps-one-find-trouble-when-one-
has-none lays huge things among other
people's eggs; he packs rocks into the load
of a person who[se load] is light.[1] (This is a
variant of the preceding entry.)

3252. *Àdàpọ̀ owó ní ḿmú ìjà wá.*
Saving money in joint accounts results in
quarrels. (Certain things should not be a
part of friendship.)

3253. *Adébipani kì í sọ̀rẹ́ ẹni.*
He who inflicts hunger on one is no friend.
(Know your enemy.)

3254. *Ajé ní ḿba ojú ọ̀rẹ́ jẹ́.*
It is money that brings a frown to the brow
of friendship. (Nothing ruins a friendship
more surely than the intrusion of money.)

3255. *Àpá kì í jòlọ̀ kó dà bí ara ẹni; ká jà ká rẹ́
ò dà bí ọ̀rẹ́ ìpilẹ̀sẹ̀.*
However smooth a scar is, it is never the
same as the original skin; a mended quarrel
is not like original friendship. (Relationships
may be mended, but it is better if they never
need mending.)

3256. *A-ríre-báni-jẹ, àgbọ̀n ìsàlẹ̀; òkú kú
láàárọ̀, àgbọ̀n-ọ́n yà kó tó dalẹ́.*
A-thing-that-shares-only-good-things-with-
one, the lower jaw; a person dies in the
morning, and the jaw separates before nightfall. (Fair-weather friends are like the lower
jaw that separates from the head as soon as
the owner dies.)

---

1. Here is an example of peculiar proverbial constructions. Instead of *ó di òkúta sẹrù ẹni tẹ́rù-u rẹ̀ẹ́ fúyẹ́*
("he packs rocks into the load of the person whose
load is light"), we have *ó di òkúta sẹrù ẹni tó fúyẹ́* ("he
packs rocks into the load of a person who is light").
The hearer, of course, understands that "light" is meant
to describe the load.

B

3257. *Bí a bá gbá ilé gbá ọ̀nà, ọ̀dọ̀ àátàn là ńdà á sí.*
After one has swept the house and the pathways, one dumps the dirt at the rubbish heap. (However long a matter is discussed, its resolution devolves to the proper agent. Compare 4857.)

3258. *Bí ijó bá di ijó àgbà, ìlù a yípadà.*
When the dance becomes a dance of elders, the drumming should change. (One must match one's behavior to one's circumstances.)

3259. *Bí ọmọdé lásọ bí àgbà, kò lè lákìísà bí àgbà.*
A youth may have as many clothes as an elder, but he will not have as many rags as an elder. (Though a youth may enjoy the same rank as an elder, he cannot match the elder in experience.)

E

3260. *Ègbé ni fún ọmọ tó ní bàbá òún kéré.*
Woe betide the child who says his or her father is insignificant. (Children who belittle their father deserve the worst fate possible.)

Ẹ

3261. *Ègbọ́n iwájú: alugbọn baba.*
One's older brother [is a suitable] substitute father. (Respect others of your elders as you would your parents.)

3262. *Ẹni tí a bá dé ìlú ò tó ẹni tí a dé ìlú mọ̀.*
The person with whom one came to a town is not as important as the person one came to know after arriving in the town. (A current friend or benefactor is more important than a sometime friend or benefactor.)

3263. *Ẹni tí a bá nídìí àbà ní ńjẹ́ baba.*
The person one finds settled at the granary is the lord of the place. (One should give due ragard to those who have been to places, or accomplished things, before one's time. Compare 3326 and 3456.)

I

3264. *Ìjà ò mègbọ́n.*
A quarrel does not know who is the elder. (In a quarrel one is likely to forget all proprieties.)

3265. *Ìkonkoso-ó tiiri pa eku, iwọ̀-ó tiiri pa eja, ọkàa bàbà-á tiiri wo olóko; bí ọmọdé ó báá àgbà jẹun títiiri ní ńtiiri.*
The mousetrap leans to one side to kill the mouse; the hook bends in order to kill the fish; the guinea corn leans sideways to watch the farmer; if a child will eat with an elder, it is proper for the child to lean to the side. (One must defer to one's elders and superiors and not be too forward in their company.)

3266. *Ipa abẹ́rẹ́ lokùn ńtọ̀.*
It is the path blazed by the needle that the thread follows. (One should emulate one's elders.)

K

3267. *Ká dòbálẹ̀, ká pa ìgbònwọ́ mọ́: ó ní ohun tí ńṣe fúnni.*
To prostrate oneself and bring one's hands together: there are certain things one gains from so doing. (Paying due homage to one's elders brings good things one's way.)[2]

---

2. The posture described is the Yoruba man's way of showing respect to his elders.

O

3268. *"Ó ṁbọ̀!" ló yẹ baba; bí babá bá dé, ọ̀rán tán.*
"Watch out, here he comes" is what befits the patriarch; after he has arrived, there is no more threat. (Fear of what a person might do is often a more powerful deterrent than what the person is actually capable of doing. Compare 1081.)

Ọ

3269. *Ọmọdé féẹ́ kú, o ní ẹnu àgbà ṅrùn.*
A child seeks death [when] he says the mouth of an elder stinks. (Disrespect for elders is a death wish.)

3270. *Ọmọdé kì í wò sọ̀sọ̀ níbùjókòó àgbà.*
A youth does not stare when in the company of elders. (Etiquette demands that youth avert its eyes from age, or at least look deferentially at it.)

3271. *Ọ̀-pani-nítàn ní ṅfi ojúlé ẹni hanni.*
It is the person who tells one one's own history that shows one the doorway to one's own home. (We would do well to pay attention to the words of the sages who know more than we do about our own lineage.)

3272. *Ọ̀rọ̀ tí a pé kí baba má gbọ̀ọ́, baba ní ṅparí è.*
A matter that one tries to keep from the ears of the patriarch will eventually come before the patriarch for resolution. (The elders have a right to be privy to all important matters, because keeping order and peace is their responsibility.)

3273. *Ọ̀rọ̀ tí oníkọlàá bá sọ, abẹ́ gé e.*
Whatever statement the circumciser makes is cut off by a razor.[3] (When the person in charge has spoken, the discussion is over. The following is a variant.)

3274. *Ọ̀rọ̀ tí ọbá bá sọ, abẹ́ gé e.*
Whatever the king says is severed by a razor. (The king's word is final. See the previous entry.)

---

3. The expression *abẹ́ gé e*, literally "it is severed by a razor," is employed to indicate finality. In this case the proverb plays on the idea that the circumciser uses a sharp razor to ply his trade.

On relationships with friends and acquaintances

A

3275. *A kì í bá ẹrú mulẹ̀, ká bá olúwa mulẹ̀, ká má da ẹnìkan.*
One cannot make a pact with the slave and make a pact with the master and not betray one of them. (One cannot enter into alliance with people whose interests are in conflict.)

3276. *A kì í dúpẹ́ ara ẹni.*
One does not give thanks to oneself. (Gratitude is superfluous among close friends or relatives.)

3277. *A kì í fi ibi sú olóore.*
One does not return evil to one's benefactor. (Never render evil for good.)

3278. *A kì í fi òtítọ́ sínú gbàwìn ìkà.*
One does not leave truthfulness inside to purchase wickedness on credit. (Never go out of your way to injure others.)

3279. *A kì í fi ọ̀ràn-an pápá lọ ẹja; a kì í fi ọ̀ràn-an odò lọ àfẹ̀.*
One does not invite a fish to the grassland; one does not entice the field mouse to the stream. (Do not expect people to destroy themselves at your bidding.)

3280. *A kì í gba àkàkà lọ́wọ́ akítì; a kì ígba ilée baba ẹni lọ́wọ́ ẹni.*
One does not deny the monkey the habit of squatting; one does not wrest a person's father's home from him. (Respect others' rights.)

3281. *A kì í gbà lọ́wọ́-ọ "Mé rì í."*
One does not take from "I do not have." (Never seek to take from the destitute the little they do have.)

3282. *A kì í rí a-rẹ́-má-jà; a kì í rí a-jà-má-rèẹ́.*
No one ever sees friends who do not quarrel; no one ever sees people who quarrel and never make up. (Friendship and quarrels cannot go on forever, unbroken.)

3283. *A kì í ṣe ọ̀rẹ́ èrò ká yọ̀; èrò yó relé bó dòla.*
One does not befriend a sojourner and rejoice; the sojourner will leave for home come tomorrow. (Permanent ties are to be preferred to fleeting ones.)

3284. *A kì í sìpẹ̀-ẹ "Nàró" fábuké.*
One does not give the advice "Stand up straight" to a humpback. (Do not impose impossible conditions on others.)

3285. *À ńdáhùn sí gbèsè; góńgó orí ẹ̀ la kì í kán.*
One may intervene in the discussion of a debt, but one does not break its spike. (Though one may discuss others' debts, one has no obligation to settle them.)

3286. *Abanijẹ́ ba ara ẹ̀ jẹ́.*
A detractor injures his own reputation. (A person who maligns other people re-

flects badly on his own character. See the following entry.)

3287. *Abanijẹ́ ò níí gbayì.*
A detractor will not earn a good reputation. (This is a variant of the previous entry.)

3288. *A-báni-jẹ-má-bàáni-ṣe, ìfà èèyàn; ẹní jẹ dídùn ní ńjẹ kíkan.*
He-who-shares-one's-food-but-does-not-share-one's-tasks [is a] freeloader; he who eats the sweet should also eat the sour. (People should not be fair-weather friends.)

3289. *Abánikú ọ̀rẹ́ sọ̀wọ́n; abánikú, ogun ní ńbani lọ.*
A friend who would die with one is rare; he who would do so accompanies one even to war. (Few friends will risk death by accompanying one to a war that they have no interest in.)

3290. *Abánirẹ́ fi àfo ìjà sílẹ̀.*
A person who befriends another should make allowances for quarrels. (It is realistic to expect that a friendship will not be without occasional quarrels.)

3291. *Àdánù ńláńlá ni fún ẹni tó fẹ́ni, tí a ò fẹ́.*
What a great loss it is for a person who loves you but that you do not love. (Unrequited love is a painful thing.)

3292. *Àdàpọ̀mọ́ obìnrin ò ṣéé yanjú.*
A congress of women [or with women] is not easy to unravel. (Problems in certain relationships defy intervention from outside.)

3293. *Adáríjini ní ńṣètẹ́ ẹjọ́.*
He who forgives takes the wind out of the case's sails. (To forgive is to be magnanimous.)

3294. *Adìẹ dà mí lóògùn nù; mo fọ́ ọ léyin.*
The chicken spilled my medicine; I broke its eggs. (One pays back tit for tat.)

3295. *A-dùn-ún-jẹ bí àjẹpọ̀.*
A delight to eat, like something one shares with others. (It is more delightful to share food than to eat alone.)

3296. *Afinisẹ̀sín àlè, ó ní òun ó jẹ ìbẹ́pẹ.*
Concubine-who-would-disgrace-one says she would like some papaya. (True love and true friendship make no impossible demands. This is a variant of 3322.)

3297. *Afínjú méjì kì í wo òjìji wọn nínú agada.*
Two fops will not share the same mirror. (Arrogance leaves no room for rivalry.)

3298. *Àfohunwéohun, àfọ̀rànwéọ̀ràn; fi ọ̀ràn jì ká lè yinni.*
Recalling-similar-matters-of-the-past, recalling-similar-problems-of-the-past, forgive an offense and earn praise. (One should forgive and not keep recalling past offenses. See 1554 and the following entry.)

3299. *À-fi-ọ̀rọ̀-wé-ọ̀rọ̀ ò jẹ́ kí ọ̀rọ̀ tán bọ̀rọ̀.*
Allowing-a-current-matter-to-remind-one-of-similar-matters-in-the-past prevents a quarrel from ending easily. (This is similar to the previous entry.)

3300. *Afọ́jú onílù; atiro àrìnjó; bàtá ògèdè; ṣaworo òkòtó.*
A blind drummer; a lame dancer; *bàtá* drum made from banana stem; bells made of snail shells. (All of a kind.)[1]

3301. *Àgùntàn tó bá ajá rìn á jẹgbẹ́.*
A sheep that fraternizes with dogs will eat

---

1. The banana stem is no substitute for the *ọmọ* usually used to make this type of drum, and snail shells are poor substitutes for the usual brass bells.

excrement. (One inevitably assumes the habits of one's constant company.)

3302. *Àgbà ò sí nílùú ọ̀kẹ́rẹ́.*
There are no elders in the town of squirrels. (Some cultures lack proper regard for age. Compare 4224.)

3303. *Àgbà tí kò fọ̀ mọ́ni níkùn kì í fọ̀ mọ́ni lórí.*
An elder who does not make an impression on one's stomach does not make an impression on one's mind. (If a venerable elder cannot feed you, he may not command you, either.)

3304. *Àgbà tí kò yáni légbàá ìkòkò, bó bá dáṣẹ ilé sílẹ̀ a kì í lọ.*
An elder who does not secretly lend one six pence: if he embarks on building a house, one does not show up to help. (One returns favor for favor.)

3305. *Àgbà tó bú èwe lèwe ḿbú.*
It is an elder who insults a youth that a youth insults. (Elders earn respect only if they respect others. Compare the following two entries.)

3306. *Àgbà tó gba gbàdù, ó gba ìtùnú.*
An elder who has experienced a disaster has earned commiseration. (Be sensitive to other people's difficulties.)

3307. *Àgbà tó gbin èbù ìkà, orí ọmọ-ọ rẹ̀ ni yó hù sí.*
An elder who plants yams of wickedness will see them sprout on the head of his child. (The wickedness of the father will be visited on the children. Compare 702 and 1306.)

3308. *Àgbà tó jẹ à-jẹ-ì-wẹ̀hìn ni yó ru ẹrù-u rẹ̀ délé.*
The elder who eats with abandon will carry his own load to the house. (If an elder offers no food to the youth around him, he cannot expect any help from them.)[2]

3309. *Àgbàlagbà kì í méku dání kó di amùn-rín.*
An elder does not hold a rat and see it turn into a lizard. (One should be able to rely on an elder.)

3310. *Àgbàlagbà ńfibínú lọ sÍlọrin, a ní kó ra tìróò bọ̀.*
An elder is on his way to Ìlọrin in anger, and we ask him to bring back galena for us.[3] (Be sensitive to others' problems. Compare the following entry.)

3311. *Àgbàlagbà ńfìrójú ròrun, a ní kó kílé kó kọ́nà; ojú rere ló fi ńlọ?*
An elder is making his way to heaven with great reluctance, and we ask him to give our regards to all and sundry; is he departing cheerfully? (One should be sensitive to other people's predicaments. This is a variant of the preceding entry.)

3312. *Àgbàrá òjò-ó bánijà, ó bá ojúde ẹni lọ.*
The rain flood quarrels with one yet passes in front of one's house.[4] (In spite of disagreements, people must still act in concert when necessary.)

---

2. *Àjẹìwẹ̀hìn* literally means "eating without looking back": in other words, eating without considering what is proper. What is proper is for elders to leave a little of their food for the young people. That gesture is rewarded by the youths, who will stop the elder from doing any task and do it themselves. If the elder omits this gesture, he loses the consideration and respect of the youth.

3. Galena is used as a cosmetic on the eyelashes and eyebrows.

4. In Yoruba etiquette, people who meet or pass must exchange greetings, whether they know each other or not, but quarrels do make people ignore this rule. Since rainwater cannot exchange greetings with the owners of the homes it flows past, it is here construed as having a quarrel with them.

3313. *Àgbèjẹ-ẹ́ gbà wọ́n là tán, wọ́n ní ká pa á ní pánṣá.*
After the pumpkin had saved them (in a famine), they ordered that it be cut into ordinary calabash. (Never forget those who stick by you in your times of difficulty.)

3314. *Àìfinipeni, àìfèèyànpèèyàn lará oko-ó fi ńsán ìbàntẹ́ wọlú.*
Lack-of-regard-for-anyone, lack-of-regard-for-people makes the bush dweller enter the town in his loincloth. (Self-respect implies respect for others.)

3315. *Ajá kì í gbàgbé olóore.*
A dog never forgets a benefactor. (One will, or should, always remember one's benefactor.)

3316. *Ajá kọ imí ẹlẹ́dẹ̀; ẹlẹ́dẹ̀-ẹ́ kọ imí ajá.*
The dog snubs the pig's excrement; the pig snubs the dog's excrement. (Neither party in a relationship will accept disrespect from the other.)

3317. *Ajá tó yó kì í bá àìyó ṣeré.*
A satiated dog does not frolic with a hungry dog. (Avoid levity in the company of benighted people.)

3318. *Ajẹgbodò ńwá ẹni kúnra.*
The-eater-of-new-yams seeks people to join him. (A culprit always wants company. Compare 4912.)

3319. *Àjọjẹ ò dùn bí ẹnìkan ò ní; bí a bá ní là ńṣe àjọjẹ.*
Sharing of food is not pleasant if one participant has nothing; it is when one has something that one shares. (Those who share expect something in return.)

3320. *Àjọsùn ní ńmú iná wá sáṣọ.*
Sleeping together infects clothes with lice. (One takes on some of the blemishes of one's associates.)

3321. *Àkàsù bàmbà lósù àgà, iṣu gbọọrọ lẹ́jọ̀dún.*
A sizable corn loaf in the month before the harvest, a long yam in the month of the harvest. (A good turn when it is needed will be repaid with accretion. Compare 3240.)

3322. *Àlè tí yó fini ṣèsín ní ńbèrè ìbépẹ.*
It is a concubine who wishes to disgrace one that demands pawpaw. (Those who deliberately force one into compromising behavior seek to disgrace one. This is a variant of 3296.)

3323. *À-múró-yaró ò jẹ́ kí ọ̀rọ̀ ó tán.*
Repaying-injury-with-injury prevents the settlement of disputes. (As long as a wronged person insists on revenge, a quarrel will not be settled.)

3324. *Àpáńtètè ńbẹ láyé; kò sí lọ́nà ọ̀run.*
"Let's see who will be first to get there" is found on this earth; it is not found on the way to heaven.[5] (No one vies to be the first in heaven.)

3325. *A-pọ́n-ori-kéré ò gbọ́n bí a-yọwó-má-rà.*
The-person-who-skimps-on-his-or-her-merchandise is not as clever as the would-be-customer-who-prices-the-merchandise-but-resists-buying. (The seller may attempt to scalp, but the buyer may refuse to buy.)

3326. *Àràbà ni bàbá; ẹni a bá lábà ni baba.*
The silk-cotton tree is the father; the person one finds at the hut is the lord. (Just as the silk-cotton tree sways over all other trees, the person who is first in a place holds sway over all others. Compare 3263 and 3456.)

---

5. *Àpáńtètè* is a game children on an errand play when there are alternate routes to their destination. The children split into two groups, each party taking one route and trying to arrive first.

3327. *Àrífín ilé-ìgbé, tí ḿmú ọmọdé wo ìhòòhò àgbà.*
The disgrace that comes of using a communal latrine exposes an elder's nakedness to the young. (The contingencies of living in a group sometimes expose one to insults one would otherwise avoid.)

3328. *Àrífín tí ejò-ó fi yán ahun.*
Lack of proper regard makes a snake bite a tortoise. (It is adding insult to injury for a person to be belittled by someone far below him or her.)

3329. *À-rí-ìgbọdò-wí, ẹran ilé tí ńfojú dọdẹ.*
Something-seen-but-unmentionable: a domestic animal that disdains a hunter. (The domestic animal may strut with impunity before a hunter.)

3330. *À-ríni-mọni ni à-kíni-mọni.*
Seeing-one-with-a-person is greeting-one-with-a-person. (The sort of reception one receives depends on the sort of company one is in.)

3331. *A-rojú-fúnni-láwìn-ojà-á sàn ju a-rojú-sinni-lówó lo.*
One-who-reluctantly-sells-to-one-on-credit is preferable to one-who-reluctantly-asks-for-his-money. (Someone who reluctantly gives one something increases one's stock nonetheless; someone who reluctantly takes from one decreases one's stock. See the next entry also.)

3332. *A-rójú-fúnni-lóhun-ún sàn ju a-rójú-gbà-á lo.*
One-who-reluctantly-gives-one-something is preferable to one-who-reluctantly-takes-it-back. (See the preceding entry.)

3333. *Asínwín Ìká, aṣiwèrè Ìlúká, wọn dáríjọ, wó ní àwọn ńsòrẹ.*
The mad people of Ìká and the imbeciles of Ìlúká got together and said they were all friends. (Like people keep like company.)

3334. *Àsọtélẹ̀ kò jé kí ìwòfà di ẹrú olówó.*
A standing arrangement keeps the pawn from becoming a slave of the creditor. (To agree beforehand is to prevent misunderstandings later.)

3335. *Aṣiwèrè èèyàn ní ńwípé ẹgbón ò tó; ẹni a bá níwájú ní ńṣe baba fúnni.*
Only an imbecile says that those older than he or she are of no account; those who came before one can fill the role of father. (Never disdain an elder.)

3336. *Aṣọ kan-án kángun sára eégún ju òkan lo.*
One cloth is closer to the masquerader's body than others. (Some friends or relatives are dearer than others.)

3337. *A-tòrun-wáá-dọbè-síná, eégún-un sálà.*
One-who-comes-all-the-way-from-heaven-to-upset-stew-on-the-fire: masquerader of the Muslim day of worship. (The masquerader who disrupts one's projects is an unwelcome visitor from heaven.)

3338. *Awo ní ńperí awo.*
Only mysteries can communicate with mysteries. (Only the initiate can gain access to mysteries and their import.)

3339. *Àwówówó ni ti irínwó; ìdòbálẹ̀ ni tèbìtì; bájá bá gbé egungun a dòbálẹ̀ gbooro.*
Crashing completely is the mark of four hundred; lying prone is the mark of the snare; when a dog finds a bone, it lies down flat. (The proper posture before one's elders is a prone position.)[6]

---

6. The proverb evokes images of things that lie prone in order to indicate to the person to whom the proverb is addressed what is expected of him, or to

3340. *Bí a bá ńdíje níbi iṣé, ọwọ́ a máa yáni.*
If people compete at a task, the task is soon done. (Competition promotes efficiency.)

3341. *Bí a bá rí ọlọ́rọ̀ eni, sọ̀rọ̀-sọ̀rọ̀ là ńdà.*
When one sees one's confidant, one runs at the mouth like a spout. (In the right company, one is uninhibited.)[7]

3342. *Bí a bá torí igi gba odì, a ṣe iná fúnni yá.*
If one makes enemies because of wood, it should make fire for one to warm oneself. (One should have something to show for one's pains.)

3343. *Bí a kò bá fìjà pàdé, a kì í fìjà túká.*
If people did not come together in a quarrel, they should not part in a quarrel. (Friendship should not be permitted to turn to enmity.)

3344. *Bí a kò bá jà a kì í ré.*
If we have not quarreled, we cannot be friends. (Friends do not appreciate each other until after a quarrel.)

3345. *Bí a kò bá pàdé lókè, a ó pàdé lódò.*
If we do not meet up on high, we will meet down below. (Paths that have crossed will somewhere, somehow, cross again.)

3346. *Bí a kò bá rí ohun fún òrìṣà èrò, a kì í gba torí-i rè.*
If one has nothing to offer the god of trav-

elers, one does not take from him what he has. (If one has nothing to give another person, one should not take what that person has.)

3347. *Bí àgbàlagbà kò bá ríbi jókòó, gbédìí-gbédìí a gbé ọmọdé.*
If an elder can find no place to sit, lift-bottom-lift-bottom lifts the youth. (If a youth does not voluntarily show respect to elders, forces beyond his control will compel him.)

3348. *Bí àgbàlagbà-á bá ńsọ̀rọ̀, tọ́mọdé ò yájú, bó pé títí á mọ ohun tí wọ́n ńṣe.*
If elders confer and the youth does not exceed his station, sooner or later he will know what they conferred about. (The well-behaved youth will learn the way of the elders.)

3349. *Bí ará ilé eni bá foríṣo, tí a kò bá mọ̀ ọ́ kí, ìjà ní ńdà.*
If a member of one's household bumps his or her head and one is careless in expressing one's sympathy, a quarrel results. (Sympathy extended the wrong way leads to quarrels.)

3350. *Bí aṣáájú ò bá mọ̀ọ́ rìn, ìgbé lará èhìn ńwọ̀.*
If the leader does not know his way, the follower winds up in the bush. (The incompetence of the leader spells disaster for the followers.)

3351. *Bí èèyàn-án bá ṣeun ká sọ pé ó ṣeun; bí èèyàn-án bá ṣèèyàn ká sọ pé ó ṣèèyàn; nítorípé, ohun tí a ṣe, ó yẹ kó gbeni.*
If a person deserves gratitude, we should say that he deserves gratitude; if a person is kindly, we should say that he is kindly, because one should reap the rewards of one's actions. (A person's goodness should be publicly acknowledged.)

---

indicate acceptance of the posture one knows one must assume.

7. The word *dà,* "to become," is indistinguishable from *dà,* "to spill." If one assumes the first meaning, then *sòròsòrò* is "one who speaks [a great deal]"; however, with the second meaning, *sòròsòrò* becomes an onomatopoeic representation of the sound of pouring water.

3352. *Bí ekòló bá júbà ilẹ̀, ilẹ̀ á lanu.*
If the worm pays homage to the earth, the earth opens for it. (The proper approach will open any door.)

3353. *Bí ewé bá pẹ́ lára ọṣẹ, á dọṣẹ.*
If a leaf remains long enough around soap, it becomes part of the soap.[8] (People who remain long enough in association eventually become alike.)

3354. *Bí ẹbìtì ò pa eku, a kó eyìn fẹ́léyìn.*
If the snare does not kill the rat, it returns the kernel bait to the owner. (If a performer will not carry out a task for which he or she has received payment, he or she returns the payment.)

3355. *Bí ẹlẹ́dẹ̀-ẹ́ bá pàfọ̀ tán, ẹni rere ní m̀máa-á wá fi yí lára.*
After a pig has wallowed in the mud, it seeks a good person to soil with the mud. (Evil people always look for virtuous people to implicate. Compare 3739.)

3356. *Bí iná bá wọlé, òkùnkùn a paradà.*
When light enters the house, darkness removes itself. (When one's superiors arrive, one yields authority to them.)

3357. *Bí kò tó ẹ̀rù, kò tó ìsájú?*
If it does not strike fear, does it not merit deference? (If one would not do a thing out of fear, could one not do it out of respect or as a favor?)

3358. *"Bí o bá ṣe mí mà ṣe ọ́" nigi oko-ó fi ńdádé.*
"If you injure me, I will injure you in return"; it is thus that trees in the forest sprout crowns. (Rivalry or antagonism is often the spur for glorious achievements.)

3359. *Bí ó ti ńṣe iṣu ọ̀bẹ ló yé; bí ó ti ńṣèyàwó ọkọ-ọ rẹ̀ ló mọ̀; bí o ti ńṣe mí ẹ bi ọ̀rẹ́-ẹ̀ mi.*
How the yam feels is known only to the knife; how the wife feels is known only to the husband; for how I feel, ask my friend. (The people closest to a person know best that person's condition.)

3360. *Bí ó ti wù kí Olúkòtún gbójú tó, Ajagùnnà ni bàbá-a rẹ̀.*
However brave the *Olúkòtún* might be, the *Ajagùnnà* is his father.[9] (However great the son turns out to be, he must still defer to his father; however successful the youth, he owes respect to the elders.)

3361. *Bí ó ti wù kí ọmọdé tètè jí tó, ọ̀nà ni yó bàá kùkùté.*
However early the youth may rise from the bed, he will find the stump already on the road. (In some respects, the youth cannot compete with his elders.)

3362. *Bí orí kan-án sunwọ̀n, a ran igba.*
If one head is fortunate, it will affect others. (One person's good fortune spills over to his or her associates.)

3363. *Bí orogún ìyá ẹní bá ju ìyá ẹni lọ, ìyá là ńpè é.*
If one's mother's co-wife is older than one's mother, one calls her mother. (One shows the same respect to all elders as one would show to one's parents.)

3364. *Bí owó bá pọ̀ ọ̀rẹ́ àtèrò a pọ̀; bówó bá tán gbogbo wọn a wábi gbà lọ.*
If money is plentiful, friends and guests are plentiful; when the money is gone, all of them will find other places to go. (People will swarm around the rich but disappear when reverses occur.)

---

8. The traditional soap is wrapped in leaves.

9. These terms are chieftaincy titles.

3365. *Bí ọmọdé bá máa só, a wo iwájú; bí àgbàà bá máa só, a wo èhìn.*
If a youth wants to fart, he looks ahead; if an elder wants to fart, he looks behind. (The youth should consider what his elders will make of his actions, whereas the elder should consider what example his actions set for the youth. Compare 881.)

3366. *Bí ọmọdé bá ḿbá àgbà jẹun, títiiri ní ḿmáaá tiiri.*
If a youth eats with an elder, he must show great diffidence. (In the company of elders, the youth must be well-behaved.)

3367. *Bí ọmọdé bá ní baba òun ò tó ẹni tí à ńsáré bá, bàbá-a rẹ̀ a ní ọmọ òun ò tó ẹni tí à ńdúró dè.*
If a youth says that his father is not worth catching up with, the father will say that his son is not worth waiting for. (A person who rejects his or her parents deserves to be disowned by them.)

3368. *Bí ọmọdé bá ṣu imí búburú, èsìsì la fi ńnù ú nídìí.*
If a youth expels foul excrement, one wipes his anus with nettle leaves. (A grievous offense deserves adequate punishment.)

3369. *Bí ọtí bá ńpani, ṣé òòrùn ńpa bọ̀tí; oró táa dá ọkà lọkà ńdáni san.*
If wine intoxicates one, the fermented corn was beaten by the sun also; it is the pain one inflicted on the corn that is being avenged. (If one is wronged by the person one has wronged, one has no ground for complaint.)

3370. *Bí yó ṣe èmi, bí yó ṣe ìwọ, kì í jé ká ṣu sóko a-lâi-rójú.*
It-might-happen-to-me, it-might-happen-to-you stops one from defecating on the farm of the person who has no time to tend it. (One does not take advantage of the

weak, for one does not know what might happen to one in the future.)

3371. *Bó-mọ-gín-ń-gín-ní-eegun-ní-ńlọ tí ḿbá ọmọ-ọ rẹ̀ pín ìrè; Bó-mọ-jẹ́mpẹ́-orí-ní-ńtani tí ḿbá baba-a rẹ̀ pín agbọ̀n rù.*
However-tiny-it-may-be-it-goes-to-the-bones shares a cricket with his son; However-light-it-may-be-it-makes-one's-skull-smart shares the carrying of the basket with his father. (A father who does not treat his son with generosity will not receive much regard from the son.)[10]

3372. *"Bùn mi mbùn ọ" lòpòló ńké.*
"Give to me and I will give to you" is the cry of the toad. (Reciprocity is best in human relations.)

3373. *Búni-búni, a-bèébú-wọ̀ntì-wọ̀ntì.*
The person who insults others: a-person-whose-nature-deserves-many-insults. (The person with many flaws is typically the most ready to insult others.)

D

3374. *Dídùn ló dùn tí à ḿbọ́rẹ̀-ẹ́ jẹkọ; tilé oge-é to oge-é jẹ.*
It is because a relationship is pleasant that one eats corn loaf with one's friend; what each dandy has at home is enough food for him. (If a friendship sours, each friend will survive without the other. Compare 2103.)

E

3375. *Èèyàn búburú ba èèyàn rere jé.*
Evil people give good people a bad name. (A

---

10. The cricket is so small that the father should leave it to the son; a son must not permit his father to carry any load.

good person in the company of bad people shares their reputation.)

3376. Èèyàn loògùn èèyàn.
People are the antidote for people. (People may be a bane, but they may also be a succor; with people behind one, one can withstand much from other people.)

3377. Èkùró lalábàákú èwà.
Palm kernel is inseparable company for beans. (Wherever one sees a certain person, one is sure to see another certain person.)

3378. Eléérú ní ńsoko alátà; wón bímo wón so ó ní Òwó-sòkan.
An ash seller marries a seller of atà wood; on having a child they name it The-trades-are-united. (The people concerned are all of a kind.)

3379. Epinrin ní ńwú epinrin sílè; òkú ògá-láńtá ní ńwú òkú ògolonto.
It is epinrin [a secret] that exposes epinrin; it is a half-shrouded corpse that exposes a shroudless corpse. (Exposure of one secret calls for the exposure of another; the person whose secret is exposed will expose the exposer's secret.)

E

3380. "E kú àtijó" mo ara-a won rí.
"It's been a long time" signals previous acquaintance. (How people behave toward one another can be explained by what went on between [or among] them in the past. Compare 2482.)

3381. Egbé búburú ní ḿba ìwà rere jé.
Bad company ruins good character. (The reputation of one's company rubs off on one.)

3382. Eni a bíni bí ńdani, áḿbòńtórí òré.
The person born of the same parents with one might betray one, let alone one's friends. (Trust no one, neither relatives nor friends.)

3383. Eni a fé kì í lárùn lára.
A person one loves is never afflicted with a disease. (One is always blind to the flaws of those one loves. Compare the following entry.)

3384. Eni a fé kì í sìwàhù.
A beloved person can do nothing wrong. (To be loved is to be infallible. Compare the preceding entry.)

3385. Eni a fé kì í té; sùgbón ká má sàsejù níbè.
A beloved person never suffers disgrace, but he or she must not overstep bounds. (A favored person retains the favor only as long as he or she behaves decorously.)

3386. Eni a féràn ní ńríni fín.
It is a person one loves who acts with dis-respect toward one. (It is those to whom one permits familiarity who take liberties in one's presence.)

3387. Eni à ḿbá mu tábà kó yò; ehín ní ńpónni.
The person whose snuff one shares should be happy; all one gets from it is stained teeth. (He whose favor one accepts should know that even the acceptance of the favor has its burdens.)

3388. Eni à ḿbárìn là ńfìwà jo.
It is the person whose company one keeps that one emulates. (One should match one's comportment to one's company.)

3389. Eni bí akàn ní ńhe akàn.
Only crablike people gather crabs. (Like attracts like. Compare 4927 and 4928.)

3390. Ẹni tí a bá fẹ́ràn là ńtijú fún.
It is people one likes that one takes care
not to offend. (One's consideration should
be for one's friends, not for indifferent
people.)

3391. Ẹni tí a bá ròde là ḿbá relé; ẹni ajá bá
wá lajá ḿbá lọ.
One returns home with the person one went
out with; the dog departs with the person
it came with. (One should not drop one's
partner or collaborator in the midst of an
engagement. Compare 3393.)

3392. Ẹni tí a bá sùn tì là ńjarunpá lù.
It is the person with whom one sleeps that
one thrashes against in restless sleep. (One
should confine one's affairs to people with
whom one keeps company.)

3393. Ẹni tí ajá bá wá sóde lajá ḿbá relé.
Whoever the dog came out with is the person the dog returns home with. (One should
remain faithful to one's companions. This is
a variant of 3391.)

3394. Ẹran ní ḿmúni jẹ ìdin; ọ̀rẹ́ ẹni ní ḿmúni
ru ẹrù ọ̀tá ẹni.
It is meat that makes one eat maggots; it is
one's friend that makes one carry an enemy's
load. (To please those one likes and respects, one often has to do things one finds
distasteful.)

3395. Ẹrú kan ní ḿmúni bú igba ẹrú.
A single slave causes one to insult two
hundred slaves. (The misbehavior of one
member of a group brings dishonor to all
members of the group. Compare 3186.)

F

3396. Fírífírí lojú ńrímú.
The eyes glimpse the nose only indistinctly.

(A statement that someone is all but impossible to see or find.)[11]

I

3397. Igi à bá fẹ̀hìntìí légùn-ún; ẹni à bá fìnú
hàn ńkajó ẹni.
The tree one would lean on has thorns; the
person one would confide in is spreading
evil stories about one. (There is no one to
trust but oneself.)

3398. Igi tó tó erin lerin ńfara rò.
It is a tree that is as mighty as the elephant
that the elephant leans on. (One should seek
a worthy enough person to rely on.)

3399. Ìka tó tọ́ símú là ńnà símú.
It is a finger proper for the nose that one
pokes at the nose. (One should know the
proper way to approach others—according
to their status. Compare 564.)

3400. Ìsúnmọ́ni nìmọni; èèyàn gbé òkèèrè
níyì.
One knows a person by being close to the
person; those who live afar enjoy high regard. (One's true nature reveals itself at close
quarters. Compare 3024.)

3401. Ìwàà jọ ìwà ní ńjẹ́ ọ̀rẹ́ jọ ọ̀rẹ́.
Compatibility of character means compatibility in friendship. (Friendship succeeds
only when the friends are compatible in
their habits.)

3402. Ìyá egbẹ́ mọ oye ọmọ tí òun bí.
The matron knows just how many children
she gave birth to. (When the chips are down,
one gives priority to one's own interests.)[12]

---

11. The proverb is usually addressed to people one
sees only once in a very long while.

12. Ìyá egbẹ́, which translates as "matron," literally

3403. *Ìyá odó òun ọmọ ẹ̀ ò níjà; àgbẹ̀ ló dájà sílẹ̀ fún wọn; ọmọ odó kì í na ìyá ẹ̀ lásán.*
The mortar and the pestle have no quarrel between them; it is the farmer that has caused the quarrel; the pestle would not pound the mortar otherwise. (Said when extraneous matters cause a rift between two friends.)

3404. *Ìyá ọbá tóó pè ní ìyá ẹbọ; ìyá-a baálẹ̀-ẹ́ tóó pè ní ìyá àjẹ́; Olúṣẹyẹ́ tóó pè ní Olúfàya.*
The king's mother is worthy of the designation "mother of mysteries"; the chief's mother is worthy of the appellation "mother of witches"; Olúṣẹyẹ [He who makes merry] can also be named Olúfàya [He who tears things apart]. (Those brought together by merrymaking may be dispersed by dissension.)

K

3405. *Ká báni jẹ ò ní ká má bàáni wá ọ̀ràn.*
Sharing one's food with others does not stop them from getting one into trouble. (You cannot trust people simply because you fraternize with them.)

3406. *Ka èèwọ̀ fún mi kí nka èèwọ fún ẹ.*
Tell me your taboos and I will tell you my taboos. (When friends know and avoid what friends dislike, the friendship will last.)

3407. *Ká jà ká rẹ́ kò dàbí ọ̀rẹ́ ìpilẹ̀ṣẹ; àpá kì í jinná kó dàbí ara ẹni.*
Friendship made up after a quarrel is not like the original friendship; the scar left by a sore cannot be like virgin skin. (Anything that was spoiled and then repaired can never return to its original state.)

3408. *Káàkiri là ńṣégi, ojú kan là ńdì í.*
Firewood is gathered from all over, but it is all tied together at one place. (After all members of an assembly have voiced their opinions, the leader of the group puts it all together in a statement.)

3409. *Kétépé ló rí: ẹṣin òtá ẹni.*
"It is a miserably scrawny thing": one's enemy's horse. (One is always inclined to belittle one's enemy's accomplishments.)

3410. *"Kí ni Lágbájá lè ṣe?" Ìjà ní ḿbẹ níbẹ̀?*
What can So-and-So do? A quarrel brought it about. (Quarrels are the usual reasons for one person to question the worth of another.)

3411. *Kì-í-jẹ-ilá-kì-í-jẹ-ìlasa: ilé ẹ̀ ní ńgbé.*
He-will-not-eat-okro-and-he-will-not-eat-okro-leaves keeps to his or her own home. (A person who will not do what others do will have no one for company.)

3412. *Kò sí ohun tó dùn bí ọ̀rẹ́ òtítọ́; kò sí ibi tí a lè fi wé ilé ẹni.*
There is nothing quite as pleasing as true friendship; there is no place comparable to one's own home. (True friendship is a rare blessing, and one's home is one's paradise.)

3413. *Kò sí ohun tó pọ̀ tó esú; bó bá ẹni nílé a bá ẹni lóko.*
There is nothing as plentiful as locusts; if they catch up with one at home, they also catch up with one on the farm. (Said of a person or people one cannot get away from, no matter what one does.)

M

3414. *Mọ ìwà fóníwà loògùn òré.*
Knowing and accepting each person's character for what it is is the medicine for friend-

---

means "mother of the society." Although in that role the matron seeks the welfare of the group, in a crisis she will favor her own children.

ship. (Mutual tolerance is indispensable in friendship.)

O

3415. *Ogún ọmọdé kì í ṣeré gba ogún ọdún.*
Twenty children will not play together for twenty years. (All relationships end sometime.)

3416. *Ogún pa ará, odò-ó gbé iyèkan lọ, àjọbí ṣọnù lónà Ìkòròdú, a ò tún réni bá rìn mọ́, àfi ẹni tí ńtanni.*
Death took one's kin; the river carries off one's siblings; one's blood relations disappear on the road to Ìkòròdú; one has nobody left to keep one company save those intent on deceiving one. (An expression of the statement that one has lost all those one could rely on.)

3417. *Ohun mẹ́ta la kì í wípé kọ́rèẹ́ ẹni má ṣe: a kì í wí pé kọ́rèẹ́ ẹni má kòọlé; a kì í wí pé kọ́rèẹ́ ẹni má nìí obìnrin; a kì í wí pé kọ́rèẹ́ ẹni má lọ sídàálẹ̀.*
Three things one does not tell one's friend not to do: one does not tell a friend not to build a house; one does not tell a friend not to take a wife; one does not tell a friend not to travel. (One does not deny a friend the good things of life.)

3418. *Ohun tí akátá jẹ ló fi ńlọ èrò ọ̀nà.*
It is what the squirrel eats that it invites the wayfarer to share.[13] (One will inevitably be smeared by the blemish on those whose company one keeps.)

3419. *Olóhun ò níí gbèsan, aáwọ̀ ò sì níí tán.*
The owner will not accept compensation,

but the grumbling will never end. (Used for situations in which a person ruins the property of another person who is very close; the owner cannot properly accept replacement or compensation, yet he will never stop grumbling about his loss.)

3420. *Olówó ńjẹ́ Arógan; Ìwòfà ńjẹ́ Agúnmátẹ̀; ebè tí wọ́n bá kọ ẹ̀hìn ni wọn ó fi tú u ká.*
The creditor is named Arógan; the pawned servant is named Agúnmátẹ̀; the heap they make they will scatter with their backs.[14] (Any venture in which there are two masters will end in disaster.)

3421. *Oníbàtà ní ńfojú dẹ̀gún; ẹni a bá ńfẹ́ ní ńfojú dini.*
It is someone wearing shoes who can take thorns lightly; it is a person one loves who dares take one lightly. (We are more likely to take advantage of people close to us than those we do not know.)

3422. *Oníṣègùn ló lè ṣọkọ Ẹ̀bẹ̀; aláwàdà ló lè ṣọkọ ọ̀sónú.*
Only a medicine man can be a husband to Ẹ̀bẹ̀;[15] only a person with a sense of humor can be the husband of a surly woman. (A successful partnership depends on the compatibility of those involved.)

3423. *Orí ló ńdúró fún àgbọ̀n mumi.*
The head must remain still to enable the chin to drink. (Without the aid and sacrifice of another person, one would be incapable of achieving what one has achieved.)[16]

14. *Arógan* means "One who stands bolt upright," and *Agúnmátẹ̀* means "One who is ramrod straight and never bends." Obviously, if neither will give, there will be a lot of fighting.

15. *Ẹ̀bẹ̀*, a name that means "Plea," obviously once belonged to a real person.

16. "*Dúró fún*," literally "Stand up for," is used in the proverb in the sense of "Stand still for"; the

13. The proverb refers to the fact that from up in the branches squirrels drop bits of whatever they are eating in the path of wayfarers.

O

3424. *Òbùn ba irú aṣọ jẹ́.*
The filthy person destroys the appeal of a
style of clothing. (Anything a filthy person
touches is ruined for others.)

3425. *Ogbọ́n ní ńpẹ́ kó tó ran ẹni; wèrè kì
í gbèé ran èèyàn; wèrè Ìbàdàn ló ran ará
Ògbómọ̀ṣọ́.*
Only wisdom takes a long time to rub off
on others; imbecility does not take long to
affect others; it is the imbecility plaguing
Ibadan people that rubbed off on the people
of Ògbómọ̀ṣọ́.[17] (If you keep a person's company, you sooner or later will be infected
with the person's bad habits.)

3426. *Ogbọọgbọ̀n là ńrọ ìjánu, òkòòkan là
ńmọ ìwà èèyàn; à bá mọ ìwà èèyàn, à bá bùn
ọ o ò fẹ́ ẹ; adunnijojo bí abájo.*
In the thirties one manufactures bridles;
one by one one learns people's character;
had I known a certain person's character
when she was offered to me, I would not
have married her: a situation that hurts like
"had I known." (If it were possible to know
people's character beforehand, one would
more easily choose those one would have
anything to do with.)

3427. *Ojọ́ tó bá burú là ńmọ ẹní fẹ́ni.*
It is on bitter days that one knows who loves
one. (A friend in need is a true friend.)

3428. *Ọkọ bí ẹmọ́; aya bí àfẹ̀; alárìnà bí àgó.*
Husband like a field mouse; wife like a
spotted grass mouse; go-between like the
àgó rat. (Three of a kind.)

---

real intention, though, is to stand up for, or support,
somebody.

17. Ògbómọ̀ṣọ́ is a town near Ibadan; they are
closely related in culture and history.

3429. *Ọmọ aráye kì í fẹ́ ká rún ọbẹ̀ láwo.*
The people of this world never wish that one
eat stew in a dish. (People seldom like to see
others prosper.)

3430. *Ọmọ aráye ò báni jẹ owó kan ìyà; owó
kan èwà ni wọ́n ńbáni jẹ.*
The people of this world never join one in
enduring a little bit of suffering; it is only
a little bit of black-eyed peas that they will
join one to enjoy. (People will share your
good fortune, not your misfortune.)

3431. *Ọmọ arúgbó ò jẹ́ ká sàánú arúgbó.*
The aged person's child stops one from extending charity toward the aged person.
(The character of one's close relatives often
determines how people act toward one.)

3432. *Ọna là ńpàdé fẹrè.*
It is on the pathway that people meet fleet-
ingly. (One should not be too eager to take
one's leave when one visits other people at
home.)

3433. *Ọ̀pèrèkẹ́tẹ̀ ńdàgbà, inú adámọ̀ ńbàjẹ́; a
di baba tán inú ńbí wọn.*
The small palm tree grows bigger, and the
cutter of palm leaves becomes angry; we
grow in greatness, and they become angry.
(People are consumed with jealous anger
when they see others prosper.)

3434. *Òràn ṣeni wò, ká mọ eni tó fẹ́ni.*
Misfortune should befall one so one might
know who really loves one. (We know our
true friends only when we are in trouble.)

3435. *Òrẹ́ abánikú sòwọ́n.*
Friends who will die with one are rare. (Do
not expect a friend to die for you or with
you.)

3436. *Òrẹ́ alábẹ́rẹ́ kì í gbé òtún.*
The friend of a needle wielder does not sit

to his or her right. (One should know, and allow for, the idiosyncrasies of one's close friends.)

3437. Ọ̀rẹ́ díẹ̀, ọ̀tá díẹ̀, ní ńṣe ikú pani.
A little friendship, a little enmity, is what kills people. (Intermittent friendship does not make for peace of mind.)

3438. Ọ̀rẹ́ èké, èké ọ̀rẹ́; olè, olè.
A false friend, a friendly fraud: both are like thieves. (Never have anything to do with friends who prove false and frauds who act friendly.)

3439. Ọ̀rẹ́ eni ní ḿmúni ru ẹrù ọ̀tá eni.
It is a friend that makes one carry an enemy's load. (Obligations one owes a friend may sometimes entail doing things one would otherwise not contemplate.)

3440. Ọ̀rẹ́ là ńwá kún ọ̀rẹ́, a kì í wá ọ̀tá kún ọ̀tá.
One seeks to add friends to friends, not enemies to enemies. (Always look for more friends and fewer enemies.)

3441. Ọre ńjẹ́ ọre, ọ̀tà ńjẹ́ ọ̀tà; a kì í dúpẹ́ẹ "Mo ta ọ̀pọ."
A gift is one thing, and a sale is quite a different thing; one does not thank "I sold it to you cheap." (Selling cheap is not the same as making a gift.)

3442. Ọ̀rẹ́ ò fẹ́ ẹlẹ̀ta, elẹ̀jì lọ̀rẹ́ gbà.
Friendship does not accommodate a third person; it accommodates only a second person. (Two is company; three is confusion.)

3443. Ọ̀rẹ́ ò fẹ́ iró; awo ò fẹ́ ìtànjẹ.
Friendship does not brook lying; secret covenants do not brook deceit. (Always be true and honest in your dealings with those close to you.)

3444. Ọ̀rẹ́ ọdún méta ò ṣéé finú hàn tán; Júdáàsì-í bá Jésù sọ̀rẹ́ ọdún méta, ó ta á níjàṁbá.
A friend of three years is not to be trusted completely; Judas was a friend to Jesus for three years, yet he played him false. (Never place your complete trust in a friend, no matter how long your friendship.)

3445. Ọ̀rẹ́ pọ̀; ìwà àtìkà inú-u wọn ò dọ́gba.
Friends abound, but their character and their wickedness are very different. (Friendship does not mean compatibility or mutual good will.)

3446. Ọ̀rẹ́ purọ́ kan, èmi pàkan; ọ̀rẹ́ ní kí ngbé apá ẹjò lájà, mo ní kó gbé itan eja ní pẹpẹ.
My friend engaged in some deviousness, and I responded with my own deviousness; my friend told me to help myself to the arm of a snake on his rafters, and I asked him to help himself to the thigh of a fish on my shelf. (One should meet cunning with cunning.)

3447. Ọ̀rẹ́ tí àkàrà ḿbá epo ṣe ò kéré.
The friendship that àkàrà maintains with palm oil is not something to take lightly.[18] (Said of friendship that is obsessive and problematic.)

P

3448. Pòpóòrò àtèṣí kì í ba olóko dìgbàro.
Last year's cornstalk will not stand erect as long as the farmer. (The closest of friends and companions eventually go their separate ways.)

---

18. Àkàrà, black-eyed-bean fritters, are fried in palm oil.

R

3449. *Rẹ́rẹ́ ojú; ojú ni afẹ́ni, ṣùtì lẹ́hìn.*
Friendship that depends on presence offers
friendship in one's presence but despises one
when one is absent. (Friendship that does
not persist in one's absence is not worth
much.)

Ṣ

3450. *Ṣàṣà èeyàn ní ńfẹni lẹ́hìn bí a ò sí nílé;
tajá tẹran ní ńfẹ́ni lójú ẹni.*
Few people love one when one is absent;
every dog and goat loves one when one is
present. (Never trust that those who show
you affection in your presence will express
the same sentiments in your absence.)

3451. *Ṣe-fún-mi-kí-nṣe-fún-ọ loògùn ọ̀rẹ́.*
You-do-me-a-favor-and-I-do-you-a-favor is
the medicine for friendship. (Reciprocity is
essential in friendship. Compare the following entry.)

3452. *Ṣe-mí-kí-mbi-ọ́ loògùn ọ̀rẹ́.*
You-offend-me-and-I-talk-the-matter-over-
with-you is the medicine for friendship.
(Friendship is maintained by talking problems out, not by holding grudges. Compare
the preceding entry.)

T

3453. *Togbó togbó là ńrí agogo.*
The bell is always seen in the company of its
ringer. (Said of things or people that always
go together.)

On relationships with strangers

A

3454. *À ńgira sè fún àlejò jẹ, ó ní "Ilé yìí mà dùn láé!"*
One extends oneself to feed a visitor, and he remarks, "What abundance exists in this home!" (The visitor has no way of knowing the extent to which the host incurs debt for his, the visitor's, benefit. Compare proverb 474.)

3455. *Àjòjì tó bú baálẹ̀-ẹ́ di ẹrù tan.*
A stranger who insults the chief has packed his load. (A defenseless person who provokes the greatest power in the vicinity authors his or her own disaster.)

B

3456. *Baálé àlejò ni baba àlejò.*
The visitor's host is the visitor's father. (The host is father to the visitor. Compare 3263 and 3326.)

3457. *Baálé lọlọ́ràn awo.*
The landlord is the proper keeper of secrets. (One should not keep one's secret problems from the head of one's household.)

3458. *Bí ilẹ̀-ẹ́ bá rorò, tó pa ọ̀wẹ̀, orí olóko ni yó dàá lé.*
If the earth is unkind and kills a helper on the farm, the responsibility falls on the owner of the farm. (The host is responsible for the guest.)

Ẹ

3459. *Ẹni tí ó ńríni là ńrín; èèyàn tí kò rín èèyàn, a ò gbọdọ̀ rín in; èrín di méjì a dìjà.*
You may laugh only at a person who laughs at you, not at a person who does not laugh at you; when laughter becomes two, a quarrel results. (One seeks a quarrel when one laughs at others with whom one does not share a joking relationship.)

M

3460. *"Máa lọ, àlejò" kì í ti ẹnu onílé wá.*
"Stranger, it is time you departed" does not come from the mouth of a host. (Visitors should know when they have used up their welcome; a host should be gracious, even when the visitor is an insensitive boor.)

O

3461. *Omi àjèjì tó wọlú, píparẹ́ ní ńparẹ́.*
Whatever strange water enters a town inevitably disappears. (A newcomer to a community must adapt to its ways or face disaster.)

S

3462. *"Sún mọ́hùn-ún, a féẹ́ ṣọrò ilé-e wa," kì í jẹ́ kálejò di onílé.*
"Move aside; we are about to perform some

secret rites of our lineage" keeps a sojourner from becoming a member of the household. (Exclusion from intimate affairs will remind the visitor that he or she does not belong.)

On relationships with the less fortunate

3463. *A kì í bá baba ta ifòn tán ká tún ba ọmọ ta eṣinṣin kúrò.*
One does not lance an abscess for a father and then help the son chase flies away [from open wounds]. (One should not be expected to be a benefactor to one generation and to the next one also.)

3464. *A kì í dá ọmọ òkú lóró; a kì í ṣe ìkà fún ọmọ òrukàn.*
One does not misuse an orphan; one does not act cruelly to one's blood brother. (One should be considerate of those in need and also of one's relatives.)

3465. *Afúniję kì í fúni tà.*
The person who will give one food to eat will not give one food to sell. (There is a limit to charity.)

3466. *Àgbàtán là ńgbọ̀lẹ: bí a dáṣọ fóle à pa á láró; bí a lani níjà à sìn ín délé.*
One should go the whole way in rescuing a lazy person: if one makes a garment for him, one should also dye it; if one extricates him from a fight, one should also walk him home. (Never do things by halves.)[1]

3467. *Àì-dúpé-oore-ànà mú ooré súnií ṣe.*
Failure-to-show-gratitude-for-yesterday's-favor dissuades benefactors from extending favors. (If one shows no gratitude for previous kindnesses, one stops receiving favors. Compare 878.)

3468. *Ara ò ni ìwòfà bí onígbọ̀wọ́; a-bánikówó lara ńni.*
The pawn is never as troubled as his guarantor; it is the person who stands for another who is apprehensive. (The guarantor has more reason to worry than the debtor.)

3469. *Àríṣe làríkà; àríkà baba ìrègún.*
What-one-is-able-to-do is what-one-has-to-list; what-one-has-to-list gives one ground for recrimination. (If one does another a favor, one has some ground to reproach the recipient if he deserves it.)

3470. *"Ata-à mi dandan, iyò-ọ̀ mi dandan," olórí èpè.*
"My pepper indeed, my salt indeed": the most formidable of curses. (Never do evil to your benefactor.)[2]

3471. *À-wín-ì-san ò rí owó wín.*
The-borrower-who-does-not-repay finds no money to borrow. (He who defaults on a loan forfeits his opportunities for other loans.)

---

1. The lazy person is unlikely to wash his clothes; dyeing them will conceal the dirt. And until the lazy coward is safely within his own walls, he could be attacked again by his assailants.

2. The curse of a person whose salt and pepper the cursed person has eaten is most dangerous.

3472. *Bí aṣiwèrè-é bá se àṣè, ọlọgbọ́n a jẹ ẹ́.*
If an imbecile prepares a feast, the wise person will eat it. (The fool is there for the wise to take advantage of.)

3473. *Èkúté ilé ní tẹni tó pa òun ò dun òun bí ẹni tó gbé òun ṣánlẹ̀.*
The house mouse says he is not as hurt by the person who killed him as by the person who dashed him on the floor. (I may forgive the person who vanquished me but not the person who took advantage of me afterward.)

FOUR

Human Nature

On fate (and reciprocity)

A

3474. *À báà ṣẹbọ; à báà ṣòògùn; bí a ti pé a ó rìí láyé là ńrí.*
Even though one makes sacrifices, and even though one procures charms, however one is covenanted to turn out on earth is how one will turn out. (Neither sacrifices nor charms will alter a person's destiny.)

3475. *A bímọ lÓwu, wọ́n ní "akọ mbábo?" Èwo ni yó ṣọmọ níbẹ̀?*
A child is born in Òwu and people inquire, "Boy or girl?" Which can be expected to turn out well?[1] (A sentiment that Òwu people are uniformly worthless; a suggestion, therefore, that all members of a certain group are uniformly worthless.)

3476. *A bímọ nílé ọgbọ́n, a mú u relé ìmọ̀ràn lọ wò, nígbàtí ó ńbọ̀ ó pàdé òye lọ́nà; ọgbọ́n ni kò níí gbọ́n ni, tàbí òràn ni kò níí mọ̀; tàbí òye ni kò níí yé e?*
A child is born into the house of wisdom, is sent to the house of discernment for upbringing, and while returning comes upon intelligence; can he lack wisdom, can he lack discernment, or can he lack intelligence? (A child is never better or worse than the sort of upbringing he receives. Compare 2737.)

3477. *A kì í pé kí ọmọdé má fẹ ehín gan-gan-ran bó bá tù ú; ètè ni kò rí fi bò ó.*
One does not order a child not to expose his buckteeth if doing so soothes him; what he lacks are enough lips to cover them. (Do not force people to act against their nature.)

3478. *A kì í rí búburú lẹ́hìn Agà.*
One never sees misfortune after *Agà*, the month of May. (A time comes when all one's problems will be over.)[2]

3479. *A kì í rí ọmọ ọba ká má rìí àmì ọba lára è.*
One never sees a prince or princess without seeing his or her mark of royalty. (People show their worth and breeding by their comportment. Also, a person from an illustrious lineage should not be seen going about in rags or in bad company.)

3480. *A kì í yin ará Ìjẹ́mọ̀ pé ó mọ asẹ́-ẹ hun; a ní "Àmònímànà alẹ́ àná ni mo fi pète ìdí ẹ̀."*
One does not praise an Ìjẹ́mọ̀ person as an expert at weaving sieves, for then he will boast, "Only last night did I start on it!" (Compare 639.)

3481. *A kúnlẹ̀ a yànpín; a dáyé tán ojú ńyánni.*
We kneel and choose our destiny, but on reaching earth we are disillusioned. (However unfortunate, one's destiny is one's own choice.[3] Compare 3496 and 4612.)

---

1. Òwu is an ancient Ègbá Yoruba town.

2. May is the month of harvest; thereafter, any dearth of food ends and festivals and celebrations commence. (See also note 13 at 3531.)

3. At the basis of the proverb is the Yoruba belief

3482. *"A ò mọ eyí tí Ọlọ́run ó ṣe" ò jẹ́ á bínú kú.*
"We know not what God will do" stops one from committing suicide. (As long as one lives, one may hope.)

3483. *A ṣé ẹtu, a ò ṣé ẹtu, oparún gbá a nídìí; òràn ẹtu ni bí?*
We shot and missed the antelope; we shot and did not miss the antelope, and the bamboo hits its rear; is the antelope at fault? (One cannot always determine one's own fate.)

3484. *A sọ ọmọ ní Ṣódé, ó lọ síbi ó dé; a sọ ọmọ ní Ṣóbọ̀, ó lọ sájò ó bọ; a wá sọ ọmọ ní Ṣórìnlọ, ó lọ sájò kò dé mọ́, à ńsọ. Ta ni kò mọ̀ pé ilé lọmọ-ọ́ ti mú orúkọ ànù lọ?*
A child named Ṣódé goes on a journey and returns; a child named Ṣóbọ̀ travels afar and returns; then a child named Ṣórìnlọ travels away and does not return, and people wonder why. Who does not know that the child left home with a name that assures his loss?[4] (An expression of the belief that people act according to their names. Give a dog a bad name . . .)

3485. *A ṣe àlapà lọ́sọ̀ọ́ kò yẹ ẹ́; a ṣe ohun gbogbo fúngi, o yẹ igi.*
We decorate a bare, freestanding wall; the result is not pleasing, but whatever decoration a tree receives becomes it. (Efforts at improvement are wasted on some people.)[5]

3486. *Ààfáà-á sọ̀rọ̀ òjò-ó kù; ó ní Ọlọ́runún jẹ́rìí òun.*
The Muslim priest makes a statement, and thunder rumbles; he says God is bearing him witness. (The opportunist will turn everything to his or her advantage.)

3487. *Àbíjọ là ńmọ ìtan.*
It is through resemblance that one knows those who are related. (People show their affinity by their similar behavior or appearance.)

3488. *Àbíkú ńlọ, ìyá ẹ̀ ńpè é.*
A child destined to die is on its way [to dying]; its mother is calling it back.[6] (No one can stop fate.)

3489. *Àdàbà ò wá oúnjẹ sẹ́nu òrofó; oníkálukú ní ńwá oúnjẹ sẹ́nu ara-a rẹ̀.*
The dove does not put food into the mouth of the fruit pigeon; each person finds food for his or her own mouth. (Each person is responsible for his or her own welfare.)

3490. *Àgbìgbò ló mórí ìyà wáyé; orí tó máa gbeni ò dẹ́rù pani.*
It is *àgbìgbò* that chose an evil destiny for itself; the head that will be one's succor will not weigh one down. (A thing that will be one's salvation will not also torment one.)[7]

3491. *Agbojọ́ kì í gba ọjọ́ kan tì.*
What is destined to occupy one's day will not fail to consume it. (Fate cannot be averted.)[8]

---

that before incarnation, each person kneels before the Creator to choose his or her destiny on earth.

4. The names mean, respectively, Ọṣó (someone connected with certain mysteries) arrives, Ọṣó returns, and Ọṣó walks away.

5. A bare wall left standing after the collapse of a house will not show off decorations to advantage, whereas carvings on a tree look good.

6. *Àbíkú* (see note 3 to 2639), children the Yoruba believe to have made a pact before birth that they will die before maturity, are an explanation for the high incidence of infant mortality.

7. *Àgbìgbò* is a bird with an unusually big head. The proverb shifts from *orí*, the physical head, to *orí*, the embodiment of one's destiny.

8. There is no day on which death cannot take its intended victim.

3492. *Àìdé ikú là ńso àájà mọ́rùn; bíkú bá dé a já àájà sílẹ̀ a gbé aláàjà lọ.*
It is when death has not come calling that one ties charms around one's neck; when death comes calling, it rips the charm away and carries its wearer off. (This proverb is essentially the same as 3982.)

3493. *Àjíbòwábá là ńbá ilà àtẹ́lẹwọ́; a ò mọ ẹni tó kọ ọ́; àjíbòwábá lowó àdásan; a ò mọ ẹni tó jẹ ẹ́.*
The lines of the palm are things that pre-exist the owner's awareness; no one knows who made them; a debt the whole community must contribute to repay is an ageless debt; no one knows who incurred it. (Certain things defy human knowledge, and the sins of fathers are sometimes visited on their offspring generations later. Compare 3503.)

3494. *Àkèré pète ìyé; ìyá olódò ni ò gbà fún un.*
The frog tried for wings; it was the river-mother that refused her consent. (But for the forces of Nature, frogs would fly.)

3495. *Àkọ́dá oró ò dàbí àdágbẹ̀hìn.*
The first injury is nothing like the last. (The injury one inflicts is nothing compared to the injury one will receive in retaliation. Compare 4785.)

3496. *Àkúnlẹ̀yàn làdáyébá; a kúnlẹ̀ a yan ìpín; a dáyé tán ojú ńroni.*
What-was-chosen-on-the-knees is what-is-encountered-on-earth; one kneels and chooses a destiny, but on reaching earth one is disconsolate. (A person's fortunes on earth result from the person's choices at his or her creation; however much one might lament one's fortunes on earth, they are one's choice and responsibility. Compare 3481.)

3497. *Àlùmọ́nì: ó ní ẹni tí òún bá wà lọ́wọ́-ọ rẹ̀ ló ni òun.*

Prosperity: it says that the person in whose possession it is found is its owner. (Good fortune is no respecter of persons; it stays with whoever gets his or her hands on it.)

3498. *Àníyàn ladìẹ fi imú ṣe; adìẹ kì í fọnkun.*
A chicken's nose is merely obligatory; a chicken does not blow its nose. (Certain things one endures as a matter of obligation; one can easily do without them.)

3499. *Àránsí Ọlọ́run ò séni; ọkọ̀ ìbàjẹ́ ò sélẹ̀.*
Whatever God sends in your direction will not miss you; a vehicle destined for disaster will not escape it. (One cannot escape one's destiny.)

3500. *Asùngbè-oyún lọmọ ńjọ.*
It is the person who sleeps next to a pregnant woman that her child resembles. (A person will inevitably manifest the traits of his or her pedigree.)

3501. *Aṣégi-í ṣe wẹ́rẹ́-wẹ́rẹ́ wọ igbó; wàwà lọdẹ ńṣe tọ okùn ọ̀nà; kò sóhun tórí ò lè fini ṣe; orí ẹni ní ńmú ni jọba.*
The wood gatherer walks stealthily into the bush; the hunter stalks briskly through the bush path; there is nothing one's head cannot make one do; it is one's head that makes one a king. (One's destiny may lead one astray, and one's destiny may bring one good fortune.)

3502. *Aṣọ pupa kì í bá òkú ròrun.*
Purple cloth never accompanies the dead to heaven. (One individual has no part in another individual's fate.)

3503. *Àtẹ́wọ́ la bá ilà; a ò mọ ẹni tó kọ ọ́.*
The lines of the palm were always there; no one knows who drew them. (One's destiny is hidden from one. This is a variant of 3493.)

3504. *Àti kékeré làràmàjà-á ti ńlalé kọ́.*
It is from its youth that the crab learns to build its house. (The nature of the adult is apparent in the child.)

3505. *Àyànmọ́ ò gbóògùn.*
Destiny does not respond to medicine. (No medicine can cure fate.)

3506. *Ayésanmí ò se gbèdu; èèyàn lásán ò ní làárì; ọba ni làárì ẹni.*
Being prosperous does not entitle one to *gbèdu* drums; an ordinary person has no regality; it is in a king that regality resides. (Certain qualities are congenital, not to be acquired in life.)

3507. *Ayọ̀ ò rúbọ.*
Happiness offers no sacrifices. (When one is happy and contented, one has no need of sacrifice.)

B

3508. *Bániwí kì í báni débè.*
The counselor does not share the consequences [of one's choices] with one. (The adviser has no responsibility; only the doer does.)

3509. *Bí a bá bẹ oṣó oṣó á gbọ́; bí a bá bẹ àjẹ́ àjẹ́ á gbọ́; sùgbọ́n kí-ni-ngó-jẹ kì í gbọ́.*
If one pleads with a wizard, the wizard should be appeased; if one pleads with a witch, the witch should be appeased; but what-will-I-eat is never appeased. (One does not assuage hunger with pleas.)

3510. *Bí a bá ńfi èèpo ẹpà sú ọtí, ẹní máa yó á yó.*
[Even] were one to sell wine by the peanut-shell measure, those who will be intoxicated will be intoxicated. (Even in the midst of dearth, those who are destined to prosper will prosper. Compare the next entry.)

3511. *Bí a bá ńgúnyán nínú ewé, tí à ńsebẹ̀ nínú èèpo ẹpà, ẹní máa yó á yó.*
Even though one makes pounded yams in a leaf and cooks stew in a peanut shell, who will be full will be full. (Even in the midst of dearth, those destined to prosper will prosper. Compare the preceding entry.)

3512. *Bí adìẹ bá se ogún, tó se ọgbọ̀n, àgò ni yó dè é.*
Whether chickens number twenty or thirty, they will yield to being covered by the coop. (Certain fates cannot be averted by numbers alone.)

3513. *Bí alẹ́ ẹni yó ti rí, òwúrọ̀ ẹni ni yó fi hàn.*
How a person's night will be is revealed by the person's morning. (A person's nature reveals itself from youth.)

3514. *Bí inú ti rí lobì ńyàn.*
The omen revealed by the divinatory kola is determined by the nature of one's heart.[9] (The gods respond to one according to the goodness of one's heart.)

3515. *Bí ológbòó bá pámi pámi, yó wọ ọ́.*
A cat may skirt the water for a long time, but in the end it will enter the water. (An inevitability may be delayed but will not be avoided.)

3516. *Bí Ọlọ́run ńse rere, à ní Ó ńse ibi.*
When God is doing good, someone says he is doing evil. (Those who do not understand God's grand design fault some of his actions.)

3517. *Bí Ọlọ́run ò pani, ẹnìkan ò lè pani.*
If God does not kill one, nobody can kill one. (Only God can order people's fates. A variant is *Bí Ọlọ́run ò pani ọba ò lè pani*: "If

9. Kola nuts are used in divination; the way they lie after being cast reveals the omen or message.

God does not kill one, the king cannot kill one.")

3518. *Bí yó balè̩, bí yó balè̩ ni labalábá fi ń̩wogbó lo̩; araàìbalè̩ ni tàwòdì.*
As though it would land, as though it would land is the way a butterfly enters into the bush; restlessness is the lot of the eagle. (Although it might seem otherwise, a person headed for disaster will not escape it.)[10]

E

3519. *E̩ṣú á je̩, e̩ṣú á mu, e̩ṣú á lo̩; níbo ni alátampoko ó wò̩?*
The locusts will eat, the locusts will drink, and the locusts will depart; where will the grasshopper hide? (After the despoiler has done his or her damage, will the heirs not reap the consequences?)

3520. *Ewúré̩ tó je̩ s̩ílè̩ kan pò̩ mó̩ eèrí je̩ àdùbás̩ì ojó̩ mé̩ta.*
The goat that eats a shilling along with corn bran has eaten for three days in advance. (Whoever squanders valuable resources will pay with privation.)

E̩

3521. *È̩dá ń̩lùlù ìbàjé̩; O̩ló̩run ni ò̩ jé̩ kó dún.*
Humans beat the drum of disgrace, but God prevents it from making a sound. (Others seek one's disgrace, but God has foiled their plan.)

3522. *È̩hìn-in kete lòfò̩ ń̩ṣe.*
It is the back of the calabash that loses out on all good things. (It is some people's fate always to get the short end of things.)

3523. *E̩ni tí yó bàjé̩ ti bàjé̩ tán; e̩ni tí yó bàlùmò̩ ló kù.*
The person whose lot it is to be spoiled is spoiled already; only the person whose lot is to rot remains to be seen. (One wastes one's effort in attempting to improve an incorrigible person.)

3524. *E̩ni tó ń̩rínni ò ní ìbáwí; orí e̩ni ní ń̩pé ká rínni.*
Those who laugh at one have no blame; it is destiny that places one in a position of being laughed at. (One should blame not others but one's own fortune for whatever fate one suffers.)

3525. *È̩rè̩ké̩ oló̩kùnrùn: á wú kó tó bé̩.*
The cheeks of the diseased person will swell before they burst. (Things will get a great deal more painful before there is any relief.)

3526. *È̩rúkó̩, orí aaka; è̩rú àáké, orí aaka; aaka nìkan nigi tó wà nígbó ni?*
For a haft for the hoe, the choice is the *aaka* tree; for a haft for the axe, the choice is the *aaka* tree; is the *aaka* tree the only one in the forest?[11] (A person should not be the one to whom every offense or crime is traced.)

3527. *E̩sè̩ tí yó bù, pè̩lé̩ ò̩ ràn án.*
A gashed foot that will fester is not helped by "Easy does it!" (Mere expression of sympathy is of little use to a person in desperate straits.)

3528. *E̩ṣin kì í wó kó mú è̩kàn-an rè̩ rò̩run.*
A horse does not fall and take its tethering post to heaven with it.[12] (One suffers one's fate alone; one cannot share it with others.)

---

10. This proverb is among the many that are used primarily in incantations; this one would make it impossible for a person to avoid disaster.

11. *Aaka* is *Lecaniodiscus cupaniodes* (Sapindaceae); see Abraham 40.

12. In this construction, falling is a euphemism for dying.

F

3529. *"Fínná fún mi!" "Ng ò fínná fún o!" ní ńdájà sílè láro.*
"Blow the furnace for me!" "I will not blow the furnace for you!" results in a fight at the forge. (If responsibilities are not clearly specified among friends, quarrels result.)

Gb

3530. *"Gba àkàsù bàmbà" lósù agà ni "Gba isu gbooro" léèjòdún.*
"Have a huge loaf [of corn meal] in May" translates to "Have a long yam" after the harvest. (A favor one does a person who is in difficulty is not forgotten. The four following entries are variants.)

3531. *"Gba àkàsù bàmbà" lósù agà ni "Gbé ńnú agánrán" léèjòdún.*
"Have a huge loaf [of corn meal]" during May translates to "Take some of my *agánrán* yams" after the harvest. (A person whom one helps out of difficulty will remember to reward one when he or she comes into some fortune. The preceding entry and the following three entries are variants.)[13]

3532. *"Gba àkàsù" ní àbojà ni "Gba isu bòòkù" ní àmódún.*
"Take a loaf [of corn meal]" on returning from the market translates to "Take a huge yam" a year hence. (A good turn will attract a good turn in return. The preceding two and following two entries are variants.)

3533. *"Gba isu fún Omolàńké" nílé ni "Gba iyò fún Òsoko" lóko.*

---

13. *Osù agà*, the month of May, is hard on farmers because it comes after the last year's harvest has been exhausted and before the new harvest.

"Take this yam for Omolàńké" at home translates to "Take this salt for Òsoko" on the farm. (A favor one does when one has the advantage will be rewarded when one is in need. The preceding three entries and the following entry are variants.)

3534. *Gbà mí lójò kí ngbà o léèrùn.*
Aid me in times of rain so I can aid you in times of drought. (A person who extends aid to those in difficulty will receive aid from them when he or she is in difficulty. The preceding four entries are variants.)

I

3535. *Ibi tí a ti jeun ogóji, ka sòrò okòó.*
Where one eats food worth 40 cowries, one should make a speech worth 20 cowries. (One should make some effort to earn one's keep.)

3536. *Ibi tí àgbà-á bá pin sí lomodé ti ńbá a.*
Wherever age comes to rest, there youth will catch up with it. (Sooner or later the youth of today will put on the mantle of the elders and become just like them.)

3537. *Igí gbe níjù ó dègbé.*
The tree dries up in the forest and it becomes worthless. (When one has lost the qualities that make one desirable, one is done for.)

3538. *Ìkà kì í fi oníkà sílè.*
Wickedness never leaves the wicked. (The wicked person can never change his or her nature.)

3539. *Ilé ni aláso-ó jókòó sí tí òkùkù-ú wolé tò ó.*
The weaver was at home when the woof entered to seek him or her out. (The good

destined to come one's way will find one even if one does not venture out of the house.)

3540. *Ilé tó bá máa wó kì í gbọ́ ti igi ayègèrè; ohun tó bá máa ṣeni kì í ní àkókò kan.*
A house that is destined to collapse will not be saved by slipping posts; disaster that is destined to befall one is not daunted by what season it is. (No one can deflect fate.)

3541. *Iná ilé lẹranko ńyá gbèhìn, àfi èyí tó bá ringbó kú.*
It is the household fire that warms [or roasts] an animal in the end, except for those that die wandering in the bush. (The person who besmirches the good name of his or her community when he or she is abroad must return home eventually to give an account.)

3542. *Iná ni yó jàá bàtà tádìẹ̀ wò.*
It is fire that will remove the shoes a chicken wears.[14] (A foolish person will sooner or later reap the reward of his or her folly.)

3543. *Inú ẹ-ẹ́ dára ò ńyọ̀; orí ẹ-ẹ́ dára ná?*
Because you harbor good will toward others, you are happy; has good fortune come your way? (One is not necessarily fortunate simply because one harbors good will toward others. Compare the next entry.)

3544. *Inú rere ò jọ orí rere.*
Good nature (or good will toward others) is not the same as good fortune. (The good person is not necessarily safe from misfortune. Compare the preceding entry.)

3545. *Ìpín ọ̀go kì í tẹ́; baarú lórí rere nínú ẹsin.*
A person destined for glory will not suffer

---

14. The reference is to the practice of searing the skin on a chicken's legs before peeling it off.

disgrace; an exceptionally powerful horse is fortunate among horses. (A person destined to shine will not fail to do so.)

3546. *Ìpín òjẹun kì í jé kíná kú.*
The destiny of the person who will eat will keep the fire from going out. (Providence will take care of one's needs.)

3547. *Ire ẹni kì í kọjá ẹni.*
The good fortune destined for one will not pass one by. (One's destined good fortune will not be deflected.)

3548. *Ìrìn Àṣàké ò papò mọ́ ti Ọwọ́olú; Àṣàké ńlọ ilé ọkọ, Ọwọ́olú ńre òrun.*
Àṣàké's path is not the same as Ọwọ́olú's path; Àṣàké is bound for her spouse's home, whereas Ọwọ́olú is bound for heaven. (Different people have different destinies.)

3549. *Irù tó bà lé ẹni nípàkọ́ ò ní òun ò ní gbéni mì; Ọlọ́run ọba ni ò jé kí ipá è ká a.*
The gadfly that alighted on one's occiput is not reticent about swallowing one; only God Almighty denied it the power to do so. (One's enemies are unrelenting in their effort to do harm; only God has thwarted them.)

3550. *Iṣe tí èfúùfù-lèlè ńṣe òrun, bí kò wó, bí kò ya, Ọlọ́run ọba ni kò jé.*
The way the wind belabors the sky, that the sky does not collapse or tear into pieces is thanks to God Almighty. (Only the gods have kept one from falling into the hands of one's enemies.)

3551. *Iṣẹ́ ò mojú; ìyà ò màwọ̀; ebí pa àlejò, ojú tó ilé, ojú á tóko.*
Poverty cares not who owns which eyes; suffering does not pay attention to skin complexion; when hunger grips the stranger, the eyes that have seen the house will see the farm. (Hard times do not spare anyone; every person must gird himself or herself.)

3552. *Ìwò tí à ńwo àparò bíi ká fi dálá, orí ẹyẹ ni ò pẹyẹ.*
The way one eyes a partridge betrays one's wish to cook it in okro stew; it is the bird's head [or providence] that kept death from the bird. (One's enemies would like to see one dead, but one's destiny will not let them have their way.)

K

3553. *Ká fi ẹfun tọ́ ile aje, ká fosùn tọ́lé ìlẹ̀kẹ̀; àkọ́dá orí kì í gbé ìsàlẹ̀ ọjà.*
Let us whitewash the house of riches and paint that of beads with camwood; the head created at the beginning of time does not languish at the marketplace. (Whoever is destined to prosper will not fail to do so.)

3554. *Kángun-kàngùn-kángun á kángun síbìkan.*
Reckless, uncontrolled to-and-froing will inevitably wind up someplace.[15] (Recklessness leads to disaster).

3555. *Kì í ṣe ẹjọ́ eléhín gan-gan-ran; òrìṣà ló dá a tí kò fi awọ bò ó.*
The blame does not belong to the person with protruding teeth; it was the god who created him or her that failed to cover them with enough skin. (One should not be faulted for things over which one has no control.)

3556. *Kò sí alábàárò tó ju orí ẹni.*
There is no commiserator that surpasses one's head. (The best support one has is one's own head, one's protective spirit.)

3557. *Kò sí ìgbà tí ọmọ awo ò níí ṣawo.*
There is no escaping the time when a person born into a cult must become initiated into its mysteries. (One cannot avoid one's ordained calling.)

3558. *Koṣé-koṣé kan kì í kọ iṣẹ́ Ọlọ́run.*
No recalcitrant person ever refuses God's errand. (No one can refuse to do God's bidding.)

L

3559. *Lílọ ní ńkéhìn-in bọ́í.*
Departure is the inevitable fate of the houseboy. (However much a servant may be made to feel like family, he should know that his eventual separation is inevitable.)

M

3560. *Màkàn-màkàn loyè ńkàn.*
Chieftaincy titles go around in turns. (One's good fortune will come one's way in due time.)

3561. *Mú orí lọ, má mùú ẹwà lọ; òòjọ́ lẹwà ńdẹ̀hìn, orí ní ńbáni gbélé ọkọ.*
Go with your head, not with your beauty; beauty abandons one in a day, but one's head remains with one in the marital home.[16] (A woman should care more about good character than about beauty.)

---

15. The word *kángun* means "to end up somewhere," whereas the ideophone *kángun-kàngùn-kángun* is used to describe the staggering sort of movement one would associate with drunkenness. The two expressions are not etymologically linked, but their phonological commonalities permit a play on the expressions for semantic effect.

16. Again, *orí*, the agency that controls a person's fortune, is identified with the head; hence its designation by the same word.

3562. *Ní inú ilẹ̀kú lOrò ńjẹ.*
Where the dead are buried, there Orò feeds. (Some people's misfortune is other people's good fortune.)

3563. *Níní owó kàdárà ni; àìní owó kàdárà ni.*
Being blessed with money is a matter of destiny; not having money is also a matter of destiny. (One's earthly fortune is a matter of destiny beyond one's control.)

3564. *Ó wu àgùàlà kó mọ́lẹ̀ bí òṣùpá, Ọlọ́run ọba ni ò jẹ́.*
The planet Venus would like to be as bright as the moon, but God the King would not permit it to be. (Everyone wishes to be as great as the greatest person, but each individual's destiny is decisive. The following three entries are variants.)

3565. *Ó wu aṣiwèrè kó ru igbá-a rẹ̀ dọ́jà, ará ilé ẹ̀ ni ò jẹ́.*
The mad person would wish to carry her calabash as far as the market, except that the members of her household would not let her. (Communal constraints are to be thanked for curbing people's propensity to indulge in licentious behavior. The preceding entry and the following two are variants.)

3566. *Ó wu ewúrẹ́ kó bímọ ẹ̀ ní òbúkọ, Ọlọ́run ọba ni ò fun; ó wu àgùntàn bọ̀lọ̀jọ̀ kó bímọ ẹ̀ lágbò, Ọlọ́run ọba ni ò fún un; ó wu adìẹ òkòkó kó bímọ ẹ̀ lákùkọ, Ọlọ́run ọba ni ò fún un.*
The goat would wish that its kid was a he-goat, only God the King did not consent; the robust sheep would wish its lamb was a ram, only God the King would not agree; the big hen would wish its chick was a cock, only God the King would not grant her wish. (Everybody wishes for great things, but God does not grant all wishes. The preceding two and the following are variants.)

3567. *Ó wu ẹtu kó gbé ogún ọdún nígbó, ṣùgbọ́n ó wu onípàkúté kó dọ́jà lóla.*
The antelope would like to live for twenty years in the bush, but the setter of snares would like it to reach the market on the morrow. (Different people's interests often conflict. The preceding three entries are variants.)

3568. *Òfò ò jẹ́ kí ọlọ́rọ̀ ó pọ̀.*
Gainless ventures limit the ranks of the rich. (Everybody craves success, but not all are favored by fortune.)

3569. *Òkèté ní tòun ló bá òun tí oun-ún fẹ̀hìn tiná.*
The giant bush rat says a misfortune befell it and caused it to sit warming itself by the fire. (It was a grave disaster that caused one to be found in disgraceful or embarrassing circumstances.)

3570. *Olóríburúkú kì í re oko ikàn; bó bá re oko ikàn, ilá ní ńká wálé.*
An ill-fated person does not go to a locust-bean farm; if he should go to a locust-bean farm, he will return home with okra. (A person destined to fail will always find a way to fail.)

3571. *Omi lèèyàn; bó bá ṣàn wá a tún ṣàn padà.*
Humans are streams; they flow forth and flow back. (People are not fixed in one location; no one knows where he or she will find himself or herself in the future.)

3572. *Omi tí a máa mu kì í ṣàn kojá ẹni.*
The water one is destined to drink will

not flow past. (One's destiny will not pass one by.)

3573. *Òmùgòó lè sìse kó dogbón; orí yàtò sórí.*
The fool may commit a blunder that comes to seem as wisdom; heads differ from one another. (Although some pay dearly for their mistakes, others benefit from mistakes that fortuitously prove fortunate; it is all a matter of chance.)

3574. *Òní la rí, kò séni tó mòla.*
Today is all we see; nobody knows tomorrow. (No one knows what the future will bring.)

3575. *Orí burúkú lòbó ní; òbọ ò lénu bí ẹsin.*
What the monkey has is ill luck; the monkey does not have a mouth like a horse's. (It is ill luck that brings unusual or unnatural misfortunes.)[17]

3576. *Orí burúkú tí ṁmú ọmọdé pín itan eran.*
[It is] a great misfortune that entitles a young person to the thigh of an animal. (Used when adverse circumstances force people to do ordinarily unacceptable things.)[18]

3577. *Orí inú kì í jé kí tòde sunwòn.*
The unseen head prevents the visible head from prospering. (A person's chosen [evil] destiny will always keep him from prospering.)

3578. *Orí la fi mméran láwo.*
It is one's luck that determines the piece

of meat one takes from a plate.[19] (How one fares in life depends on luck.)

3579. *Orí ló mọ ibi ẹsè ńrè.*
The head alone knows where the feet will go. (One never knows where one's destiny will lead.)

3580. *Orí lonísẹ; èdá lèrè.*
The head acts; one's nature determines one's reward. (People act as their heads direct them; their reward is according to their nature.)

3581. *Orí tí kò níí rún àgbàdo sùn ní ńgbéni ko elérù iṣu kan.*
A head [destiny] that will not chew corn for supper brings a certain bearer of yams one's way. (When matters seem hopeless, a way out will surely materialize for the fortunate person.)

3582. *Orí tí yó gbeni kì í pani lérù.*
A head that will make one prosper will not prove too heavy for one to carry. (Whatever is destined to make one prosper will not cause inconvenience.)

3583. *Orí tó máa dádé, nínú agoroodẹ ní ńti-í yọ ó wá; ọrùn tí yó lo èjìgbà ìlẹ̀kẹ̀, nínú agoroodẹ ní ńti-í yọ ó wá; bèbè-ìdí tí yó lo mósàajì, aṣọ ọba tó kóná yanran-yanran, nínú agoroodẹ ní ńti-í yọ ó wá.*
The head that will wear a crown is so destined from before the birth of the gods; the neck that will be adorned with beads is so destined from before the birth of the gods; the waist that will wear *mósàajì*, the cloth of kings that is soft and shiny, is so destined from before the birth of the gods. (One only lives a course that was predetermined before one's birth.)

---

17. The monkey is restrained, or saddled, as a pet, even though no one wants to ride it.

18. When an animal is killed for food, the thigh usually goes to the oldest person in the household. The youth gets the share in this case because all the elderly people have died off.

---

19. When people eat from a communal dish, no one can be sure what piece of meat will fall to his or her lot.

3584. *Orí tó máa je ògèdè sùn kì í gbó; bí wón bá ńgbéyán bò wá fun, yó fóó ni dandan.*
A head destined to eat plantains for supper will not escape that destiny; if pounded yam is being brought, it [the dish] will unfailingly break. (There is no antidote or cure for ill luck.)

3585. *Òrìsà tí Sàngó ò bá lè mú, eré ló lè sá.*
Whatever god Sango cannot catch must indeed be fleet of foot. (Only extraordinarily good fortune can save people from fate.)

3586. *Òrìsà tó dá enu níbùú mo ohun tí òun ó fi sí i.*
The god who made the mouth horizontal knows what [food] he will put in it. (The gods have a plan and a reason for whatever they have created.)

3587. *Òwú tí ìyá gbòn lomo ńran.*
It is the cotton that the mother fluffs that the daughter spins. (Children take after their parents.)

Ọ

3588. *Okàn eni làlùfáà eni.*
One's heart is one's priest. (The quality of one's heart determines how good one's fortune will be.)

3589. *Olórun ló gbe Ìgbìrà gesin.*
It was God that placed an Ìgbìra man on a horse. (One should not be angry at the upstart who makes it big and becomes garrulous; the blame is God's.)[20]

3590. *Omo aráyé ò fé ká rerù ká sò; orí eni ní ńsoni.*
The people of this world never want to see

one carry a load and later set it down; only one's guardian spirit helps one set the load down.[21] (People do not offer to help others out of difficulties; only providence does.)

3591. *Òpá ò lè pa agogo; abínú eni ò lè pa kádàrá dà.*
A stick cannot kill a bell; ill wishers cannot alter a person's destiny. (No amount of ill will by others will change God's plan for a person.)

3592. *Òpò èèyàn ló wù kó kowó bàpò, kádàrá ni ò jé.*
Many people would wish to dip their hands into their pockets, but destiny prevents their doing so. (Everybody wishes to be rich, but destiny says otherwise.)[22]

3593. *Òtá ńlùlù ìbàjé, Olórun ò jé kó dún.*
One's enemy is beating the drum of defamation, but God won't let it make a sound. (God has frustrated the schemes of one's enemies.)

R

3594. *Rìkísí ò gbó oògùn; Olórun ní ḿbáni sèté-e rìkísí.*
Intrigue cannot be combatted with medicine; only God can help one conquer intrigue. (Only God can help one overcome one'e enemies.)

S

3595. *Sa orí má sa oògùn; oògùn ní ojó ìpónjú, orí lójó gbogbo.*

---

20. The Yoruba consider Ìgbìrà people to be bumpkins.

21. *Orí* here refers to the mystical force that determines each person's destiny. Chance would equate to fortune or luck.

22. The gesture of dipping the hand into the pocket is for the purpose of pulling out money.

Trust in your head and not in medicine; medicine is for the day of hardship, but your head is for every day. (It is better to trust in one's genius than in medicinal charms.)

Ṣ

3596. *Ṣátánì ló mú àtọ̀sí ààfáà wá; ẹlẹ́hàá kì í jáde, ààfáà kì í yànlè.*
Satan is to blame for the imam's gonorrhea; the wife confined in the harem does not venture outdoors, and the imam does not keep an illicit lover. (One has to be most inventive to explain away a problem for which there can be no one else to blame.)

T

3597. *Ta ní ńfẹ́ ká jí? Aráyé ò fẹ́ni fọ́rọ̀, àforí ẹni.*
Who ever wants one to wake up? People never wish wealth for one, only one's head does. (People seldom wish that others prosper.)

3598. *Tẹní máa sunwọ̀n kì í gbó.*
No one can block the path of good fortune for someone destined to prosper. (No one can stop another's destiny.)

W

3599. *Wíwò téwúrẹ́ ńwo alápatà bíi kó kú; orí ẹni ni ò pani.*
The look the goat gives the butcher wishes death for the latter; only one's head does not deliver one to death. (Those adversely affected by year lawful duties may hate you, but your head will protect you from their machinations. Compare the following entry.)

3600. *Wíwò tí à ńwàparò, bíi ká fi dálá, orí ẹyẹ ni ò pẹyẹ.*
The way one eyes a partridge betrays a desire to cook it in okro stew; only the bird's head says no to death. (One's enemies look at one with death in their eyes, but one's destiny says no to their desires. Compare the preceding entry.)

3601. *Wọ́n ní ọ̀nà-á wà níbìkan, o ò bèèrè lọ́wọ́ orí.*
They say a path is open somewhere, and you did not ask your head [guiding spirit]. (Always seek the guidance of your guiding power.)

On human vulnerability and limitations

A

3602. *A fẹ́ ẹ nílé, a fẹ́ ẹ lóko; bọ́mọ́ bá ti lóyún, kò parí ná?*
She is courted at home; she is courted on the farm; once the girl becomes pregnant, will there not be an end to courting? (However attractive and desirable a woman may be, once she becomes pregnant, she no longer attracts suitors.)

3603. *A ká àgbìgbò mọ́ orí igi; ó ku bí eyẹ́ ti máa fò.*
The bird *àgbìgbò* is treed; we shall see how it will manage to escape.[1] (The game is up.)

3604. *A kì í gbé àárín ojì èèyàn ká má sì wí.*
One cannot live amid forty people and never misspeak. (It is impossible to live in a group and never cause offense.)

3605. *A kì í mọ ilẹ̀ ojà-á gbá.*
One never knows how to sweep a market. (If there is a multitude to please, one will always leave some people disgruntled.)

3606. *A kì í mọ̀ọ́ gún mọ̀ọ́ tẹ̀ kíyán ewùrà má lẹ̀ẹ́mọ.*
One is never so good at pounding and smoothing that the pounded yams one makes with *ewùrà* yams [also water yams] will not be lumpy. (Certain tasks defeat even the experts.)

3607. *A kì í mọ̀ọ́ wẹ̀ ká káyéjá; bòròkìnní kan ò wà á já; báa ṣoore títí á kù síbìkan.*
One is never so expert a swimmer that one swims the whole world; no great man ever swam it; no matter how much good one does there will be some omission. (No one can be all-wise in worldly matters.)

3608. *A kì í nàró ká ọdún.*
One cannot stand upright year-round. (Everybody falls sometime.)

3609. *A kì í ríwà oníwà ká fọwọ́ jurí.*
One does not see other people's behavior and make the hand gesture indicating the warding-off of abomination from one's head. (Do not rush to judge other people's behavior without knowing their reason.)[2]

3610. *A kì í ṣe ọmọ ju ọmọọ́lé; a kì í ṣe ọmọ òrìṣà ju ààfín.*
One cannot be a better child than the gecko; one cannot be a more favored child of the gods than the albino. (No matter how hard one tries, one cannot, as an outsider, displace the favorite.)[3]

---

1. This bird's large head presumably might interfere with its flight. If the bird is well and truly treed, then, of course, it cannot escape.

2. The gesture as described is intended to ward off any impending evil.

3. *Ọmọọ́lé* (gecko) means, literally, "child of the house," and the gecko is always to be found on the walls of houses; the albino is among those afflicted people who are considered special wards of the gods.

3611. *A kì í wáyé ká màà lárùn kan lára; ìjà-ìgboro làrùn Ìbàdàn.*
One does not come into this world and not have a disease; street fighting is the disease of Ibadan people. (Ibadan people cannot help street fighting; other people have other peculiar second natures.)

3612. *A lè gbé omi léná de elégbò, ṣùgbón a ò lè wẹ ẹṣẹ̀ dè é.*
One may heat water in preparation for the person with an ulcer, but one cannot clean the ulcer until he or she arrives. (There is a limit to the help one can render another person, especially a person who will not make an effort on his or her own behalf.)

3613. *A ní kí ohun tó wuni wá, ohun tó dára-á bọ́ sílẹ̀; bó dára tí kò wuni ǹkọ́?*
We call for something to which we are attracted, and something beautiful presents itself; what if we are not attracted to it despite its beauty? (Beauty is in the eyes of the beholder.)

3614. *A ní kó múwá, ó ní kò sí; ahun ni lójú alágbe.*
He is asked for alms and says he has nothing to give; to the beggar he appears as a miser. (People are often unmindful of the fact that other people have their own problems.)

3615. *À ńkọ́lé ikin, à ńyọ̀dèdè imọ̀, hòrò ni ilé àgbékẹ́hìn.*
Though we build houses of thatch, though we make corridors of palm leaves, it is to a grave that we will retire in the end. (Whatever a person's riches, in the end he or she winds up in a grave.)

3616. *A pe ẹléfọ́ọ̀-ọ tẹtẹ̀, o ni, "Tàatàn kọ́."*
We hail a spinach seller, and she protests that her spinach is not from the dung heap. (The evildoer's conscience will betray him or her.)

3617. *A rìn fàà lójú akẹ́gàn; a yan kàṣà lójú abúni; abúni ò ní okòó nílé.*
One strolls nonchalantly before a detractor; one struts proudly before a slanderer; the slanderer has not 20 cowries at home. (One need not pay a worthless detractor any mind.)

3618. *A ṣe ohun gbogbo tán; ti ẹlẹ́nu ló kù.*
We have done all we can do; what detractors will say is another matter. (Even after doing one's best, one cannot control what critics will say.)

3619. *Ààlà-á tó, ìmàle ò dúró de ara-a wọn.*
The time for ablutions arrives; Muslims do not wait for one another. (Each person bears his or her own responsibility.)

3620. *Àánú ojú ò jé ká fọwọ́ bojú; ìbẹ̀rù ejò ò jé ká tẹ ọmọ ejò mọ́lẹ̀.*
Compassion keeps one from covering one's eyes; fear of the snake keeps one from stepping on its young. (One's good behavior may be due to goodness or to fear of what repercussions misbehavior might entail.)[4]

3621. *Àáyá ṣéjú, ọmọ-ọ rẹ̀-ẹ́ ki ọwọ́ bọ́ ọ.*
The colobus monkey blinks, and its child pokes its fingers into the monkey's eyes. (Children are a handful for their parents, who cannot always be quick enough to stop their mischief.)

3622. *Abanilóríjẹ́: ilé-e rẹ̀ ní ńtií mú abẹ wá.*
He who will deface one's head brings his razor from his own house.[5] (Detractors do

---

4. *Àánú ojú,* translated as "compassion," literally means either "kindness that resides in the eyes," or "kindness toward the eyes" (hence compassion for the eyes). The play on the expression therefore permits the understanding of the first part of the proverb as stating that one's compassion for the eyes keeps one from covering them.

5. *Abanilóríjẹ́* literally means "spoiler of another's

not depend on the cooperation of those they malign.)

3623. *Abarapá ti gbogbo èèyàn; òkùnrùn tẹnìkan ṣoṣo.*
Sprightliness is everybody's; indisposition is one person's alone. (People will fraternize with a lively person; nobody fraternizes with a sickly person.)

3624. *Àbàtá ta kété bí ẹnipé kò bá odò tan.*
The marsh stands apart as though it is not related to the river. (It is futile to deny responsibility for, or knowledge of, an event when the evidence of the truth is obvious and incontrovertible. Some people sometimes find it expedient to deny any relationship with relatives.)

3625. *Abẹrẹ jádìí, àkísà ńyọ̀ sẹ̀sẹ̀; ó rò pé òyìnbó ò gún mọ́.*
The needle's eye breaks, and the cloth rejoices; it thinks the white man has ceased making needles. (Do not rejoice at your formidable adversary's temporary discomfiture.)

3626. *Àbíkẹ́hìn-in gbẹ̀gẹ̀ tí ńyọ olóko lẹ́nu.*
The last born of the brown monkey: the nemesis of the farmer. (Said of a problem that defies easy solution.)[6]

3627. *Àbíkú ṣọ olóògùn dèké.*
A child that is born to die makes a quack out of the medicine man. (No amount of effort to the contrary will prevent what is ordained. Compare 2747.)

---

head" but in this instance suggests spoiling the cut of one's hair.

6. The youngest of a brood of monkeys is characteristically a brat. The construction is technically a descriptive phrase that has no main verb, literally, "The last born of the monkey, that infuriates the farmer." The word *tí* (that) is understood in this case to be equivalent to *ni* (it is that).

3628. *Abínúẹni kò sẹ́ òràn deni.*
He who wants no good for one does not plead one's innocence in one's absence. (Expect no kindness from an enemy.)

3629. *Àbọ̀ là ńya ilé òrẹ́ tí kò wuni.*
It is on one's way back home from a trip that one stops at the home of a friend one does not like. (One will always find ways to temporize on an unpalatable obligation.)

3630. *A-bo-eégún ò réégún; abọ̀rìsà ò rórìsà; ìmàlé foríbalẹ̀ kò rÓlórun.*
The worshiper of *eégún* does not see *eégún*; the worshiper of a god does not see the god; the Muslim bows to the ground [at prayer] but does not see the High God. (One often does not see the person one serves.)

3631. *A-bojú-gòdògbà kì í ríran lọ́nà méjì.*
A person with huge eyes does not see in two directions at once. (The size of the eyes offers no special advantage.)

3632. *Abuké ló ru ẹrù òrìsà má sò.*
A humpback carries a god-imposed burden that cannot be laid down. (Congenital conditions cannot be easily vacated.)

3633. *Abuké sùnkákà bí ẹní ta sínà.*
The humpback sleeps all spread out like one bloated in a fire. (Deformity prevents graceful sleeping postures.)

3634. *A-búni-lọ́lẹ ò mọ ohun tí ńṣeni.*
The person who calls one a lazy person does not know what one's problem is. (No one knows others' private woes.)

3635. *Àdábá nìjà; ẹni tí ìjà ò bá ní ńpera-a rẹ̀ lọ́kùnrin.*
Fights are uninvited plagues; it is he who is not visited by a fight that boasts about his

manhood. (Manliness is sometimes a matter of good fortune.)[7]

3636. *Àdàbà ò náání à ńkùngbẹ́; iná jó, ẹyẹ fò lọ.*
The dove is not bothered that one sets fire to the brush; the fire rages, and the bird flies away. (One cannot be hurt by eventualities to which one is immune.)

3637. *Adánilóró ò ṣéé fẹ̀hìntì.*
A person who habitually causes others pain is no one to trust. (Know your enemy.)

3638. *Adáramáṣu ò sí.*
There is no one so beautiful or handsome that she or he never has to empty her or his bowels. (Even the most illustrious person is still human.)

3639. *Adìẹ bà lókùn; ara ò rọ okùn, ara ò rọ adìẹ.*
The chicken alighted on a rope; the rope cannot relax, and the chicken cannot relax. (One person's problems are problems also for those close to him or her.)

3640. *Adìẹ ìbá lókó, ìbá fi àátàn ṣe n-ǹkan.*
Had the chicken a hoe, it would have worked wonders with the dung heap.[8] (One's accomplishments are often limited by one's means rather than by one's aspirations.)

3641. *Adìẹ ńlàágùn; ìhùùhù ni ò jẹ́ ká mọ̀.*
The chicken sweats, but its down prevents us from knowing. (Everybody has his or her problems, although strangers may not guess. Compare 4041.)

7. The combination *àdábá* (uninvited problem) and *ìjà* (fight) suggests *ìjàmbá* (disaster).

8. Judging by what the chicken does to the dung heap with its talons alone, perhaps it is a good thing that it does not have a hoe.

3642. *Adìẹ òpìpì kì í rápá gun orílé.*
The flightless chicken never has the wings to fly to the top of the roof. (One's enemies will not have the means to injure one; or, a person will never have the means to thrive.)

3643. *Adití woni lẹ́nu sùn-ùn.*
The deaf person stares fixedly at people's mouths. (One acts according to one's capabilities.)

3644. *Afẹ́fẹ́ ńgbá eruku lálá; èfúùfù ńmi ewé àgbọ́n jìà-jìà.*
The wind whips the dust into a storm; the strong breeze whips the coconut leaves to a frenzy. (Everyone is beset with problems.)

3645. *Àgádá mádìẹ dòlẹ.*
The grass shelter makes the chicken lazy. (Too much ease discourages resourcefulness.)

3646. *Agílítí, a-bara-yíyi.*
Lizard, thick-skinned creature. (To each his or her flaws.)

3647. *Àgùntàn ò ìtîí kú à ńwì í níná; bóbá wá kú ńkọ́?*
The sheep is not yet dead, and it is already being massaged with fire to burn the hair off its skin; what will happen then after its death? (If people do evil to a person when the person is present, what can one expect them to do when the person is not?)

3648. *Àgùntàn ò pa aṣọ èṣí dà.*
The sheep does not change its clothing from year to year. (Old habits die hard.)

3649. *Àgùntàn pòpó ṣe ońdè lọ́rùn: oníkáluku a-bi-tiè-lára.*
Sacrificial sheep with leather charms around its neck: each person has his or her own problems. (To each his or her problems.)

3650. *Àgbà Ìjèṣà ò lè ṣàìjobì.*
An Ìjèṣà elder cannot refrain from chewing kola nuts. (Do not begrudge people what they crave.)

3651. *Agbádá ya lọ́rùn, ó bàjẹ́.*
The grand traditional garment rips around the neck and becomes ruined. (An object that loses its utility loses it value.)

3652. *A-gbáhéré-yáná ni a-gbénú-oko-yá-òòrùn.*
Person-who-sits-by-the-fire-inside-the-hut is one-who-suns-himself-on-the-farm. (One's habits follow one, whether at home or on the farm.)

3653. *Àgbè roko roko, wọn kà ṣàì gbàgbé ewé kan sébè.*
However thoroughly a farmer might weed his farm, he will not fail to overlook some leaf on a mound. (No one can achieve perfection.)

3654. *Agbọ́nmi ní ńwólé eja; apàjùbà ní ńwólé àparò; òlùgbóńgbó tìnlà ni wọ́n fi ńṣégun ògúlùtu.*
Who drains the stream destroys the home of the fish; who clears the forest for farming destroys the home of the partridge; a huge cudgel is the weapon for conquering what is left of a wall. (Each situation has its proper medicine, and each person his or her nemesis.)

3655. *Ahún bu òkèlè, ọmọ-ọ rẹ̀-ẹ́ lanu, ó ní ó gbọ́ bẹ̀ẹ̀ òun rí?*
Tortoise takes a morsel of food and its child opens its mouth; Tortoise asks wherever did the child hear such a report about it? (Never expect a person to act contrary to his or her nature.)[9]

3656. *Ahun tó yọkùn, omi ló mu yó.*
A miser who has a potbelly got it by drinking water. (A shiftless person's prosperity comes by unwholesome means.)[10]

3657. *Àìmọ̀ kì í pa ọmọ.*
Ignorance does not kill a child. (There are worse things in a child than ignorance.)

3658. *Àìmọ̀-ójó ni kì í jẹ́ kí àlejò ó jó.*
It is ignorance about dancing that keeps a stranger from dancing. (Ignorance about the customs of a place keeps the outsider from full integration.)

3659. *Àìtètèjí inú òtá ńdùn, a jí tán inú ḿbí wọn.*
One's lateness in getting up in the morning makes one's enemies happy; once one is up and about, they become angry. (One's enemies always rejoice at the prospect of one's demise.)

3660. *Ajá ẹgbẹ̀rún ò gbọ́ orúkọ.*
A dog bought for 1,000 cowries does not recognize or heed its name. (One cannot teach a cheap dog anything. One gets what one pays for.)

3661. *Ajá ní ńlá omi lébàà-lébàà; ẹsinsin ò kún àtẹ ilẹ̀kẹ̀; ọmọrí igbá ò fidí kalẹ̀ kó gún régí-régí.*
It is a dog that licks water with its tongue; flies will not fill a tray for beads; the lid of a calabash cannot sit straight upright. (Certain things are characteristic of certain people; each has his or her limitations.)

3662. *Ajá òyìnbó dára, ó ku àtiṣọdẹ.*
The white man's dog is beautiful, but it lacks

---

9. Another reference to *ahun*, tortoise, as embodying miserliness, so that its name has come to mean "miser."

10. The Yoruba regard a potbelly as evidence of rich feeding and therefore of prosperity. The miser, of course, is too stingy with his money to spend it on food.

the ability to hunt. (A beautiful thing that has no use is nothing to be desired.)

3663. *Ajá tó pa ikún lónìí m̀bọ̀ wá pa òyà lóla; ká má fibínú pajá.*
A dog that kills a squirrel today will kill a cane rat tomorrow; one should, therefore, not kill the dog in anger. (One should not write anybody off because the person has suffered one setback.)

3664. *Àjàpá ní bí òún bá jẹ, tí òún mu, tí òún yó, ara òun a yá; ṣùgbọ́n ìgbà tí òún bá rántí irán ìdí òun, òun a bú sékún pèrè.*
Tortoise says when it has eaten and drunk to its fill, it becomes cheerful, but when it remembers its coccyx, it breaks into tears. (Even in the best of circumstances one is left with some blemish.)

3665. *Àjẹ́ ò lè jẹ òkú.*
A witch cannot eat the dead. (A person dies only once and, once dead, is safe from witches and enemies.)

3666. *Ajẹ́dẹ́jẹ kì í jẹ òkan mọ.*
A-person-who-sneakily-eats-shrimps does not stop after eating only one. (Small transgressions tend to become a habit.)

3667. *Akátá m̀dífá, ẹta m̀dìbò, ìkamùdùn m̀yìnbọn ìdí; wọ́n ní kí ní m̀rùn?*
The *akátá* bird is consulting the oracle, the civet cat is casting lots, and the stink ant is expelling gas; yet people ask what is smelling. (Certain phenomena have their unmistakable signs.)[11]

3668. *Akáyín ò mọ efùrù-ú pè.*
A person with a missing tooth does not

know how to pronounce *efùrù.*[12] (One is limited by one's nature.)

3669. *Akọ́kọ́dájọ́ lòtá ẹléjọ́.*
The first judge is the enemy of the litigant. (Few people take criticism kindly.)

3670. *Akọkọlúkọ ẹbọ ní m̀pa igún lérù.*
It is a veritable masculine [high-quality] offering that weighs down the vulture. (Certain obligations make one regret taking them on.)[13]

3671. *A-kọ́ni-ká-bàjẹ́ ò ṣe tiẹ̀ bẹ́ẹ̀.*
He-who-coaches-one-into-ruin does not manage his own affairs the same way. (People who will preside over the destruction of others know how to protect themselves.)

3672. *Àkùkọ́ kì í pamọ.*
A rooster does not hatch eggs. (There is a limit to what one can expect of people; certain things are contrary to nature.)

3673. *Alágbèdé ò fẹ́ kí ogun tán láyé.*
The blacksmith [who makes weapons] does not wish for an end of wars on earth. (Self-interest is paramount.)

3674. *Alákàrà kì í fẹ́ kí ẹnìkejì gbé agbada.*
The seller of bean fritters does not wish that another person acquire a deep-frying pot. (No trader wants competition.)

3675. *Alákàsù ò fẹ́ kí ẹni tó rà á yó.*
The seller of corn-meal loaves does not

---

11. Given the circumstances, the stink is inevitable; the cause is obvious. The three creatures named are reputed for their smell.

12. *Efùrù* is a type of yam. A gap in the teeth makes pronouncing the "f" sound difficult.

13. The proverb is often found in the form of an exclamation at an oppressive duty, but in that case the *ni* (*ní*) is replaced with *tí.* The proverb refers to Vulture's volunteering to take an offering to heaven to induce God to send rain and then being caught in the deluge on its way back (see note 72 to 1003).

wish buyers to be full. (Self-interest is paramount.)

3676. *Aláṣo dúdú lòtá ayé; èèyàn bí àparò layé ńfẹ́.*
The person in black is begrudged by humankind; humankind loves people like partridges. (People love those they can take advantage of.)[14]

3677. *Àpọ́n tọrọ ọbẹ̀; kò mọ oye à ńkọ́lá.*
The bachelor begs for stew; he does not know how much okro costs. (A person ignorant of a trade does not appreciate its difficulties.)

3678. *Àròyé niṣẹ́ ìbakà; kí niṣẹ́ eye lóko?*
Chattering is the burden of the Senegal canary; what is the trait of the birds on the farm? (Said of a talkative or idle person.)

3679. *Asòtítọ́ ò gbé ilẹ̀ Èyọ̀; purópurọ́ ò gbé ilẹ̀ Awúsá.*
Speakers-of-the-truth do not live in the land of Èyọ̀ (Àwórì); speakers-of-lies do not live in Hausaland. (Certain peoples are characterized by certain ethnic qualities.)

3680. *Àṣá ò kú, ara ńta ẹtù; àwòdì á wo ìgbín kòrò.*
The kite does not die, and the partridge is anxious; the eagle watches the snail from the corner of its eye. (If one's nemesis thrives, one is anxious, especially when one has no means of defense or retaliation.)

3681. *Aṣọ èṣín ò yẹni, bíi ti aṣọ ẹ̀wọ̀n kọ́.*
Last year's clothing is not proper for people, but that does not apply to prison uniforms. (Adverse circumstances may force people to live by conditions they would normally shun.)

3682. *Aṣọ tuntun ní ńṣe olúwa-a rẹ̀ tòde-tòde.*
A new dress impels its owner to roam outdoors. (One is ever eager to show off one's new acquisitions.)

3683. *Aṣọ-ọ́ lọ́wọ́ kò ní èékánná; èèyàn-án lọ́wọ́ kò ní ìbàlẹ̀.*
Cloths have arms but no nails; humans have arms but no reaching-the-ground. (Every creature has some failing.)[15]

3684. *A-ti-kékeré-ṣẹrú ò mọyì ọmọlúwàbí.*
One-who-has-been-a-slave-since-childhood does not appreciate being a freeborn. (A stranger to freedom does not appreciate it.)

3685. *À-tò-ìṣíwọ́ là ńmòkóbó.*
Urinating-without-ceasing is what betrays the eunuch. (One's secret flaws have ways of making themselves public.)

3686. *Awo Eégún lobìnrín lè ṣe, awo Gẹ̀lẹ̀dẹ́ lobìnrín lè wò; bóbìnrín bá fojú kan Orò, Orò á gbé e.*
Only the mystery of *Eégun* is accessible to women; it is only the mystery of *Gẹ̀lẹ̀dẹ́* that women may watch; if a woman catches a glimpse of Orò, Orò will make an end of her. (Only certain rites are allowed to certain people; the rest are proscribed.)

3687. *Àwọn lẹ wò, ẹ ò lè rí eégún.*
The netting is all you can see; you cannot see the masquerader himself. (Some mysteries are available only to the initiate.)[16]

---

14. Black clothing is invulnerable to stain, but the partridge has a reputation for being a ready victim.

15. The Yoruba say of a cloth wider than usual that it has arms, *ó lọ́wọ́*, and of a wider-than-usual wrapper that it has the quality of reaching to the floor, *ó ní ìbàlẹ̀* (or *ìbalẹ̀*).

16. The masquerader's visor is made of netting that

3688. A-wọ́n-bí-ọgbọ́n, aṣòroódà bí àgbà.
Scarce-as-wisdom, difficult-to-become-as-an-elder. (Wisdom is not common; achieving the traits of a sage is not easy.)

3689. Àyè ìlẹ̀kẹ̀ ò sí nídìí adìẹ.
There is no room for beads on the waist of a chicken. (Not every person can wear finery to good effect.)

3690. Ayé lè pa fìtílà ẹ̀yẹ.
The world is capable of snuffing one's lamp of glory. (People are capable of damaging one's good reputation.)

B

3691. Baálé di mẹ́ta, itan adìẹ dàròyé.
Husbands number three; a chicken's thigh becomes a bone of contention. (Too many claims on meager resources result in dissension.)

3692. Bí a bá máa gbàwìn là ńṣe ojú àánú; bí a bá yó tán à di ọmọ ọba.
When one wants to make a purchase on credit, one wears a friendly look; after one has satisfied oneself, one becomes a prince. (Pleasantness lasts no longer than one's need for favors.)

3693. Bí a kò bá forí sọ, a kì í mọ ìrẹ̀-ẹ́ bẹ̀.
If one has not butted one's head against a beam, one does not learn to stoop. (Nothing teaches caution like a mishap.)

3694. Bí a kò bá pa ìjì han ìjí, ẹrù kì í ba ìjí.
Unless one kills a brown monkey and shows it to a brown monkey, the brown monkey does not learn fear. (People seldom learn caution until danger has brushed by them.)

---

permits the wearer to see but remain unidentifiable by spectators.

3695. Bí a kò bá ṣubú, a kì í mọ ẹrù-ú dì.
If one has not fallen, one does not learn how best to pack one's load. (One learns only after one has erred.)

3696. Bí àwòdì ò kú, adìẹ ò lè sinmi.
If the kite does not die, the chickens cannot relax. (As long as danger persists, one must be vigilant.)

3697. Bí Básè ò sè, kí ni Bálá ó làá?
If Help-Cook does not cook, what will Help-Lick lick? (If nothing is available, one cannot expect anything.)

3698. Bí ebí bá ńpa ejò, ahun kì í yan; àtahun àtejò, ẹran jíjẹ.
If a snake is hungry, a tortoise should not go strutting by; both snake and tortoise are edible meat. (One should always be vigilant and stay away from dangerous situations.)

3699. Bí ẹsú bá jẹ oko tán ẹsú á lọ, a ku alátanpopo.
Having devoured the farm, the locusts will depart, leaving the cricket behind. (When one has surmounted one's greatest obstacle, the little ones will remain to claim one's attention.)

3700. Bí etí kò gbọ́ yìnkìn, inú kì í bàjẹ́.
If the ears do not hear bad news, the mind does not become unhappy. (Depression does not occur for no reason; it follows bad tidings.)

3701. Bí ìgbá ò so kúdu-kùdu, kí lọmọ ẹrankó ó jẹ?
If the bitter tomato does not fruit abundantly, what will young animals eat? (If the provider does not provide, the dependents suffer.)

3702. Bí ikú bá tìlẹ̀kùn, ebi ní ńṣí i.
If death locks a door, hunger will open it.

(The disconsolate mourner will sooner or later yield to hunger.)

3703. *Bí ilé kò bá kan ilé, wọn kì í jó àjóràn.*
If houses do not abut, they do not catch fire from one another. (Unless one is associated with a person in trouble, one does not share in it.)

3704. *Bí ilé ńjó, bí olè ńjà, ẹni ebi ńpa yó máa wí.*
If the house is on fire, if a burglar is at work, the hungry person will say his or her piece. (One's private woes take precedence over public disasters.)

3705. *Bí ìrònú bá pọ̀, bí ikú ò tẹ̀le, àrùn ńkọ́?*
If brooding is excessive, and if death does not result, what about disease? (Excessive brooding is not healthy.)

3706. *Bí iṣu bá tán lóko, obìnrin a di àwòdì; a ní rírà lòún tún ńrà jẹ kiri òo.*
When there are no more yams on the farm, one's woman becomes a hawk; she says she is now reduced to going around to buy food.[17] (In lean times, one's dependents often fail to hide their disappointment in one's capacity as a provider.)

3707. *Bí iwín bí iwín ní ńṣe ọlÓya; bíi wèrè bíi wèrè ní ńṣe elÈṣù; àjótàpá àjópòyì ní ńṣe oníṢàngó.*
Like imbecility, like imbecility is the action of the Oya worshiper; like madness, like madness is the action of the Èṣù worshiper; dancing-with-kicking, dancing-and-spinning is the hallmark of the Ṣango worshiper. (Each occupation has its peculiar habits.)[18]

---

17. The proverb plays on the verb *rà*, which can mean either "buy" or "hover," the latter being applied to the hawk's predatory tactic.

18. The saying could be part of an incantation to invoke madness in a person.

3708. *Bí ìyà ńlá bá gbéni sánlẹ̀, ké-kè-ké a máa gorí ẹni.*
When a great misfortune floors us, small ones climb on us. (People who would otherwise not dare to will take advantage of a person who is down.)

3709. *Bí kò sí tọ̀mọ̀, kí là ńwá ní fùrọ̀ onífùrọ̀.*
Were it not on account of children, what business would one have with another person's genitals? (Necessity imposes obligations.)

3710. *Bí ó bá di ibi yíyan, ògòǹgò a súnkì.*
When it comes to frying, the palm weevil will contract. (If the disaster is big enough, the strongest person feels the effect.)

3711. *Bí o bá fẹ́ bọ̀rọ̀kìnní-í tẹ́, jí relé-e rẹ̀ láfẹ̀ẹ̀mójúmọ́; wo ẹní tó tẹ́ sùn; wo aṣọ tó fi ńbora.*
If you wish to deflate a dandy, go to his home in the early dawn; look at the mat he sleeps on, and look at the sheet he covers himself with. (The dandy abroad is often filthy at home.)

3712. *Bí ó ti wù ká ṣe Ìbàdàn tó, apá kan ìlú là ńrí.*
However long one lives in Ibadan, one sees only one part of the city. (No one can know all about the affairs of a city or person.)

3713. *Bí òjò ò rò, bí àgbàdo ò gbó, kí ni ọmọ aráyé ó jẹ?*
If rain does not fall, and corn does not mature, what will humans eat? (If the powers people rely on do not fulfill their obligations, the masses face peril.)

3714. *Bí òru bí òru ní ńṣe aláṣọ dúdú.*
Eager anticipation of nightfall is the mind-set of the person wearing black-colored garments. (One always seeks operating conditions conducive to one's circumstances.)

3715. *Bí ọmọdé bá lówó, ìgbéraga ní ńdà lójú àgbà.*
If a youth is wealthy, his actions seem like pride in the eyes of the elders. (Older people are not beyond being jealous of youthful success.)

3716. *Bí ọ̀pọ̀lọ́ bá fẹ̀hìn lélẹ̀, nǹkan ló ńṣe é.*
If a toad lies on its back, something is the matter with it. (If a person does the unexpected, there must be a reason.)

3717. *Bí pépéyẹẹ́ bá jẹ òkúta, omi ni yó fi ṣu.*
If a duck eats stones, it evacuates them in the form of water. (No matter what the circumstances, some people cannot change their nature or habits.)

E

3718. *Ebi ò mọ̀ pé oókan ò sí nílé; bí ojú bá mọ́, ebi a máa pani.*
Hunger does not care that there is not one single cowrie shell in the home; when morning breaks, hunger assails one. (Hunger does not leave one alone simply because one is poor.)

3719. *Eégún débi, kò ṣéé gbá lójú.*
The masquerader judges one guilty, and yet one dares not slap him. (Against some people one has no recourse.)[19]

3720. *Èèmọ̀ ní Ìmọ̀: Onímọ̀-ọ́ sòpá, ayaa rẹ̀-ẹ́ dégbò.*
Unspeakable abomination: the ruler of Imọ contracts hydroceles, and his wife develops a sore. (Even those people to whom one would look up are blighted.)

3721. *Èèyàn bí àparò layé ńfẹ́.*
Humankind favors only partridgelike people. (People warm only to those less fortunate than themselves.)[20]

3722. *Èèyàn gígùn ò ṣé-é bọ òrìṣà méjì.*
A tall person is not enough sacrifice for two gods. (The mightiest person is still one person. Compare 3750.)

3723. *Èèyàn kan ní ńrọ kangara mọ́ni lọ́wọ́.*
It is a person who fashions a billhook and thrusts it into one's hand. (Impositions do not materialize by themselves; there is always human agency behind them.)

3724. *Èèyàn ní ńkọ́ni ká gùn; èèyàn ní ńkọ́ni ká kúrú.*
People teach one to be tall [or long]; people teach one to be short. (One soon learns from experience how to cope with the devious ways of humans.)

3725. *Egbinrin ọ̀tẹ̀: à ńpàkan, òkan ńhù.*
Plots like wild vegetables: one eliminates one, and another sprouts. (Some problems are so resistant that they are virtually impossible to resolve.)

3726. *Eji wẹ́rẹ́-wẹ́rẹ́ ní ńlé ọmọ wọlé; àgbàrá ọ̀jọ̀ ńlá ní ńmi ọgọ̀rọ̀ tìtì lẹ́sẹ̀.*
It is a light rain that chases a child indoors; it is a raging torrent that shakes the raffia palm to its roots. (Every person, however lowly or mighty, has his or her nemesis.)

3727. *Ejò ò kó ọmọ ẹ̀ lẹ́hìn jẹ̀ yoo-yọ̀ọ̀-yoo kánú igbó.*
A snake does not wander in the bush with all its young in train. (Each person pursues his or her destiny singly.)

---

19. It is because they are believed to be the embodiments of the spirits of departed ancestors that the *eégún* are sacrosanct.

20. The partridge's inelegant plumage suggests poverty.

3728. Èké ní ńrojọ́; ìkà ní ńdá a.
The person stating a case is devious; the person judging it is evil. (One's adversary and the person one looks to for justice are in league together.)

3729. Èlùbọ́ sẹ̀gbodò rí; ẹrú sọmọ rí nílé-e bàbá è.
Yam flour was once fresh yam; a slave was once a child in his father's house. (No one is immune to a change in fortune.)

3730. Erín kú màngúdú fi jẹ; ẹfọn-ọ́n kú màngúdú fi jẹ; màngúdú kú kò réni jẹun.
The elephant dies and màngúdú devours it; the buffalo dies and màngúdú devours it; màngúdú dies but finds no one to devour it. (The person or thing that serves the needs of all others usually has no one or nothing to serve his, her, or its own needs.)[21]

3731. Èsù ìbá ti là, akówó-ẹbọ ni ò jẹ́.
Èsù would have prospered, but the people who remove the money from sacrifices have thwarted him. (Hard though one may work, others may block the way of one's success.)[22]

3732. Etí kì í tóbi kó gbọ́ òrò méje lẹ́èkan sọsọ.
Ears are never so large that they can hear [decipher] seven messages all at once. (There is an existential limit to human capabilities.)

3733. Etí lobìnrín fi ńgbóhùn Orò.
Only with her ears does a woman hear the voice of Orò. (The sight of Orò is forbidden to a certain class of people.)

---

21. Màngúdú is apparently a word designating only the person or thing that serves all others.

22. Èsù is a god who receives sacrifice either in his own right or as an intermediary between people and their gods. The sacrifice, often left at crossroads, usually includes some palm oil and some money. People whose need is greater than their fear of the god scoop up the money when they come upon such sacrifices.

3734. Ẹ̀bìtì ò peèrà; ará ilé ẹni ní ńpani.
A trap does not kill an ant; people of one's household engineer one's death. (The enemy within is the one to fear. Compare 3747.)

3735. Ẹ̀bùn Ọlọ́run ò kan ọgbọ́n.
God's gift has nothing to do with wisdom. (Natural gifts are nothing to take credit for.)

3736. Ẹ̀hìnkùlé lòtá wà; ilé lasẹni ńgbé.
One's back yard is where one's enemy is to be found; it is in one's home that the person who means one harm lives. (One's most dangerous enemies are those closest to one.)

3737. Ejọ́ bá ọ, bí òràn ikúnlẹ̀-ẹ́ bá arọ.
Trouble has found you, just as the compulsion to kneel has found the cripple. (You have just as much chance of escaping trouble as the cripple has of avoiding crawling.)

3738. Ejọ́ ní ńbá mo-kó-mo-rò wa.
"I will tell all I know" results from a dispute. (If there were no dispute, one would not be required to explain; when one lands in an unfortunate situation, inconveniences are piled on.)

3739. Ẹlẹ́dẹ̀-ẹ́ pàfọ tán, ó ńwá ẹni rere tí òun ó fara yí.
The pig, after wallowing in the mud, goes looking for a decent person to rub bodies with. (Evil people are always on the prowl for decent people to corrupt. Compare 3355.)

3740. Ẹni à bá fẹ̀hìntìí jẹ elégùn-ún; ẹni à bá finú hàn-án jẹ aláròkiri.
The person one would lean on turns out to be thorny; the person one would confide in turns out to be a blabbermouth. (There are few people one can really trust.)

3741. Ẹni a gbójú olókùn lé kì í ṣeni ẹgba.
The person for whom one has readied a
rope is not one for whom a whip is appropriate. (The person one has been spoiling to
destroy turns out to be beyond one's reach.)

3742. Ẹni à ńpète pèrò ká sọwọ́-ọ rẹ̀ dilẹ̀,
pípele ní ńpele sí i.
The person we keep plotting to bring to destruction nevertheless continues to grow in
prosperity. (The machinations of enemies
have no effect on the fortunes of a certain
person.)

3743. Ẹni a rí la mọ̀; ẹni a mọ̀ rí a gbàgbé.
We know only those whom we see; those we
saw in the past we forget. (Only those who
are present command people's attention.)

3744. Ẹni a rí ṣígun: ó ní fèrè lòun ó fọn.
The person on whose arrival one advances
against the enemy: he says all he will do is
blow the bugle. (The person one reposed all
one's hopes in turns out to be a disappointment.)

3745. Ẹní bá rí ibi ṣu a dawọ́ bolẹ̀.
A person who finds a place to relieve himself
or herself will rest his or her palms on the
ground. (Once one's pressing needs are met,
one begins to seek luxuries.)[23]

3746. Ẹní bá ru àjèjé ọdẹ kì í là.
Whoever serves as funerary carrier for a
hunter's paraphernalia never prospers.
(The person whose lot it is to perform the
meanest duties seldom prospers.)[24]

3747. Ẹni ẹni ní ńṣeni; ẹbìtì ò peèrà.
One's own relatives constitute one's bane;
the ant does not fall victim to a snare.
(Those closest to one are best placed to
cause one injury. Compare 3734.)

3748. Ẹní fi ẹ̀kẹ̀sẹ́ kan orí, ìba rí obì a fi bọ ọ́.
He who hits his head with his fist: could he
find kola nuts, he would sacrifice them to his
head. (Whoever is in desperate straits would
clutch at any remedy to extricate himself.)[25]

3749. Ẹní géwọ́ gésẹ̀-ẹ́ bù gé tán.
A person whose arms have been amputated
and whose legs have been amputated has
lost just about everything amputable. (A
person who has lost everything has nothing
else to lose.)

3750. Ẹni gígùn kì í kú lẹ́ẹ̀mejì.
A tall person does not die twice. (However
great a person can be, he or she remains yet
only one person; however great a person is,
he or she shares the same destiny with all
human beings. Compare 3722.)

3751. Ẹni ìjà ò bá ní ńpe ara ẹ̀ lókùnrin.
It is the person not faced with a fight who
boasts about his manliness. (One can always
boast when one is certain there will be no
need for proof.)

3752. Ẹni mọ́tò-ó pa-á re ọ̀run ìyà; ẹni
rélùwéè-é pa-á re ọ̀run èsín.
Whoever is killed by a motor vehicle dies a
miserable death; whoever is killed by a train

---

23. The proverb is based on the practice of walking
into the bush to relieve oneself. An area frequented by
many people for that purpose will yield few clear spots
to crouch. A person who is fortunate to find such a
spot also seeks enough space as well to rest the arms for
support.

24. Part of the funerary observance for a hunter's
death is to appoint a person who will carry the dead

hunter's hunting paraphernalia (charms and so forth)
in a ritual procession for burial in the bush. The task is
not attractive, for the charms are invested with dangerous powers. The assumption is that whoever has had to
perform the duty is thereafter blighted.

25. Striking one's head with one's fist is a sign of
desperation; kola nuts are sacrificed in propitiation to
the force guiding one's destiny, which is believed to
reside in the head.

dies a disgraceful death. (It is better to be killed by a motor vehicle than by a train, but neither way of death is becoming.)

3753. Ẹni ọká bá ṣán: bí kò kú, a di elégùn ejò.
When a person is bitten by a cobra and he does not die, he becomes a devotee of the snake's cult. (Whoever survives a great calamity has no further reason to fear its like.)

3754. Ẹní ra filà fún akàn-án fowó ṣòfun; níbo ni yó de sí?
Whoever buys a cap for a crab wastes money; where will it place the cap? (One should not waste one's resources on foolish ventures.)

3755. Ẹni tí à bá fínú hàn ní ńṣe elénìní ẹni.
The person in whom one would confide is the author of one's ruin. (There is hardly anyone a person can confidently trust.)

3756. Ẹni tí a bá ní ní ńgbani.
The champion one has is the one who comes to one's aid. (A champion should not default just when his or her aid is needed.)

3757. Ẹni tí a kọ́ níkà tó gbà, ó ti ní tìrẹ̀ nínú tẹ́lẹ̀.
A person who is receptive to the advice to do evil was predisposed to evil. (Only those willing to be corrupted can be corrupted.)

3758. Ẹni tí a sọ òkò lùú ní kí á sọ ìdàrọ.
The person at whom one throws stones urges one to throw iron dross. (The target of one's punishment, rather than being impressed, urges one to do one's worst.)

3759. Ẹni tí ebi ńpa ò gbọ́ ìwàásù.
A starving person hears no preaching. (Expect nothing from a starving person. Compare 4918.)

3760. Ẹni tí ikú ńpa ò tó nkan; gbogbo ayé lebi ńpa.
The number of people subject to [immediate] death is tiny; everybody is subject to hunger. (Hunger is a greater and more general affliction than death.)[26]

3761. Ẹni tí ò mú nnkan wá sáyé ò lè mú nnkan lọ sọ́run.
People who brought nothing into this world cannot expect to depart from it with something. (We came into this world naked, and we shall depart naked.)

3762. Ẹni tí ò rí ehín fi jẹ ẹja tútù ò lè jẹ gúgúrú.
Whoever lacks teeth to eat fresh fish cannot eat popcorn. (A person who fails at an easy task will not succeed at a difficult venture.)

3763. Ẹni tí òjò-ó pa, tí Ṣàngó ò pa, kó máa dúpẹ́.
The person who is caught in the rain but is not struck by Ṣango, god of lightning, should be thankful. (If one suffers a small misfortune, one should remember that it could have been much worse.)

3764. Ẹni tó bá ogun níbodè-é bá iṣẹ́.
Whoever walks in on a battle at the town gate walks in on a tough assignment. (If one walks in on trouble, one's task is cut out.)

3765. Ẹni tó gba ọmọ ẹni ò ní òun ò níí gba aya.
The person who makes off with one's daughter will think nothing of making off with one's wife. (One should expect no quarter from an adversary who has proved himself or herself ruthless and unscrupulous.)

---

26. The force of the proverb derives from the common verb used in describing the effects (actions) of both death and hunger: *pa* (literally "to kill").

3766. Ẹni tó kàn ló mọ̀.
It is the person a calamity has befallen who knows how it feels. (No amount of sympathy can give one firsthand experience of other people's woes.)

3767. Ẹni tó láyà ní ńṣòwò òtẹ̀.
Only a person who is bold makes conspiracy his trade. (Those who conspire must have the spine to take on the consequences.)

3768. Ẹni tó mọ ìhín ò mọ òhún; alágbèdẹ ò roko.
The person who is familiar with this place is not familiar with the other place; the blacksmith does not till a farm. (No one person can know it all, or do it all.)

3769. Ẹni tó mọ̀ ọ́ kò kò ọ́; ẹni tó kò ọ́ kò mọ̀ ọ́.
Those who know him do not meet him; those who meet him do not know him. (People often fail to appreciate the qualities of those they encounter.)

3770. Ẹni tó mọ ọ̀ràn tán di Olódùmarè.
The person who knows everything has become God Almighty. (No human being can know everything.)

3771. Ẹni tó sọ pé láti ìgbà tí òun-ún ti dáyé ìyà ò jẹ òun rí, ohun tí ìyà ńjẹ lẹ́nu ni kòì tíì kúnná.
The person who says since he came to this world he or she has never been in the teeth of suffering: it is simply because suffering has not yet chewed up what it already has in its teeth. (Everybody comes to know suffering in time.)

3772. Ẹni tó tàkìtì lÉkòó, tó balẹ̀ nÍbàdàn: wọ́n ní Abẹ́kùúta ńkọ́? Ó ní káfò ó.
The person who somersaulted from Lagos and landed in Ibadan is asked, "What about Abẹ́òkúta?"[27] He responds, "Let us skip that." (When earthshaking problems arise, it is no time to dwell on trifles. Compare 3934.)

3773. Ẹni tó tejúmọ́lẹ̀-ẹ́ mọ ohun tí òun ńwa.
The person who fixes his eyes on the ground knows what he is looking for. (No one does anything without a good reason, even if it is not readily apparent to others.)

3774. Ẹnìkan kì í gbọ́n tán.
Nobody is all wise. (Everybody can learn something from others.)

3775. Ẹnu aláìsàn ló fi ńpe ikú.
The sick person summons death with his or her own mouth. (The person who despairs often ensures his or her own hopelessness.)[28]

3776. Ẹnu ehoro ò gba ìjánu.
The rabbit's mouth is not suited for a bridle. (However accomplished one might be, there are certain tasks one will be incapable of doing. Also, some treatments are not proper for some people.)[29]

3777. Ẹnu ẹyẹ ò lè yán òkúta.
A bird's beak cannot snap up a rock. (There are certain tasks that are beyond a person's capabilities.)

3778. Ẹnu kò gbọ́ "Mo jẹ rí."
The mouth does not say, "I ate once before." (Hunger is not something one assuages once and for all.)

---

27. Èkó is the Yoruba name for Lagos; Abẹ́òkúta is a city midway between Ibadan and Lagos.

28. A Yoruba form of lamentation that a despairing sick person might resort to is Mo kú o! ("Oh, I am dead!"). The Yoruba believe that such talk invites its own fulfillment.

29. Swift though the rabbit is, it cannot emulate a horse.

3779. Èpa ò bá oró mọ́.
The antidote can no longer catch up with the poison. (Matters have gone past the possibility of redress.)

3780. Èrò pèsè-pèsè, kò mọ̀ bí ara ǹkan ìgbín.
The charm to ensure ease does not care how much the snail hurts.[30] (People seldom stop to consider what effects their selfish actions have on others.)

3781. Èrú gba ẹdùn, ominú ǹkọ igi.
The axe is slipped onto the haft; the tree become anxious. (When danger threatens, the vulnerable become apprehensive.)

3782. Ẹrù kì í pa òsùká; ẹlérù lẹrù ǹpa.
The load does not weigh down the carrying pad; it is the owner [carrier] of the load that the load weighs down. (Much as one may give aid to a person in trouble, one cannot assume the trouble.)

3783. Ẹsè ǹtẹlè, inú ḿbí aráyé.
The feet tread the ground, and people are angry. [Some] people will begrudge others simply for living. Compare 4035.)

3784. Ẹsín dára ó ku aré; èèyán dára ó ku ìwà; ajá òyìnbó dára ó ku àtidẹ.
The horse looks great but lacks speed; the man is handsome but lacks character; the European dog is good-looking but cannot hunt. (Looks are nothing compared to substance or utility.)

3785. Ẹsin eni kì í ga lójú òtá ẹni.
One's horse is never tall in the eyes of one's enemy. (Whatever one does, one cannot impress an enemy. Compare the next entry.)

3786. Ẹsin òtá eni kì í ga lójú ẹni; à ní bíi kétékété ló rí.
One's enemy's horse is never tall in one's sight; one says it is just like an ass. (One always minimizes an enemy's accomplishments. Compare the preceding entry.)

3787. Ètù ò sí ìbọ́n dòpá; baba ọmọ́ kú ọmọ́ dẹyọ.
Without gunpowder the gun becomes a stick; the father dies, and his children become disconnected individuals. (When the main support is removed, the greatest edifice collapses.)

3788. Èwà ìkákùré ò nà tán; awo eni ò lè ṣe awo rere tán.
Ìkákùré bean does not stretch out completely;[31] one's charm cannot be absolutely infallible. (There is no absolute perfection anywhere.)

3789. Eye ǹwú bà-ǹ-kù ba-n-ku, ìyẹ làsírí è.
The bird swells to a huge dimension, but the secret is in its feathers. (A person's impressive appearance is not always backed by substance.)

G

3790. Gagalo-ó ṣubú, ọwọ́ tẹ apákó.
The stilt walker falls; planks become available. (When a person loses control, his or her belongings become fair game.)

---

30. Èrò pèsè-pèsè, meaning "exceeding softness" or "exceeding ease," is a charm for which the juice obtained by cracking a snail shell is an essential ingredient.

---

31. Ìkákùre beans have curly pods.

Gb

3791. *"Gbà kún tìrẹ" ò bí ọmọ aráyé nínú.*
"Take this and add it to yours" does not
offend humankind. (People are ever receptive to aggrandizement.)

3792. *"Gbà mu" ò tán ibà.*
"Take this and drink it" does not end a fever.
(Seemingly simple problems are seldom
easily resolved.)[32]

3793. *"Gbà pamọ́" fún olè ní ṁmú olè jà.*
"Take this for safekeeping" addressed to a
thief encourages thievery. (The person who
places temptations in another's path is partly
responsible for whatever goes amiss.)

3794. *"Gbà ràn mí" di ẹlẹ́rù; ajínifẹ́ di ọkọ
ẹni.*
"Help me with this load" becomes the owner
of the load; the cuckolder becomes the husband. (Temporary expedients sometimes
become permanent conditions. Compare the
following entry.)

3795. *"Gbà tọ́wò-ọ́" gbé ipọn mì; "Gbà ràn
mí lẹ́rù-ú" di ẹlẹ́rù; "Bá mi gún èlùbọ́" fi ègbé
gún èèkàn.*
"Taste this" swallows the spoon; "Help me
with this load" becomes the owner of the
load; "Help me pound these dried yams"
impales herself on a wooden peg. (One
should not be more zealous as a helper than
the person one is helping. Compare the
preceding entry.)

3796. *Gbẹ́nà-gbẹ́nàá gbẹ tán; ó ku gbẹ́nu-
gbẹ́nu.*

The carpenter has done his job; now comes
the braggart's turn. (People of little accomplishment are often more vociferous in their
own praise than are great achievers.)[33]

H

3797. *"Háó fọ dúù" lòyìnbó fi ńjẹ̀bà lÓrígo.*
"How for do?" [What else can one do?] is
the white man's rationalization for eating
cassava meal at Orígo. (When in dire straits,
one will do things one would normally not
stoop to.)[34]

I

3798. *Ìbànújẹ́ sọ orí àgbà kodò.*
Sadness bows the head of the most venerable
elder. (No one outgrows sadness.)

3799. *Ibi ènì là ṁpa ọmọ alákàrà sí.*
The child of the bean-fritters seller usually
gets killed in disputes over how much of the
food will be added to the purchase as gratuity.[35] (Disastrous quarrels often arise over
matters that are really not worth fighting
about.)

3800. *Ibi iṣẹ́ la ti ṁmọ ọlẹ.*
It is at his or her trade or occupation that

---

32. The proverb possibly results from the traditional
experience that fevers were not to be taken lightly. It is
also quite likely to derive from the belief that no illness
is purely physiological and that the treatment cannot
exclude psychic ministering.

33. The Yoruba word that designates a carpenter
exemplifies one of the language's methods for word
formation, the reduplication of the activity: in this case
gbẹ ọna, contracted to *gbẹ́nà*, is the profession, and one
engaged in it is *gbẹ́nà-gbẹ́nà*. *Gbẹ ẹnu* means "hone the
mouth."

34. Orígo is a very small village on the railway line
in the Yoruba area; *èbà* is considered a poor person's
meal even for the Yoruba.

35. The underlying idea seems to be that although
the *àkàrà* seller herself would have freely granted the
bonus, the child she leaves in temporary charge would
not feel as free to do so, causing the expectant customer
to fly into a rage.

one knows the shirker. (To really know the hard worker or the shirker, one must see him or her at work.)

3801. *Igí gbun nígbó à ńsò; òpòlopò èèyàn ló gbun láàrin ìlú.*
We complain that a tree grows crooked in the forest, yet a great many people are crooked in the town. (When one has skeletons in one's own closet, one should not find fault with others.)

3802. *Ìgbàgbé ò lóògùn.*
Forgetting knows no antidote. (Anyone is likely to forget something sometime.)

3803. *Ìgbòó wá ilé eyekéye tú.*
Àgbìgbò takes delight in raiding the nests of other birds. (Said of a person who enjoys introducing disharmony into other people's affairs.)

3804. *Ijó ńbe nínú aro, esè ni ò sí.*
There is a lot of dance in the cripple; what he or she lacks are legs. (If one had the wherewithal, one would perform wonders.)

3805. *Ikán ńje orù; kèrègbè paramó.*
Termites are consuming the small earthen pot; gourds had better beware. (If an evil fate befalls those who are more formidable than you are, look out.)

3806. *Ikùn baba òrìsà.*
The stomach [is the] father of all gods. (One can less afford to neglect one's stomach than one's gods. Compare 3911.)

3807. *Ikún ní bí òun-ún bá pé nílé, òràn ilé á bá òun; bí òun-ún bá sì pé lóde, òràn òde a bá òun.*
The squirrel says if it stays too long at home, it is beset by the problems of home; if it stays long outside instead, it is plagued by problems of the outside. (No matter where one turns, there is trouble aplenty.)

3808. *Ilè kì í gba ògèdè kó so ìdì méjì.*
The soil is never so nourishing for the banana plant that it brings forth two bunches at once. (Nature places limits on everyone and everything.)

3809. *Ilè tí kò ti ojú eni sú, a kì í mo òkùnkùn-un rèé rìn.*
One never knows how to negotiate the darkness of a night that did not fall in one's presence. (One cannot know all the intricacies of a matter that developed outside one's knowledge.)

3810. *Ìlérí ilé ò mo ti à ńjagun; kùfè-kùfè ò mo ìjà; ojó táa rógun là ńmojo.*
Boasting within the house is no proof of bravery in battle; rearing in anticipation is no proof of prowess in a fight; the day that war breaks out is when one knows who is a coward. (Valor is a matter not of speech but of deed.)

3811. *Ìlú kì í kéré kó má nìí ààtàn.*
A town is never so small that it does not have a dung hill. (Everybody has his or her flaws, or skeletons in the closet.)

3812. *Ìlú òsí nilé ìjàpá; bí a bá mú ahun lo sílùú orò yó padà wá sílù-ú òsì-i rè.*
The town of misery is the domicile of the tortoise; if one takes the tortoise to a town of prosperity, it will return to its town of misery.[36] (Nothing will cure the ill-fated person of his or her misery.)

3813. *Ìnùkínù ní ńmú ìwákúwàà wá; esín sonù à ńwá a nínú igbá Ifá.*
Inexplicable loss occasions senseless searching; a horse is lost and one searches for it in an Ifá divining bowl. (Baffling occurrences lead one to strange behavior.)

---

36. The proverb is based on the character of *ahun* (*àjàpá*), the Yoruba trickster.

3814. *Inúnibíni ò kan àì-mòwà-rere-éhù.*
Malice toward others does not result from
not knowing how to be good. (Evil behavior
is a matter of will, not of nature.)

3815. *Iró ní ńjé "Mo kú tán."*
The exclamation "I am dead!" is a lie. (A
person who can still lament has not reached
the height of suffering.)

3816. *Işé ní ḿmú ahun je eèrí; eèrí kì í şe
oúnje ahun.*
It is destitution that brought the tortoise
to eating corn bran; bran is no food for the
tortoise. (Misfortune reduces one to doing
things one would rather not do.)

3817. *Işé tán, òwó pin, òwú ò kún kéké; ara
gbogbó le bí ìtì ògèdè.*
The work is done, the trading is over, the
cotton does not fill the barrow; the body
remains as firm as a banana trunk. (One has
done what one is called upon to do, but the
desired goal is not yet achieved, and one
would rather continue to work if one only
could.)

3818. *Ìşeńşe tó şe dé ìhín kì í tán lórò-o
panşágà.*
The sort of behavior that brought her to her
present condition never leaves the prostitute. (One cannot change one's nature.)

3819. *Ìyà méta a-fàdá-pa-ikún: ikún lo, àdá
nù, aládàá ní òun ó gba àdá òun.*
Three misfortunes that befell the person
who would kill a squirrel with a cutlass: the
squirrel escaped, the cutlass was lost, and the
owner of the cutlass demanded its return.
(Said when problems climb on problems.)

3820. *Ìyà méta ògànjó: bi a feşè kó imí, à fowó
bà á, à fi runmú.*
Three outrages of a dark night: if one steps
into excrement, one feels it with one's hand,

and then one takes a sniff at it. (One who
is not careful about what he or she does or
the company he or she keeps will endure
unpleasant consequences.)

3821. *Ìyàn ní ḿmúni je èso igi-kígi.*
It is famine that brings one to eating the
fruits of all sorts of trees. (Hard times force
one to unbecoming behavior.)

3822. *Ìyàwó tí a gbé lójú ijó, onílù ni yó bàá
lo.*
The wife one met at a dance will eventually
elope with a drummer. (People cannot shed
their innate habits.)

K

3823. *Ká rí owó ra elééyó ò dàbí-i kó yeni.*
Having the means to buy the cloth *elééyó*
is nothing like having it look good on one.
(Having money is nothing like knowing how
to use it well.)

3824. *Kì í şe ejó ajá: eni tó so ó ni ò só ore; eni
tó só só ore: okùn ni ò yi; okùn-ún yi: orúko
ajá ló ro ajá tó fi ńjá.*
The dog is not to blame: it was the person
who tied it up that did a poor job; the person who tied it up did a good job: it was
the rope that was brittle; the rope was not
brittle: the dog was simply acting according to its name when it broke loose.[37] (In
spite of any preemptive efforts, a person will
eventually show his or her true colors.)

3825. *Kí ni a fi ńpa lára ìka tí à ńwí pé ó tó
màyànkàn-mayankan?*
What wound would one sustain on one's
finger that one would say was huge and gap-

---

37. The pun is based on the fact that the word *ajá*
(dog) is construed to mean "one who breaks loose"
(*a-já*).

ing? (There is a limit to which anyone or anything can be at risk.)

3826. *Kí ni a ó ti ṣe Ẹrú tí kò ní hùwà ẹrú?*
What could one do to Ẹrú [Slave] to keep him or her from behaving like a slave? (Nothing one does will ever keep a person from acting according to his or her nature.)

3827. *Kí ni òkóbó ńwò tí kò gbé nǹkan mì?*
What is the eunuch considering that keeps him from swallowing poison? (A worthless person has little cause to cling tenaciously to life.)

3828. *Kí ọmọdé tó gbọn, ìwà-a ẹ́ á bàjẹ́.*
Before a child learns wisdom, he or she will have earned a bad reputation. (One seldom learns wisdom before one has made some blunders.)

3829. *Kiní kan-án ba àjàò jẹ́: apá ẹ̀-ẹ́ pọ̀ ju itan ẹ̀ lọ.*
Àjàò [a nocturnal bird] has one blemish: its wing is heftier than its thigh. (Said of an essentially good person who, however, has an unfortunate serious flaw.)

3830. *"Kiní yìí, ng kò lè jẹ ẹ": kí Ọlọrun má dà à sí agbada ẹni.*
This thing is something I cannot eat: may God not pour it into my vat. (May God keep away from me the problems I cannot handle.)

3831. *"Kò mọ̀ọ́ tà kò mọ̀ọ́ rà" tí ńgun ẹṣin lórí àpáta.*
He-knows-not-how-to-sell-and-he-knows-not-how-to-buy who rides a horse on the rock. (Said of people who misuse valuable things which other people must pay for and care for — vandals, in one word.)

3832. *"Kò pa ẹtu kò jẹ́ kí ẹtu jẹ̀," tí ńfaṣọ funfun ṣọdẹ.*

He-will-not-kill-antelopes-and-he-will-not-let-antelopes-forage who hunts in white attire. (Said of people who will neither do something nor get out of the way of others willing to do it: dogs in the manger. See 3837.)

3833. *Kò run ẹni, kò run ẹni, ó wa ńdòyì ka ẹni.*
It does not destroy one, it does not destroy one, yet it persists in circling one. (Said of needling problems that persist despite one's efforts to get rid of them.)

3834. *Kò sí bí a ti lè ṣe ebòlò tí kò níí rùngbẹ́.*
There is nothing one can do to the vegetable *ebòlò* that will make it not smell of the wild. (One cannot cure people of their innate habits. Compare the next two entries.)

3835. *Kò sí bí a ti lè ṣe ẹlẹ́dẹ̀ tí kò níí pàfọ̀.*
There is nothing one can do to the pig to keep it from wallowing in the mud. (People cannot be cured of their natures. Compare the preceding entry and the one following.)

3836. *Kò sí bí a ti lè ṣe Ifá kó má hùwà èkùrọ́.*
There is nothing one can do to Ifá that will keep him from behavior suggestive of palm kernels.[38] (There is no curing people of their natures. Compare the preceding two entries.)

3837. *Kò ṣe, kò jólúrè ṣe.*
He or she will not act, and he or she will not permit others to act. (Compare 3832.)

3838. *Kó wó, kó wó lojú aṣeni.*
That things would collapse, that things would collapse is the expectation of the ill-wisher. (One's enemies always wish for one to fail.)

---

38. *Èkùrọ́* (palm kernels) are used in consulting Ifá, the Yoruba oracle divinity.

3839. *Kòkòrò jewé-jewé, kòkòrò jobì-jobì: kò-kòrò tí ńjewé ara ewé ní ńgbé; kòkòrò tí ńjobì ara obì ní ńwà.*
Leaf-eating insect, kola-nut-eating insect: the insect that eats leaves lives on leaves; the insect that feeds on kola nuts sticks to the kola nut. (One should remain where one is supposed to be, or where one's living is.)

3840. *Kòtò ayé, kòtò obìnrin, àti kòtò ikú, òkan ò yàtò.*
The pit dug by the world, the one dug by a woman, and the one dug by death: they are all the same. (The world, women, and death are equal in their portent.)

3841. *Kúkúrú ye ijó.*
Shortness is an asset in dancing. (Being short is not all bad.)

3842. *Kùkùté àgbon ò lè sorú.*
The stump of a coconut palm cannot sprout leaves. (A person down and out cannot excel.)

L

3843. *Làmílóye, aláje Ìmòbà; ó ní ilé ló jó ni, tàbí olè ló jà?*
Làmílóye, the trial-by-ordeal officer of Ìmòbà town, asked, did the house burn down or was it burgled? (Trust a dunce to ask stupid questions.)[39]

3844. *Lílo-ó yá fún oníbodè tí wón kó nífá lo.*
It is quitting time for the gatekeeper whose divining tray has been stolen. (When one's

surest weapon has been neutralized, one had better make one's escape.)

3845. *"Lo fún mi nílé yìí" kó ni "Lo fún mi níbòmíràn."*
"Get out of my sight in this house" is not "Get out of my sight elsewhere." (If one is shut out of one opportunity, one can usually find another elsewhere.[40] The following entry is a variant.)

3846. *"Lo kúrò nílé mi" kì í se "Kúrò láyé."*
"Get away from my home" is not the same as "Get out of this life." (Divorce is not a death sentence. Compare the preceding entry.)

3847. *Lójú àwòdì òkè, bí-i kádìe lo sórí àpáta.*
In the eyes of a kite aloft, the wish is that the chicken would venture onto a rock. (One always wishes that one's intended victims would render themselves more vulnerable.)

M

3848. *Má rìí igbo loògùn-un wèrè; bó bá rígbó á kó wò ó.*
Not seeing a bush is the only remedy for a madman; if he sees a bush, he will head for it. (The best remedy for a weak-willed person is not to bring temptation his or her way.)

3849. *Mélòó la ó kà léhín Adépèlé? Tinú orún, tòde òjo; òjìlénírínwó èrìgì ló forí mulè láìyo.*
How many will one count among Adépèlé's teeth? The inner row numbers 100, the outer row 160, and 440 molars are embedded in the gums without showing. (Instances or examples [of defects] are far too numerous to enumerate.)[41]

---

39. The name Làmílóye means "Explain to me" or "Make me understand." *Aláje* is the official who presides at ordeals by boiling oil. The proverb suggests that the two events he names are so far apart as not to qualify as possible alternative explanations for a crime. But note the tone play in the shift from *ilé ló jó* to *olè ló jà*.

40. This is a woman's usual response to being discarded by her husband.

41. The name Adépèlé suggests surfeit.

3850. *"Mò ḿbò!" "Máa bò!" Àwọn méjèèjì lèrù ḿbà.*
"Here I come!" "Come on already!" Both of them are afraid. (Both the person bluffing and the person calling the bluff are secretly apprehensive.)

3851. *"Mo ròkè ogbà mo tètè bò": a lè fi wé tẹni tí ò lọ? "Àkèekèé ta mí kò tù mí": a lè fi wé ẹni tí sèbé bùjẹ?*
"I went to my nearby farm and returned early": can one compare such a person to a person who went nowhere? "A scorpion stung me and the pain is unrelenting": can one compare such a person to a person bitten by a viper? (Misfortunes vary in their severity.)

3852. *"Mo yó lánàá" ò kan tebi.*
"I ate my fill yesterday" does not relieve hunger. (Each day brings its own cares.)

N

3853. *"Ng óò gúnyán, ng óò bùn ọ́ jẹ"; ibi èsun la ti ḿmò ó.*
"I will prepare pounded yam and share it with you"; one will see the signs of its likelihood in connection with roasted yams. (People's behavior in circumstances of no consequence is a good indication of how they will behave in circumstances that matter.)

3854. *Ní ojọ́ tí ọbùn-ún bá wè lara ńyún un.*
It is on the day that the filthy person takes a bath that his or her whole body itches. (Evil people never feel comfortable with virtuous things.)

3855. *Ní ojọ́-ọ ṣíṣu ni fùrò ńlà.*
It is on the day one must defecate that the anus must open. (Some obligations permit no options.)

O

3856. *Ó di ojọ́ tí aláró bá kú ká tó mọ oye aṣọ tó gbà rẹ.*
It is on the day of the dyer's death that one knows how many pieces of cloth she had taken in to dye. (When one dies, one's every secret becomes public knowledge.)

3857. *Ó wuni ká jẹran pẹ́ lẹ́nu, olóńfà ni ò jẹ́.*
One would like to chew a piece of meat for a long time, but a downward pulling force will not allow. (Contingencies often limit how long one can relish a boon.)

3858. *Ó yé ọmọ tí ńsunkún, ó sì yé ìyá ẹ̀ tí ḿbẹ̀ ẹ́.*
The crying child knows why it is crying, and the mother consoling it knows why she is doing so. (Each person is privy to the motivation for his or her actions.)

3859. *Obìnrin kì í ròhìn àjò tán.*
A woman is never done telling about the trip she took. (Some people never cease talking about an experience.)

3860. *Obìnrin kì í tóbi kÓrò má gbèe e.*
A woman is never so large that Orò cannot carry her off. (There are certain offenses a woman cannot get away with.)

3861. *Obìnrin ò ṣéé finú hàn.*
A woman is not suitable to expose one's secrets to. (Women cannot be relied on.)

3862. *Obìnrin-ín tẹ ìlú, ó tú.*
A woman founds a town, and it scatters. (A woman is not a fit mainstay of a community.)

3863. *Obìnrin tí a fi ijó fẹ́, ìran ni yó wò lọ.*
The woman one marries on account of her dancing will leave one by losing herself

watching [dancers]. (People's habits seldom leave them.)

3864. *Obìnrín torí ọ̀rọ̀ rodò.*
Women go to the stream only in search of gossip. (Women will do anything for the opportunity to gossip.)

3865. *Òbò ò jọba, ìlú ò dàrú.*
[If] the vagina does not become king, the town does not descend into chaos. (Affairs in the hands of women inevitably become chaotic.)

3866. *Òbúkọ-ọ́ ní àìsàn àgbẹ̀ olówó òun yìí ḿba òun lẹ́rù; bí àìsàn náà-á bá pọ̀ si, baba-láwo a ní kí wọ́n lọ mú òbúkọ wá láti fi ṣe ètùtù fún un; bó bá sàn, àwọn ọmọ ẹ a ní wọn ó mùú òbúkọ fi wewu àmódi.*
The he-goat says the illness of his owner, the farmer, frightens him: if the illness worsens, the diviners will ask that a he-goat be brought and offered as a propitiatory sacrifice on the farmer's behalf; if the illness lessens, the children will vow to sacrifice a he-goat as a thank offering. (One is in a predicament whose every possible outcome is disastrous.)

3867. *Odò-ó gbé Láwálé lọ, ẹ̀ ḿbèrè-e Lábọ́-lùú.*
The river carried off Láwálé, and you ask about Lábọ́lùù's fate. (When the person at the least risk comes to grief, it is pointless to ask what fate befell the person most at risk.)[42]

3868. *Ògúnná gbòǹgbò tí ńdátọ́ lẹ́nu ìgbín!*
Mighty faggot that dries up the dribble in the snail's mouth! (An exclamation on being confronted with an overwhelming problem or stupefying situation.)

3869. *Ògbójú ò tẹ ara ẹ̀ nÍfá; ọ̀mọ̀ràn ò fara ẹ̀ joyè; ọbẹ tó mú ò gbé ẹkù ara ẹ̀.*
The intrepid person does not consult the Ifá oracle on his own behalf; the sagacious person does not enthrone himself; the sharpest knife does not carve its own hilt. (No matter how powerful and accomplished one might be, one will need other people for some things.)

3870. *Ohun mẹ́ta ní ńfi ara wọn rẹ́rìn-ín: aṣọ tó ya ńfi abẹ́rẹ́ rẹ́rìn-ín; àbíkú tí yó kùú ńfi oníṣègùn rẹ́rìn-ín; obìnrin tí yó kọ ọkọ ńfi onípẹ̀ rẹ́rìn-ín.*
There are three things that laugh at their mates: a torn piece of cloth laughs at the needle; an *àbíkú* bound to die laughs at a medicine man; a woman intent on leaving her husband laughs at a conciliator. (Some problems mock any person who attempts to solve them.)

3871. *Ohun tí a bá ńwá ní ńgbọ́n juni lọ.*
Whatever one is searching for always seems wiser than the searcher. (Nothing is ever more difficult to find than whatever one is searching for.)

3872. *Ohun tí afọ́jú fojú ẹ̀ rí kó tó fọ́ ló rí mọ; kò tún rí òmíràn mọ́.*
Whatever the blind person sees before going blind is all he or she will ever see; he or she will never see another thing. (One should seize all opportunities before it is too late.)

3873. *Ohun tí ó tánni ní ìdùn ní ńtánni lówó.*
Whatever exceeds the limits of one's capacity to endure is the same thing that will exhaust one's supply of money. (Serious problems wreak havoc on one's resources.)

---

42. The name Láwálé (Ọláwálé) means "The illustrious one comes home," whereas Lábọ́lùù (Ọlábọ́lùù) means "The illustrious one has plunged into it." Names are believed to influence their bearers' fates.

3874. *Ohun tí ojú rí ní Mákún ò ṣéé délé wí.*
What one's eyes saw at Mákún is not something one can relate on returning home.[43] (Some experiences are too frightful to speak about.)

3875. *Ohun tó nù ní mọ́sálásí rékojá-a sálúbàtà.*
What has gone missing in a mosque is far more than some slippers.[44] (A problem is weightier than people suppose.)

3876. *Òjò ńlá ní ńtẹrí ikin balẹ̀.*
It is a heavy rain that beats the lemon grass to the earth. (It is a mighty misfortune that can prostrate even the most resilient person.)

3877. *Òjó ńrọ̀ sí kòtò, gegele ńbínú.*
The rain fills up the gully, and the hill becomes envious. (When fortune smiles on some, others become envious.)

3878. *Òjò ò dá, ìrì ò da; eji wẹ́rẹ́ gba ọjó alásọ.*
The rain does not stop, and the drizzle does not stop; the gentle precipitation takes the day away from the cloth seller. (A succession of inconsiderable but persistent problems keeps one from attending to important matters.)

3879. *Òjò tó rọ̀ ló mú pẹ̀tẹ̀-pẹ́tẹ̀ wá.*
The rain that fell is what brought about much mud. (Some unfortunate incident has resulted in an unpleasant situation.)

3880. *Òjò-ó pa alágundi, iyán domi; ìyàwó ńretí agundi, ọkọ́ sùn sóko.*
The *agundi* purveyor is caught in the rain,

and the pounded yam becomes like water; the wife awaits *agundi*, but the husband spends the night on the farm. (Adverse circumstances will cause the best-laid schemes to go awry.)

3881. *Òjò-ó pa wèrèpè ó dẹni à ńkọlù.*
Rain beats the cow-itch and renders it something one can walk into.[45] (Misfortune renders one vulnerable to abuse from people who otherwise would not dare displease one.)

3882. *Òjò-ó rọ̀ lánàá a rí esẹ̀-ẹ kòrikò; ilẹ̀-ẹ́ mọ a fẹ́ orimáwo nù; ta ni ò mọ̀ pé kòrikò àná ló gbé e lọ téfé-téfé?*
Yesterday it rained and we saw the tracks of a hyena; in the morning we look in vain for *orimáwo*; who cannot tell that it was yesterday's hyena that made off with it? (When a crime is committed just after a suspicious person makes his appearance, one can be certain that the suspicious stranger is the culprit. Compare 4685.)

3883. *Ojú aboyún ò tó fùrò; ojú òṣìkà ò tó ọla.*
The eyes of a pregnant woman cannot see her genitals; the eyes of the wicked cannot see the future. (The wicked do not know when they will reap what they have sown.)

3884. *Ojú elégbò legbò-ó ti ńkẹ̀.*
It is to the knowledge of the person with a sore that the sore festers. (Some reverses one can do nothing to prevent. Compare 3890.)

3885. *Ojú layé ńjẹ; bí a yísẹ̀ padà wọn a pẹ̀gàn.*
Humans serve only the eyes; when one is absent, they ridicule one. (It is human nature to love you in your presence and smear you in your absence.)

---

43. This is a reference to the Mákún war between the Ègbá and the Ìjèbú in the early years of the twentieth century.

44. A reference to the fact that worshipers are required to remove their shoes before entering a mosque.

45. When its hairs are wet, the stinging effect of cow-itch is practically nil.

3886. *Ojú mọ́n a ò gbọ́ poro-poro odó; ọ̀gànjọ́ gàn a ò gbọ́ wọ̀sọ̀-wọ̀sọ̀-ọ kọ̀ǹkọ̀sọ̀.*
The day dawns and we fail to hear the sound of the mortar; noontime came and we heard no sound of sifting. (One sees and hears no sign of life where one had expected it.)

3887. *Ojú olóbì ni kòkòró ti ńwọ̀ ọ́ lọ.*
It is in the presence of the kola-nut seller that worms enter the kola nut. (Some developments one can in no way prevent. Compare 3890.)

3888. *Ojú olójú là ńrí; ẹni ẹlẹ́ni ní ńrí tẹni.*
One can see only other people's eyes; only other people can see one's eyes. (You can always see other people's flaws, but only other people see your flaws. Compare 378.)

3889. *Ojú ọ̀run ò hu koóko, ilẹ̀pa ò jẹ́ kókù-ú bẹ ọ̀nà wò.*
The sky does not grow grass; the soil of the graveyard does not afford the dead an opportunity to read trails. (Some phenomena offer people no helpful clues to understand them.)

3890. *Ojú-u baba àtọmọ ni làpálàpá ti ńmú ọmọ lórí.*
It is with the knowledge of both father and child that ringworm attacks the child's head. (There are some vicissitudes nothing one can do will avert. Compare 3887.)

3891. *Ojúgun-ún dé ojú eékún paré; ọ̀ná dé orí àpata pòrúrù.*
The shin arrives at the knee and disappears; the path arrives at the rock and becomes confused. (The problem one faces is most intractable.)

3892. *Ojúgun-ún mú odò fọhùn.*
The shin forces the stream to speak out. (A matter one cannot ignore forces one to take action.)

3893. *Òkè ìhín ò jẹ ká rí tòún.*
The nearer hill prevents one from seeing the farther one. (Urgent obligations keep one from attending to less urgent ones.)

3894. *Ókété fẹ́ẹ́ jẹyán, ilé ò gbodó.*
The giant bush rat wishes to eat pounded yams, but its home is not large enough for the mortar. (One's capacity does not match the feats one would wish to perform.)

3895. *Òkú àfín ba àkàlà lẹ́rù.*
The albino's corpse strikes terror into the vulture. (Response to an affair that stupefies even the most unflappable person.)

3896. *Òkú ajá kì í gbó; òkú àgbò kì í kàn.*
A dead dog does not bark; a dead ram does not butt. (Once a person is dead, he or she can do nothing.)

3897. *Olórí lorí ńsán; kì í sán akàn lókè odò.*
Only a person who has a head suffers from headaches, not a crab on the bank of the river. (If one does not have the amenities, one will not suffer the inconveniences that go with them.)

3898. *Òmùwẹ̀ lodò ńgbé lọ.*
It is the expert swimmer that is carried off by the river. (Whatever one is addicted to doing is likely to be one's death.)

3899. *Oníkálukú, a-bèèmọ̀-nílé.*
Everybody [is] someone who has something unmentionable at home. (Everyone is hiding some secret.)

3900. *Oníkáluku a-bi-tiẹ̀-lára.*
Everybody [is] someone with his or her own flaw. (No one is without some flaw.)

3901. *Oníkọ́ ò sá pamọ́.*
A person with a cough does not hide.

(People too much in the public eye cannot be incognito.)

3902. *OníṢàngó ò mọ ẹni ọba; òjò ò mẹni ọ̀wọ̀; òjò ìbá mẹni ọ̀wọ̀ kò pa oníṢàngó àtọlÓya.*
The Ṣango worshiper does not countenance the king's man; the rain does not know who deserves deference; had the rain any idea who deserved respect, it would not have beaten the Ṣango worshiper or the Ọya worshiper. (Nobody gets any special treatment. Compare 3966.)

3903. *Ooru-ú gba aṣọ lọ́wọ́ onílé; ó fi abẹ̀bẹ̀ lé àlejò lọ́wọ́.*
Heat takes the garment off the host and hands a fan to the guest. (Excessive heat forces people out of ceremonious pretenses.)

3904. *Oówo ńlá sọ ọ̀mọ̀ràn lẹ́nu.*
An almighty boil has attacked the mouth of the sage. (An unheard-of situation has preempted action by even the most capable.)

3905. *Ọ̀pọ̀ fúú, ìyà Ọ̀yọ́; ọ̀pọ̀ ò tajà láwìn; àwìn ò tajà lọ́pọ̀.*
Unrequited effort, the misfortune one finds in Ọ̀yọ́ town: the person who sells her wares cheap does not sell on credit; the person who sells on credit does not sell cheap. (Two people must deal with each other but cannot see eye to eye.)

3906. *Ọpó tí à bá fẹ̀hìn tì-í fi gbogbo ara ṣègún; ẹni tí à bá finú hàn-án jẹ́ aláròkiri ẹni.*
The post one would lean on is completely covered with spikes; the person one would confide in turns out to be a talkative backbiter. (One has no one to look to for help or counsel.)

3907. *Orí àgbò-ó sunwọ̀n; àgbò ni yó ba orí ara è jẹ́.*
The ram has a good head; it is the ram itself

that will ruin its head.[46] (People are often responsible for their own misfortune.)

3908. *Orí Olúkànmbí kì í gẹṣin; ìpín àjàpá kì í sọ̀sọ́; a sòlèkè máhun lọ́rùn, ahun-ún wọgbó.*
Olúkànmbí's destiny does not include riding a horse; the tortoise's fate is never to know splendor; people adorn the tortoise's neck with beads, and it heads for the bush. (If one gives something of value to people incapable of recognizing value, they will instantly ruin it.)[47]

3909. *Orí pò ní Mògún; ìpín àìṣè ló pò níbẹ̀.*
There are heads aplenty in the grove where Ògún receives sacrifice; most numerous are those of innocent people. (Even innocence does not always guarantee safety or justice.)

3910. *Orin kan tí adití bá gbọ́ kó tó dití ní ńtẹnu mọ́ láé-láé.*
The one song the deaf person heard before going deaf is the one he will sing repeatedly forever. (It is difficult to move people fixated on one thing to something else.)

3911. *Òrìṣà bí ọ̀fun ò sí; ojoojúmọ́ ní ńgbẹbọ.*
There is no god like the gullet; it received sacrifices daily. (No one can be anything without food. Compare 3806.)

3912. *Òtòmpòrò-ó jókòó gaga-gúgú; alára ló mọ̀ pé kò le.*
Òtòmpòrò sits upright and in splendor; only the owner of the body knows it is unwell. (A person's outward appearance is not always a good indication of his or her true condition.)

---

46. *Orí ẹẹ́ bàjẹ́* ("Your head is ruined"), *Orí ẹ ò sunwọ̀n,* and *Orí ẹ ò dára* ("Your head is no good") are all insults. The proverb refers to the ram's habit of butting against hard objects, such as other rams' heads.
47. Olúkànmbí was apparently a real person, one who did not appreciate good things.

3913. *Òtòṣì-í rìn tolè tolè.*
The poor person walks with the mien of a thief. (A poor person is ever under suspicion of being susceptible to stealing.)

3914. *Owó tí àpọ́n fi ra iyọ̀, ó tó-ó ra eṣin.*
The money the bachelor paid for salt is enough to buy a horse. (A novice in a venture is bound to commit huge blunders.)

3915. *Owó tó pa Ajéníyà ló pa Àpatì; owó tó pa Agbájé ló pa Kútere.*
The trade that killed Ajéníyà is the same one that killed Àpatì; the trade that killed Agbájé is the same that killed Kútere. (No one can escape the influence of money.)[48]

Ọ

3916. *Ọbe kì í mú títí kó gbé ẹkù ara è.*
A knife is never so sharp that it carves its own handle. (Everybody needs other people sometime.)

3917. *Ọdún méfà-a jàbú, bí ọgọ́rùn-ún ọdún ni.*
Six years of wading in the river is like a hundred years. (Hardship that actually lasts a brief time seems to the sufferer to last forever.)

3918. *Ọ́fììsì ní ńréhìn akòwé.*
The office will be the death of the clerk. (Each occupation has its peculiar hazard. Compare 4542, 4544, and 5190.)

3919. *"Ọ̀gá ńbọ̀, ọ̀gá ńbọ̀!" ni yó pa ọmọṣé.*
"Here comes the boss, here comes the boss!"

will be the death of the apprentice. (Fear of discovery, not diligent working, will be the nemesis of the shirker.)

3920. *Ọ̀gèdẹ́ gbé odò so sìn-sín; eja gbé inú omi dára.*
The banana plant grows by the river and prospers; the fish live in the water and look beautiful. (One prospers only to the extent that one's living situation is hospitable.)

3921. *Ọkọkíkú lòsì obìnrin.*
The husband's death is the bane of a woman. (Nothing is worse for a woman than to be widowed.)

3922. *Ọlọ́run ìbá dá kan-in-kan-in tóbi tó eṣinṣin, àtapa ni ì bá ta èèyàn.*
Had God made the black ant as large as a fly, it would have stung humans to death. (It is by the grace of God that the wicked lack the power to do as they otherwise would. See the following variant.)

3923. *Ọlọ́run ò dá kan-in-kan-in kó lésè ńlá bí eṣin; àtapa ni ì bá máa ta èèyàn; eni tí yó fi èèyàn ṣèsín, Ọlọ́run kì í jẹ́ kó níláárí.*
God did not create the black ant to have limbs as big as horses'; otherwise, it would have kicked humans to death; the person who would ridicule people has been denied prosperity by God. (By the grace of God one's adversaries are powerless to injure one. Compare the preceding entry.)

3924. *Ọmọ ẹkùn laja ńpa.*
It is the young of a leopard that a dog kills. (It is only while one is still vulnerable that one's enemies can get the better of one.)

3925. *Ọmọ ológòdò-ó ní òun kú lónìí, ọla baba ọnì ńkọ́?*
A child afflicted with yaws says today is his death; what about tomorrow, father of today? (A doomed person may think his

---

48. The first name in each of the two halves of the proverb includes the word *ajé*, which could mean "money" or "riches," indicating that the bearer was obsessed with the pursuit of wealth. The proverb suggests, therefore, that it is not only people so blatantly obsessed who are thus affected by money.

current woes are unsurpassable, but he has not seen what is in store for him.)

3926. *Ọmọ tí ò léwà, òdèdè ìyá è ní ńpé sí.*
A woman without beauty lasts long on her mother's porch. (Plain women are not soon married.)

3927. *Ọmọ kú lọ́wọ́ adití; ọ̀rọ́ di káti-kàti.*
A child dies in the care of a deaf person; matters become a muddle. (Coming to an understanding with a person beyond communication is a formidable task.)

3928. *Ọnà òfun ò gba kòkò òdù; ọnà òfun ì bá gba kòkò òdù, òmìrán ì bá ti gbé òkan mì, ara ọlọ́tí a dá.*
The throat cannot accommodate a large pot; were the throat able to accommodate such a pot, the giant would have swallowed one, causing the wine seller to wallow in her loss. (Only the limits Nature places on the greedy person limit the damage he can do to others' property.)

3929. *Ọ̀ọ̀rọ̀gọ̀jìmọ̀ ẹkùn, tí ńkọ ọdẹ lọ́mìnú.*
A frightfully huge leopard: it paralyzes the hunter with fear and anxiety. (A huge problem stumps even the most resourceful of people.)

3930. *Ọpá ìbúmbú ṣẹ́ àgbò níwo.*
A horizontal stick knocks off the ram's horns. (An unexpected problem has got the better of a person.)

3931. *Ọpálábá, imú ẹ-ẹ́ ṣe rí báyìí? Ò ní sùù-u è lòun ńwò.*
Broken bottle, why is your nose the way it is? It responds that it is itself contemplating the matter. (Said when one cannot explain a situation that people assume one would be able to explain.)

3932. *Ọpẹ́ lọpẹ́ àtàrí tí ò jẹ́ kí oòrùn ó pa àgbọ̀n ìsàlẹ̀.*
Much gratitude is due the skull that kept the sun from beating down on the chin below. (Even as one laments one's fate when confronted by adversity, one should be grateful for little mercies. The following is a variant.)

3933. *Ọpẹ́ lọpẹ́ èjìká tí ò jẹ́ kí ẹwù ó bọ́.*
Much gratitude is due the shoulders that kept the garment from falling off. (Said when one has experienced extreme adversity and has come through by the grace of God. See the previous entry.)

3934. *Ọpọ̀lọ́ ní bí a bá sọ̀rọ̀ débi ìrù, ká fọ̀ ó.*
The toad says when conversation turns to the matter of tails, let's skip it. (A person with a blemish is always uncomfortable when such blemishes become the subject of conversation. Compare 3772.)

3935. *Ọ̀ràn burúkú tòun tẹ̀rín.*
A terrible disaster is always confronted with laughter. (The laughter that greets a disaster is not one of merriment.)

3936. *Ọ̀ran kan ẹnìkan kénìkan má yọ̀; bó ṣe ogún ọdún, ti olúwarè ńbọ̀ wá bá a.*
When trouble befalls someone, let at another person not rejoice; it may take twenty years, but that other person will experience his or her own trouble. (It does not pay to rejoice at other people's misfortune, for we are all subject to misfortune.)

3937. *Ọ̀ràn kì í báni ju bí a ti mọ lọ.*
No problem affects one beyond one's capacity to be affected. (One is liable only to the extent that one is vulnerable.)

3938. *Ọ̀ràn ò bá ojúgun, ó ní òun ò léran.*
The shin has not yet got into trouble, and therefore it says it has no flesh. (Until one

gets into trouble, one always thinks one is invulnerable.)

3939. Ọ̀ràn tí ńdunni làròkàn ẹni.
Whatever problem troubles one is what one talks to other people about. (One's pressing problems always preoccupy one's consciousness.)

3940. Ọ̀ràn tí olóko-ó fi ńṣe ẹkún sun ni àpárò-ó fi ńṣe èrín rín.
The matter that causes the owner of the farm to burst into tears is the same that causes the partridge to burst into laughter. (Some people's disasters are other people's good fortune.)

3941. Ọ̀ràn-an hùn-hùn ò tán nínú ẹlẹ́dẹ̀.
The compulsion to grunt is never ended where the pig is concerned. (Said of people who are irrevocably wedded to some tendency.)

3942. Ọ̀rẹ́ burú ju ọ̀tá, Olùwa ló lè yọni.
Friends are more terrible than enemies; only God can protect one. (Friends can be more dangerous than enemies.)

3943. Ọ̀rọ̀ àtọjọ́mọ́jọ́ ò lè ṣí ni létí bí ọ̀rọ̀ titun.
Stale news cannot pique one's attention as new news can. (People are ever more interested in something new than in familiar things.)

3944. Ọ̀rọ̀ tí akúwárápá bá sọ, ará ọrun ló sọ ọ́.
Whatever an epileptic says is said by someone bound for heaven. (An observation that what a certain person is saying is not worth listening to.)

3945. Ọ̀rọ̀-ọ́ pọ̀ nínú ìwé-e kọ́bọ̀, epo-o tọ́rọ́ la fi ńkà á.
The one-penny newspaper is chock-full of words, so much so that one needs three-

pence oil to read it all. (There is a great deal to be said on the matter under discussion, and there may not be enough time to say it all.)

3946. Ọrun àkùrọ̀ làparò ńkú sí.
The partridge meets its death on the dry-season-marsh farm. (Danger often finds one while one fulfills unavoidable obligations.)

3947. Ọ̀ṣọ́ ilé ò jọ obìnrin lójú.
Preening that is confined to the home does not appeal to a woman. (Women always wish to go outside the home in order to advertise their beauty.)

3948. Ọ̀tá ọrun ò gba ẹbọ.
An implacable enemy does not respond to sacrifices. (There is nothing one can do to win over a sworn enemy.)

3949. Ọ̀tẹ̀ ní ńdààmú Ọlọ́run-ún-tó-ó-wò; Ọlọ́runúntóówò kì í ṣe ajákájá.
It is the season that has taken its toll on Ọlọ́runúntóówò; Ọlọ́runúntóówò is not really a worthless dog. (Adverse circumstances sometimes make people do unbecoming things they would not normally do.)

3950. Ọtí ò yà fún omi.
Wine does not differ from water.[49] (Matters that will have horrendous effects on people seldom appear different from innocuous matters.)

3951. Ọ̀tọ̀ọ̀tọ̀ là ńwọgbẹ́ ìṣẹ́.
People enter the jungle of misery in different ways. (People take different paths toward ruination.)

3952. Ọ̀wá ò ní pàlàkà.
The palm-leaf midrib does not have nodes from which branches may emerge. (Said of

---

49. Read Ọtí ò yàtọ̀ sómi.

people who cannot conceivably be of any use to others.)

3953. Ọ̀wàrà òjò ní ḿba oníléọgbà lérù.
A torrential deluge is what strikes terror into the heart of a person who lives in a house made of thatch. (People who are vulnerable to any sort of danger have reason to tremble if it should threaten.)

3954. Ọwọ́ adẹ́tẹ̀-ẹ́ kó òjì ọ̀wọ̀wọ̀, kò tún gba èkùrọ́.
The leper's hands scoop up forty grains of boiled dry corn; there is no room left for palm kernels. (People with disadvantages are limited in their capabilities.)

3955. Owọ́ ahọ́n kì í tó imú.
The reach of the tongue is never as far as the nose. (There is a limit to what a person can accomplish.)

3956. Ọ̀wọ́n owó là ńro owó níní; ọ̀wọ́n omi là ńde ìsun; ọ̀wọ́n oúnjẹ là ńpé jẹ yànmù.
It is when money is scarce that one is pre-occupied with the thought of money; it is when water is scarce that one keeps watch by the spring; it is when food is scarce that one joins a crowd to scramble for food. (Scarcity reduces people to unseemly behavior.)

3957. Oyé ńfẹ́ o ò funfun, ìrì ńsẹ̀ o ò jọlọ̀, oníṣègùn ni yó fi owó ẹ po ori mu.
The harmattan rages, and your skin does not go white; the drizzle falls, and your skin does not soften; your money will end up paying for the medicine man's meal. (A person affected by natural phenomena in a way different from others will enrich doctors.)

3958. Oyé ò sán àrá, kùru-kùru ò tan mọ̀nà-mọ́ná; akọ àparò, abo àparò ò lágbe lórí sán-sán-sán.
The harmattan does not come with thunder; haze does not come with lightning; neither the male nor the female partridge has a prominent comb on its head. (Everybody has some deficiency.)

P

3959. Pàkìtì-í kọ ìrìn àjò, gbágùúdá kọ ilé àna kò lọ; àsẹ̀hìnwá àsẹ̀hìnbọ̀ gbágùúdá filé àna ṣèsimi.
A coarse mat does not go on a journey; cassava refuses to go to the in-law's home; in the end, though, cassave makes the in-law's home its final resting place. (One is some-times forced to take up what one had earlier refused.)[50]

3960. Pátákò efọ̀n, kaka ní ńti ajá lẹ́nu.
The hoof of the buffalo is a tough thing in a horse's mouth. (Said of problems that are difficult to tackle.)

3961. Pípá tórí igún pá, kì í ṣe ti erù rírù.
The baldness that afflicts the vulture did not result from its carrying heavy loads. (One cannot presume to know the reasons for other people's conditions.)

R

3962. Rẹ́dẹ-rèdẹ lára alámọ̀ọ́di tó ní omi ejá korò.
Matters have gone rather badly for the sick person who says fish broth is bitter. (When a person sees only putrefaction in priceless things, he or she is really far gone.)

3963. Rírò ni tèèyàn, ṣíṣe ni tỌlọ́run.
It is people's province to propose; it is God's

---

50. One would take one's most presentable pos-sessions along on a journey: in this case, a fine mat. Cassava is a poor person's food, compared with yams, for example, so one would not offer cassava to one's in-laws if one could afford better.

fiat to dispose. (Man proposes, but God disposes.)[51]

3964. *Rógódó ìdí igbá ò jẹ́ kó jókòó-o re.*
The protrusion at the base of the calabash keeps it from sitting straight. (An obstacle prevents one from acting as one might wish.)

Ṣ

3965. *Ṣakatá ní ńdá wòn-wòn ni Bèse.*
The bog represents a troublesome obstacle for the people of Bèse. (A stubborn and inevitable problem is an impediment one must learn to live with.)

3966. *Ṣege ò mọ ẹni ọba, òjò ò mẹni ọwọ̀.*
The tall prickly grass does not care who is a royal personage; rain does not care who is a venerable person. (Natural phenomena do not distinguish among human ranks. Compare 3902.)

3967. *Ṣíṣán ló dá èkọ lára.*
Being eaten without any condiments is the misfortune of the corn meal. (It is a misfortune to have to do without what is needed for comfortable living.)

3968. *Ṣó-ń-ṣó méjì kì í forí kan orí.*
Two pinnacles can never touch heads. (Two irreconcilables can never be brought together.)

T

3969. *Ta ní tó Olọ́run? Ẹdá tó mòla ò sí.*
Who is as great as God? No human being

knows tomorrow. (No one is as great or knowledgeable as God.)

3970. *Tìmùtìmù-ú kó ẹgbin dà sínú.*
The footstool-cushion fills itself with rubbish. (Said of people who must put up with a lot of rubbish or annoyance.)

3971. *Túlàsì kaya-n-doro, tíná fi ḿbọ́ bàtà lẹ́sẹ̀ adìẹ.*
Irresistible compulsion, with which fire strips the scaly skin off a chicken's legs. (When the problem is unmanageable, even the toughest person hasn't a prayer.)

3972. *Túlàsì-í ní òun ó bàá ọ gbé, o ní kò sáàyè; góńgó imú ẹ ńkọ́?*
An unpreventable disaster says it will lodge with you, and you say you have no room for it; what about the tip of your nose? (Everybody can make room for disaster.)

W

3973. *"Wá jẹún" kúrò ní teégún.*
"Come and eat" is out of the question for a masquerader.[52] (Because of their natural limitations some people cannot hope to enjoy certain privileges.)

3974. *Wọ́n ní, "Adétẹ̀, o ò gbènì àkàrà." Ó ní wọn ò gbàdúrà pé kí tọwọ́ òun ba òun délé ná.*
They said, "Leper, won't you stop and receive your extra [gratuity of] fried bean fritters?" He responded by asking if they should not rather pray that what he already has in his hands will go home safely with him. (Covetousness can turn out to be a drain on one's resources.)

---

51. This is very likely a borrowing from the European proverb treasury.

52. The *eégún* masquerader cannot eat because he is completely covered and must not reveal his identity (his face) to the public.

3975. *Wọ́n ní, "Amúkùnún, èru ẹ́ mà wọ́ọ̀." Ó ní "Ìsàlẹ̀ ló ti wọ́ wá."*
People said, "Cripple, your load is crooked." He responded that the crookedness was from the ground up. (In considering a problem, one must look at the root causes, not only the manifestations.)

3976. *Wọ́n ní ká faró palé, a faró palé, ìtalẹ̀-ẹ́ tún ńjẹni; wọ́n ní ká fitọ̀ pajà a fitọ̀ pajà, jẹsèjẹsè-ẹ́ tún ńjẹ èèyàn.*
One is told to scrub one's floor with indigo dye; one scrubs the floor with indigo dye, yet mud-floor worms persist in biting one. One is told to wash the market stall with urine, and one washes the stall with urine, yet foot-eating worms continue to eat one. (All one's efforts to master a problem have proved futile.)

3977. *Wọ́n ní kí ni wọ́n sọnù, wọ́n ní ẹran; wọ́n ní kí ni wọ́n ńje, wọ́n ní eegun.*
When asked what they lost, they said meat; when asked what they were eating, they said bones. (In the face of misfortune, one makes do with what one has.)

Y

3978. *Yọyọ lẹnu ayé ńdà.*
The world runs endlessly at the mouth. (People can be relied upon to spread tales irresponsibly about others.)

On mortality

3979. *A kì í pé láyé ká má fi ilè bora.*
One does not live so long on this earth that one does not eventually cover oneself with earth. (Everybody dies in the end.)

3980. *A kì í sunkún a-nìkàn-para-è.*
One does not weep for a person who took his or her own life. (Do not pity anyone who invites disaster on his or her own head.)

3981. *Àgbà kì í subú yègè kó da ti ikùn-un rè sílè; ohun a bá je ní mbá ni ílo.*
An elderly person does not stumble and spill what is in his stomach; what one has eaten goes with one. (All that one will take to heaven is what one has eaten on this earth.[1] See 4834.)

3982. *Àìdé ikú là mbo Ògún; àìdé ikú là mbo òrìsà; bíkú bá dé ikú ò gbébo.*
It is when death has not called that one sacrifices to Ògún; it is when death has not called that one sacrifices to gods; when death comes calling, death does not heed sacrifices. (There is no medicine or sacrifice to stop death when its time comes. See also 3492.)

3983. *Àìsàn kan ò lè kó ogbòn ikú lo.*
One illness cannot bear thirty deaths away.

(One person's illness or death will not indemnify others against death.)

3984. *Ajá kú ó feegun sílé ayé; adìe funfun-ún kú ó tu ìhùùhù gbugbu; ìgbín kú ó gbàgbé ikaraun.*
The dog dies and leaves bones on earth; the white chicken dies and loses its down; the snail dies and forgets about its shell. (One cannot take anything with one to heaven.)

3985. *Ajogún-Ifá ní kí òun má kù-ú; eni tó kó tè é dà?*
He who inherited the Ifá priesthood prays that he not die; where is his predecessor as priest? (Everyone dies, willy-nilly.)

3986. *Ako ajá lólá; àgùàlà niyì osù.*
The male dog is glorious; the planet Venus is the glory of the moon. (One can tell who is illustrious from mere appearance.)

3987. *Aláwo á kú; onísègùn á ròrun; adáhunse ò níí gbélè.*
The diviner will die; the medicine man will go to heaven; the sorcerer will not remain forever on earth. (Death is the lot of everyone. Compare 3992.)

3988. *Àtàrí wo òrun momo bí enipé kò ní ibè-é rè; oye ojú tó wo ayé ni yó wo òrun.*
The skull stares at the sky as though it would not wind up there; every eye that looks upon the earth will also see heaven. (One cannot avoid one's destiny.)

---

1. Just as no one can take away what one has eaten, so one cannot take earthly possessions to heaven. In other words, one should enjoy this life while one has the chance.

3989. Àtèmákùú ò sí nÍfá.
Consulting-without-ever-dying is not a feature of Ifá oracle. (Even the priest of Ifá is not immune from dying.)

3990. Àtiwáyé ò dàbí àtiròrun.
Coming-to-earth is nothing like going-to-heaven. (Life is a pleasurable experience until one thinks of dying.)

3991. Àwáyé-àìkú ò sí; èrù lásán la fi ńdá ba ara-a wa.
There is no living without dying; we only scare ourselves [with death]. (Death is inevitable, and there is no point in dreading it.)

B

3992. Babaaláwo á ku; oníṣègùn á ròrun; adáunṣe ò níí gbélè.
The diviner will die; the medicine man will go to heaven; the sorcerer will not remain forever on earth. (Death comes to all in the end. This is the same as 3987.)

3993. Bí a bá dàgbà, tí a gbó, bó pé títí ojú á kájó.
If one lives long and grows old, in time one's eyes will encompass all. (Age is experience.)

3994. Bí a bá forí solè tí a kò kú, ohun tí a ó ṣe-é kù.
If one dives headfirst onto the ground and does not die, one must still have things to accomplish in life. (Providence has plans for one who fails in a suicide attempt.)

3995. Bí ikú bá dé, kò sí lóyà tó lè ṣojú eni.
When death comes, no lawyer can represent us. (We cannot hide from death behind well-wishers.)

Ẹ

3996. Ẹbọ-ọ́ le, kò ju òkú lọ.
The sacrifice is formidable; it is not worse than death. (No suffering extends beyond death.)[2]

3997. Ẹní féẹ́ rí òkú kó sùn; àtúnrarí dojú álá.
Whoever wants to see the dead should go to sleep; such encounters happen only in the realm of dreams. (Once people die, they cannot be seen again in this life.)

3998. Ẹni tó kú àti ẹni tó sọnù: wọ́n lè pàdé.
The dead person and the lost person: both could meet. (A person lost to his community is no different from a dead person.)

3999. Ẹni tó ó sùn-ún sàn ju ẹni tó kú lọ.
The sleeping person is better off than the dead person. (Conditions that superficially seem the same may in fact be very different; sleep is preferable to death.)

4000. Ẹrú kú ìyá ò gbọ́; ọmọ kú ariwó ta.
A slave dies, and the mother does not learn of the death; a freeborn dies, and lamentations erupt. (People are not all equal, nor are they valued equally.)

4001. Ẹṣín ta ta ta ó kú; èèyán rìn rìn rìn ó sọnù.
A horse kicks and kicks and kicks and dies; a person walks and walks and walks and gets lost. (The fate of humans, as of animals, is to keep striving until death.)

---

2. The proverb could also be construed to mean that no protective sacrifice can be more efficacious than the protection the dead can offer — this in keeping with the Yoruba belief that departed ancestors vigilantly protect those they have left behind.

Gb

4002. *Gbèsè nikú; kò séni tí kò níí pa.*
Death is a debt; there is no one it will not
kill. (Death is a debt everyone owes and
everyone must repay.)

I

4003. *Ìbí ò ju ìbí; bí a ti bí ẹru la ti bí ọmọ.*
No birth is worthier than another; just as the
slave was born, so was the scion born. (All
humans start out equal.)

4004. *Ìgbà mélòó làá fi ńkú? Àfi àìráyè
ṣàìsàn.*
How long does it take to die? The problem
is not having the time to be sick. (The good
thing about sudden disasters is that they are
not preceded by protracted anxieties.)

4005. *Igba ọ̀kẹ́ là ńra ẹ̀mí.*
The price one pays for life breath is 4 million
cowries. (Life is priceless.)[3]

4006. *Ikán ńjẹlé àgbà ńsọ; àgbà náà oúnjẹ
ikán.*
Termites eat up the house, and the old person complains; but the old man or woman
himself or herself is food for termites. (If a
certain fate awaits one, one should not make
futile efforts to protect others from it.)

4007. *Ikú lorúkọ àjẹ́pẹ̀kun.*
Death is the name one bears at the last.
(Death is everybody's ultimate fate.)

4008. *Ikú ńpa aláwọ ẹkùn, káláwọ agílíńtí ó
múra.*
Death kills the person clothed in leopard
skin; the person clothed in lizard skin had
better prepare himself or herself. (When the
mighty fall, lesser people should take heed.)

4009. *Ikú tí ńpa ojúgbà ẹni ńpòwe fúnni.*
The death that kills one's age mate is send-
ing one a message in proverbs. (One should
learn from others' fate. Compare the following entry.)

4010. *Ikú tó pa òwè ńpòwe fún ẹdun.*
The death that killed the black monkey
sends a proverbial message to the colobus
monkey. (What happened to a person in a
position similar to yours may well happen to
you. Compare the preceding entry.)

4011. *Ikú tóbi lóba; àrà tó wu ikú nikú ńda.*
Death is a mighty king indeed; whatever
it chooses to do, that it does. (There is no
force that can stop death.)

4012. *Ilé ayé, à-fọwọ́-bà-fi-sílẹ̀.*
This world [is] something to be handled
momentarily and then let go of. (All life is
ephemeral.)

4013. *Ilẹ̀-ẹ́ mọ́, ilẹ̀-ẹ́ ṣú, ọlójọ́ ńkà á.*
The day dawns, the day ends, and the owner
of days keeps count. (Time passes relent-
lessly on.)

4014. *Ìrù ẹsin kì í pẹ́ di ìrù èèyàn; bẹ́sín bá kú
a fìrù sílẹ̀ lọ.*
A horse's tail soon becomes a person's tail;
when a horse dies, it leaves its tail behind.
(Other people eventually inherit one's property.)[4]

---

3. Before the arrival of the British, 4 million cowries
represented wealth of almost unimaginable magnitude.
When a rate of conversion to British currency was imposed, that amount became a paltry £50 sterling, or
about $150.

---

4. Horses' tails are used as whisks, especially as part
of the ceremonial paraphernalia of kings.

4015. *Irun dúdú ní ńṣíwájú ewú.*
Black hair is the forerunner of white hair.
(Old age comes inexorably after youth.)

M

4016. *Má fọrun yọ̀ mí; gbogbo wa la jọ ńlọ.*
Do not taunt me with heading for heaven;
we will all end up there eventually. (The
living should remember that they will follow
the dead to heaven in the end.)

O

4017. *Ogbó ò lóògùn.*
Aging has no antidote. (We all grow old,
willy-nilly.)

4018. *Òjòjò kan ò lè ju tẹni tó kú.*
No illness can be more grave than that of the
person who died. (Some problems have no
equal.)

4019. *Ojúmọ́ mọ́ à ńyọ̀; ọjọ́ ikú ńdínkù.*
The day dawns and we rejoice; one's dying
day approaches closer. (Every new day
brings death closer.)

4020. *Òkú ńsunkún òkú; akáṣọléri ńsunkún
ara-a wọn.*
The dead are weeping for the dead; carriers
of cloth bundles are weeping for themselves
[and for one another].[5] (The survivor weeping for the dead soon dies himself or herself;
death takes everybody in the end.)

4021. *Olè ké-kè-ké ni wọ́n ńpè kúnlẹ̀; ta ní jẹ́
wí pé kí ọmọ Aríọrí ó wá sí gba-n-gba kó wá
wí tirẹ̀?*
Only small-time thieves are called to ac-

count on their knees; who dares summon
the son of Aríọrí to come out in the open
and render an account? (Small-time criminals alone are brought to book; the really
big criminals go scot-free.)[6]

4022. *Òní orí fífọ́; òla, ẹ̀dọ̀ rírìn; ìgbà wo ni
Mákùú ò níí kú?*
Today a headache, tomorrow a liver ailment;
how will Mákùú escape death? (A person
dogged by ailments will surely die, despite
all efforts to prevent that fate.)[7]

4023. *Òní, Òyèkúbàrà; òla, Òyèkúbàrà; nínú
ètè àtèrò nikú ńbáni.*
Today, a death-dodging strategy; tomorrow,
a death-dodging strategy; death comes even
as one finds ever more ways of dodging it.[8]
(Death comes to all, willy-nilly.)

4024. *Òwú là bá gbìn, a ò gbin idẹ; òwú là bá
gbìn, a ò gbìnlèkè; àtidẹ àtìlèkè, òkan kì í báni
dé hòrò òkú; ọjọ́ a bá kú aṣọ ní ńbani lọ.*
Cotton is what one should plant, not brass;
cotton is what one should plant, not beads;
as for brass and beads, neither goes with one
to the grave; on the day one dies, only cloth
accompanies one. (When we die, our jewelry
is of no use to us.)

Ọ

4025. *Ọjọ́ a bá kú là ńdère, èèyàn ò sunwọ̀n
láàyè.*
It is on the day one dies that one becomes
an idol; no one is appreciated when alive.

---

5. A woman mourner would roll up her headgear
and place it atop her head.

6. Aríọrí is obviously a historical figure and a
formidable criminal.

7. The name Mákùú means "Do not die."

8. The term *Òyèkú*, which heads a subchapter of
the Ifá divination corpus, means, roughly, "a means of
deflecting death." The ending *bàrà* expresses a mode of
dodging.

(People are often more glorious in death than in life.)

4026. *Ọrun ò dùn; ẹni tó kú ò padà wáyé.*
Heaven may turn out not to be a pleasant place, but the dead cannot come back to earth. (Once one is dead, one is done.)

P

4027. *Pá-ń-sá ilẹ̀-ẹ́ láriwo nínú; àjà-ilẹ̀-ẹ́ ba àgbà lẹ́rù.*
A tomb is attended by crying; a grave strikes terror into elderly people. (People are always sobered by reminders of their mortality.)

T

4028. *Tikú tikú là ńro àgbà; àgbà ní ńpète àìkú.*
People always look at aged people with death in their eyes; the aged are the ones who strive to stay alive. (Each person is the most reliable guardian of his or her own well-being.)

On inscrutability

4029. *A kì í kóni níkà bí a ò bá níká nínú; ta ní ńkóni ká ṣe rere?*
Nobody teaches one to be wicked if one does not have wickedness in one; whoever teaches one to be good? (Goodness and wickedness are not learned but are part of one's nature.)

4030. *A kì í mòràn mòràn ká mọ oyún ìgbín nínu ìkaraun.*
One is never so knowledgeable that one can detect the pregnancy of a snail in its shell. (Certain things are beyond the ken of even the wisest of people.)

4031. *A kí ìyàwó kò dáhùn; a fun ní tóró ó nawó.*
One greets the new bride, but she does not respond; one offers her three pence, and she extends her hand. (Minor inconveniences, or observance of form, will not rob one of one's judgment.)[1]

4032. *A mọ aláré, a mọ eléki; aláṣìsọ ló kù.*
The entertainer we know; the praise singer we know; the misspeaker is all that is left. (There is no doubt about the intentions of the entertainer and the praise singer, but there may be doubt about the intentions of a person whose utterances are offensive.)

4033. *A ní ká rójú jẹkọ òbùn, ó ńdá ẹkọ ẹ̀ kéré.*
One resolves to make an effort to buy and eat corn meal prepared by a filthy person, and the person skimps on the measure. (The person does not realize that her customers will be only too happy not to patronize her.)[2]

4034. *À ńjọ-ọ́ rìn, a kò mọ orí olówó.*
Though we might travel as a group, we do not know who is destined to prosper. (No one can tell who among a company is most likely to succeed.)

4035. *À ńrìn nílẹ̀ inú ṁbéléṣin; à ńfò lókè inú ṁbéléyẹ; à ńwọ àkísà inú ṁbáláṣọ; à ńjẹfó òsùn inú ṁbéléran.*
One walks on the ground, and the horse rider is angry; one flies in the air, and the bird keeper is angry; one wears rags, and the dealer in cloth is angry; one feeds on vegetables, and the meat seller is angry. (Whatever one does, one will incur some people's displeasure. Compare 3783.)

4036. *A ò mọ ẹsẹ̀ òsìkà lónà.*
One cannot tell who is wicked by his or her footprint. (By their deeds they shall be known.)

---

1. New brides are expected to demonstrate extreme diffidence on arrival at their new homes, but that does not prevent them from receiving gifts offered as part of the marriage festivities.

---

2. The use of the feminine gender here is deliberate because the trade in question is exclusive to women.

4037. A ṣe é lébù, o ṣe ìkòkò; a fún un ládìe sìn, ó pa iṣu síná.
He is given planting-yam pieces, and he prepares a cooking pot; he is given a chicken to raise, and he begins to cook yams. (Some people cannot be relied on.)[3]

4038. Abínú ẹní foore ṣegi nígbó; ó ní kẹranko mu jẹ.
He who wants no good for one does a favor for trees in the forest; he invites animals to share the favor. (Expect no favors from an enemy.)

4039. Àdán so orí kodò, ó ńwòṣe eyẹ gbogbo.
The bat hangs its head and contemplates the doings of birds. (The quiet person sees more than the loudmouth.)[4]

4040. Afiniṣe kì í jé ká fòun ṣe.
He-who-exploits-others never permits himself to be exploited. (The evil person is always on his guard.)

4041. Ahun ńmí; igbá ẹhìn-in rẹ̀ ni ò jé ká mò.
The tortoise breathes; only its shell conceals the fact. (Whatever appearances might be, no human is essentially different from another. Compare 3641.)

4042. Ahùwà-ìbàjé ṣe bí tòun là ńwí; aṣe-burúkú o kú ara fífun.
The person of evil character thinks he is the subject of discussion; the evildoer is plagued by suspiciousness. (Evil acts breed uneasy consciences.)

4043. Ara la mò, a ò mọ inú.
It is the body that one knows; one does not know what lies inside. (No one can see into the mind of another.)

4044. A-sáré-ṣá-ṣá-nínú-ègún ò sá lásán; bí kò lé nǹkan, nǹkan ńlé e.
One-who-runs-wildly-through-a-thorn-bush does not run for no reason; if he or she is not after something, something is after him or her. (A person who behaves in an unusual manner must have some reason.)

4045. Aṣòràn ní ńṣe aájò.
The guilty person is the one who commiserates. (The guilty person often tries to conceal his or her culpability by being the most solicitous.)

4046. A-ṣòràn-ìbàjé ṣe bí tòun là ńwí; a-ṣe-búburú o kú ara fífun.
The-person-who-has-done-something-bad thinks people are discussing him or her; evildoer, we acknowledge your guilty conscience. (A guilty conscience is an uneasy conscience.)

4047. Awọ féẹ́rẹ́ bo inú, kò jé ká rí ikùn aṣeni.
A thin skin covers the stomach and prevents one from seeing inside the evildoer. (One cannot tell friends from enemies simply by looking at them.)

4048. Ayé lòkun, èèyàn lòsà; a kì í mò-ọ́ wẹ̀ ká káyéjá.
The world is a sea, and the people in it are a lagoon; no matter how well one knows how to swim, one cannot swim the world. (The world and the people in it are as dangerous as the sea; no matter what one does, one cannot be entirely safe from them.)

---

3. The indication is that the recipient of the yam pieces and the chicken will put them to uses other than the ones the giver intended; such actions are inauspicious and suspicious.

4. The bat's habit of hanging upside down is here regarded as a contemplative pose.

B

4049. *Bí a bá gúnyán fún Kòníífẹ́, kò níí fẹ́; bí a bá rokà fún Kòníífẹ́, kò níí fẹ́.*
If one makes pounded yams for Kòníífẹ́ [meaning "He-will-not-like-it"], he will not like it; if one cooks yam-powder meal for Kòníífẹ́, he will not like it. (There is no pleasing a grouch.)

4050. *Bí a kò bá tẹ̀lé wèrè, a kì í mọ ilé tí yó wọ̀.*
Unless one follows an imbecile, one does not know which house he will enter. (There is no anticipating an unpredictable person.)

4051. *Bí alẹ́ yó ṣe rí, ọwọ́ ẹlẹ́dàà ló wà.*
What the evening of life will be like is in the hands of the Creator. (Only God knows how one's life will end.)

4052. *Bí aráyé bá ṣìkà tán, wọn a tún báni dárò.*
After people have acted wickedly, they then sympathize with their victims. (People are not to be trusted.)

4053. *Bí inú kò bá ní odì, odì a nínú.*
Even if one's mind harbors no enmity, one's enemy keeps one in mind. (You may harbor no ill will toward others, but others may harbor ill will toward you.)

4054. *Bí o ní iyùn, ní èjìgbà, tí o ní sègi pẹ̀lú, ata wẹ́ẹ́rẹ́ ni lójú abúni.*
If you have *iyùn* beads and have *èjìgbà* beads, even *iyùn* beads also, they are all like small peppers to the detractor. (Nothing one has or does impresses one's detractor.)

D

4055. *Dẹ̀ngẹ́ tutù lẹ́hìn, ó gbóná nínú.*
Maize porridge is cool on top but steaming

hot inside. (A person who appears docile may be a firebrand underneath.)

4056. *Dùlúmọ̀ ẹ̀pà lọ́rùn-un sèsé: ajẹbi-ọ̀ràn-wò tiiri.* *Sèsé* beans cause trouble for peanuts: the-guilty-one-that-wears-an-innocent-look. (The person who drags others into trouble is often adept at escaping the responsibility.)

E

4057. *Èéfín nìwà; kò ṣé-é bò mọ́ra.*
Character is smoke; one cannot conceal it under one's clothing. (Character will show.)

4058. *Eégún mọni, èèyàn ò mọ̀ ọ́.*
The masquerader knows one, but one does not know him. (A masquerader may recognize you, but you cannot recognize him, since he is under a shroud. The sage, or better-placed people, have the advantage over you.)[5]

4059. *Eèrà ò fẹ́ pòpóòrò dénú; kí-ń-kín-ní layé ńfẹni mọ.*
The ant harbors no deep love for the cornstalk; people love others only minimally.[6] (Never take people's professed love at face value.)

4060. *Èèyàn ìbá ṣe bí Ọlọ́run kò bunni lómi mu.*
Were man in the same position as God, he would not provide humans with water to drink. (Trust placed in human goodness is trust misplaced.)

---

5. This is usually a comment one makes to a person who recognizes one but whom one does not recognize; it says, in effect, "You have the advantage of me."

6. The ant's fondness for dry cornstalk is here assumed to be a profession of love, whereas it actually damages the host.

4061. *Èèyàn ńwojú; Olórun ńwọkàn.*
Human beings keep their gaze on the face;
God looks into the heart. (Human beings
can see only what a face reveals; only God
know what is in the heart.)

4062. *Èké ò pe ara-a rẹ̀ lórúkọ; ìkà ò pe ara-a rẹ̀ níkà.*
The devious person does not call himself or
herself devious; the wicked person does not
call himself or herself wicked. (Evil people
do not admit being evil.)

4063. *Èkúté ilé ò fibi àjà han ara wọn.*
House mice do not point the way to the
rafters to one another. (Each person for
himself or herself.)

4064. *Eléte ò pá a lójú ẹni; ẹ̀hìn ẹni là ńgbìmòràn ikà.*
Plotters do not hatch their plots in one's
presence; evil plots are hatched when the
victim is not about. (One is always in the
dark about one's enemies' machinations.)

Ẹ

4065. *Ẹni à bá ní kó kínni léhìn-ín fẹgún sọ́wọ́; ẹni à bá ní kó féni lójú fata sénu.*
The person one would ask to scratch one's
back fills his hand with thorns; the person
one would ask to blow into one's eyes fills
his mouth with pepper. (Those in whom one
would wish to place one's trust are not to be
trusted.)

4066. *Ẹni a fẹ́ la mọ̀; a ò mọ ẹni ó féni.*
We know only those we love; we know
not who loves us. (We know our disposition toward others, not their disposition
toward us.)

4067. *Ẹni a ní ká fẹhìntì ká mu dídùn ọsàn, kíkan ní ńka fúnni mu.*

The person one hoped to lean upon to eat
the sweetest of oranges plucks only sour
oranges for one to eat. (It is courting disappointment to place one's hope in other
people.)

4068. *Ẹní réjò ńsá; ejò ńsá.*
The person who sees a snake flees; the snake
also flees. (Two adversaries confront each
other, but neither has the will to make a
move.)

4069. *Ẹni tí a bá pète àti ra ẹṣin ní ńfẹ́ sọni di olóko ẹṣin.*
The person with whom one plans to buy a
horse is the same person scheming to trade
one for a horse. (Presumed friends may turn
out to be deadly enemies.)

4070. *Ẹni tó rí ojú ikún mọ̀ pé yó jẹ oko.*
Whoever looks at the face of the squirrel
will know that it will eat farm crops. (If one
studies people well, one can predict what
they are capable of.)

4071. *Ẹni tobìnrin ò kí lọ̀rẹ́-ẹ rẹ̀.*
It is the person a woman does not greet that
is her lover. (A woman's behavior toward a
man often belies her true feelings for him.)

4072. *Ẹnu èèyàn lẹbọ.*
People's mouths are the things to offer sacrifices to. (One need fear nothing as much as
what people say.)

4073. *Ẹnu kò jẹun kan mọ, tí yó sọ ọ̀rọ̀ kan mọ.*
The mouth is not limited to one type of
food or one type of speech. (One cannot be
certain of what the mouth will say; a tool
may be used for more than one task.)

4074. *Ẹsẹ̀ gìrì-gìrì nílé àńjòfẹ́; òfẹ́ tán, ẹsẹ̀-ẹ́ sì dá.*
Thundering footsteps in the home of free

gifts: the free gifts are all gone, and the foot-steps cease. (People will congregate around a person who has a lot to give but only as long as he or she has something left to give.)

Gb

4075. *Gbogbo aláǹgbá ló dakùn délè: a ò mọ èyí tí inú ǹrun.*
All lizards have their stomachs to the ground: no one knows which among them is suffering from stomachache.[7] (One cannot tell from looks alone the worries anyone is concealing behind a cheerful mien.)

4076. *Gbogbo lodì; bóo lówó odì, gbogbo lodì; bóò lówó odì.*
Everything can incite enmity: if you have money, you incite enmity; all things can in-cite enmity: if you lack money, you incite enmity. (There is no pleasing people; what-ever one is or does can earn one enemies.)

I

4077. *Ibi ajá la ti ńmọ oǹrorò àpón.*
It is from his treatment of his dog that one can tell which unmarried man will be a ter-ror to live with. (One can tell much about a person's character from how he or she acts with regard to seemingly inconsequential matters.)

4078. *Ibi tí Ng-ó-pa-á-gbé ńbẹ, ibè ni Ng-ó-gbà-á sì wà.*
Where one finds I-will-kill-him-for-sure, even there too will one find I-will-save-him. (Just as there are people who bear one ill will, so there are those who have good will toward one.)

4079. *Ibi tó sòro lójú eégun, àwọn-ón bò ó.*
The most problematic part of the masquer-ader's front [or face] is concealed behind a net.[8] (The most embarrasing part of a matter has so far remained unrevealed.)

4080. *Ìkà ò jé sẹ ọmọ è béè.*
The wicked would not treat his or her own child the same way [the way he or she treats the children of others]. (The wicked always protect their own interests.)

4081. *Ilé bo ilé lójú; òrùlé bo àjà mólè; awọ fééré bo inú kò jé ká ríkùn aṣeni.*
One house obscures another; the roof con-ceals the ceiling; a thin layer of skin covers the stomach, making it impossible to see inside the evildoer. (One cannot discern a person's character by simply looking. Compare 4097.)

4082. *Inú ìkòkò dúdú lèkọ funfún ti ńjáde.*
It is from the black pot that the white corn meal comes. (An evil person may sire a good person.)

4083. *Ìsòràn ni ìṣe aájò.*
The extent of one's culpability is the ex-tent of one's commiseration. (The person secretly responsible for a disaster is often the one who shows the greatest sympathy and concern.)

N

4084. *Ní ojó eré là ńjiyàn ohun.*
It is at play that one argues about weighty issues. (Playful arguments sometimes hide deadly serious disagreements.)

---

7. One of the ways to relieve stomachache is to lie on one's stomach.

8. The "net" is the visor that permits the masquer-ader to see yet not be recognized.

4085. *Òbírípo layé; ìmùlè̩ ò̩ré̩ a máa dòtá.*
Life is something that goes in cycles; sworn friends do become enemies. (There is no condition that cannot change.)

4086. *Odíde̩ré̩ kì í rí ojú atùkó.*
The parrot never sees the face of the person who plucks its tail feather. (One seldom knows the identity of one's enemies and detractors.)

4087. *Ohun tí a wá lo̩ si Ìparà, a ba ní párá.*
What one sought all the way to Ìparà one finds in the rafters; one's problem is solved.[9] (One sometimes expends unnecessary effort in the quest for things that one could have simply for the asking.)

4088. *Ojú onílá nilá s̩e n̄kó.*
It is in the presence of the okro planter that the fruits become fibrous. (The negligent person will watch as his or her affairs go to ruin.[10] Compare 4585 and 4586.)

4089. *Ojúbánire̩ ò dékùn e̩ni; as̩è̩hìndeni ò wó̩po̩; sàsà èèyàn ní n̄fé̩ni lé̩hìn bí a ò sí nílé; tajá te̩ran ní n̄fé̩ni lójú e̩ni.*
Outward expression of love does not come from within; people who will look after others' interests in their absence are few; only a few people love one when one is absent, though every dog and goat loves a person in his presence. (One cannot trust that those who love one in one's presence will love one when one is absent.)

4090. *Omi inú-u kàn-n̄-ga: kò s̩éé dúró mu, kò s̩éé be̩rè̩ mu.*
The water in a well: one cannot stand and reach it to drink, neither can one stoop to reach it. (Some problems are so difficult as almost to defy solution.)

4091. *Oníkùn ló mò̩kà; oníbàntè̩ ló moye òun-ún dì sí i.*
The owner of the stomach alone knows what wickedness lurks inside; the owner of the loin money pouch alone knows how much money she has tied up in it. (No one knows what secret lies buried inside other people. Compare the following variant.)

4092. *Oníkùn ló mò̩kà; ò̩jeun ló mo̩wó̩-ó̩ lá.*
Only the owner of the stomach knows how he will practice wickedness; only the person eating knows how to lick his fingers. (One should not from a position of ignorance attempt to second-guess a person who has all the information and the initiative. Compare the preceding entry.)

4093. *Onítìjú e̩ni lobìnrin e̩ni.*
The woman who is coy in one's presence is the one destined to be one's wife. (People's interractions in public often give away their private relationships.)

4094. *Orí as̩é̩gità-á lè yí bìrí kó di o̩ló̩rò̩.*
The fortune of the seller of firewood might suddenly change, and he or she might become prosperous. (Fortune is likely to change unexpectedly.)

4095. *Orí ò mo̩ ibùsùn; ì-bá mò̩ ó̩ a tún ilè̩ ibè̩ s̩e.*
The head does not know where it will eventually rest in sleep; had it known, it would have tidied up the place. (If one knew where one's destiny would lead, one would do whatever one could to cultivate the place.)

---

9. The proverb is based on the pun available from the repetition of the syllables *párá* in the name of the town, even though the accents differ. Ìparà is a Yoruba town.

10. Okro seeds if not harvested in time become fibrous and inedible.

4096. *Orúko méta là ńpèyàwó: Olórùn-lélé; Olá-yóko-sílè; Olá-bóko-lo.*
A new wife has three names: Olórùnlélé [She of the slender neck]; Oláyókosílè [She who sneaks off, leaving the husband behind]; Olábókolo [She who goes with her husband]. (One cannot predict the actions of a beautiful wife; she may sneak off with other men, but, again, she may remain faithful to her husband.)

4097. *Òrùlé bo àjà mólè; asó bo ese ìdí; awo fééré bonú kò jé ká ríkùn aseni.*
The roof covers the ceiling; the cloth covers the buttocks; a thin layer of skin covers the stomach and prevents one from seeing inside a wicked person. (Nobody knows what wickedness lurks inside others. Compare 4081.)

O

4098. *Òlàjà ò pò bí amújàwú.*
Quarrel settlers are not as plentiful as quarrel aggravators. (People are more likely to add to your troubles than help you end them.)

4099. *Omo aráyé le; wón lè di agbe kí wó ní ká má tèlè aró.*
Human beings are hardhearted; they may become tanager birds and decree that we must not tread on indigo-covered earth.[11] (People can be wicked and inconsiderate.)

4100. *Òpè òyìnbó fi dídùn sewà, ó fègún bora, oró inú è egbèje.*
The pineapple derives its beauty from sweetness; the wickednesses [dangerous spines on the leaves] it harbors number 1,400. (What is beautiful may be deadly also.)

4101. *Òsòòrò tó mú ajá: owó èko olúwa è ló dínkù.*
The dysentry that attacks a dog saves its owner the cost of providing corn meal for it. (Every misfortune has its positive aspect.)

P

4102. *"Pèlé" láko, ó lábo.*
"Take it easy" can be either masculine or feminine. (Even a greeting or word of caution can be said in either an aggressive or a placatory manner.)

4103. *Pòòkó nídìi, ó fihà jókòó.*
The coconut shell has a bottom but rests on its side. (Unconventional people will always do things differently.)

---

11. The vividly blue touraco is considered to have sole proprietary ownership of indigo dye.

On inequality

A

4104. *A gbọ́ pé ẹjọ́ ọmọdé jàre ná; ó ku ẹni ti yó bàá a wí i.*
Let us grant that the youth has a just claim, but who will press it for him? (The culture favors age over youth, even when youth is in the right.)

4105. *A gbọ́ tajá, a gbọ́ tẹran; èwo ni tàgùntàn lórí àga?*
A dog, yes, even a goat, yes; but who ever heard of a sheep sitting on a chair? (One can be flexible and grant exceptions to certain individuals from a prohibition, but there is a point beyond which one refuses to go. Compare 561.)

4106. *A gbọ́ ti elélùbọ́; èwo ni ti ọlọ́rùn-únlá?*
The seller of yam flour we know, but who ever heard of the seller of dried okra? (People will do well to know where they fit in the social hierarchy.)[1]

4107. *À ńjọ-ọ́ rìn, a kò jọ ara wa.*
Though we travel in the same group, we are not therefore alike. (Everybody in a group is unique.)

4108. *"À ńjù wọ́n" ò ṣéé wí léjọ́; ìjà ìlara ò tán bọ̀rọ̀.*
"We are driven by envy of them" is not a good case to make; a quarrel born of jealousy does not end easily. (Jealousy is a difficult motive to acknowledge.)

4109. *Ààfáà bọ̀rọ̀kìnní: bí Ọlọ́run ò bá ṣeni lágbà, a kì í fiyànjú ṣe bí àgbà.*
Wealthy, famous Muslim priest: if God has not made one an elder, one does not become one simply by striving. (The achievement of status is a gift from God. Certain things are out of human hands.)

4110. *Ààfáà-á jóná, ẹ̀ ńbèrè irùgbọ̀n; kí ló fa sábàbí?*
The Muslim priest is consumed in a fire, and you ask about his beard; what do you think was the cause of the problem? (When the mighty fall, it is idle to wonder what happened to lesser beings. This is a variant of 4846.)

4111. *Àáké wọ igbo, a gbọ́ òkìkí.*
The axe enters into a forest, and we hear reports of its doings. (When an illustrious person acts, his deeds are noised about.)

4112. *Áásìkí tí a fún ẹyẹ ọ̀sìn a ò fún igún; áásìkí ẹrú ò sí lọ́dọ̀ ọmọ.*
The regard that a domestic bird enjoys is denied the vulture; the regard a slave receives is not the same as a freeborn enjoys. (People are not uniformly fortunate.)

4113. *Àáyá ní ohun tí a bá mọ̀-ọ́ ṣe, bí ẹni ńṣeré ni; ó ni bí òun bá ńlọ lóko ẹpà, òkòòkan a máa bọ́ sí òun lẹ́nu.*

---

1. The seller of yam flour has some stature among traders; the seller of dried okro has no such status and should keep his or her peace in an assembly.

The colobus monkey says that one's specialty is like child's play; it says that when it walks through a peanut farm, peanuts continually pop into its mouth. (Some chores are ridiculously easy, sometimes even suspiciously easy, especially for the expert.)

4114. Àdá lẹnu tálákà; igbó la ó fi ṣán.
The poor person's mouth is a machete; its use is to clear the bush. (A poor person's voice carries no weight.)

4115. Àdàbà ò jẹpà; kanna-kánná ò jẹ sèsé.
The dove does not eat peanuts; the crow does not eat yam beans. (To each its dislikes.)

4116. A-dÍfá-bí-ẹní-ṁmùjè-ẹ́ dÍfá kò rí mu; Amùṣùà aya rè-ẹ́ ní òun ó fòjò wè.
He-who-consults-Ifá-as-though-he-were-drinking-blood consults Ifá but finds nothing to drink; his spendthrift wife says she will bathe in rainwater. (When even the mighty suffer deprivation, humble people aspire to plenty in vain.)[2]

4117. Afínjú ò dóko; òjòwú ò dígbèsè; òmú-murà ni yó bẹ́kọ-ọ rè dálè.
The preener does not go to the farm; the jealous woman does not get into debt; it is a woman with forbearance that finds a concubine for her husband. (Different people have different habits and qualities.)

4118. Àgún-ì-jẹ ní ṁpa ẹrú.
Pounding-[food]-without-partaking-of-it is the death of the slave. (The slave's labor is not unheard of, but he derives no benefit from it.)

4119. Àgbà létù; àlàárì lọba aṣọ.
The ẹtù cloth is the elder; the reddish dyed

cloth is the king of cloths. (There is a hierarchy even in the textile realm.)

4120. Agbára odó kò jọ agbára ìkòkò; bí a gbé odó kaná a jó; bí a sì gúnyán nínú ìkòkò a lu.
The strength of the mortar is not similar to the strength of the pot; if one places a mortar on the fire, it burns; if one pounds yams in a pot, it breaks. (To each his or her particular qualities.)

4121. Agbe ló laró; àlùkò ló losùn.
To the Blue Touraco belongs indigo dye; to the àlùko belongs camwood stain. (Each individual has his or her unique qualities.)[3]

4122. Àgbò méjì kì í mumi nínú-u koto kan.
Two rams cannot drink [at the same time] from the same water pot. (Two masters cannot coexist in the same household. Compare the following entry.)

4123. Àgbò méjì kì í pàdé lórí afárá.
Two rams will not meet on a narrow bridge. (Two contrary and uncompromising forces will never come to an accommodation. Compare the preceding entry.)

4124. Àìgùn kò ní àìdàgbà; gudugudu kì í sẹgbé-ẹ dùndún.
Deficiency in height is not deficiency in years; a gudugudu drum is no peer of a dùndún drum.[4] (A person's worth is a matter of substance, not of appearance.)

4125. Àìjẹunsùn àkàlàmàgbò, a ò lè fi wé ti àtíòro.
Àkàlàmàgbò's lack of supper is not compa-

---

2. There is obviously a drought—no time to bathe in rainwater, if any could be found.

3. As the touraco's blue color suggests the blue of indigo dye, àlùkò's purple suggests camwood stain.

4. The short gudugudu drum is used especially on state occasions, the longer dùndún on more popular occasions.

rable to that of àtíòro.[5] (A noble person's poverty is not the same as an ordinary person's. Compare this with the following five entries.)

4126. Àìjẹunsùn ẹkùn, a ò lè fi wé ti ajá.
The leopard's lack of supper is not comparable to that of the dog. (A powerful person's setback does not make him the equal of a nobody. Compare the preceding and the following four entries.)

4127. Àìlọ́ràá àkàlàmàgbò, a ò lè fi wé ti àtíòro.
The ground hornbill's lack of fat is not to be compared with that of the allied hornbill. (A renowned person's inconvenience does not make him the equal of a peon. Compare the preceding two and the following three entries.)

4128. Àìlọ́ràá ògòngò, a ò lè fi wé ti agílítí.
The ostrich's lack of fat is not to be compared with that of the lizard. (A rich person's lack of ready cash does not make him the equal of a poverty-stricken person. Compare the preceding three and following two entries.)

4129. Àìlówó Olówu, a ò lè fi wé ti asẹgità.
Olówu's poverty is not to be compared with that of the wood seller.[6] (An august person's inconvenience is not the same as a poverty-stricken person's. Compare the preceding four and the following entry.)

4130. Àìlówó Ọrúnmìlà, a ò lè fi wé ti Ẹlẹ́gbára.

Ọrúnmìlà's poverty is not to be compared with that of Ẹlẹ́gbára. (An illustrious person, however hard up, will still be better off than the nonentity. Compare the preceding five entries.)[7]

4131. Àìmọ̀ọ́jó là ńtàkìtì; ijó-ò mí ju àntọ bọ́.
It is deficiency as a dancer that induces one to somersault; my dancing goes beyond cartwheeling. (Overexertion betrays a lack of competence.)

4132. Àì-mọ-orín-ín-rùn kọ́ làsá fi pọ́n léhín; Ọlọ́run ló sẹdá-a rẹ̀ bẹ́ẹ̀.
It is not ignorance about how to clean the teeth that causes the kite's teeth [beak] to be red; God it was that created it so.[8] (One cannot help one's nature.)

4133. Àì-rí-oǹjẹ-jẹ ológbò kọ́ ni kò fi tó ajá.
It is not the cat's failure to find food that makes it smaller than a dog. (Great size is not a measure of one's striving.)

4134. Àjà ló lẹrù iró ni pẹpẹ ńpa.
To the rafter belongs the load; the shelf is a mere pretender. (Others may strive, but only certain special people have the means to carry out a task.)

4135. Àjànàkú kúrò léran à ńfajá dẹ.
The elephant is beyond the sort of animal one hunts with a dog. (One should not approach formidable tasks with levity.)

4136. Àjànàkú ló nìgbẹ́; iró ni gbogbo ẹranko ńpa.
To the elephant belongs the forest; all other animals are mere pretenders. (There is no disputing a person's preeminence. See also 276.)

---

5. Àkàlàmàgbò is the ground hornbill, a much more sprightly and resourceful bird than its cousin àtíòro (atíálá), the allied hornbill, which is sluggish and slow.

6. Olówu is one of the traditional crowned rulers of Yorubaland.

7. Note the similar import of entries 4125–4130.

8. The Yoruba refer to birds' beaks as teeth.

4137. *Àjẹkùlóko àgbẹ lọba ńjẹ lórí ìtẹ́.*
It is the leavings from the farmer's farm table that the king eats on his throne. (Each profession fills a unique need. See 738.)

4138. *Àjùlọ ò pin sọ́dọ̀ ẹnikan.*
Preeminence does not end with any one person. (No one has a corner on excellence.)

4139. *Ajunilọ́ lè juni nù.*
A person who is greater than one can do away with one.[9] (People are at the mercy of those greater than they are.)

4140. *Akàn-án ní òún dúpẹ́ àìlórí; gbogbo ẹní lórí lorí ńfọ́.*
The crab says it gives thanks that it lacks a head, for whoever has a head also suffers headaches. (There is no adversity without its positive aspect.)

4141. *Akíkanjú wọgbó, o sọ̀wò igba ẹ̀ẹyàn.*
An illustrious person enters the forest and does enough trade for two hundred people. (One illustrious person accomplishes enough for many ordinary people.)

4142. *Akíni-kúusẹ́ ńjiyán yó; apòyì-kábà ńyá iwòfà; olóko ńpa ẹgbàa-gbèẹdógún kó tó jẹun.*
The person who greets one while one is working eats pounded yams to his fill; the person who perambulates around the hut employs a pawn; the farmer himself must earn 15,000 cowries before he can eat. (Idlers and hangers-on have the easiest of times, whereas a person working for his living must eat of his sweat.)

4143. *Àkókó kun osùn ó kun orí; arèré kun osùn ó kun àyà; olóbùró kun osùn ó kun òfun.*
The woodpecker takes camwood and stains its head; the custard-apple tree takes camwood and stains its breast; *olóbùró* takes camwood and stains its throat. (Each has a different notion of self-adornment.)

4144. *Àkùkọ ńlá ò jẹ́ kí kékeré ó kọ.*
The big rooster prevents the small rooster from crowing. (Those in authority prevent their subordinates from asserting themselves.)

4145. *Àkùkọ́ tó lógbe ò ní ìreré; èyí tó ní ìreré ò ní ògàn.*
The cock that has a comb lacks tail plumes; the one that has tail plumes lacks spurs. (Every person has his or her failings.)

4146. *Alágìdí lògá alákàrà.*
The seller of corn-meal loaf is the master of the seller of bean-fritter cakes.[10] (The person who has what one cannot do without has some control over one.)

4147. *Aláńgbá jọ ònì, agbára wọn ló yàtọ̀.*
The lizard resembles the crocodile; it is their strength that is different. (Look-alikes are not necessarily equals.)

4148. *Àlùkẹ́ḿbù, baba asa.*
Stirrup, father of the saddle. (The stirrup is more important than the saddle.)

4149. *Àlùmọ́nì méjì kì í gbé ọwọ́ ẹnikan.*
Two treasures will not reside with one person. (A person cannot have everything.)

4150. *Apá ọmọdé ò ká oyè-e bàrà.*
A youth's resources are not adequate for the chieftaincy of the royal mausoleum. (A

---

9. The proverb plays on the word *jù:* in combination with *lọ* (literally "go"; in this instance "pass") it would by itself mean "surpass," the combination meaning "surpass completely"; in combination with *nù* (literally "off") it would by itself mean "throw," the combination meaning "lose."

---

10. *Àkàrà* is a desirable accompaniment for *àgìdí.*

youth cannot take on the responsibilities of an elder.)[11]

4151. *Àparò ò ṣàìmọ ibi tí lékèé-lékèé ti ńfọṣọ; Olórun ni ò ṣe àparò láláṣọ-mímọ́.*
The partridge is not ignorant of the place where the egret washes its clothes; it is only that God did not wish the partridge to have clean clothes.[12] (Nothing one can do will alter one's nature.)

4152. *Àpón sàn ju òkóbó; bó pé títí àpón yó fẹ́ẹ́ obìnrin.*
A bachelor is better off than a eunuch; sooner or later a bachelor will take a wife. (Some ills are better than others.)

4153. *Aró ḿbẹ lÓṣogbo; àtàtà èèyàn ḿbẹ nÍbàdàn.*
There is indigo dye aplenty at Òṣogbo; there are numerous illustrious people in Ibadan. (Certain qualities are synonymous with certain places.)

4154. *Àrùn mììràn-án kù lẹ́hìn-in wárápá; wárápá nìkan kọ́ ní ńgbéni sánlẹ̀.*
There are other diseases besides epilepsy; it is not only epilepsy that knocks people to the floor. (Nothing and no one can claim to be the ultimate in any regard.)

4155. *Àrùn òtòṣì ní ńsàn lóòjó; tolówó a máa sàn díẹ̀-díẹ̀.*
It is a poor person's disease that is cured in a day; a rich person's disease mends only gradually. (Protracted illness is too great a luxury for a poor person to afford.)

4156. *Àrùn tí ńṣe aláárùn-ún ò ṣe eléèta.*
The disease that attacks the person with five does not attack the person with three. (Each person with his or her own problems.)

4157. *Àrùn tí ńṣòbọ ò ṣegún: igún pá lórí; òbọ hùrù.*
The disease that afflicts the monkey does not afflict the vulture: the vulture is bald on its head; the monkey grows a tail. (Different people, different aches. See also the next entry.)

4158. *Àrùn tí ńṣòbọ ò ṣegún: igún pá lórí; òbọ pá nídìí.*
The disease that afflicts the monkey does not afflict the vulture: the vulture is bald on its head; the monkey is bald on its buttocks. (Different problems for different people. This is a variant of the preceding entry.)

4159. *Àsísorí ò ní ikùn bí àgbá; òtòṣì ò lówó bí olórò.*
A pistol does not have a bore like a cannon's; a poor person does not have the money of a wealthy person. (There is no equality in people's fortunes.)

4160. *Aṣọ abilà gbogbo ló lórúkọ.*
Every striped cloth has a name. (Every person has a name; an offender has a name to be mentioned.)

4161. *Àti kékeré àjànàkú leerin-ín ti pọ̀ ju efòn lo.*
It is from childhood that the elephant was greater than the buffalo. (Regardless of age, an elephant is greater than a buffalo.)

4162. *Àti ogún ọdún tí èkọ́ ti ńlo aṣọ, ìhòòhò làkàrà-á wà.*
In the twenty years that the corn meal has been wearing clothes, the bean fritters have

---

11. *Bàrà* is the royal mausoleum of Òyó kings, and important coronation ceremonies take place there.

12. This is a response to the proverb *Ibi tí lékèélékèé ti ńfọṣọ, Olórun ò fi ibẹ̀ han ọmọ àparò* ("The place where the egret washes its clothes, God has kept hidden from the clan of partridges").

always been naked.[13] (One's better standing than one's rival's is not a recent development.)

4163. *Àwa ara wa la ríra-a wa: ológìnní rí ọmọ ẹkùn.*
All of us assembled here are of a type; the cat comes face to face with the offspring of the leopard. (When equals come together, none has anything to fear from any other.)

4164. *Àwòròsàsà ní ńjẹ ajá Ògún.*
Only the most powerful of priests eats dogs sacrificed to Ògún. (Only a select few can perform formidable tasks.)

B

4165. *Bákan-náà lomọ ńsorí léhìn ìyá-a rẹ̀.*
Babies' heads lie the same way on their mothers' backs. (Natural habits die hard. Also, one baby is no different from another baby.)

4166. *Bí a bá bi àgbà tó kúrú mọ́lẹ̀, yóò rí wí.*
If one asks the elder that is short and close to the ground, he will have something to say. (There is always an explanation for a person's condition, if we will only ask.)

4167. *Bí alákẹdun-ún bá rò, tó fọwọ́ sẹ́; agbọn la ó fi kó ọmọ òwè níbẹ̀.*
If the colobus monkey breaks its arm while suspended from a tree, it is by the basketful that black monkeys will be scooped off the place. (When an expert comes to grief doing something, novices will fail at it in their hundreds.)

4168. *Bí ehoro ò lè sáré bí ìgalà, bìí ká fi wé ti ìjàpá kọ́.*
If a rabbit cannot run as fast as the deer, that does not make it comparable to a tortoise. (One's worth depends on the standard by which one is judged.)

4169. *Bí igún ti ní ìlasa, bẹ̀ẹ̀ ni àwòdí sì ní bòbo.*
As the vulture has okro leaves, so the hawk has *bòbo* leaves.[14] (Each person has his or her assets.)

4170. *Bí igbá bá wọ odò a lé té-ń-té.*
If a calabash falls into the stream, it floats on top. (Nothing can prevent the illustrious person from shining.)

4171. *Bí inú ti ńbí àjànàkú, bẹ̀ẹ̀ ní ńbí eèrà.*
Just as the elephant may be angered, so an ant may be angered. (Even the least of people has feelings.)

4172. *Bí iyán ti ńfún lóko ẹgàn, bẹ̀ẹ̀ náà ní ńfún ní ti etílé.*
As pounded yam is white on a farm deep in the forest, so it is white on the farm near the town. (A commodity does not change its nature according to its location.)

4173. *Bí lékèélékèé ò bá rómi wẹ̀, a dẹgbé àparò.*
If the egret cannot find water to bathe in, it becomes like the partridge. (When a great person loses his resources, he becomes like ordinary people.)

4174. *Bí Olúgbọ́n ti gbọ́n, bẹ̀ẹ̀ ni Arẹsà-á gbọ́n pèlú.*
As the *Olúgbọ́n* is clever, so also is the *Arẹsà*

---

13. Corn meal is wrapped in leaves, whereas bean fritters are not wrapped.

14. The plant *Solanium duplosinuatum* is known as *bòbo àwòdì; àwòdì* means "hawk."

clever.[15] (Each person is wise in his or her
own way.)

4175. *Bó ti ṁbẹ lára adẹ́bọ, bẹ́ẹ̀ ní ṁbẹ lára
a-dá-má-rùú.*
As it is with the person who offers a sacrifice, so it is with the person who refuses
to make a sacrifice. (Each person makes
his or her own choice and also bears the
consequences.)

4176. *Bó ti wà ní Líkí, bẹ́ẹ̀ ní ṁbẹ ní Gbà-ǹ-
ja.*
As it is in Líkí, so it is in Gbàǹja. (Matters
are fundamentally the same everywhere.)

4177. *Bó ti wá ni yó lọ; ọ̀gbẹ̀rì ò jẹ iyán odù.*
As he came, so will he depart; the uninitiated person will not eat the pounded yams
of Ifá. (An outsider will not be included in
the benefits of exclusive groups.)

4178. *Bọ́mọdé bá ní okun tó ọ̀bọ, kò lè ní
gẹlẹ̀tẹ̀ àyà-a rẹ̀.*
Even though a youth has as much strength
as a monkey, he cannot have a chest as huge
as the monkey's. (A person who is a match
for another in one regard may be deficient in
others.)

4179. *Bọ̀rọkìnní ba ọlọ́rọ̀ nínú jẹ́.*
The person of exemplary character angers
the rich person. (People do not admire those
who steal the show from them.)

4180. *Bọ̀rọkìnní ìletò ni akéde ìlú ńlá.*
The celebrated dandy in the village is a street
crier in a large town. (When people are few,
anybody may be important. Compare 4184.)

D

4181. *Dágunró yàtọ̀ sí tẹ̀tẹ̀, kò ṣéé jẹ.*
Star-burr is different from spinach; it is inedible.[16] (A thing may resemble another and
yet lack its good qualities.)

4182. *Dúdú lẹ̀gbón, pupa làbúrò.*
Black is the elder; light brown is the younger.
(A dark complexion is more desirable than a
light one.)

E

4183. *Erèé òtòṣì lọlọ́rọ̀-ọ́ fi ńṣe èkuru jẹ.*
It is of the poor person's beans that the rich
man makes bean meal to eat. (The rich will
take from the poor the little they have.)

4184. *Erin ibòmín-ìn, èlírí ibomín-ìn.*
An elephant in one place; a tiny mouse in
another. (What people make much of in one
place is of no account in another. Compare
4180.)

4185. *Erín ńtú eruku; ẹfọn ńtú eruku; títú
eruku àjànàkú bo tẹfọn mọ́lẹ̀.*
The elephant raises a cloud of dust; the buffalo raises a cloud of dust; the elephant's
ability to raise dust far surpasses the buffalo's. (Certain people or things are beyond
all competition.)

4186. *Erin-ín wó wọ́n fiwo-o rẹ̀ gbẹ́ ike; ẹfọn-
ọ́n wó wọ́n fiwo-o rẹ̀ tẹ poolo; àgbá-ǹ-réré wó
wọ́n fiwo-o rẹ̀ kùn lósùn rúbú-rúbú.*
An elephant dies, and its tusks are carved
into ivory; a buffalo dies, and its horns are
made into a *poolo;*[17] an antelope dies, and its

---

15. The identity of Olúgbón is unclear. Arẹsà is the
title of the king of Ìrẹsà (two towns are so named in
Yorubaland).

16. Star-burr is *Acanthospermum hispidum* (see
Abraham 123).

17. Supposedly a representative image of Poolo,

horns are anointed with camwood. (Some people are more fortunate than others.)

4187. *Eṣinṣín kọ ikú àpabérí; yànmù-yánmú kọ ikú àpalàdọ̀.*
The fly is immune to death by beheading; the mosquito is immune to death caused by the splitting of the liver. (Some fates are impossible for some people or things.)

4188. *Èsúó ti ńlògbà kéwúrẹ́ tó dáyé.*
The red-flanked ducker was already enjoying life before the goat came into being. (A person or thing was already long established before the upstart came about.)

4189. *Ewé ńlá kì í rú wéwẹ́.*
Large leaves do not sprout small. (A person destined to be great will not fail to be great.)

4190. *Èwo ni kò tó "Hì hì" lára ìnàkí?*
What baboon is incapable of sounding "Hee hee"? (Certain things are within the capability of everyone.)

4191. *Ewúrẹ́ ilé ò mọdẹ; ìbá ṣàgbọ̀nrín a gbọfà léhìn ṣan-ṣan.*
The domesticated goat has no regard for the hunter; were it a deer it would sport arrows prominently on its back. (As the domestic goat's protected status makes it misbehave when a hunter is around, so a sheltered person gets away with much that less fortunate people dare not attempt.)

Ẹ

4192. *Èfúùfù-ú gbé ológìì lọ; oníyẹ̀fun ni ẹgbè yán-yán.*
The wind blows away the corn-gruel seller;

the seller of corn powder is hopelessly doomed. (When illustrious ones fall, lesser people have no hope.)

4193. *Ègún ò gún ọmọ lẹ́sẹ̀ ká yọ ọ́ lẹ́sẹ̀ ẹrú.*
When a thorn lodges in the foot of a child, one does not remove it from a slave's foot. (However privileged one might be, there are certain things one must do oneself.)

4194. *Egbàafà-á tóó pè ní igbá Ifá.*
Twelve thousand cowries are enough to be called an Ifá divination calabash. (Two things or people are of a kind.)[18]

4195. *Ẹgbẹ́ erin ò wọ́n lÁlò.*
The equal of an elephant is not difficult to find in Álò. (There is little difficulty in finding a substitute for a common thing or an ordinary person.)

4196. *Ẹgbẹ́ iṣu kọ́ niyán.*
The pounded yam is not the equal of the yam. (A refined product is superior to the raw version.)

4197. *Ẹgbẹ̀rún ibalùwẹ̀ ò lè tó sánmà.*
A thousand bath enclosures are no equal for the sky.[19] (Possession of a tiny amount of a substance does not make one an equal of the person who controls its supply.)

4198. *Ẹgbẹ̀rún ìràwọ̀ ò lè mọ́lẹ̀ tó òṣùpá.*
A thousand stars cannot give as much light as the moon. (One cannot exceed one's possibilities.)

---

18. The proverb's effect derives from the similarity in sounds of *ẹgbàafà* and *igbá Ifá*. Besides, 12,000 cowries signifies a considerable sum in pre–European Yoruba currency, enough to purchase the expensive divination calabash.

19. The proverb apparently compares the amount of moisture available in the two.

---

believed to be a cave-dwelling, witch-executing demon (see Abraham 556).

4199. Ẹké òtòṣì kì í tó ilé lówùúrò.
The poor person's forked pole never touches
the house in the morning. (A poor person's
counsel is never welcome in the early stages
of deliberation.)[20]

4200. Elésin-ín ṣe oògùn ejò tán: elésin-ín wà
lókè, ejò-ó wà nílè.
The horse rider has the surest antidote for
snakebite: the rider is up above; the snake is
on the ground. (A person beyond the reach
of his or her adversary need not fear the
adversary.)

4201. Eni a lè mú là nlèdí mó.
It is against a person one can handle that
one is aggressive. (One usually picks a fight
only when one is sure of victory.[21] Compare
1522.)

4202. Ẹní Abá ò tọ́ bí ẹní òré; ẹní abá ò ṣéé
ká; rírún ní nrún wómú-wómu.
Abá mat does not last as long as òré mat; the
former cannot be folded, as it disintegrates
completely in the attempt. (Some things are
better and more desirable than others.)

4203. Ẹní bá pa àfè ìmòjò kó mú-u re Òyó;
edá lará oko nje.
Whoever kills a spotted grass mouse should
take it to Òyó; the brown bush rat is good
enough food for a bush person. (Only certain people can appreciate, and therefore
deserve, the choicest prizes.)

4204. Ẹní jẹ Olúwo, ká yìn ín; sàṣà èèyàn ló lè
jẹ Bara.
Whoever takes the title Olùwo deserves

commendation; few people can take the
Bara title.[22] (Whoever has performed an
extraordinary feat deserves people's recognition and praise.)

4205. Ẹní jù ló máa gbéra mì nínú ajá àti
òkéré.
The more formidable will triumph over the
other in a contest between the dog and the
squirrel. (The weakling will not triumph
over the powerful person.)

4206. Ẹní lágbára juni ní nfi ọwọ́ ẹni gbáni
lénu.
Only a stronger person can use one's own
hand to slap one in the mouth. (Only those
who have authority over you can make you
act against your own interest, or injure you
and add insult to the injury.)

4207. Ẹní lọ́wọ́ rere ò róbìrin fi pa lára.
The person who has worthy hands can
find no woman to caress. (People with the
best endowments have nothing to show for
them.)[23]

4208. Eni nlá ní nṣe ohun nlá; Àjànàkú pa
erin bọ Ifá.
Only a mighty person can perform mighty
deeds; Àjànàkú killed an elephant as an
offering to the Ifá oracle.[24] (Only the mighty
can perform mighty deeds. Compare the
following entry.)

---

20. The idea is that people have brought forked
poles to contribute to the effort of building a house;
what the poor person brought will have to wait until
what the rich brought has been used up.

21. Often addressed to a person to whom one would
say, "Why not pick on someone your own size?"

22. Olúwo (Olú awo) is one of the the two highest
Ògbóni titles; Bara is a high Ifá title.

23. We are to understand the omitted words "let
alone those with no endowments to speak of."

24. This is an example of a binary proverb, comprising the proverb proper plus the explanation or an
illustration of its usage. As a whole the second part
becomes the analogy for the occasion or context. There
is also some play involved: Àjànàkú is a proper name
but also a designation (primarily honorific) for the
elephant.

4209. Ẹni ńlá ní ńṣe ohun ńlá, baálẹ̀-ẹ Jìnìbà: ó gbé àká mì, ó fọmọrí odó tayín.
Only the mighty can perform mighty deeds; so it was for the chief of Jìnìbà: he swallowed a whole granary and picked his teeth with a pestle. (From an eccentric person one can expect anything. This is a variant of the preceding proverb, with the exception that in this case the application is ironic. The deed referenced is not to be admired but perhaps to be amazed by. Compare the preceding entry.)

4210. Ẹni tí a ò tó là ńgàn; agánrán ńgan ọdẹ.
People disparage only those worthier than themselves; the parrot disparages the hunter. (Disparagement is an indication of helpless envy; the parrot's only weapon against the hunter is ineffectual disparagement.)

4211. Ẹni tí ńkun osùn ò dàbí ẹni tí ńkun ata.
The person rubbing himself or herself with camwood does not compare with the person rubbing himself or herself with hot pepper. (Things may look alike without being the same.)

4212. Ẹni tó gbọ́ Ifá ò mọ Ọ̀fà; ẹni tó mọ Ọ̀fà ò gbọ́Fá, bẹ̀ẹ̀ ni Ifá tà lỌ́fà.
The person versed in Ifá does not know the way to Ọ̀fà; the person who knows the way to Ọfà is ignorant of Ifá; and yet knowledge of Ifá is lucrative at Ọfà.[25] (The talent and the opportunity are available, but they are mismatched; nobody has everything.)

4213. Ẹni tó ní àgbàdo ò léhín; ẹni tó léhín ò lágbàdo.
The person who has corn has no teeth; the person who has teeth has no corn. (Need

and supply are often mismatched. Compare the following three entries.)

4214. Ẹni tó ní ẹẹ̀wàá ò níwà; ẹni tí ó níwà ò ní ẹẹ́wàá.[26]
The person who has good character does not have 10 cowries; the person who has 10 cowries does not have good character. (Character and means seldom go together. Compare the preceding and the following two entries.)

4215. Ẹni tó ní èjìká ò léwù; ẹni tó léwù ò léjìká.
The person who has a shoulder has no garment; the one who has a garment has no shoulder. (Need and supply are often mismatched. Compare the preceding two and the following entries.)

4216. Ẹni tó ní orí ò ní fìlà; ẹni tó ní fìlà ò lórí.
The person who has a head has no hat; the person who has a hat has no head. (Need and fortune are often mismatched. Compare the preceding three entries.)

4217. Ẹni tó wà láyé ní inú òun-ún bàjẹ́; ẹni tó ti kú ńkọ́?
The person who is alive says he or she is sad; what about the person who is dead? (As long as one has life, one should consider oneself fortunate.)

4218. Ẹni tó wáyé ò tó asinniwáyé.
People who came to the world are far fewer than people who came as companions. (There are fewer people with a purpose than people without a purpose.)

4219. Ẹnu àgbà lobì ńgbó.
It is only in the mouth of the elder that the

---

25. The proverb obviously gains much from the play on Ifá, the Yoruba divination system, and Ọ̀fà, a northern Yoruba town.

26. Part of the charm of the proverb is its play on ìwà and ẹẹ́wàá.

kola nut is ripe. (The last say in a matter belongs to the elder who is present.)

4220. Ẹranko bí ọ̀bọ ò sí lóko, àfi ìjímèrè tí ńpe ara-a rẹ̀ ní olóògùn.
There is no animal in the bush like the monkey, except for the brown (Pataguenon) monkey calling itself a medicine man. (Nobody can vie with a certain person; those who try deceive themselves.)[27]

4221. Ẹranko tó gbọ́n bí ajá ò sí, èyí tó wèrè bí ẹsin ò wọ́pọ̀; ajá bímọ-ọ rẹ̀ sílẹ̀ ó ńlọ ki ọmọ èkùlù mólẹ̀; ẹsín bímọ tirẹ̀ sílẹ̀ ó ńfi èhìn pọn ọmọ elòmíràn re oko.
Animals as wise as the dog are nonexistent; those as stupid as the horse are rare; the dog gives birth to its children but goes and pounces on the children of the crested duiker; the horse gives birth to its own children but carries others' children on its back to the farm. (The wise put their own interests before all else.)

4222. Ẹrù tí onígẹ̀gẹ̀ẹ́ rù tí ó ńṣomilójú, abuké kọ́ ni yó pàǹtète-e rẹ̀.
The load that draws tears from the eyes of the carrier with a goiter is not one for the humpback to carry nonchalantly, with arms swinging freely. (A burden that prostrates a formidable person is not one for a spineless person to tackle lightly.)

4223. Ẹ̀rúkọ́ lórí; kò ní mùndùn-múndùn.
The hoe shaft has a head but no marrow. (One cannot get something from where there is nothing, just as one cannot get marrow from a skull.)

4224. Ẹyẹlé kì í ní àgògo, kìkì àrupẹ̀.
Pigeons never grow to giant size; they are all dwarfish. (There is no rank distinction among a certain group of people.[28] Compare 3302.)

G

4225. Gagalo-ó ṣíṣẹ̀ méjì, ó bá ará iwájú.
The stilt walker takes only two steps, and he catches up with those who had long gone ahead. (The person referred to has extraordinary capabilities, surpassing all others.)

4226. Gégé ṣe gégé; onígẹ̀gẹ̀ tó fẹ́ atiro.
Two well-matched things have come together: a person with a goiter has married a cripple. (Two or more people are both, or all, all of a kind.)

4227. Gèlè ò dùn bíi ká mọ̀ọ́ wé; ká mọ̀ọ́ wé ò dùn bíi kó yẹni.
Head scarf is no good if one does not know how to tie it; knowing how to tie it is no use if it does not look good on one. (Having an asset is not as important as knowing how to use it; knowing how to use it is not as important as knowing how to use it profitably. Compare the following two variants and 4988.)

4228. Gèlè ò dùn bíi ká mọ̀ọ́ wé; ká rówó ra eléyàá ò dàbíi kó yẹni.
Head scarf is no good unless one knows how to tie it; having money to afford Ẹléyàá cloth is no good if it does not look good on one. (This is a variant of the preceding and following entries.)

4229. Gèlè ò dùn bíi ká mọ̀ọ́ wé; oúnjẹ ò dùn bíi ká mọ̀ọ́ jẹ.
Head scarf is no good if one does not know how to tie it; food is no good if it is some-

---

27. Ìjímèrè, a small brown (Pataguenon) monkey, is considered a clown among the species.

28. This proverb is sometimes used to order someone to prostrate himself before the speaker as a mark of respect.

thing one does not eat. (This is a variant of the preceding two entries.)

Gb

4230. *Gbajúmò-ó ju owó lọ; àyà níní ju oògùn lótò.*
Popularity is better than money; bravery is far better than magical charms. (Better fame than riches; better fortitude than magic.)

4231. *Gbogbo ọdún ni tọba; gbogbo èsìn ni tìjòyè.*
All festivals belongs to the king; all weekly worship belong to the chief. (The more important one's stature, the more important one's responsibility.)

4232. *Gbo-gbọ-gbọ lọwọ́ ńyọ ju orí.*
Loftily, loftily, loftily the raised hand reaches above the head. (The person blessed with extraordinary qualities will always stand out in a group.)

I

4233. *Ibi tí àjànàkú ti fi ẹsẹ̀ tẹlẹ̀ ni gbogbo ẹrankó ti ńmu.*
Where the elephant once planted its foot, there the rest of the animals come to drink. (The feats of the mighty bestow some boon on the humble. Compare the variant at 4244.)

4234. *Ibi tí lékèélékèé ti ńfọsọ, Ọlọ́run ò fi han ọmọ àparò.*
The place where the cattle egret washes its clothes has not been revealed by God to the partridge.[29] (The secret of some people's suc-

cess is fortunately not common knowledge to all.)

4235. *Igi gbogbo ní ńso owó, òtò ni tobì.*
All trees grow money, but the kola-nut tree surpasses all others.[30] (Among illustrious people, some will still stand out.)

4236. *Ìgún iyán ò jọ ti èlùbọ́; mímú niyán ńmú, kíki lèlùbọ́ ńki.*
The consistency of pounded yam is different from that of yam-flower meal; pounded yam is smooth, while yam-flower meal is elastic. (Each thing or person is good in a different way.)

4237. *Ìgbà tí ajá ti ńṣe ilé, ọbọ ò ì tíì ti oko bọ.*
The dog was master of the home long before the monkey came from the farm. (The upstart or Johnny-just-come must not be garrulous in the presence of well-established old-timers.)[31]

4238. *Ìgbà tí ìkẹtẹ́ òì tíì dáyé, oníbgó ti ńjẹ ìkẹtẹ́.*
Long before the thick sediment of the palm oil came to earth, the lord of the forest had been eating it.[32] (Said to claim that one does not need another person's favors but had always gotten along very well without that person's help. Compare the following entry.)

4239. *Ìgbà tí ìsín òì dódò, Oníbarà-á ti ńjeja.*
Long before the minnows showed up in the stream, the king of Ìbarà [a riverside quarter

29. The egret is spotless white, whereas the partridge seems always dirty.

30. Kola nuts are considered such a valuable commodity that no other tree can compare to the kola-nut tree.

31. Dogs were pets long before anybody thought of monkeys as such.

32. *Ìkẹtẹ́*, the thick sediment left in the process of making palm oil, is something of a delicacy; but before people began to make palm oil out of the fruits of the palm, the fruits had been rotting in the forest, making, in effect, *ìkẹtẹ́* for the spirits of the forest.

of Abẹ́òkúta] had been eating fish. (Said to assert that one got along very well without help from another and does not need that person's aid. Compare the preceding entry.)

4240. Ìgbín ò dùn, kò ṣéé fi wé pọ̀nmọ́.
The snail is not delicious; it cannot be compared to boiled cow hide. (Some foods are more delicious than others.)

4241. Igbó biribiri, òkùkùn biribiri; òkùkùn ni ó ṣẹ̀tẹ́ igbó.
The forest is as dark as ever, and the night is as dark as ever, but the darkness of the night puts that of the forest to shame. (Greatness is not without gradation.)

4242. Ìka ò dọ́gba.
The fingers are not equal. (People are not equally endowed.)

4243. Ilé Ifẹ̀ ló ladé; fìlà ni ti baálẹ̀ ibòmíràn.
To Ilé Ifẹ̀ belongs the crown; hats are the lot of the chiefs of other places. (The king of Ilé Ifẹ̀ is preeminent over all other kings.)

4244. Ilẹ̀ tí àjànàkú ńtẹ̀, níbẹ̀ lọmọ ẹrankó ti ńjẹun.
The ground the elephant treads is the same place from which the clan of animals eat. (Lesser people can benefit from the actions and leavings of great people. Compare the variant 4233.)

4245. Ìrèké lẹ́wà ju eèsún; igikígi kì í ṣomi síní lẹ́nu.
The sugarcane has more appeal than the elephant grass; no other tree fills one's mouth with juice. (Some things are of surpassing merit and are incomparable to others.)

4246. Ìrìn ò papọ̀; eni tó ru ọ̀ọ́dúnrún èbù àtẹni tó gun ẹsin.
The paths being taken are not the same; one person is carrying three hundred yam seed-lings, and the other is mounted on a horse. (The expectations and experiences of the servant and the master are never the same.)

4247. Irọ́ ni Lébé ńpa; kò mọ eré bíi Eyéba.
Lébé is merely deceiving himself; he cannot match the agility of Eyẹ́bà. (Said of a person who is no match for an opponent but does not know it.)[33]

4248. Ìrònú ò papọ̀; ebi ló jọ ńpani.
Different people have different minds, even though all are hungry. (All people may be hungry alike, but each person will have a different approach to solving the problem.)

4249. Ìrù ẹsin ò ṣe déédé; bákannáà kọ́ la mórí wáyé.
Horses' tails are not of equal length; we did not all come to earth with identical heads. (Different people have different destinies.)

4250. Iṣe tí igbà ńṣe ọpẹ, ìbá ṣe àgbọn kò léwé lórí.
What the climbing rope does to the palm tree, had it done the same to the coconut tree it would have no leaves left. (Some people are better able to withstand vicissitudes than others.)

4251. Ìsòwò-ó wà lóòrùn; náwónáwó wà níbòji.
The trader [who makes the money] is in the sun; the person who spends the money is in the shade. (Said of people who lift not a finger to help the worker but yet get the best of the benefits of his or her efforts.)

4252. Iwájú lojúgun ńgbé.
The front part is where the shinbone lives. (The person with leadership qualities will always shine above the rest.)

---

33. Lébé and Eyẹ́bà are both acrobatic masquer-aders, but Lébé is by far the less agile of the two.

4253. *Ìyà àdá pọ̀ ju ti àkọ̀; nígbàtí àdá ńṣiṣẹ́, àkọ́ sùnlọ.*

The suffering the cutlass endures is greater than that of the sheath; while the cutlass works, the sheath sleeps. (Some people have to bear burdens greater than others'.)

4254. *Ìyà ni tọmọrí ìṣasùn; ìyá ńjẹ dídùn, ọmọ ńjẹ ooru.*

The lot of the pot lid is a bad one: the mother enjoys delicacies, while the child only suffers from the heat. (Some people have all the luck; others bear all the suffering.)[34]

4255. *Iyán ni oúnjẹ, ọkà loògùn, àìkórira là ńjẹ̀kọ, kẹ́nu má dìlẹ̀ ni tẹ̀wà, kẹ́mìí ó má baà bọ ni tẹ̀bà.*

It is pounded yam that is food; corn-flour meal is medicine; corn loaf one eats to prove absence of ill will; black-eyed peas are for snacking; and cassava meal is simply for keeping life going. (People or friends, like food, are not of equal value or appeal.)

J

4256. *Jíjọ ló jọ ọ́; ọ̀ṣùpá ò lè rí bí ọ̀sán.*

It is only resemblance; moonlight cannot be like noontime. (Some phenomena are without equal.)

K

4257. *Ká tó rí erin ó dìgbó; ká tó réfọn ó dòdàn; ká tó rí ẹyẹ bí ọ̀kín ó di kése.*

Before one can see the elephant, one must go to the bush; before one can see the buffalo, one must go to the wilderness; before one can see another bird like the egret, one must await the end of time. (Comment

that the likes of a given person are rare indeed.)

4258. *Kékeré àjànàkú kì í ṣe egbé efọn; gbogbo wọn ní ńjẹ́ erin.*

A young elephant is not in the same league as the buffalo; all of them [elephants] merit the designation "elephant." (Regardless of size or any other consideration, the person referenced is far superior to all competitors.)

4259. *Kí esú yin ẹyẹ; esu fò lójọ́ kan ṣoṣo, ìyẹ́ è-é re.*

The locust should praise the bird; the locust flew only one day and lost its wings. (One should credit those who perform feats that others cannot approach.)

4260. *Kì í ṣe gbogbo aṣọ là ńsá lóòrùn.*

It is not all cloths that one dries in the sun. (Some matters require more delicate handling than others.)

4261. *Kí ni ìyẹ́ etutu-ú jámọ́ nínú ìyẹ́ ọ̀sìn?*

What value has the wing of the tiny flying ant compared to that of the vulturine fish eagle? (One should not assign inordinate value to worthless things, especially in comparison with much more valuable things.)

4262. *Kìnìún fìtọ̀ gba ijù; kìnìún gba ijù láìlápó.*

The lion claims the forest; the lion claims the forest without a quiver of arrows. (The mighty do not always need to put themselves out or acquire weapons in order to secure advantages.)

4263. *Kìnìún kì í ṣegbé ẹran kẹran nínú igbó.*

The lion is more than the equal of any other sort of animal in the bush. (There is a hierarchy among animals and humans.)

---

34. The pot is the mother; the lid is the child.

4264. *Kò sí ẹyẹ méjì tí ńjẹ́ àkùkọ.*
There are not two birds known as the cock.
(The likes of some persons are rare.)

4265. *Kò sí ìlù tó lè borí-i bẹ̀m̀bẹ́.*
There is no drum that can surpass the
bẹ̀m̀bẹ́. (The greatest entity will not lose its
preeminence to minor ones.)

4266. *Kò sí òrìṣà tó ju Olóde lọ.*
Thre is no god greater than Olóde.[35] (Certain
forces are more potent than others.)

4267. *Kò sí òrìṣà tó lè ṣe bí Ògún lágbẹ̀dẹ.*
There is no *òrìṣà* that can do as Ògún, [god
of metals and the forge], can do at the
smithy. (No one else can attempt the feats
that the person referred to can accomplish.)

L

4268. *Láká-ǹ-láká tòyìnbó; làkúrègbé
tòyìnbó.*
Limping is the white man's habit; rheuma-
tism is the white man's ailment. (Different
people have their peculiar traits.)

M

4269. *Mímú aró ò tó ti abẹ, ìkà ẹṣin ò tó
tèèyàn; ẹṣín fọmọ ẹ̀ sílẹ̀ ó ńfẹ̀hìn gbé ọmọ
olómọ kiri.*
The keenness of a dye is not comparable
to that of a knife, and a horse's cruelty is
nothing compared with a human's; the horse
neglects its own children and carries other
people about on its back.[36] (There are sig-

nificant differences among people and their
behavior. Compare the following proverb.)

4270. *Mímú oòrùn ò jọ mímú abẹ.*
The sun's sharpness is not comparable to
a knife's. (Even things or people described
with the same words are not necessarily
alike. Compare the preceding proverb.)

4271. *Mo dáṣáṣá àgbẹ̀, bí ọbọ ìlú ló rí.*
The smartest of farmers seems like the idiot
of the city. (Farm-smartness does not translate into city [or street] smarts.)

O

4272. *Ó dorí igbá; a kì í mú àwo lọ sódò lọ
ponmi.*
Problems converge on the calabash; no one
takes a china plate to the stream to draw
water. (People should not be approached
with matters that are inappropriate for
them.)[37]

4273. *Ó wu ìràwọ̀ kó mọ́lẹ̀ tó òṣùpá, Ọlọ́run
ni ò jẹ́.*
The star would wish to be as bright as the
moon; it is God that would not permit. (God
determined individual possibilities, and it is
futile to attempt to transcend them.)

4274. *Òbu ò tó iyọ̀.*
Saltpeter does not equal salt. (An inferior
substitute is never like the real thing.)[38]

4275. *Ògìdán kì í ṣegbé ajá.*
The leopard is not the equal of the dog.

---

35. Olóde, literally "the owner of the outdoors," is
the euphemistic designation for Ṣòpònnọ́, the god of
smallpox.

36. The play is on the adjective *mímú,* here translated as "keenness," which is the same Yoruba descrip-

tion (or adjective) for dye that is of the highest staining
quality and for a knife's sharpness.

37. This is also an incantatory statement to ward
misfortune away from oneself.

38. Òbu was the seasoning in use before salt was
introduced.

(Some powers surpass others. See the following two entries.)

4276. *Ògìdán kì í ṣegbé-ẹ lágídò.*
The leopard is not the equal of the monkey. (Some powers are superior to others. See the preceding and following entries.)

4277. *Ògìdán lọlọ́là ijù.*
The leopard is undisputed lord of the wild.[39] (A way of asserting a person's preeminence, or of conceding it. Compare the preceding two entries.)

4278. *Ògìdìgbó parí ìlù gbogbo.*
The *ògìdìgbó* is the ultimate among all drums.[40] (An assertion or concession of a person's or thing's preeminence.)

4279. *Ogbe tákùkọ́ fi ńṣakọ ni kọ̀lọ̀kọ̀lọ̀-ọ́ fi ńpanu.*
The cock's comb, which the cock flaunts, is the same thing the fox eats as a snack. (One person's prized possession is another person's trash.)

4280. *Ohun gbogbo ní ńyẹ arẹwà; bó yọkun lémú a dàbí òjé.*
Everything looks good on a good-looking person; if mucus flows down his or her nostrils, it looks like molten lead [or silver].[41] (One is always inclined to be indulgent toward the failings of those one likes.)

4281. *Ohùn là ńta ọ̀fàfà; ìdí igi là ḿbá a.*
It is in the direction of the tree bear's voice that one shoots; it is at the bottom of a tree that one finds it. (No matter how they might

try, some people, because of their greatness, cannot conceal the fact of their presence.)

4282. *Ohun tí ojú àgbà-á rí tó fi jìn; bí tọmọdé bá rí i á fọ́.*
That which the elder's eyes saw and became sunken, if a youth's eyes see it, they will go blind. (What an elder can easily endure will destroy a youth. Compare 4284, 4285, and 4286.)

4283. *Ohun tó ńṣe Lémbájé ò ṣe ọmọ ẹ̀; Lémbájé nwówó, ọmọ ẹ̀ ńwọ́mọ.*
Lémbájé's problem is different from his son's; Lémbájé is striving for riches, but his son is striving for children.[42] (Different people have different priorities.)

4284. *Ohun tó ṣe àgùntàn tó fi kó òtútù; bó ṣe ewúrẹ́ á ṣe aláìsí.*
The condition that gave a sheep a cold, if it befell a goat, would result in its death. (Some people are more resilient than others. Compare the two proverbs that follow.)

4285. *Ohun tó ṣe àgbìgbò tó fi dékun ẹrín, bó ṣe igúnnugún a wankoko sórí ẹyin.*
The affliction that caused the *àgbìgbò* bird to stop laughing would have paralyzed the vulture while brooding on her eggs. (Some people are more resilient than others. Compare the preceding and following entries and 4282.)

4286. *Ohun tó ṣe igún tó fi pá lórí ló ṣe àkàlà tó fi di alákìisà.*
The disaster that befell the vulture and made it bald is the same that befell the ground hornbill and reduced its covering to tatters. (Some are better able to withstand adversity than others. Compare the two preceding entries and 4282.)

---

39. *Ọlọ́lá* literally means "a wealthy person."

40. The *ògìdìgbó* is a hollow log beaten with sticks, but only during an annual dance by the *Aláàfin* of Ọ̀yọ́ and the Baṣọ̀run, his chief minister.

41. Lead is sometimes used for such ornaments as necklaces or bangles.

42. The name Lémbájé can be translated "Pursue me until I come upon riches."

4287. *Ohun tó ṣe ilá tó ṣe kó, bó bá ṣe ikàn á wèwù ẹjẹ̀; ohun tó ṣe olówó tó fi ńrojú, bó bá ṣe tálákà wọ́n á ti gbàgbé ẹ; ohun tó ṣe igún tó fi pá lórí, bó bá ṣe àgbò wọ́n a ti yọ̀wo è.*
The disaster that befell okro and caused it to become wooden, if it had befallen *ikàn*, it would have taken on a hue of blood; the woe that befell the rich person and caused him or her to scowl, if it had befallen a poor person, he or she would have been long forgotten; the problem that came upon the vulture and made it bald, if it had come upon the ram, he would long ago have lost his horns. (The reverses that illustrious people can endure and weather will easily destroy people of little substance.)

4288. *Ohùn-un kéjiró ò dé ọ̀run.*
The voice of the *kéjiró* bird does not rise to reach the sky. (A sentiment that a person's voice carries no weight.)

4289. *Òjò ńrọ̀, ìwọ̀fà ńyọ̀; ojú olówó kan ó ju ìbó.*
It is raining, and the pawned laborer is re-joicing, but the look on the creditor's face is as sour as can be. (Some people's fortune is other people's misfortune. Compare the next entry.)

4290. *Òjò òwúrọ̀ tí ḿbí olówó nínú: olówó gẹlẹtẹ, ìwọ̀fà gẹlẹtẹ.*
The morning rain angers the creditor: the creditor lolls about, and his pawn lolls about. (It is an annoying situation that pre-vents one from enjoying what is due one. Compare the preceding entry.)

4291. *Òjòjò ńṣe ìwọ̀fà wọ́n ní ó kó iṣe è dé; bó bá ṣe ọmọ-ọ wọn, wọ-n a máa náwó, wọn a máa nára.*
An illness takes hold of the pawned ser-vant, and they say he has resorted to his habitual tricks; if it were their own son, they would commit their money and their effort

[to healing him]. (One is always indulgent toward one's own children while having no patience with others' children.)

4292. *Ojú abẹ́rẹ́ ò nípin; ibalùwẹ̀-ẹ́ gbòrò kò gba ọkọ̀.*
The eye of a needle does not ooze matter; the bath place is broad but not enough for a boat. (Comparisons between two different things are valid only up to a point.)

4293. *Ojú ọkùnrin lobìnrín ti ńníyì.*
It is only in the eyes of a man that a woman is desirable. (Different people have their proper attractions.)[43]

4294. *Òkèlè àkọ́bù tí ńre ògangan ìdí.*
The first morsel of food sinks down to the base of the backbone. (Said of a thing that makes an incomparable impression, just as the first morsel makes a powerful impression on a starving person.)

4295. *Òkò ńlá ṣe alángbá pìnsín; ẹni tó juni lọ ní ńṣekú pani.*
A huge stone missile flattens the lizard; a person with more power will be the death of you. (Those who are in positions of power are likely to use their power to crush the less powerful.)

4296. *Òkun lọba omi.*
The ocean is the king of all waters. (A cer-tain thing or person is without rivals.)

4297. *Ológìnní tó fẹ́ẹ́ ṣe bí ẹkùn, ó najú ni.*
The cat that attempts to emulate the leopard merely fools itself. (One should know one's limits.)

4298. *Ológìnní ò ṣéé bọ ìrókò; erin ò ṣéé pa fún Iléyá.*

---

43. Yoruba culture does not acknowledge homo-sexual attractions.

A cat is nothing to sacrifice to the *írókò* tree; an elephant is not a thing to kill for the feast of *Id el Fitr*. (Provide for the occasion what is proper for the occasion.)

4299. *Ológbo ni baba arókin.*
The court poet is the father of the court rhapsodist.[44] (Certain functions are more important than others.)

4300. *Olóko lègbón alágbàro.*
The owner of the farm is the master of the hired tiller. (The employee is subservient to the employer.)

4301. *Olórí yan orí; alámò-ó gbé amò.*
He to whose lot the head fell chose the head;[45] the one to whose lot the clay fell picked up his clay. (Different lots to different people; each person must live with his or hers.)

4302. *Olówó dénú ègún kò roko; ìwòfà-á tinú ègún bèrè.*
The rich man gets to the thorn patch and stops hoeing; the pawned servant starts his hoeing from the thorn patch. (The rich can afford to leave the worst assignments for those beholden to them.)

4303. *Olówó féé sin odò; tálákà ngbon orí.*
The rich man wishes to sacrifice to the river, and the poor man shakes his head in refusal. (If one has no standing, one might as well keep one's opinion to oneself.)

4304. *Olówó ìlú kan, tálákà ìlú mìíràn.*
The rich man of one town is the pauper of another. (Everything is relative.)

---

44. Both the *ológbo* and the *arókin* are court poets attached to the palace of Òyó and other locations.

45. Yet another allusion to the head as the repose of one's chosen fate, which is received from the Creator, Olódùmarè. (See note 1 to 4613.)

4305. *Olówó làgbà; olówó sòrò enu è nyoná.*
The rich person is the eldest of all; the rich person speaks, and fire shoots out of his mouth. (No one compares with a rich person; nothing is beyond a rich person.)

4306. *Olówó lògá-a tálákà; Olórun lògá-a gbogbo-o wa.*
The rich person is the master of the poor; God is the master of all. (The rich may lord it over the poor, but even they must answer to God.)

4307. *Olówó nsòrò enu è ndùn; òtòsì nsòrò enu è nró sáka-sàka.*
The rich person speaks, and his mouth sounds sweet; the lazy person speaks, and his mouth sounds like unbearable noise. (The sound of a rich man's voice is music to the ears; that of a poor person is merely grating noise.)

4308. *Omi ni yó paná.*
Water is the thing that will quench fire. (Each person has his particular nemesis.)

4309. *Òní lègbón òla; ìrìwòwò lègbón òjò.*
Today precedes tomorrow in age; the drizzle precedes the rain in age. (There is order in Nature, such that certain things always precede others, never the reverse.)

4310. *Oníyàwó ngbéyàwó, Abídogun nkó eèpè.*
The groom is welcoming his new bride; Abídogun is carrying sand. (Some suffer while others enjoy life.)

4311. *Orí ajá lekùn ó fàbò sí.*
It is to the matter of the dog that the leopard will finally turn. (The weakling may tease the bully with impunity for a while, but the bully will find time for him in the end.)

4312. *Orí esin ò see fi wé tòkéré.*
The horse's head is not comparable to that

of the squirrel. (Some people are more
fortunate than others.)

4313. *Orí lègbọ́n ara.*
The head is an elder sibling to the body.
(Certain entities are unquestionably su-
perior to their associates.)

4314. *Òrìṣà bí Ògún ò sí; ojú lásán ni gbogbo
wọn ńyá.*
A god to rival Ògún does not exist; all the
others are only being impudent. (A certain
person is without peer among humans, just
as Ògún is without equal among the gods.)

4315. *Òrìṣà ní ńṣọlà; ọba ní ńṣọlá.*
It is for the gods to confer greatness; it is
for the king to enjoy greatness. (The king's
greatness is at the behest of the gods.)

4316. *Oró mú ju oró lọ; ọká gbé paramọ́lẹ̀ mì.*
Some venoms are more deadly than others;
the viper swallows the adder. (Some people
or things are more formidable than others.)

4317. *Òrùlé fara wé ẹṣin; a gùn ún, kò lè rìn.*
A roof looks like a horse; one mounts it, but
it cannot walk. (Things that may look similar will prove themselves quite different.)

4318. *Oyin ò nífìwé nínú adùn.*
There is nothing that compares with honey
in sweetness. (Some things are simply incomparable.)

Ọ

4319. *Ọba kì í dòbálẹ̀ fólórí abúlé.*
The king does not prostrate before the head
of a village. (The person of superior rank
does not pay obeisance to a person in an
inferior position.)

4320. *Ọba ò ní fìlà, adé ló ní.*
The king has no hat; he has only crowns.

(The king is not to be compared with ordinary people.)

4321. *Ọ̀bùn-ún ṣubú lójà a fẹ̀rín si; bí afínjú
ṣubú àá gbọ́ ariwo.*
The filthy person falls in the market, and we
burst into laughter; if a fashionable person
falls, there will be loud exclamations. (Few
people care what misfortune befalls a lousy
person; everybody cares about the welfare of
a fashionable person.)

4322. *Ọgá ni ìgbò tí ńṣe sójà nínú ẹyẹ.*
The *ìgbò* bird is a boss, a soldier among
birds. (Said of a person whose notable deeds
have earned him or her renown among the
people.)

4323. *Ọgán ńṣe nǹkan díẹ̀.*
The great one is showing off. (Said of a person doing impressive things to show his or
her prowess.)

4324. *Ọgọ́rùn-ún ẹsinsin ò dá màlúù dúró.*
One hundred flies will not stop an elephant.
(A multitude of little people will not prevent
a great man from doing what he wishes.)

4325. *Ọjá kan ò dàbí ọjá òróòro; òkè kan
ò dàbí Òkèe Gbadi; Òkèe Gbadií sunwọ̀n
sunwọ̀n, o fi ibi ṣ́óńṣó ṣe àrà; ọnà kan ò dàbí
ọnà-a sàréè.*
No sash compares with the red sash; no hill
compares with Gbadi Hill; Gbadi Hill is
so beautiful that it adorns itself with a tall
peak; no path compares with the path to
the grave. (Some things are incomparable in
their quality. The following is a variant.)

4326. *Ọjá kan ò dàbí ọjá òróòro; òkè kan ò
dàbí Òkèe Gbadi; ọmú kan ò dùn bí ọmú ìyá
ẹni.*
No sash compares with the red sash; no hill
compares with Gbadi Hill; no breast milk is
as delicious as one's mother's breast milk.

(Certain things have no rivals in value. See the previous entry.)

4327. *Ọká ojú ọ̀nà tí ńlé guuru kó-kó-kó.*
The pathway gaboon viper defiantly occupies the whole path. (Said of a tough person who defies all would-be opponents.)

4328. *Òkín ọba ẹyẹ; ọ̀kín ẹléwà àlà.*
Egret, king of birds; egret whose beauty is in whiteness. (Praise for people of exemplary qualities.)

4329. *Ọ̀lẹ̀lẹ̀-ẹ́ ti ráṣọ wọ̀, tàkàrà ló sọ̀rọ.*
The steamed, seasoned bean mash is already blessed with clothes to wear; it is the case of the fried-bean fritters that constitutes a problem.[46] (Some people are naturally blessed, while others have to struggle for every advantage.)

4330. *Ọlọ́mkọsíkàtà baba àgbàdo.*
The corncob with irregular rows of grains on it is the father of all corn. (The unconventional person is a person to be reckoned with among people.)

4331. *Ọlọ́run ò pín in dọ́gba; sajiméjòọ ju kòròfo.*
God did not distribute things equally; the seargeant major is more important than the plain soldier. (God did not create people equal in importance.)

4332. *Olòtọ̀ kékeré là ńfọwọ́ tẹ̀ níkùn.*
It is an insignificant wealthy person whose stomach one pokes with one's finger. (One can take liberties with people of sudden wealth.)[47]

4333. *Ọmọ òtòṣì-í ṣubú lọ́jà a fẹ̀rín sí i; ọmọ olówó ṣubú ariwó ta: "Yéè! Pẹ̀lé! Pẹ̀lé! Pẹ̀lé!"*
The child of a poor man falls in the market, and people burst into laughter; the child of a rich man falls, and there is a huge outcry: "Great heavens! Easy does it! Easy does it! Easy does it!" (If you are poor, you are on your own; if you are rich, the whole world is in your corner.)

4334. *Ọmọ ọlọ́lá lọlá yẹ.*
It is the offspring of a famous person that greatness befits. (Parents' greatness rubs off on their children.)

4335. *Ọmọ ọlọ́rọ̀ ìṣíwájú ní ńta ìlẹ̀kẹ̀ fún ọmọ ọlọ́rọ̀ ìkẹhìn.*
The child of the first rich person sells beads to the child of the latest rich person. (Those who precede one in greatness will always take precedence.)

4336. *Ọmọ ọlọ́rọ̀ ní ńjẹ ẹyin awó.*
It is the child of a wealthy person that eats guinea-fowl eggs. (Only the wealthy enjoy rare things.)

4337. *Ọ̀pọ̀lọ́ ò ga ju ara wọn lọ, àfi èyí tó bá gun ebè.*
No one toad is taller than another, except one that climbs a heap. (Said of people who, despite the affectations of some of them, are indistinguishable in stature and worth.)

4338. *Ọ̀pọ̀lọ́ ò jẹ gbèsè ju ara wọn lọ; tìe okòó, tèmi okòó, tàwa okòó, tèyin okòó, okokòó.*
Toads are not in greater debt than one another: yours 20 cowries, mine 20 cowries, ours 20 cowries, theirs 20 cowries, 20 cowries all around. (None of us is better off than the others.)

4339. *Ọ̀pọ̀lọ́ ò jẹ́ kí kọ̀-ǹ-kọ̀-ọ́ dún; ẹni tó juni ò jẹ́ ká sọ̀rọ̀.*
The toad will not let the frog make a sound;

---

46. *Ọ̀lẹ̀lẹ̀* is wrapped in leaves (clothing) before being steamed; *àkàrà* are simply deep-fried and displayed unadorned for sale.

47. The gesture would be made to call attention to his well-fed stomach.

a mightier person prevents one from speaking. (One often must hold one's tongue for fear of mightier people.)

4340. Ọ̀rán sàn ju òràn; adétè-ẹ́ rí wèrè, ó kán lùgbé, ó ní "Ng ò níí jẹ́ kí kiní yìí bùmíjẹ ojàre."
Some misfortunes are worse than others; the leper sees the mad person and dashes into the bush, saying, "I'll be hanged if I will let that creature take a bite out of me!" (Even the afflicted know that some people have even worse afflictions.)

4341. Ọ̀rán sàn ju òràn; ti àpọ́n sàn díẹ̀ ju ti òkóbó.
Some problems are better than others; a bachelor's plight is somewhat better than a eunuch's. (Misfortunes come in different degrees of seriousness.)

4342. Ọ̀wọ́nrín, baba Ifá.
The Ọ̀wọ́nrín chapter is the father of Ifá. (Said of a thing or person preeminent among all others.)

P

4343. Pàtàkì orò ò ju ilé Àjànà.
The greatest authority within the Orò cult is not to be sought beyond the Àjànà's home.[48] (Said of a person or thing that is not surpassed in importance. The following entry is a variant.)

4344. Pàtàkì òjẹ̀ ò ju ilé Alápìíni lọ.
The chief authority among the òjẹ̀ masqueraders is not to be sought beyond the home of the Alápìíni.[49] (Nothing could be of greater importance than the subject of the discussion. Compare the foregoing entry.)

4345. Pé-ń-pé làṣá wà tó fi ńṣe ọkọ adìẹ.
The kite is modest in size, and yet it is the terror of chickens. (A person's importance is not a matter of his or her size.)

T

4346. Tijó tayọ̀ ní ńṣe ìdin; wùyè-wùyè ní ńṣe ìgòngò; à ńjó, à ńyọ̀, ọmọ bọna-bọ́ná ńre oko igi.
The maggot is addicted to dancing and rejoicing; the worm is addicted to wriggling; we dance, we rejoice, and the wood-boring insect goes in search of wood. (The laboring poor person must keep working even while others are relaxing and rejoicing.)

---

48. Àjànà is the title of the head of the Orò cult.
49. Alápìíni is the chief of the egúngún cult.

FIVE

Rights and Responsibilities

On the right to life

A

4347. *A kì í sùn sílé ẹni ká fọrùn ṣẹ́.*
One does not sleep in one's own home and break one's neck. (A person does not get into trouble while minding his or her own business.)

4348. *Àìkú ẹkìrì, a kì í fi awọ-ọ rẹ̀ se gbẹ̀du.*
The skin of a live wild goat cannot be made into a *gbẹ̀du* drum.[1] (As long as one is alive, one will be able to protect one's interests. Compare 4409.)

B

4349. *Bí a kò bá kú lógún ọdún, baba ẹnìkan o lè gbéni sin.*
If one does not die in twenty years, nobody's father can bury one. (If one does not die, nobody can stop one from living.)

4350. *Bí ẹtu ò bá kú, ta ni yó fi awọ-ọ rẹ̀ tọ́ ọsán? Bí ẹkìrì ò bá kú, ta ni yó fi awọ-ọ rẹ̀ dá bàtà? Bí olórìṣà ò bá kú, ta ni yó gba ìbọ̀-o rẹ̀ bọ̀?*
If the antelope does not die, who would make bowstrings of its hide? If the wild goat does not die, who would make shoes from its skin? If the priest does not die, who would usurp his casting of lots? (As long as one lives, no one may alienate one's rights.)

Ọ

4351. *Ọmọ kì í pa ọmọ jayé.*
A child does not kill another child as a means to prosper. (There are certain things that one simply may not do to other people, however great one might be.)

---

1. The large *gbẹ̀du* drum, made from the skin of a wild goat, is used on state occasions or during ceremonies of Ògbóni, the ancient Yoruba secret society.

On freedom to be oneself

A

4352. *A kì í kí ayaba kó doyún; èrèkè kó lokó wà.*
One does not greet a queen and thereby impregnate her; the cheek is not the place where the penis is located. (Innocent actions should not get one in trouble.)

4353. *A kì í torí-i gbígbó pa ajá; a kì í toríi kíkàn pa àgbò; a kì í torí-i wérewère pa òbúkọ.*
One does not kill a dog for barking; one does not kill a ram for butting; one does not kill a he-goat because of randiness. (Do not punish people for doing what they cannot help doing.)

4354. *Àgbè tó nísu lọ́gbà tó ńjẹ ẹgé, ohun tó fẹ́ ló ńṣe.*
A farmer who has yams in his barn but eats cassava is doing as he pleases. (It is good fortune to have the right to choose.)[1]

4355. *Aṣọ tí a bá lára eégún, ti eégún ni.*
Whatever costume one finds on the masquerader belongs to him. (No one can or should begrudge a person what rightfully belongs to him or her. Compare 797.)

B

4356. *Bí a bá ni eégún-un baba ẹni ó jòó, tí kò jó, ọ̀ràn kọ́.*

If one said that one's father's masquerader would dance and he fails to, there is no crime committed. (Inability to make good on a promise is no crime.)

E

4357. *Ekòló ḿmì gbàgò, inú ḿbí adìẹ sùú-sùú.*
The worm crawls nonchalantly, and the chicken is consumed with anger. (One's enemies are never pleased by one's prosperity.)

Ẹ

4358. *Ẹnu kì í rírí kí ẹlẹ́nu má lè fi jẹun.*
The mouth is never so filthy that its owner cannot eat with it. (A person is always comfortable with his or her own bad habits and shortcomings. See the following variant.)

4359. *Ẹnu kò súnwọ̀n, ẹlẹ́nuú pón-ọn lá.*
The mouth is not appealing; the owner licks it. (One is not put off by one's own blemish. See the foregoing entry.)

G

4360. *Gegele ló bí gegele; kòtò ló bí kòtò; òjò-ó rò sí kòtò gegele ḿbínú.*
The mound was sired by a mound; the pit was sired by a pit; rain falls into a pit, and the mound becomes angry. (Each person is

---

1. Normally, one would prefer yams to cassava.

different; one should not envy what others have.)

I

4361. *Ìbáà ṣorí pàlàbà kó ṣorí pàbó, ṭeni ní ńjẹ́ ṭeni.*
Be his or her head oversized or deformed, one's own thing is one's own. (One treasures what one has, however defective it might be.)

4362. *Ilé ẹni la ti ńjẹ òkété onídodo.*
It is within one's home that one eats a field rat with a tumor. (One may do what one pleases in the fastness of one's home.)

K

4363. *Kantíkantí ò ní ọ̀ràn akèrègbè lórùn.*
Sugar ants have no feud with the gourd.[2] (One does a thing because one chooses to, not because one must.)

4364. *Kán-ún ni ọmọ Hausa; asárá ni ọmọ òyìnbó; gòmbó lọmọ Onírè.*
Potash seasoning is the fetish of the Hausa; snuff is the fetish of the white man; facial marks are the fetish of the Ìrè person. (Different peoples have their different habits.)

4365. *Kí Lámọnrín ṣe bí ẹni, ìjà ní ńdà.*
Demanding that such and such a person emulate one exactly leads to a fight. (One should not expect others to be just like oneself.)

4366. *Kò-jí-kò-wí kò wí pé kí olóhun má lọ ohun ẹ̀.*
He-did-not-steal-and-he-will-not-tell can-

not tell the person not to broadcast his or her stolen thing. (One must not be impatient with people agitated by some loss they have sustained.)

O

4367. *"Ò báà rí, o ò gbọdọ̀ wí" ní ńpa akoni.*
"Even though you see it you must not make a sound" is what kills the intrepid man. (Vain people go to their death even when judiciously calling for help in the face of danger would have saved them.)

4368. *Odò kì í kọ iwẹ̀, kó kọ ìtù, kó tún kọ à-padà-relé.*
A river does not prevent one from swimming across it, prevent one from rowing across it, and yet prevent one from returning home. (If a goal proves unattainable, one can always let go of it.)

4369. *Ohun tó wu ọ̀bùn ló ńfowó ẹ̀ rà; bí ẹrú bá tagi tán a fowó bu iṣu jẹ.*
Whatever pleases the bumpkin is what he spends his money on; when the slave sells his load of firewood, he uses the money to buy yams to eat. (What one spends one's money on is what one pleases to spend it on. Compare the following variant.)

4370. *Ohun tó wu ọ̀bùn ló ńfowó ẹ̀ rà; ohun tó wu afínjú ló ńfowó ẹ̀ ṣe.*
The bumpkin spends his money on whatever he pleases; the fop likewise spends his money on whatever he pleases. (One does what one pleases with one's possessions. Compare the preceding proverb.)

4371. *Oko ni tàgbè; gègé ni talákòwé.*
To the farmer belongs the farm; to the bookish person belongs the pen. (Each person or profession has its proper preserves.)

2. Sugar ants cluster at the mouth of the gourd containing palm wine in order to get at the sugar.

4372. *Onímàle Ìbàdàn, bí oníṢàngó Ìlọrin.*
The Muslim from Ibadan is like a Ṣango
worshiper from Ìlọrin. (Different people
practice their religion differently.)

Ọ

4373. *Ọbá lè sòfin olè kí adìẹ má jẹ lósùpá?*
Can the king interdict stealing and thus stop
a chicken from scratching for food in the
moonlight? (No law or authority has the
right to stop people from conducting their
normal lives.)

4374. *Ọbọ tàkìtì ọbọ ò ró, inàkí ṣe "Ha!" ní
igọ̀ igi; ọbọ́ ní, "A kì í bánijà ti nnkan ẹni."*
The monkey somersaulted and failed to
land erect, and the gorilla resting among the
roots of a large tree exclaimed, "Ha!" The
monkey responded, "Nobody has a right to
fault one over how one performs one's signature stunt." (One is free to do one's thing
as one wishes.)

4375. *Ọká bímọ-ọ rẹ̀ ó mọ rébété; òjòlá bí tirẹ̀
ó gùn gbàlàjà.*
The gaboon viper has its child, and it is of
moderate length; the python has its child,
and it is very long indeed. (Children take
after their parents.)

4376. *Ọká ló bí paramọ́lẹ̀; ìkà ló bí ìkà sílẹ̀;
ẹni tó bíni là ńjọ.*
The gaboon viper sired the serpent; the
wicked person is born of a wicked person;
one takes after one's parent. (Wickedness is
an inherited trait.)

4377. *Ọmùtí ò ṣe wèrè, owó ẹ̀ ní ńná.*
The drunkard is not an imbecile; it is his
money he is spending. (The drunk has a
right to spend his money as he pleases. The
following entry is a variant.)

4378. *Ọmùtí ò yan àpà; owó ẹ̀ ní ńná.*
The drunkard is no spendthrift; he is spending his own money. (One may do as one
pleases with one's property. See the previous
entry.)

4379. *Ọnà kan ò wọ ọjà.*
It is not one road only that leads to the
market. (There are many different ways to
approach a problem.)

S

4380. *Sèsé ò lè so bí èwà.*
The yam bean cannot produce fruits like the
black-eyed peas. (One can only act according to one's nature.)

Ṣ

4381. *Ṣàngó Iṣaga, aṣọ àgìdì ní ńfìí bòdí jó.*
The Ṣango of Iṣaga town chooses to wrap
his waist with canvas cloth for dancing. (The
unconventional person will always finds
ways to be different.)[3]

4382. *"Ṣe é báyìí" ní ńkọ́ aya ẹ̀ lọ́bùn.*
"Do it this way" is the one who teaches filthy
habits to his wife. (Do not impose your own
instructions on people who know better
than you do what they are doing.)

4383. *Ṣòkòtò òyìnbó ò lókùn; apá ni wọ́n fi
ńkọ́.*
The white man's trousers have no strings;
they are suspended from the shoulders.
(Different people, different fashions.)

---

3. Canvas is not the prescribed or usual fabric for
Ṣango worshipers. Iṣaga is an Ẹ̀gbá town.

4384. *Ta ní ḿbá adélébọ̀ ṣe ejọ́ oyún?*
Who would take a married woman to task
for being pregnant? (One should not fault
people for doing what is expected of them.)

4385. *"Tèmí yémi," tí ńfi inú iṣu ẹ̀ gbin ọkà.*
"I know what I am doing" plants corn
among his yams. (Said of a person who
thinks he knows it all but who will learn
only from the consequences of his folly.)

4386. *Tèfètèfèé yọ owó ọjà.*
Permanent loss patronized the merchant.
(All one's labor has gone for nought.)

4387. *Wàrà ní ḿmú ọmọ Fúlàní dàgbà; iyán
ní ḿmú ọmọ oko sanra.*
It is cottage cheese that nurtures the Fulbe
child to adulthood; it is pounded yams that
make the farm dweller fat. (Different people
depend on different things for nurturing.)

4388. *Wọ̀nṣàn-wọ̀nṣàn ò mú ehín gbórín; bí
kò jù ṣẹ́kí, a ó máa fi rún àgbàdo.*
Loud chewing does not increase the size of
one's teeth; if one's teeth are short, one can
at least chew corn with them. (One does not
need to prove that one is great; no matter
how lowly one might be, there is much one
can accomplish.)

On the right to human dignity

A

4389. *A kì í fi àìlépọ̀n di ẹrù asòpá.*
One does not become afflicted with elephantiasis of the scrotum despite having no testicles. (One cannot be deprived of an amenity and yet be subjected to the cares of enjoying it. Compare 4521.)

4390. *A kì í kó owó ra ẹsin, ká kówó ra yàgòlọ́nà.*
One does not spend one's money purchasing a horse and then spend more money purchasing "Get out of the way." (Once one has done one's part, one is entitled to expect others to do theirs.)

4391. *Àáyá ò gọ̀ bíi ká fà á nírù.*
The colobus monkey is not so stupid as to permit its tail to be pulled. (Even the most foolish people are wise to certain things.)

4392. *Àgùàlà ḿbá osù rìn, wọ́n rò pé ajá-a rẹ̀ ni.*
The planet Venus follows the moon across the sky, and people think it is the moon's dog.[1] (Every man is a king in his home, even though some might not think so.)

4393. *Àjànàkú fojú ìsẹ́ wòbọ, ọbọ ò tọrọ je.*
The elephant looks at the monkey with the eyes of disdain, but the monkey does not beg food to eat. (Each person has his

or her worth; even the lowly monkey has its dignity, since it is not beholden to the elephant.)

4394. *Akẹ̀sán lòpin Ọ̀yọ́; ibi a báni lọ́wọ̀ ni ilé ẹni.*
Akẹsan is the boundary of Ọ̀yọ́; the place where one is found in dignity is one's home.[2] (Home is wherever one is welcome and accorded dignity.)

B

4395. *Bí a kò fẹ́ ẹni nílùú, a kì í tó abẹ́rẹ́.*
If one is not wanted in a town, one is worth less than a needle. (An unwanted person enjoys no regard.)

4396. *Bí ikú yó pani á gbọ́ tẹnu ẹni; òpìtàn ní ńfi ìtàn gba ara-a rẹ̀ kalẹ̀.*
If death will kill one, it should listen to what one has to say; he who tells tales may by that means deliver himself. (One should not impose punishment before hearing from the offender.)

---

1. Another name for the planet is *Ajá osù*, moon's dog.

2. Akẹ̀sán, the king's market in Ọ̀yọ́, was traditionally at the edge of the city. The expression translated as "the end" or "boundary" could also mean "the ultimate place," a translation that would also be appropriate here, inasmuch as the market was the focus of important events in the life of the city. The proverb is still applicable, therefore, even though the city has grown far beyond the market.

E

4397. *Eégún ni baba lórun; Pààká ni baba nígbàlè.*
The masquerader is the father figure in heaven; *Pààká* is the father figure in the masquerader's secret grove. (There is no disputing the preeminence of a person among his or her peers.)

4398. *Ejò-ó kéré kò kéré, kò șéé dì ní ìgbànú.*
However small a snake may be, it cannot be used as a belt. (However mean or weak a person may be, there is a limit to what one can do to him or her.)

Ẹ

4399. *Ẹni tí a tìràn mọ́ ò lè dáké; ẹni tí a pè lólè ò lè fojú rere woni.*
A person one has falsely accused will not remain quiet; a person one has called a thief will not look kindly on one. (One who causes others injury should not expect them to be indifferent.)

4400. *Ẹni tí kò kú yó họra.*
A person who is not dead will be able to scratch where he itches. (So long as one has life, one can act in one's own interest.)

4401. *Ẹrú kì í șe ọmọ igi; èèyàn ló bí ìyá-a rẹ̀.*
A slave is not born of a tree; his or her mother was the offspring of a human being. (Even a slave deserves the consideration due every human being; misfortune does not rob people of their humanity. Compare the following entry.)

4402. *Ẹrú șe ọmọ nílé ìyá-a rẹ̀ rí.*
A slave was once a freeborn person in his or her mother's house. (A person who is down on his or her luck was once in better circum-

stances; people's circumstances do change. Compare the preceding entry.)

I

4403. *Ilé ahun là ńpa ahun sí.*
It is inside the tortoise's own house that one kills it. (One should make a stand in defense of one's rights and property, even to the death.)

4404. *Ilé là ḿbá onímọ́tò gbé; oní-báísíkùlù, má tẹ̀ wá mọ́lè pa.*
One is able to share a home with the owner of a motor vehicle; owner of a bicycle, do not crush us to death. (People with little advantages should not throw their weight around, especially when truly great people are considerate of others. Compare the next entry.)

4405. *Ìlú là ḿbá ọba gbé, kí ìjòyè má tẹ̀ wá mọ́lè pa.*
One is able to live in the same town with the king; the chief should not stomp us to death. (The minor official should not impose on people more than the important officials do. Compare the preceding entry.)

K

4406. *Kì í burú fún èèyàn ká lọ fi ajá wa.*
A person is never so down on his or her luck that one sends a dog to seek him or her out. (A person, however disgraced, still deserves to be treated like a human being.)

4407. *Kíkéré labẹ́rẹ́ kéré, kì í șe mímì adìẹ.*
A needle may be small, but that does not make it something a chicken can swallow. (One should not underestimate people simply because they seem unimpressive.)

M

4408. *Má fi òdù fọ́ mi ní àdó; má fi ẹṣin tẹ̀ mí lágùntàn pa.*
Do not break my tiny gourdlet with your large pot; do not use your horse to trample my sheep to death. (Do not take advantage of me, even though you are wealthier and more powerful than I.)

O

4409. *Ó di ẹ̀hìn ìgbín ká tó fikaraun ẹ̀ họ igbá.*
Not until the demise of the snail can one use its shell to scoop out the inside of a calabash. (As long as one is still around, one does not permit one's interests to be assaulted without making a scene. Compare 4348.)

4410. *Ojú ẹrú ò gbé ìpàkọ́; a-bojú-níwájú bí ọmọ.*
The slave's eyes are not at the back of his head; his eyes are in front just like a freeborn child's. (A slave is just as human as the freeborn child.)

4411. *Ojú kì í pọ́n òkú kó má nasẹ̀ tọ́tọ́.*
A corpse is never so benighted that it cannot stretch its legs. (Even in the worst of circumstances, one can still count some blessings.)

4412. *Ojú kì í pọ́nni ká má nìí aṣọ kan.*
One is never so poor that one does not own one single item of clothing. (Suffering is never absolute.)

4413. *Olówó ẹni kì í rorò kó ní ká má ṣu.*
One's master cannot be so tyrannical that he orders one not to shit. (Even servants have some rights.)

4414. *Owó tí kò sí, ọba ò lè gbà á.*
Money that does not exist, no king can take from you. (One cannot be at risk for what one does not own.)

Ọ

4415. *Ọba kì í kọ obìnrin sílẹ̀ kí tálákà lọ gbé e sílé.*
A king does not divorce a woman, only for her to be married then by a pauper. (A disgraced person is not necessarily without some residual dignity and standing.)

4416. *Ọmọdé hu irùngbọ̀n, ó ní òun òì tó baba òun; baba rẹ̀ẹ́ hu jọ̀jọ̀ àgbò?*
A youth grows a beard and yet claims he has not achieved the same status as his father; did his father grow a dewlap? (One should not contrive to defer adult responsibilities.)

P

4417. *Pàṣípààrọ̀ obìnrin ò ṣeé ṣe.*
One cannot take a woman back for an exchange. (Wives are not like commodities purchased at the market.)

4418. *Pátá-pátá kọ́ nìjàpá ò níru.*
It is not completely that a tortoise lacks a tail. (A poor person is not absolutely bereft of means.)

T

4419. *Tolè tolè ni mẹ̀kúnnùú fi ńrìn lójú olówó.*
Ever with a propensity to steal is the appearance of a simple person's movement in the eyes of the wealthy. (The well-off are ever suspicious that the worse-off are after their wealth.)

W

4420. *Wón so ajá mólè, wón so ekùn mólè,
wón firù ekùn lé ajá lówó.*
They tied down the dog; they tied down the leopard; and then they delivered the leopard's tail into the dog's paws. (One's enemies have conspired to make one vulnerable to people who otherwise would not have dared to confront one.)

On the right to one's patrimony and to property

A

4421. *A kì í bá eku du igbó, a kì í ba efòn du òdàn, a kì í bá Olúkóre du ipò-o baba-a rè.*
One does not dispute the bush with the rodent; one does not dispute the grassland with the buffalo; one does not dispute Olúkóre's patrimony with him. (One should not seek to deny people their God-given rights.)

4422. *A kì í gbé ọmọ Ọbà fún Ọ̀ṣun.*
One does not give the child of the Ọbà river to the Ọ̀ṣun river. (Do not rob Peter to pay Paul.)

4423. *A kì í lé ẹlénu rírùn níbi àmù ìyá ẹ̀.*
One does not chase a smelly-mouthed person away from his or her mother's water pot. (Even problem people have their rights.)

4424. *A kì í pa igún jẹ ká sé; kì í ṣe ẹyẹ baba ẹnìkan.*
One does not kill a vulture for food and deny doing so; it is not a bird that belongs to anybody's father. (Never be afraid to own up to taking advantage of something or someone nobody favors.)

4425. *A kì í pé ojú ọbá fó ká má pe ẹléfòó mọ́.*
One cannot, simply because the king is blind, stop hailing the vegetable seller. (Fear of a touchy authority figure should not rule one's life.)[1]

4426. *A kì í ṣúpó aláàyè.*
One does not inherit the wife of a living man. (Do not attempt to wrest property or a right from its owner while the owner is still around.)

4427. *A sẹbẹ̀ fún Fádípè, Fájẹbẹ̀-ẹ́ fá a lá; ọlóbẹ̀ ló lábẹ̀.*
We prepared stew for Fádípè, and Fájẹbẹ̀ ate it; the person who deserved the stew got it. (If the legitimate owner snatches an article from the illegitimate owner, no crime has been committed.)[2]

4428. *Àkọ́bí ẹléran kì í já mọ́ wọn lọ́wọ́.*
The first foal of the owner of the herd does not slip from his fingers.[3] (People deserve to hold on to what is rightfully theirs. See the following entry.)

4429. *Àkọ́bí ni ti ẹléran.*
The firstborn belongs to the owner of the animal.[4] (To the owner of an object belongs the largest right to it. This is a variant of the preceding entry.)

---

also happens to constitute the term *èfó*, meaning "vegetable."

2. The name Fádípè means "Ifá [the oracle] commiserates"; the name Fájẹbẹ̀ means "Ifá eats stew." The latter obviously has better claim to the stew.

3. The reference is to the first offspring of the owner's livestock.

4. People sometimes give animals to others to keep for them. If any of those animals have offspring, the first is customarily the owner's to dispose of.

---

1. The proverb plays on the syllable *fó*, the verb that means "to go blind" when it refers to eyes but

4430. *Aṣọ tá a bá rí lára igún, ti igún ni.*
Whatever cloth one finds on the vulture belongs to it. (The vulture may lack feathers,
but it does not borrow from other birds.)

4431. *Aya òlẹ là ńgbà, a kì í gbọmọ ọlẹ.*
It is a lazy person's wife that one may take;
one may not take a lazy person's child. (Even
the lazy person has some rights. Compare
4445.)

B

4432. *Bí oògùn ò bá jẹ́, owó ẹ̀ á jíṣẹ́.*
If the medicine does not work, the money
expended on it must explain why. (One has
a right to the service one has paid for or an
explanation for the withholding of it.)

E

4433. *Eégún mọ̀ọ́ jó kò mọ̀ọ́ jó; yó gba owó
ọjà-a rẹ̀.*
Whether the masquerader knows how to
dance or does not, he will receive his market
fee. (People in authority will receive their
reward whether they perform well or ill.)

4434. *Èèyàn lásán ò ní gòbì; olówó ò ní ìlàrí.*
An ordinary person does not have a throne
room; a wealthy man does not have royal
courtiers. (Each position has its proper
privileges.)

4435. *Èkúté ilé ò lẹ́nu bá alákàà wíjọ́.*
The house mouse has no mouth to dispute
a case with the owner of the granary. (A
known culprit cannot successfully plead
innocence.)

4436. *Èwo nìjà nínú "Ògún dá rèké"? Ṣe bí
Ògúndárèkẹ́ ló ni ìrèké-e rẹ̀?*
Where is the problem in *"Ògún dá rèké"*
[Ògún breaks sugarcane]? Is Ògúndárèkẹ́

not the owner of the sugarcane?[5] (One may
do with one's property as one wishes.)

Ẹ

4437. *Ẹja ló nibú.*
To the fish belongs the deep. (People should
not be begrudged what is rightfully theirs.)

4438. *Ẹlẹ́nu là ḿbi ká tó gbá a.*
It is from the owner of the mouth that one
asks leave before one slaps it. (One should
not take liberties with a thing without the
permission of its owner.)

4439. *Ẹni tó gba ọ̀nà ẹ̀bùrú wá ta ojì: wọ́n ní
a kì í gba ọ̀nà ẹ̀bùrú wá ta ojì; ó ní ṣé a lè gba
ọ̀nà ojúlé? Wọ́n ní bẹ́ẹ̀ ni.*
A man who came on the sly to confront his
cuckolder was told one does not confront
one's cuckolder on the sly; he asked if one
could do so frontally and was told, yes. (If
one's cause is just, one should press it boldly
and openly.)

F

4440. *Fúlàní ló ni pàpá-a daran-daran.*
To the Fulbe man belongs the cattle-herding
staff. (The objects people favor are good
indicators of their occupations.)

I

4441. *Ìran Awúsá ní ńjẹ góròò, ehín a pọ́n
koko.*

---

5. The proverb is an elaborate pun. The statement
"*Ògún dárèké*" says that the god of iron has broken
the cane. But since the shortened form of the name
Ògúndárèkẹ́ (which can be a person's name) is Ògún,
one also says that the person Ògún[dárèkẹ́] has broken
a cane. The proverb says Ògúndárèkẹ́ is the owner of
the sugarcane, in which case, when one says the god has
broken the cane, there is no problem.

It is the lineage of the Hausa that eats kola nuts; their teeth are brilliantly red. (Inherited habits leave their indelible marks. Compare the next entry.)

4442. *Ìran Ìbàdàn ní ńjàmàlà; iyán ni tÌjèṣà.*
It is Ibadan's lineage that eats *àmàlà;* pounded yams are what the Ìjèṣà eat. (Different people have different habits. Compare the foregoing variant.)

4443. *Ìṣé kì í mú ọkọ mú aya kó má ran ọmọ.*
Suffering does not grip the husband and grip the wife but spare the child. (The dependent cannot escape the hardship that befalls his or her benefactors.)

4444. *Ìwòfà àjọyá, orí è ní ńkún.*
A person pawned to several creditors is the one whose hair overgrows. (Everybody's responsibility is nobody's responsibility.)

4445. *Ìyàwó ọlẹ là ńgbà, a kì í gba ọmọ ọlẹ.*
The shiftless man's wife one may take from him, but one may not take his children. (Everybody has some inalienable rights. Compare 4431.)

K

4446. *Kàkà kí eku má jẹ sèsé, a fi ṣe à-wà-dànù.*
Rather than leave the yam beans uneaten, the rat will scatter them. (If one cannot have access to one's property, one would rather destroy it than permit others to have access.)

4447. *Kò sí ohun tí Alágbaà ò lẹ̀ ṣe nígbàlẹ̀ eégún.*
There is nothing the Alágbaà cannot do in the *eégun* grove. (The person invested with absolute authority can do as he or she wishes.)

O

4448. *Ohun tó wu olówó ní ńfi owó ẹ̀ rà.*
It is whatever the wealthy person wishes that he or she does with his or her money. (One can do as one wishes with one's property.)

4449. *Ojú kì í pọ́n àáfáà kó má nìí tèṣùbáà kan ṣoṣo.*
A Muslim priest is never so hard up that he does not have a solitary string of telling beads [prayer beads]. (Whatever condition one may be in, one will always have something to fall back on.)

4450. *Ojú kì í pọ́n Kurumá kó má nìí ṣíbí ìjẹun kan.*
A crew man is never so destitute that he does not have a single spoon.[6] (One is never so destitute as to have absolutely nothing.)

4451. *Oko ti ikún, ilẹ̀ ti èpà; a kì í bá àlùkẹrẹṣẹ du ilé-e baba-a rè.*
The farm is the domain of the squirrel; the ground is the domain of the groundnut; one does not dispute its father's house with the plant *àlùkẹrẹṣẹ.* (Each person has the right to enjoy his or her patrimony in peace.)

4452. *Olórùká gbòrùka, ọwọ́ àwé dòfo.*
The owner of the ring has taken back his ring; the fingers of the friend are now empty. (When the owner takes his property back, the flaunting of it by the borrower comes to an end.)

4453. *Olówó ṣe bí tòun là ńná.*
The rich person thinks it is his money other people are spending. (The rich would begrudge others any money of their own.)

---

6. *Kurumá* is the Yoruba rendering of "crew man," designating a member of the crew on any of the trading ships that plied the West African coast.

4454. *Olówó ṣe bí tòun là ńwí; òtòṣì ò jẹ iyanrìn.*
The rich person believes that it is he everybody thinks and talks about, [but] the poor person does not eat sand. (There are other people in the world besides the rich, even if the rich do not think so.)

4455. *Òṣùpá ò mòde òtòṣì; bó bá délé olórò á dé tèmi.*
The moon does not know which yard belongs to a poor man; if it reaches a wealthy man's abode, it will reach mine also. (With regard to Nature, all people are equal.)

4456. *Oye tó bá wuni là ńta Ifá ẹni pa.*
Whatever amount one pleases is what one demands for one's Ifá paraphernalia. (One is at liberty to do as one pleases with what one owns.)

Ọ

4457. *Ọmọ àjànàkú kì í ya arárá; ọmọ erín bí erin ní ńjọ.*
An elephant's baby will not turn out to be dwarfish; the baby sired by an elephant resembles nothing but an elephant. (People take after their parents.)

4458. *Ọmọ Aláké ní ńjoba lÁké, ọmọ olóko ní ńjoba lóko, àkóbí Onjo ní ńjoba nÍjèbú Òde.*
It is the firstborn of the Aláké [king of Abéòkúta] that inherits the throne of Aké; it is the firstborn of the farmer who rules on the farm; it is the firstborn of Onjo who inherits the throne at Ìjèbú Òde.[7] (The right to certain privileges is determined by set precedence, not at random.)

---
7. Johnson (76) identifies the Onjo (of Òkèehò) as a kingling of one of the provinces of the Òyó kingdom, the Èkún Òtún.

4459. *Ọmọ alápatà-á jogún ọbẹ.*
The son of the butcher inherits a knife. (One takes after one's parent's trade.)

4460. *Ọmọ erin-ín jogún ọlá.*
An elephant's child inherits greatness. (One takes after one's parents.)

4461. *Ọmọ ẹni ì ba jọni à bá yò; ọmọ tí Gàmbàrí bí okùn ni yó ran.*
Were one's child to resemble one, one would rejoice; the child of a Hausa man takes up the rope-weaving trade. (One always hopes that one's offspring will take after one. Compare 4465 and 4466.)

4462. *Ọmọ ọlẹ ní ńlágbára; ọmọ alágbára ní ńlẹ.*
The child of a lazy person is usually strong; the child of a strong person is usually lazy. (Children often turn out as opposites to their parents.)

4463. *Ọmọ tí a jí adìẹ bí, yó jìí adìẹ ju ìyá è lọ.*
A child born while the mother is a habitual chicken stealer will steal chickens even more compulsively than its mother. (Children take after their parents. The following is a variant.)

4464. *Ọmọ tí a pòn lọ yọ òmùnù-un koóko, yó yọ òmùnù-un koóko ju ìyá è lọ.*
The child carried on the mother's back while the mother plucks young grass proposes to pluck more young grass than its mother. (This is a slam at anyone who presumes to do better than those who enable him or her to do anything at all. See the previous entry for comparison.)

4465. *Ọmọ tí àgbè-é bí, oko ni yó ro; ọmọ tí Gàmbàrí bí, okùn ni yó ran.*
The child sired by a farmer will engage in farming; the child sired by a Hausa man will

engage in rope weaving. (People usually take up their lineage profession. Compare 4461 and the following entry.)

4466. *Ọmọ tí ẹjá bí ẹja ní ńjọ; ọmọ tí ẹkùn-ún bí ẹkùn ni yó yà; ọmọ tí Fúlàní bí okùn ni yó ran.*
The child spawned by a fish resembles a fish; the child sired by a leopard resembles a leopard; the child born to a Fulbe person will weave ropes. (One takes after one's parents. Compare 4461 and the preceding entry.)

4467. *Ọtá elésùúsú yó kòó tiẹ̀.*
The enemy of the person in charge of the saving scheme will collect when his or her turn arrives. (People's rights do not depend on whether one likes them or not.)

Ṣ

4468. *Ṣòkòtò ní ńjogún ìdí; ọmọ ní ńjogún-un baba.*
To the trousers belong the heritage of the buttocks; to the child belongs the patrimony of the father. (Children survive and inherit from their father, just as the trousers survive and inherit from the buttocks.)

T

4469. *Ta ní ńbá adẹ́tẹ̀ du ońjẹ jẹ?*
Who would scramble for food in the same plate with a leper? (People are unlikely to expose themselves voluntarily to abominations.)

4470. *Ta ní ńbá kọ̀-ń-kọ̀ṣọ̀ du èlùbọ́ kù?*
Who would dispute with the sieve the function of sifting yam flour? (No one can or should deprive people of what is rightfully theirs.)

4471. *Ta ní ńbá yímí-yímí du ìyípo?*
Who would ever wish to take over the dung beetle's habit of rolling dung? (There are certain things one should have no aspiration whatsoever of achieving.)

4472. *Tẹni ntẹni, àÀtàn ló làkísà.*
One's property belongs to one; to the dung heap belongs the rag. (No one should begrudge a person what is rightfully his or hers.)

On subservience to authority

A

4473. *A kì í gbèjà èèwọ̀; èèwọ̀ ní yó gbèjà ara è.*
One does not fight on behalf of a taboo; the taboo will fight its own fight. (It is unnecessary to try to keep people from committing crimes; the system will seek out offenders.)

4474. *Ayé lòyìnbó ńjẹ kú.*
Lifelong luxury is the lot of the white man. (The white man enjoys nothing but the best all his life long.)

Ẹ

4475. *Ẹni tó bá bú ọba lẹ́hìn, tó dójú ọba tó sẹ́, èrù ọba ló bà.*
The person who insults the king in the king's absence and denies doing so in the king's presence shows his fear of the king. (People's behavior in one's presence counts more than their behavior in one's absence, at least as an index of their fear. Compare 1378 and 1379.)

4476. *Ẹni tó gba ọtí fún eégún, òun náà ní ńgba obì fún ọ̀gbèrì.*
The person whose office is to bring wine to the masquerader is the same who will bring kola nuts to the novices.[1] (The servant can-

not choose whom he or she will serve and whom he or she will not.)

4477. *Ẹni tó ránni níṣẹ́ là ḿbẹ̀rù, a kì í bẹ̀rù ẹni tí a ó jẹ́ẹ́ ẹ fún.*
One fears the person who sent one with a message; one does not fear the person to whom one will deliver it. (The messenger need not fear the recipient of his or her message, since he or she is not responsible for its content; one's duty is to one's master, not to those one serves on his or her behalf.)

F

4478. *Ibi tó wu èfúùfù lèlè ní ńdarí ìgbé sí; ibi tó wu olówó ẹni ní ńranni lọ.*
The stiff breeze bends the bush in whichever direction it pleases; the person in control may send one wherever he or she wishes. (A person under authority has no choice but to obey the orders of the powers over him or her.)

Ọ

4479. *Ọba ló nilẹ̀.*
The king is the owner of the land. (There is no higher authority on earth than the king.)

4480. *Ọba ní ńgba owó ibodè.*
It is the king who receives customs dues.

---

1. The *eégún* are attended during their outing by novices, or the uninitiated. When they visit dignitaries, they receive gifts: wine for the masqueraders and kola nuts for the attendants.

(The wealth of the community belongs to the king.)

4481. Ọba ní ńjẹ ọrọ̀.
It is the king who enjoys all prosperity. (It is the king's lot to prosper.)

4482. Ọba tó ni apá ọ̀tún ló ni apá òsì.
The king who owns the area to the right also owns the area to the left. (The lord of all has authority over all.)

On just deserts

A

4483. *A kì í sìnni ká má nìí àpèjúwe.*
One does not escort a traveler and lack a description. (The helper must be acknowledged and rewarded.)

4484. *Ààbà ò ṣéé kàn mọ́ ẹni lésẹ̀, àfi ẹni tí ńṣe búburú.*
Stakes are not meant for people's legs, only for the legs of evildoers. (One who has not committed an offense does not deserve punishment.)

4485. *Agídí páálí òun ìyọnu; akùrẹtẹ̀ òun ìyà.*
Unalloyed obstinacy with its attendant troubles; lowly birth with its attendant suffering. (Each condition imposes its woes.)

4486. *A-gúnyán-sanyán kì í bẹ̀rù òkèlè.*
He-who-will-pound-yam-to-repay-pounded-yam is not bashful about morsels. (One can be as free as one chooses with a loan one will repay.)

4487. *Àgbà tí kò bá dáwó, omitooro ọbẹ̀ ni yó jẹ.*
An elder who does not contribute money will eat the watery remnants of the stew. (Nothing goes for nothing.)

4488. *Àgbà tí kò mú iṣu wá sábà ò níí jẹ iyán alẹ́.*
An elder who does not bring yams to the hut will not eat pounded yams at supper time. (One may not reap where one has not sown.)

4489. *Agbèfọ́ba kì í jẹbi fún un.*
The king's spokesman does not bear the king's guilt. (The servant is not liable for the master's misdeeds.)

4490. *Àìtà ni àdánù onígi.*
Failure to make a sale is the loss of the firewood seller. (Every exertion is worthwhile as long as it is rewarded.)[1]

4491. *Ajá kì í kọsẹ̀ ibi sí àtàn; bí kò bá tútù a bá gbígbẹ.*
A dog never encounters an ill omen (like stubbing its toe) on its way to the dung heap; if it does not find fresh dung there, it will find dry. (Whatever the circumstance, one cannot be left entirely without some asset.)

4492. *Ajá tó lọ sílé ẹkùn tó bọ̀, ká kí i kú ewu.*
A dog that goes to a leopard's home and returns: one should congratulate it on surviving the ordeal. (One should acknowledge and praise unusual feats.)

4493. *A-jí-ṣeṣé-lódèdè ní ńjẹun ju a-jí-gbọn-enini.*
He-who-wakes-in-the-morning-and-works-

---

1. The proverb plays on the word *dá*, meaning "break": the firewood seller goes to the forest to break dry branches to sell as firewood. The word also occurs as one syllable in *àdánù*, translatable as "breaking for nought" but meaning "loss." If the seller makes some money, he has not lost.

on-the-porch usually eats more than He-who-wakes-in-the-morning-and-brushes-against-morning-dew. (Those who have it easier often also receive the larger rewards.)

4494. *Akátá ję̀yìn ó ṣu ihá; ohun a bá ję là ńṣu.*
The civet cat ate palm fruits and excreted palm-fruit pericarp; one excretes what one eats. (One should not be surprised at the logical consequences of one's actions.)

4495. *Akéde ò ję iyán gbígbóná.*
The town crier does not eat steaming pounded yam. (Every obligation has its toll.)

4496. *Akèsán lòpin Ọ̀yọ́; ilé ọkọ nibìsinmi obìnrin.*
Akèsán is the frontier of Ọ̀yọ́; a spouse's home is a woman's place of rest. (Just as Akèsan is Ọyọ's city limit, so a spouse's home is a woman's final destination.)

4497. *Aláàárù tí ńję̀ran ńję awọ orí-i rè̩.*
A hired carrier who eats meat eats skin off his skull. (The laborer eats of his sweat; the laborer with a luxurious taste pays for it with his sweat. Compare 4499.)

4498. *Alákatampò-ó bojú wòkè.*
The user of a crossbow casts his eyes upward. (One's trade imposes certain behaviors.)

4499. *Alápatà tí ńję̀ran, ẹran orí-i rè̩ ló ńję.*
The butcher who eats meat eats the skin off his skull. (One eats of one's labor. Compare 4497.)

4500. *Àpáàdì-í bá wọn dín àgbàdo kò rí rún; ọkọ́ tó bá wọn ṣá oko-ó sùn lébi.*
The potsherd makes itself available for popping corn but gets no share of it; the hoe that helped to clear the farm sleeps in hunger. (The fate of some is to work so that others might thrive.)

4501. *À-pa-ì-délé ò jẹ́ ká mọ̀ pé ológbò ńṣọdẹ.*
Failure to bring home its kill denies the cat recognition as a hunter. (Secret accomplishments are like no accomplishments at all. Compare 4688.)

B

4502. *Baálè̩ Ìròkò-ó yan tiè̩ té̩lè̩; ó ní bí ẹ rókùnrin ẹ ṣá a; bí ẹ róbìnrin ẹ ṣá a.*
The chief of Ìròkò made his pronouncement beforehand; he said, "If you come upon a man, slash him, and if you come upon a woman, slash her." (The law does not distinguish between man and woman, or between one offender and another.)

4503. *Bí a bá bu omi sórí, ó ńwá ẹsè̩ bò̩.*
If one pours water on one's head, it comes looking for the legs. (Actions have their inevitable consequences; matters will not be resolved until they have reached their conclusions.)

4504. *Bí a bá pẹja tán, lébé eja la fi ńhá eja lénu.*
After killing a fish, one stuffs its tail fin into its mouth. (An offender furnishes the means of his or her own punishment.)

4505. *Bí a ó lọ nílùú, a ó mọ ohun tí ńléni.*
If one must flee a town, one should know what is chasing one off. (One must know the cause of one's suffering or punishment.)

4506. *Bí àrígiṣégi-í bá ṣégi, orí ara-a rè̩ ní ńfií rù ú.*
After the twig-cutting insect cuts twigs, it carries them on its own head. (The disaster a person causes descends on his own head.)

4507. *Bí egbò ò bá pa elégbò, kì í pa ẹni tí ńwẹ̀ ẹ́.*
If an ulcer does not kill the person who has

it, it will not kill the person who treats it. (Each person suffers his or her own woes.)

4508. *Bí ẹkọ bá ní kókó, kì í ṣẹjọ alágbàdo.*
If the corn meal is lumpy, the fault does not lie with the corn seller. (The person who furnished the raw material is not responsible for the flaws of the finished product.)

4509. *Bí ìyàwó bá sọjú ẹni, tó tún ṣẹ̀hìn ẹni, ó ní láti ní èrè tí yó jẹ níbẹ̀.*
If a wife honors one's wishes in one's presence and also honors one's wishes in one's absence, some reward is certainly due her. (The ever-faithful mate deserves some rich reward.)

4510. *Bí owó bá ti mọ ni oògùn ńmọ.*
The limit of the money is the limit of the medicine. (One gets only as much as one's money can buy.)

4511. *Bí ọmọ bá ti rí là ńṣe àna-a rẹ̀.*
The considerations one offers to the parents and relatives of one's fiancée are always commensurate with the quality of the fiancée. (One offers equal value in exchange for whatever one procures.)

Ẹ

4512. *Èèmejì lojú ahun ńpọn.*
The miser's eyes redden twice.[2] (One is often paid back in one's own coin.)

4513. *Èfọ́ kì í sún èfọ́ sọ́hùn-ún.*
Vegetables do not push vegetables out of the way. (One must respects others' claims as one asserts one's own.)

---

2. The miser's eyes redden at the fear that others wish to share what he or she has; they redden again when others, remembering that refusal to share, deny the miser a share of what *they* have.

4514. *Ègàn ni "Hẹ̀."*
A sneer is a mere indication of jealousy. (Let us acknowledge achievements when we see them and not sneer in envy.)

4515. *Ègàn ò pé kóyin má dùn.*
Detraction does not rob honey of its sweetness. (People's failure to acknowledge one's achievements does not detract from their value; one's ability to thrive does not depend on other people's approval.)

4516. *Ẹní da eérú leérú ńtọ̀; eléte lète ńyé; oun a bá ṣe ní ńyéni.*
Ashes blow toward the thrower; the plotter alone knows what he or she is plotting; one is privy only to that which one is involved in. (Evil recoils on those who plot evil, and those who are visited with evil must know what actions of theirs caused it. Compare 2485.)

4517. *Ẹní fúnni légbàá ò ṣeun bí ẹni a fún.*
The person who gives six pence deserves less praise than the person to whom it is given. (Whoever gives a trifle as a gift is less to be valued than the person who accepts such a gift.)

4518. *Ẹni tí a bá ṣe lóore tí kò dúpẹ́, bí a bá ṣe é níkà kò níí dùn ún.*
The person who shows no gratitude when he or she is done a favor will feel no hurt when he or she is done an injury. (Ungrateful people deserve to be deliberately hurt.)

4519. *Ẹni tí a kò fẹ́ là ńgàn.*
People we do not like are the ones we sneer at. (One can always find fault with people one does not like.)

4520. *Ẹni tí kò kíni "Kú àbọ̀"-ọ́ pàdánùú "Kúule."*
The person who does not give one "Welcome" forfeits the arriving person's saluta-

tion to those already there. (Courtesies and discourtesies are repaid in kind. Compare 302.)

4521. Ẹni tí kò níyàwó kì í bí àbíkú.
A man who has no wife does not father born-to-die children. (Misfortunes have their fortunate aspects. Compare 4389.)

4522. Ẹni tó bá dẹ ẹbìtì kágbó ní ńpa orí kágbó.
The person who sets traps all over the forest is the one who has to wander all over the forest. (One will have to live with the consequences of one's actions.)

4523. Ẹni tó fẹ́ni ní àfẹ̀ìlówó, iwọ ní ńfúnni jẹ.
A woman who marries one even though one paid no dowry feeds one nothing but gall. (One cannot expect much from something one acquires free or too cheaply. Compare 963.)

4524. Ẹni tó lẹrú ló lẹrù.
The owner of the slave also owns the luggage [he carries]. (Appendages go with the main item.)

4525. Ẹni tó mọ iyì-i wúrà là ńta á fún.
One sells gold only to those who appreciate its value. (Do not squander treasure on those incapable of appreciating it.)

4526. Ẹni tó na àjànàkú ládàá nídìí ṣe aájò ajé.
The person who smites an elephant on its rump with a machete makes at least a gesture toward riches. (However modest the effort, it should be acknowledged.)[3]

4527. Ẹni tó pa èèyàn ni yó ru òkú; ẹni tó fọ́ koto ejò ni yó gbèé e.
It is the person who kills another person who will carry the corpse; it is the person who breaks the gourd housing a snake who will carry the snake. (Each person is responsible for the consequences of his or her actions.)

4528. Ẹni tó rí Aláké, tí ó ńyínmú, jorí-jorí ní ńjẹ é.
Whoever sees Aláké and wrinkles his or her nose in a sneer has got a worm in his or her nose.[4] (It is futile to sneer at an illustrious person.)

4529. Ẹni tó ṣe ọbẹ̀ tí kò dùn, a ní kí òrìṣá pa á; ẹni tí kò sè ńkọ́?
The person who makes a stew that is not delicious, we ask the gods to kill; what about the person who did not cook anything? (We should not overreact to other people's minor flaws.)

4530. Ẹni tó ṣe òràn òtùfù ní ńkíyè sí ẹ̀hìnkùlé.
It is a person who has done something that calls for the torch [light] who must keep a close watch on his back yard. (If one has done something underhanded, one has good reason to be apprehensive.)

4531. Ẹnu asọsọkọ́ kì í tó òrò.
The mouth of the person whose garment is a loincloth is never welcome in a discussion. (A shiftless person has no privileges in the community.)

4532. Ẹ̀pà pẹ̀lú olúwa-a rẹ̀ ní ńfojú winá.
Both the peanut and its owner will feel the effects of the fire. (The person belaboring others will also suffer from the exertion.)

---

3. The person cannot kill the elephant with his puny blows and therefore will not have it to sell, but he has at least tried.

4. Aláké is the title of the king of the Ẹgbá.

4533. Ẹran tó jẹ èbù ló ní ká gbé olówó-o rẹ̀ yílẹ̀.
The goat that ate the yam cut for planting caused its owner to be flung to the ground. (One may be blameless and yet be dragged into trouble by the actions of those one is responsible for.)

4534. Ẹsin pòpóòrò kì í sáré ju ẹni tó gùn ún lọ.
A cornstalk horse does not gallop faster than its rider. (The limit of one's effort is the limit of one's reward.)

I

4535. Ibi òjó pa igún dé, yó rò fún ẹni tó rán-an níṣẹ́.
The extent to which the rain beat the vulture, it will recount to the person who sent it on an errand.[5] (The servant has a right to let his or her master know the hardships endured in doing the master's bidding.)

4536. Ìgbẹ́ lẹtu mbá erin gbé.
The antelope shares the forest with the elephant as its home. (The lowliest creature has a claim to some space just as the mightiest has.)

4537. Ìkà a máa gbó; ìkà a máa tọ́; àtisùn ìkà ni kò sunwọ̀n.
The wicked may live long, and the wicked may survive long, but the end of the wicked is never pleasant. (However long the wicked succeeds, he or she comes to grief in the end.)

4538. Ìkà ò jẹ́ kí paramọ́lẹ̀ ó dàgbà: ì bá gùn tó ọká, ì bá gùn tó erè; a yó gbọ-gbọ bí iṣan.
Wickedness kept the night adder from full development: it would have been as long as the cobra; it would have been as long as the python; it would have been as thick as sinews. (Wickedness takes its toll on the wicked also.)

4539. Ìkàtè-é forí gbùsì; oun tí ńpeja-á wà nísàlẹ̀ omi.
The stick to which the fishhook line is tied receives the curses on its head, but what kills the fish is under the surface of the water. (Sometimes one's position makes one bear the blame for others' misdeeds.)

4540. Ìkòkò tí ńse eyìn, eyìn ni yó fọ́ọ o.
The pot used for cooking palm fruits will be broken by palm fruits in the end. (Those who live dangerously die dangerously.)

4541. Ikú ẹwà ní ńpọ̀kín; ikú ara-ríré ní ńpa odíde.
It is the death of beauty that kills the egret; it is the death of swaggering that kills the parrot. (Calling attention to one's enviable assets invites trouble and ultimately disaster.)[6]

4542. Ikú ogun ní ńpa akíkanjú; ikú odò ní ńpa òmùwẹ̀; ikú ara-ríré ní ńpa arẹwà, màjà-màsá ní ńpa onítìjú; ọwọ́ tádàá bá mọ̀ ní ńká àdá léhín.
It is death related to warfare that kills the warrior; it is the death associated with the river that kills the swimmer; it is the death attendant on preening that kills the beautiful person; wondering whether to stand and fight or run kills the easily embarrassed person; the trade that the cutlass knows knocks out its teeth. (Each person's bane is closely

---

5. See note 72 to 1003 for the traditional vulture story.

6. The egret and the parrot stand out among birds for their attractiveness and therefore invite the attention of humans far more than other birds do.

connected to his or her calling. Compare 3918, 4544, and 5190.)

4543. *Ikú ọmọ ní ńpa ayíntalẹ̀.*
It is death that comes of having children that kills the grub. (Some obligations carry deadly risks with them.)[7]

4544. *Ikú tí yó pọdẹ ńbẹ nínú igbó; ikú tí yó pàgbẹ̀ ńbẹ lọ́rùn ebè; ikú tí yó pa ajókakanfa ńbẹ lọ́jà tó wé gèlè ga-n-ga.*
The death that will kill the hunter is in the forest; the death that will kill the farmer is coiled around the heap; the death that will kill the dancer to the *kakanfa* drums is in the market, sporting gargantuan headgear. (One's favorite addiction is likely to be one's undoing. Compare 3918 and 4542.)

4545. *Imú kì í tóbi kó gba ọ̀rọ̀ ẹnu sọ.*
The nose cannot get so big that it takes the speech out of the mouth. (No one, however mighty, may usurp tthe rights of others.)

4546. *Ìpín àìṣẹ̀ ni yó pa aláròká.*
The protective mystical force of the innocent will kill whoever speaks ill about him or her. (Whoever spreads scandal about an innocent person will answer to the powers of the universe.)

4547. *Ìrà nìtà.*
Buying determines selling. (How one goes about acquiring something will determine one's manner of expending it or disposing of it.)

4548. *Ìṣẹ́ ibi, èrè ibi á tálẹ́.*
The suffering that results from doing evil, the rewards for doing evil, will last until

nighttime [i.e., until old age]. (The reward for wickedness is not fleeting.)

4549. *Ìsòkú ni ìjogún.*
One's manner of performing the burial determines how one inherits. (One's claim to inheritance is dependent on how worthy a survivor one proves oneself.)

4550. *Iṣu ẹni ní ńki ọwọ́ ẹni bọ epo.*
It is on account of one's yams that one's fingers come to be soiled by palm oil. (Said when one is forced to endure some indignity because of the behavior of others close to one.)

4551. *Ìtà a ta olè là ńta adóhunmọ́.*
The terms with which one sells the thief are the same as those one applies to the false accuser. (The thief and the perjurer deserve the same fate.)

4552. *Ìtàdógún kù sí dèdè; ọjọ́ ẹlẹ́sìn-ín kòla.*
The seventeenth day is at hand; the day [of reckoning] for the person who deserves ridicule is one day away. (The day approaches when the shiftless person will be exposed.)[8]

4553. *Ìtàdógún làjọ Ègbá.*
The plenary gathering of the Ègbá is every seventeenth day.[9] (The day of reckonning approaches inexorably.)

4554. *Ìwà adìẹ ní ńwípé ká tu ìyẹ́ ẹ̀.*
It is the chicken's behavior that caused its wing feathers to be plucked. (People by their

---

7. Ayíntalẹ̀ are supposedly grubs that invade the mud floors of homes in order to lay eggs; people kill them because they are a nuisance.

8. The seventeenth-day sabbath of the gods (day of worship) calls for elaborate sacrificing and feasting; on that occasion the shiftless person who lacks the required means is exposed to public ridicule.

9. In the Ègbá mutual saving system, èésú, each person makes his or her contribution at the meeting that falls every seventeenth day.

own habits suggest what restrictions should be placed on them.)

4555. *Ìwà awó ní ńpe awó lẹ́tù.*
It is the guinea fowl's behavior that makes one know it as a guinea fowl.[10] (By their habits shall people be known. Compare 3054.)

4556. *Ìwòfà ẹgbàá àtolúwa-a rẹ̀ ní ńsin ẹrú.*
The person pawned for 2,000 cowries [six pence in old British currency] will share the slave labor with the creditor. (One cannot expect a great deal of service from something acquired on the cheap.)

4557. *Ìwòfà tí kò wá ní ńjẹ́ òkú-ùgbé lójú olówó.*
The pawn who does not come to work is the one the creditor regards as a deadbeat. (A person who does what is expected of him or her avoids criticism.)

4558. *Ìyá kà, ọmọ́ kà ni òwò.*
Mother counts and then the child [or daughter] counts; such is the practice in trading. (In a joint venture each person involved must do his or her share.)

4559. *Iyán díkókó, kì í ṣejọ́ onísu; ọkàá mẹrẹ, kì í ṣejọ́ elélùbọ́.*
If the pounded yam is lumpy, the fault does not belong to the seller of the yams; if the yam-flour meal is ill cooked, the fault does not belong to the seller of the yam flour. (One should not blame those from whom one obtained materials if in the end one botched their use.)

4560. *Ìyàwó tí a gbé lósù agà, tó ńfi iyán molé, Yóbaníbẹ̀ lọmọ è ńjẹ́.*

The wife who was married during the lean month of May and who plasters pounded yams on the walls: the child she bears will be named Her-comeuppance-awaits her. (Said of nonproducing but wasteful people.)

4561. *Iye ajá bí lajá ńṣọ́.*
The dog looks after whatever the number of pups in its litter. (One is entitled only to what one owns.)

J

4562. *Jagun-jagun ní ńjẹ obì; àgbẹ̀ jẹ awùsá ṣẹnu yángí-yángí.*
It is the warrior that eats kola nuts; the farmer eats only *awùsá* nuts, which make the mouth bitter. (To the valiant belong the best of the spoils; the rest get only the leavings.)

K

4563. *Ká fi inú ṣèkà, ká fòde sòótọ́, kan-kan lara ńnini; ohun tí ńbini kò níí ṣàì bini wò.*
If one is kind outwardly but secretly wicked, one is beset by unease; whatever is supposed to call one to account will not fail to do so. (Wickedness, however well concealed, will not go unpunished.)

4564. *Kàkà ká fi ọmọ oyè jọyè, wọ́n ńwá ọmọ aṣẹ́wé.*
Instead of placing the legitimate heir on the throne, they go in search of the son of a seller of leaves. (Said of people who bypass gems in preference for pebbles.)

4565. *Kí ikú má pa ẹni tí ńdáni lóro; kí òrìṣà má jẹ́ẹ́ kí ǹkan ṣe ẹni tí ńṣe èèyàn níkà; bó pẹ́ títí orí ẹni a dáni.*
May death not take the person who deprives one of the things one needs; may the gods

---

10. *Ẹtù* and *awó* are different names for the same bird.

not permit anything to happen to the person who does wicked things to one; sooner or later one's head will vindicate one. (One should let evil people do their evil without seeking revenge; eventually they will reap what they have sown.)

4566. *Kò tètè dé ò níí tètè lọ; ẹni ò tètè dáyé ò níí tètè lọ sọ́run.*
The person who was not early in arriving will not be early in departing; the person who did not come into this world early will not go early to heaven. (Older people should die before younger ones.)

L

4567. *Lámbẹ́ lè yàgbàdo lóko ká wá gbá ìbejì lójú nílé?*
Because a monkey cut some corn on the farm, can one slap a twin in the house? (One cannot punish a person for another person's crimes, however closely the two may be related.)[11]

M

4568. *Má sọ ọ́ lófin, òfin ní ńsọ ara ẹ̀.*
Do not lay down the law; the law will lay itself down. (One does not need to be a vigilante for the wrongdoer to come to grief.)

4569. *Méjì kì í ko ọ̀bẹ́mu; bí kò bá rí mu yó rìí tà; bí kò bá rí tà yó rìí mu.*
Two misfortunes will not befall a palm-wine tapster; if there is not enough to drink, there will be enough to sell; if there is not enough to sell, there will be enough to drink. (Every

misfortune has its consolation. Compare the next entry.)

4570. *Méjì ni ìlẹ̀kùn; bí kò ṣí sínú a ṣí sóde; bí kò tì sínú a tì sóde.*
Doors come in two different dispositions; if they do not open inward, they will open outward; if they do not shut inward, they will shut outward. (One always has an option in the face of any difficulty. Compare the preceding entry.)

4571. *Mọ̀ọ́ gún, mọ̀ọ́ tẹ̀, oníṣu ló niyán.*
One may be an expert at pounding and mashing, but the pounded yam belongs to the owner of the yams. (The owner's claim is always superior to the helper's.)

N

4572. *Ní ọjọ́ tí ìjímèrè-é bá fi ojú kan Aláàpíni lòràn inú ẹ̀ ńtán.*
The day the brown monkey meets the Aláàpíni [head of the *egúngún* cult] is the day all his troubles will end. (Whenever one encounters one's savior, one's troubles are over.)[12]

O

4573. *Obìnrin kì í gba owó àlè tán kó ní gìnìsà ńṣe òun.*
A woman does not take a lover's money and then complain of menorrhagia. (One should perform obligations for which one has received payment.)

4574. *Obìnrín ńdá gbèsè a ní ká ba wí, ẹ ní tọmọ ẹ̀ ni ká wò; èyí tí ńyá ìwòfà fún ọkọ ẹ̀ ńbí ìtì igi bí?*

---

11. The Yoruba usually refer to twins as ẹdun, the name for the colobus monkey, believing in an affinity between twins and that animal; *lámbẹ́* is another name for the same animal.

12. The assumption is that there is a secret pact between the brown monkey and the eégún (egúngún) cult.

A woman keeps incurring debts, and we propose to caution her; you advise that we consider only the fact that she has borne some children; does the one [wife] who procures pawns for her husband give birth to logs of wood? (A person's performance of a certain duty does not relieve him or her of responsibility in all other regards.)

4575. *Òfò lomi èfó ńṣe.*
To be tossed away is the fate of the liquid squeezed from vegetables.[13] (An expression that the person addressed or referred to is fated for destruction, or a curse or wish to the same effect.)

4576. *Ogun ní ńṣi ẹni mú; èpè kì í ṣi ẹni jà.*
A war might capture a person by mistake; a curse never affects one by mistake. (More often than not one's misfortunes are the clear results of curses, not simply happenstance.)

4577. *Ohun ìdí là ńtà ra ìdí; bóbìnrín bá gba owó àlè a fi ràlèkè sídìí.*
It is something that pertains to the buttocks that one sells to buy buttocks; if a woman receives money from her paramour, she uses it to buy beads for her waist. (The profit from a venture should go to promoting that venture.)

4578. *Ohun tí a sọ síwájú là ḿbá; ohun tí a gbìn là ńwà; nígbàtí a ò sọ síwájú, tí a ò gbìn séhìn, kí la ó bàá?*
Whatever one throws ahead is what one comes upon; whatever one plants is what one reaps; when one does not throw anything ahead and does not plant anything, what can one expect to find later? (One can expect no profit without investment.)

---

13. This is a reference to the cooking practice of parboiling vegetables and squeezing them dry before using them for stew.

4579. *Ohun tí a wá là ńrí.*
One finds what one seeks. (Whatever befalls, it has most likely been invited.)

4580. *Ohun tó dé ló ní ká wáá wo òun.*
It is the phenomenon that occurred which summoned people to come witness it. (If something did not attract people's attention, they would not assemble to watch it.)

4581. *Ojú àánú ti fó tìkà ló kù.*
Merciful eyes have gone blind; only wicked ones remain. (The time for mercy is past; now is the time for hardheartedness.)

4582. *Ojú kì í rí arẹwà kó má kìí i.*
The eyes never see a beautiful person without acknowledging him or her. (Things that deserve one's attention should receive it.)

4583. *Ojú kì í ti ọkọ kó má bàá ìyàwó è sòrò.*
A husband can never be so bashful that he cannot speak to his wife. (However reticent one might be, some duties one must perform.)

4584. *Ojú ní ńyin-ni kẹ́ni ó sèmín-ìn.*
It is the eyes that praise one and cause one to do even better. (Approving eyes are an encouragement to do even better.)

4585. *Ojú olóko làgbàdó ṣe ńgbó.*
The corn matures in the presence of the farmer. (An incantation or a prayer that the fruition of one's efforts will happen in one's lifetime. Compare the next entry and 4088.)

4586. *Ojú oníkàn nikàn-án ṣe ńwèwù èjè.*
It is in the presence of the locust-bean planter that the locust bean puts on a cloth of blood [or ripens]. (One will know of the consequences of one's actions. Compare the preceding entry and 4088.)

4587. *Òkú kú a ní ká wá oúnje fún àwon omodé ilé; àgbà ilé ló pa á bí?*
A person dies, and the concern is expressed that the young ones of the household be fed; are the elders of the household responsible for the death? (In a disaster one should be mindful of the needs of all concerned, not only of the youngest, the weakest, or the most helpless.)

4588. *Okùn-ún mú eléèdà.*
The noose has caught a trickster. (A person is hoist with his own petard.)

4589. *Olókùnrùn tó je iyán ogójì, tòun tiwon ní ńre ogun.*
The invalid who eats pounded yams worth 40 cowries: both he and the warriors will head for the war. (One cannot have a healthy appetite and also complain of ill health.)

4590. *Omi kì í wón ká má fi fún òde mu.*
Water is never so scarce that one does not give some to the outdoor earth to drink. (However hard up one is, one will do those things that are essential.)

4591. *Onídìí gègèrè ni yó gba egbàà; ohun e bá rí e féléegun.*
The person with a hefty backside is the one who deserves 2,000 cowries [six pence]; whatever else you can afford, give it to the bony person. (The better-endowed woman is the one to spend money on.)

4592. *Oníyà ni yó je èyí tó jù.*
The person who earned the punishment will bear most of it. (The person responsible for a problem will suffer most of its consequences.)

4593. *Òòjó là ńsu imí àgbagbà.*
The shit from a plantain meal comes on the same day. (The consequences for certain actions are virtually immediate.)

4594. *Orí è ló kún tí à ḿbá a fá a.*
It is his head that has grown bushy and that we are helping him to groom. (It is because a person has erred that he is being lectured for his own good.)

4595. *Orí la bé; àyà la là; ibi tí orí bá wá ni yó bàá lo.*
The head is what was severed; the chest is what was split open; the manner of the head's coming will be the manner of its going. (The condition in which a person becomes involved in a venture will determine the way he emerges at the end of it.)[14]

4596. *Orí òpómù: ó kó ajá lódè; ajá mode tán ó pa orí òbo je.*
The monkey's fortune: he taught the dog hunting; the dog became adept at hunting and killed the monkey for food. (A person one has helped may turn around to plot one's destruction.)

4597. *Òròmo-adìe ò lè nù kí eégún gba òbúko.*
A young chick that goes missing cannot thereby justify the presentation of a he-goat to the masquerader as replacement. (The replacement or compensation for a thing must be commensurate with that thing.)

O

4598. *Ògá ni oníjó, ògá ni arìnnà, ògá ni àtè tó mú eye lésè tí kò lè lo.*
The dancer is honorable; the wayfarer is honorable; also honorable is the birdlime that catches a bird and prevents it from flying off. (Anybody who performs a commendable feat deserves honor.)

---

14. The reference to beheading and chest splitting suggests criminality and, thus, that the person's criminal propensities will lead him to a terrible end.

4599. *Ọgá tà, ọgá ò tà, owó aláàárù á pé.*
Whether the master's wares sell or not, the porter's fees must be paid in full. (Whether you use the services well or not, the provider's fee must be paid. See the next entry.)

4600. *Ọgọ́ tà, ọgọ̀ ò tà, owó aláàárù á pé.*
Whether the foolish trader profits or not, the porter's fees must be paid in full. (One's folly will not absolve one of obligations. See the preceding entry.)

4601. *Ojọ́ gbogbo ni tolè, ojọ́ kan ni tolóhun.*
Every day belongs to the thief; one day belongs to the owner. (The evildoer may enjoy prolonged success, but the day he is exposed is the one that matters.)

4602. *Ọ̀kọ̀ṣẹ́ ò gbà jẹ.*
A person who refuses to run errands does not receive gifts of food. (Never expect rewards if you never offer help.)

4603. *Ọ̀kọ̀ṣẹ́ ò mọ ìpè búburú, kò mọ ìpè rere.*
A shirker does not know which summons will be taxing and which will be rewarding. (People who will answer no call cannot know which is profitable.)

4604. *Ọmọ kì í forí pẹkàn kó mú bàbá ẹ̀ dání; iye ọmọ lọmọ ḿmú lọ.*
A child does not emerge from a womb with its father in tow; the child emerges all by itself. (A child who gets in trouble cannot depend on his father to bear the consequences.)

4605. *Ọmọ ọba tó kú lọ́yọ̀ọ́ ò léjọ́; ọmọ ọba tó kú níbòmíràn lo ní aápọn.*
The prince's death in Ọ̀yọ́ entails no difficulty; it is the prince's death elsewhere that demands explanations.[15] (If a matter

in one's charge goes wrong, one cannot be blamed, so long as one was doing as one was supposed to do.)

4606. *Ọmọ tó na Ọ̀yẹ̀kú ńláti rí ìjà Ogbè.*
A child that whips Ọ̀yẹ̀kú will undoubtedly face repercussion from Ogbè.[16] (Never victimize a person who has a powerful champion.)

4607. *Ọmọdé kì í wọ oko èèsì kó má jo.*
A child does not venture into a bush of stinging nettles and escape being stung. (One cannot escape the consequences of one's actions.)

4608. *Ọtí pani, oòrún pa bọ̀tí; oró tí a dá ọkà lọkà ńdáni san.*
Wine intoxicates people; the sun beats down on the malt; the suffering that people inflicted on the corn is what the corn is avenging.[17] (When one suffers, one is accounting for an earlier misdeed.)

4609. *Ọwọ́ kékeré la fi ńgba ńlá.*
It is with a small hand that one provokes a big one. (A weakling should take care not to attract the attention of a bully through provocative behavior.)

4610. *Ọwọ́ kì í pẹ́ níhò àkèekèe, àfi bí a ò bá bá a nílé.*
The hand does not stay long in a scorpion's hole unless the scorpion is not at home. (Unless he is somehow incapacitated, a vindictive person does not delay before extracting vengeance; unless the world has

---

15. The *Aláàfin* (king) of Ọ̀yọ́ is preeminent among all Yoruba rulers. If an Ọ̀yọ́ prince dies outside of Ọ̀yọ́,

the ruler of the place where the event occurs will surely feel some anxiety.

16. Ọ̀yẹ̀kú is one of the junior headings of the Ifá corpus, whereas Ogbè is the senior heading.

17. The ingredients for making malt liquor are dried in the sun in the process.

turned upside down, retribution for certain offenses is swift.)

T

4611. *Tàkúté Ọlọ́run, kò sẹ́ni tí kò lè mú; bó májá, a mẹ́ran, a sì mú adìẹ òkókó.*

No one is beyond being caught in God's mousetrap; it catches the dog, catches the goat, and catches even the strapping chicken. (No one is beyond God's judgment.)

SIX

Truisms

Miscellany

A

4612. *À bá mọ̀ a kò ṣe é; a ṣé tán ó di aápọn.*
Had one known, one would not have done
it; having been done, it becomes a bother.
(If one knew what the consequences of certain actions would be, one would avoid
them, but hindsight does not diminish the
consequences. See 3481.)

4613. *À bá rí kàdárà, kedere là bá róhun tí
ńṣeni.*
Were one able to discern what lot one had
chosen, plainly would one see the source of
one's problems.[1] (Clairvoyance removes all
mystery from one's misfortune).

4614. *À bá sọ pé omi ni yó ṣe eja jinná, à pé
irọ́.*
Had anyone said that water would cook fish,
one would have argued the opposite. (Water
is the natural medium for fish; who would
have thought that it could also be the death
of fish?)

4615. *A bọ́ ike lọ́wọ́ ọ̀tún, a fi bọ ọwọ́ òsì; lọ́wọ́
lọ́wọ́ niké wà.*
One removes an ivory bangle from one's
right wrist and slips it onto the left wrist; for
all that, the bangle remains on one's wrist.
(The gesture or effort has not significantly
altered the status quo ante.)

---

1. The underlying idea here is the Yoruba belief that
each person chooses at creation what lot he or she will
endure in life but that the information is deleted from
the person's memory at birth.

4616. *A bú ológbò ní a-bẹ̀rẹ̀kẹ́-kangiri; a ha
purọ́ mọ́ ọ?*
We insult the cat as being bulge-cheeked;
do we misspeak? (The insult is a justified
description of a cat.)

4617. *A kì í dé ìgbàro èṣí ká fẹ́ ohun okòó kù.*
One does not get to last year's farm and not
find things worth 20 cowries. (One cannot
become so destitute that one is left with
absolutely nothing. Compare 1659 and
2183.)

4618. *A kì í dé ilé arúgbó lọ́fẹ̀ẹ́.*
One does not go to an old person's home for
nothing. (Nothing in life is free.)

4619. *A kì í dé ilé ikú ká fẹ́ orí kù; bí a ò bá
tútù, a ó bàá gbígbẹ.*
One does not get to Death's home and fail to
find heads; if one does not find fresh ones,
one will find dry ones. (The sole custodian
of a commodity is unlikely to experience a
lack of it.)

4620. *A kì í dẹ igbó ká peja; a kì í gbọ́n odò
ká pa àfè.*
One does not hunt in the bush and kill fish;
one does not drain a river and kill a grass
mouse. (Some occurrences would be impossible and unexpected in certain places.)

4621. *A kì í dó oko dá gbèsè; ọmọ la fi ḿbí.*
One does not make love to a person and
get into debt; it is childbirth that results. (A

routine and pleasurable activity should not lead to disaster.)

4622. *A kì í dùn yùngbà ká fi wé ìbòsí ìgárá.*
One does not make a joyful noise that can be compared to the alarm that announces a theft. (Joyousness should express itself differently from disaster.)

4623. *A kì í fi ojoojúmọ́ rókọ ẹni; ọmọ ẹni kì í ní ọbàkan.*
One does not see one's husband every day; one's child does not have a half-brother. (Never expect the impossible.)

4624. *A kì í gbélé mọ ẹni ogún pa.*
One cannot remain at home and know who has been killed in battle. (There is no knowledge like firsthand knowledge.)

4625. *A kì í gbélé mọ ogun tí ò níí dùn.*
One does not stay at home and know which battle will be unpleasant. (Only an eye-witness knows the truth of an affair.)

4626. *A kì í gbin àlùbọ́sà kó hu ẹ̀fọ́.*
One does not plant onions and have [the ground] yield spinach. (What one plants is what one reaps.)

4627. *A kì í gbọ́ búburú lẹ́nu Abọrẹ.*
One never hears evil from the mouth of Abọrẹ. (Only good issues from the mouths of the gods.)[2]

4628. *A kì í há ẹran kí òróòro má gba tiẹ̀.*
One does not butcher and share out an animal's meat without the gallbladder taking its share. (Never seek to do rightful claimants out of what they deserve.)

4629. *A kì í já lórí ọ̀pẹ ká tún jọba nísàlẹ̀.*
One does not fall from atop a palm tree and

then become a king below. (One does not reap glory from disgrace.)

4630. *A kì í jà nígbó ráhùn ọpa.*
One does not fight in the bush and lament a lack of sticks. (There can be no drought in a deluge.)

4631. *A kì í jẹ aládùn méjì pọ̀.*
One does not enjoy two pleasures at the same time. (One cannot have everything at once.)

4632. *A kì í jẹ ejò ká jẹ ogún inú ẹ̀.*
One does not eat a snake and eat the un-born snakes inside it. (It is not done to have an affair with a mother and also with her daughter.)

4633. *A kì í jẹ méjì lábà Àlàdé; ẹní jẹyán ò gbọdò jẹsu.*
One does not eat two things on Àlàdé's farm; whoever eats pounded yams may not eat yams. (One must choose among alterna-tives, not have everything. See the following variant.)

4634. *A kì í jẹ méjì lóko Ǹtọfà; ẹní bá jẹyán kì í jẹ èkọ; ẹní bá jẹ isu kì í jẹ àmàlà.*
One does not eat two things on Ǹtọfà's farm; the person who eats pounded yams may not eat corn-meal loaf; whoever eats yams may not eat yam-flour loaf. (One cannot have all amenities. Compare the preceding entry.)

4635. *A kì í jẹ òkèlè léri òkèlè.*
One does not eat one morsel [or mouthful] atop another. (Do things at a seemly pace, not in a rushed manner.)

4636. *A kì í kó imí tán kó tún máa rùn.*
One does not remove excrement and yet en-dure its stink. (Once a problem is resolved, there should be an end to its attendant bad blood.)

---

2. Abọrẹ is a god worshiped in Ile Ifẹ.

4637. *A kì í lápá-a bàbá ká má nìí ti ìyá.*
One does not have relatives on the father's side and not have relatives on the mother's. (There is complementarity in all things.)

4638. *A kì í rí ewú lọ́sàn-án.*
One does not see the nocturnal bush rat at high noon. (Everything at its proper time.)

4639. *A kì í rí idà lọ́rùn eṣinṣin.*
One does not see a sword at the neck of a fly. (It is unnecessary to use a sledge hammer to kill a fly. Also, some approaches are improper in tackling certain problems.)

4640. *A kì í rí kékeré ẹkùn.*
One never sees an insignificant leopard. (Never minimize any danger.)

4641. *A kì í ro rere ká má ro búburú.*
One does not think of the good without thinking also of the bad. (There is not good without evil.)

4642. *A kì í ṣe méjì ní Mékà: a kì í kírun ní Mékà, ká tún nájà ní Mékà.*
One does not do two things in Mecca: one does not worship in Mecca [performing the *hadj*] and also trade in Mecca. (Always concentrate on one major project at a time.)

4643. *A kì í tèhìn akiṣalẹ̀ wúre.*
One cannot make good-luck charms without the *akiṣalẹ̀* plant. (No venture can succeed in the absence of the condition most essential for its success.)

4644. *A kì í wáyé ká má da nǹkan; oun a ó dà la ò mọ̀.*
One does not come into this world without becoming something; what one does not know is what one will become. (Everybody has a future, but no one knows what it is ahead of time.)

4645. *À ńdín i, kò dùn ni à ńwí pé adìẹ ní itan mẹ́ta.*
It is when one fries a chicken but it does not taste good that one says it had three thighs. (A bad cook quarrels with his ingredients.)

4646. *A ní ká jẹ ìrọ̀ kó rọni, ó tún ńfúnni lọ́rùn.*
We decide to eat *ìrọ̀* so that one might enjoy some ease, and yet one chokes on it.[3] (What one turns to for relief can turn out to be the source of more difficulties.)[4]

4647. *A ò mọ ibi orí ńbá ẹsẹ̀-ẹ́ rè.*
No one knows where the head will accompany the feet. (The future is hidden from us.)[5]

4648. *A ò mọ iṣu tí yó kẹ̀ẹ́hìn ọgbà.*
No one knows which yam will be the last in the barn. (Parents do not know which child will survive them.)

4649. *A pa ìgbín a ò bá ẹpọ́n; a pa ìrẹ̀ a ò kan ẹ̀jẹ̀.*
We kill a snail but find no red matter; we kill a cricket and find no blood.[6] (One cannot expect to get blood out of a turnip; not all creatures are alike.)

---

3. *Ìrọ̀*, a meal made by steaming ground and seasoned corn, is also known as *àbàrì*.

4. The proverb features a play on the name of the food, because its second syllable, *rọ̀*, means "soft" or "be soft" (i.e., softness or ease).

5. *Orí* in this instance is again not the physiological head but the repository of a person's destiny. The proverb, despite its wording, actually means that no one knows where *orí* will guide or conduct the feet. It can, of course, also be used to suggest that although *orí* directs one's destiny, it is the feet that do the walking, and they may conduct *orí* wherever it suits them.

6. Neither a snail nor a cricket has red blood. The suggestion is that one is disappointed at not finding what one expended considerable effort in seeking.

4650. *A rí èèmọ̀ lÉréko; ajá wẹ̀wù ó rósọ.*
We saw an abomination at Eréko: a dog wore a blouse and wore a wrapper around its waist.[7] (The world is full of wonders.)

4651. *A tẹ́ní bẹẹrẹ kò sí oǹdá; a pàjùbà bẹẹrẹ kò sí oǹko.*
We spread the divination mat wide, but there is no client; we clear the field for planting, but there is no tiller. (Some human aspirations come to nought.)

4652. *A ti oko ìroko de oko ìrokòtò.*
We have gone from hoeing a farm to hoeing a gully. (Matters have gone from bad to worse.)

4653. *Àbálé lòràn ìpilẹ̀ ḿbá ògiri.*
It is one after the other that problems of foundation-building befall walls. (Problems have a way of piling on one another.)[8]

4654. *Àbàtàbútú ojú ọ̀run ò hu koríko.*
The wide expanse of the sky grows no grass.[9] (Certain things can never be.)

4655. *Abẹ̀bẹ̀ ní ḿbẹ ikú; abẹ̀bẹ̀ ní ḿbẹ ọ̀ràn; bi oorú bá mú, abẹ̀bẹ̀ ní ḿbẹ̀ ẹ́.*
It is an intercessor that pleads with death; it is an intercessor that pleads with trouble; when one is beset with sweat, it is a fan that intercedes for one.[10] (There is a means of dealing with any sort of difficulty.)

4656. *Abẹ́rẹ́ bọ́ lọ́wọ́ adẹtẹ̀ ó dète; ọ̀rán balẹ̀ ó dèrò.*
A needle drops from a leper's hand and presents an impossible problem; a grievous matter hits the ground and imposes deep contemplation. (Certain problems defy easy solution.)

4657. *Abiyamọ ló mọwọ́ ọ̀já.*
It is a nursing mother that is adept at tying the child-support strip. (One cannot beat an expert at his or her trade.)

4658. *Adùn-únṣe bí àlejò omi.*
Painless hospitality, like one requiring only the offering of water. (A good deed that entails hardly any cost is easily and cheerfully performed.)

4659. *Afàkàràjèkọ, ó ní òún gbé ata mì.*
He-who-eats-corn-meal-with-bean-fritters says he has swallowed pepper. (Every venture has its hazards.)[11]

4660. *Àfẹ́dànù ni tìyàngbò.*
To-be-blown-away-in-the-wind is the fate of fallen leaves. (The person this incantational proverb is directed at will not escape an evil fate, just as fallen leaves cannot avoid being blown about by the wind.)

4661. *Aféfé lele ò jẹ́ ká gbé orí igi; àgbàrá òjò ò jẹ́ ká gbé ilẹ̀-ẹ́lẹ̀.*
Turbulent winds dissuade one from living atop a tree; flash floods dissuade one from living on the ground. (Life offers no risk-free options.)

---

7. Eréko is a market ward in Lagos. It is tempting to suspect that the reference is to the covers that colonial British people placed on their dogs in the relatively chilly periods of the tropics. No African, certainly, would dream of clothing a dog.

8. The mud for building foundations is piled up with a hoe, one scoop after the other. The comment is that one's troubles pile up one atop the other. In incantations this would be a curse that troubles pile up on someone.

9. *Àbàtàbútú* is an onomatopoeic suggestion of vastness.

10. This proverb plays on the word *abẹ̀bẹ̀*, which means "fan" but also "one who pleads" or "intercessor." The second meaning comes from the formation of the word as *a* (one who) *bẹ̀* (begs, a peculiar rendition of "makes") *ẹ̀bẹ̀* (plea).

11. The dish *àkàrà*, bean fritters, usually includes chopped hot peppers—sometimes whole ones.

4662. *Afèfójiyán di imíi rè ládìre.*
A person who eats pounded yam with vegetable stew makes batik of his or her excrement.[12] (No action is without its consequences.)

4663. *Afínjú egbò ní ńgba ewé iyá; àgbàlagbà egbò ní ńgba ègbèsì; òkánjúwà egbò ní ḿmúni ní san-san ojúgun.*
It is the elite among ulcers that is treated with *iyá* leaves;[13] it is a venerable ulcer that develops urticaria; it is a covetous ulcer that afflicts one right at the front of one's shin. (Ailments came in different forms.)

4664. *Àfowórọ́wó laláròóbọ̀-ọ́ fi là; àfowórọ́wó sì laláròóbọ̀-ọ́ fi dígbèsè.*
It is by reinvesting his profits that the retailer makes his fortune; it is also by reinvesting his profits that the retailer gets into debt. (Commerce is subject to uncertainty and luck.)

4665. *Àgùntàn kì í yọwo.*
Sheep never sprout horns. (Certain things can, and should, never be.)

4666. *Àgbà-ì-kà lolè ńgbowó.*
Snatching-without-counting is the way a thief takes money. (The evildoer seldom has peace of mind.)

4667. *Agbárí ò ní mùdùn-múdùn.*
The skull has no marrow. (One cannot get blood out of a turnip.)

4668. *Àgbásí mú àatàn gélé.*
Constant addition of garbage makes a mountain of the garbage dump. (Little things add up.)

4669. *Àgbélémọ̀ kan ò sí; awo ní ńsọ fúnni.*
There is no medicine that enables one to know, without leaving home, what is taking place abroad; only compacts [with those who know] enlighten one. (There is no substitute for being there.)

4670. *Àgbéró lọmọdé ńgbé agà; àkànmọ́lè ni ti èèkàn; bí a bá gbé ọmọ odó à fidí-i rè so.*
It is upright that a youth carries a ladder; it is straight into the ground that one drives a stake; when one lifts a pestle, one stands it straight on the ground. (The proper way to hold something is erect.)[14]

4671. *Àgbè gbin ohun gbogbo má gbin iyọ̀.*
A farmer plants everything but not salt. (Desirable as salt is, one cannot grow it.)

4672. *Àgbè ló dájà sílè; ọmọ odó kì í lu ìyá-a rè lásán.*
It was the farmer that sowed dissension between them; the pestle would otherwise have no cause to beat the mortar.[15] (Circumstances often force actions that one would rather avoid.)

4673. *Àgbè ni baba onísòwò.*
The farmer is the father of the trader. (No profession is as venerable as farming.)

4674. *Àgbè ò moko àrolà; onísòwò ò mọ ọjà ànápèkún.*
A farmer does not know which planting will bring prosperity; a trader does not know which transaction will be his last. (No one knows the future.)

---

14. This is actually an incantation to make someone stand still, rooted to a spot, although it has its proverbial application.

15. The name for pestle is *ọmọ odó*, literally "the child of the mortar"; in Yoruba society, of course, it is practically taboo for a child to beat its parent. The farmer planted the yam or corn that needs pounding.

---

12. Pounded yam remnants will emerge whitish; vegetable stew remnants will emerge blackish.

13. African *Copaiba balsam* (see Abraham 352).

4675. *Àgbìgbò ló̩ba eye.*
The hornbill is the king of birds. (Some people are superior to others.)

4676. *Agbò dúdú kojá odò ó di funfun.*[16]
The black ram crosses the river and becomes white.[16] (Propitious events can drastically change a person's fortunes for the better.)

4677. *Agbó̩n ńsé̩; oyin ńsé̩; ojú o̩mo̩ olóko ló wú yìí.*
The wasp denies responsibility; the bee denies responsibility; yet here is the farmer's son with his eyes all swollen. (A crime has obviously been committed, yet all possible culprits deny responsibility.)

4678. *Ahéré ní ńké̩hìn oko; ààtàn ní ńké̩hìn ilé.*
At the demise of the farm the hut survives; at the demise of the house the garbage dump survives. (When the ephemeral is gone, the permanent remains.)

4679. *Àìfárí kì í se o̩bo̩ ní túúlu; àìje̩un lèèwò̩-o̩ rè̩.*
Want of a shave is no headache to the monkey; it is want of food that it cannot abide. (Certain things are luxuries; certain things are essentials.)

4680. *Àìgbó̩Fá là ńwòkè; Ifá kan ò sí ní párá.*
It is ignorance about Ifá that causes one to stare upward; Ifá is not to be seen on the ceiling. (It is an admission of defeat for one to cast about for excuses or to beat around the bush.)[17]

4681. *Àìpò̩ ìlú là ńmò̩le̩; bí a bá dé Ìlo̩rin a ò níí mò̩le̩.*
It is because a town is small that one knows who is lazy there; if one goes to Ìlo̩rin, one will be unable to tell who is lazy. (There is anonymity in numbers.)[18]

4682. *Àì-rí è̩è̩yàn ní Té̩pò̩nà, wó̩n fi kàríò̩rán je̩ ìyálóde.*
On failing to find a human being, Té̩pò̩nà people made a *kàríò̩rán* [a person from Ilé̩sà] their *Ìyálóde* [the highest female officer in the community]. (Better any human being at all than an Ilé̩sà person for a high position, but when candidates are scarce, any available person will do.)[19]

4683. *Àjànàkú kì í sòpá kínú bí o̩ló̩de̩.*
The elephant's development of hydrocele does not anger the hunter. (One cannot be dismayed because one's enemy has been visited by disaster.)

4684. *Àjànàkú ò lé̩kàn; o̩ba tí yó mùú erin so ò tíì je̩.*
The elephant tolerates no stakes; the king that will tether the elephant has not been crowned. (Some people are beyond anybody's control.)

4685. *Àjé̩ ké lánàá, o̩mó̩ kú lónìí; ta ni ò mò̩ pé àjé̩ aná ló po̩mo̩ je̩?*
A witch announced her presence yesterday, and a child dies today; who does not know that yesterday's witch killed the child? (When the evidence suggests an obvious conclusion, one should not shy away from it. Compare 3882.)

---

16. This is also a riddle whose solution is soap; the traditional soap, when dry, is blackish in color.

17. The reference is to the recitation from rote of Ifá divination verses. The diviner who forgets them and searches the ceiling (while racking his brain) will not find the verses written there.

18. Ìlo̩rin is a northern Yoruba town. As the proverb indicates, other branches of the Yoruba family have a low opinion of Ìlo̩rin people.

19. *Kà rí o̩ rán* is a way of saying in Ìjè̩sà, "Come here a minute."

4686. Àjẹ́ lápo, ojúu rẹ̀-ẹ́ rò.
The witch licks palm oil and becomes calm.
(A balm masters wild dispositions.)

4687. Àjẹ́ ò lólúwa méjì, lẹ́hìn-in Poolo.[20]
The witch has no other lord besides Poolo.[20]
(For every force there is a check.)

4688. À-jẹ-ì-padà-wálé ò jẹ́ ká mọ ọdẹ adìẹ.
Its foraging-without-returning-home prevents people from knowing what a hunter
the chicken is. (Without seeing the kill,
people will not credit the hunter. See also
4501.)

4689. Àkàṣù ò níbìí rè lágbọ̀n.
The corn meal has nowhere to go in the
basket. (A treasure is not lost in a safe.)

4690. Akéèrà kì í roko ìrà kó sanwó.
The dealer in ìrà products does not pay for
cutting the tree.[21] (One does not pay for
using public property.)

4691. Àkéte kékeré ò gba èèyàn méjì.
A tiny bed will not accommodate two
people. (Some deficiencies cannot be fi-
nessed.)

4692. Àkèhìnsí onígẹ̀gẹ́, bí eni tí ńkébòsí.
The back view of a person with goiter gives
the impression that he or she is hailing
someone. (Seeing something from a disadvantageous perspective is likely to mislead.)

4693. Ako ikú tí ńpa ojú àrùn mọ́.
Masculine death, that which closes the eyes
of a disease. (It is a determined death that
sees the end of an illness.)

4694. Ako ológbò-ó mú owó rá.
A male cat renders the money invested on it
unprofitable. (One cannot expect kittens of
tomcats.)

4695. Àkọsẹ̀bá, èyí tí ńjẹ ìfà.
An unexpected find: free booty. (Unantici-
pated good fortune is free for the taking.)

4696. Àkúdin ò kọminú àáké.
The heartwood fears no axe. (Hardy souls
need fear no adversaries.)

4697. Àkùkọ gàgàrà ní ńdájọ́ fúnni láàrin
ògànjọ́.
It is a mature rooster that settles disputes for
people in the dead of night.[22] (Incontrovertible evidence settles all disagreement.)

4698. A-kú-má-tòó-elèjì-rù, ó dérù pa ẹnikan.
He-who-dies-but-is-too-small-for-two-
people-to-carry constitutes a load that
weighs down one person. (A matter that
falls in the crack between two categories is a
troublesome thing.)

4699. Àlà funfun, ọ̀rẹ́ òrìṣà.
White cloth, friend of the gods. (Each occasion has its special requirements.)

4700. Aláàfáà, ìmàlé adodo; ó ní bí òun ò bá
dé ibú òun ò mu.
Muslim priest, inhabitant of the conical
house, vows that until he reaches the deep,
he will not drink. (It is a choosy priest who
will drink nothing but water from the deep-
est part of the sea.)

4701. Àlàárì, baba aṣọ.
Reddish hand-woven cloth, father of all
cloths. (No cloth is more glorious than
àlàárì.)

---

20. Poolo is the god that exposes and executes
witches; compare note 17 at 4186.

21. Products of the tree ìrà are used for tanning and
for treating fired clay pots.

22. The crowing rooster marks the hours for people,
thus settling disputes as to what time of night it is.

4702. *Alágbàtà ní ńso ọjà-á dọwọ́n.*
It is the retail merchant who makes merchandise dear. (Caretakers are often more punctilious and stingy than owners. Compare 1703.)

4703. *Alágbe ò kú lÓyọ̀ọ́.*
A beggar does not die in Ọ̀yọ́. (Other people's generosity will save the destitute from starvation.)

4704. *Alájàpá ò lẹ́ran láyà.*
The tortoise has no flesh on its chest. (It is futile to seek meat on a turtle's chest.)

4705. *Alápámálẹ̀sịsẹ́, baba ọ̀lẹ.*
A person with sturdy arms but no will to work is the laziest of creatures. (Strong arms that will not work are lazy arms.)

4706. *Aláròyé, olókotoro, onítìjú àwòko tí ńgbónu nínú oko; ó délé tán ó ṣẹnu mẹ́rén.*
Loquacious, forward person, bashful bird that boasts on the farm; on reaching home it keeps its peace. (Boasting is easy where no one will dare one to prove oneself.)

4707. *Alásẹ mọ̀ pé ó ńjò kó tó rà á; ẹní hún mò pé ó ńjò kó tó tà á; isẹ́-ẹ jíjò ni wọ́ fi ńṣe.*
The owner of the sieve knew that it leaked before buying it; the weaver of the sieve knew that it leaked before selling it; after all, it is used for tasks that call for leaking. (If the particulars of a transaction are not kept secret, no party involved has grounds for complaint. And, differences are proper, for circumstances and needs are not the same.)

4708. *Aláyìn-ínsí ò lódó; ẹnu gbó-ń-gbó lodó-o wọn.*
The interfering person owns no mortar; his mortar is his overactive mouth. (The interfering person's only asset is his mouth.)

4709. *Àlejò tí kò wá là ńpa àgbà àgùntàn dè.*
It is a visitor who fails to show up in whose

honor one killed a large sheep. (A safe lie is one no one can disprove.)

4710. *Àlejò tó fòru wọlú, "Igí dá!" ni yó jẹ.*
A visitor who enters the town in the middle of the night will have "What a misfortune!" for dinner. (One should not visit when circumstances will make hospitality impossible.)

4711. *A-le-koko-bí-ọsán: egbòó jinná, ohùn ò jinná.*
A thing as resistant as bowstring: the ulcer heals, but a spoken word does not heal. (Words are as tough as bowstrings; while wounds may heal, the marks words leave do not heal.)

4712. *Alẹ́ tí kò ti ojú ẹni lé, a kì í mọ òkùnkùn-un rẹ̀ẹ́ rìn.*
A night that does not fall in one's presence, one never knows how to walk in its darkness. (A person who does not know the origin of an affair will surely err if he attempts to intervene in it.)

4713. *Àlòkùàdá ò jọ obìnrin lójú.*
A secondhand machete does not impress a woman. (Newness is all-important to a woman, even when the newness does not mean greater efficiency.)

4714. *Àlọ la rí; a ò rábọ̀.*
The departure is all we saw; we did not see the return. (Much was made of the beginning of a project, but that was the last anyone heard of it. This is an abbreviated version of 66.)

4715. *Àlùkò-ó fínní; ìbọn rè-ẹ́ fínní.*
Àlùkò is well groomed, and his gun is well groomed. (The person concerned is painstaking and particular about his affairs.)

4716. *A-mòòkùn-ṣolè, bí ọba ayé ò rí ọ, tòrun ńwò ọ́.*

Person-who-lies-low-to-do-evil: if the king on earth does not see you, the king of heaven is looking at you. (Nothing one does is hidden from God.)

4717. *Àmọ́dún ò ríírìì; ká múra ká ṣiṣẹ́.*
One year hence is not unforeseeable; let us gird ourselves and set to work. (A year of grace is soon over; one should conscientiously do what is expected of one.)

4718. *Amọ́nilójú ò bániwí; kọ̀bì-kọ̀bì ló ńwò.*
A-person-who-looks-disdainfully-at-one but says nothing: it is simply that there is something the matter with his or her sight. (Disdainful looks cannot kill; what is more, they do not become the looker.)

4719. *A-mòràn-mòwe ní ńlàdí ọ̀rọ̀.*
It is a-sage-who-knows-proverbs that resolves disputes. (Proverbs are a means of settling differences.)

4720. *Àmù tí a fi ńse iṣu ò lè mọ̀ọ́ wẹ̀ bí èyí tí a fi ńpọnmi.*
The pot used for cooking yams cannot know swimming as well as the pot used for drawing water. (In one's métier one is master.)

4721. *Amúniṣèsín ètè tí ńmúni lógangan imú.*
A-thing-that-exposes-one-to-ridicule, leprosy that attacks one on the tip of one's nose. (A disfigurement that afflicts one in the most conspicuous place will surely be laughed at.)

4722. *Anígò-ń-gọ́ tí ńká obì, tí ńká awùsá, bó bá ká ìdì eyìn á fàya.*
The hooked pole that plucks kola nuts and plucks *awùsá* fruits, if it attempts to pluck the palm-fruit cluster, will break.[23] (Some tasks are beyond some tools.)

4723. *Àpáàdì ní ńṣíwájú ọ̀fọnná.*
It is the potsherd that precedes the live coal

gatherer. (Events should take their proper order, and people should observe the proper order of precedence.)

4724. *Àparò, aṣọ-ọ̀ rẹ́ ṣe pọ́n báyìi? O ní ìgbà wo ni aṣọ òun ò níí pọ́n? Òsán jíjẹ, òru sísùn, oúnjẹ ò ṣéé fi sílẹ̀ lọ́sàn-án; orun ò ṣéé fi sílẹ̀ lóru.*
Partridge, how come your dress is so red [dirty]? He said, how would his dress not be red [dirty]? In the afternoon grubbing for food, at night sleeping: one cannot leave off food in the afternoon, and one cannot leave off sleep at night. (The priorities of the self-indulgent are always inverted.)

4725. *Àparò ńgba ikú oníkú kú, ámbọ̀ntorí ikú ara-a rè.*
The partridge falls prey to the death meant for others, let alone a death meant for it. (A person whose destiny is to be a habitual victim will not escape his or her fate.)

4726. *Àparò ò ga ju ara-a wọn lo, àfi èyí tó gun ebè.*
No partridge is taller than another except for those [standing] on earth mounds. (Said of people among whom there is nothing to choose.)

4727. *Apata-á ríkú kẹ̀hìn si í; apata ní ńgbani lógun.*
The shield sees death and presents its back to it; it is the shield that saves one in battle. (There is nothing like the shield when it comes to defying death.)

4728. *Ará Ànko ò tún ṣe oògùn ìkà mọ́; ọmọ méfà-á ku ọ̀kan.*
The people of Ànko have given up evil charms; of six children only one is left.[24] (Disaster teaches people to mend their ways.)

---

23. *Awùsá* is *Tetracarpidium conophorum*, a climber (Abraham 82).

24. The proverb refers to the sacking of Ànko by Fulani forces in the nineteenth century, which caused the people to move to Èrúwà.

4729. *Àrán nìparí òṣọ́.*
Velvet is the ultimate in finery. (There is no cloth more resplendent than velvet.)

4730. *A-rí-erin-láte ò moyì erin.*
One-who-sees-an-elephant-on-a-tray does not appreciate an elephant. (Those who have not seen you on your home ground cannot appreciate you.)

4731. *A-rí-je-níjà ò níṣẹ́ mìíràn àfi ìjà.*
The person who profits from quarrels has no other pursuit than quarreling. (It is most difficult to wean people from their bad habits.)

4732. *Àrò kì í gbónà kalẹ́.*[25]
The cooking hearth does not stay hot until nighttime. (There is no difficulty that does not have its moments of release. There is no difficulty without an end. Compare 4734.)

4733. *Àrò kì í jóni lẹ́sẹ̀ lásán; ọmọ aráyé ní ńfanná sí i.*
A cooking hearth does not burn one's feet on its own; it is people who stoke fire in it. (There is no misfortune behind which one will not find other people's machination.)

4734. *Àrò kì í rẹrù kó má sò.*
A cooking hearth does not bear a load without eventually setting it down. (There is no problem that does not come to an end. Compare 4732.)

4735. *Àrokò-ó ti bàjẹ́ láti Ilésà wá; wọ́n ní kí wọ́n mú ẹrú fún Lọ́wá, kí wọ́n gbé obì fún Ọòni.*
The tribute was wayward right from Ilésà; they said the slave should be presented to *Lọ́wá,* and the kola nuts to the *Ọòni.* (Attend to causes, not to symptoms.)[26]

4736. *Àròyé ò kún àjọ.*
A lengthy explanation will not fill the till. (Excuses are a poor substitute for fulfilling one's obligations.)

4737. *Arọ ni ìdènà òrìṣà.*
The cripple is the gatekeeper of the gods. (The cripple, though handicapped, is the chosen one of the gods.)[27]

4738. *Arọ tí ńbú ogun, orí ẹlẹ́sẹ̀ méjì ló bú u lé.*
The cripple who incites war incites it on those who have two legs. (A person of no means who incurs obligations for the whole community causes problems for the people with means.)

4739. *A-róba-má-sàá pàdé a-róba-má-yà; pẹkí ko pẹkí.*
He-who-never-runs-from-the-king meets him-who-never-makes-way-for-the-king; trouble comes face to face with trouble. (When two obstinate people meet, trouble is in the offing.)

4740. *Arugudu òjò tí ńṣú laàrin òru.*
The problematic rain: its clouds gather in the middle of the night. (It is a formidable visitation that descends when one is least prepared.)

4741. *Arúgbó ẹrú ò jẹ́ òfé; òtòṣì oba ò singbà; ìwọ̀fà kan ò dàgbà dàgbà kó ní òun ò sin olówó mọ́.*
An old slave does not go for nothing; a poor king does not pawn himself; however old a pawn may be, he may not refuse to serve the creditor. (Every station has its obliga-

---

25. *Àrò* is also spelled *Àdìrò.*
26. The *Ọòni* is the superior of all Yoruba kings;

Lọ́wá is one of his subordinate's chieftaincy titles, and Ilésà is one of the traditional tributary kingdoms.

27. This proverb is consistent with the Yoruba belief that like the albino, handicapped people are favored by the gods.

tions and its limits; prosperity, poverty, and duties are relative to one's position.)

4742. *Arúgbó ẹṣín sàn ju bàtà-a ṣílè mẹ́wàà lo.*
An old horse is preferable to a ten-shilling shoe.[28] (However poor the mount, the rider is better off than the well-shod pedestrian.)

4743. *Àrùn ní ńmúni jẹun ọ̀tá.*
It is disease that makes one eat food offered by one's enemy. (When one is prostrated by a formidable misfortune, one is forced to do many things one would rather not do.)

4744. *Àsá;rébá ní ńmú ìrìn yá.*
It is running-to-overtake-those-ahead that speeds a journey. (One should strive to match those ahead of one, not behind.)

4745. *Asọ̀ baba ìjà.*
Quarrelsome criticism is the father of a fight. (Ill-natured criticism is likely to lead to a fight.)

4746. *Asọ̀rọ̀kẹ́lẹ́ bojú wògbé; ìgbé ò délé sọ fẹ́nìkan; ẹni a ńbá wí ní ńwíni kiri.*
The whisperer glances at the bush; the bush does not go home to expose one's secret; it is the person one talks to who spreads one's secret about. (Secrets do not expose themselves; those who know about them reveal them.)

4747. *Àsúnmọ́ dẹ̀tẹ́; èèyàn gbókèèrè níyì.*
Closeness breeds contempt; the person who lives afar is made much of. (To be close by is to be unappreciated; to be far away is to be valued. See the next two entries also.)

4748. *Àsúnmọ́ dẹ̀tẹ́; òkèèrè ní ńdùn.*
Closeness breeds contempt; distance is best.

(This is a variant of the preceding and following entries.)

4749. *Àsúnmọ́ là ńmọ ìṣe ẹni; èèyàn gbókèèrè níyì.*
Only by living close does one know another's nature; the person who lives far away enjoys much respect. (Distance is a good cloak for a person's flaws. See the two preceding entries.)

4750. *Àṣá gbé mi ládìẹ kò dúró, nítorí ó mọ ohun tó ṣe.*
The kite snatched my chicken and did not tarry, because it knew what it had done. (The guilty person has his or her conscience to contend with.)

4751. *Àṣá kékélùké, àdàbà kékélùké, kò sí ọjà tí wọn ò ná.*
The tiny kite, the tiny dove: there is no market they do not patronize. (Certain things seem insignificant but are good for many uses.)[29]

4752. *Àṣá ni baba ẹyẹ.*
The kite is the father of birds. (There is no bird to match the kite.)

4753. *Àṣá ńtà, àwòdì ńrà; àwòdì tí ńgbé adìẹ lósàn-án ò sanra to igún; bỌ́lọ́run ò pa igún, ohun tí igún bá rí a máa je.*
The kite sells and the eagle buys; the eagle that snatches chicks in broad daylight is no fatter than the vulture; if God spares the vulture, it will feed on whatever it can find. (The powerful may live luxuriously; the weak, by the grace of providence, will find something to live on.)

4754. *Àṣá tó gbé adìẹ òtòṣì-í gbé ti aláróòyé.*
The kite that snatches a poor person's chick

---

28. The proverb obviously harks back to the days when British currency was in use and, moreover, when ten shillings was a lot of money.

29. This is primarily a riddle whose solution is money. Though small, money (in the form of a coin) is welcome everywhere.

provokes endless complaint. (A poor person never ceases bewailing a small loss.)

4755. *Àṣàdànù, àṣàdànù lọmọdé ńṣa òkúta ìta baálè.*
Picking-and-throwing-away, picking-and-throwing-away is the way a child picks stones in the chief's front court. (The stones a child picks playfully never arrive home with the child.)[30]

4756. *Aṣápẹ́ fún wèrè jó, òun àti wèrè ẹgbéra.*
The person who claps for an imbecile to dance and the imbecile are no different. (Any person who has time for unworthy people is himself or herself unworthy.)

4757. *Àṣàwí ẹjọ́ ẹnìkan-án ṣàre.*
The doctored case of the only side heard in a dispute is always just. (If one's opponent has no say, one's case is just by default.)

4758. *Aṣẹ́ ni ikọ̀ oyún; àtọ̀ ni ikọ̀ ọmọ; rírà lódèdè ni ikọ̀ àwòdì tí ńjá ọmọ léhìn adìẹ.*
Menstruation heralds pregnancy; sperm heralds children; hovering in the yard signals the presence of the kite that snatches chicks from their mothers. (Momentous events send their omens before them.)

4759. *Aṣẹní ṣe ara-a rè; asánbàǹtẹ́ sán ara-a rè lókùn.*
He-who-would-hurt-others hurts himself; he who wraps himself in a loincloth ties himself in a rope.[31] (He who would hurt others hurts himself also.)

4760. *Àṣèṣèjáde akàn, a ò mọ ibi tí ó ńlọ.*
The newly emerged crab gives no indication of where it is headed. (It is futile to attempt to predict the unpredictable.)

4761. *Àṣèṣèwọlú àlejò, jolojolo lojú ńṣeni.*
On first entering a town, the stranger's eyes are restless. (The eyes of a stranger do not rest on anything for long.)

4762. *Àṣetán ló níyì; a kì í dúpẹ́ aláṣekù.*
Completing-a-job is what is appreciated; one does not express gratitude for something half done. (What is worth doing is worth finishing.)

4763. *Àṣìṣe ò kan ọgbón.*
Mistakes have nothing to do with wisdom. (To be mistaken is not necessarily to be unwise.)

4764. *Aṣiwèrè-é yẹ ìlú, kò yẹ ẹni ẹni.*
An imbecile is acceptable in a town but not among one's kin. (No one wants an imbecile for a relative.)

4765. *Àṣìwí ò tó àṣìṣe; àṣìṣe ò tó ká múra òrun.*
To misspeak is not as bad as to commit a blunder; to commit a blunder is not as bad as making ready to go to heaven. (Errors are not all equally grave.)

4766. *Aṣooregbèṣù: baba àdánù.*
Doing-a-favor-and-receiving-wickedness-in-return: father of losses. (Receiving evil in return for good is the worst sort of loss.)

4767. *A-ṣoore-má-ṣìkà; ẹní ṣooré ṣe é fúnra-a rè; ẹní ṣìkàá ṣe é fúnra-a rè.*
Doer-of-good-who-does-no-evil; who does good does it for himself or herself; who does evil does it for himself or herself. (Good deeds and evil deeds will come home to roost.)

4768. *A-ṣòro-ó-bini, ìjà àná.*
Difficult-to-ask-about, yesterday's quarrel.

---

30. This proverb is used as an incantation to make the target person lose whatever assets he or she possesses.

31. The point about the loincloth is that a rope is a rope is a rope.

(A festering quarrel is a difficult issue to broach.)

4769. *Aṣòroófinúhàn bí èké.*
Difficult-to-confide-in like an unreliable person. (An untrue friend is not one to confide in.)

4770. *Aṣòroógbé bi agò-ọ Masiada; báa bá gbe níwájú a balẹ̀ lẹ́hìn; báa bá gbe lẹhìn a balẹ̀ níwájú.*
Difficult-to-wear like the costume of the Masiada masquerade; if one lifts it in front, it drags at the back; if one lifts it at the back, it drags in front. (In certain circumstances, nothing one does turns out right.)

4771. *Aṣòroóṣe bí ohun tỌ́lọ́run ò fẹ́; adùn-únṣe bí ohun tỌ́lọ́run-ún ṣe tán.*
Difficult-to-accomplish like something God disapproves of; easy-to-accomplish like something God is ready to do. (What does not please God is difficult to do; what pleases God is easily accomplished.)

4772. *Aṣòroówí bí àrùn ìdílé.*
Difficult-to-discuss like a hereditary disease. (Discussing the congenital disease of a family is a delicate matter.)

4773. *Ata loògùn ẹ̀mí; ẹ̀mí tí kò jata, ẹ̀mí yẹpẹrẹ.*
Pepper is the medicine for life; a soul that does not eat pepper is an insignificant soul. (The benefits of pepper cannot be overestimated.)

4774. *Ata ò mọ̀ pé òun ó dèélé.*
Pepper had no idea it would end up in the house. (One cannot foretell what lies in one's future.)

4775. *Ataepo àti araepo ló mọ ohun tí wọ́n fi ńnuwọ́.*
The seller of palm oil and the buyer of palm oil both know what they use to wipe their hands. (People who share the same trade or secrets understand one another.)

4776. *Àtàmpàkò baba ìka.*
Thumb, father of fingers. (The thumb is the chief among the fingers.)

4777. *Àtàmpàkò ò ṣéé júwe òkánkán.*
The thumb is useless for pointing straight ahead. (Even an important tool is not proper for every task.)

4778. *Àtàrí àjànàkú kì í ṣerù ọmọdé.*
An elephant's head is no load for a child. (There is a limit to what youth can accomplish.)

4779. *Àtàtàkurá: ẹnu eye ò ran òkúta.*
An impossible task: the bird's beak avails nothing against a rock. (The rock has nothing to fear from the bird.)

4780. *Àtè peye méye kú.*
Birdlime kills birds and causes the death of birds. (Birdlime is the nemesis of birds.)

4781. *Atètèdélé ní ńjoyè ẹrú.*
The-first-to-arrive-home assumes the ownership of slaves. (The race is to the swift.)

4782. *Àtètègbà làtètèsan.*
Early-arrival-at-terms means early payment. (Too-long haggling defers the enjoyment of the acquisition.)

4783. *Àtètèlóbìnrin ò kan ọmọ bíbí.*
Taking-a-wife-early has nothing to do with having children. (Marrying early does not guarantee having children early.)

4784. *Àtètèsùn làtètèjí; ẹní tètè kú ló múlẹ̀ lọ́run.*
Going-to-sleep-early is rising early; the first

to die is the homesteader in heaven. (The first arrival has the richest choice.)

4785. *Atètèságbẹ́ kì í mọ ogbẹ́-ẹ́ ṣá bí aṣánisan.*
The-first-to-wound-with-a-machete does not know how to wound like the-person-who-wounds-in-retaliation. (Retaliation is usually more severe than the provocation. Compare 3495.)

4786. *Àtègbé lẹsẹ̀ ńtẹ ọnà.*
Stepping-upon-without-repercussion is the way the foot steps on the path. (The path has no recourse against the foot that steps on it.)

4787. *Àtélẹsẹ̀ àwẹ̀nù tó dojú ara-a rẹ̀ délẹ̀.*
The washed-in-vain sole sets its face down on the ground. (Avoid inconsistencies or senseless efforts.)

4788. *Àtélẹsẹ̀ ní ńjẹ̀gbin ọnà.*
It is the sole that eats the filth on the path. (One's responsibilities often expose one to unwarranted abuse.)

4789. *Àtèyún àtèwá là ńtẹ èkùrọ́ ojú ọnà.*
Stepping-on-while-going, stepping-on-while-returning is the way one steps on the kernel in the path. (The ill-fated person can hope for no respite.)

4790. *Àtidé onígbàjámọ̀ là mmọ̀, a kì í mọ àtilọ.*
One knows only of the arrival of the barber, not of his departure. (Once one has served one's purpose, one is soon forgotten.)

4791. *Àtijẹ awùsá kò tó àtimumi.*
Eating *awùsá* nuts is nothing like drinking water afterward. (Pleasures often have bitter aftertastes.)[32]

---

32. The nuts of *awùsá* leave a bitter aftertaste that is aggravated by water.

4792. *Àtijẹun, ọ̀tọ̀tọ̀ ọ̀ràn.*
Finding a means of livelihood, a formidable problem. (Earning a living is no mean matter.)

4793. *Àtìkà àtoore, ọ̀kan kì í gbé.*
Be it good or evil, neither goes for nought. (Good as well as evil will be requited.)

4794. *Àtilọ-ọ lámi-lámi là ńrí, a kì í rí àtibọ̀.*
One sees only the departure of the dragon-fly, never its return. (The boastful person proclaims his accomplishments beforehand, but is usually silent when he falls short.)

4795. *Àtíòro-ó jẹgbá jẹlá, ó ní òun ò kú; ó ní bí gbogbo ẹyẹ ayé ti ńfò náà ni òun ńfò yí.*
The allied hornbill eats garden eggs and eats okro and proclaims that it has not died; it says that just as other birds on earth fly around, so it also does. (However tough the times, whoever will survive will survive.)

4796. *Àtípìjí, a-wúwo-bí-àtẹ-ìbànújẹ́; ìbànújẹ́ dorí àgbà kodò.*
A mighty problem, heavy-as-a-tray-of-sadness; sadness causes an elder to hang his head. (Heavy sadness prostrates even an elder.)

4797. *Àtiràbọn ò tó àtirẹ̀tù; ojọ́ kan là ńra ìbọn; ojoojúmọ́ là ńrẹ̀tù.*
Buying-a-gun is nothing like buying gun-powder; one buys a gun only on one day, but one buys powder every day. (Making an impressive purchase is one thing; being able to maintain the thing purchased is quite another.)

4798. *Àtiwáyé ìlẹ̀kè alágídígba ò ṣẹhìn èkùrọ́.*
The incarnation of the *lágídígba* bead will not be in the absence of the palm kernel. (Nothing can be done in the absence of a person whose consent is all-important, or

a commodity whose availability is crucial. You cannot make stew without the ingredients.)[33]

4799. *Atúmálòóyún, aràmásèdin, agbẹmánìisèépẹ́.*
It-bursts-without-pus, it-rots-without-maggots, it-dries-without-scales. (It is never as one would expect but stops halfway.)

4800. *Atúnnise ò pọ̀ bí abanijẹ́.*
Those-who-groom-people are not as many as those-who-soil-people. (There are far more detractors than praisers.)

4801. *Àwàilọ-ọ́ lọ́ sílé Asèmásò.*
A-person-who-visits-and-does-not-leave goes to the house of A-person-who-cooks-and-does-not-remove-the-food-from-the-fire. (Two contrary characters are in a contest of wills.)

4802. *Awo kan ò sí nínú awo ẹ̀wà.*
There is nothing inscrutable about beans. (Common knowledge is nobody's monopoly.)

4803. *Awo ò mọ̀ pé òun ó jata.*
The plate did not know that it would eat pepper. (Some boons one does not work for or anticipate.)

4804. *Àwòdì ìbá kú, aládìẹ ò sunkún.*
Were the hawk to die, the owner of chickens would not shed a tear. (The death of one's enemy is no loss.)[34]

4805. *Àwòdì jẹun ẹpè sanra.*
The hawk feeds fat on accursed food. (One

cannot worry too much about offending people.)[35]

4806. *Àwòdì ńrà, inú aládìẹ bàjẹ́.*
The hawk hovers, and the owner of chickens becomes unhappy. (The appearance of one's enemy never fails to displease.)

4807. *Àwòdì ò náání à ńkùngbẹ́; igí wó eyẹ́ fò lọ.*
The hawk is not bothered that the forest is being burned; the tree crashes, and the bird flies away. (Some people are immune to certain perils.)

4808. *Àwòdì ò sí ńlé, kan-na-kán-ná ńse bí ọba lóko.*
The hawk is away, and the crow behaves like a king on the farm. (In the absence of the hawk, the crow is king.)

4809. *Àwòdì tí ńre Ìbarà, èfúùfù-ú gba nídìi, ó ní isẹ́ kúkú yá.*
The hawk that is bound for Ìbarà is lifted at the tail by the breeze; it says, "Now to business." (An order that one should do what one wants to do is nothing but an encouragement.)

4810. *Àwòdì tó bà lé òrùlé; ojú tólé, ojú tóko.*
The hawk that alights on a roof: the eyes see the home and the eyes see the farm. (One perched on high can see near and far.)

4811. *Àwòdì-í lọ re ìyẹ́, wọ́n ní eyẹ́ sá lọ.*
The hawk goes to molt, and they say the bird has fled. (Those who do not know why one does what one does choose the explanation they prefer.)

4812. *Àwòdì-í sọ olówó adìẹ di wèrè.*
The hawk makes a maniac of the owner of

---

33. The suggestion here is that the palm kernel is an essential ingredient in making the beads used to adorn the waist.

34. *Àwòdì* is another designation for *àsá*, the hawk.

35. A reference to the curses that attend the hawk's snatching of chicks.

chicks. (The imperative of protecting one's property sometimes makes one do strange things.)

4813. *Àwòkó, wón ní o bú ọba; ó ní ìgbà wo lòún ráyè bú ọba, kí òun tó kọ igba láàárò, igba lósànán; igba lálé?*
Àwòko, they say you insulted the king; it replies, when would I have the time to insult the king, given the task of singing two hundred songs in the morning, two hundred in the afternoon, and two hundred at night? (Too elaborate alibis call for a close look.)

4814. *Àwòmójú kì í pọ̀tá; mójú-mójú lọrùn ńdùn.*
Disdainful looks do not kill an enemy; it is the looker who suffers neck strain. (If there is nothing one can do to one's enemy, looking at him disdainfully is no substitute.)

4815. *Awoníní kọjá àlùkùráni.*
Possession of charms is more efficacious than carrying a Koran. (A sure medicine is preferable to faith in religion.)

4816. *Àwòrán sètè kólóbó, igi tá-a bá gbé léhìn ò lè bunijẹ.*
An image with its small lips, a piece of wood whose teeth one carved cannot bite one. (A sculpture one carves with one's hands cannot do harm.)

4817. *Àwòsùn-ùn, awònù lẹkùn ńwẹyẹ òkè.*
It is a frustrated stare and pointless watching that the leopard directs at the bird flying high above. (When a person is beyond one's control or discipline, all one can do is stare at him or her.)

4818. *Awọ nídìí àdá ò wí pé kí àdá má kànán.*
Wrapping the hilt in leather will not keep a machete from breaking. (There is a limit to what one can do to prevent occupational disasters.)

4819. *Awọni ní ńfidí ara-a rẹ̀ lànà fún ẹni tí ńwọ́ lọ.*
He who drags a person uses his buttocks to clear the bush for the person he is dragging. (Victimizing another person does not leave oneself unscathed. See 1693.)

4820. *Àwúyéwúyé, àròyé òtè; wọ́n ní kí wọ́n tún ìlú ṣe, wọ́n féé tú ìlú.*
Clandestine whispering, the devious conversation of plotting; they were urged to improve conditions in the town, but they would rather destroy it. (Clandestine plotters would rather engage in secret designs to ruin the community than work for its improvement.)

4821. *Àyà ọmọdé ni wèré dì sí; ọ̀rẹ́ la fi ńjá a.*
Insanity is bunched on the chest of the child; it is a whip that one uses to dislodge it. (A whip is the surest cure for a child's misbehavior.)

4822. *Aya-méè-rọ́mọ-rí ní ńtanna wo oyún ọ̀gànjó.*
Wife-I-have-never-seen-a-child-before is the one who lights a lamp in the middle of the night to look at a pregnancy. (A person new to a privilege is usually not noted for moderation in its exercise.)

4823. *Ayé àgbè bí àjẹròrun.*
A farmer's lifestyle is like something out of this world. (Farm dwellers know no social constraints.)

4824. *Ayé àkámarà! Ayé lè pa ìràwọ̀ dà.*
Untrustworthy humankind! Humankind can alter people's destiny. (People are not to be trusted.)

4825. *Ayé di lẹhẹ-n-hẹ: ẹyin adìẹ tòkè wá fọ́ ìpọn.*
The world has turned awry: a chicken egg drops from above and breaks a wooden

spoon below. (When a raw egg breaks a spoon, the world has turned upside down.)

4826. *Ayé jìn, kò lópin; ibi tí ẹsẹ̀ ò dé lógún ọdún ò ló-n̄-kà.*
The world is so vast that there is no end to it; the places a person's feet cannot reach in twenty years are uncountable. (No one can claim to know all there is of the world.)

4827. *Ayé kì í di pọlọru ká fẹsẹ̀ rọrí sùn.*
The world is never so disrupted that one rests one's head on one's legs to sleep. (However the world turns, a person does not suffer the same fate as a chicken.)

4828. *Ayé kì í di pọlọru kádìẹ má fẹsẹ̀ rọrí sùn.*
The world is never so disrupted that the chicken does not rest its head on its legs to sleep.[36] (However the world goes, the fate of the chicken will not change.)

4829. *Ayé le; bí o bá a o pa á; bí o ò bá a o bù ú lẹ́sẹ̀.*
Humankind is awesome: if you catch up with him, kill him; if you are unable to, put a hex on his footprint. (Humans' evil machinations are formidable; people will explore all means to injure others.)

4830. *Ayé le, èèyàn-án burú ju ẹkùn.*
The world is tough; people are more evil than the leopard. (Living among people is full of peril.)

4831. *Ayé ńretí ẹléyà; níbo ni wọ́n fi ti Olúwa sí?*
The world waits expectantly for one's disgrace; to what place have they relegated God's purpose? (People hope for a person's

disgrace without considering what God might wish.)

4832. *Ayé ò fẹ́ ká ru ẹrù ká sọ̀; orí ẹni ní ńsọni.*
The world does not wish that one rid oneself of the burden one carries; it is one's head that relieves one. (Other people do not wish one good fortune; each person's guardian spirit ensures his or her good fortune. See also the next entry.)

4833. *Ayé ò fẹ́ni fọ́rò̀, àfi orí ẹni.*
The world does not wish one to prosper; only one's own head does. (Only one's guardian spirit, not other people, wishes one to prosper. Compare the preceding entry.)

4834. *Ayé ò lóràà: ojọ́ a rí kéré ká jẹ kéré; ojọ́ a rí wọ̀mù ká jẹ wọ̀mù; àgbà kì í subú yẹ̀gẹ̀ kó da ti ikùn sílẹ̀; oun a bá jẹ ní ḿbani lọ.*
There is no fat to this world: when one has only a little, one should eat only a little; when one has a great deal, one should eat a great deal; an elder does not fall and spill what is in his stomach; it is what one has eaten that goes with one. (The future is uncertain; one should therefore live according to one's present circumstances; the only thing that can go with one in death is what one has already enjoyed. Compare 3981.)

4835. *Ayé ò ríni nígbà tí a sun ògèdè jẹ; ìgbà tí a fi ẹ̀gúsí sebẹ̀ tó pọ́n bí edé layé ríni.*
The world pays no attention when one has to roast plantains for food; it is only when one cooks melon-seed stew that is as pink as shrimps that the world pays attention. (People have time only for those whose stars are ascending.)

4836. *Ayò kì í jẹ ká yè ẹ́.*
One does not hit the jackpot in the game of *ayò* and refuse to collect. (One does not turn one's back on good fortune.)

---

36. This is a reference to the way dressed chickens are trussed.

4837. *Ayo òtòsì lọlọrọ ńfọwọ́ tẹ̀ níkùn.*
It is a satiated poor person that a rich person may poke in the stomach with a finger. (The poor person's abundance does not impress a wealthy person.)

4838. *Ayọ̀ abaratíńtín.*
Happiness, a thing with a frail constitution. (Happiness is fickle.)

4839. *Àyòká, ọmọ ẹnìkan ló kù.*
Universal happiness: only a certain person is left out. (The happiness in question is all-embracing, leaving out only the unfortunate.)

4840. *Ayọnilẹ́nu ọkùnrin ló ní òun ó jẹ ìrọ̀.*
It is the burdensome man who says he would eat steamed corn-meal. (A person with uncommon tastes is a great bother.)[37]

4841. *Àyúnbọ̀ lọwọ́ ńyún ẹnu.*
Going-and-returning is the manner of the hand's journey to the mouth. (The hand that lifts food to the mouth always returns safely.)

B

4842. *"Bá mi na ọmọ-ọ̀ mi" ò dénú ọlọ́mọ.*
"Whip my child for me" does not come from deep inside the mother. (No mother is enthusiastic in delivering her child to deserved punishment.)

4843. *Baálẹ̀ tó sọ ọmọ ajá di ẹgbàá, ọmọ tirẹ̀ á wọ́n níbẹ̀.*
The chief who raised the price of a puppy to 200 cowries, his own child will pay the price. (The child will reap some of what the father sowed.)

4844. *Bábá bo bábá; bàbà bo bàbà; ewé ọ̀pọ̀tọ́ bo ewé òròmbó.*
Bábá covers *bábá*; guinea corn overhangs guinea corn; the leaves of the fig tree overarch those of the orange tree. (Although people supposedly are of equal stature, some are to be preferred over others.)[38]

4845. *Baba ẹnìkan ò gbin yánrin; baba ẹnìkan ò gbin tẹ̀tẹ̀; fúnra-a rẹ̀ ní ńhù.*
Nobody's father plants *yánrin* [a wild vegetable], and nobody's father plants wild spinach; they grow by themselves. (No one may lay an exclusive claim to public property.)

4846. *Babá joná ẹ̀ ńbèrè irùngbọ̀n; kí ló fa sábàbí?*
The old man is consumed in flames, and you ask about his beard; what led to the disaster in the first place? (If the hardiest things succumb to a misfortune, there is no point in asking about the frail. Compare 4110.)

4847. *Ba-owò-jẹ́, obì tí ńso lẹ̀rùn.*
Ruiner-of-trade, kola nut that fruits in the dry season. (Plants that yield out of their season undermine the market.)

4848. *"Báríkà" lónìí; "Báríkà" lóla; "Ẹ kú ìrójú" ò jìnnà síbẹ̀.*
"Congratulations on surviving a disaster" today; "Congratulations on surviving a disaster" the next day; "Accept my condolences" is not far away. (Persistent close shaves sooner or later become real disasters.)

4849. *Bàtá dún kò dún, á tan ilẹ̀kú kanlẹ̀ kanlẹ̀.*
Whether or not the *bàtá* drum sounds well, it will do its part in the funeral obsequies.

---

37. The food *àbàrí*, or *ìrọ̀*, takes a great deal of effort to make.

38. Part of the appeal of the proverb derives from the reduplication of *bá* syllables. The word *bábá* refers to nothing in particular.

(What matters is that a thing serve its purpose, not that one like it.)

4850. *Bàtà la fi ńsagbára láàrin ègún.*
Shoes make for fearlessness amid thorns.
(Who has shoes may strut even over dangerous ground.)

4851. *Bàtà ò jé ká mọ agésè òyìnbó; a sé aṣọ létí kò jé ká mọ ẹni tí ńfaṣọ ìyà bora.*
Shoes keep one from knowing which white man has lost his toes; hemming dresses keeps people from knowing who is clothed in wretchedness. (Outward appearances often belie private woes.)

4852. *Bàtáakoto, atiro àrìnjó, ṣaworo ògèdè, gbogbo wọn bákan-náà bákan-náà.*
The *bàtáakoto* drum, a lame itinerant dancer, a rattle made of bananas, all are the same. (The enumerated things are three of a kind, all defective.)

4853. *Bé màrìwò, bé ògèdè, ojó kan-náà ni wón ńyo.*
Cut off palm fronds and cut down a banana tree; they sprout anew the same day. (Said of things that share the same characteristics.)

4854. *Bèbè ìdí ni yó lo kíjìpá gbó.*
The large beads adorning the waist will wear out the durable home-woven cloth in the end. (One always pays somehow for one's pleasures and vanities.)

4855. *Bẹbẹ ò tán léhìn-in bẹbẹ.*
One celebration does not end all celebrations.[39] (The accomplishment of one feat does not prevent the accomplishment of another.)

4856. *Bèwè kó-o rókòṣé; ṣagbe kó-o ráhun.*
Seek help and find out who is recalcitrant;

---

39. *Bẹbẹ* is the elaborate celebration that the *Aláàfin* of Ọyọ́ performs after a momentous achievement.

beg for alms and find out who is a miser. (One does not know one's friends until one needs help.)

4857. *Bí a bá bójú tí a bónu; ìsàlè àgbòn là ńparí-i rè sí.*
After one has washed one's face and one's mouth, the ablution concludes at the underside of the chin. (After discussing a matter back and forth, one rests it with the proper person to decide on it. Compare 3257.)

4858. *Bí a bá gé igi nígbó, gbohùn-gbohùn á gbà á.*
If one fells a tree in the forest, the echo carries the sound. (Not even things done in secret can be long concealed.)

4859. *Bí a bá máa jẹun dun ọmọdé, híhàn la fi ńhàn án.*
If one wishes to hurt a child by eating something he wants, one shows it to him first. (If one intends to hurt a person, one should be sure the person knows of one's actions.)

4860. *Bí a bá ńféràn ọmọdé ní ilèkú, à mò pé a féé fi sofà ni.*
If a child is being made much of at a funeral (presumably of his father), it is obvious that he is about to be pawned. (Favors done for an orphan have ulterior motives.)

4861. *Bí a bá ńjiyàn sípàá, à sí aṣọ kúrò.*
If there is any dispute about hydrocele, let us strip away all clothing. (There is no point in carrying on protracted arguments when a simple and incontrovertible means of resolving the issue is available. Compare 606.)

4862. *Bí a bá ńrérìn-ín hèn-hèn, tí à ńgúnni lóbẹ, kò ní kó má wọnú.*
If one laughs while stabbing another, that does not keep the dagger from piercing the

skin. (A person killed with kindness is just as dead.)

4863. *Bí a bá ńṣẹ́ gègé ìjà, ká mú ti ológbò kúrò; ọba lọba ńjẹ́.*
If people cast lots to determine the best fighter, a cat should be set aside; a king is a king. (The cat is undisputed king where wrestling is concerned.)

4864. *Bí a bá pọn omi, tó dànù, tí agbè ò fọ́, à tún òmíràn pọn.*
If one draws water and it is spilled but the gourd is unbroken, one refills the gourd. (As long as one has a capacity to act, temporary setbacks are of little consequence.)

4865. *Bí a bá sọ idà sílẹ̀ lẹ́ẹ̀mẹwàá, ibi pẹlẹbẹ ni yó dà délẹ̀.*
If one throws a sword down ten times, it will come to rest on its side. (However long one worries a case, the facts will not change.)

4866. *Bí a bá yọ ipin lójú, ojú la fi ńhàn.*
If one removes secreted matter from the eye, one shows it to the eye. (One discusses an offense with the offender, not other people. This is a variant of 4892.)

4867. *Bí a kò rí ọkọ̀, a ò lè dé Èkó.*
Without a boat, one cannot get to Lagos.[40] (Without the means, the end is out of reach.)

4868. *Bí a kò ṣe àsẹnù, a ò lè ṣe àṣẹjẹ.*
If one has never labored for nought, one does not gain from one's labor. (Disappointment comes before fulfillment.)

4869. *Bí afẹ́fẹ́ bá ńfẹ́, koríko a máa jó.*
If the wind blows, the grass dances. (Certain orders cannot be ignored.)

---

40. Before the construction of bridges, boats were of course the only means of getting to Lagos Island.

4870. *Bí àgbàlagbà-á bá ńti orí jẹ àkèré, kọ́mọdé má nìírètí ati jẹ níbẹ̀.*
If an elder begins eating a frog from its head, a youth should not hope to have any share of it. (One can expect no help from a person whose actions reveal his or her own desperation.)

4871. *Bí agbọ́n bá máa sọrò, a kìdí bọlè; bí idà-á bá máa sọrò, a ki ẹkù bọ àkọ̀.*
When the wasp is about to fight, it dips its tail in the ground; when a sword is about to fight, it dips its hilt into the scabbard. (Before engaging in a demanding task, one makes the proper preparations. Also, momentous events are presaged by warning signs.)

4872. *Bí ajá bá ńwọ agbádá iná, tí àmọ̀tẹ́kùn ńwẹ̀wù ẹ̀jẹ̀, tí ológìnnì ńsán àkísà jìnnì mọ́dìí, egbẹ́ apẹranjẹ ní ńṣe.*
If the dog wears a garment of fire, and the leopard wears a dress of blood, while the cat ties a tattered rag around its waist, it is nevertheless a member of the clan of carnivores. (Innate quality, not clothing, is what matters.)

4873. *Bí àjànàkú jẹ tí kò yó, ìgbẹ́ lojú ó tì.*
If the elephant eats and is not full, the shame belongs to the forest. (To the person unable to fulfill his or her obligations belongs the shame, not to the disappointed person.)

4874. *Bí alágbèdẹ-ẹ́ bá ńlurin lójú kan, ojú àmì ló wà níbẹ̀.*
If a blacksmith keeps hitting the iron on the same spot, it is because there is a mark or blemish there. (There is a reason for every action.)

4875. *Bí alápatà-á bá pa ẹran, alágbàtà a bù ú ní àjàn.*
When a butcher kills an animal, meat hawkers cut it up for sale. (Each person does his or her bit when it is his or her turn.)

4876. *Bí aṣọ bá pẹ́ lápò, á bu.*
If a cloth remains too long in the sack, it goes moldy. (If a person stays long enough in one place, he or she acquires the traits of that place.)

4877. *Bí ayé bá já, kò ṣéé so.*
Once life has snapped, it cannot be mended. (A lost life is irretrievable.)

4878. *Bí eégún ò bá ṣe ohun tó tóbi, atọ́kùn-un rẹ̀ kì í tú u wò.*
If a masquerader has not done something unprecedented, his attendant does not open his mask for inspection. (Only extraordinary actions call for extraordinary reactions.)

4879. *Bí ẹran bá balẹ̀, ojú a yán ọdẹ.*
When an animal falls to the ground, the hunter's eyes lose their wildness. (At the end of the chase, ennui sets in.)

4880. *Bí igí bá dá, igi a yẹrí; bí èèyàn bá kú, a ku èèyàn ṣàà-ṣàà nílẹ̀; bí ẹni orí ẹní bá kú, ẹni ilẹ̀ẹ́lẹ̀ a di ẹni orí ẹní.*
If a tree breaks, other trees make way; if a person dies, other people will remain; if the person on the mat dies, the person on the bare floor becomes the person on the mat. (As one generation passes, another generation succeeds it; life goes on regardless.)

4881. *Bí ilẹ̀-ẹ́ gbe òṣìkà, tí kò gbe olóòótọ́, oore a súni ṣe.*
If the earth succors the wicked but not the good person, one tires of good deeds. (If the wicked prosper while good people flounder, one is discouraged about doing good.)

4882. *Bí iná bá jó lóko, màjàlà a fò wá sílé.*
When there is a fire in the forest, the soot flies home. (Events that happen afar send their news back home.)

4883. *Bí iná kò bá láwo nínú, kì í gun òkè odò.*
If a fire is not endowed with mysterious powers, it does not jump rivers. (When matters take unprecedented turns, they are driven by unusual forces.)

4884. *Bí inú ẹnìkan ò bàjẹ́, inú ẹnìkan kì í dùn.*
If one person does not become sad, another person does not become happy. (One person's sadness is another person's happiness.)

4885. *Bí kò bá nídìí, obìnrin kì í jẹ́ Kúmólú.*
If there is no unusual circumstance, a woman is not named Kúmólú.[41] (Unusual circumstances necessitate unusual actions.)

4886. *Bí kò bá sí lójú, kì í kàn sáyà.*
If it is not visible to the eyes, it does not weigh on the mind. (What the eyes do not see does not cause terror.)

4887. *Bí kò bá sí ohun tó ṣe èṣé, èṣé kì í ṣé.*
If the fist is not provoked, the fist does not fight. (For every quarrel there must be some reason.)

4888. *Bí kò sí bó ti rí, ìrẹ̀ kì í ṣé nítan.*
Were things not as they were, the cricket's thigh would not have snapped. (Unavoidable adversity caused a calamity.)

4889. *Bí kòn-nòn-ǹ-gó bá ṣe méjì a làlú já.*
If *kònnònǹgó* drums number two, they will encompass the whole town.[42] (Two of a certain type of person would be too much for a town.)

4890. *Bí kúkúrú ò gbọ́n, èyí gbogboro ńkọ́?*
If the short person is unwise, how about the tall person? (A group cannot be uniformly stupid.)

---

41. This name, meaning "Death has taken the headman," is usually restricted to males.

42. *Kònnònǹgó* drums are part of the *dùndún* drum ensemble.

4891. *Bí ogún bá lọ, ogún á bọ̀; bí kò ṣe bẹ́ẹ̀, ìbòsí ìgárá là ńké.*
If twenty go, twenty should return; otherwise, one raises an alarm that one has been defrauded. (Welching is not a good practice in dealing with others.)

4892. *Bí ojú bá ṣọbùn ojú là á fi í hàn; bí a bá yọpin lójú, à fi han ojú.*
If the eyes produce filth, one shows it to the eyes; if one takes secreted matter out of the eyes, one shows it to the eyes. (It is with the perpetrator of an offense that one discusses it. This is a variant of 4866.)

4893. *Bí òkú bá kú láyé, àkàlà a mọ̀ lọ́run.*
When the dead dies on earth, the ground hornbill knows in heaven. (A momentous event cannot be kept quiet.)

4894. *Bí ológìnní bá lọ sájò tó bọ̀, inú èkúté a bàjé.*
If the cat goes on a journey and returns, the mouse becomes sad. (The oppressed always bemoan their oppressor's good fortune.)

4895. *Bí olÓrò-ó májá, owó oúnjẹ olówó-o rẹ̀ ló dínkù.*
If the secret cult impounds a dog, it is the owner's food expense that is lessened. (There is a bright side to every misfortune.)

4896. *Bí Onírese ò fíngbá mọ́, èyí tó ti fín ò lè parun.*
If Onírese stops carving calabashes, those he has carved will not perish. (Whatever one has accomplished cannot be undone, even after one has lost the capacity to accomplish more.)

4897. *Bí oṣù-ú bá lé, gbogbo ojú ní ńrí i.*
When the moon appears, all eyes see it. (A public event cannot be hidden from people.)

4898. *Bí òyìnbó bá máa lọ lógbà, a ba ọgbà jẹ́.*
When a white man prepares to take his leave from a yard, he ruins it. (The white man on taking his leave from a place creates a shambles. See the following entry.)

4899. *Bí òyìnbó bá máa lọ nílùú, a ṣu sága.*
When a white man prepares to leave a town, he defecates in the chair. (The white man on departing a place creates a mess to leave behind. See the previous entry.)

4900. *Bí ọba ò kú, ọba ò jẹ.*
If a king does not die, a king is not crowned. (There is a certain order to events, and every event has its purpose.)

4901. *Bí ọ̀bẹ ò bá mú, òun ìpọ́nrin ni yó mọ̀.*
If a knife is not sharp, both it and the honing stone will know. (The solution of a problem is between the person involved and the person who will help to solve it.)

4902. *Bí ọdún bá burú, èṣí làgbẹ̀ ńyìn.*
If a year is bad, the farmer speaks well of the previous year. (Present hardships make one appreciate past comforts.)

4903. *Bí ọkọ̀-ọ́ re òkun, bó re ọ̀sà, a forílé èbúté.*
After a boat has plied the oceans and plied the lagoon, it returns to harbor. (After much traveling, one returns home in the end.)

4904. *Bí ọ̀lẹ́ bá lẹ, ìgbòrò-o rẹ̀ á gbójú.*
If a lazy person engages in his lazy ways, his farm will be neglected. (The affairs of a lazy person will not prosper.)

4905. *Bí Ọlọ́rún bá páni lórí, a fi irùngbọ̀n dípò-o rẹ̀.*
If God makes one bald, he gives one a beard as compensation. (There is a bright side to every misfortune.)

4906. *Bí ọ̀pọ̀ èèyàn-án bá kúrò légbẹ́, ọ̀pọ̀ a dáni lára yá.*
If many people leave a company, many people cheer one up. (The departure of many people from a company should not stop the rest from pursuing their aims.)

4907. *Bí yó ti rí ni yó rìí; alágbẹ̀dẹ ò lè gbé ọmọ owú mì.*
Whatever threatens to happen will have to happen; the blacksmith cannot swallow his hammer. (Come what may, one will not do what one has no intention of doing.)

4908. *Bíbà ló bà; kò ì tíì bàjẹ́.*
It has only settled; it is not yet ruined. (The damage is still salvageable.)[43]

4909. *Bìrí bìrí layé ńyí; ìgbà kan ò lo ilé ayé gbó.*
Round and round the earth turns; one season does not mark the end of the world. (The times are always changing.)

4910. *Bọ̀rọ̀kìnní òun ọlọ́rọ̀ egbẹ́ra; òbùn òun asiwèrè ọ̀kan-ùn; ọ̀kánjúà òun olè déédé ni wọ́n já sí.*
The dandy and the wealthy person are equal; the filthy person and the imbecile are alike; the covetous person and the thief amount to the same thing. (Being fashionable is as desirable as being wealthy; filthiness is comparable to imbecility; covetousness is kin to thievery.)

4911. *Bùtù-bútú ọ̀nà Ìjẹ̀sà lọmọdé fi ńṣeré; bí kò kọ́mọ ní rírìn ẹsẹ̀, a kọ́mọ ní yíyan.*
It is in the fine sand on the road to Ilẹ́ṣà that the child is playing; if it does not teach the child how to walk, it will teach him how to stride. (Nobody comes out of an encounter with a difficult force without having learned some lesson.)

D

4912. *Dà bí mo ti dà layé ńfẹ́.*
Become-as-I-am is what the world wants. (People always want others to share their misfortunes. Compare 3318.)

4913. *Dan-dan kì í sélẹ̀.*
A necessity cannot be ignored. (Whatever must be done cannot be left undone.)

4914. *Dì ẹ̀ńdì lòpin-in sinimá.*
"The end" marks the end of a film show. (When a thing or a relationship is over, it is over.)

4915. *Dídùn là ḿbá láfárá oyin.*
One finds only sweetness in a honeycomb. (A certain person's affairs will always be characterized by pleasantness.)

4916. *Díẹ̀-díẹ̀ là ḿmọ àpẹrẹ.*
Portents make themselves known only gradually. (From little things one learns the true nature of someone or something.)

4917. *Dín-dín-dín là ḿbólú; dín-dín-dín là ḿbáwò; dín-dín-dín là ḿbá olóòṣà tòun tèkó orí-i rẹ̀.*
Robust as ever is how one finds the queen termite; fresh as ever is how one comes upon skin complexion; healthy as ever is how one finds the cult worshiper complete with a parrot's tail feather in his hair. (This person's lot will always be good health.)[44]

---

43. The construction takes advantage of the similarity of two unrelated words: *bà* (to alight or settle) and *bàjẹ́* (to spoil).

44. Such proverbs as this find their usual application in prayer contexts.

4918. *Ebi kì í wọnú kóró míràn-án wò ó.*
Hunger does not enter into a person and leave room for other matters. (A hungry person is a distracted person. Compare 3759.)

4919. *Ebi ní ńpani bákan-náà; òràn kì í dunni bákan-náà.*
Hunger affects people the same way, but disasters do not hurt people the same way. (Different people have different vulnerabilities.)

4920. *Eégún ní òún féé jó; òjò-ó ní òún féé rò; ọmọ-ó ní òún féé ṣe bẹbẹ.*
The masquerader says he wants to dance; the rain says it wants to fall; and the child says he wants to perform wonders. (Conflicting desires pose a difficult problem.)[45]

4921. *Eégún tí ńbẹ ọmọ lórí kì í dérù ba ọmọ-ọ tirè.*
The masquerader that beheads people does not pose a threat to his own child.[46] (People who are uncompromisingly strict with the children of others are usually permissive with their own.)

4922. *Èèmò lukutupébé; ìyàwó lóyún ó bí ajá.*
Unspeakable abomination: the bride becomes pregnant and gives birth to a puppy. (The occurrence under reference is such as the world has never seen before. The following entry is a variant.)

4923. *Èèmò lukutupébé; ìyàwó lóyún tán òna ò gba ọkọ.*

Unspeakable abomination: the wife becomes pregnant, and the doorway cannot accommodate the husband. (The person with a problem shows no adverse effects, but the bystander does. Compare the preceding entry.)

4924. *Èèmò lukutupébé, sòbìyà Àjàyí, èyí tó dá a lésè tó ńro ó léhìn.*
Unspeakable abomination: Àjàyí's guinea worm, which attacks his foot and causes his teeth to ache. (It is a strange affliction whose effects are wholly at variance with experience.)

4925. *Èèmò-ọ kí lèyí? Ẹni a bẹ́ lórí géni jẹ.*
What sort of abomination is this? The person one has beheaded bites one. (Unnatural events defy explanation.)

4926. *Èésú ò lérè; oye a dá là ńkó.*
Pooled contributions earn no profit; one winds up with only how much one contributed.[47] (Certain pursuits or obligations are necessary or expedient but thankless.)

4927. *Èèyàn bí ahun ní ńhe ahun; èèyàn bí aṣọ kì í jé kó kùtà.*
Only tortoiselike people find tortoises; it is people who are attracted to particular cloths that save them from being unsalable. (Everything has its champions. Compare the following entry and 3389.)

4928. *Èèyàn bí ìgbín ní ńhe ìgbín; èèyán bí ahun ní ńhe ahun.*
Only tortoiselike people find tortoises; only snaillike people find snails. (People with like temperaments are inevitably drawn together. Compare the preceding entry and 3389.)

---

45. Masqueraders cannot dance in the rain. The wonder the child wants to perform is to lavish money on the dancing masquerader.

46. The executioner was traditionally a masquerader.

47. This refers to a mutual saving systems; see note 2 to 2899.

4929. Èèyàn búburú pò ó jùgbẹ́; ẹni reré wọ́n ju ojú lọ.
Evil people are as common as feces; good people are dearer than eyes. (Evil people are a dime a dozen; good people are a rarity.)

4930. Èèyàn yin-ni yin-ni kẹ́ni ó ṣe òmíràn.
People's unstinted praise encourages one to perform further feats. (To be praised is to be urged on to further accomplishments.)

4931. Ehoro tó jẹsu, tó dùn mọ, a tún padà wá.
The rabbit that eats yams and enjoys them will return for more. (People remember good experiences and seek their repetition.)

4932. Eku-kéku kì í rùn borí asín.
No rat surpasses asín [a vicious rat with a pointed snout and strong smell] in stink. (Certain people are unique, or unsurpassable, in certain ways.)

4933. Èpè ńrò kó tó jà.
Curses delay a while before taking effect. (Retribution may not be swift, but that does not mean that it will never come.)

4934. Erín wó sílù-ú àìlóbẹ.
An elephant collapses in a town without knives. (An unmanageable problem has arisen.)

4935. Eruku gbágbá ọmọ ìyá ọ̀dá; ìrì wọ̀wọ̀ ọmọ ìyá òjò.
Billowing dust, sibling of drought; showering sprinkle, sibling of rain. (Certain phenomena are symbols of other realities; certain people have qualities that recall those of legendary people.)

4936. Èwo ló sàn nínúu "Ó di ìjẹsàn-án tí ọmọ́ ti ńṣu," àti "Ó di ìjẹsàn-án tí ọmọ ò ti lè ṣu"?
Which can one say is the better statement:

"It has been nine days now that the child has been having the runs" or "It has been nine days now that the child has been unable to shit"? (An indication that one has been presented with a form of Hobson's choice.)

4937. Ewúrẹ́ wo alápatà bíi kó kú.
The goat eyes the butcher as though it would kill him with looks. (If one's adversary is too formidable, one is reduced to ineffectual gestures.)

Ẹ

4938. Ẹ ti pé yó ríi, nígbàtí ọmọ olè ńgun ìbaka?
What do you expect, when the scion of a thief rides a camel? (If a person lives conspicuously beyond his or her means, one may legitimately suspect some hanky-panky.)

4939. Èbè là ńbẹ Ṣàngó; obìnrin kì í wọ ṣòkòtò.
One's only option before Ṣango is to plead; it is taboo for a woman to wear trousers. (Certain things are irrevocable and must be accommodated, like the prohibition of trousers for women).

4940. Ẹ̀bìtì tí yó pa erè, ojú-u rẹ̀ á pón.
The trap that will kill a python will grow red in the eyes.[48] (Whoever attempts the near-impossible will labor greatly.)

4941. Ẹdá ní kó má torí òun dá; ológùn-ṣẹṣèé ní kó má torí òun ṣè; ọkàa bàbàá ní kó má torí òun bàjẹ́.
Ẹ̀dá says that it must not break in his time; ológùn-ṣẹṣè says it must not occur in its time; guinea corn says it must not spoil in

---

48. The expression translated as "grow red in the eyes" is an idiom for suffering.

its time. (Evil will not occur during a certain person's watch.)[49]

4942. Èdá ò làròpin.
A human being does not have a write-off point. (Never write anyone off.)

4943. Ègún ò bése ré.
Thorns do not make friends with the soles of the feet. (Certain people are by constitution incompatible with others, just as certain actions are unsuitable for certain situations.)

4944. Ègbìn kì í jo èló; opó kì í jo àtowófé.
What one plants is not like what one grafts; an inherited wife is not like one married by choice. (Something thrust on one is never the same as something acquired of one's free will.)

4945. Èjá kì í já kó pé.
A fragment, after being broken off, cannot be reattached perfectly. (Once something has been damaged, it can no longer return to its pristine state.)

4946. Èjè ahun ò kúnni lówó.
The blood of the tortoise does not fill one's palm. (There is very little one can expect from a miser.)[50]

4947. Ejó ni àlè mbáni rò bí yó kani.
When a concubine begins to argue with one, it is a sure sign that she intends to expose one. (When one's accomplice in a crime begins to be unfriendly and contentious, one should look out.)

4948. Èkàn gbarigidí wolè; ògbágárá wolé ó ku àtiyo.
An enormous root has bored into the ground; the heated iron borer has entered [the trunk], and pulling it out becomes a problem. (A person, or thing, is so well established that there is no dislodging him, her, or it.)[51]

4949. Èmú (ni) baálè àgbède.
Pliers [are] chief of the smithy. (A certain object or person is more to be reckoned with than others in a certain context.)[52]

4950. Ení bá bá Ìjèbú sorò-ó bá Olórun se.
Whoever makes a pact with an Ìjèbú person makes a pact with God. (No relationship is more auspicious than one with an Ìjèbú person.)[53]

4951. Ení bá rí se lòtá ayé.
Whoever finds success is the enemy of humankind. (People always begrudge successful people their good fortune.)

4952. Ení bá rìn jìnnà á fi odó ibúlè jeun.
Whoever travels far will eat food pounded in a horizontal mortar. (Whoever looks well beyond his or her immediate environment will be exposed to unusual habits; the more one travels, the more one learns.)

---

49. This incantation/proverb displays the Yoruba belief in a mystical connection between objects and forces embedded in or suggested by their names. The second syllable of Èdá (dá) means "break"; the last syllable in ológùn-sesè (sè) means "occur" (as in selè); and the last syllable in bàbà is the first in the expression bàjé, which means "spoil." Ológùn-sesè is the tree Erithrina senegalensis (Papilonaceae); see Abraham 470.

50. Since ahun means both "tortoise" and "miser," the proverb works on both the literal and figurative levels, because a butchered tortoise gives off little blood.

51. The proverb is commonly applied by a woman in a polygamous situation to warn her co-wives of the futility of trying to get rid of her.

52. The proverb often takes the form of an exclamation without the verb: Èmú, baálè àgbède! (Pliers, chief of the smithy!).

53. This is an obvious coinage by an Ìjèbú person, and variants of it can be found naming other Yoruba groups.

4953. Ẹní bá tàjò wá ní ńpurọ́ fárá ilé.
It is the person who has just returned from a journey that tells tall tales to those who stayed at home. (A person with wide experiences has the advantage of those with narrow ones.)

4954. Ẹní fi ẹ̀wù fábuké wọ̀ ló ní kó ròde kó má tètè dé.
Whoever gave the humpback a garment to wear is to blame for his going on an outing from which he will be long in returning. (The person who suddenly comes into the sort of fortune he or she never dreamed of is sure to be ostentatious in showing it off.)

4955. Ẹní fúnni lọ́mọ-ọ́ parí oore.
Whoever gives one a child [to marry] has gone the limit in conferring favors. (There is no greater favor a person can do than to give another his daughter in marriage. One should acknowledge extraordinary gestures. See 2653.)

4956. Ẹní su-ú lè gbàgbé; ẹni tó kó o ò níí gbàgbé.
The person who defecates may forget; the person who cleans the feces off will not forget. (A person who offends may soon forget, but the person wronged will not soon forget.)

4957. Ẹní tí kò gbọ́ tẹnu ẹ̀gà ló ńní ẹ̀gà ńpàtótó.
It is a person who does not understand what the weaver bird is saying who says it is chattering. (Unless one is privy to people's thoughts, one does not know why they do what they do.)

4958. Ẹní tí òràn-án dùn, a kì í fi òràn lọ̀ ọ́.
The person most aggrieved is not the one to ask for mediation in the case. (A partisan is not a good judge.)

4959. Ẹni tí Sàngó bá ti ojú-u rẹ̀ wọlẹ̀ ò níí bú Ọya lékèé mọ́.
Whoever witnesses Sango enter the ground [i.e., sees lightning strike] will never again say that Ọya lies.[54] (Once one has seen the feat a person can perform, one stops being a skeptic.)

4960. Ẹni tí yó kọ igba lóko, ìrìn ẹsẹ̀-ẹ rẹ̀ là ńwò.
The person who vows to make two hundred heaps on the farm: one should pay attention to how he walks. (How a person behaves reveals more about his or her capabilities than what the person says.)

4961. Ẹni tí yó pẹ̀gàn òrìṣà ni yó pèé àfín kò fín tó; ó fẹ́ kó bó lára ni?
It is a person who wishes to scorn the gods who will say that the albino is not bleached enough; would the person prefer that the albino have no skin? (It is silly to find fault with perfection.)[55]

4962. Ẹni tó bí arẹwà-á bí ìyọnu.
Whoever gives birth to a beautiful girl gives birth to trouble. (A beautiful girl will eventually cause her parents a great deal of unease or disturbance. This is a variant of the next entry.)

---

54. According to legend, Ṣango, king of Ọ̀yọ́, hanged himself when his people turned against him. The only witness was Ọya, his wife. As the people were lamenting the dead king's fate, lightning struck, and they heard his voice saying he had ascended to heaven and harnessed the power of lightning. In order to enjoy his protection they were to broadcast the news Ọba kò so (the king did not hang); whoever said otherwise would be struck by lightning. Thereafter, his followers made certain that if anyone said Ṣàngó did hang, his or her house was secretly torched.

55. The òrìṣà here is Ọbàtálá (Òrìṣà Ńlá), the fashioner of human beings, believed to create albinos and people who are deformed as a way of demonstrating his freedom to fashion as he pleases.

4963. Ẹni tó fẹ́ arẹwà-á fẹ́ ìyọnu; gbogbo ayé ní m̀bá wọn tan.
Whoever marries a beautiful woman marries trouble; the whole wide world [of men] claims kinship with him. (Whoever marries a beautiful woman will have the whole world of scheming men to fend off. See the preceding entry.)

4964. Ẹni tó mọ èyí tí yó gbẹ̀hìn ọ̀rọ̀ là ńpè lágbà.
Only the person who knows the last word in a matter deserves the title of elder. (An elder earns his status by his effectiveness in settling disputes.)

4965. Ẹni tó sọ pé òkúta a máa dàgbà ò puró; ẹni tó sọ pé òkúta kì í dàgbà ò puró.
The person who says that rocks age does not lie; the person who says that rocks do not age does not lie. (Two people can see the same situation in different but equally valid ways.)[56]

4966. Ẹni tó wáyé dáràn.
Whoever comes into the world comes into trouble. (Life is a pain.)

4967. Ẹni tó yínbọn sí ahoro, ó ti mọ̀ pé alámù lòun òó rí pa níbẹ̀.
The person who shoots a gun into a deserted house knows that he will kill only lizards therein. (A person who engages in a pointless gesture is reconciled to emptiness.)

4968. Ẹnu ni Ifá wà.
The Ifá oracle is in the mouth. (There is no oracle as powerful as the word the mouth pronounces.)

4969. Ẹnu oníhìn ni ìhìn-ín ti ńdùn.
It is in the mouth of the person who has the news that the news is interesting. (One should not take the news out of the mouth of the bearer.)

4970. Ẹran ọba ló fìṣu ọba jẹ.
It is the king's goat that has eaten the king's yams. (The offender and the offended are virtually one and the same; there is no need for punishment. Compare 3187.)

4971. Ẹrán kú, ẹ̀rẹ̀kẹ́ yọ̀.
An animal dies; the cheeks rejoice. (A person's misfortune is another person's fortune.)

4972. Ẹrín mú ẹ̀rẹ̀kẹ́ dùn; ẹkún ba ẹnu jẹ́.
Laughter sweetens the cheeks; crying disfigures the mouth. (Laughter is more agreeable than crying.)

4973. Ẹ̀rìndínlógún àgbọn ò ṣeé dá nÍfá.
Sixteen coconuts are useless for casting [consulting] Ifá. (Everything has its limitations as well as its uses.)[57]

4974. Ẹrù àgbà kì í ní òṣùká; baba, ẹ kú ẹrù àgbà.
An elder's load is without the luxury of a carrying pad; elders, we acknowledge the load you bear. (Elders bear a great many difficult and thankless responsibilities.)

4975. Ẹṣin kì í kọ eré àsárélé.
A horse never refuses a homeward gallop. (Nobody refuses an exertion that has a great reward at its conclusion.)

4976. Ẹṣín rí ogun jó; òkò-ó rí ogun yọ̀.
The horse sees war and dances; the spear sees war and rejoices. (The most distasteful of tasks have their enthusiasts.)

---

56. Aging may be taken to mean enduring for more than one moment in time, but it may also mean passage through the biological process that culminates in death.

57. Ifá divination is done with kola-nut pieces; coconuts are useless for the purpose.

4977. Ẹ̀tẹ́ awo ni ẹ̀tẹ́ ọ̀gbẹ̀rì.
The disgrace of the initiated is the disgrace of the novice. (When one member of the group is disgraced, every member is disgraced.)

4978. Ẹwìrì ní ńfẹ́ná lágbẹ̀dẹ.
It is the bellows that fans the furnace at the smithy. (Difficult tasks demand the proper tools.)

4979. Ẹ̀wọ̀n kì í já kó pé.
A chain once broken is no longer whole. (Lost innocence can never be retrieved.)

4980. Ẹyẹ kì í fò kó forí sọ igi.
A bird in its flight does not collide with a tree. (One does not blunder while doing what is second nature.)

4981. Ẹyin ní ńdi àkùkọ.
It is an egg that becomes a cock. (Great things and great people start small. Compare 5127.)

F

4982. "Fi ojú kàn mí" àna kì í ṣe lásán; bí kò fẹ́ẹ́ gba owó, ó fẹ́ẹ́ sọ nǹkan.
A parent-in-law's "Come see me briefly" is not for nothing; if he or she is not after money, there must be something to discuss. (People seldom do things for others without having ulterior motives.)

4983. Fi òní kú, fi òla jí, ojọ́ kan ní ńkú tán.
Die one day, return to life the next; one day the dying will be for good. (Intermittent maladies eventually become permanent.)

4984. Fi oore lọ ọ̀sìn, fi ibi lọ ọ̀sìn; àti oore àti ìkà ọkan kì í gbé.
Show kindness to a ward, show wickedness to a ward; kindness or wickedness, neither

goes unrewarded. (One is eventually rewarded in kind for the way one treats one's dependents.)

4985. Fi ọmú fọ́mọ, fi ọmọ fọ́mú; bí ọmọ́ bá ti mu ọmú, kò bùṣe?
Take the breast to the child, take the child to the breast; as long as the child is nursed, is that not all that matters? (There is no point in arguing over trifles.)

4986. Fífẹ́ ni yiyìn oṣù; méjì-i rẹ̀ kì í lé lójú ọ̀run.
Adulation for the moon is a mark of admiration for it; there are never two of them in the sky. (People or things that are peerless deserve to be so acknowledged.)

4987. Fífò ni iṣe ẹyẹ; ògúnná gbígbọn ni òwò olókùnrùn.
The bird's habit is to fly; fetching glowing faggots is the trade of the invalid.[58] (Different people and situations have different preoccupations and requirements.)

4988. Fìlà ò dùn bí-i ká mọ̀ọ́ dé; ṣòkòtò ò dùn bí-i kà mọ̀ọ́ wọ̀.
A hat is of little use if one does not know how to wear it well; pants are of little use if one does not know how to wear them well. (Having assets is one thing; knowing how to use them effectively is another. Compare the Gèlè ò dùn sequence at 4227, 4228, and 4229.)

4989. Fìrífìrí ò jọ kolombo; ìhòòhò ò jọ awọ.
Vaguely is not like clearly; nakedness is not like leather. (It is better to be clear about something than to be vague, better to be clothed in leather than to be naked.)

---

58. Ògúnná gbígbọn, literally "faggot shaking," refers here to an invalid's gathering of glowing coals, or making a fire, to warm himself or herself.

4990. *Funfun leye ńsu, kì í su dúdú.*
White is the color of bird's droppings, never
black. (Certain things one can rely on to
happen in certain set ways.)

4991. *Funfun ni iyì eyín; ó gún régé ni iyì
orùn; omú sìkí-sìkí ni iyì obìnrin.*
Whiteness is the pride of the teeth; straight-
ness is the pride of the neck; firm, pointed
breasts are the pride of a woman. (There
is a proper and ideal form for everything.
Compare 2723.)

G

4992. *Gàárí olóóyò; ó ti ládùn télè, àgbéré ni
súgà ńgbé.*
Sifted cassava grits are sweet by themselves; sugar is simply strutting for nothing.
(Natural endowments need no validation
or acknowledgment by detractors; and, the
self-sufficient person needs no help from
others.)

4993. *Gùdù-gudu ò séé bé èlùbó.*
Poisonous yam is nothing to make yam flour
with. (A certain object or person is of no use
to anyone.)

4994. *Gùdù-gudu ò séé sè; ó ko àwàsunje.*
Poisonous yam cannot be cooked for food; it
defies being roasted to eat. (A certain thing
or person is of no use to anyone.)

4995. *Gùdù-gudu-ú fi ojú jo èsúrú, béèni kò
séé je.*
Poisonous yam looks like *èsúrú* yam, yet it
is not edible.[59] (What looks inviting is often
quite deadly.)

---

59. *Èsúrú* yam is *Dioscorea dumetorum* (Abraham
324); *gùdù-gudu* is a variety.

Gb

4996. *"Gba akosu" ni "Gba ewùrà"; gbà lénu
òfón-òn ni gbà lénu agánrán.*
"Have a prime-quality yam" equals "Have
a water yam";[60] snatching something out of
a rat's mouth is no different from snatching
something from the mouth of a green parrot. (All gift giving is of a kind; all property
husbanding is of a kind.)

4997. *"Gbà lénu asín ni gbà lénu èkúté.*
Taking something from a malodorous rat's
mouth is the same as taking something
from a mouse's mouth. (All inappropriate
behavior is of a kind.)

4998. *Gba-n-gba-á dekùn, kedereé bè e wò:
òrò ìkòkò ò sí níbè.*
A leopard is trapped in open space; clear
sight gets a good look at it; the matter does
not admit of secrets. (Once a secret is leaked,
it can no longer be hidden.)[61]

4999. *Gbé oyún lo kó o gbómo bò.*
Leave with a pregnancy and return with
a baby. (However long the journey, the
traveler eventually returns home.)[62]

5000. *Gbogbo ohun tí a bá ńse lónìí, ìtàn ni
lóla.*
Whatever one does today is a story tomor-

---

60. Water yam is *Dioscorea alata*.

61. *Gbangba* (open space) and *kedere* (clear sight)
are here personified as the agents that have caught
the leopard in the open. A leopard thus caught is easy
prey to any hunter. The proverb refers to the traditional custom of burying the dead within the family
compound.

62. This proverb is usually addressed to people who
cause some offense as they depart a place; it would remind such people that however long their return may
be delayed, they will return, and the consequence of
their behavior will be waiting.

row. (Whatever the event, however grandiose or earthshaking, it eventually passes into memory.)

5001. *Gbogbo ohun tí okó bá ńṣe, òbò ní ńgbà á.*
Whatever effort the penis might put forth, it is the vagina that reaps the reward. (A prayer or incantation that a person be the beneficiary of his her efforts, and even of those of others.)

5002. *"Gbómọ wá kí mi," owó ní ńnáni.*
"Come and visit me with your new baby" is a costly invitation. (A person who makes expensive propositions should be prepared to bear the cost.)[63]

H

5003. *Há a, há a, há a, ẹran Iléyá tán.*
Share it out, share it out, share it out; that way nothing is left of the *Id el Fitr* sacrificial animal.[64] (Too many claims soon deplete the most plentiful store.)

5004. *Há-ń-há lòpòló fi ga ju alámù lọ.*
Only by bloating itself does the toad come to be taller than the lizard. (There is really nothing to choose among certain rivals.)

5005. *Híhó là ńhó tọ olè léhìn.*
It is with clamorous insults that a crowd pursues a thief. (A person who disgraces himself or herself deserves public humiliation.)

---

63. When mothers are invited by friends and relatives to bring their babies to visit, it is customary for the hosts to make gifts to the babies and, indirectly, to the mothers.

64. *Id el Fitr* is a Muslim festival the celebration of which calls for killing and feasting on rams. Each person who kills an animal is expected to send a little of the meat to relatives and friends.

5006. *Hùn hùn hùn inú ẹlédè inú ẹlédè ní ńgbé.*
The [meaning of the] grunting of a pig does not go beyond the pig. (The ranting and raving of a worthless person are not worth one's attention.)

I

5007. *Ìbàjẹ́ ìkòkò, gba-n-gba ni lójú Olúwa.*
Wickedness perpetrated in secret is open knowledge to God. (No secret wickedness can be hidden from God.)

5008. *Ibi a bá pè lórí ní ńhurun.*
It is the place named the head that grows hair. (People and objects should live up to expectations.)

5009. *Ibi tí Gàmbàrí ti ńje obì bò kó tó pọn léhín, ọná jìn.*
The time the Hausa person began chewing kola such that all his or her teeth are now red is far in the past. (Present conditions had their origins long ago.)

5010. *Ibi tí ó tòrò ò mu agbè; ibi tó mu agbè-é léwu.*
The place where the water is clear is not deep enough for the gourd; the place where the water is deep enough, though, is dangerous. (There is no boon without its dangers.)

5011. *Ibi tí ọká pẹbu sí lọńje è ńbò wá bá a.*
Wherever the viper makes its lair, there its food will come to find it. (Whatever is destined to come one's way will do so without one's lifting a finger.)

5012. *Ibi tí ọmọ ńrè lọmọ ò mò, ọmọ́ mọ ibi tó ti wá.*
What the child does not know is where he or she is headed; the child knows where

he or she came from. (The future may be a mystery, but the past is not.)

5013. *Ibìkan ṣoṣo kọ́ la ti ńrí ọ̀run.*
It is not only at one location that one can see the sky. (There are few opportunities that do not have alternatives.)

5014. *Ibikíbi tí a bá Alágbaà nìgbàle ẹ̀.*
Wherever one finds the chief priest of the *egúngùn* cult, there his secret grove is. (A person's authority attaches to his or her person, not to the insignia.)[65]

5015. *Ìbọkúbọ lọmọdé ńbọ kórikóto; ìgbàkúgbà ní ńgbà á.*
Children's manner of sacrificing to their guardian spirit is nonchalant, and its way of heeding their worship is also nonchalant. (How one approaches others determines how they respond.)

5016. *Ìbù-ùbú là ńtu òkun; odò-odò là ńtu òsà; ibi tí a bá fẹ́ là ńtu Ọ̀yán.*
One rows in the ocean along the shore; in the [Lagos] lagoon one rows down the channel; as for the Ọ̀yán river, one rows as one pleases. (Each situation has its peculiar difficulties and demands, which must be accommodated.)

5017. *Ìdálùú ni ìṣe ìlú; eégún ní ńgba owó òde lÓṣogbo.*
The customs of a town are established on the establishment of the town; at Òṣogbo, tax collecting is the duty of masqueraders. (Different people have different responsibilities.)

5018. *Ìdí funfun ò níran, àfi bí àgbè tó bá fi tiẹ̀ yí eèpè.*

A white buttock is not a natural condition; for a farmer it happens when he rubs his buttocks in the dirt. (One should not mistake temporary setbacks or afflictions for permanent conditions.)

5019. *Ìdí nikú ìgbín; orí nikú ahun.*
The rear end is the death of the snail;[66] the front end is the death of the tortoise. (Each person is vulnerable in a different way. Compare 360.)

5020. *Ìdìkudì là ńdi ẹrù ikùn.*
Indifferently is one's manner of tying the load destined for the belly. (One does not need to worry overmuch about details where matters never exposed to public scrutiny are concerned.)

5021. *Ìdọ̀tí ò mátà; woléwolé lejọ́ bá wí.*
Dirt does not matter; only the sanitary inspector fusses.[67] (The subject under discussion is not of great import.)

5022. *Ifá ńlá ní ńya olúwa ẹ̀ lápò.*
It is an extraordinary [useless] Ifá that rips the owner's sack. (It is a strange charm that ruins the owner instead of benefiting him or her.)

5023. *Ìgbà iyán ò jọ ìgbà ìyàn; yíyó là ńyó nígbà iyán, rírù là ńrù nígbà ìyàn.*
The days of pounded yam are different from the days of famine; one enjoys a full stomach on the days of pounded yam, while one grows lean during the days of famine. (Life is made up of different seasons.)

5024. *Ìgbà kì í yí padà kéwúrẹ́ bí màlúù.*
Times cannot so change that a goat will give

---

65. The *Alágbaà* can perform the rites required of him anywhere, although properly they belong in the secret grove.

66. Snails are usually killed by cracking the bases of their shells and letting out the fluid.

67. *Ìdọ̀tí ò mátà* is a parody in Yoruba of "It doesn't matter," the Yoruba rendition stating that for the white man, dirt does not matter.

birth to a calf. (Certain things in life are immutable.)

5025. Ìgbà lasọ, ìgbà lèwù, ìgbà lòdèrée-kókò nÍlọrin.
The season prescribes cloth; the season prescribes clothes; the season determines the presence of the Senegal dove in Ìlọrin. (Everything in its proper time or season.)[68]

5026. Ìgbà ò lọ bí òréré.
Time does not go on endlessly. (Life is short. Compare 5207.)

5027. Ìgbà tí ìlú bá ńdùn jù, à mọ̀ pé yó tùú.
When a town becomes too happy a place, one should know that it is on the verge of breaking up. (Excess of even good things brings disaster.)

5028. Ìgbèhìn laláyò ńta.
It is at the end of the game that the real champion shines. (Early advantages do not ensure final victory.)

5029. Ìgbèhìnwá ayé ò ní ìmọ̀; ó dá fún ẹni tí òì tíì kú.
The manner of life's end is unknown; the oracle is directed at those who have not died. (Said as consolation to people suffering misfortune or reverses; it says fortunes may change for the better.)

5030. Ìgbékẹ̀lé èèyàn, asán ni.
Trust placed in humans is misplaced. (One should be wary about trusting people.)

5031. Igi ìbàjé layé ńsáré gùn.
It is the tree of defamation that the world hurries to climb. (People are ever more eager

to seek the ruination of others than to seek their elevation.)

5032. Igi tí a bá torí è gbodì, ó ye kó ṣená fúnni yá.
The tree on account of which one makes enemies should at least kindle fire for one to warm oneself. (One deserves some recompense for one's sacrifices.)

5033. Igi tí a fèhìntì tí ò gbani dúró, bó wó luni kò lè pani.
A tree that one leans on but that cannot support one's weight, if it falls on you it will not crush you. (A person whose support is ineffectual cannot do one any ill by his or her opposition. Compare 2076.)

5034. Igi tí baba ẹní bá lọ́, a kì í fà á tu, bíi tègé kọ́.
A tree that one's father plants one does not uproot, but that does not apply to cassava. (One must treat tradition and patrimony with reverence, but one should know when exceptions are called for.)[69]

5035. Igi tí yó pani lódúnnìí, kì í ṣe bòtujè èhìnkùlé ẹni.
The tree that will kill one this year will not be the Jatropha plant in one's back yard.[70] (A person of absolute insignificance in relation to one cannot be one's effective adversary.)

5036. Igi tó hù lójú ẹni kì í dá pani.
A tree that sprouts while one is alive cannot fall and crush one. (Upstarts whose beginnings one knows cannot have supreme power over one.)

---

68. The Senegal dove or laughing dove (*Stigmatopelia senegalensis*) is to Ìlọrin as the swallow is to Capistrano (Abraham 449).

69. Cassava (manioc) is food, but one would be foolish to apply to it the general rule regarding preserving one's heritage.

70. *Bòtujè* (*làpálàpá*) is a fragile plant with stems made up of substantial "marrows" inside very thin, hard stalks that are not even practical as whips.

5037. *Igúnnugún kì í kú séwe.*
The vulture never dies young. (A wish or prayer that a person may live long.)[71]

5038. *Igúnnugún kì í ṣe eye "Gbà je."* The vulture is not a fowl in reference to which one says, "Take and eat this." (Not all things are available for exploitation.)[72]

5039. *Igbó ńla la ti nrí eye-kéye.*
It is in a huge forest that one finds all sorts of birds. (Multitude offers variety.)

5040. *Igbó ńla ní ńmu eni mu orí.*
It is a huge forest that swallows a person, including the person's head. (It is a great task that makes great demands on one.)

5041. *Ìháhá tó há ṣórùn òpe, orí araa è ló fi ńrù ú.*
The pericarp of the palm fruit that is wedged atop the palm tree is a burden that the palm tree itself must bear. (Whatever ill will one wishes others recoils on oneself.)

5042. *Ìhìn ojà là ńgbó nájà.*
It is the report one hears about a market that induces one to trade in it. (A person's or a thing's reputation determines how people will act toward it.)

5043. *Ìhó odòó bo ìhó igba èèyàn mólè.*
The roar of a river drowns the roar of two hundred people. (One illustrious person makes a greater impression than a multitude of worthless people.)

5044. *Ìjà kì í lo lásán kóníjà má fara pa.*
A fight does not end without those involved showing some mark from it. (The aftermath of a fight or quarrel is never like the time before the fight or quarrel.)

5045. *Ìjà ní ńjé "Ìlú ṁpè ọ́"; gbogbo wọn ló lórúkọ.*
It is when there is a quarrel that the message says, "The town demands your presence"; everybody [in the town] has a name. (When communication with acquaintances becomes cryptic, something is amiss.)

5046. *Ìjà ò bímọ kó rò.*
A fight or quarrel never fathers a child that is docile. (The aftermath of a fight or quarrel is always troublesome.)

5047. *Ìjá tán lóko àropò; ẹgbón tẹ Ifá, àbúrò-ó gbéyàwó.*
There is no more cause for a fight on the communal farm; the elder brother has taken up Ifá divination, and the younger has gone to get married. (The principals in a feud are too preoccupied with other pressing problems to carry on the feud.)

5048. *Ìjàgbòn léhìn eni tí ò kú; ẹní kú bọ́ lọ́wọ́ aápọn.*
Constant worries are the lot of the person who has not died; only those who have died are free from worries. (Only death saves humans from the need to worry.)

5049. *Ìjàṁbá ṣolè, onílé tají.*
A great disaster befalls the burglar: the homeowner wakes up unexpectedly. (Said of an evildoer who is beset with his or her comeuppance.)

5050. *Ìjẹ ni ìsu.*
As one eats, so one excretes [or what you eat is what you excrete]. (One reaps what one sows.)

5051. *Ìjèbú kì í jé Òjó.*
The Ìjèbú never bear the name Òjó. (Certain things one must never do.)

---

71. Because vultures are bald, they all look aged.
72. It is taboo to eat a vulture.

5052. Ìkà ìbá là a bàlújẹ́; ẹrú ìbá jọba èèyàn ìbá kùkan.
Were the wicked to prosper, they would ruin the town; were a slave to be made king, there would be no one left in the town. (To put the affairs of a community in the hands of wicked or careless people is to destroy the community.)

5053. Ìkaakà là ḿbá ọmọrí igbá.
Face up is the way one always finds the calabash lid. (Some things are ordained to be certain ways always.)

5054. Ìkórítamẹ́ta ọ̀nà Èṣù.
The point where three roads meet: Èṣù's pathway. (Evil colonizes the place it finds hospitable.)[73]

5055. Ìkórítamẹ́ta tí ńdààmú àlejò.
The fork in the road throws a stranger into a quandary. (Those who know not the secrets of a process have no way to solve its puzzles.)

5056. Ìkótí ò jẹ́ nǹkan lẹ́rù ìyàwó.
A hairpin does not add much to the luggage of a bride. (A little chore is of no consequence in addition to an immense task.)

5057. Ìkòkò ayé yá ju ìkòkò ọ̀run lọ.
The obscurity of this earth is far better than the obscurity of heaven. (Not knowing what is what in this life is better than not knowing what is in store for one in heaven.)

5058. Ikú ẹgbẹ̀rún kan ò payé rẹ́; bí èèyán ṣe ńkú làwọn mìíràn ńwá sáyé.
The death of any one thousand people will not obliterate the world; as some people die, so others come to life. (Humankind will survive the most deadly disasters.)

5059. Ikú ẹja ní ḿmú ẹja mọ̀lú; ẹja Ògùn ìbá ṣe dé Akèsán?
It is the death of the fish that makes it know the town; what else would have brought a fish from the Ògùn river to Akèsán market? (A mishap is likely to bring other mishaps in its wake.)

5060. Ikú kì í jẹun ẹni kó pani; àrùn kì í jẹun ẹni kó ṣeni.
Death does not eat one's food and then kill one; disease does not eat one's food and then afflict one. (Those who enter into covenants are obliged to fulfill their part of the bargain.)

5061. Ikú ò jẹ́ kẹ́ni ó lọ sógun; ìfà ò jẹ́ kẹ́ni ó fòyè sílẹ̀.
Death keeps one from going to war; spoils keep one from giving up one's chieftaincy. (Thoughts of the advantages of a position make one reluctant to contemplate giving it up.)

5062. Ikú pa olówó; odò-ó gbé ìwòfà; sònpònnón pa onígbòwó; ẹni tó mọ oye owó ṣè ḿbùṣe.
Death killed the lender; a river carried off the pawn; the guarantor died of smallpox; there is hardly anyone left who knows the amount of the debt. (Said of a matter that occurred so long ago that hardly anyone remains who remembers the circumstances.)

5063. Ikú tí yó pani kì í peni lórúkọ.
The death that will kill a person does not call the person by name. (Disasters do not announce their approach.)

5064. Ikú wọnú ahoro ṣákálá.
Death enters an abandoned home in vain. (A person who has lost everything has nothing else to lose.)

---

73. This exclamation could be used when some inexplicable evil has befallen someone.

5065. *Ikun ní ḿbá ẹkún wá; kèlèbè ní ḿbá "tùè" wá.*
Mucus is what accompanies crying; phlegm is what accompanies a cough. (Each affliction has its particular misery.)

5066. *Ikún ńwá ònà àtilọ, wọ́n ní ẹrú àna ẹ́ẹ́ sá; àwòdì ńre Ìbarà èfúùfù-ú ta á nídìi pá; ó ní isẹ́ kúkú yá.*
The squirrel is waiting for an excuse to get away and is told that its parents-in-law's slave has escaped; the eagle prepares to depart for Ìbarà, and the breeze lifts its tail feathers; time, it says, to get going. (A person straining to do a certain thing is grateful for any excuse offered him or her.)

5067. *Ilé ni adìẹ ńya òpìpì; ìbá ṣe àparò, ọmọ aráyé a mú u jẹ.*
It is in the household that a featherless chicken is shunned; were it a partridge, humans would have killed it for food. (One very often does not appreciate the value of what one has.)[74]

5068. *Ilé ọba tó jó, ẹwà ló bù sí i.*
The conflagration that destroyed the king's palace only makes it more palatial.[75] (There are blessings hidden in every disaster.)

5069. *Ilé tí a fi itọ́ mọ, ìrì ni yó wo.*
A house built with saliva will be demolished by the dew. (Ventures based on shaky foundations will not withstand even the flimsiest of tests.)

5070. *Ilé tí a gbá èèyàn létí wò, bó pé títí a ó gbàá èèyàn létí jáde níbẹ̀.*

---

74. *Òpìpì* is a chicken that has lost its feathers and therefore is not considered proper to eat. The partridge does not have many more feathers than the *òpìpì*, but it is not shunned for that reason, just because it is not a home dweller.

75. The palace will be rebuilt on a grander scale.

A home one is able to enter only after one has slapped someone in the ears: sooner or later one will have to slap someone in the ears in order to get out of it. (A transaction that has a fractious beginning will end in a fractious way.)

5071. *Ilè ìjàmbá kì í ṣu.*
The day of disaster is never done. (Disaster can befall anyone anytime.)

5072. *Ìlú tí a ò ti rímú rí ní ḿmú imú ẹni tó àká.*
It is in a town where no one has ever seen a nose that one's nose seems as capacious as a granary. (A person seeing an ordinary thing for the first time always overestimates its importance or significance.)

5073. *Ìmàdò ìbá ṣe bí ẹlédẹ̀ a bàlújẹ́; ẹrú ìbá jọba èèyàn kì bá kùkan.*
Were the warthog to enter the town, it would ruin the town; were a slave to become king, there would be no citizens left. (Trusting matters to the hands of an unfit person guarantees disaster.)

5074. *Ìmàdò kì í dé odò kó tòrò.*
A warthog does not arrive at the stream and leave it unmuddied. (A boorish person's intervention in a matter always muddies the water.)

5075. *Iná dilè lẹ́hìn asunṣuje.*
The fire earns some rest after the person roasting yams to eat is done. (Peace descends after the departure of a troublemaker.)

5076. *Iná jí ó gbé aṣọ epo mú; oòrún jí ó gbẹ́wù òṣèrìṣẹrì bọrùn; òṣùpá jí ó gbáwọ̀-ọ yìnyín.*
Fire wakes up and takes up a cloth of palm oil; the sun rises and puts on a dazzling dress; the moon rises and dons a skin of hailstones. (Each phenomenon has its spe-

cial qualities. Or, comment in praise of an exceptional person.)

5077. *Iná jó lóko kò jó erùpè ilè; òràn tí ńṣeni ò ṣolùkù eni.*
Fire consumes the forest but not the earth; what plagues one does not plague one's friends. (Nobody shares one's fate.)

5078. *Iná orí ò jó aṣọ; àbàtà reere ò gbọkọ̀.*
Fire-of-the-head [head lice] cannot burn one's clothing; floating mud will not accommodate [or support] a boat. (Each task or occasion has its specific requirements.)

5079. *Ìpín àìṣè, ìpín àìrò ní ńpa aláròká.*
The destiny of the innocent, the destiny of the person who thought no ill, will be the death of the person who spreads evil reports about another person.[76] (The evil that one does to innocent people will rebound on one.)

5080. *Ìpọn-ọ́n ríkú ki orí bọ̀ ọ́.*
The wooden spoon sees death and plunges into it. (Comment on the death-defying behavior of an intrepid person.)

5081. *Ìrì kékeré ní ńdi odò; ìrì wàwà ní ńdi òjò; bómọdé méje-é bá kọ oúnje alé, a dìjà àgbàlagbà.*
Tiny dewdrops soon become a river, and heavy dews soon become rain; if seven children refuse their dinner, a fight ensues among adults. (Seemingly unimportant matters soon mushroom into unmanageable problems.)

5082. *Ìrírí ní ḿmúni gbọ́n.*
It is experience that makes one wise. (Experience is the best teacher.)

5083. *Irúkan-ùn, ọbè iwọ.*
All of a kind, stews made with brimstone tree leaves.[77] (Said of people who have no real individual identities outside of the group.)

5084. *Ìsọ̀rọ̀ nìgbèsì.*
How one speaks is how one receives a response. (People respond in kind to the way one addresses or behaves toward them.)

5085. *Ìṣe èèyàn nìṣe eranko.*
As animals behave, so do humans. (One may learn much about humans by watching animals.)

5086. *Ìṣe tí a fi he àdá lóko igbó ni yó ṣe sọnù lóko ẹgàn.*
What caused one to find a cutlass in the forest will cause one to misplace it in the wilderness. (Easy come, easy go.)

5087. *Iṣẹ́ ḿbẹ nílé, iṣẹ́ ḿbẹ lóko: ìwọ̀fà ọ̀pọ̀ló.*
"There is work at home, and there is work on the farm," said the frog that was pawned. (No matter where one goes, there is work to be done.)

5088. *Ìṣẹ́ ò dún, iyà ò fohùn ká mọ ẹni tí ìyà ńdùn lára.*
Destitution does not make a sound, and suffering does not speak to let people know who is plagued by suffering. (One cannot tell from just looking who is in the grip of suffering.)

5089. *Isú paradà ó diyán, àgbàdó paradà ó dèkọ.*
Yam changes its state and becomes pounded yam; corn changes its state and becomes steamed corn meal. (People and things can change for the better.)

---

76. *Ìpín* here refers to the mystical guardian spirit each person has that directs and regulates his or her fate.

77. The medicinal decoction made from these leaves is quite bitter.

5090. Ìtì ọ̀gẹ̀dẹ̀ẹ́ bọ́ lọ́wọ́-ọ gbẹ́nàgbẹ́nà.
The banana trunk is safe from the carpenter.
(One is safe from those who have no use for
whatever one has.)

5091. Iwájú iwájú là ḿbá ọ̀nà.
One always finds that the road is ahead of
one [one can never walk past it]. (Said as a
prayer that a person may never fall behind
his or her peers, or as a boast that one will
ever be ahead of one's peers.)

5092. Iwájú iwáju lọpá ẹ̀bìtì ńré sí.
The ẹ̀bìtì snare always springs forward when
tripped. (Used in the context of a prayer to
wish someone continuous progress.)

5093. Iwájú lalákàn ńfà sí.
Forward is the direction in which the crab
crawls. (A wish that a person's fortunes will
always improve.)

5094. Ìwọ̀fà tó gun ẹṣin lọ sódò, owó ní ńgun
owó.
The pawn who rides the horse to the stream:
money is riding on money. (Said to indicate
that the people referred to, though seemingly different, are really indistinguishable.)

5095. Ìwọ̀sí loko etílé; ìyà loko ẹgàn ńje.
A farm hard by the town brings insults; a
farm far away in the wilds suffers neglect.
(Every pursuit has its drawbacks.)

5096. Ìyà méjì kì í je òkú; bí kò bá ráṣọ bora,
a rílẹ̀ bora.
Two misfortunes will not befall a corpse; if it
lacks a shroud, it will not lack earth to cover
itself. (If one's first option fails, there will
always be a fall-back alternative.)

5097. Ìyá tó bí Alárá ló bí Ajerò, ló sì bí
Ọ̀ràngún Ìlá.
The mother who gave birth to the Alárá
[king of Ará] gave birth to the Ajerò [king

of Ìjerò] and the Ọ̀ràngún of Ìlà.[78] (All referents are of a kind. Compare the following
two entries.)

5098. Ìyá tó bí aṣọ ló bí ẹwù.
The mother who gave birth to the cloth
also gave birth to the shirt. (Two or more
seemingly different things are essentially the
same. Compare the preceding and following
entries.)

5099. Ìyáa ṣòkòtò ló bí bàǹté.
The mother of the trousers also gave birth to
the loincloth. (Though apparently different,
the two entities are virtually indistinguishable. Compare the preceding two entries.)

5100. Iyán ogún ọdún a máa jóni lọ́wọ́.
Twenty-year-old pounded yams can still
scald one's fingers. (One can still remember
favors or injuries twenty years after they
were done.)

5101. Ìyàwó fi àparò dá ilá; ọkọ́ je iyán àìjẹkù.
The wife cooks a partridge stew, and the
husband eats the pounded yam without
leaving a morsel. (It is difficult to restrain
oneself in the face of something powerfully
appealing.)

5102. Iyì lọbá fi orí bíbẹ́ ṣe; ọba kì í mu ẹ̀jẹ̀.
A king derives only awe from beheading
people; the king does not drink blood. (One
does certain things out of duty and not from
desire.)[79]

---

78. These are all related sovereigns in Yorubaland.

79. Orí bíbẹ́ means both "beheading" and military-
style salute. Taking the second meaning, the proverb
would suggest that the respect other people show to
a person does not materially enrich the person, and
therefore that he or she would not miss it if it were
withheld.

J

5103. *Ję kí nję kì í pa ayò.*
You win and I win does not make for defeat in a game. (When both sides are evenly matched, there will be no winner; cooperation makes for harmony.)

5104. *Ję kí nję ní ḿmú ayò dùn.*
You win and I win is what makes a game exciting. (Sharing alike makes for a harmonious relationship.)

5105. *Jìgìjìgì ò ṣéé fà tu.*
A firmly rooted plant cannot be uprooted. (Whatever is based on a sound foundation will not be easily dismantled.)

K

5106. *Ká kú ní kékeré ká fẹsin ṣe ìrèlè ẹni, ó sàn ju ká dàgbà kú láìní adìẹ ìrènà.*
To die young and have a horse sacrificed to ease one's passage to the beyond is better than to reach old age before dying but with not even a chicken sacrificed to ease one's passage. (Better to die young and prosperous than to die old and destitute.)

5107. *Ká ọwọ́ fún mi kí nká ẹsẹ̀ fún ẹ.*
Move your hands out of the way for me, and I will move my legs out of the way for you. (Consideration earns consideration in return.)

5108. *Kàkà kí ewé àgbọn rò, pípele ní ńpele sí i.*
The coconut palm's leaves instead of wilting only become even stiffer. (The opposite of what one has been hoping for is what keeps happening.)

5109. *Kán-un-kàn-un ìlù ìgbàgbọ́.*
Bereft of rhythm and bereft of coherence is the sound of Christians drumming. (The matter or person referred to lacks any sense of coherence.)[80]

5110. *Keese-keese lẹ rí, kàásà-kàásà ḿbọ̀ léhìn; kàásà-kàásà baba keese-keese.*
Something evil is all you have seen, but behind it comes something extremely evil; Kàásà-kàásà is the father of all keese-keese. (What people are complaining about does not compare in terror to what is in the offing.)

5111. *Kékeré nìmàlé ti ńkọ́mọ láásọ.*
It is from youth that the Muslim teaches a child how to engage in disputes. (People develop problem characteristics from youth.)[81]

5112. *Kì í pẹ́ títí kí eji ọdún má rò.*
No matter how long it takes, the annual rain will eventually fall. (What is ordained to happen eventually will, however long it might take.)

5113. *Kì í ṣe títí ayé ni Ọrúnmìlà ò níí ję àgbàdo mọ́.*
It is not forever that Ọrúnmìlà will abstain from eating corn. (Even though one is enjoying plenty, lean times may come around.)

5114. *Kí ilẹ̀ tó pa òṣìkà, ohun rere gbogbo á ti bàjẹ́.*
Before Earth kills the wicked, a great many good things will have been ruined. (God's justice may eventually prevail, but by then a lot of evil will have been done.)[82]

---

80. Christian music, or Western music in general, made little sense to the Yoruba when they first encountered it.

81. This proverb bears witness to the non-Muslim Yoruba belief that Muslims are obstinate.

82. The Yoruba often advise people to leave the wicked, especially if they are powerful, to the good Earth to punish; Earth, they believe, will not permit the wicked to prosper.

5115. *Kí ni à ńje tí kì í tan? Kí ni ó ńkù sílẹ̀ tí kì í dòla?*
What does one eat that one does not eventually finish? What does one leave aside that does not keep until the morrow? (A person who knows no thrift deprives himself or herself of a future; the person who puts something aside today will have something to use in the future.)

5116. *Kí ni àǹfàní orógbó? A pa á kò láwẹ; a jẹ ẹ́ ó ńkorò; a ní ká figi ẹ̀ dáná, Ṣàngó ní ọmọ ìyá òun ní ńṣe.*
Of what use is the bitter kola? One splits it, but it lacks naturally separated lobes; one eats it and it is bitter; one attempts to use its wood for fire, and Ṣàngo says both [he and the tree] were born of the same mother.[83] (Why should one put oneself out for something or someone from which or whom one can expect no appreciation or reward?)

5117. *Kí òràn ó lè sú ọlọ́ràn la fi ńsọ pé a ò rí irú èyí rí; kò sí irú ohun tí ojú ò rí rí.*
It is only so that the offender might know the enormity of the offense that one says one has never seen the likes of it before; there is nothing the likes of which the eyes have never seen. (There is nothing a person does that others have not done before, even though one might say the contrary in order to regulate people's behavior.)

5118. *Kíjìpá kì í ṣe awo.*
Durable hand-woven cloth is not leather. (One should not overestimate the quality of one's possessions or make too much of one's position.)

5119. *Kò sí ẹni tó mọ bí omí ṣe ńdénú àgbọn.*
Nobody knows how water gets into the coconut. (No one knows the mysteries of nature.)

5120. *Kò sí "Fi sílẹ̀" mọ́; gbogbo ayé di "Mú u re!"* There is no more "Let him or her be"; all of life is now "Hold him or her tight!" (The world no longer knows mercy.)

5121. *Kò sí obìnrin òfé; bó ṣe akúwárápá, owó ni.*
No woman is available free; even if she has epilepsy, she costs money. (One must have the means if one means to take a wife.)

5122. *Kò sí ohun tí a ńjẹ tí kò tán, àfi ọlá Ọlọ́run.*
There is nothing one eats that is never finished except the grace of God. (One should never forget that whatever material things one has will eventually be gone.)

5123. *Kò sí ohun tí ò nítàn.*
There is nothing without a history. (Every phenomenon, as well as every condition, has its explanation.)

5124. *Kò sí ohun tí owó pa tí kò kú.*
There is nothing money kills that does not die. (Money accomplishes all.)

5125. *Kò sí orin kan tó borí aráyé.*
There is no song that surpasses "People of this world." (Said when all that needs to be said has been said. Also, there is nothing one needs to be more wary of than people.)

5126. *Kò tó iṣẹ́ ikú; arẹwà ló ńpa.*
One cannot put it [anything] past death; it kills beautiful people. (Even beautiful people are not beyond the notice of death.)

5127. *Kòkòrò ní ńdi labalábá.*
It is an insect that becomes the butterfly. (The youth of today will be the elders of tomorrow. Compare 4981.)

---

83. One would not want to offend Ṣango, the god of thunder and lightning, in any way.

5128. *Kòsínkan òun nnkan ní njo nrìn.*
There-is-no-problem always travels in the company of problem. (Even when there is no problem, problems are never far away.)

5129. *Kòtónilérù tí ntani lórí.*
A-thing-that-is-not-a-big-enough-load-for-one hurts one's head nevertheless. (Said of an insignificant thing that nevertheless constitutes a persistent nuisance.)

5130. *Kòlòkòlò tí ngbé adìe ò jé ká mo olè.*
The fox that steals chickens prevents one from knowing about the thief. (Said of circumstances in which offenders are able to hide behind fortuitous occurrences.)

5131. *Kòlòkòlò tí ngbe adìe ò sanra bí igún.*
The fox that steals chickens is not as fat as the vulture. (A criminal has not profited visibly from his or her crimes.)

L

5132. *Lójú òtá, bí kí ìdálè di òrun ni.*
For one's enemy, the wish is that one's journey would lead to heaven. (One's enemies never wish one well.)

M

5133. *Mo gbójú wo ewé ìgbá, ng ò rí èyí tó gba àkàsù níbè.*
I looked up at the leaves of the acacia tree, but I did not see any that would do for wrapping corn meal. (However precious a thing might be, if it will not serve one's end, it is of little value.)

N

5134. *Nnkan kì í dùn ko tún pò.*
A thing is never both pleasant and plentiful. (One cannot have things all ways.)

O

5135. *Ò báà sín iyùn egbàá, kóo sín sègi pèlú, ata wèerè ni lójú abúni.*
Even if you wore coral beads and tubular beads in addition, to a detractor they are just like red peppers. (Nothing one does impresses detractors.)

5136. *Ó kù dèdè ká kó iwì wo Akèsán, oba tí à ó yìn-ín térí gbaso.*
We were just about to enter Akèsán market with our praise-singing performance when the king we would honor gave up the ghost. (One's gifts or services may be too late to be of any use to the recipient.)

5137. *Obìnrin kì í jé Òjó.*
No woman ever bears the name Òjó. (There are certain things a person may not do, simply because of who he or she is.)[84]

5138. *Obìnrin kì í ní iná kí torogún è má jòó.*
A woman's having fire does not stop her co-wife's from burning. (One's fierceness does not stop one's rivals from being fierce also.)

5139. *Obìnrín pò lójà, gbogbo won ló lóko.*
Women are plentiful at the market, but all of them have husbands. (There are few things out there that have not been spoken for.)

5140. *Òbírí lokò ndà; yíyí layé nyí.*
It is all of a sudden that a boat capsizes; turning is what the world does. (Nobody can predict the future.)

---

84. Òjó is invariably a male name.

5141. *Ogún ọdún kì í ṣe títí láé.*
Twenty years hence is not the same as the
infinite future. (The furthest day arrives in
time. Compare the entry that follows.)

5142. *Ogún ọdún ḿbọ̀ wá kòla.*
Twenty years hence will soon become
tomorrow. (No matter how distant, the
future sooner or later arrives. Compare the
preceding entry.)

5143. *Ohun ẹlẹgẹ́ kì í gbẹ̀ é bàjẹ́.*
An excessively delicate thing is easy to ruin.
(One cannot be too careful with delicate
matters.)

5144. *Ohun ẹyẹ́ ńjẹ lóko lẹyẹ ńgbé fò.*
Whatever the bird eats on the farm is what
it takes with it in flight. (One always devotes
great attention to protecting what is dear to
one.)

5145. *Ohun ńlá-ńlá tó ròkè, ilẹ̀ ní ḿbọ̀.*
The mighty thing that rose into the heavens
will wind up back on earth. (However long
the diversion, a matter eventually winds up
before the tribunal charged with adjudicat-
ing it.)

5146. *Ohun tí a bá ní là ńnáání; ọmọ àgbẹ̀
ńnáání ewùrà; ọmọ aṣégità ńnáání èpo igi;
ọmọ alápata ńnáání èdọ̀ ẹran; ọmọ ọdẹ
ńnáání ẹran gbígbẹ.*
Whatever one has [in abundance] is what
one disparages; the child of the farmer disparages the water yam; the firewood seller
attaches little value to the bark of firewood;
the child of the butcher belittles cow liver;
the son of the hunter disdains dried bush
meat. (One never attaches much value to
articles one has in plenty.)

5147. *Ohun tí kòì délẹ̀ yó tàn-án; èyí tó ti dé
tán nìyẹn.*
Whatever is in the offing will end in time;

that applies only to what has already arrived.
(One can know the nature of only those
things one has experienced.)

5148. *Ohun tó bá dunni là ńjagun mú lógun.*
Whatever one craves most painfully is what
one takes as booty in a war. (One's greatest
need is always uppermost in one's preoccupation.)

5149. *Ohun tó bá wuni ní ńpọ̀ lórọ̀ ẹni; ológún
ẹrú kú, aṣọ ẹẹ́ ku òkan ṣoṣo.*
Whatever one most values will be the most
abundant component of one's wealth; the
owner of twelve slaves dies and leaves only
one garment. (One spends one's wealth on
whatever one most likes.)

5150. *Ohun tó wà léhìn èfà-á ju èje lọ.*
What comes after six is a lot more than
seven. (People seldom realize how serious
the consequences of their actions could be.)

5151. *Òjò àkọ́rọ̀ kì í rọ̀ lósàn-án; ejidún kì í
palẹ̀ lóru.*
The first rain never falls in the afternoon;
the annual downpour does not soak the
soil in the middle of the night. (There is a
proper time for everything.)

5152. *Òjò iwájú kì í pa ahun; òjò ẹ̀hìn kì í pa
ìgbín; léhìn léhìn lolóbẹ ńso.*
The rain ahead does not beat the tortoise;
the rain behind does not soak the snail; ever
to the rear does the *olobe* grow its fruits.
(Incantation to ward off evil.)

5153. *Òjò lọko àgbàdo.*
Rain is the lord of the corn. (Without one's
source of sustenance one is nothing.)

5154. *Òjò ò bénìkan ṣọré, ẹni eji rí leji ńpa.*
The rain plays favorites with no one; whomever the rain finds, it drenches. (Misfortune
is not selective.)

5155. Òjò pa gbòdògì ró wòrò-wòrò.
The rain pounds the *gbòdògì*, producing a
loud noise.[85] (Certain behaviors by others
force comments out of the mouths of even
normally recalcitrant people.)

5156. Òjò tó rò lásìkò ní ńjẹ́ ejidún.
It is rain that falls at its proper time that is
known as the annual heavy rain. (Windfalls
that come when one cannot take advantage
of them are of no value.)

5157. Òjò-ó kò òjò ò rò mọ́; Olórun-ún fi tèèsó
lé àgbàdo lóko.
The rains become adamant and stop falling; God has inflicted *tèèsó* on the corn in
the fields.[86] (Adverse conditions make it
impossible for people to thrive.)

5158. Ojoojúmọ́ kọ́ lobìnrin ńrí ńnkan oṣù.
It is not every day that a woman sees her
monthly thing [i.e., menstruation]. (Not
every day is Christmas. The next entry is a
variant.)

5159. Ojoojúmọ́ kọ́ lobìnrin ńrí ọkọ ẹ̀.
It is not every day that a woman sees her
husband.[87] (Compare the preceding entry.)

5160. Ojú kì í mọ́ kéji òwúrọ̀ má rò.
A day does not dawn without formation of
the morning dew. (A prayer that one might
always find blessing, just as the morning is
always blessed with the dew.)

5161. Ojú kì í pa ojú jẹ.
An eye does not kill an[other] eye for food.
(Staring eyes pose no danger. Compare the
following entry.)

5162. Ojú kòkòrò kì í pa ojú kòkòrò jẹ.
An envious eye cannot kill an envious eye
for food. (One person's envy can't stare
down another person's. This is a variant of
of the preceding entry.)

5163. Ojú ò léjè, omi ní ńsun.
The eyes have no blood; they only ooze
tears. (One can seldom tell from mere
appearance what another person's inner
state is.)

5164. Ojú ológbò òun ẹ̀gún; àmòtékùn òun
ẹkùn; òkánjúwà òun olè; déédé ni wọ́n.
The scarlet love-bean plant and thorns, the
àmòtékùn big cat and the leopard, greed and
thievery: they are equivalents.[88] (A greedy
person is no different from a thief.)

5165. Ojú tí a fi ata bọ̀; màjò-màjò-ó tán níbẹ̀.
The eyes into which pepper has been thrown:
there one finds the ultimate in frantic jump-
ing about. (Where one finds the greatest
disaster, one will also find the greatest
lamentation.)

5166. Òkìtì bàábà ní ńpẹkun òpópó.
It is usually a large hill that marks the end of
a straight avenue. (Nothing goes on forever.)

5167. Òkò tí a bá sọ ságbọn làgbọn ńsọ síni.
The stone one throws at a coconut palm is
the same as the coconut palm throws back.
(One's evil deeds are likely to recoil on one.)

5168. Òkú ẹjọ́ lọlọ́jà ńdá.
It is a dead case that the ruler adjudicates.[89]

---

85. *Gbòdògì* is a plant with broad leaves, *Sarco-*
phrynium (Marantaceae); see Abraham 246.
86. *Tèèsó* is a juju that causes an adulterer to lose
his erection as soon as he penetrates a woman.
87. In polygamous settings the wives take turns to
"see" the husband.

88. *Ojú ológbò* is *Abrus precatorius* (Papilonaceae;
Abraham 463); *àmòtékùn* is always identified as a type
of leopard.
89. *Olójà* means literally "owner of the market" but
is also another designation for the ruler of a community, because the market is usually outside his palace.
In his role as ruler he adjudicates and resolves disputes
among his subjects.

(A matter that has come before a conciliatory body is no longer urgent.)

5169. *Òkú ò lè sin baba.*
A dead person cannot serve the patriarch. (One cannot expect service from a corpse.)

5170. *Olè lọmọ olè ńfiwà jọ.*
A thief's child takes after him. (One takes after one's parents.)

5171. *Olè ní ḿmọ ẹsẹ̀ olè-é tọ̀ lórí àpáta.*
Only a thief can find the tracks of a thief on a rock. (It takes a thief to catch a thief.)

5172. *Olè ńpolè lólè; ìkà ńpèkà níkà.*
The thief calls another thief a thief; a wicked person calls another wicked person wicked. (The pot is calling the kettle black.)

5173. *Olè-é ta ohun lópọ̀; ewúrẹ́ mẹ́ta ẹgbẹ̀ta; àgùntàn mẹ́fà ẹgbẹ̀fà.*
A thief sells everything cheap: three goats for 600 cowries; six sheep for 1,200 cowries. (A person who did not work for something is never reluctant to discard it for little or nothing.)[90]

5174. *Olóòlà kì í wọlú kó má fọwọ́ kan ẹ̀jẹ̀.*
A circumciser does not enter a town and not get his fingers bloody. (One cannot avoid the fallout of one's profession.)

5175. *Omi, baálé àlejò.*
Water: the lord and master of the visitor. (Water is the ultimate thing with which one welcomes a visitor.)

5176. *Omi titún dé, eja titún wọ̀ ó.*
A new stream arrives, and new fish enter into it. (Each era brings its own fashion.)

5177. *Òní ló bo ọ̀la lójú.*
It is today that obscures tomorrow. (Tomorrow arrives before one knows it.)

5178. *Oníbàjẹ́ ò wọ́n; awọ́ngógó bí atúnniṣe; atúnnìṣe ò pọ̀ bí abanijẹ́.*
Detractors are not scarce; nothing is more difficult to find than reputation menders; reputation menders are far fewer than detractors. (Most people are more interested in running others down than in building them up.)

5179. *Onígbàjámọ̀-ọ́ fẹ́ẹ́ kiri télẹ̀.*
The itinerant barber always intended to get on the road. (One needs little goading to do what one wanted to do anyway.)

5180. *Oògùn tí a ò bá fowó ṣe, ẹ̀hìn àdìrò ní ńgbé.*
Medicine on which one spent no money usually winds up behind the cooking hearth. (One seldom places any value on things that come easy and cheap.)

5181. *Oorun ò mọ ikú.*
Sleep does not know death. (A sleeping person does not know when death comes.)

5182. *Orí kì í burú kó má lọ̀ọ́rùn.*
A head is never so unfortunate that it does not have a neck.[91] (No matter how bad one's situation, there will be some redeeming factor.)

5183. *Orí-i Táyé yàtọ̀ sí ti Kẹ́hìndé.*
Táyé's destiny is different from Kẹ́hìndé's.[92] (No two people, however close or similar, have identical destinies.)

---

90. In the conversion of the traditional monetary system to British currency, 300 cowries equaled one penny.

91. The Yoruba use the concept *orí bíburú* or *orí burúkú*, literally "bad head," for ill luck.

92. Táyé is the name automatically given to the firstborn of twins and Kẹ́hìndé to the second.

5184. *Òrìṣà kì í gba méjì lọ́wọ́ ìmẹ̀lẹ́; bó bá gba apá a fún un lẹ́nu.*
The gods do not deprive the shirker of two gifts; if they take his arms, they endow them with a mouth. (People whose arms are feeble always have overactive mouths.)

5185. *Orísìírísìí ọbẹ là ńrí níjọ́ ikú erin.*
One sees all sorts of knives on the day an elephant dies. (Extraordinary events prompt extraordinary behavior.)

5186. *Orúkọ eni ni ìjánu eni.*
One's name is one's bridle. (The means of controlling people, or getting their attention, is their names.)

5187. *Òtìpí ìjí, a-wúwo-bí-àtẹ-ìbànújẹ́.*
Huge baboon, as heavy as a tray of sadness. (Sadness is a heavy burden to bear.)

5188. *Òwe lẹsin ọ̀rọ̀; bí ọ̀rọ̀-ọ́ bá sọnù, òwe la fi ńwá a.*
Proverbs are the horses of communication; if communication is lost, proverbs are what one uses to find it. (Effective discourse is impossible without resort to proverbs.)

5189. *Owó obì; obì owó.*
Money, kola nut; kola nut, money. (Money and kola nuts are equal in importance.)[93]

5190. *Òwò tí àdá bá mọ̀ ní ńká àdá léhín.*
The trade the cutlass knows is the one that knocks out its teeth. (The dangers to which one is most vulnerable are those attached to one's profession. Compare 3918, 4542, and 4544.)

5191. *Owó tí ò lè dáni ní gbèsè ò lè lani.*
Money that is not enough to make one a debtor is not enough to make one prosper either. (Insignificant amounts of money, or of anything else, cannot much affect one, one way or another.)

5192. *Òwúrọ̀ la ti ńmọ̀ bí alẹ́ yó ti sanni sí.*
It is from the morning that one knows how good one's night will be. (From youth one can tell how pleasant one's old age will be.)

Ọ

5193. *Ọba mẹ́wàá, ìgbà mẹ́wàá.*
Ten kings, ten eras. (Each generation has its peculiar fashions and tastes.)

5194. *Ọbẹ tó dùn kì í pẹ́ nísàsùn.*
A delicious stew does not last long in the pot. (Desirable commodities are soon used up.)

5195. *Ọdọọdún là ńrí yemẹtì.*[94] (A
It is annually that one sees *yemẹtì*. prayer that good fortune will annually be a person's lot, just as the *yemẹtì* insect is seen annually. Compare the following three variants.)

5196. *Ọdọọdún lẹ̀wà ńwà.*
It is annually that black-eyed beans are available. (May good fortune be ours each year. See the preceding and following two entries.)

5197. *Ọdọọdún ni ṣákúwé ńrúwe; ọdọọdún lewúro ńyọ ewé.*
It is every year that the *ṣákúwé* plant sprouts leaves; it is yearly that the bitterleaf plant sprouts leaves. (A wish that a desired annual event will never fail to occur. See the preceding two and following entries.)

5198. *Ọdọọdún nìrèké ńso.*
The sugarcane flourishes annually. (Prayer

---

93. Equal where hospitality is concerned.

94. *Yemẹtì* is an insect found on the cotton plant.

for perennial good fortune. See the preceding three entries.)

5199. *Ọ̀gá ńtà, ọ̀gá ńrà.*
The master is selling; the master is buying. (It takes a buyer and a seller to make a deal.)

5200. *Ọjà ojú-u sánmà lókè, àwọn ẹyẹ ni yó na.*
The market holding in the sky aloft is for the birds alone to ply. (Only people with the requisite qualifications can engage in certain trades.)

5201. *Ọ̀já osùn ní ńfi-í hàn pé a bí ọmọ titun.*
It is a camwood-stained baby strap that announces that one has a newborn baby. (Some events are announced by their accompanying behavior.)

5202. *Ọjà Òyìngbò ò mọ̀ pénìkan ò wá.*
Òyìngbò market does not know [or care] that someone is absent.[95] (An insignificant person will not be missed in an assembly. The following entry is a variant.)

5203. *Ọjà ọba ò mọ̀ pé ẹnìkan ò wá.*
The king's market does not know that a person is absent. (An individual's input, if withheld, will not disrupt the project of the community. The preceding entry is a variant.)

5204. *Ọjọ́ kan òjò-ó borí ọ̀dá.*
The rain of one day conquers the drought. (However long the deprivation, relief is welcome when it comes.)

5205. *Ọjọ́ kì í pẹ títí kó má pèé; ojọ́ kì í jìnnà jìnnà kó má kò.*
The day is never so distant that it does not arrive; the future is never so far that it does

not arrive. (A thousand days are soon over. Compare the following two variants.)

5206. *Ojọ́ kì í ríírìi kó má pèé.*
A day is never so distant that it does not arrive. (The furthest future soon becomes the present. See the preceding and following entries.)

5207. *Ojọ́ kì í tọ́ lọ bi òréré.*
Days do not go on straight like an avenue. (Life is not without curves. This is a variant of the preceding two entries.)

5208. *Ojọ́ tí atá bá bọ́ sójú ní ńba ẹwà ojú jẹ́; ojọ́ tína bá fojú ba ètù ni ètù ńgbà.*
The day pepper enters the eye is the day it ruins the beauty of the eye; the day fire catches a glimpse of gunpowder is the day the gunpowder does its bidding. ("No" is not an option as a response to the inevitable.)

5209. *Ojọ́ tí ọmọ́ bá fi ojú kan ayé lojú ẹ̀ ńlà.*
The day a child first glimpses [comes into] the world is the day its eyes open. (The business of living begins on the day one is born.)

5210. *Ọ̀kákárá re ilé òkokoro.*
Destitution goes to the home of distress. (Troubles pile on trouble.)

5211. *Ọ̀kan sọsọ ẹkùn, ó ba igba ọdẹ jẹ́.*
One single leopard sows confusion among two hundred hunters. (A formidable problem defies the efforts of many experts.)

5212. *Ọ̀kọ́lé ò mú u ràjò.*
The person who builds a house does not travel with it. (Even though one owns a house, one will still have to be a lodger if one travels.)

5213. *Ọmoge ńrelé ọkọ pẹ̀lú-u májèlé, alárẹnà-a rẹ̀-ẹ́ mú apó dání, ọkọ ìyàwó di ẹ̀bìtì sílẹ̀; ká wá wo irú ọmọ tí wọn ó bìí.*

---

95. Òyìngbò is an area on the Lagos mainland where a large market once thrived.

A young woman leaves for her groom's home carrying poisons; her intermediary carries a quiver, and the husband awaits them with a snare; let us see what sort of children they will produce. (One can predict the outcome of a collaborative venture from the nature of those involved.)

5214. *Ọmọ eja lejá ńje sanra.*
It is the children of fishes that fishes eat and grow fat upon. (It is the nature of things that people who prosper do so at the expense of other people.)

5215. *Ọmọ kékeré la fi ńse oògun ògbójú.*
It is a small child that serves as an ingredient for a charm for bravery. (Even small things can effect large consequences.)

5216. *Ọmọdé kékeré kì í ṣe àkọ́pa ikú.*
A small child is not death's first victim. (Children have been dying since the beginning of time.)

5217. *Ọmọ́yẹ-ẹ́ ti rìnhòòhò dọ́ja; aṣọ ò bá Ọmọ́yẹ.*
Ọmọ́yẹ has arrived at the market naked; clothes are too late for Ọmọ́yẹ.[96] (Matters past remedy are past care.)

5218. *Ọpẹ Ìjàyè là bá bi ní ìhìn ogun Ògún-mọ́lá.*
It is the palm tree of Ìjàyè that one should ask about the battle with Ògúnmọ́lá. (Said of a disaster that leaves no survivors.)[97]

5219. *Ọpọ̀lọpọ̀ òjò ló ti rọ̀ tílẹ̀-ẹ́ ti fimu.*
A great deal of rain has fallen, which the

earth has soaked up. (Much more has happened than one could ever recount.)

5220. *Ọ̀rán dé; ọ̀tá yọ̀.*
Problems arrive; enemies rejoice. (One's enemies rejoice at one's misfortune.)

5221. *Ọ̀rán ìhùùhù ní ńdun aládìẹ.*
It is the matter of the down feathers that troubles the owner of the fowl. (Delicate tasks are far more taxing than routine ones.)[98]

5222. *Ọ̀rẹ́ eni ní ńbáni pilẹ̀ ọrọ̀; ará ilé eni ní ńkófà-a rẹ̀.*
Friends help one lay the foundation for wealth; one's relatives reap the benefit. (Friends are in some regards more valuable than kin.)

5223. *Ọwọ́ kì í sìnà ẹnu.*
The hand never misses the way to the mouth. (Actions that are second nature will not go awry.)

5224. *Ọwọ́ tó wẹ̀, ilẹ̀ ló fi nù.*
The hand that he washed, he had to wipe on the ground. (Said of people frustrated in their expectations.)[99]

P

5225. *Palaku-n-gọ palaku-n-gọ: ìpàkọ́ igún bí ẹrú àáké; bẹ̀ẹ̀ni kò sẹ́ẹ́ lagi.*
Protruding, protruding: the occiput of the vulture seems like an axe's handle, yet one cannot split wood with it. (Said of a thing

---

96. Ọmọ́yẹ is the shortened form of the name Ọmọ́yẹni, which means "a child [that] bestows decorum [propriety, or what one desires] on one."

97. Ògúnmọ́lá was an Ibadan general in the war that city waged against Ìjàyè in 1860–62, in which Ìjàyè was defeated and destroyed.

98. The down feathers are more trouble because they are more difficult to remove than the main feathers when the fowl is being plucked for cooking.

99. Since etiquette demands that one wash one's hands before sitting down to a meal, the person in question was apparently expecting to be invited to eat.

that may look impressive but is really useless.)

5226. *Pani-pani kì í jẹ́ ká mú idà kọjá nípàkọ́ òun.*
The murderer would never let people carrying swords pass behind him. (The evildoer is always afraid of his shadow.)

5227. *Pẹ́tẹ-pẹ̀tẹ là ḿbá ibalùwẹ̀.*
Ever in a muddy state is how one finds the bath place. (Said to invoke a filthy fate on a person.)

R

5228. *Rẹ́rẹ́ rún.*
A delicate thing has disintegrated. (A problem has arisen.)

Ṣ

5229. *Ṣàn-ǹ-gbá tú sépo.*
The bean cake has disintegrated in the oil. (A misfortune has occurred.)

T

5230. *Ta ló gbọ́ ikú ẹbọra? Ẹnìkan kì í gbọ́ ikú Olódùmarè.*
Whoever heard of the death of a spirit? No one ever hears of the death of the Almighty.

(God endures forever; this is also a wish for longevity.)

5231. *Tàlùbọ̀ ni iyèkan afọ́jú.*
Tàlùbọ̀ is the blood sibling of the blind. (Said of things that are always to be found in the company of one another.)[100]

5232. *Tibi tire làfọn ńrọ̀.*
The fruit of the baobab tree drops without regard for good or foul weather. (A prayer that a pregnant woman might deliver without hardship.)

5233. *Tòjò tẹ̀rùn, omi kì í gbẹ níhò akàn.*
Be it the rainy season or the dry, the crab's hole is never short of water. (A wish that one may never be short of the good things of life, whatever the season. The following is a variant.)

5234. *Tòjò tẹ̀rùn, omi kì í wọ́n ọmọ oníròjo-ròjo.*
Whether in the rainy season or in the dry, the *oníròjoròjo* child never lacks water. (A prayer for unceasing blessings. Compare the foregoing entry.)

W

5235. *Wúńdíá: abọkojọjọ.*
The unmarried woman: one whose husbands are legion. (The potential husbands of an unmarried woman are uncountable.)

---

100. Tàlùbọ̀ is an insect that flies into people's eyes, but the word can also mean a walking stick.

References

Abiodun, Rowland. Preface. *A History of Art in Africa.* By Monica Blackmun Visonà et al. New York: Abrams, 2000. 10–13.

Abraham, R. C. *Dictionary of Modern Yoruba.* London: U of London P, 1958.

Abrahams, Roger. "Proverbs and Proverbial Expressions." *Folklore and Folklife: An Introduction.* Ed. Richard M. Dorson. Chicago: U of Chicago P, 1972. 117–27.

Adéẹ̀kọ, Adélékè. *Proverbs, Textuality, and Nativism in African Literature.* Gainesville: UP of Florida, 1998.

Ajayi, J. F. Ade, and Robert S. Smith. *Yoruba Warfare in the 19th Century.* London: Cambridge UP, 1964 (in association with the Institute of African Studies, U of Ibadan).

Apperson, G. L. *English Proverbs and Proverbial Phrases: A Historical Dictionary.* London: J. M. Dent, 1929. Reprinted by Gale Research Company, Detroit, 1969.

Atanda, J. Adebowale. "The Yoruba People: Their Origin, Culture and Civilization." *The Yoruba: History, Culture and Language.* J. F. Odunjo Memorial Lectures Ser. 5. Ibadan: Ibadan UP, 1996. 3–34.

Babalola, S. A. *The Content and Form of Yoruba Ijala.* Oxford: Clarendon, 1966.

Bamgbose, A. "The Assimilated Low Tone in Yoruba." *Lingua* 16.1 (1966): 1–13.

———. *A Grammar of Yoruba.* West African Language Monographs 5. Cambridge: Cambridge UP, 1966.

Bascom, William. "Four Functions of Folklore." *The Study of Folklore.* Ed. Alan Dundes. Englewood Cliffs NJ: Prentice, 1965. 279–98.

———. *The Yoruba of Southwestern Nigeria.* New York: Holt, 1969.

Boadi, Lawrence A. "The Language of the Proverb in Akan." *African Folklore.* Ed. Richard Dorson. New York: Anchor, 1972. 183–91.

Brunvand, Jan Harold. *The Study of American Folklore: An Introduction.* New York: Norton, 1978.

"The Dangers of Proverbial Philosophy." *Spectator* 87.3,828 (1901): 694.

Dundes, Alan. "On the Structure of the Proverb." *The Wisdom of Many: Essays on the Proverb.* Ed. Wolfgang Mieder and Alan Dundes, 43–64. New York: Garland, 1981.

———. "Some Yoruba Wellerisms, Dialogue Proverbs, and Tongue-Twisters." *Folklore* 75 (1964): 113–20.

Eagleton, Terry. *Literary Theory: An Introduction.* Minneapolis: U of Minnesota P, 1983.

Firth, Raymond. "Proverbs in Native Life, with Special Reference to Those of the Maori." *Folklore* 37 (1926): 134–53, 245–70.

Greenway, John. *Literature among the Primitives.* Hatboro PA: Folklore Associates, 1964.

Gyekye, Kwame. *An Essay on African Philosophical Thought: The Akan Conceptual Scheme.* Cambridge: Cambridge UP, 1987.

Hallen, Barry. *The Good, the Bad, and the Beautiful: Discourse about Values in Yoruba Culture.* Bloomington: Indiana UP, 2000.

Hallgren, Roland. *The Good Things in Life: A Study of the Traditional Religious Culture of the Yoruba People*. Lund Studies in African and Asian Religions 2. Lund, Swed.: Plus Ultra, 1991.

Hodgkin, Thomas. *Nigerian Perspectives: An Historical Anthology*. London: Oxford UP, 1975.

Hulme, Edward F. *Proverb Lore*. 1902. Detroit: Gale, 1968.

Johnson, S. *The History of the Yorubas*. Lagos: CMS, 1921.

Ladipo, Duro. *Ọba Kò So* (The king did not hang). Opera. Transcribed and translated by R. G. Armstrong, Robert L. Awujoola, and Val Olayemi from a tape recording by R. Curt Wittig. Ibadan: Institute of African Studies, U of Ibadan. 60.

Lerner, Gerder. *The Creation of Patriarchy*. New York: Oxford UP, 1986.

Mbembe, Achille. "Ways of Seeing: Beyond the New Nativism." *African Studies Review* 44.2 (2001): 1–14.

Messenger, John. "The Role of Proverbs in a Nigerian Judicial System." *Southwestern Journal of Anthropology* 15 (1959): 64–73.

Mieder, Wolfgang. "Modern Paremiology: In Retrospect and Prospect." *Embracing the Baobab Tree: The African Proverb in the 21st Century*. Comp. Willem Saayman. CD-ROM, 1996.

———. *The Prentice-Hall Encyclopedia of World Proverbs*. New York: MJF, 1986.

Nietzsche, Friedrich. *The Genealogy of Morals. The Birth of Tragedy and the Genealogy of Morals*. Trans. Francis Golffing. Garden City NY: Doubleday Anchor, 1956.

Nussbaum, Stan, ed. *The Wisdom of African Proverbs: Collections, Studies, Bibliographies*. CD-ROM. Vers. 1.2. Colorado Springs CO: Global Mapping International, June 1998.

Oduyoye, Dupe. "Traditional African Proverbs and African Christian Identity." *The Wisdom of African Proverbs*. Ed. John S. Pobee. CD-ROM, 1996.

Ojoade, J. Olowo. "African Proverbs on Proverbs." *Folklore Forum* 10.3 (1977): 20–23.

Okpewho, Isidore. *African Oral Literature*. Bloomington: Indiana UP, 1992.

Olatunji, Olatunde O. *Features of Yoruba Oral Poetry*. Ibadan: Ibadan UP, 1984.

Owomoyela, Oyekan. *A Kì í: Yoruba Proscriptive and Prescriptive Proverbs*. Lanham MD: UP of America, 1988.

———. "The Sociology of Sex and Crudity in Yoruba Proverbs." *Proverbium* 20 (1972): 751–58.

Pachocinski, Ryszard. *Proverbs of Africa: Human Nature in the Nigerian Oral Tradition*. St. Paul MN: PWPA, 1996.

Raji-Oyelade, Aderemi. "Postproverbials in Yoruba Culture: A Playful Blasphemy." *Research in African Literatures* 30.1 (1999): 74–82.

Spectator. London: The Spectator, 1901.

Taylor, Archer. "Problems in the Study of Proverbs." *Journal of American Folklore* 47.183 (1934): 1–21.

———. "The Wisdom of Many and the Wit of One." *The Wisdom of Many: Essays on the Proverb*. Ed. Wolfgang Mieder and Alan Dundes. New York: Garland, 1981. 3–9.

Turner, Victor. "Liminality and the Performative Genres." *Rite, Drama, Festival, Spectacle: Rehearsals toward a Theory of Cultural Performance*. Ed. John J. MacAloon. Philadelphia: ISHI, 1984.

Wiredu, Kwasi. *Philosophy and an African Culture*. Cambridge: Cambridge UP, 1980.

Yankah, Kwesi. *Speaking for the Chief: Okyeame and the Politics of Akan Royal Oratory*. Bloomington: Indiana UP, 1995.